PROFESSIONAL

Android™ 2 Application Development

Reto Meier

WILEY

Wiley Publishing, Inc.

Professional Android™ 2 Application Development

Published by
Wiley Publishing, Inc.
10475 Crosspoint Boulevard
Indianapolis, IN 46256
www.wiley.com

Copyright © 2010 by Wiley Publishing, Inc., Indianapolis, Indiana

ISBN: 978-0-470-56552-0

Manufactured in the United States of America

10 9 8 7 6 5 4

For general information on our other products and services please contact our Customer Care Department within the United States at (877) 762-2974, outside the United States at (317) 572-3993 or fax (317) 572-4002.

Wiley also publishes its books in a variety of electronic formats. Some content that appears in print may not be available in electronic books.

Library of Congress Control Number: 2009943638

PROFESSIONAL
ANDROID™ 2 APPLICATION DEVELOPMENT

To Kristy

ABOUT THE AUTHOR

RETO MEIER is originally from Perth, Western Australia, but now lives in London.

He currently works as an Android Developer Advocate at Google, helping Android app developers create the best applications possible. Reto is an experienced software developer with more than 10 years of experience in GUI application development. Before Google, he worked in various industries, including offshore oil and gas and finance.

Always interested in emerging technologies, Reto has been involved in Android since the initial release in 2007. In his spare time, he tinkers with a wide range of development platforms, including Google's plethora of developer tools.

You can check out Reto's web site, The Radioactive Yak, at `http://blog.radioactiveyak.com` or follow him on twitter at `http://www.twitter.com/retomeier`.

ABOUT THE TECHNICAL EDITOR

MILAN NARENDRA SHAH graduated with a BSc Computer Science degree from the University of Southampton. He has been working as a software engineer for more than seven years, with experiences in C#, C/C++, and Java. He is married and lives in Buckinghamshire, United Kingdom.

CREDITS

ACQUISITIONS EDITOR
Scott Meyers

PROJECT EDITOR
William Bridges

TECHNICAL EDITOR
Milan Narendra Shah

PRODUCTION EDITOR
Rebecca Anderson

COPY EDITOR
Sadie Kleinman

EDITORIAL DIRECTOR
Robyn B. Siesky

EDITORIAL MANAGER
Mary Beth Wakefield

ASSOCIATE DIRECTOR OF MARKETING
David Mayhew

PRODUCTION MANAGER
Tim Tate

VICE PRESIDENT AND EXECUTIVE GROUP PUBLISHER
Richard Swadley

VICE PRESIDENT AND EXECUTIVE PUBLISHER
Barry Pruett

ASSOCIATE PUBLISHER
Jim Minatel

PROJECT COORDINATOR, COVER
Lynsey Stanford

PROOFREADER
Kyle Schlesinger, Word One

INDEXER
Robert Swanson

COVER IMAGE
© Linda Bucklin/istockphoto

COVER DESIGNER
Michael E. Trent

ACKNOWLEDGMENTS

Most importantly I'd like to thank Kristy. Your support makes everything I do possible, and your generous help ensured that this book was the best it could be. Without you it would never have happened.

A big thank-you goes to Google and the Android team, particularly the Android engineers and my colleagues in developer relations. The pace at which Android has grown and developed in the past year is nothing short of phenomenal.

I also thank Scott Meyers for giving me the chance to bring this book up to date; and Bill Bridges, Milan Shah, Sadie Kleinman, and the Wrox team for helping get it done.

Special thanks go out to the Android developer community. Your hard work and exciting applications have helped make Android a great success.

CONTENTS

INTRODUCTION

Now is an exciting time for mobile developers. Mobile phones have never been more popular, and powerful smartphones are now a popular choice for consumers. Stylish and versatile phones packing hardware features like GPS, accelerometers, and touch screens, combined with fixed-rate, reasonably priced data plans provide an enticing platform upon which to create innovative mobile applications.

A host of Android handsets are now available to tempt consumers, including phones with QVGA screens and powerful WVGA devices like the Motorola Droid and the Google Nexus One. The real win though, is for developers. With much existing mobile development built on proprietary operating systems that restrict the development and deployment of third-party applications, Android offers an open alternative. Without artificial barriers, Android developers are free to write applications that take full advantage of increasingly powerful mobile hardware and distribute them in an open market.

As a result, developer interest in Android devices has exploded as handset sales have continued to grow. In 2009 and the early parts of 2010 more than 20 Android handsets have been released from OEMs including HTC, Motorola, LG, Samsung, and Sony Ericsson. Android devices are now available in over 26 countries on more than 32 carriers. In the United States, Android devices are available on all four major carriers: T-Mobile, Verizon, AT&T, and Sprint. Additionally, you can now buy the unlocked Google Nexus One handset directly from Google at `http://www.google.com/phone`.

Built on an open source framework, and featuring powerful SDK libraries and an open philosophy, Android has opened mobile phone development to thousands of developers who haven't had access to tools for building mobile applications. Experienced mobile developers can now expand into the Android platform, leveraging the unique features to enhance existing products or create innovative new ones.

Using the Android Market for distribution, developers can take advantage of an open marketplace, with no review process, for distributing free and paid apps to all compatible Android devices.

This book is a hands-on guide to building mobile applications using version 2 of the Android software development kit. Chapter by chapter, it takes you through a series of sample projects, each introducing new features and techniques to get the most out of Android. It covers all the basic functionality as well as exploring the advanced features through concise and useful examples.

Google's philosophy is to release early and iterate often. Since Android's first full release in October 2008, there have been seven platform and SDK releases. With such a rapid release cycle, there are likely to be regular changes and improvements to the software and development libraries. While the Android engineering team has worked hard to ensure backwards compatibility, future releases are likely to date some of the information provided in this book.

Nonetheless, the explanations and examples included here will give you the grounding and knowledge needed to write compelling mobile applications using the current SDK, along with the flexibility to quickly adapt to future enhancements.

WHOM THIS BOOK IS FOR

This book is for anyone interested in creating applications for the Android mobile phone platform using the SDK. It includes information that will be valuable, whether you're an experienced mobile developer or you're making your first foray, via Android, into writing mobile applications.

It will help if readers have used mobile phones (particularly phones running Android), but it's not necessary, nor is prior experience in mobile phone development. It's expected that you'll have some experience in software development and be familiar with basic development practices. While knowledge of Java is helpful, it's not a necessity.

Chapters 1 and 2 introduce mobile development and contain instructions to get you started in Android. Beyond that, there's no requirement to read the chapters in order, although a good understanding of the core components described in Chapters 3 through 7 is important before you venture into the remaining chapters. Chapters 8 through 15 cover a variety of optional and advanced functionality and can be read in whatever order interest or need dictates.

WHAT THIS BOOK COVERS

Chapter 1 introduces Android, including what it is and how it fits into existing mobile development. What Android offers as a development platform and why it's an exciting opportunity for creating mobile phone applications are then examined in greater detail.

Chapter 2 covers some best practices for mobile development and explains how to download the Android SDK and start developing applications. It also introduces the Android developer tools and demonstrates how to create new applications from scratch.

Chapters 3 through 7 take an in-depth look at the fundamental Android application components. Starting with examining the pieces that make up an Android application and its life cycle, you'll quickly move on to the application manifest and external resources before learning about Activities, their lifetimes, and their life cycles.

You'll then learn how to create user interfaces with layouts and Views, before being introduced to the Intent mechanism used to perform actions and send messages between application components. Internet resources are then covered before a detailed look at data storage, retrieval, and sharing. You'll start with the preference-saving mechanism before moving on to file handling and databases. This section finishes with a look at sharing application data using Content Providers.

Chapters 8 to 14 look at more advanced topics. Starting with maps and location-based services, you'll move on to Services, background Threads, and using Notifications.

Next you'll learn how your applications can interact with the user directly from the home screen using widgets, live folders, Live Wallpaper, and the quick search box. After looking at playing and recording multimedia, and using the camera, you'll be introduced to Android's communication abilities.

The telephony API will be examined as well as the APIs used to send and receive SMS messages before going on to Bluetooth and network management (both Wi-Fi and mobile data connections).

Chapter 14 examines the sensor APIs, demonstrating how to use the compass, accelerometers, and other hardware sensors to let your application react to its environment.

Chapter 15 includes several advanced development topics, among them security, IPC, advanced graphics techniques, and user–hardware interactions.

HOW THIS BOOK IS STRUCTURED

This book is structured in a logical sequence to help readers of different development backgrounds learn how to write advanced Android applications.

There's no requirement to read each chapter sequentially, but several of the sample projects are developed over the course of several chapters, adding new functionality and other enhancements at each stage.

Experienced mobile developers with a working Android development environment can skim the first two chapters — which are an introduction to mobile development and instructions for creating your development environment — and dive in at Chapters 3 to 7. These cover the fundamentals of Android development, so it's important to have a solid understanding of the concepts they describe. With this covered, you can move on to the remaining chapters, which look at maps, location-based services, background applications, and more advanced topics such as hardware interaction and networking.

WHAT YOU NEED TO USE THIS BOOK

To use the code samples in this book, you will need to create an Android development environment by downloading the Android SDK, developer tools, and the Java development kit. You may also wish to download and install Eclipse and the Android Developer Tool plug-in to ease your development, but neither is a requirement.

Android development is supported in Windows, MacOS, and Linux, with the SDK available from the Android web site.

You do not need an Android device to use this book or develop Android applications.

 Chapter 2 outlines these requirements in more detail as well as describing where to download and how to install each component.

CONVENTIONS

To help you get the most from the text and keep track of what's happening, I've used various conventions throughout the book.

 Notes, tips, hints, tricks, and asides to the current discussion are offset and placed in italics like this.

As for styles in the text:

➤ I show URLs and code within the text like so: `persistence.properties`.

➤ To help readability, class names in text are often represented using a regular font but capitalized like so:

Content Provider

➤ I present code in two different ways:

```
I use a monofont type with no highlighting for most code examples.
I use bold highlighting to emphasize code that's particularly important
in the present context.
```

➤ In some code samples, you'll see lines marked as follows:

```
[ ... previous code goes here ... ]
```

or

```
[ ... implement something here ... ]
```

This represents an instruction to replace the entire line (including the square brackets) with actual code, either from a previous code snippet in the former case, or your own implementation in the latter.

➤ To keep the code sample reasonably concise, I have not always included every `import` statement required in the code samples. The downloadable code samples described below include all the required `import` statements.

SOURCE CODE

As you work through the examples in this book, you may choose either to type in all the code manually or to use the source code files that accompany the book. All the source code used in this book is available for download at `www.wrox.com`. Once at the site, simply locate the book's title (either by using the Search box or by using one of the title lists), and click the Download Code link on the book's detail page to obtain all the source code for the book.

> *Because many books have similar titles, you may find it easiest to search by ISBN; this book's ISBN is 978-0-470-56552-0.*

Once you download the code, just decompress it with your favorite decompression tool. Alternatively, you can go to the main Wrox code download page at `www.wrox.com/dynamic/books/download.aspx` to see the code available for this book and all other Wrox books.

ERRATA

We make every effort to ensure that there are no errors in the text or in the code. However, no one is perfect, and mistakes do occur. If you find an error in one of our books, like a spelling mistake or faulty piece of code, we would be very grateful for your feedback. By sending in errata you may save another reader hours of frustration, and at the same time you will be helping us provide even higher quality information.

To find the errata page for this book, go to www.wrox.com and locate the title using the Search box or one of the title lists. Then, on the book details page, click the Book Errata link. On this page, you can view all errata that have been submitted for this book and posted by Wrox editors. A complete book list including links to each book's errata is also available at www.wrox.com/misc-pages/booklist .shtml.

If you don't spot "your" error on the Book Errata page, go to www.wrox.com/contact/techsupport .shtml and complete the form there to send us the error you have found. We'll check the information and, if appropriate, post a message to the book's Errata page and fix the problem in subsequent editions of the book.

P2P.WROX.COM

For author and peer discussion, join the P2P forums at p2p.wrox.com. The forums are a web-based system for you to post messages relating to Wrox books and related technologies and interact with other readers and technology users. The forums offer a subscription feature to e-mail you topics of interest of your choosing when new posts are made to the forums. Wrox authors, editors, other industry experts, and your fellow readers are present on these forums.

At http://p2p.wrox.com, you will find a number of different forums that will help you not only as you read this book, but also as you develop your own applications. To join the forums, just follow these steps:

1. Go to p2p.wrox.com and click the Register link.
2. Read the terms of use and click Agree.
3. Complete the required information to join as well as any optional information you wish to provide, and click Submit.
4. You will receive an e-mail with information describing how to verify your account and complete the joining process.

 You can read messages in the forums without joining P2P, but in order to post your own messages, you must join.

Once you join, you can post new messages and respond to messages other users post. You can read messages at any time on the Web. If you would like to have new messages from a particular forum e-mailed to you, click the "Subscribe to This Forum" icon by the forum name in the forum listing.

For more information about how to use the Wrox P2P, be sure to read the P2P FAQs for answers to questions about how the forum software works as well as many common questions specific to P2P and Wrox books. To read the FAQs, click the FAQ link on any P2P page.

1

Hello, Android

WHAT'S IN THIS CHAPTER?

➤ A background to mobile application development

➤ What Android is (and what it isn't)

➤· An introduction to the Android SDK features

➤ What devices Android runs on

➤ Why develop for mobile and Android?

➤ An introduction to the SDK and the Android development framework

Whether you're an experienced mobile engineer, a desktop or web developer, or a complete programming novice, Android represents an exciting new opportunity to write innovative applications for mobile devices.

Despite the name, Android will not help you create an unstoppable army of emotionless robot warriors on a relentless quest to cleanse the earth of the scourge of humanity. Instead, Android is an open-source software stack that includes the operating system, middleware, and key mobile applications along with a set of API libraries for writing mobile applications that can shape the look, feel, and function of mobile handsets.

Small, stylish, and versatile, modern mobile devices have become powerful tools that incorporate cameras, media players, GPS systems, and touchscreens. As technology has evolved, mobile phones have become about more than simply making calls, but their software and development platforms have struggled to keep pace.

Until recently, mobile phones were largely closed environments built on highly fragmented, proprietary operating systems that required proprietary development tools. The phones themselves often prioritized native applications over those written by third parties. This has introduced an artificial barrier for developers hoping to build on increasingly powerful mobile hardware.

In Android, native and third-party applications are written with the same APIs and executed on the same run time. These APIs feature hardware sensor access, video recording, location-based services, support for background services, map-based activities, relational databases, inter-application communication, and 2D and 3D graphics.

Using this book, you will learn how to use these APIs to create your own Android applications. In this chapter you'll learn some mobile development guidelines and be introduced to the features available from the Android development platform.

Android has powerful APIs, excellent documentation, a thriving developer community, and no development or distribution costs. As mobile devices continue to increase in popularity, this is an exciting opportunity to create innovative mobile phone applications no matter what your development experience.

A LITTLE BACKGROUND

In the days before Twitter and Facebook, when Google was still a twinkle in its founders' eyes and dinosaurs roamed the earth, mobile phones were just that — portable phones small enough to fit inside a briefcase, featuring batteries that could last up to several hours. They did however offer the freedom to make calls without being physically connected to a landline.

Increasingly small, stylish, and powerful mobile phones are now as ubiquitous as they are indispensable. Hardware advancements have made mobiles smaller and more efficient while including an increasing number of peripherals.

After first getting cameras and media players, mobiles now include GPS systems, accelerometers, and touch screens. While these hardware innovations should prove fertile ground for software development, the applications available for mobile phones have generally lagged behind the hardware.

The Not-So-Distant Past

Historically, developers, generally coding in low-level C or C++, have needed to understand the specific hardware they were coding for, generally a single device or possibly a range of devices from a single manufacturer. As hardware technology and mobile Internet access has advanced, this closed approach has become outmoded.

More recently, platforms like Symbian have been created to provide developers with a wider target audience. These systems have proven more successful in encouraging mobile developers to provide rich applications that better leverage the hardware available.

These platforms offer some access to the device hardware, but require the developer to write complex C/C++ code and make heavy use of proprietary APIs that are notoriously difficult to work with. This difficulty is amplified for applications that must work on different hardware implementations and those that make use of a particular hardware feature, like GPS.

In more recent years, the biggest advance in mobile phone development was the introduction of Java-hosted MIDlets. MIDlets are executed on a Java virtual machine, a process that abstracts the underlying hardware and lets developers create applications that run on the wide variety of devices that supports the Java run time. Unfortunately, this convenience comes at the price of restricted access to the device hardware.

In mobile development it was considered normal for third-party applications to receive different hardware access and execution rights from those given to native applications written by the phone manufacturers, with MIDlets often receiving few of either.

The introduction of Java MIDlets expanded developers' audiences, but the lack of low-level hardware access and sandboxed execution meant that most mobile applications are regular desktop programs or web sites designed to render on a smaller screen, and do not take advantage of the inherent mobility of the handheld platform.

The Future

Android sits alongside a new wave of mobile operating systems designed for increasingly powerful mobile hardware. Windows Mobile, the Apple iPhone, and the Palm Pre now provide a richer, simplified development environment for mobile applications. However, unlike Android, they're built on proprietary operating systems that in some cases prioritize native applications over those created by third parties, restrict communication among applications and native phone data, and restrict or control the distribution of third-party apps to their platforms.

Android offers new possibilities for mobile applications by offering an open development environment built on an open-source Linux kernel. Hardware access is available to all applications through a series of API libraries, and application interaction, while carefully controlled, is fully supported.

In Android, all applications have equal standing. Third-party and native Android applications are written with the same APIs and are executed on the same run time. Users can remove and replace any native application with a third-party developer alternative; even the dialer and home screens can be replaced.

WHAT IT ISN'T

As a disruptive addition to a mature field, it's not hard to see why there has been some confusion about what exactly Android is. Android is **not**:

➤ **A Java ME implementation** Android applications are written in the Java language, but they are not run within a Java ME virtual machine, and Java-compiled classes and executables will not run natively in Android.

➤ **Part of the Linux Phone Standards Forum (LiPS) or the Open Mobile Alliance (OMA)** Android runs on an open-source Linux kernel, but, while their goals are similar, Android's complete software stack approach goes further than the focus of these standards-defining organizations.

➤ **Simply an application layer (like UIQ or S60)** While Android does include an application layer, "Android" also describes the entire software stack encompassing the underlying operating system, the API libraries, and the applications themselves.

➤ **A mobile phone handset** Android includes a reference design for mobile handset manufacturers, but there is no single "Android phone." Instead, Android has been designed to support many alternative hardware devices.

➤ **Google's answer to the iPhone** The iPhone is a fully proprietary hardware and software platform released by a single company (Apple), while Android is an open-source software stack produced and supported by the Open Handset Alliance and designed to operate on any handset that meets the requirements. Google has now released its first direct-to-consumer handset, the Nexus 1, but this device remains simply one hardware implementation running on the Android platform.

ANDROID: AN OPEN PLATFORM FOR MOBILE DEVELOPMENT

Google's Andy Rubin describes Android as:

> *The first truly open and comprehensive platform for mobile devices, all of the software to run a mobile phone but without the proprietary obstacles that have hindered mobile innovation. (http://googleblog.blogspot.com/2007/11/ wheres-my-gphone.html)*

Put simply, Android is a combination of three components:

➤ A free, open-source operating system for mobile devices

➤ An open-source development platform for creating mobile applications

➤ Devices, particularly mobile phones, that run the Android operating system and the applications created for it

More specifically, Android is made up of several necessary and dependent parts, including the following:

➤ A hardware reference design that describes the capabilities required for a mobile device to support the software stack.

➤ A Linux operating system kernel that provides low-level interface with the hardware, memory management, and process control, all optimized for mobile devices.

➤ Open-source libraries for application development, including SQLite, WebKit, OpenGL, and a media manager.

➤ A run time used to execute and host Android applications, including the Dalvik virtual machine and the core libraries that provide Android-specific functionality. The run time is designed to be small and efficient for use on mobile devices.

➤ An application framework that agnostically exposes system services to the application layer, including the window manager and location manager, content providers, telephony, and sensors.

➤ A user interface framework used to host and launch applications.

➤ Preinstalled applications shipped as part of the stack.

➤ A software development kit used to create applications, including tools, plug-ins, and documentation.

What really makes Android compelling is its open philosophy, which ensures that you can fix any deficiencies in user interface or native application design by writing an extension or replacement. Android provides you, as a developer, with the opportunity to create mobile phone interfaces and applications designed to look, feel, and function exactly as you imagine them.

NATIVE ANDROID APPLICATIONS

Android phones will normally come with a suite of generic preinstalled applications that are part of the Android Open Source Project (AOSP), including, but not necessarily limited to:

- ➤ An e-mail client
- ➤ An SMS management application
- ➤ A full PIM (personal information management) suite including a calendar and contacts list
- ➤ A WebKit-based web browser
- ➤ A music player and picture gallery
- ➤ A camera and video recording application
- ➤ A calculator
- ➤ The home screen
- ➤ An alarm clock

In many cases Android devices will also ship with the following proprietary Google mobile applications:

- ➤ The Android Market client for downloading third-party Android applications
- ➤ A fully-featured mobile Google Maps application including StreetView, driving directions and turn-by-turn navigation, satellite view, and traffic conditions
- ➤ The Gmail mail client
- ➤ The Google Talk instant-messaging client
- ➤ The YouTube video player

The data stored and used by many of these native applications — like contact details — are also available to third-party applications. Similarly, your applications can handle events such as incoming calls or new SMS messages.

The exact makeup of the applications available on new Android phones is likely to vary based on the hardware manufacturer and/or the phone carrier or distributor.

The open-source nature of Android means that carriers and OEMs can customize the user interface and the applications bundled with each Android device. Several OEMs have done this, including HTC with the Sense UI, Motorola with MotoBlur, and Sony Ericsson's custom UI.

It's important to note that for compatible devices, the underlying platform and SDK remain consistent across OEM and carrier variations. The look and feel of the user interface may vary, but your applications will function in the same way across all compatible Android devices.

ANDROID SDK FEATURES

The true appeal of Android as a development environment lies in the APIs it provides.

As an application-neutral platform, Android gives you the opportunity to create applications that are as much a part of the phone as anything provided out of the box. The following list highlights some of the most noteworthy Android features:

- ➤ No licensing, distribution, or development fees or release approval processes
- ➤ Wi-Fi hardware access
- ➤ GSM, EDGE, and 3G networks for telephony or data transfer, enabling you to make or receive calls or SMS messages, or to send and retrieve data across mobile networks
- ➤ Comprehensive APIs for location-based services such as GPS
- ➤ Full multimedia hardware control, including playback and recording with the camera and microphone
- ➤ APIs for using sensor hardware, including accelerometers and the compass
- ➤ Libraries for using Bluetooth for peer-to-peer data transfer
- ➤ IPC message passing
- ➤ Shared data stores
- ➤ Background applications and processes
- ➤ Home-screen Widgets, Live Folders, and Live Wallpaper
- ➤ The ability to integrate application search results into the system search
- ➤ An integrated open-source HTML5 WebKit-based browser
- ➤ Full support for applications that integrate map controls as part of their user interface
- ➤ Mobile-optimized hardware-accelerated graphics, including a path-based 2D graphics library and support for 3D graphics using OpenGL ES 2.0
- ➤ Media libraries for playing and recording a variety of audio/video or still image formats
- ➤ Localization through a dynamic resource framework
- ➤ An application framework that encourages reuse of application components and the replacement of native applications

Access to Hardware, Including Camera, GPS, and Accelerometer

Android includes API libraries to simplify development involving the device hardware. These ensure that you don't need to create specific implementations of your software for different devices, so you can create Android applications that work as expected on any device that supports the Android software stack.

The Android SDK includes APIs for location-based hardware (such as GPS), the camera, audio, network connections, Wi-Fi, Bluetooth, accelerometers, the touchscreen, and power management. You can explore the possibilities of some of Android's hardware APIs in more detail in Chapters 11 through 14.

Native Google Maps, Geocoding, and Location-Based Services

Native map support lets you create a range of map-based applications that leverage the mobility of Android devices. Android lets you create activities that include interactive Google Maps as part of your user interface, with full access to maps that you can control programmatically and annotate using Android's rich graphics library.

Android's location-based services manage technologies like GPS and Google's GSM cell-based location technology to determine the device's current position. These services enforce an abstraction from specific location-detecting technology and let you specify minimum requirements (e.g., accuracy or cost) rather than choosing a particular technology. They also mean that your location-based applications will work no matter what technology the host handset supports.

To combine maps with locations, Android includes an API for forward and reverse geocoding that lets you find map coordinates for an address, and the address of a map position.

You'll learn the details of using maps, the Geocoder, and location-based services in Chapter 8.

Background Services

Android supports applications and services designed to run invisibly in the background.

Modern mobiles are by nature multifunction devices; however, their limited screen sizes means that generally only one interactive application can be visible at any time. Platforms that don't support background execution limit the viability of applications that don't need your constant attention.

Background services make it possible to create invisible application components that perform automatic processing without direct user action. Background execution allows your applications to become event-driven and to support regular updates, which is perfect for monitoring game scores or market prices, generating location-based alerts, or prioritizing and prescreening incoming calls and SMS messages.

Learn more about how to get the most out of background services in Chapter 9.

SQLite Database for Data Storage and Retrieval

Rapid and efficient data storage and retrieval are essential for a device whose storage capacity is limited by its compact nature.

Android provides a lightweight relational database for each application using SQLite. Your applications can take advantage of this managed relational database engine to store data securely and efficiently.

By default each application database is *sandboxed* — its content is available only to the application that created it — but Content Providers supply a mechanism for the managed sharing of these application databases.

Databases and Content Providers are covered in detail in Chapter 7.

Shared Data and Interapplication Communication

Android includes three techniques for transmitting information from your applications for use elsewhere: Notifications, Intents, and Content Providers.

Notifications are the standard means by which a mobile device traditionally alerts users. Using the API you can trigger audible alerts, cause vibration, and flash the device's LED, as well as control status bar notification icons, as shown in Chapter 9.

Intents provide a mechanism for message-passing within and between applications. Using Intents you can broadcast a desired action (such as dialing the phone or editing a contact) system-wide for other applications to handle. Intents are an important core component of Android and are covered in depth in Chapter 5.

Finally, you can use *Content Providers* to give managed access to your application's private databases. The data stores for native applications, such as the contact manager, are exposed as Content Providers so you can create your own applications that read or modify this data. Chapter 7 covers Content Providers in detail, including the native providers, and demonstrates how to create and use providers of your own.

Using Widgets, Live Folders, and Live Wallpaper to Enhance the Home Screen

Widgets, Live Folders, and Live Wallpaper let you create dynamic application components that provide a window into your applications or offer useful and timely information directly on the home screen.

If you offer a way for users to interact with your application directly from the home screen, they get instant access to interesting information without needing to open an application, and you get a dynamic shortcut into your application.

You'll learn how to create application components for the home screen in Chapter 10.

Extensive Media Support and 2D/3D Graphics

Bigger screens and brighter, higher-resolution displays have helped make mobiles multimedia devices. To help you make the most of the hardware available, Android provides graphics libraries for 2D canvas drawing and 3D graphics with OpenGL.

Android also offers comprehensive libraries for handling still images, video, and audio files, including the MPEG4, H.264, MP3, AAC, AMR, JPG, PNG, and GIF formats.

2D and 3D graphics are covered in depth in Chapter 15, while Android media management libraries are covered in Chapter 11.

Optimized Memory and Process Management

Android's process and memory management is a little unusual. Like Java and .NET, Android uses its own run time and virtual machine to manage application memory. Unlike with either of these other frameworks, the Android run time also manages the process lifetimes. Android ensures application responsiveness by stopping and killing processes as necessary to free resources for higher-priority applications.

In this context, the highest priority is given to the application with which the user is interacting. Ensuring that your applications are prepared for a swift death but are still able to remain responsive, and to update or restart in the background if necessary, is an important consideration in an environment that does not allow applications to control their own lifetimes.

You will learn more about the Android application life cycle in Chapter 3.

INTRODUCING THE OPEN HANDSET ALLIANCE

The Open Handset Alliance (OHA) is a collection of more than 50 technology companies, including hardware manufacturers, mobile carriers, and software developers. Of particular note are the prominent mobile technology companies Motorola, HTC, T-Mobile, and Qualcomm. In their own words, the OHA represents the following:

> *A commitment to openness, a shared vision for the future, and concrete plans to make the vision a reality. To accelerate innovation in mobile and offer consumers a richer, less expensive, and better mobile experience.* (`http://www.openhandsetalliance.com/`)

The OHA hopes to deliver a better mobile software experience for consumers by providing the platform needed for innovative mobile development at a faster rate and with higher quality than existing platforms, without licensing fees for either software developers or handset manufacturers.

WHAT DOES ANDROID RUN ON?

The first Android mobile handset, the T-Mobile G1, was released in the United States in October 2008. By the end of 2009 over 20 Android-compatible handsets had been launched or announced in more than 26 countries on 32 different carrier networks.

Rather than being a mobile OS created for a single hardware implementation, Android is designed to support a large variety of hardware platforms, from WVGA phones with hard keyboards to QVGA devices with resistive touchscreens.

Beyond that, with no licensing fees or proprietary software, the cost to handset manufacturers for providing Android handsets, and potentially other Android-powered devices, is comparatively low. Many people now expect that the advantages of Android as a platform for creating powerful applications will encourage device manufacturers to produce increasingly tailored hardware.

WHY DEVELOP FOR MOBILE?

In market terms, the emergence of modern mobile smartphones and *superphones* — multifunction devices including a phone but featuring a full-featured web browser, cameras, media players, Wi-Fi, and location-based services — has fundamentally changed the way people interact with their mobile devices and access the Internet. Mobile-phone ownership easily surpasses computer ownership in many countries; 2009 marked the year that more people accessed the Internet for the first time from a mobile phone rather than a PC.

The increasing popularity of modern smartphones, combined with the increasing availability of flat-rate, affordable data plans and Wi-Fi, has created a growth market for advanced mobile applications.

The ubiquity of mobile phones, and our attachment to them, makes them a fundamentally different platform for development from PCs. With a microphone, a camera, a touchscreen, location detection, and environmental sensors, a phone can effectively become an extension of your own perceptions.

With the average Android user installing and using around 40 apps, mobile applications have changed the way people use their phones. This gives you, the application developer, a unique opportunity to create dynamic, compelling new applications that become a vital part of people's lives.

WHY DEVELOP FOR ANDROID?

If you have a background in mobile application development, you don't need me to tell you that:

➤ A lot of what you can do with Android is already possible.

➤ But doing it is painful.

Android represents a clean break, a mobile framework based on the reality of modern mobile devices designed by developers, for developers.

With a simple and powerful SDK, no licensing fees, excellent documentation, and a thriving developer community, Android represents an excellent opportunity to create software that changes how and why people use their mobile phones.

From a commercial perspective Android:

➤ Requires no certification for becoming an Android developer

➤ Provides the Android Market for distribution and monetization of your applications

➤ Has no approval process for application distribution

➤ Gives you total control over your brand and access to the user's home screen

What Has and Will Continue to Drive Android Adoption?

Android is targeted primarily at developers, with Google and the OHA betting that the way to deliver better mobile software to consumers is to make it easier for developers to write it themselves.

As a development platform, Android is powerful and intuitive, letting developers who have never programmed for mobile devices create useful applications quickly and easily. It's easy to see how innovative Android applications could create demand for the devices necessary to run them, particularly if developers write applications for Android because they *can't* write them for other platforms.

Open access to the nuts and bolts of the underlying system is what's always driven software development and platform adoption. The Internet's inherent openness and neutrality have seen it become the platform for a multibillion-dollar industry within 10 years of its inception. Before that, it was open systems like Linux and the powerful APIs provided as part of the Windows operating system that enabled the explosion in personal computers and the movement of computer programming from the arcane to the mainstream.

This openness and power ensure that anyone with the inclination can bring a vision to life at minimal cost.

What Does It Have That Others Don't?

Many of the features listed previously, such as 3D graphics and native database support, are also available in other mobile SDKs. Here are some of the unique features that set Android apart:

➤ **Google Map applications** Google Maps for Mobile has been hugely popular, and Android offers a Google Map as an atomic, reusable control for use in your applications. The Map View lets you display, manipulate, and annotate a Google Map within your Activities to build map-based applications using the familiar Google Maps interface.

➤ **Background services and applications** Background services let you create an application that uses an event-driven model, working silently while other applications are being used or while your mobile sits ignored until it rings, flashes, or vibrates to get your attention. Maybe it's a streaming music player, an application that tracks the stock market, alerting you to significant changes in your portfolio, or a service that changes your ringtone or volume depending on your current location, the time of day, and the identity of the caller.

➤ **Shared data and interprocess communication** Using Intents and Content Providers, Android lets your applications exchange messages, perform processing, and share data. You can also use these mechanisms to leverage the data and functionality provided by the native Android applications. To mitigate the risks of such an open strategy, each application's process, data storage, and files are private unless explicitly shared with other applications via a full permission-based security mechanism detailed in Chapter 15.

➤ **All applications are created equal** Android doesn't differentiate between native applications and those developed by third parties. This gives consumers unprecedented power to change the look and feel of their devices by letting them completely replace every native application with a third-party alternative that has access to the same underlying data and hardware.

➤ **Home-screen Widgets, Live Folders, Live Wallpaper, and the quick search box** Using Widgets, Live Folders, and Live Wallpaper, you can create windows into your application from the phone's home screen. The quick search box lets you integrate search results from your application directly into the phone's search functionality.

Changing the Mobile Development Landscape

Existing mobile development platforms have created an aura of exclusivity around mobile development. Whether by design or as a side effect of the cost, complexity, or necessity for approval involved in developing native applications, many mobile phones remain almost exactly as they were when first purchased.

In contrast, Android allows, even encourages, radical change. As consumer devices, Android handsets ship with a core set of the standard applications that consumers demand on a new phone, but the real power lies in users' ability to completely change how their devices look, feel, and function.

Android gives developers a great opportunity. All Android applications are a native part of the phone, not just software that's run in a sandbox on top of it. Rather than writing small-screen versions of software that can be run on low-power devices, you can now write mobile applications that change the way people use their phones.

While Android will still have to compete with existing and future mobile development platforms as an open-source developer framework, the strength of the development kit is very much in its favor. Certainly its free and open approach to mobile application development, with total access to the phone's resources, is a giant step in the right direction.

INTRODUCING THE DEVELOPMENT FRAMEWORK

With the PR job done, it's time to look at how you can start developing applications for Android. Android applications are written with Java as a programming language but executed by means of a custom virtual machine called Dalvik rather than a traditional Java VM.

Later in this chapter you'll be introduced to the framework, starting with a technical explanation of the Android software stack, a look at what's included in the SDK, an introduction to the Android libraries, and a look at the Dalvik virtual machine.

Each Android application runs in a separate process within its own Dalvik instance, relinquishing all responsibility for memory and process management to the Android run time, which stops and kills processes as necessary to manage resources.

Dalvik and the Android run time sit on top of a Linux kernel that handles low-level hardware interaction, including drivers and memory management, while a set of APIs provides access to all the underlying services, features, and hardware.

What Comes in the Box

The Android software development kit (SDK) includes everything you need to start developing, testing, and debugging Android applications. Included in the SDK download are:

➤ **The Android APIs**   The core of the SDK is the Android API libraries that provide developer access to the Android stack. These are the same libraries used at Google to create native Android applications.

➤ **Development tools**   So you can turn Android source code into executable Android applications, the SDK includes several development tools that let you compile and debug your applications. You will learn more about the developer tools in Chapter 2.

➤ **The Android Virtual Device Manager and Emulator**   The Android Emulator is a fully interactive Android device emulator featuring several alternative skins. The emulator runs within an Android Virtual Device that simulates the device hardware configuration. Using the emulator you can see how your applications will look and behave on a real Android device. All Android applications run within the Dalvik VM, so the software emulator is an excellent environment — in fact, as it is hardware-neutral, it provides a better independent test environment than any single hardware implementation.

➤ **Full documentation**   The SDK includes extensive code-level reference information detailing exactly what's included in each package and class and how to use them. In addition to the code documentation, Android's reference documentation explains how to get started and gives detailed explanations of the fundamentals behind Android development.

➤ **Sample code**   The Android SDK includes a selection of sample applications that demonstrate some of the possibilities available with Android, as well as simple programs that highlight how to use individual API features.

➤ **Online support**   Android has rapidly generated a vibrant developer community. The Google Groups at `http://developer.android.com/resources/community-groups.html` are active forums of Android developers with regular input from the Android engineering and developer relations teams at Google. StackOverflow at `http://www.stackoverflow.com/questions/tagged/android` has also become a popular destination for Android questions.

For those using the popular Eclipse IDE, Android has released a special plug-in that simplifies project creation and tightly integrates Eclipse with the Android Emulator and debugging tools. The features of the ADT plug-in are covered in more detail in Chapter 2.

Understanding the Android Software Stack

The Android software stack is composed of the elements shown in Figure 1-1 and described in further detail after it. Put simply, a Linux kernel and a collection of C/C++ libraries are exposed through an application framework that provides services for, and management of, the run time and applications.

➤ **Linux kernel**   Core services (including hardware drivers, process and memory management, security, network, and power management) are handled by a Linux 2.6 kernel. The kernel also provides an abstraction layer between the hardware and the remainder of the stack.

➤ **Libraries**   Running on top of the kernel, Android includes various C/C++ core libraries such as libc and SSL, as well as:

  ➤ A media library for playback of audio and video media

  ➤ A surface manager to provide display management

  ➤ Graphics libraries that include SGL and OpenGL for 2D and 3D graphics

  ➤ SQLite for native database support

  ➤ SSL and WebKit for integrated web browser and Internet security

➤ **Android run time**   What makes an Android phone an Android phone rather than a mobile Linux implementation is the Android run time. Including the core libraries and the Dalvik virtual machine, the Android run time is the engine that powers your applications and, along with the libraries, forms the basis for the application framework.

  ➤ **Core libraries**   While Android development is done in Java, Dalvik is not a Java VM. The core Android libraries provide most of the functionality available in the core Java libraries as well as the Android-specific libraries.

  ➤ **Dalvik virtual machine**   Dalvik is a register-based virtual machine that's been optimized to ensure that a device can run multiple instances efficiently. It relies on the Linux kernel for threading and low-level memory management.

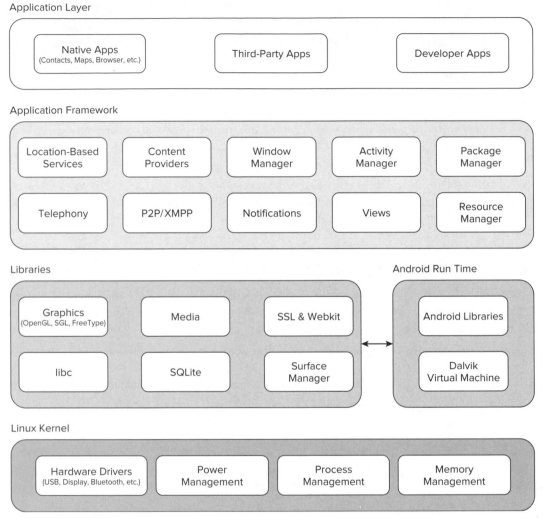

FIGURE 1-1

> ➤ **Application framework** The application framework provides the classes used to create Android applications. It also provides a generic abstraction for hardware access and manages the user interface and application resources.

> ➤ **Application layer** All applications, both native and third-party, are built on the application layer by means of the same API libraries. The application layer runs within the Android run time, using the classes and services made available from the application framework.

The Dalvik Virtual Machine

One of the key elements of Android is the Dalvik virtual machine. Rather than use a traditional Java virtual machine (VM) such as Java ME (Java Mobile Edition), Android uses its own custom VM designed to ensure that multiple instances run efficiently on a single device.

The Dalvik VM uses the device's underlying Linux kernel to handle low-level functionality including security, threading, and process and memory management. It's also possible to write C/C++ applications that run directly on the underlying Linux OS. While you *can* do this, in most cases there's no reason you should need to.

If the speed and efficiency of C/C++ is required for your application, Android now provides a Native Development Kit (NDK). The NDK is designed to enable you to create C++ libraries using the libc and libm libraries, along with native access to OpenGL.

This book focuses exclusively on writing applications that run within Dalvik using the SDK. If your inclinations run toward exploring the Linux kernel and C/C++ underbelly of Android, modifying Dalvik, or otherwise tinkering with things under the hood, check out the Android Internals Google Group at `http://groups.google.com/group/android-internals`

While use of the NDK is encouraged where needed, details of its use have not been included within this book.

All Android hardware and system service access is managed using Dalvik as a middle tier. By using a VM to host application execution, developers have an abstraction layer that ensures they never have to worry about a particular hardware implementation.

The Dalvik VM executes Dalvik executable files, a format optimized to ensure minimal memory footprint. You create .dex executables by transforming Java language compiled classes using the tools supplied within the SDK. You'll learn more about how to create Dalvik executables in the next chapter.

Android Application Architecture

Android's architecture encourages the concept of component reuse, enabling you to publish and share Activities, Services, and data with other applications, with access managed by the security restrictions you put in place.

The same mechanism that lets you produce a replacement contact manager or phone dialer can let you expose your application components to let other developers create new UI front ends and functionality extensions, or otherwise build on them.

The following application services are the architectural cornerstones of all Android applications, providing the framework you'll be using for your own software:

- ➤ **Activity Manager** Controls the life cycle of your Activities, including management of the Activity stack described in Chapter 3.

- ➤ **Views** Used to construct the user interfaces for your Activities, as described in Chapter 4.

- ➤ **Notification Manager** Provides a consistent and nonintrusive mechanism for signaling your users, as described in Chapter 9.

- ➤ **Content Providers** Let your applications share data, as described in Chapter 7.

- ➤ **Resource Manager** Supports non-code resources like strings and graphics to be externalized, as shown in Chapter 3.

Android Libraries

Android offers a number of APIs for developing your applications. Rather than list them all here, I refer you to the documentation at `http://developer.android.com/reference/packages.html`, which gives a complete list of packages included in the Android SDK.

Android is intended to target a wide range of mobile hardware, so be aware that the suitability and implementation of some of the advanced or optional APIs may vary depending on the host device.

SUMMARY

This chapter explained that despite significant advances in the hardware features available on modern mobile phones, the software has lagged. Hard-to-use development kits, hardware-specific APIs, and a lack of openness have stifled innovation in mobile software.

Android offers an opportunity for developers to create innovative software applications for mobile devices without the restrictions generally associated with the existing proprietary mobile development frameworks.

You were shown the complete Android software stack, which includes not only an application layer and development toolkit but also the Dalvik VM, a custom run time, core libraries, and a Linux kernel, all of which are available as open source.

You also learned:

➤ How handsets with an expanding range of hardware features have created demand for tools that give developers better access to these features.

➤ About some of the features available to developers using Android, including native map support, hardware access, background services, interprocess messaging, shared databases, and 2D and 3D graphics.

➤ That all Android applications are built equal, allowing users to completely replace one application, even a core native application, with another.

➤ That the Android SDK includes developer tools, APIs, and comprehensive documentation.

The next chapter will help you get started by downloading and installing the Android SDK and setting up an Android development environment in Eclipse.

You'll also learn how to use the Android developer tools plug-in to streamline development, testing, and debugging before creating your first Android application.

After learning about the building blocks of Android applications, you'll be introduced to the different types of applications you can create, and you'll start to understand some of the design considerations that should go into developing applications for mobile devices.

2

Getting Started

WHAT'S IN THIS CHAPTER?

➤ How to install the Android SDK, create a development environment, and debug your projects.

➤ Understanding mobile design considerations and the importance of optimizing for speed and efficiency and designing for small screens and mobile data connections.

➤ Using Android Virtual Devices, the emulator, and developer tools.

All you need to start writing your own Android applications is a copy of the Android SDK and the Java development kit. Unless you're a masochist, you'll probably want a Java IDE — Eclipse is particularly well supported — to make development a little easier.

Versions of the SDK, Java, and Eclipse are available for Windows, MacOS, and Linux, so you can explore Android from the comfort of whatever OS you favor. The SDK tools and emulator work on all three OS environments, and because Android applications are run on a virtual machine, there's no advantage to developing from any particular operating system.

Android code is written with Java syntax, and the core Android libraries include most of the features from the core Java APIs. Before they can be run, though, your projects must first be translated into Dalvik byte code. As a result, you get the benefits of using Java while your applications have the advantage of running on a virtual machine optimized for mobile devices.

The SDK download includes all the Android libraries, full documentation, and excellent sample applications. It also includes tools to help you write and debug your applications, like the Android Emulator to run your projects and the Dalvik Debug Monitoring Service (DDMS) to help debug them.

By the end of this chapter you'll have downloaded the Android SDK, set up your development environment, completed two new applications, and run and debugged them with the DDMS using the emulator running on an Android Virtual Device.

If you've developed for mobile devices before, you already know that their small-form factor, limited power, and restricted memory create some unique design challenges. Even if you're new to the game, it's obvious that some of the things you can take for granted on the desktop or the Web aren't going to work on a mobile.

As well as the hardware limitations, the user environment brings its own challenges. Mobile devices are used on the move and are often a distraction rather than the focus of attention, so your applications need to be fast, responsive, and easy to learn and use.

This chapter examines some of the best practices for writing mobile applications to help overcome the inherent hardware and environmental challenges. Rather than try to tackle the whole topic, we'll focus on using the Android SDK in a way that's consistent with good mobile design principles.

DEVELOPING FOR ANDROID

The Android SDK includes all the tools and APIs you need to write compelling and powerful mobile applications. The biggest challenge with Android, as with any new development toolkit, is learning the features and limitations of its APIs.

If you have experience in Java development you'll find that the techniques, syntax, and grammar you've been using will translate directly into Android, although some of the specific optimization techniques may seem counterintuitive.

If you don't have experience with Java but have used other object-oriented languages (such as C#), you should find the transition straightforward. The power of Android comes from its APIs, not from Java, so being unfamiliar with all the Java-specific classes won't be a big disadvantage.

What You Need to Begin

Because Android applications run within the Dalvik virtual machine, you can write them on any platform that supports the developer tools. This currently includes the following:

➤ Microsoft Windows (XP or later)

➤ Mac OS X 10.4.8 or later (Intel chips only)

➤ Linux

To get started, you'll need to download and install the following:

➤ The Android SDK

➤ Java Development Kit (JDK) 5 or 6

You can download the latest JDK from Sun at `http://java.sun.com/javase/downloads/index.jsp`

 If you already have a JDK installed, make sure that it meets the version requirements listed above, and note that the Java runtime environment (JRE) is not sufficient.

Downloading and Installing the SDK

The Android SDK is completely open. There's no cost to download or use the API, and Google doesn't charge (or require review) to distribute your finished programs on the Android Market or otherwise.

You can download the latest version of the SDK for your development platform from the Android development homepage at `http://developer.android.com/sdk/index.html`

 Unless otherwise noted, the version of the Android SDK used for writing this book was version 2.1 r1.

The SDK is presented as a ZIP file containing only the latest version of the Android developer tools. Install it by unzipping the SDK into a new folder. (Take note of this location, as you'll need it later.)

Before you can begin development you need to add at least one SDK Platform; do this on Windows by running the "SDK Setup.exe" executable, or on MacOS or Linux by running the "android" executable in the tools subfolder. In the screen that appears, select the "Available Packages" option on the left panel, and then select the SDK Platform versions you wish to install in the "Sources, Packages, and Archives" panel on the right. The selected platform will then be downloaded to your SDK installation folder and will contain the API libraries, documentation, and several sample applications.

The examples and step-by-step instructions provided are targeted at developers using Eclipse with the Android Developer Tool (ADT) plug-in. Neither is required, though — you can use any text editor or Java IDE you're comfortable with and use the developer tools in the SDK to compile, test, and debug the code snippets and sample applications.

If you're planning to use them, the next sections explain how to set up Eclipse and the ADT plug-in as your Android development environment. Later in the chapter we'll also take a closer look at the developer tools that come with the SDK, so if you'd prefer to develop without using Eclipse or the ADT plug-in you'll particularly want to check that out.

 The examples included in the SDK are well documented and are an excellent source for full, working examples of applications written for Android. Once you've finished setting up your development environment it's worth going through them.

Developing with Eclipse

Using Eclipse with the ADT plug-in for your Android development offers some significant advantages.

Eclipse is an open-source IDE (integrated development environment) particularly popular for Java development. It's available for download for each of the development platforms supported by Android (Windows, MacOS, and Linux) from the Eclipse foundation homepage: `www.eclipse.org/downloads/`

There are many variations available; the following is the recommended configuration for Android:

- ➤ Eclipse 3.4 or 3.5 (Galileo)
  - ➤ Eclipse JDT plug-in
  - ➤ WST

WST and the JDT plug-in are included in most Eclipse IDE packages.

Installing Eclipse consists of uncompressing the download into a new folder. When that's done, run the `eclipse` executable. When it starts for the first time, create a new workspace for your Android development projects.

Using the Eclipse Plug-In

The ADT plug-in for Eclipse simplifies your Android development by integrating the developer tools, including the emulator and .class-to-.dex converter, directly into the IDE. While you don't have to use the ADT plug-in, it does make creating, testing, and debugging your applications faster and easier.

The ADT plug-in integrates the following into Eclipse:

➤ An Android Project Wizard that simplifies creating new projects and includes a basic application template

➤ Forms-based manifest, layout, and resource editors to help create, edit, and validate your XML resources

➤ Automated building of Android projects, conversion to Android executables (`.dex`), packaging to package files (`.apk`), and installation of packages onto Dalvik virtual machines

➤ The Android Virtual Device manager, which lets you create and manage virtual devices hosting emulators that run a specific release of the Android OS and with set memory constraints

➤ The Android Emulator, including control of the emulator's appearance and network connection settings, and the ability to simulate incoming calls and SMS messages

➤ The Dalvik Debug Monitoring Service (DDMS), which includes port forwarding, stack, heap, and thread viewing, process details, and screen-capture facilities

➤ Access to the device or emulator's file system, enabling you to navigate the folder tree and transfer files

➤ Runtime debugging, so you can set breakpoints and view call stacks

➤ All Android/Dalvik log and console outputs

Figure 2-1 shows the DDMS perspective within Eclipse with the ADT plug-in installed.

Installing the ADT Plug-In

Install the developer tools plug-in by following these steps:

1. Select **Help ➪ Install New Software...** from within Eclipse.

2. In the resulting dialog box enter the following address into the **Work With** text entry box and press Enter: `https://dl-ssl.google.com/android/eclipse/`

3. Eclipse will now search for the ADT plug-in. When finished it will display the available plug-in, as shown in Figure 2-2. Select it by clicking the checkbox next to the Developer Tools root node, and click **Next**.

4. Eclipse will now download the plug-in. When it's finished, ensure both the Android DDMS and Android Developer Tools plug-ins are selected and click **Next**.

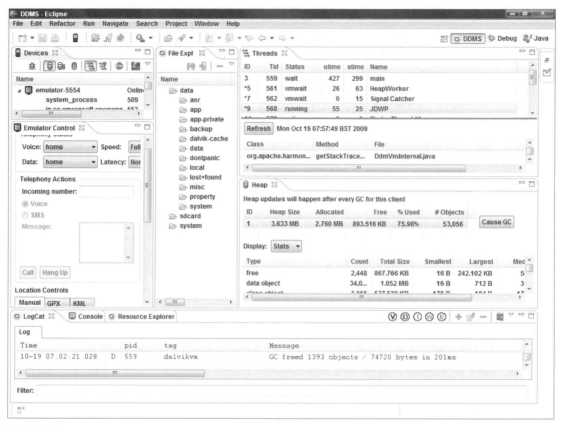

FIGURE 2-1

5. Read and then **Accept** the terms of the license agreement, and click **Next** and then **Finish**. As the ADT plug-in is not signed, you'll be prompted before the installation continues.

6. When installation is complete you'll have to restart Eclipse and update the ADT preferences. Restart and select **Window** ➪ **Preferences...** (or **Eclipse** ➪ **Preferences** for MacOS).

7. Then select **Android** from the left panel.

8. Click **Browse...** and navigate to the folder into which you unzipped the Android SDK; then click **Apply.** The list will then update to display each of the available SDK targets, as in Figure 2-3. Click **OK** to complete the SDK installation.

 If you download a new version of the SDK and place it in a different location, you will need to update this preference to reflect the SDK with which the ADT should be building.

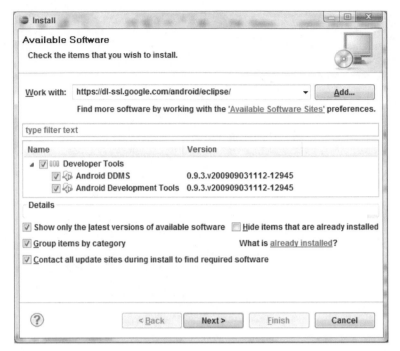

FIGURE 2-2

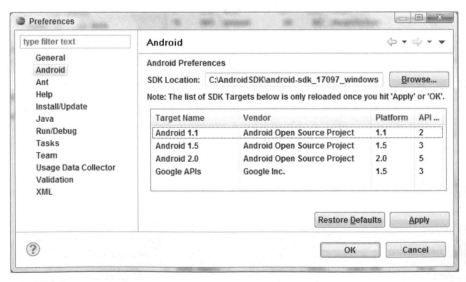

FIGURE 2-3

Updating the Plug-In

As the Android SDK matures, there are likely to be frequent updates to the ADT plug-in. In most cases, to update your plug-in you simply:

1. Navigate to **Help** ➪ **Check for Updates.**

2. If there are any ADT updates available, they will be presented. Simply select them and choose **Install.**

Sometimes a plug-in upgrade may be so significant that the dynamic update mechanism can't be used. In those cases you may have to remove the previous plug-in completely before installing the newer version as described in the previous section.

Creating Your First Android Application

You've downloaded the SDK, installed Eclipse, and plugged in the plug-in. You're now ready to start programming for Android. Start by creating a new project and setting up your Eclipse run and debug configurations.

Starting a New Android Project

To create a new Android project using the Android New Project Wizard, do the following:

1. Select **File** ➪ **New** ➪ **Project.**

2. Select the **Android Project** application type from the Android folder and click **Next.**

3. In the dialog that appears (shown in Figure 2-4), enter the details for your new project. The "Project name" is the name of your project file; the "Package name" specifies its java package; Create Activity lets you specify the name of a class that will be your initial Activity; and the "Application name" is the friendly name for your application. "Min SDK Version" lets you specify the minimum version of the SDK that your application will run on.

Selecting the minimum SDK version requires you to choose between gaining functionality provided in newer SDK releases and making your application available to a larger group of Android devices. Your application will be available from the Google Android Market on any device running the specified build or higher.

Android version 1.6 (Donut) is version 4 — at the time of going to print, the majority of Android devices were currently running at least version 4. The 2.0 (Eclair) SDK is version 5, while 2.1 is version 7.

4. When you've entered the details, click **Finish.**

FIGURE 2-4

If you selected **Create Activity** the ADT plug-in will create a new project that includes a class that extends `Activity`. Rather than being completely empty, the default template implements Hello World. Before modifying the project, take this opportunity to configure launch configurations for running and debugging.

Creating a Launch Configuration

Launch configurations let you specify runtime options for running and debugging applications. Using a launch configuration you can specify the following:

- ➤ The Project and Activity to launch
- ➤ The virtual device and emulator options to use
- ➤ Input/output settings (including console defaults)

You can specify different launch configurations for running and debugging applications. The following steps show how to create a launch configuration for an Android application:

1. Select **Run Configurations...** or **Debug Configurations...** from the **Run** menu.

2. Right-click **Android Application** on the project type list, and select **New**.

3. Enter a name for the configuration. You can create multiple configurations for each project, so create a descriptive title that will help you identify this particular setup.

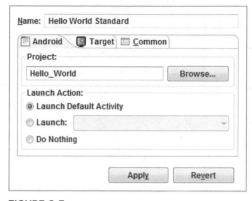

FIGURE 2-5

4. Now choose your start-up options. The first (**Android**) tab lets you select the project to run and the Activity that you want to start when you run (or debug) the application. Figure 2-5 shows the settings for the project you created earlier.

5. Use the **Target** tab shown in Figure 2-6 to select the default virtual device to launch on, or select manual to select a device or AVD each time. You can also configure the emulator's network connection settings and optionally wipe the user data and disable the boot animation when launching a virtual device. Using the command line textbox you can specify additional emulator start-up options if needed.

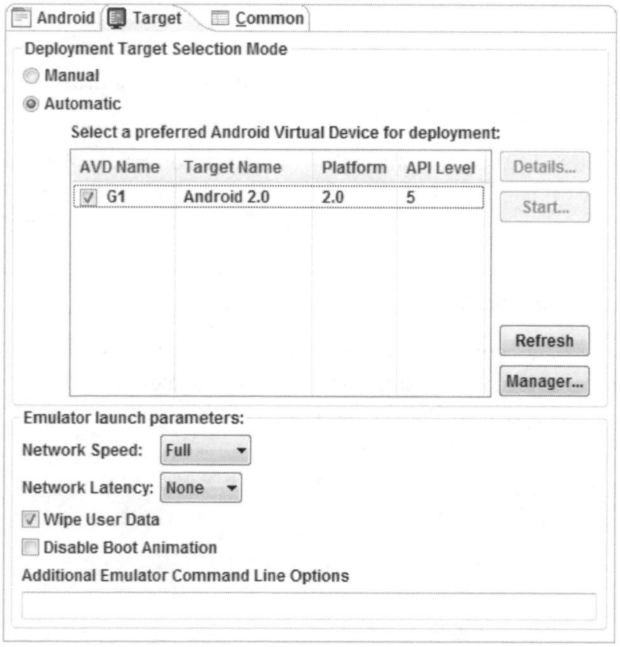

FIGURE 2-6

The Android SDK does not include a default virtual machine. You will need to create a virtual machine before you can run or debug your applications using the emulator. If the virtual device selection dialog in Figure 2-6 is empty, click **Manage...** *to open the SDK and Virtual Machine Manager and create one. The SDK and Virtual Machine Manager is described in more detail later in this chapter.*

6. Finally, set any additional properties in the **Common** tab.

7. Click **Apply**, and your launch configuration will be saved.

Running and Debugging Your Android Applications

You've created your first project and created the run and debug configurations for it. Before making any changes, test your installation and configurations by running and debugging the Hello World project.

From the **Run** menu select **Run** or **Debug** to launch the most recently selected configuration, or select **Run Configurations...** or **Debug Configurations...** to select a specific configuration to use.

If you're using the ADT plug-in, running or debugging your application does the following:

➤ Compiles the current project and converts it to an Android executable (.dex)

➤ Packages the executable and external resources into an Android package (.apk)

➤ Starts the selected virtual device (if you've selected an AVD and it's not already running)

➤ Installs your application onto the target device

➤ Starts your application

If you're debugging, the Eclipse debugger will then be attached, allowing you to set breakpoints and debug your code.

If everything is working correctly you'll see a new Activity running in the emulator, as shown in Figure 2-7.

Understanding Hello World

Let's take a step back and have a real look at your first Android application.

`Activity` is the base class for the visual, interactive components of your application; it is roughly equivalent to a Form in traditional desktop development. Listing 2-1 shows the skeleton code for an Activity-based class; note that it extends `Activity`, overriding the `onCreate` method.

LISTING 2-1: Hello World

```
package com.paad.helloworld;

import android.app.Activity;
import android.os.Bundle;
```

```
public class HelloWorld extends Activity {

  /** Called when the activity is first created. */
  @Override
  public void onCreate(Bundle savedInstanceState) {
    super.onCreate(savedInstanceState);
  }
}
```

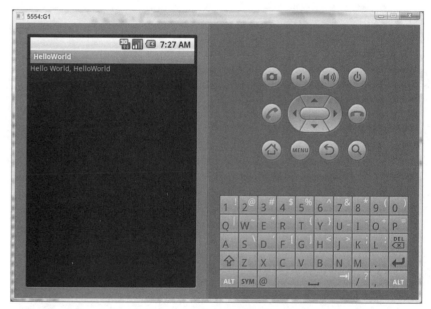

FIGURE 2-7

What's missing from this template is the layout of the visual interface. In Android, visual components are called *Views*, which are similar to controls in traditional desktop development.

The Hello World template created by the wizard overrides the onCreate method to call setContentView, which lays out the user interface by inflating a layout resource, as highlighted below:

```
@Override
public void onCreate(Bundle savedInstanceState) {
  super.onCreate(savedInstanceState);
  setContentView(R.layout.main);
}
```

The resources for an Android project are stored in the res folder of your project hierarchy, which includes drawable, layout, and values subfolders. The ADT plug-in interprets these resources to provide design-time access to them through the R variable, as described in Chapter 3.

Listing 2-2 shows the UI layout defined in the `main.xml` file created by the Android project template.

LISTING 2-2: Hello World layout resource

```xml
<?xml version="1.0" encoding="utf-8"?>
<LinearLayout xmlns:android="http://schemas.android.com/apk/res/android"
  android:orientation="vertical"
  android:layout_width="fill_parent"
  android:layout_height="fill_parent">
  <TextView
    android:layout_width="fill_parent"
    android:layout_height="wrap_content"
    android:text="Hello World, HelloWorld"
  />
</LinearLayout>
```

Defining your UI in XML and inflating it is the preferred way of implementing your user interfaces, as it neatly decouples your application logic from your UI design.

To get access to your UI elements in code, you add identifier attributes to them in the XML definition. You can then use the `findViewById` method to return a reference to each named item. The following XML snippet shows an ID attribute added to the Text View widget in the Hello World template:

```xml
<TextView
  android:id="@+id/myTextView"
  android:layout_width="fill_parent"
  android:layout_height="wrap_content"
  android:text="Hello World, HelloWorld"
/>
```

And the following snippet shows how to get access to it in code:

```java
TextView myTextView = (TextView)findViewById(R.id.myTextView);
```

Alternatively (although it's not generally considered good practice), you can create your layout directly in code, as shown in Listing 2-3.

LISTING 2-3: Creating layouts in code

```java
public void onCreate(Bundle savedInstanceState) {
    super.onCreate(savedInstanceState);

    LinearLayout.LayoutParams lp;
    lp = new LinearLayout.LayoutParams(LayoutParams.FILL_PARENT,
                                       LayoutParams.FILL_PARENT);

    LinearLayout.LayoutParams textViewLP;
    textViewLP = new LinearLayout.LayoutParams(LayoutParams.FILL_PARENT,
                                               LayoutParams.WRAP_CONTENT);

    LinearLayout ll = new LinearLayout(this);
    ll.setOrientation(LinearLayout.VERTICAL);

    TextView myTextView = new TextView(this);
    myTextView.setText("Hello World, HelloWorld");
```

```
        ll.addView(myTextView, textViewLP);
        this.addContentView(ll, lp);
    }
```

All the properties available in code can be set with attributes in the XML layout. As well as allowing easier substitution of layout designs and individual UI elements, keeping the visual design decoupled from the application code helps keep the code more concise.

You'll learn how to create complex layouts and about the Views used to populate them in Chapter 4.

Types of Android Applications

Most of the applications you create in Android will fall into one of the following categories:

➤   **Foreground**   An application that's useful only when it's in the foreground and is effectively suspended when it's not visible. Games and map mashups are common examples.

➤   **Background**   An application with limited interaction that, apart from when being configured, spends most of its lifetime hidden. Examples include call screening applications and SMS auto-responders.

➤   **Intermittent**   Expects some interactivity but does most of its work in the background. Often these applications will be set up and then run silently, notifying users when appropriate. A common example would be a media player.

➤   **Widget**   Some applications are represented only as a home-screen widget.

Complex applications are difficult to pigeonhole into a single category and usually include elements of each of these types. When creating your application you need to consider how it's likely to be used and then design it accordingly. Let's look more closely at some of the design considerations for each application type.

Foreground Applications

When creating foreground applications you need to carefully consider the Activity life cycle (described in Chapter 3) so that the Activity switches seamlessly between the foreground and the background.

Applications have little control over their life cycles, and a background application with no running Services is a prime candidate for cleanup by Android's resource management. This means that you need to save the state of the application when it is no longer in the foreground, to let you present the exact same state when it is brought to the front.

It's also particularly important for foreground applications to present a slick and intuitive user experience. You'll learn more about creating well-behaved and attractive foreground Activities in Chapters 3 and 4.

Background Services and Intent Receivers

These applications run silently in the background with very little user input. They often listen for messages or actions caused by the hardware, system, or other applications, rather than rely on user interaction.

It's possible to create completely invisible services, but in practice it's better form to provide at least some sort of user control. At a minimum you should let users confirm that the service is running and let them configure, pause, or terminate it as needed.

Services and Intent Receivers, the driving forces of background applications, are covered in depth in Chapters 5 and 9.

Intermittent Applications

Often you'll want to create an application that reacts to user input but is still useful when it's not active in the foreground. Chat and e-mail apps are typical examples. These applications are generally a union of visible Activities and invisible background Services.

Such an application needs to be aware of its state when interacting with the user. This might mean updating the Activity UI when it's visible and sending notifications to keep the user updated when it's in the background, as seen in the section on Notifications and Services in Chapter 9.

Widgets

In some circumstances your application may consist entirely of a widget component. Using widgets, described in detail in Chapter 10, you can create interactive visual components that users can add to their home screens.

Widget-only applications are commonly used to display dynamic information such as battery levels, weather forecasts, or the date and time.

DEVELOPING FOR MOBILE DEVICES

Android does a lot to simplify mobile-device software development, but it's still important to understand the reasons behind the conventions. There are several factors to account for when writing software for mobile and embedded devices, and when developing for Android in particular.

In this chapter you'll learn some of the techniques and best practices for writing efficient Android code. In later examples, efficiency is sometimes compromised for clarity and brevity when new Android concepts or functionality are introduced. In the best tradition of "Do as I say, not as I do," the examples you'll see are designed to show the simplest (or easiest-to-understand) way of doing something, not necessarily the best way of doing it.

Hardware-Imposed Design Considerations

Small and portable, mobile devices offer exciting opportunities for software development. Their limited screen size and reduced memory, storage, and processor power are far less exciting, and instead present some unique challenges.

Compared to desktop or notebook computers, mobile devices have relatively:

➤ Low processing power

➤ Limited RAM

➤ Limited permanent storage capacity

➤ Small screens with low resolution

➤ High costs associated with data transfer

➤ Slow data transfer rates with high latency

➤ Unreliable data connections

➤ Limited battery life

Each new generation of phones improves many of these restrictions. In particular, newer phones have dramatically improved screen resolutions and significantly cheaper data tariffs. However, given the range of devices available, it is good practice to design to accommodate the worst-case scenario.

Be Efficient

Manufacturers of embedded devices, particularly mobile devices, generally value small size and long battery life over potential improvements in processor speed. For developers, that means losing the head start traditionally afforded thanks to Moore's law (the doubling of the number of transistors placed on an integrated circuit every two years). In desktop and server hardware this usually results directly in processor performance improvements; for mobile devices it instead means smaller, more power-efficient mobiles without significant improvement in processor power.

In practice, this means that you always need to optimize your code so that it runs quickly and responsively, assuming that hardware improvements over the lifetime of your software are unlikely to do you any favors.

Since code efficiency is a big topic in software engineering, I'm not going to try to capture it here. Later in this chapter you'll learn some Android-specific efficiency tips, but for now just note that efficiency is particularly important for resource-constrained environments like mobile devices.

Expect Limited Capacity

Advances in flash memory and solid-state disks have led to a dramatic increase in mobile-device storage capacities (though MP3 collections still tend to expand to fill the available storage). While an 8 GB flash drive or SD card is no longer uncommon in mobile devices, optical disks offer over 32 GB, and terabyte drives are now commonly available for PCs. Given that most of the available storage on a mobile device is likely to be used to store music and movies, most devices offer relatively limited storage space for your applications.

Android devices offer an additional restriction in that applications must be installed on the internal memory (as opposed to external SD cards). As a result, the compiled size of your application is a consideration, though more important is ensuring that your application is polite in its use of system resources.

You should carefully consider how you store your application data. To make life easier you can use the Android databases and Content Providers to persist, reuse, and share large quantities of data, as described in Chapter 7. For smaller data storage, such as preferences or state settings, Android provides an optimized framework, as described in Chapter 6.

Of course, these mechanisms won't stop you from writing directly to the file system when you want or need to, but in those circumstances always consider how you're structuring these files, and ensure that yours is an efficient solution.

Part of being polite is cleaning up after yourself. Techniques like caching are useful for limiting repetitive network lookups, but don't leave files on the file system or records in a database when they're no longer needed.

Design for Small Screens

The small size and portability of mobiles are a challenge for creating good interfaces, particularly when users are demanding an increasingly striking and information-rich graphical user experience.

Write your applications knowing that users will often only glance at the (small) screen. Make your applications intuitive and easy to use by reducing the number of controls and putting the most important information front and center.

Graphical controls, like the ones you'll create in Chapter 4, are an excellent means of displaying a lot of information in a way that's easy to understand. Rather than a screen full of text with lots of buttons and text-entry boxes, use colors, shapes, and graphics to convey information.

If you're planning to include touch-screen support (and if you're not, you should be), you'll need to consider how touch input is going to affect your interface design. The time of the stylus has passed; now it's all about finger input, so make sure your Views are big enough to support interaction using a finger on the screen. There's more information on touch-screen interaction in Chapter 15.

Android phones are now available with a variety of screen sizes including QVGA, HVGA, and WVGA. As display technology advances, and Android expands beyond mobile devices, screen sizes and resolutions will continue to increase. To ensure that your app looks good and behaves well on all the possible host devices it's important to design for small screens, but also make sure your UIs scale well on larger displays. You'll learn some techniques for optimizing your UI for different screen sizes in Chapter 3.

Expect Low Speeds, High Latency

In Chapter 5 you'll learn how to use Internet resources in your applications. The ability to incorporate some of the wealth of online information in your applications is incredibly powerful.

The mobile Web unfortunately isn't as fast, reliable, or readily available as we'd often like, so when you're developing your Internet-based applications it's best to assume that the network connection will be slow, intermittent, and expensive. With unlimited 3G data plans and citywide Wi-Fi, this is changing, but designing for the worst case ensures that you always deliver a high-standard user experience.

This also means making sure that your applications can handle losing (or not finding) a data connection.

The Android Emulator lets you control the speed and latency of your network connection. Figure 2-8 shows the emulator's network connection speed and latency, simulating a distinctly suboptimal EDGE connection.

Experiment to ensure seamlessness and responsiveness no matter what the speed, latency, and availability of network access. In some circumstances you might find that it's better to limit the functionality of your application or reduce network lookups to cached bursts, based on the network connection(s) available. Details on how to detect the kind of network connections available at run time, and their speeds, are included in Chapter 13.

At What Cost?

If you're a mobile owner, you know all too well that some of the more powerful features on your mobile can literally come at a price. Services like SMS, some location-based services, and data transfer can sometimes incur an additional tariff from your service provider.

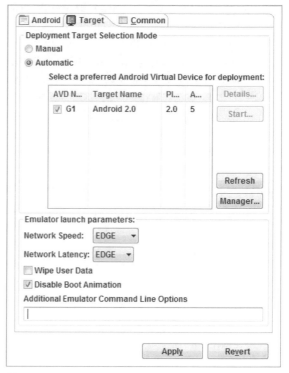

FIGURE 2-8

It's obvious why it's important that any costs associated with functionality in your applications be minimized, and that users be aware when an action they perform might result in their being charged.

It's a good approach to assume that there's a cost associated with any action involving an interaction with the outside world. In some cases (such as with GPS and data transfer) the user can toggle Android settings to disable a potentially costly action. As a developer it's important that you use and respect those settings within your application.

In any case, it's important to minimize interaction costs by doing the following:

➤ Transferring as little data as possible

➤ Caching data and GPS results to eliminate redundant or repetitive lookups

➤ Stopping all data transfers and GPS updates when your activity is not visible in the foreground and if they're only being used to update the UI

➤ Keeping the refresh/update rates for data transfers (and location lookups) as low as practicable

➤ Scheduling big updates or transfers at "off-peak" times using alarms, as shown in Chapter 9

➤ Respecting the user's preferences for background data transfer

Often the best solution is to use a lower-quality option that comes at a lower cost.

When using the location-based services described in Chapter 8, you can select a location provider based on whether there is an associated cost. Within your location-based applications, consider giving users the choice of lower cost or greater accuracy.

In some circumstances costs are hard to define, or they're different for different users. Charges for services vary between service providers and contract plans. While some people will have free unlimited data transfers, others will have free SMS.

Rather than enforcing a particular technique based on which seems cheaper, consider letting your users choose. For example, when downloading data from the Internet, you could ask users if they want to use any network available or limit their transfers to times when they're connected via Wi-Fi.

Considering the Users' Environment

You can't assume that your users will think of your application as the most important feature of their device.

While Android is already starting to expand beyond its core base as a mobile phone platform, most Android devices are still mobile phones. Remember that for most people, such a device is first and foremost a phone, secondly an SMS and email communicator, thirdly a camera, and fourthly an MP3 player. The applications you write will most likely be in the fifth category of "useful mobile tools."

That's not a bad thing — they'll be in good company with others including Google Maps and the web browser. That said, each user's usage model will be different; some people will never use their mobiles to listen to music, and some phones don't include a camera, but the multitasking principle inherent in a device as ubiquitous as it is indispensable is an important consideration for usability design.

It's also important to consider when and how your users will use your applications. People use their mobiles all the time — on the train, walking down the street, or even while driving their cars. You can't make people use their phones appropriately, but you can make sure that your applications don't distract them any more than necessary.

What does this mean in terms of software design? Make sure that your application:

> **Is well behaved** Start by ensuring that your Activities suspend when they're not in the foreground. Android triggers event handlers when your Activity is suspended or resumed so you can pause UI updates and network lookups when your application isn't visible — there's no point updating your UI if no one can see it. If you need to continue updating or processing in the background, Android provides a Service class designed to run in the background without the UI overheads.

> **Switches seamlessly from the background to the foreground** With the multitasking nature of mobile devices, it's very likely that your applications will regularly move into and out of the background. It's important that they "come to life" quickly and seamlessly. Android's nondeterministic process management means that if your application is in the background, there's every chance it will get killed to free resources. This should be invisible to the user. You can ensure seamlessness by saving the application state and queuing updates so that your users don't notice a difference between restarting and resuming your application. Switching back to it should be seamless, with users being shown the exact UI and application state they last saw.

➤ **Is polite**   Your application should never steal focus or interrupt a user's current activity. Use Notifications and Toasts (detailed in Chapter 9) instead to inform or remind users that their attention is requested, if your application isn't in the foreground. There are several ways for mobile devices to alert users. For example, when a call is coming in, your phone rings; when you have unread messages, the LED flashes; and when you have new voice mail, a small "mail" icon appears in your status bar. All these techniques and more are available through the notification mechanism.

➤ **Presents a consistent user interface**   Your application is likely to be one of several in use at any time, so it's important that the UI you present is easy to use. Don't force users to interpret and relearn your application every time they load it. Using it should be simple, easy, and obvious — particularly given the limited screen space and distracting user environment.

➤ **Is responsive**   Responsiveness is one of the most important design considerations on a mobile device. You've no doubt experienced the frustration of a "frozen" piece of software; the multifunctional nature of a mobile makes this even more annoying. With the possibility of delays caused by slow and unreliable data connections, it's important that your application use worker threads and background services to keep your activities responsive and, more importantly, to stop them from preventing other applications from responding promptly.

Developing for Android

Nothing covered so far is specific to Android; the preceding design considerations are just as important in developing applications for any mobile. In addition to these general guidelines, Android has some particular considerations.

To start with, it's worth taking a few minutes to read the design best practices included in Google's Android developer guide at `http://developer.android.com/guide/index.html`

The Android design philosophy demands that applications be designed for:

➤ Performance

➤ Responsiveness

➤ Seamlessness

➤ Security

Being Fast and Efficient

In a resource-constrained environment, being fast means being efficient. A lot of what you already know about writing efficient code will be just as applicable to Android, but the limitations of embedded systems and the use of the Dalvik VM mean you can't take things for granted.

The smart bet for advice is to go to the source. The Android team has published some specific guidance on writing efficient code for Android, so rather than rehash their advice, I suggest you visit `http://developer.android.com/guide/practices/design/performance.html` and take note of their suggestions.

You may find that some of these performance suggestions contradict established design practices — for example, avoiding the use of internal setters and getters or preferring virtual classes over using interfaces. When writing software for resource-constrained systems like embedded devices, there's often a compromise between conventional design principles and the demand for greater efficiency.

One of the keys to writing efficient Android code is not to carry over assumptions from desktop and server environments to embedded devices.

At a time when 2 to 4 GB of memory is standard for most desktop and server rigs, typical smartphones feature around 200 MB of SDRAM. With memory such a scarce commodity, you need to take special care to use it efficiently. This means thinking about how you use the stack and heap, limiting object creation, and being aware of how variable scope affects memory use.

Being Responsive

Android takes responsiveness very seriously.

Android enforces responsiveness with the Activity Manager and Window Manager. If either service detects an unresponsive application, it will display the dreaded "Sorry! Activity is not responding" message — often reported by users as a *Force Close* error. This is shown in Figure 2-9.

This alert is modal, steals focus, and won't go away until you hit a button or your application starts responding. It's pretty much the last thing you ever want to confront a user with.

Android monitors two conditions to determine responsiveness:

➤ An application must respond to any user action, such as a key press or screen touch, within five seconds.

➤ A Broadcast Receiver must return from its `onReceive` handler within 10 seconds.

The most likely culprits in cases of unresponsiveness are network lookups, complex processing (such as the calculating of game moves), and file I/O. There are a number of ways to ensure that these actions don't exceed the responsiveness conditions, in particular by using Services and worker threads, as shown in Chapter 9.

FIGURE 2-9

 The "Force close" dialog is a last resort of usability; the generous five-second limit is a worst-case scenario, not a target. Users will notice a regular pause of anything more than half a second between key press and action. Happily, a side effect of the efficient code you're already writing will be more responsive applications.

Developing Secure Applications

Android applications have access to networks and hardware, can be distributed independently, and are built on an open-source platform featuring open communication, so it shouldn't be surprising that security is a significant concern.

For the most part, users need to take responsibility for the applications they install and the permissions requests they accept. The Android security model restricts access to certain services and functionality by forcing applications to declare the permissions they require. During installation users are shown the application's required permissions before they commit to installing it. (You can learn more about Android's security model in Chapter 15 and at `http://developer.android.com/guide/appendix/faq/security.html`)

This doesn't get you off the hook. You not only need to make sure your application is secure for its own sake, you also need to ensure that it can't be hijacked to compromise the device. You can use several techniques to help maintain device security, and they'll be covered in more detail as you learn the technologies involved. In particular, you should do the following:

➤ Require permissions for any Services you publish or Intents you broadcast.

➤ Take special care when accepting input to your application from external sources such as the Internet, Bluetooth, SMS messages, or instant messaging (IM). You can find out more about using Bluetooth and SMS for application messaging in Chapters 12 and 13.

➤ Be cautious when your application may expose access to lower-level hardware to third-party applications.

For reasons of clarity and simplicity, many of the examples in this book take a fairly relaxed approach to security. When you're creating your own applications, particularly ones you plan to distribute, this is an area that should not be overlooked.

Ensuring a Seamless User Experience

The idea of a seamless user experience is an important, if somewhat nebulous, concept. What do we mean by *seamless?* The goal is a consistent user experience in which applications start, stop, and transition instantly and without noticeable delays or jarring transitions.

The speed and responsiveness of a mobile device shouldn't degrade the longer it's on. Android's process management helps by acting as a silent assassin, killing background applications to free resources as required. Knowing this, your applications should always present a consistent interface, regardless of whether they're being restarted or resumed.

With an Android device typically running several third-party applications written by different developers, it's particularly important that these applications interact seamlessly. Using Intents, applications can provide functionality for each other. Knowing your application may provide, or consume, third-party Activities provides additional incentive to maintain a consistent look and feel.

Use a consistent and intuitive approach to usability. You can create applications that are revolutionary and unfamiliar, but even these should integrate cleanly with the wider Android environment.

Persist data between sessions, and when the application isn't visible, suspend tasks that use processor cycles, network bandwidth, or battery life. If your application has processes that need to continue running while your Activities are out of sight, use a Service, but hide these implementation decisions from your users.

When your application is brought back to the front, or restarted, it should seamlessly return to its last visible state. As far as your users are concerned, each application should be sitting silently, ready to be used but just out of sight.

You should also follow the best-practice guidelines for using Notifications and use generic UI elements and themes to maintain consistency among applications.

There are many other techniques you can use to ensure a seamless user experience, and you'll be introduced to some of them as you discover more of the possibilities available in Android in the coming chapters.

TO-DO LIST EXAMPLE

In this example you'll be creating a new Android application from scratch. This simple example creates a new to-do list application using native Android View controls. It's designed to illustrate the basic steps involved in starting a new project.

> *Don't worry if you don't understand everything that happens in this example. Some of the features used to create this application, including* `ArrayAdapters`, `ListViews`, *and* `KeyListeners`, *won't be introduced properly until later chapters, where they'll be explained in detail. You'll also return to this example later to add new functionality as you learn more about Android.*

1. Start by creating a new Android project. Within Eclipse, select **File** ➪ **New** ➪ **Project. . .**, then choose **Android** (as shown in Figure 2-10) before clicking **Next.**

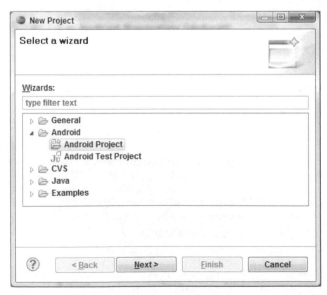

FIGURE 2-10

2. In the dialog box that appears (shown in Figure 2-11), enter the details for your new project. The "Application name" is the friendly name of your application, and the "Create Activity" field lets you name your Activity. With the details entered, click **Finish** to create your new project.

FIGURE 2-11

3. Before creating your debug and run configurations, take this opportunity to create a virtual device to test your apps with.

3.1. Select **Window ⇨ Android SDK and AVD Manager.** In the resulting dialog (shown in Figure 2-12), select **Virtual Devices** from the left panel and click the **New. . .** button.

3.2. Enter a name for your device, and choose an SDK target and screen resolution. Set the SD Card size to larger than 8 MB: enter 12 into the text-entry box as shown in Figure 2-13.

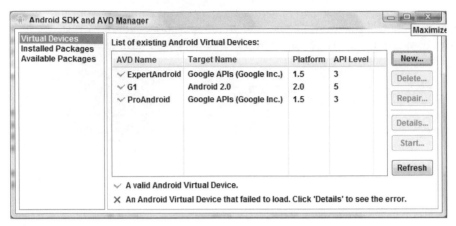

FIGURE 2-12

FIGURE 2-13

4.   Now create your debug and run configurations. Select **Run ⇨ Debug Configurations...** and then **Run ⇨ Run Configurations...** , creating a new configuration for each specifying the Todo_List project and selecting the virtual device you created in Step 3. You can leave the launch action as **Launch Default Activity**, or explicitly set it to launch the new ToDoList Activity, as shown in Figure 2-14.

5. Now decide what you want to show the users and what actions they'll need to perform. Design a user interface that will make these actions as intuitive as possible.

In this example we want to present users with a list of to-do items and a text entry box to add new ones. There's both a list and a text-entry control available from the Android libraries. (You'll learn more about the Views available in Android, and how to create new ones, in Chapter 4.)

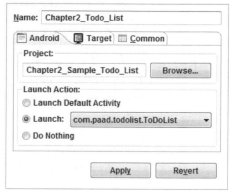

The preferred method for laying out your UI is using a layout resource file. Open the main.xml layout file in the res/layout project folder, as shown in Figure 2-15.

FIGURE 2-14

6. Modify the main layout to include a `ListView` and an `EditText` within a `LinearLayout`. It's important to give both the `Edit Text` and `List View` an ID so you can get references to them both in code.

```xml
<?xml version="1.0" encoding="utf-8"?>
<LinearLayout xmlns:android="http://schemas.android.com/apk/res/android"
  android:orientation="vertical"
  android:layout_width="fill_parent"
  android:layout_height="fill_parent">
  <EditText
    android:id="@+id/myEditText"
    android:layout_width="fill_parent"
    android:layout_height="wrap_content"
    android:text="New To Do Item"
  />
  <ListView
    android:id="@+id/myListView"
    android:layout_width="fill_parent"
    android:layout_height="wrap_content"
  />
</LinearLayout>
```

7. With your user interface defined, open the `ToDoList` Activity from your project's source folder. In this example you'll make all your changes by overriding the `onCreate` method. Start by inflating your UI using `setContentView` and then get references to the `ListView` and `EditText` using `findViewById`.

```java
public void onCreate(Bundle savedInstanceState) {
    super.onCreate(savedInstanceState);

    // Inflate your view
    setContentView(R.layout.main);
```

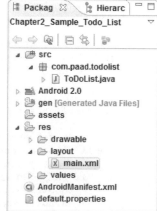

FIGURE 2-15

```
        // Get references to UI widgets
        ListView myListView = (ListView)findViewById(R.id.myListView);
        final EditText myEditText = (EditText)findViewById(R.id.myEditText);
    }
```

8. Still within `onCreate`, define an `ArrayList` of Strings to store each to-do list item. You can bind a `ListView` to an `ArrayList` using an `ArrayAdapter`, so create a new `ArrayAdapter` instance to bind the to-do item array to the `ListView`. (We'll return to `ArrayAdapters` in Chapter 5.)

```
    public void onCreate(Bundle savedInstanceState) {
        super.onCreate(savedInstanceState);
        setContentView(R.layout.main);

        ListView myListView = (ListView)findViewById(R.id.myListView);
        final EditText myEditText = (EditText)findViewById(R.id.myEditText);

        // Create the array list of to do items
        final ArrayList<String> todoItems = new ArrayList<String>();
        // Create the array adapter to bind the array to the listview
        final ArrayAdapter<String> aa;
        aa = new ArrayAdapter<String>(this,
                                      android.R.layout.simple_list_item_1,
                                      todoItems);
        // Bind the array adapter to the listview.
        myListView.setAdapter(aa);
    }
```

9. The final step to make this to-do list functional is to let users add new to-do items. Add an `onKeyListener` to the `EditText` that listens for a "D-pad center button" click before adding the contents of the `EditText` to the to-do list array and notifying the `ArrayAdapter` of the change. Then clear the `EditText` to prepare for another item.

```
public void onCreate(Bundle savedInstanceState) {
    super.onCreate(savedInstanceState);
    setContentView(R.layout.main);

    ListView myListView = (ListView)findViewById(R.id.myListView);
    final EditText myEditText = (EditText)findViewById(R.id.myEditText);

    final ArrayList<String> todoItems = new ArrayList<String>();
    final ArrayAdapter<String> aa;
    aa = new ArrayAdapter<String>(this,
                                  android.R.layout.simple_list_item_1,
                                  todoItems);
    myListView.setAdapter(aa);

    myEditText.setOnKeyListener(new OnKeyListener() {
        public boolean onKey(View v, int keyCode, KeyEvent event) {
            if (event.getAction() == KeyEvent.ACTION_DOWN)
                if (keyCode == KeyEvent.KEYCODE_DPAD_CENTER){
                    todoItems.add(0, myEditText.getText().toString());
                    aa.notifyDataSetChanged();
                    myEditText.setText("");
                    return true;
```

```
        }
      return false;
    }
  });
}
```

10. Run or debug the application and you'll see a text entry box above a list, as shown in Figure 2-16.

11. You've now finished your first "real" Android application. Try adding breakpoints to the code to test the debugger and experiment with the DDMS perspective.

All code snippets in this example are part of the Chapter 2 To-do List *project, available for download at Wrox.com.*

As it stands, this to-do list application isn't spectacularly useful. It doesn't save to-do list items between sessions, you can't edit or remove an item from the list, and typical task-list items like due dates and task priority aren't recorded or displayed. On balance, it fails most of the criteria laid out so far for a good mobile application design.

You'll rectify some of these deficiencies when you return to this example in later chapters.

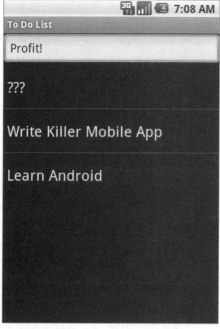

FIGURE 2-16

ANDROID DEVELOPMENT TOOLS

The Android SDK includes several tools and utilities to help you create, test, and debug your projects. A detailed examination of each developer tool is outside the scope of this book, but it's worth briefly reviewing what's available. For more detail than is included here, check out the Android documentation at `http://developer.android.com/guide/developing/tools/index.html`

As mentioned earlier, the ADT plug-in conveniently incorporates most of these tools into the Eclipse IDE, where you can access them from the DDMS perspective, including:

➤ **The Android SDK and Virtual Device Manager**   Used to create and manage Android Virtual Devices (AVD) and SDK packages. The AVD hosts an emulator running a particular build of Android, letting you specify the supported SDK version, screen resolution, amount of SD card storage available, and available hardware capabilities (such as touchscreens and GPS).

➤ **The Android Emulator**   An implementation of the Android virtual machine designed to run within a virtual device on your development computer. Use the emulator to test and debug your Android applications.

➤ **Dalvik Debug Monitoring Service (DDMS)**   Use the DDMS perspective to monitor and control the Dalvik virtual machines on which you're debugging your applications.

➤ **Android Asset Packaging Tool (AAPT)**   Constructs the distributable Android package files (`.apk`).

➤ **Android Debug Bridge (ADB)**   A client-server application that provides a link to a running emulator. It lets you copy files, install compiled application packages (.apk), and run shell commands.

The following additional tools are also available:

➤ **SQLite3**   A database tool that you can use to access the SQLite database files created and used by Android.

➤ **Traceview**   A graphical analysis tool for viewing the trace logs from your Android application.

➤ **MkSDCard**   Creates an SD card disk image that can be used by the emulator to simulate an external storage card.

➤ **Dx**   Converts Java .class bytecode into Android .dex bytecode.

➤ **activityCreator**   A script that builds Ant build files that you can then use to compile your Android applications without the ADT plug-in.

➤ **layoutOpt**   A tool that analyzes your layout resources and suggests improvements and optimizations.

Let's take a look at some of the more important tools in more detail.

The Android Virtual Device and SDK Manager

The Virtual Device and SDK Manager is a tool used to create and manage the virtual devices that will host instances of your emulator. You can use the same tool both to see which version of the SDK you have installed and to install new SDKs when they are released.

Android Virtual Devices

Android Virtual Devices are used to simulate the software builds and hardware specifications available on different devices. This lets you test your application on a variety of hardware platforms without needing to buy a variety of phones.

 The Android SDK doesn't include any pre-built virtual devices, so you will need to create at least one device before you can run your applications within an emulator.

Each virtual device is configured with a name, a target build of Android (based on the SDK version it supports), an SD Card capacity, and screen resolution, as shown in the "Create new AVD" dialog in Figure 2-17.

Each virtual device also supports a number of specific hardware settings and restrictions that can be added in the form of NVPs in the hardware table. These additional settings include:

➤ Maximum virtual machine heap size

➤ Screen pixel density

FIGURE 2-17

➤ SD Card support

➤ The existence of DPad, touchscreen, keyboard, and trackball hardware

➤ Accelerometer and GPS support

➤ Available device memory

➤ Camera hardware (and resolution)

➤ Support for audio recording

Different hardware settings and screen resolutions will present alternative user-interface skins to represent the different hardware configurations. This simulates a variety of mobile device types. To complete the illusion, you can create a custom skin for each virtual device to make it look like the device it is emulating.

SDK Manager

Use the installed and available package tabs to manage your SDK installations.

Installed Packages, shown in Figure 2-18, displays the SDK platforms, documentation, and tools you have available to use in your development environment. When updating to a new version you can simply click the **Update All...** button to have the manager update your SDK installation with the latest version of each component.

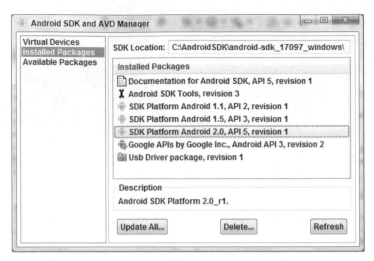

FIGURE 2-18

Alternatively, Available Packages checks the Android SDK repository for any source, packages, and archives available but not yet installed on your system. Use the checkboxes, as shown in Figure 2-19, to select additional SDK packages to install.

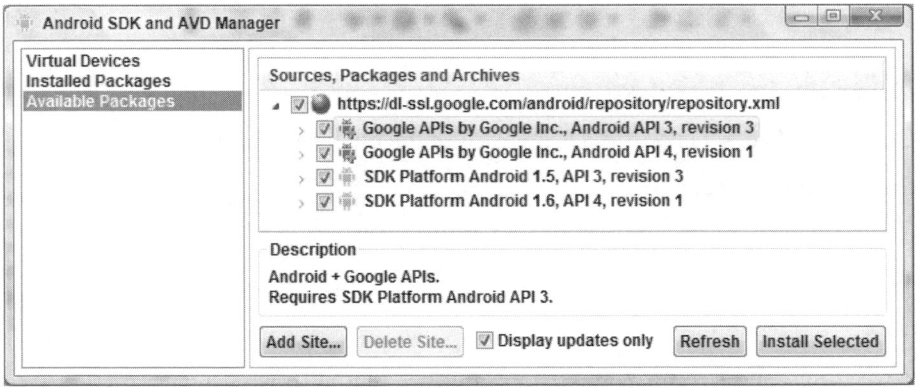

FIGURE 2-19

The Android Emulator

The emulator is the perfect tool for testing and debugging your applications.

The emulator is an implementation of the Dalvik virtual machine, making it as valid a platform for running Android applications as any Android phone. Because it's decoupled from any particular hardware, it's an excellent baseline to use for testing your applications.

Full network connectivity is provided along with the ability to tweak the Internet connection speed and latency while debugging your applications. You can also simulate placing and receiving voice calls and SMS messages.

The ADT plug-in integrates the emulator into Eclipse so that it's launched automatically within the selected AVD when you run or debug your projects. If you aren't using the plug-in or want to use the emulator outside of Eclipse, you can telnet into the emulator and control it from its console. (For more details on controlling the emulator, check the documentation at http://developer.android.com/guide/developing/tools/emulator.html)

To execute the emulator you first need to create a virtual device, as described in the previous section. The emulator will launch the virtual device and run a Dalvik instance within it.

 At this time, the emulator doesn't implement all the mobile hardware features supported by Android. It does not implement the camera, vibration, LEDs, actual phone calls, the accelerometer, USB connections, audio capture, or battery charge level.

Dalvik Debug Monitor Service (DDMS)

The emulator lets you see how your application will look, behave, and interact, but to really see what's happening under the surface you need the Dalvik Debug Monitoring Service. The DDMS is a powerful debugging tool that lets you interrogate active processes, view the stack and heap, watch and pause active threads, and explore the file system of any connected Android device.

The DDMS perspective in Eclipse also provides simplified access to screen captures of the emulator and the logs generated by LogCat.

If you're using the ADT plug-in, the DDMS is fully integrated into Eclipse and is available from the DDMS perspective. If you aren't using the plug-in or Eclipse, you can run DDMS from the command line and it will automatically connect to any running device or emulator.

The Android Debug Bridge (ADB)

The *Android debug bridge (ADB)* is a client-service application that lets you connect with an Android Emulator or device. It's made up of three components: a daemon running on the emulator, a service that runs on your development hardware, and client applications (like the DDMS) that communicate with the daemon through the service.

As a communications conduit between your development hardware and the Android device/emulator, the ADB lets you install applications, push and pull files, and run shell commands on the target device. Using the device shell you can change logging settings, and query or modify SQLite databases available on the device.

The ADT tool automates and simplifies a lot of the usual interaction with the ADB, including application installation and updating, file logging, and file transfer (through the DDMS perspective).

To learn more about what you can do with the ADB, check out the documentation at http://developer.android.com/guide/developing/tools/adb.html

SUMMARY

This chapter showed you how to download and install the Android SDK, create a development environment using Eclipse on Windows, Mac OS, or Linux platforms, and create run and debug configurations for your projects. You learned how to install and use the ADT plug-in to simplify the creation of new projects and streamline your development cycle.

You were introduced to some of the design considerations involved in developing mobile applications, particularly the importance of optimizing for speed and efficiency when increasing battery life and shrinking sizes are higher priorities than increasing processor power.

As with any mobile development, there are considerations involved in designing for small screens and potentially slow, costly, and unreliable mobile data connections.

After creating an Android to-do list application, you were introduced to Android virtual devices and the emulator, as well as the developer tools you'll use to test and debug your applications.

Specifically, in this chapter you:

- ➤ Downloaded and installed the Android SDK
- ➤ Set up a development environment in Eclipse and downloaded and installed the ADT plug-in
- ➤ Created your first application and learned how it works
- ➤ Set up run and debug launch configurations for your projects
- ➤ Learned about the different types of Android applications
- ➤ Were introduced to some mobile-device design considerations and learned some specific Android design practices
- ➤ Created a to-do list application
- ➤ Were introduced to Android Virtual Devices, the emulator, and the developer tools

The next chapter focuses on Activities and application design. You'll see how to define application settings using the Android manifest and how to externalize your UI layouts and application resources. You'll also find out more about the Android application life cycle and Android application states.

3

Creating Applications and Activities

WHAT'S IN THIS CHAPTER?

➤ An introduction to the Android application components and the different types of Android applications you can build with them

➤ The Android application life cycle

➤ How to create and annotate the application manifest

➤ How to use external resources to provide dynamic support for locations, languages, and hardware configurations

➤ How to implement and use your own Application class

➤ How to create new Activities

➤ Understanding an Activity's state transitions and life cycle

Before you start writing your own Android applications, it's important to understand how they're constructed and to have an understanding of the Android application life cycle. In this chapter you'll be introduced to the loosely coupled components that make up Android applications and how they're bound together by the Android manifest. Next you'll see how and why you should use external resources, before getting an introduction to the Activity component.

In recent years there's been a move toward development frameworks featuring managed code, such as the Java virtual machine and the .NET Common Language Runtime.

In Chapter 1 you learned that Android also uses this model, with each application running in a separate process on its own instance of the Dalvik virtual machine. In this chapter you'll learn more about the application life cycle and how it's managed by the Android run time. This leads to an introduction of the application process states. These states are used to determine an application's priority, which in turn affects the likelihood of an application's being terminated when more resources are required by the system.

Mobile devices come in a large variety of shapes and sizes and are used across the world. In this chapter you'll learn how to externalize resources to ensure your applications run seamlessly on different hardware (particularly different screen resolutions and pixel densities), in different countries, and supporting multiple languages.

Next you'll examine the Application class, and learn how to extend it to provide a place for storing application state values.

Arguably the most important of the Android building blocks, the `Activity` class forms the basis for all your user interface screens. You'll learn how to create new Activities and gain an understanding of their life cycles and how they affect the application lifetime.

Finally, you'll be introduced to some of the Activity subclasses that simplify resource management for some common user interface components such as maps and lists.

WHAT MAKES AN ANDROID APPLICATION?

Android applications consist of loosely coupled components, bound by an application manifest that describes each component and how they all interact, as well as the application metadata including its hardware and platform requirements.

The following six components provide the building blocks for your applications:

➤ **Activities**   Your application's presentation layer. Every screen in your application will be an extension of the `Activity` class. Activities use Views to form graphical user interfaces that display information and respond to user actions. In terms of desktop development, an Activity is equivalent to a Form. You'll learn more about Activities later in this chapter.

➤ **Services**   The invisible workers of your application. Service components run in the background, updating your data sources and visible Activities and triggering Notifications. They're used to perform regular processing that needs to continue even when your application's Activities aren't active or visible. You'll learn how to create Services in Chapter 9.

➤ **Content Providers**   Shareable data stores. Content Providers are used to manage and share application databases. They're the preferred means of sharing data across application boundaries. This means that you can configure your own Content Providers to permit access from other applications and use Content Providers exposed by others to access their stored data. Android devices include several native Content Providers that expose useful databases like the media store and contact details. You'll learn how to create and use Content Providers in Chapter 7.

➤ **Intents**   An inter-application message-passing framework. Using Intents you can broadcast messages system-wide or to a target Activity or Service, stating your intention to have an action performed. The system will then determine the target(s) that will perform any actions as appropriate.

➤ **Broadcast Receivers**   Intent broadcast consumers. If you create and register a Broadcast Receiver, your application can listen for broadcast Intents that match specific filter criteria. Broadcast Receivers will automatically start your application to respond to an incoming Intent, making them perfect for creating event-driven applications.

➤ **Widgets**   Visual application components that can be added to the home screen. A special variation of a Broadcast Receiver, widgets let you create dynamic, interactive application components for users to embed on their home screens. You'll learn how to create your own widgets in Chapter 10.

➤ **Notifications**   A user notification framework. Notifications let you signal users without stealing focus or interrupting their current Activities. They're the preferred technique for getting a user's attention from within a Service or Broadcast Receiver. For example, when a device receives a text message or an incoming call, it alerts you by flashing lights, making sounds, displaying icons, or showing messages. You can trigger these same events from your own applications using Notifications, as shown in Chapter 9.

By decoupling the dependencies between application components, you can share and interchange individual pieces, such as Content Providers, Services, and even Activities, with other applications — both your own and those of third parties.

INTRODUCING THE APPLICATION MANIFEST

Each Android project includes a manifest file, `AndroidManifest.xml`, stored in the root of the project hierarchy. The manifest lets you define the structure and metadata of your application, its components, and its requirements.

It includes nodes for each of the components (Activities, Services, Content Providers, and Broadcast Receivers) that make up your application and, using Intent Filters and Permissions, determines how they interact with each other and with other applications.

The manifest also offers attributes to specify application metadata (like its icon or theme), and additional top-level nodes can be used for security settings, unit tests, and defining hardware and platform support requirements, as described below.

The manifest is made up of a root `<manifest>` tag with a `package` attribute set to the project's package. It usually includes an `xmlns:android` attribute that supplies several system attributes used within the file.

Use the `versionCode` attribute to define the current application version as an integer. This value is used internally to compare application versions. Use the `versionName` attribute to specify a public version number that is displayed to users.

A typical manifest node is shown in the following XML snippet:

```
<manifest xmlns:android=http://schemas.android.com/apk/res/android
          package="com.my_domain.my_app"
          android:versionCode="1"
          android:versionName="0.9 Beta">
          [ ... manifest nodes ... ]
</manifest>
```

The `<manifest>` tag includes nodes that define the application components, security settings, test classes, and requirements that make up your application. The following list gives a summary of the available `<manifest>` node tags, and an XML snippet demonstrating how each one is used:

➤ `uses-sdk` This node lets you define a minimum, maximum, and target SDK version that must be available on a device in order for your application to function properly. Using a combination of `minSDKVersion`, `maxSDKVersion`, and `targetSDKVersion` attributes you can restrict which devices your application can run on, based on the SDK version supported by the installed platform.

The minimum SDK version specifies the lowest version of the SDK that includes the APIs you have used in your application. If you fail to specify a minimum version one will be assumed and your application will crash if it attempts to access APIs that aren't available on the host device.

The maximum SDK version lets you define an upper limit you are willing to support. Your application will not be visible on the Market for devices running a higher platform release. It's good practice *not* to set the maximum SDK value unless you know your application will definitely not work on newer platform releases.

The target SDK version attribute lets you specify the platform against which you did your development and testing. Setting a target SDK version tells the system that there is no need to apply any forward- or backward- compatibility changes to support that particular version.

```
<uses-sdk android:minSdkVersion="4"
          android:targetSdkVersion="5">
</uses-sdk>
```

The supported SDK version is not equivalent to the platform version and cannot be derived from it. For example, Android platform release 2.0 supports the SDK version 5. To find the correct SDK version for each platform use the table at `http://developer.android.com/guide/appendix/api-levels.html`

➤ `uses-configuration` Use `uses-configuration` nodes to specify each combination of input mechanisms supported by your application. You can specify any combination of input devices that include:

  ➤ `reqFiveWayNav` Specify `true` for this attribute if you require an input device capable of navigating up, down, left, and right and of clicking the current selection. This includes both trackballs and D-pads.

  ➤ `reqHardKeyboard` If your application requires a hardware keyboard specify `true`.

  ➤ `reqKeyboardType` Lets you specify the keyboard type as one of `nokeys`, `qwerty`, `twelvekey`, or `undefined`.

  ➤ `reqNavigation` Specify the attribute value as one of `nonav`, `dpad`, `trackball`, `wheel`, or `undefined` as a required navigation device.

> ➤ reqTouchScreen   Select one of notouch, stylus, finger, or undefined to specify the required touchscreen input.

You can specify multiple supported configurations, for example a device with a finger touchscreen, a trackball, and either a QUERTY or twelve-key hardware keyboard, as shown here:

```
<uses-configuration android:reqTouchScreen=["finger"]
                    android:reqNavigation=["trackball"]
                    android:reqHardKeyboard=["true"]
                    android:reqKeyboardType=["qwerty"/>
<uses-configuration android:reqTouchScreen=["finger"]
                    android:reqNavigation=["trackball"]
                    android:reqHardKeyboard=["true"]
                    android:reqKeyboardType=["twelvekey"]/>
```

When specifying required configurations be aware that your application won't be installed on any device that does not have one of the combinations specified. In the above example a device with a QWERTY keyboard and a D-pad (but no touchscreen or trackball) would not be supported. Ideally you should develop your application to ensure it works with any input configuration, in which case no uses-configuration *node is required.*

> ➤ uses-feature   One of the advantages of Android is the wide variety of hardware platforms it runs on. Use multiple uses-feature nodes to specify each of the hardware features your application requires. This will prevent your application from being installed on a device that does not include a required hardware feature. You can require support for any hardware that is optional on a compatible device. Currently optional hardware features include:
>
> > ➤ android.hardware.camera   For applications that require camera hardware.
> >
> > ➤ android.hardware.camera.autofocus   If you require an autofocus camera.

As the variety of platforms on which Android is available increases, so too will the optional hardware. A full list of uses-feature hardware can be found here: http://developer.android.com/guide/topics/manifest/uses-feature-element.html

You can also use the uses-feature node to specify the minimum version of OpenGL required by your application. Use the glEsVersion attribute, specifying the OpenGL ES version as an integer. The higher 16 bits represent the major number and the lower 16 bits represent the minor number.

```
<uses-feature android:glEsVersion=" 0x00010001"
              android:name="android.hardware.camera" />
```

> ➤ supports-screens   After the initial round of HVGA hardware, 2009 saw the introduction of WVGA and QVGA screens to the Android device menagerie. With future Android devices likely to feature devices with larger screens, the supports-screen node lets you specify the screen sizes your application can, and can't, support.

Exact dimensions will vary depending on hardware, but in general the supported screen sizes match resolutions as follows:

➤ `smallScreens` Screens with a resolution smaller than traditional HVGA — typically QVGA screens.

➤ `normalScreens` Used to specify typical mobile phone screens of at least HVGA, including WVGA and WQVGA.

➤ `largeScreens` Screens larger than normal. In this instance a large screen is considered to be significantly larger than a mobile phone display.

➤ `anyDensity` Set to `true` if your application can be scaled to accommodate any screen resolution.

As of SDK 1.6 (API level 4), the default value for each attribute is `true`. Use this node to specify screen sizes you do not support.

```
<supports-screens android:smallScreens=["false"]
                  android:normalScreens=["true"]
                  android:largeScreens=["true"]
                  android:anyDensity=["false"] />
```

Where possible you should optimize your application for different screen resolutions and densities using the resources folder, as shown later in this chapter. If you specify a supports-screen *node that excludes certain screen sizes, your application will not be available to be installed on devices with unsupported screens.*

➤ `application` A manifest can contain only one application node. It uses attributes to specify the metadata for your application (including its title, icon, and theme). During development you should include a `debuggable` attribute set to `true` to enable debugging — though you may wish to disable this on your release builds.

The `<application>` node also acts as a container that includes the Activity, Service, Content Provider, and Broadcast Receiver tags used to specify the application components. You can also define your own implementation of the Application class. Later in this chapter you'll learn how to create and use your own Application class extension to manage application state.

```
<application android:icon="@drawable/icon"
             android:theme="@style/my_theme"
             android:name="MyApplication"
             android:debuggable="true">
             [ ... application nodes ... ]
</application>
```

➤ `activity` An `<activity>` tag is required for every Activity displayed by your application. Using the `android:name` attribute to specify the Activity class name.

You must include the main launch Activity and any other screen or dialog that can be displayed. Trying to start an Activity that's not defined in the manifest will throw a runtime exception. Each Activity node supports `<intent-filter>` child tags that specify which Intents launch the Activity.

```
<activity android:name=".MyActivity" android:label="@string/app_name">
  <intent-filter>
    <action android:name="android.intent.action.MAIN" />
    <category android:name="android.intent.category.LAUNCHER" />
  </intent-filter>
</activity>
```

➤ `service` As with the `activity` tag, create a new `service` tag for each Service class used in your application. (Services are covered in detail in Chapter 9.) Service tags also support `<intent-filter>` child tags to allow late runtime binding.

```
<service android:enabled="true" android:name=".MyService"></service>
```

➤ `provider` Provider tags specify each of your application's Content Providers. Content Providers are used to manage database access and sharing within and between applications and are examined in Chapter 7.

```
<provider android:permission="com.paad.MY_PERMISSION"
          android:name=".MyContentProvider"
          android:enabled="true"
          android:authorities="com.paad.myapp.MyContentProvider">
</provider>
```

➤ `receiver` By adding a receiver tag, you can register a Broadcast Receiver without having to launch your application first. As you'll see in Chapter 5, Broadcast Receivers are like global event listeners that, once registered, will execute whenever a matching Intent is broadcast by the system or an application. By registering a Broadcast Receiver in the manifest you can make this process entirely autonomous. If a matching Intent is broadcast, your application will be started automatically and the registered Broadcast Receiver will be run.

```
<receiver android:enabled="true"
          android:label="My Intent Receiver"
          android:name=".MyIntentReceiver">
</receiver>
```

➤ `uses-permission` As part of the security model, `uses-permission` tags declare the permissions you've determined your application needs to operate properly. The permissions you include will be presented to the user before installation commences. Permissions are required for many of the native Android services, particularly those with a cost or security implication (such as dialing, receiving SMS, or using the location-based services).

```
<uses-permission android:name="android.permission.ACCESS_LOCATION"/>
```

➤ `permission` Third-party applications can also specify permissions before providing access to shared application components. Before you can restrict access to an application component, you need to define a permission in the manifest. Use the `permission` tag to create a permission definition.

Application components can then require permissions by adding the `android:permission` attribute. Other applications will then need to include a `uses-permission` tag in their manifests to use these protected components.

Within the `permission` tag, you can specify the level of access the permission will permit (`normal`, `dangerous`, `signature`, `signatureOrSystem`), a label, and an external resource containing the description that explains the risks of granting the specified permission.

```
<permission android:name="com.paad.DETONATE_DEVICE"
            android:protectionLevel="dangerous"
            android:label="Self Destruct"
            android:description="@string/detonate_description">
</permission>
```

➤ `instrumentation` Instrumentation classes provide a test framework for your application components at run time. They provide hooks to monitor your application and its interaction with the system resources. Create a new node for each of the test classes you've created for your application.

```
<instrumentation android:label="My Test"
                 android:name=".MyTestClass"
                 android:targetPackage="com.paad.aPackage">
</instrumentation>
```

A more detailed description of the manifest and each of these nodes can be found at `http://developer .android.com/guide/topics/manifest/manifest-intro.html`

The ADT New Project Wizard automatically creates a new manifest file when it creates a new project.

You'll return to the manifest as each of the application components is introduced.

USING THE MANIFEST EDITOR

The ADT plug-in includes a visual Manifest Editor so you don't have to manipulate the underlying XML directly.

To use the Manifest Editor in Eclipse, right-click the AndroidManifest.xml file in your project folder and select **Open With . . .** ➪ **Android Manifest Editor.** This presents the Android Manifest Overview screen, as shown in Figure 3-1. This screen gives you a high-level view of your application structure, enabling you to set your application version information and root level manifest nodes, including `<uses-sdk>` and `<uses-features>`, as described previously in this chapter. It also provides shortcut links to the Application, Permissions, Instrumentation, and raw XML screens.

Each of the next three tabs contains a visual interface for managing the application, security, and instrumentation (testing) settings, while the last tag (using the manifest's file name) gives access to the raw XML.

Of particular interest is the Application tab, shown in Figure 3-2. Use it to manage the application node and the application component hierarchy, where you specify the application components.

You can specify an application's attributes — including its icon, label, and theme — in the Application Attributes panel. The Application Nodes tree beneath it lets you manage the application components, including their attributes and any associated Intent Filter subnodes.

ci Android Manifest

▾ **Manifest General Attributes**
Defines general information about the AndroidManifest.xml

Package	com.paad.todolist	Browse...
Version code	1	
Version name	1.0	Browse...
Shared user id		Browse...
Shared user label		Browse...

Manifest Extras   Ⓤ Ⓢ Ⓟ Ⓤ Ⓤ Az   **Attributes for Uses Sdk**

Ⓤ Uses Sdk

Ⓤ The <u>uses-sdk</u> tag describes the SDK features that the containing package must be running on to operate correctly.

[Add...]
[Remove...]
[Up]
[Down]

Min SDK version	4	Browse...
Target SDK version	4	Browse...
Max SDK version		

▾ **Exporting**
To export the application for distribution, you have the following options:

- <u>Use the Export Wizard</u> to export and sign an APK
- <u>Export an unsigned APK</u> and sign it manually

▾ **Links**
The content of the Android Manifest is made up of three sections. You can also edit the XML directly.

Ⓐ <u>Application</u>: Activities, intent filters, providers, services and receivers.
Ⓟ <u>Permission</u>: Permissions defined and permissions used.

Manifest | Application | Permissions | Instrumentation | AndroidManifest.xml

FIGURE 3-1

THE ANDROID APPLICATION LIFE CYCLE

Unlike most traditional environments, Android applications have limited control over their own life cycles. Instead, application components must listen for changes in the application state and react accordingly, taking particular care to be prepared for untimely termination.

By default, each Android application runs in its own process, each of which is running a separate instance of Dalvik. Memory and process management is handled exclusively by the run time.

> *While it's uncommon, it's possible to force application components within the same application to run in different processes or to have multiple applications share the same process using the* `android:process` *attribute on the affected component nodes within the manifest.*

Android aggressively manages its resources, doing whatever it takes to ensure that the device remains responsive. This means that processes (and their hosted applications) will be killed, without warning in some cases, to free resources for higher-priority applications — generally those interacting directly with the user at the time. The prioritization process is discussed in the next section.

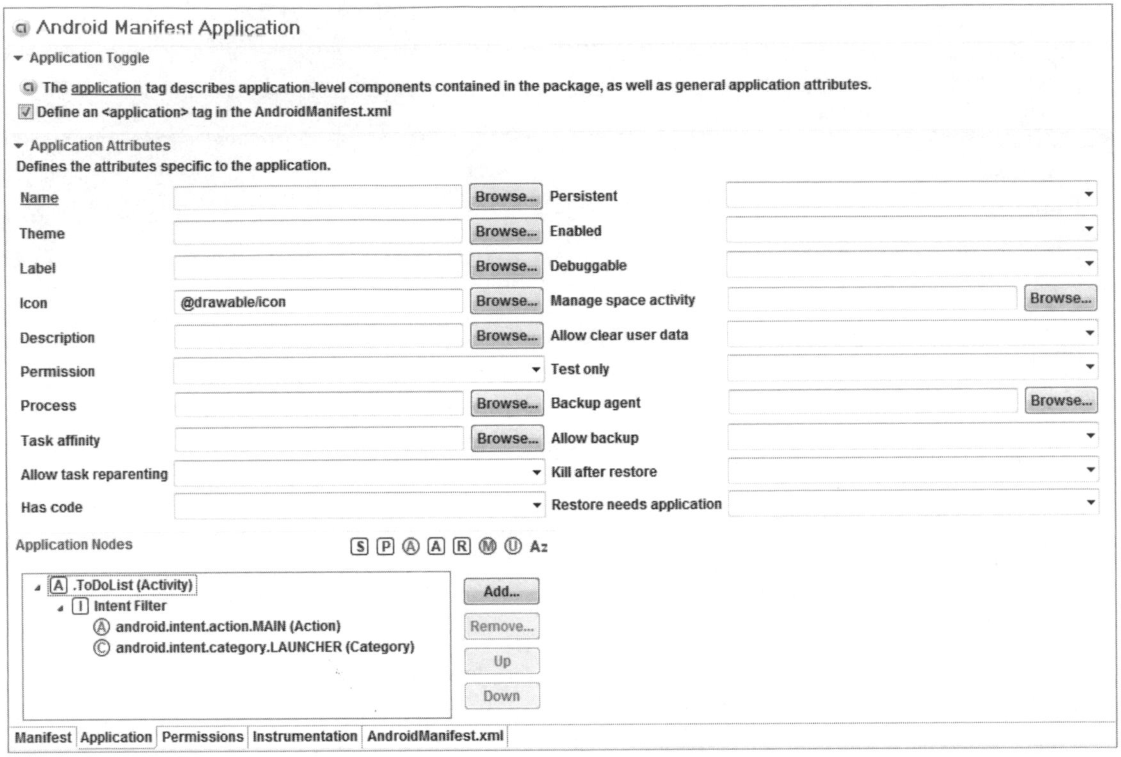

FIGURE 3-2

UNDERSTANDING APPLICATION PRIORITY AND PROCESS STATES

The order in which processes are killed to reclaim resources is determined by the priority of the hosted applications. An application's priority is equal to its highest-priority component.

If two applications have the same priority, the process that has been at a lower priority longest will be killed first. Process priority is also affected by interprocess dependencies; if an application has a dependency on a Service or Content Provider supplied by a second application, the secondary application will have at least as high a priority as the application it supports.

 All Android applications will remain running and in memory until the system needs resources for other applications.

Figure 3-3 shows the priority tree used to determine the order of application termination.

It's important to structure your application correctly to ensure that its priority is appropriate for the work it's doing. If you don't, your application could be killed while it's in the middle of something important.

The following list details each of the application states shown in Figure 3-3, explaining how the state is determined by the application components comprising it:

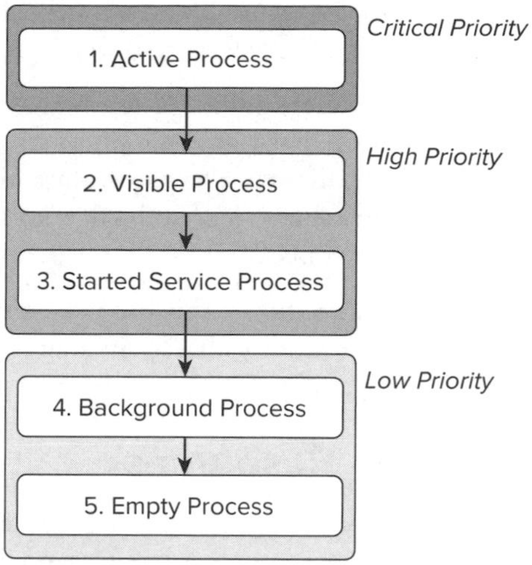

FIGURE 3-3

➤ **Active processes** Active (foreground) processes have application components interacting with the user. These are the processes Android is trying to keep responsive by reclaiming resources. There are generally very few of these processes, and they will be killed only as a last resort.

Active processes include:

➤ Activities in an "active" state; that is, those in the foreground responding to user events. You will explore Activity states in greater detail later in this chapter.

➤ Broadcast Receivers executing `onReceive` event handlers.

➤ Services executing `onStart`, `onCreate`, or `onDestroy` event handlers.

➤ Running Services that have been flagged to run in the foreground.

➤ **Visible processes** Visible but inactive processes are those hosting "visible" Activities. As the name suggests, visible Activities are visible, but they aren't in the foreground or responding to user events. This happens when an Activity is only partially obscured (by a non-full-screen or transparent Activity). There are generally very few visible processes, and they'll be killed only under extreme circumstances to allow active processes to continue.

➤ **Started Service processes** Processes hosting Services that have been started. Services support ongoing processing that should continue without a visible interface. Because background Services don't interact directly with the user, they receive a slightly lower priority than visible Activities. They are still considered foreground processes and won't be killed unless resources are needed for active or visible processes. You'll learn more about Services in Chapter 9.

➤ **Background processes** Processes hosting Activities that aren't visible and that don't have any running Services. There will generally be a large number of background processes that Android will kill using a last-seen-first-killed pattern in order to obtain resources for foreground processes.

➤ **Empty processes** To improve overall system performance, Android will often retain an application in memory after it has reached the end of its lifetime. Android maintains this cache to improve the start-up time of applications when they're relaunched. These processes are routinely killed as required.

EXTERNALIZING RESOURCES

No matter what your development environment, it's always good practice to keep non-code resources like images and string constants external to your code. Android supports the externalization of resources ranging from simple values such as strings and colors to more complex resources like images (Drawables), animations, and themes. Perhaps the most powerful externalizable resources are layouts.

By externalizing resources you make them easier to maintain, update, and manage. This also lets you easily define alternative resource values to support different hardware and internationalization.

You'll see later in this section how Android dynamically selects resources from resource trees that contain different values for alternative hardware configurations, languages, and locations. This lets you create different resource values for specific languages, countries, screens, and keyboards. When an application starts, Android will automatically select the correct resource values without your having to write a line of code.

Among other things, this lets you change the layout based on the screen size and orientation and customize text prompts based on language and country.

Creating Resources

Application resources are stored under the res/ folder of your project hierarchy. In this folder each of the available resource types are stored in a subfolder containing those resources.

If you start a project using the ADT wizard, it will create a res folder that contains subfolders for the values, drawable-ldpi, drawable-mdpi, drawable-hdpi, and layout resources that contain the default layout, application icon, and string resource definitions respectively, as shown in Figure 3-4.

Note that three Drawable resource folders are created with three different icons, one each for low, medium, and high DPI displays.

Nine primary resource types have different folders: simple values, Drawables, layouts, animations, styles, menus, searchables, XML, and raw resources. When your application is built, these resources will be compiled as efficiently as possible and included in your application package.

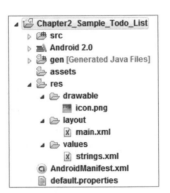

FIGURE 3-4

This process also generates an R class file that contains references to each of the resources you include in your project. This lets you reference the resources in your code, with the advantage of design-time syntax checking.

The following sections describe many of the specific resource types available within these categories and how to create them for your applications.

In all cases the resource file names should contain only lowercase letters, numbers, and the period (.) and underscore (_) symbols.

Creating Simple Values

Supported simple values include strings, colors, dimensions, and string or integer arrays. All simple values are stored within XML files in the res/values folder.

Within each XML file you indicate the type of value being stored using tags, as shown in the sample XML file in Listing 3-1.

LISTING 3-1: Simple values XML

```xml
<?xml version="1.0" encoding="utf-8"?>
<resources>
  <string name="app_name">To Do List</string>
  <color name="app_background">#FF0000FF</color>
  <dimen name="default_border">5px</dimen>
  <array name="string_array">
    <item>Item 1</item>
    <item>Item 2</item>
    <item>Item 3</item>
  </array>
  <array name="integer_array">
    <item>3</item>
    <item>2</item>
    <item>1</item>
  </array>
</resources>
```

This example includes all the simple value types. By convention, resources are separated into different files for each type; for example, res/values/strings.xml would contain only string resources.

The following sections detail the options for defining simple resources.

Strings

Externalizing your strings helps maintain consistency within your application and makes it much easier to create localized versions.

String resources are specified with the `<string>` tag, as shown in the following XML snippet.

```xml
<string name="stop_message">Stop.</string>
```

Android supports simple text styling, so you can use the HTML tags `<b>`, `<i>`, and `<u>` to apply bold, italics, or underlining respectively to parts of your text strings, as shown in the following example:

```xml
<string name="stop_message"><b>Stop.</b></string>
```

You can use resource strings as input parameters for the `String.format` method. However, `String.format` does not support the text styling described above. To apply styling to a format string you have to escape the HTML tags when creating your resource, as shown in the following.

```xml
<string name="stop_message">&lt;b>Stop&lt;/b>. %1$s</string>
```

Within your code, use the `Html.fromHtml` method to convert this back into a styled character sequence.

```java
String rString = getString(R.string.stop_message);
String fString = String.format(rString, "Collaborate and listen.");
CharSequence styledString = Html.fromHtml(fString);
```

Colors

Use the `<color>` tag to define a new color resource. Specify the color value using a # symbol followed by the (optional) alpha channel, then the red, green, and blue values using one or two hexadecimal numbers with any of the following notations:

➤ #RGB

➤ #RRGGBB

➤ #ARGB

➤ #AARRGGBB

The following example shows how to specify a fully opaque blue and a partially transparent green.

```
<color name="opaque_blue">#00F</color>
<color name="transparent_green">#7700FF00</color>
```

Dimensions

Dimensions are most commonly referenced within style and layout resources. They're useful for creating layout constants such as borders and font heights.

To specify a dimension resource use the `<dimen>` tag, specifying the dimension value, followed by an identifier describing the scale of your dimension:

➤ px (screen pixels)

➤ in (physical inches)

➤ pt (physical points)

➤ mm (physical millimeters)

➤ dp (density-independent pixels relative to a 160-dpi screen)

➤ sp (scale-independent pixels)

These alternatives let you define a dimension not only in absolute terms, but also using relative scales that account for different screen resolutions and densities to simplify scaling on different hardware.

The following XML snippet shows how to specify dimension values for a large font size and a standard border:

```
<dimen name="standard_border">5dp</dimen>
<dimen name="large_font_size">16sp</dimen>
```

Styles and Themes

Style resources let your applications maintain a consistent look and feel by enabling you to specify the attribute values used by Views. The most common use of themes and styles is to store the colors and fonts for an application.

You can easily change the appearance of your application by simply specifying a different style as the theme in your project manifest.

To create a style use a `<style>` tag that includes a `name` attribute and contains one or more `item` tags. Each `item` tag should include a `name` attribute used to specify the attribute (such as font size or color) being defined. The tag itself should then contain the value, as shown in the following skeleton code.

```
<?xml version="1.0" encoding="utf-8"?>
<resources>
  <style name="StyleName">
```

```
          <item name="attributeName">value</item>
      </style>
    </resources>
```

Styles support inheritance using the parent attribute on the <style> tag, making it easy to create simple variations.

The following example shows two styles that can also be used as a theme: a base style that sets several text properties and a second style that modifies the first to specify a smaller font.

```
        <?xml version="1.0" encoding="utf-8"?>
        <resources>
          <style name="BaseText">
            <item name="android:textSize">14sp</item>
            <item name="android:textColor">#111</item>
          </style>
          <style name="SmallText" parent="BaseText">
            <item name="android:textSize">8sp</item>
          </style>
        </resources>
```

Drawables

Drawable resources include bitmaps and NinePatch (stretchable PNG) images. They also include complex composite Drawables, such as LevelListDrawables and StateListDrawables that can be defined in XML.

Both NinePatch Drawables and complex composite resources are covered in more detail in the next chapter.

All Drawables are stored as individual files in the res/drawable folder. The resource identifier for a Drawable resource is the lowercase file name without an extension.

 The preferred format for a bitmap resource is PNG, although JPG and GIF files are also supported.

Layouts

Layout resources let you decouple your presentation layer by designing user interface layouts in XML rather than constructing them in code.

The most common use of a layout is for defining the user interface for an Activity. Once defined in XML, the layout is "inflated" within an Activity using setContentView, usually within the onCreate method. You can also reference layouts from within other layout resources, such as layouts for each row in a List View. More detailed information on using and creating layouts in Activities can be found in Chapter 4.

Using layouts to create your screens is best-practice UI design in Android. The decoupling of the layout from the code lets you create optimized layouts for different hardware configurations, such as varying screen sizes, orientation, or the presence of keyboards and touchscreens.

Each layout definition is stored in a separate file, each containing a single layout, in the `res/layout` folder. The file name then becomes the resource identifier.

A thorough explanation of layout containers and View elements is included in the next chapter, but as an example Listing 3-2 shows the layout created by the New Project Wizard. It uses a Linear Layout (described in more detail in Chapter 4) as a layout container for a Text View that displays the "Hello World" greeting.

LISTING 3-2: Hello World layout

```xml
<?xml version="1.0" encoding="utf-8"?>
<LinearLayout xmlns:android="http://schemas.android.com/apk/res/android"
  android:orientation="vertical"
  android:layout_width="fill_parent"
  android:layout_height="fill_parent">
  <TextView
    android:layout_width="fill_parent"
    android:layout_height="wrap_content"
    android:text="Hello World!"
  />
</LinearLayout>
```

Animations

Android supports two types of animation. *Tweened animations* can be used to rotate, move, stretch, and fade a View; or you can create frame-by-frame animations to display a sequence of Drawable images. A comprehensive overview of creating, using, and applying animations can be found in Chapter 15.

Defining animations as external resources enables you to reuse the same sequence in multiple places and provides you with the opportunity to present different animations based on device hardware or orientation.

Tweened Animations

Each tweened animation is stored in a separate XML file in the project's `res/anim` folder. As with layouts and Drawable resources, the animation's file name is used as its resource identifier.

An animation can be defined for changes in `alpha` (fading), `scale` (scaling), `translate` (movement), or `rotate` (rotation).

Table 3-1 shows the valid attributes, and attribute values, supported by each animation type.

You can create a combination of animations using the `set` tag. An animation set contains one or more animation transformations and supports various additional tags and attributes to customize when and how each animation within the set is run.

The following list shows some of the set tags available.

➤   `duration`   Duration of the animation in milliseconds.

➤   `startOffset`   Millisecond delay before the animation starts.

➤ `fillBefore` `true` to apply the animation transformation before it begins.

➤ `fillAfter` `true` to apply the animation transformation after it ends.

➤ `interpolator` Sets how the speed of this effect varies over time. Chapter 15 explores the interpolators available. To specify one, reference the system animation resources at `android:anim/interpolatorName`

TABLE 3-1: Animation type attributes

ANIMATION TYPE	ATTRIBUTES	VALID VALUES
Alpha	fromAlpha/toAlpha	Float from 0 to 1
Scale	fromXScale/toXScale	Float from 0 to 1
	fromYScale/toYScale	Float from 0 to 1
	pivotX/pivotY	String of the percentage of graphic width/height from 0% to 100%
Translate	fromX/to X	Float from 0 to 1
	fromY/toY	Float from 0 to 1
Rotate	fromDegrees/toDegrees	Float from 0 to 360
	pivotX/pivot Y	String of the percentage of graphic width/height from 0% to 100%

 If you do not use the `startOffset` *tag, all the animation effects within a set will execute simultaneously.*

The following example shows an animation set that spins the target 360 degrees while it shrinks and fades out.

```xml
<?xml version="1.0" encoding="utf-8"?>
<set xmlns:android="http://schemas.android.com/apk/res/android"
    android:interpolator="@android:anim/accelerate_interpolator">
  <rotate
    android:fromDegrees="0"
    android:toDegrees="360"
    android:pivotX="50%"
    android:pivotY="50%"
    android:startOffset="500"
    android:duration="1000" />
  <scale
    android:fromXScale="1.0"
    android:toXScale="0.0"
```

```
      android:fromYScale="1.0"
      android:toYScale="0.0"
      android:pivotX="50%"
      android:pivotY="50%"
      android:startOffset="500"
      android:duration="500" />
  <alpha
      android:fromAlpha="1.0"
      android:toAlpha="0.0"
      android:startOffset="500"
      android:duration="500" />
</set>
```

Frame-by-Frame Animations

Frame-by-frame animations let you create a sequence of Drawables, each of which will be displayed for a specified duration, on the background of a View.

Because frame-by-frame animations represent animated Drawables they are stored in the res/drawable folder, rather than with the tweened animations, and use their file names (without the .xml extension) as their resource IDs.

The following XML snippet shows a simple animation that cycles through a series of bitmap resources, displaying each one for half a second. In order to use this snippet you will need to create new image resources rocket1 through rocket3.

```
<animation-list
  xmlns:android="http://schemas.android.com/apk/res/android"
  android:oneshot="false">
  <item android:drawable="@drawable/rocket1" android:duration="500" />
  <item android:drawable="@drawable/rocket2" android:duration="500" />
  <item android:drawable="@drawable/rocket3" android:duration="500" />
</animation-list>
```

Menus

Create menu resources to further decouple your presentation layer by designing your menu layouts in XML rather than constructing them in code.

Menu resources can be used to define both Activity and context menus within your applications, and provide the same options you would have when constructing your menus in code. Once defined in XML, a menu is "inflated" within your application via the inflate method of the MenuInflator Service, usually within the onCreateOptionsMenu method. You will examine menus in more detail in Chapter 4.

Each menu definition is stored in a separate file, each containing a single menu, in the res/menu folder. The file name then becomes the resource identifier. Using XML to define your menus is best-practice design in Android.

A thorough explanation of menu options is included in the next chapter, but Listing 3-3 shows a simple menu example.

LISTING 3-3: Simple menu layout resource

```xml
<?xml version="1.0" encoding="utf-8"?>
<menu xmlns:android="http://schemas.android.com/apk/res/android">
  <item android:id="@+id/menu_refresh"
        android:title="Refresh" />
  <item android:id="@+id/menu_settings"
        android:title="Settings" />
</menu>
```

Using Resources

As well as the resources you create, Android supplies several system resources that you can use in your applications. The resources can be used directly from your application code and can also be referenced from within other resources (e.g., a dimension resource might be referenced in a layout definition).

Later in this chapter you'll learn how to define alternative resource values for different languages, locations, and hardware. It's important to note that when using resources you cannot choose a particular specialized version. Android will automatically select the most appropriate value for a given resource identifier based on the current hardware and device settings.

Using Resources in Code

You access resources in code using the static R class. R is a generated class based on your external resources, and created when your project is compiled. The R class contains static subclasses for each of the resource types for which you've defined at least one resource. For example, the default new project includes the R.string and R.drawable subclasses.

 If you are using the ADT plug-in in Eclipse, the R class will be created automatically when you make any change to an external resource file or folder. If you are not using the plug-in, use the AAPT tool to compile your project and generate the R class. R is a compiler-generated class, so don't make any manual modifications to it as they will be lost when the file is regenerated.

Each of the subclasses within R exposes its associated resources as variables, with the variable names matching the resource identifiers — for example, R.string.app_name or R.drawable.icon

The value of these variables is a reference to the corresponding resource's location in the resource table, *not* an instance of the resource itself.

Where a constructor or method, such as setContentView, accepts a resource identifier, you can pass in the resource variable, as shown in the following code snippet.

```java
// Inflate a layout resource.
setContentView(R.layout.main);
```

```
// Display a transient dialog box that displays the
// error message string resource.
Toast.makeText(this, R.string.app_error, Toast.LENGTH_LONG).show();
```

When you need an instance of the resource itself, you'll need to use helper methods to extract them from the resource table. The resource table is represented within your application as an instance of the Resources class.

Because these methods perform lookups on the application's resource table, these helper methods can't be static. Use the getResources method on your application context, as shown in the following snippet, to access your application's Resources instance.

```
Resources myResources = getResources();
```

The Resources class includes getters for each of the available resource types and generally works by passing in the resource ID you'd like an instance of. The following code snippet shows an example of using the helper methods to return a selection of resource values.

```
Resources myResources = getResources();

CharSequence styledText = myResources.getText(R.string.stop_message);
Drawable icon = myResources.getDrawable(R.drawable.app_icon);

int opaqueBlue = myResources.getColor(R.color.opaque_blue);

float borderWidth = myResources.getDimension(R.dimen.standard_border);

Animation tranOut;
tranOut = AnimationUtils.loadAnimation(this, R.anim.spin_shrink_fade);

String[] stringArray;
stringArray = myResources.getStringArray(R.array.string_array);

int[] intArray = myResources.getIntArray(R.array.integer_array);
```

Frame-by-frame animated resources are inflated into AnimationResources. You can return the value using getDrawable and casting the return value, as shown here:

```
AnimationDrawable rocket;
rocket = (AnimationDrawable)myResources.getDrawable(R.drawable.frame_by_frame);
```

Referencing Resources within Resources

You can also use resource references as attribute values in other XML resources.

This is particularly useful for layouts and styles, letting you create specialized variations on themes and localized strings and graphics. It's also a useful way to support different images and spacing for a layout to ensure that it's optimized for different screen sizes and resolutions.

To reference one resource from another use @ notation, as shown in the following snippet.

```
attribute="@[packagename:]resourcetype/resourceidentifier"
```

Android will assume you're using a resource from the same package, so you only need to fully qualify the package name if you're using a resource from a different package.

Listing 3-4 shows a layout that uses color, dimension, and string resources.

LISTING 3-4: Using resources in a layout

Available for download on Wrox.com

```xml
<?xml version="1.0" encoding="utf-8"?>
<LinearLayout
  xmlns:android="http://schemas.android.com/apk/res/android"
  android:orientation="vertical"
  android:layout_width="fill_parent"
  android:layout_height="fill_parent"
  android:padding="@dimen/standard_border">
  <EditText
    android:id="@+id/myEditText"
    android:layout_width="fill_parent"
    android:layout_height="wrap_content"
    android:text="@string/stop_message"
    android:textColor="@color/opaque_blue"
  />
</LinearLayout>
```

Using System Resources

The native Android applications externalize many of their resources, providing you with various strings, images, animations, styles, and layouts to use in your applications.

Accessing the system resources in code is similar to using your own resources. The difference is that you use the native Android resource classes available from `android.R`, rather than the application-specific R class. The following code snippet uses the `getString` method available in the application context to retrieve an error message available from the system resources:

```java
CharSequence httpError = getString(android.R.string.httpErrorBadUrl);
```

To access system resources in XML specify Android as the package name, as shown in this XML snippet.

```xml
<EditText
  android:id="@+id/myEditText"
  android:layout_width="fill_parent"
  android:layout_height="wrap_content"
  android:text="@android:string/httpErrorBadUrl"
  android:textColor="@android:color/darker_gray"
/>
```

Referring to Styles in the Current Theme

Using themes is an excellent way to ensure consistency for your application's UI. Rather than fully define each style, Android provides a shortcut to let you use styles from the currently applied theme.

To do this you use `?android:` rather than `@` as a prefix to the resource you want to use. The following example shows a snippet of the preceding code but uses the current theme's text color rather than an external resource.

```
<EditText
  android:id="@+id/myEditText"
  android:layout_width="fill_parent"
  android:layout_height="wrap_content"
  android:text="@string/stop_message"
  android:textColor="?android:textColor"
/>
```

This technique lets you create styles that will change if the current theme changes, without your having to modify each individual style resource.

To-Do List Resources Example

In this example you'll create new external resources in preparation for adding functionality to the To-Do List example you started in Chapter 2. The string and image resources you create here will be used in Chapter 4 when you implement a menu system for the To-Do List application.

The following steps will show you how to create text and icon resources to use for the Add and Remove menu items, and how to create a theme to apply to the application:

1. Create two new PNG images, one to represent adding a to-do list item, and one to represent removing an item. Each image should have dimensions of approximately 16 pixels by 16 pixels, like those illustrated in Figure 3-5.

    FIGURE 3-5

2. Copy the images into your project's `res/drawable-mdpi` folder and refresh your project.

3. Open the strings.xml resource from the `res/values` folder and add values for the `add_new`, `remove`, and `cancel` menu items. (You can remove the default `hello` string value while you're there.)

    ```xml
    <?xml version="1.0" encoding="utf-8"?>
    <resources>
      <string name="app_name">To Do List</string>
      <string name="add_new">Add New Item</string>
      <string name="remove">Remove Item</string>
      <string name="cancel">Cancel</string>
    </resources>
    ```

4. Create a new theme for the application by creating a new styles.xml resource in the `res/values` folder. Base your theme on the standard Android theme, but set values for a default text size.

```
<?xml version="1.0" encoding="utf-8"?>
<resources>
  <style name="ToDoTheme" parent="@android:style/Theme.Black">
    <item name="android:textSize">12sp</item>
  </style>
</resources>
```

5.   Apply the theme to your project in the manifest.

```
<activity android:name=".ToDoList"
          android:label="@string/app_name"
          android:theme="@style/ToDoTheme">
```

Creating Resources for Different Languages and Hardware

One of the most compelling reasons to externalize your resources is Android's dynamic resource-selection mechanism.

Using the directory structure described below, you can create different resource values for specific languages, locations, and hardware configurations. Android will choose from among these values dynamically at run time.

You can specify alternative resource values using a parallel directory structure within the res folder. A hyphen (-) is used to separate qualifiers that specify the conditions you're providing alternatives for.

The following example hierarchy shows a folder structure that features default string values, with French language and French Canadian location variations:

```
Project/
  res/
    values/
      strings.xml
    values-fr/
      strings.xml
    values-fr-rCA/
      strings.xml
```

The following list gives the qualifiers you can use to customize your resource values:

➤   **Mobile Country Code and Mobile Network Code (MCC/MNC)**   The country, and optionally the network, associated with the SIM currently used in the device. The MCC is specified by mcc followed by the three-digit country code. You can optionally add the MNC using mnc and the two- or three-digit network code (e.g., mcc234-mnc20 or mcc310). You can find a list of MCC/MNC codes on Wikipedia at http://en.wikipedia.org/wiki/Mobile_Network_Code

➤   **Language and Region**   Language specified by the lowercase two-letter ISO 639-1 language code, followed optionally by a region specified by a lowercase r followed by the uppercase two-letter ISO 3166-1-alpha-2 language code (e.g., en, en-rUS, or en-rGB).

➤   **Screen Size**   One of small (smaller than HVGA), medium (at least HVGA and smaller than VGA), or large (VGA or larger).

➤ **Screen Width/Length**   Specify `long` or `notlong` for resources designed specifically for wide screen (e.g., WVGA is `long`, QVGA is `notlong`).

➤ **Screen Orientation**   One of `port` (portrait), `land` (landscape), or `square` (square).

➤ **Screen Pixel Density**   Pixel density in dots per inch (dpi). Best practice is to use `ldpi`, `mdpi`, or `hdpi` to specify low (120 dpi), medium (160 dpi), or high (240 dpi) pixel density respectively. You can specify `nodpi` for bitmap resources you don't want scaled to support an exact screen density. Unlike with other resource types Android does not require an exact match to select a resource. When selecting the appropriate folder it will choose the nearest match to the device's pixel density and scale the resulting Drawables accordingly.

➤ **Touchscreen Type**   One of `notouch`, `stylus`, or `finger`.

➤ **Keyboard Availability**   One of `keysexposed`, `keyshidden`, or `keyssoft`.

➤ **Keyboard Input Type**   One of `nokeys`, `qwerty`, or `12key`.

➤ **UI Navigation Type**   One of `nonav`, `dpad`, `trackball`, or `wheel`.

You can specify multiple qualifiers for any resource type, separating each qualifier with a hyphen. Any combination is supported; however, they must be used in the order given in the preceding list, and no more than one value can be used per qualifier.

The following example shows valid and invalid directory names for alternative Drawable resources.

➤ **Valid:**

```
drawable-en-rUS
drawable-en-keyshidden
drawable-long-land-notouch-nokeys
```

➤ **Invalid:**

```
drawable-rUS-en (out of order)
drawable-rUS-rUK (multiple values for a single qualifier)
```

When Android retrieves a resource at run time, it will find the best match from the available alternatives. Starting with a list of all the folders in which the required value exists, it will select the one with the greatest number of matching qualifiers. If two folders are an equal match, the tiebreaker will be based on the order of the matched qualifiers in the preceding list.

 If no resource matches are found on a given device, your application will throw an exception when attempting to access that resource. To avoid this you should always include default values for each resource type in a folder that includes no qualifiers.

Runtime Configuration Changes

Android handles runtime changes to the language, location, and hardware by terminating and restarting each application and reloading the resource values.

This default behavior isn't always convenient or desirable, particularly as some configuration changes (like those to screen orientation and keyboard availability) can occur as easily as a user can rotate the device or slide out the keyboard. You can customize your application's response to such changes by detecting and reacting to them yourself.

To have an Activity listen for runtime configuration changes, add an `android:configChanges` attribute to its manifest node, specifying the configuration changes you want to handle.

The following list describes the configuration changes you can specify:

➤ `orientation` The screen has been rotated between portrait and landscape.

➤ `keyboardHidden` The keyboard has been exposed or hidden.

➤ `fontScale` The user has changed the preferred font size.

➤ `locale` The user has chosen a different language setting.

➤ `keyboard` The type of keyboard has changed; for example, the phone may have a 12-key keypad that flips out to reveal a full keyboard.

➤ `touchscreen` or `navigation` The type of keyboard or navigation method has changed. Neither of these events should normally happen.

In certain circumstances multiple events will be triggered simultaneously. For example, when the user is sliding out a keyboard most devices will fire both the `keyboardHidden` and `orientation` events.

You can select multiple events you wish to handle yourself by separating the values with a pipe (|).

Listing 3-5 shows an activity node declaring that it will handle changes in screen orientation and keyboard visibility.

LISTING 3-5: Activity definition for handling dynamic resource changes

```
<activity android:name=".TodoList"
          android:label="@string/app_name"
          android:theme="@style/TodoTheme"
          android:configChanges="orientation|keyboardHidden"/>
```

Adding an `android:configChanges` attribute suppresses the restart for the specified configuration changes, instead triggering the `onConfigurationChanged` method in the Activity. Override this method to handle the configuration changes, using the passed-in `Configuration` object to determine the new configuration values, as shown in Listing 3-6. Be sure to call back to the superclass and reload any resource values that the Activity uses, in case they've changed.

LISTING 3-6: Handling configuration changes in code

```
@Override
public void onConfigurationChanged(Configuration _newConfig) {
  super.onConfigurationChanged(_newConfig);

  [ ... Update any UI based on resource values ... ]
```

continues

```
    if (_newConfig.orientation == Configuration.ORIENTATION_LANDSCAPE) {
      [ ... React to different orientation ... ]
    }

    if (_newConfig.keyboardHidden == Configuration.KEYBOARDHIDDEN_NO) {
      [ ... React to changed keyboard visibility ... ]
    }
  }
```

When `onConfigurationChanged` is called, the Activity's Resource variables will have already been updated with the new values so they'll be safe to use.

Any configuration change that you don't explicitly flag as being handled by your application will cause your Activity to restart, without a call to `onConfigurationChanged`.

INTRODUCING THE ANDROID APPLICATION CLASS

Extending the `Application` class with your own implementation enables you to do three things:

1. Maintain application state

2. Transfer objects between application components

3. Manage and maintain resources used by several application components

When your Application implementation is registered in the manifest, it will be instantiated when your application process is created. As a result your Application implementation is by nature a singleton and should be implemented as such to provide access to its methods and member variables.

Extending and Using the Application Class

Listing 3-7 shows the skeleton code for extending the Application class and implementing it as a singleton.

LISTING 3-7: Skeleton application class

```
import android.app.Application;
import android.content.res.Configuration;

public class MyApplication extends Application {

  private static MyApplication singleton;

  // Returns the application instance
  public static MyApplication getInstance() {
    return singleton;
  }
```

```
    @Override
    public final void onCreate() {
      super.onCreate();
      singleton = this;
    }
  }
```

Once created, you must register your new Application class in the manifest's `<application>` node, as shown in the following snippet:

```
<application android:icon="@drawable/icon"
             android:name="MyApplication">
  [... Manifest nodes ...]
</application>
```

Your Application implementation will by instantiated when your application is started. Create new state variables and global resources for access from within the application components:

```
MyObject value = MyApplication.getInstance().getGlobalStateValue();
MyApplication.getInstance().setGlobalStateValue(myObjectValue);
```

This is a particularly effective technique for transferring objects between your loosely coupled application components, or for maintaining application state or shared resources.

Overriding the Application Life Cycle Events

The Application class also provides event handlers for application creation and termination, low available memory, and configuration changes (as described in the previous section).

By overriding these methods you can implement your own application-specific behavior for each of these circumstances:

➤ onCreate   Called when the application is created. Override this method to initialize your application singleton and create and initialize any application state variables or shared resources.

➤ onTerminate   Can be called when the application object is terminated. Note that there is no guarantee of this method handler's being called. If the application is terminated by the kernel in order to free resources for other applications, the process will be terminated without warning and without a call to the application object's onTerminate handler.

➤ onLowMemory   Provides an opportunity for well-behaved applications to free additional memory when the system is running low on resources. This will generally only be called when background processes have already been terminated and the current foreground applications are still low on memory. Override this handler to clear caches or release unnecessary resources.

➤ onConfigurationChanged   Unlike with Activities, your application object is not killed and restarted for configuration changes. Override this handler if it is necessary to handle configuration changes at an application level.

As shown in Listing 3-8, you must always call through to the superclass event handlers when overriding these methods.

LISTING 3-8: Overriding the application life cycle handlers

```java
public class MyApplication extends Application {

  private static MyApplication singleton;

  // Returns the application instance
  public static MyApplication getInstance() {
    return singleton;
  }

  @Override
  public final void onCreate() {
    super.onCreate();
    singleton = this;
  }

  @Override
  public final void onTerminate() {
    super.onTerminate();
  }

  @Override
  public final void onLowMemory() {
    super.onLowMemory();
  }

  @Override
  public final void onConfigurationChanged(Configuration newConfig) {
    super.onConfigurationChanged(newConfig);
  }
}
```

A CLOSER LOOK AT ANDROID ACTIVITIES

To create user interface screens you extend the `Activity` class, using Views to provide the UI and allow user interaction.

Each Activity represents a screen (similar to a Form) that an application can present to its users. The more complicated your application, the more screens you are likely to need.

Create a new Activity for every screen you want to display. Typically this includes at least a primary interface screen that handles the main UI functionality of your application. This primary interface is often supported by secondary Activities for entering information, providing different perspectives on your data, and supporting additional functionality. To move between screens start a new Activity (or return from one).

Most Activities are designed to occupy the entire display, but you can also create Activities that are semitransparent or floating.

Creating an Activity

Extend `Activity` to create a new Activity class. Within this new class you must define the user interface and implement your functionality. The basic skeleton code for a new Activity is shown in Listing 3-9.

LISTING 3-9: Activity skeleton code

```
package com.paad.myapplication;

import android.app.Activity;
import android.os.Bundle;

public class MyActivity extends Activity {

  /** Called when the activity is first created. */
  @Override
  public void onCreate(Bundle savedInstanceState) {
    super.onCreate(savedInstanceState);
  }
}
```

The base Activity class presents an empty screen that encapsulates the window display handling. An empty Activity isn't particularly useful, so the first thing you'll want to do is create the user interface with Views and layouts.

Views are the user interface controls that display data and provide user interaction. Android provides several layout classes, called *View Groups*, that can contain multiple Views to help you design your user interfaces.

Chapter 4 examines Views and View Groups in detail, examining what's available, how to use them, and how to create your own Views and layouts.

To assign a user interface to an Activity, call `setContentView` from the `onCreate` method of your Activity.

In this first snippet, an instance of a `TextView` is used as the Activity's user interface:

```
@Override
public void onCreate(Bundle savedInstanceState) {
  super.onCreate(savedInstanceState);
  TextView textView = new TextView(this);
  setContentView(textView);
}
```

Usually you'll want to use a more complex UI design. You can create a layout in code using layout View Groups, or you can use the standard Android convention of passing a resource ID for a layout defined in an external resource, as shown in the following snippet:

```
@Override
public void onCreate(Bundle savedInstanceState) {
  super.onCreate(savedInstanceState);
  setContentView(R.layout.main);
}
```

In order to use an Activity in your application you need to register it in the manifest. Add new `<activity>` tags within the `<application>` node of the manifest; the `<activity>` tag includes attributes for metadata such as the label, icon, required permissions, and themes used by the Activity. An Activity without a corresponding `<activity>` tag can't be displayed.

The XML in Listing 3-10 shows how to add a node for the `MyActivity` class created in Listing 3-9.

LISTING 3-10: Activity layout in XML

```
<activity android:label="@string/app_name"
          android:name=".MyActivity">
</activity>
```

Within the `<activity>` tag you can add `<intent-filter>` nodes that specify the Intents your Activity will listen for and react to. Each Intent Filter defines one or more actions and categories that your Activity supports. Intents and Intent Filters are covered in depth in Chapter 5, but it's worth noting that for an Activity to be available from the main application launcher it must include an Intent Filter listening for the MAIN action and the LAUNCHER category, as highlighted in Listing 3-11.

LISTING 3-11: Main application Activity definition

```
<activity android:label="@string/app_name"
          android:name=".MyActivity">
    <intent-filter>
        <action android:name="android.intent.action.MAIN" />
        <category android:name="android.intent.category.LAUNCHER" />
    </intent-filter>
</activity>
```

The Activity Life Cycle

A good understanding of the Activity life cycle is vital to ensure that your application provides a seamless user experience and properly manages its resources.

As explained earlier, Android applications do not control their own process lifetimes; the Android run time manages the process of each application, and by extension that of each Activity within it.

While the run time handles the termination and management of an Activity's process, the Activity's state helps determine the priority of its parent application. The application priority, in turn, influences the likelihood that the run time will terminate it and the Activities running within it.

Activity Stacks

The state of each Activity is determined by its position on the Activity stack, a last-in–first-out collection of all the currently running Activities. When a new Activity starts, the current foreground screen is moved to the top of the stack. If the user navigates back using the Back button, or the foreground Activity is closed, the next Activity on the stack moves up and becomes active. This process is illustrated in Figure 3-6.

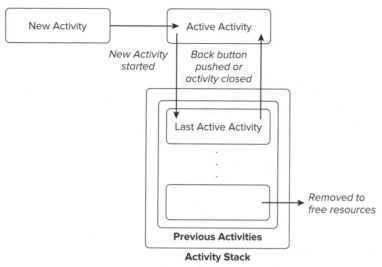

FIGURE 3-6

As described previously in this chapter, an application's priority is influenced by its highest-priority Activity. When the Android memory manager is deciding which application to terminate to free resources, it uses this stack to determine the priority of applications based on their Activities.

Activity States

As Activities are created and destroyed they move in and out of the stack shown in Figure 3-6. As they do so, they transition through four possible states:

➤ **Active** When an Activity is at the top of the stack it is the visible, focused, foreground Activity that is receiving user input. Android will attempt to keep it alive at all costs, killing Activities further down the stack as needed, to ensure that it has the resources it needs. When another Activity becomes active, this one will be paused.

➤ **Paused** In some cases your Activity will be visible but will not have focus; at this point it's paused. This state is reached if a transparent or non-full-screen Activity is active in front of it. When paused, an Activity is treated as if it were active; however, it doesn't receive user input events. In extreme cases Android will kill a paused Activity to recover resources for the active Activity. When an Activity becomes totally obscured, it is stopped.

➤ **Stopped** When an Activity isn't visible, it "stops." The Activity will remain in memory, retaining all state information; however, it is now a candidate for termination when the system requires memory elsewhere. When an Activity is stopped it's important to save data and the current UI state. Once an Activity has exited or closed, it becomes inactive.

➤ **Inactive** After an Activity has been killed, and before it's been launched, it's inactive. Inactive Activities have been removed from the Activity stack and need to be restarted before they can be displayed and used.

State transitions are nondeterministic and are handled entirely by the Android memory manager. Android will start by closing applications that contain inactive Activities, followed by those that are stopped. In extreme cases it will remove those that are paused.

 To ensure a seamless user experience, transitions between states should be invisible to the user. There should be no difference in an Activity moving from a paused, stopped, or inactive state back to active, so it's important to save all UI state and persist all data when an Activity is paused or stopped. Once an Activity does become active, it should restore those saved values.

Monitoring State Changes

To ensure that Activities can react to state changes, Android provides a series of event handlers that are fired when an Activity transitions through its full, visible, and active lifetimes. Figure 3-7 summarizes these lifetimes in terms of the Activity states described in the previous section.

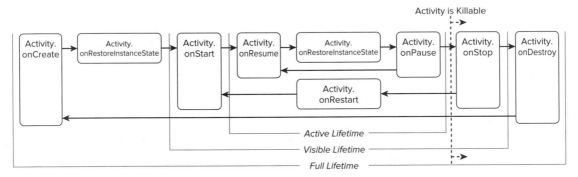

FIGURE 3-7

The skeleton code in Listing 3-12 shows the stubs for the state change method handlers available in an Activity. Comments within each stub describe the actions you should consider taking on each state change event.

LISTING 3-12: Activity state event handlers

```
package com.paad.myapplication;

import android.app.Activity;
import android.os.Bundle;

public class MyActivity extends Activity {
```

```java
// Called at the start of the full lifetime.
@Override
public void onCreate(Bundle savedInstanceState) {
  super.onCreate(savedInstanceState);
  // Initialize activity.
}

// Called after onCreate has finished, use to restore UI state
@Override
public void onRestoreInstanceState(Bundle savedInstanceState) {
  super.onRestoreInstanceState(savedInstanceState);
  // Restore UI state from the savedInstanceState.
  // This bundle has also been passed to onCreate.
}

// Called before subsequent visible lifetimes
// for an activity process.
@Override
public void onRestart(){
  super.onRestart();
  // Load changes knowing that the activity has already
  // been visible within this process.
}

// Called at the start of the visible lifetime.
@Override
public void onStart(){
  super.onStart();
  // Apply any required UI change now that the Activity is visible.
}

// Called at the start of the active lifetime.
@Override
public void onResume(){
  super.onResume();
  // Resume any paused UI updates, threads, or processes required
  // by the activity but suspended when it was inactive.
}

// Called to save UI state changes at the
// end of the active lifecycle.
@Override
public void onSaveInstanceState(Bundle savedInstanceState) {
  // Save UI state changes to the savedInstanceState.
  // This bundle will be passed to onCreate if the process is
  // killed and restarted.
  super.onSaveInstanceState(savedInstanceState);
}

// Called at the end of the active lifetime.
@Override
```

continues

LISTING 3-12 *(continued)*

```
public void onPause(){
  // Suspend UI updates, threads, or CPU intensive processes
  // that don't need to be updated when the Activity isn't
  // the active foreground activity.
  super.onPause();
}

// Called at the end of the visible lifetime.
@Override
public void onStop(){
  // Suspend remaining UI updates, threads, or processing
  // that aren't required when the Activity isn't visible.
  // Persist all edits or state changes
  // as after this call the process is likely to be killed.
  super.onStop();
}

// Called at the end of the full lifetime.
@Override
public void onDestroy(){
  // Clean up any resources including ending threads,
  // closing database connections etc.
  super.onDestroy();
}
}
```

As shown in the preceding code, you should always call back to the superclass when overriding these event handlers.

Understanding Activity Lifetimes

Within an Activity's full lifetime, between creation and destruction, it will go through one or more iterations of the active and visible lifetimes. Each transition will trigger the method handlers described previously. The following sections provide a closer look at each of these lifetimes and the events that bracket them.

The Full Lifetime

The full lifetime of your Activity occurs between the first call to onCreate and the final call to onDestroy. It's possible, in some cases, for an Activity's process to be terminated *without* the onDestroy method being called.

Use the onCreate method to initialize your Activity: inflate the user interface, allocate references to class variables, bind data to controls, and create Services and threads. The onCreate method is passed a Bundle object containing the UI state saved in the last call to onSaveInstanceState. You should use this Bundle to restore the user interface to its previous state, either within the onCreate method or by overriding onRestoreInstanceState.

Override onDestroy to clean up any resources created in onCreate, and ensure that all external connections, such as network or database links, are closed.

As part of Android's guidelines for writing efficient code, it's recommended that you avoid the creation of short-term objects. Rapid creation and destruction of objects forces additional garbage collection, a process that can have a direct impact on the user experience. If your Activity creates the same set of objects regularly, consider creating them in the onCreate method instead, as it's called only once in the Activity's lifetime.

The Visible Lifetime

An Activity's visible lifetimes are bound between calls to onStart and onStop. Between these calls your Activity will be visible to the user, although it may not have focus and may be partially obscured. Activities are likely to go through several visible lifetimes during their full lifetime, as they move between the foreground and background. While it's unusual, in extreme cases the Android run time will kill an Activity during its visible lifetime without a call to onStop.

The onStop method should be used to pause or stop animations, threads, sensor listeners, GPS lookups, timers, Services, or other processes that are used exclusively to update the user interface. There's little value in consuming resources (such as CPU cycles or network bandwidth) to update the UI when it isn't visible. Use the onStart (or onRestart) methods to resume or restart these processes when the UI is visible again.

The onRestart method is called immediately prior to all but the first call to onStart. Use it to implement special processing that you want done only when the Activity restarts within its full lifetime.

The onStart/onStop methods are also used to register and unregister Broadcast Receivers that are being used exclusively to update the user interface. You'll learn more about using Broadcast Receivers in Chapter 5.

The Active Lifetime

The active lifetime starts with a call to onResume and ends with a corresponding call to onPause.

An active Activity is in the foreground and is receiving user input events. Your Activity is likely to go through several active lifetimes before it's destroyed, as the active lifetime will end when a new Activity is displayed, the device goes to sleep, or the Activity loses focus. Try to keep code in the onPause and onResume methods relatively fast and lightweight to ensure that your application remains responsive when moving in and out of the foreground.

Immediately before onPause, a call is made to onSaveInstanceState. This method provides an opportunity to save the Activity's UI state in a Bundle that will be passed to the onCreate and onRestoreInstanceState methods. Use onSaveInstanceState to save the UI state (such as checkbox states, user focus, and entered but uncommitted user input) to ensure that the Activity can present the same UI when it next becomes active. You can safely assume that during the active lifetime onSaveInstanceState and onPause will be called before the process is terminated.

Most Activity implementations will override at least the onPause method to commit unsaved changes, as it marks the point beyond which an Activity may be killed without warning. Depending on your application architecture you may also choose to suspend threads, processes, or Broadcast Receivers while your Activity is not in the foreground.

The `onResume` method can be very lightweight. You will not need to reload the UI state here as this is handled by the `onCreate` and `onRestoreInstanceState` methods when required. Use `onResume` to reregister any Broadcast Receivers or other processes you may have suspended in `onPause`.

Android Activity Classes

The Android SDK includes a selection of Activity subclasses that wrap up the use of common user interface widgets. Some of the more useful ones are listed here:

- ➤ **MapActivity**   Encapsulates the resource handling required to support a `MapView` widget within an Activity. Learn more about `MapActivity` and `MapView` in Chapter 8.

- ➤ **ListActivity**   Wrapper class for Activities that feature a `ListView` bound to a data source as the primary UI metaphor, and exposing event handlers for list item selection.

- ➤ **ExpandableListActivity**   Similar to the List Activity but supporting an `ExpandableListView`

- ➤ **TabActivity**   Enables you to embed multiple Activities or Views within a single screen using a tab widget to switch among them.

SUMMARY

In this chapter you learned how to design robust applications using loosely coupled application components: Activities, Services, Content Providers, Intents, and Broadcast Receivers bound together by the application manifest.

You were introduced to the Android application life cycle, learning how each application's priority is determined by its process state, which is, in turn, determined by the state of the components within it.

To take full advantage of the wide range of device hardware available and the international user base, you learned how to create external resources and how to define alternative values for specific locations, languages, and hardware configurations.

Next you learned about the Application class, and how to extend it to facilitate application state management and inter-component data transfer.

You then discovered more about Activities and their role in the application framework. As well as learning how to create new Activities, you were introduced to the Activity life cycle. In particular, you learned about Activity state transitions and how to monitor these events to ensure a seamless user experience.

Finally, you were introduced to some specialized Android Activity classes.

In the next chapter you'll learn how to create user interfaces. Chapter 4 will demonstrate how to use layouts to design your UI before introducing some native widgets and showing you how to extend, modify, and group them to create specialized controls. You'll also learn how to create your own unique user interface elements from a blank canvas, before being introduced to the Android menu system.

Creating User Interfaces

WHAT'S IN THIS CHAPTER?

➤ Using Views and layouts

➤ Optimizing layouts

➤ XML Drawable resources

➤ Creating resolution-independent user interfaces

➤ The Android menu system

➤ Extending, grouping, creating, and using Views

It's vital that you create compelling and intuitive user interfaces for your applications. Ensuring that they are as stylish and easy to use as they are functional should be a top design priority.

To quote Stephen Fry on the importance of style as part of substance in the design of digital devices:

> *As if a device can function if it has no style. As if a device can be called stylish that does not function superbly. . . . yes, beauty matters. Boy, does it matter. It is not surface, it is not an extra, it is the thing itself.*
>
> — STEPHEN FRY, *The Guardian (October 27, 2007)*

Increasing screen sizes, display resolutions, and mobile processor power have made mobile applications increasingly visual. While the diminutive screens pose a challenge for those creating complex visual interfaces, the ubiquity of mobiles makes it a challenge worth accepting.

In this chapter you'll learn about the basic Android UI elements and discover how to use Views, View Groups, and layouts to create functional and intuitive user interfaces for your Activities.

After being introduced to some of the controls available from the Android SDK, you'll learn how to extend and customize them. Using View Groups, you'll see how to combine Views to create atomic, reusable UI elements made up of interacting subcontrols. You'll also learn how to create your own Views to implement creative new ways to display data and interact with users.

The individual elements of an Android user interface are arranged on screen by means of a variety of layout managers derived from `ViewGroup`. The correct use of layouts is essential for creating good interfaces; this chapter introduces several native layout classes and demonstrates how to use them and how to create your own.

With the range of Android devices rapidly increasing, the range of screen sizes and resolutions your app will be expected to run on has also increased. You'll learn how to create resolution-independent layouts and Drawables and the best practices for developing and testing your UIs so they look great on all host screens.

Android's application and context menu systems use a new approach, optimized for modern touch screen devices. As part of an examination of the Android UI model, this chapter ends with a look at how to create and use Activity and context menus.

FUNDAMENTAL ANDROID UI DESIGN

User interface (UI) design, user experience (UX), human computer interaction (HCI), and usability are huge topics that aren't covered in great depth in this book. Nonetheless, it's important that you get them right when creating your user interfaces.

Android introduces some new terminology for familiar programming metaphors that will be explored in detail in the following sections:

➤ **Views** *Views* are the base class for all visual interface elements (commonly known as *controls* or *widgets*). All UI controls, including the layout classes, are derived from `View`.

➤ **View Groups** *View Groups* are extensions of the View class that can contain multiple child Views. Extend the `ViewGroup` class to create compound controls made up of interconnected child Views. The `ViewGroup` class is also extended to provide the layout managers that help you lay out controls within your Activities.

➤ **Activities** *Activities*, described in detail in the previous chapter, represent the window, or screen, being displayed. Activities are the Android equivalent of Forms. To display a user interface you assign a View (usually a layout) to an Activity.

Android provides several common UI controls, widgets, and layout managers.

For most graphical applications it's likely that you'll need to extend and modify these standard Views — or create composite or entirely new Views — to provide your own user experience.

INTRODUCING VIEWS

As described earlier, all visual components in Android descend from the `View` class and are referred to generically as Views. You'll often see Views referred to as controls or widgets (not to be confused with home screen or App Widgets described in Chapter 10) — terms you're probably familiar with if you've previously done any GUI development.

The `ViewGroup` class is an extension of View designed to contain multiple Views. Generally, View Groups are used either to construct atomic reusable components or to manage the layout of child Views. View Groups that perform the latter function are generally referred to as *layouts*.

Because all visual elements derive from View, you will likely see both *widget* and *control* used interchangeably with *View*.

You were already introduced to a layout and two native Views — the `LinearLayout`, a `ListView`, and a `TextView` — when you created the to-do list example in Chapter 2.

In the following sections you'll learn how to put together increasingly complex UIs, starting with the Views available in the SDK, before learning how to extend them, build your own compound controls, and create your own custom Views from scratch.

Creating Activity User Interfaces with Views

A new Activity starts with a temptingly empty screen onto which you place your user interface. To assign the user interface, call `setContentView`, passing in the View instance, or layout resource, to display. Because empty screens aren't particularly inspiring, you will almost always use `setContentView` to assign an Activity's user interface when overriding its `onCreate` handler.

The `setContentView` method accepts either a layout resource ID (as described in Chapter 3) or a single View instance. This lets you define your user interface either in code or using the preferred technique of external layout resources.

Using layout resources decouples your presentation layer from the application logic, providing the flexibility to change the presentation without changing code. This makes it possible to specify different layouts optimized for different hardware configurations, even changing them at run time based on hardware changes (such as screen orientation).

Listing 4-1 shows how to set the user interface for an Activity using an external layout resource. You can get references to the Views used within a layout with the `findViewById` method. This example assumes that main.xml exists in the project's `res/layout` folder.

LISTING 4-1: Inflating an Activity layout

```
@Override
public void onCreate(Bundle savedInstanceState) {
  super.onCreate(savedInstanceState);

  setContentView(R.layout.main);
  TextView myTextView = (TextView)findViewById(R.id.myTextView);
}
```

If you prefer the more traditional approach, you can construct the user interface in code. Listing 4-2 shows how to assign a new `TextView` as the user interface.

LISTING 4-2: Creating a UI layout in code

```
@Override
public void onCreate(Bundle savedInstanceState) {
    super.onCreate(savedInstanceState);

    TextView myTextView = new TextView(this);
    setContentView(myTextView);

    myTextView.setText("Hello, Android");
}
```

The `setContentView` method accepts a single View instance; as a result, you have to use layouts to add multiple controls to your Activity.

The Android Widget Toolbox

Android supplies a toolbox of standard Views to help you create simple interfaces. By using these controls (and modifying or extending them as necessary), you can simplify your development and provide consistency between applications.

The following list highlights some of the more familiar toolbox controls:

➤ `TextView`   A standard read-only text label. It supports multiline display, string formatting, and automatic word wrapping.

➤ `EditText`   An editable text entry box. It accepts multiline entry, word-wrapping, and hint text.

➤ `ListView`   A View Group that creates and manages a vertical list of Views, displaying them as rows within the list. The simplest List View displays the `toString` value of each object in an array, using a Text View for each item.

➤ `Spinner`   A composite control that displays a Text View and an associated List View that lets you select an item from a list to display in the textbox. It's made from a Text View displaying the current selection, combined with a button that displays a selection dialog when pressed.

➤ `Button`   A standard push-button.

➤ `CheckBox`   A two-state button represented by a checked or unchecked box.

➤ `RadioButton`   A two-state grouped button. A group of these presents the user with a number of binary options of which only one can be enabled at a time.

➤ `ViewFlipper`   A View Group that lets you define a collection of Views as a horizontal row in which only one View is visible at a time, and in which transitions between visible views are animated.

➤ `QuickContactBadge`   Displays a badge showing the image icon assigned to a contact you specify using a phone number, name, e-mail address, or URI. Clicking the image will display the quick contact bar, which provides shortcuts for contacting the selected contact — including calling, sending an SMS, e-mail, and IM.

This is only a selection of the widgets available. Android also supports several more advanced View implementations, including date-time pickers, auto-complete input boxes, maps, galleries, and tab sheets. For a more comprehensive list of the available widgets, head to http://developer.android.com/guide/tutorials/views/index.html

It's only a matter of time before you, as an innovative developer, encounter a situation in which none of the built-in controls meets your needs. Later in this chapter you'll learn how to extend and combine the existing controls and how to design and create entirely new widgets from scratch.

INTRODUCING LAYOUTS

Layout managers (more generally just called *layouts*) are extensions of the ViewGroup class used to position child controls for your UI. Layouts can be nested, letting you create arbitrarily complex interfaces using a combination of layouts.

The Android SDK includes some simple layouts to help you construct your UI. It's up to you to select the right combination of layouts to make your interface easy to understand and use.

The following list includes some of the more versatile layout classes available:

> ➤ FrameLayout   The simplest of the Layout Managers, the *Frame Layout* simply pins each child view to the top left corner. Adding multiple children stacks each new child on top of the one before, with each new View obscuring the last.

> ➤ LinearLayout   A *Linear Layout* aligns each child View in either a vertical or a horizontal line. A vertical layout has a column of Views, while a horizontal layout has a row of Views. The Linear Layout manager enables you to specify a "weight" for each child View that controls the relative size of each within the available space.

> ➤ RelativeLayout   The most flexible of the native layouts, the *Relative Layout* lets you define the positions of each child View relative to the others and to the screen boundaries.

> ➤ TableLayout   The *Table Layout* lets you lay out Views using a grid of rows and columns. Tables can span multiple rows and columns, and columns can be set to shrink or grow.

> ➤ Gallery   A *Gallery Layout* displays a single row of items in a horizontally scrolling list.

The Android documentation describes the features and properties of each layout class in detail, so rather than repeat it here, I'll refer you to http://developer.android.com/guide/topics/ui/layout-objects.html

Later in this chapter you'll also learn how to create compound controls (widgets made up of several interconnected Views) by extending these layout classes.

Using Layouts

The preferred way to implement layouts is by using XML as external resources. A layout XML must contain a single root element. This root node can contain as many nested layouts and Views as necessary to construct an arbitrarily complex screen.

Listing 4-3 shows a simple layout that places a TextView above an EditText control using a vertical LinearLayout.

LISTING 4-3: Simple Linear Layout in XML

```xml
<?xml version="1.0" encoding="utf-8"?>
<LinearLayout xmlns:android="http://schemas.android.com/apk/res/android"
  android:orientation="vertical"
  android:layout_width="fill_parent"
  android:layout_height="fill_parent">
  <TextView
    android:layout_width="fill_parent"
    android:layout_height="wrap_content"
    android:text="Enter Text Below"
  />
  <EditText
    android:layout_width="fill_parent"
    android:layout_height="wrap_content"
    android:text="Text Goes Here!"
  />
</LinearLayout>
```

Note that for each of the layout elements, the constants `wrap_content` and `fill_parent` are used rather than an exact height or width in pixels. These constants are the simplest, and most powerful, technique for ensuring your layouts are screen-size and resolution independent.

The `wrap_content` constant will set the size of a View to the minimum required to contain the contents it displays (such as the height required to display a wrapped text string). The `fill_parent` constant expands the View to fill the available space within the parent View (or screen).

In Listing 4-3, the layout is set to fill the entire screen, while both text-based Views are asked to fill the full available width. Their height is restricted to that required by the text being displayed.

Later in this chapter you'll learn how to set the minimum height and width for your own controls, as well as further best practices for resolution independence.

Implementing layouts in XML decouples the presentation layer from the View and Activity code. It also lets you create hardware-specific variations that are dynamically loaded without requiring code changes.

When preferred, or required, you can implement layouts in code. When you're assigning Views to layouts in code, it's important to apply `LayoutParameters` using the `setLayoutParams` method, or by passing them in to the `addView` call, as shown in Listing 4-4.

LISTING 4-4: Simple LinearLayout in code

```java
LinearLayout ll = new LinearLayout(this);
ll.setOrientation(LinearLayout.VERTICAL);

TextView myTextView = new TextView(this);
EditText myEditText = new EditText(this);
```

```
myTextView.setText("Enter Text Below");
myEditText.setText("Text Goes Here!");

int lHeight = LinearLayout.LayoutParams.FILL_PARENT;
int lWidth = LinearLayout.LayoutParams.WRAP_CONTENT;

ll.addView(myTextView, new LinearLayout.LayoutParams(lHeight, lWidth));
ll.addView(myEditText, new LinearLayout.LayoutParams(lHeight, lWidth));
setContentView(ll);
```

Optimizing Layouts

Inflating layouts into your Activities is an expensive process. Each additional nested layout and View can have a dramatic impact on the performance and seamlessness of your applications.

In general, it's good practice to keep your layouts as simple as possible, but also to avoid needing to inflate an entirely new layout for small changes to an existing one.

The following points include some best practice guidelines for creating efficient layouts. Note that they are not exhaustive.

➤ **Avoid unnecessary nesting:** Don't put one layout within another unless it is necessary. A Linear Layout within a Frame Layout, both of which are set to FILL_PARENT, does nothing but add extra time to inflate. Look for redundant layouts, particularly if you've been making significant changes to an existing layout.

➤ **Avoid using too many Views:** Each additional View in a layout takes time and resources to inflate. A layout shouldn't ever include more than 80 Views or the time taken to inflate it becomes significant.

➤ **Avoid deep nesting:** As layouts can be arbitrarily nested, it's easy to create complex, deeply nested hierarchies. While there is no hard limit, it's good practice to restrict nesting to fewer than 10 levels.

It's important that you optimize your layout hierarchies to reduce inefficiencies and eliminate unnecessary nesting.

To assist you, the Android SDK includes the layoutopt command line tool. Call layoutopt, passing in the name of the layout resource (or a resource folder) to have your layouts analyzed and to receive recommendations for fixes and improvements.

CREATING NEW VIEWS

The ability to extend existing Views, assemble composite controls, and create unique new Views lets you implement beautiful user interfaces optimized for your application's workflow. Android lets you subclass the existing View toolbox or implement your own View controls, giving you total freedom to tailor your UI to optimize the user experience.

> *When you design a user interface it's important to balance raw aesthetics and usability. With the power to create your own custom controls comes the temptation to rebuild all your controls from scratch. Resist that urge. The standard Views will be familiar to users from other Android applications and will update in line with new platform releases. On small screens, with users often paying limited attention, familiarity can often provide better usability than a slightly shinier control.*

The best approach to use when creating a new View depends on what you want to achieve:

➤ *Modify or extend the appearance and/or behavior of an existing control* when it already supplies the basic functionality you want. By overriding the event handlers and onDraw, but still calling back to the superclass's methods, you can customize a View without having to reimplement its functionality. For example, you could customize a TextView to display a set number of decimal points.

➤ *Combine Views* to create atomic, reusable controls that leverage the functionality of several interconnected Views. For example, you could create a dropdown combo box by combining a TextView and a Button that displays a floating ListView when clicked.

➤ *Create an entirely new control* when you need a completely different interface that you can't get by changing or combining existing controls.

Modifying Existing Views

The toolbox includes Views that provide many common UI requirements, but the controls are necessarily generic. By customizing these basic Views you avoid reimplementing existing behavior while still tailoring the user interface, and functionality, to your application's needs.

To create a new View based on an existing control, create a new class that extends it, as shown in Listing 4-5.

LISTING 4-5: Extending TextView

```
import android.content.Context;
import android.util.AttributeSet;
import android.widget.TextView;

public class MyTextView extends TextView {

  public MyTextView (Context context, AttributeSet attrs, int defStyle)
  {
    super(context, attrs, defStyle);
  }

  public MyTextView (Context context) {
    super(context);
  }
```

```
        public MyTextView (Context context, AttributeSet attrs) {
          super(context, attrs);
        }
      }
```

To override the appearance or behavior of your new View, override and extend the event handlers associated with the behavior you want to change.

In the following extension of the Listing 4-5 code, the onDraw method is overridden to modify the View's appearance, and the onKeyDown handler is overridden to allow custom key-press handling.

```
public class MyTextView extends TextView {

  public MyTextView (Context context, AttributeSet ats, int defStyle) {
    super(context, ats, defStyle);
  }

  public MyTextView (Context context) {
    super(context);
  }

  public MyTextView (Context context, AttributeSet attrs) {
    super(context, attrs);
  }

  @Override
  public void onDraw(Canvas canvas) {
    [ ... Draw things on the canvas under the text ... ]

    // Render the text as usual using the TextView base class.
    super.onDraw(canvas);

    [ ... Draw things on the canvas over the text ... ]
  }

  @Override
  public boolean onKeyDown(int keyCode, KeyEvent keyEvent) {
    [ ... Perform some special processing ... ]
    [ ... based on a particular key press ... ]

    // Use the existing functionality implemented by
    // the base class to respond to a key press event.
    return super.onKeyDown(keyCode, keyEvent);
  }
}
```

The event handlers available within Views are covered in more detail later in this chapter.

Customizing Your To-Do List

The to-do list example from Chapter 2 uses TextView controls to represent each row in a List View. You can customize the appearance of the list by extending Text View and overriding the onDraw method.

In this example you'll create a new TodoListItemView that will make each item appear as if on a paper pad. When complete, your customized to-do list should look like Figure 4-1.

1. Create a new `TodoListItemView` class that extends `TextView`. Include a stub for overriding the `onDraw` method, and implement constructors that call a new `init` method stub.

```
package com.paad.todolist;

import android.content.Context;
import android.content.res.Resources;
import android.graphics.Canvas;
import android.graphics.Paint;
import android.util.AttributeSet;
import android.widget.TextView;

public class TodoListItemView extends TextView {

  public TodoListItemView (Context context, AttributeSet ats, int ds) {
    super(context, ats, ds);
    init();
  }

  public TodoListItemView (Context context) {
    super(context);
    init();
  }

  public TodoListItemView (Context context, AttributeSet attrs) {
    super(context, attrs);
    init();
  }

  private void init() {
  }

  @Override
  public void onDraw(Canvas canvas) {
    // Use the base TextView to render the text.
    super.onDraw(canvas);
  }

}
```

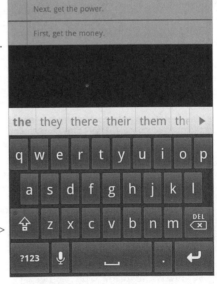

2. Create a new colors.xml resource in the `res/values` folder. Create new color values for the paper, margin, line, and text colors.

```xml
<?xml version="1.0" encoding="utf-8"?>
<resources>
  <color name="notepad_paper">#AAFFFF99</color>
  <color name="notepad_lines">#FF0000FF</color>
  <color name="notepad_margin">#90FF0000</color>
  <color name="notepad_text">#AA0000FF</color>
</resources>
```

3. Create a new dimens.xml resource file and add a new value for the paper's margin width.

FIGURE 4-1

```xml
<?xml version="1.0" encoding="utf-8"?>
<resources>
  <dimen name="notepad_margin">30dp</dimen>
</resources>
```

4. With the resources defined, you're ready to customize the `TodoListItemView` appearance. Create new private instance variables to store the `Paint` objects you'll use to draw the paper background and margin. Also create variables for the paper color and margin width values.

Fill in the `init` method to get instances of the resources you created in the last two steps, and create the `Paint` objects.

```java
private Paint marginPaint;
private Paint linePaint;
private int paperColor;
private float margin;

private void init() {
  // Get a reference to our resource table.
  Resources myResources = getResources();

  // Create the paint brushes we will use in the onDraw method.
  marginPaint = new Paint(Paint.ANTI_ALIAS_FLAG);

  marginPaint.setColor(myResources.getColor(R.color.notepad_margin));
  linePaint = new Paint(Paint.ANTI_ALIAS_FLAG);
  linePaint.setColor(myResources.getColor(R.color.notepad_lines));

  // Get the paper background color and the margin width.
  paperColor = myResources.getColor(R.color.notepad_paper);
  margin = myResources.getDimension(R.dimen.notepad_margin);
}
```

5. To draw the paper, override `onDraw` and draw the image using the `Paint` objects you created in Step 4. Once you've drawn the paper image, call the superclass's `onDraw` method and let it draw the text as usual.

```java
@Override
public void onDraw(Canvas canvas) {
  // Color as paper
  canvas.drawColor(paperColor);

  // Draw ruled lines
  canvas.drawLine(0, 0, getMeasuredHeight(), 0, linePaint);
  canvas.drawLine(0, getMeasuredHeight(),
                  getMeasuredWidth(), getMeasuredHeight(),
                  linePaint);

  // Draw margin
  canvas.drawLine(margin, 0, margin, getMeasuredHeight(), marginPaint);

  // Move the text across from the margin
  canvas.save();
  canvas.translate(margin, 0);
```

```
// Use the TextView to render the text.
super.onDraw(canvas);
canvas.restore();
}
```

6. That completes the `TodoListItemView` implementation. To use it in the To-Do List
Activity you need to include it in a new layout and pass that layout in to the Array Adapter
constructor.

Start by creating a new todolist_item.xml resource in the `res/layout` folder. It will specify
how each of the to-do list items is displayed. For this example your layout need only consist
of the new `TodoListItemView`, set to fill the entire available area.

```xml
<?xml version="1.0" encoding="utf-8"?>
<com.paad.todolist.TodoListItemView
  xmlns:android="http://schemas.android.com/apk/res/android"
  android:layout_width="fill_parent"
  android:layout_height="fill_parent"
  android:padding="10dp"
  android:scrollbars="vertical"
  android:textColor="@color/notepad_text"
  android:fadingEdge="vertical"
/>
```

7. Now open the `ToDoList` Activity class. The final step is to change the parameters
passed in to the `ArrayAdapter` in `onCreate`. Replace the reference to the default
`android.R.layout.simple_list_item_1` with a reference to the new `R.layout`
`.todolist_item` layout created in Step 6.

```java
final ArrayList<String> todoItems = new ArrayList<String>();
int resID = R.layout.todolist_item;
final ArrayAdapter<String> aa = new ArrayAdapter<String>(this, resID,
                                                         todoItems);

myListView.setAdapter(aa);
```

All code snippets in this example are part of the Chapter 4 Todo List *project, available for download at Wrox.com.*

Creating Compound Controls

Compound controls are atomic, reusable Views that contain multiple child controls laid out and wired
together.

When you create a compound control you define the layout, appearance, and interaction of the Views
it contains. You create compound controls by extending a `ViewGroup` (usually a layout). To create a
new compound control choose the layout class that's most suitable for positioning the child controls,
and extend it as shown in Listing 4-6.

LISTING 4-6: Creating a compound control

```java
public class MyCompoundView extends LinearLayout {
  public MyCompoundView(Context context) {
    super(context);
  }
```

```
        public MyCompoundView(Context context, AttributeSet attrs) {
          super(context, attrs);
        }
    }
```

As with Activities, the preferred way to design compound View layouts is using an external resource. Listing 4-7 shows the XML layout definition for a simple compound control consisting of an Edit Text View and a clear text Button to clear it.

LISTING 4-7: A compound View layout resource

```
<?xml version="1.0" encoding="utf-8"?>
<LinearLayout xmlns:android="http://schemas.android.com/apk/res/android"
  android:orientation="vertical"
  android:layout_width="fill_parent"
  android:layout_height="fill_parent">
  <EditText
    android:id="@+id/editText"
    android:layout_width="fill_parent"
    android:layout_height="wrap_content"
  />
  <Button
    android:id="@+id/clearButton"
    android:layout_width="fill_parent"
    android:layout_height="wrap_content"
    android:text="Clear"
  />
</LinearLayout>
```

To use this layout for your new View, override the View's constructor to inflate the layout resource using the `inflate` method from the `LayoutInflate` system service. The `inflate` method takes the layout resource and returns the inflated View.

For circumstances such as this, in which the returned View should be the class you're creating, you can pass in the parent View and attach the result to it automatically, as shown in Listing 4-8.

Listing 4-8 shows the `ClearableEditText` class. Within the constructor it inflates the layout resource created earlier and gets references to each of the Views it contains. It also makes a call to `hookupButton` that will be used to hook up the *clear text* functionality when the button is pressed.

LISTING 4-8: Constructing a compound View

```
public class ClearableEditText extends LinearLayout {

    EditText editText;
    Button clearButton;

    public ClearableEditText(Context context) {
      super(context);

      // Inflate the view from the layout resource.
```

continues

LISTING 4-8 *(continued)*

```
    String infService = Context.LAYOUT_INFLATER_SERVICE;
    LayoutInflater li;
    li = (LayoutInflater)getContext().getSystemService(infService);
    li.inflate(R.layout.clearable_edit_text, this, true);

    // Get references to the child controls.
    editText = (EditText)findViewById(R.id.editText);
    clearButton = (Button)findViewById(R.id.clearButton);

    // Hook up the functionality
    hookupButton();
  }
}
```

If you'd prefer to construct your layout in code, you can do so just as you would for an Activity. Listing 4-9 shows the ClearableEditText constructor overridden to create the same UI defined in the XML used in Listing 4-8.

LISTING 4-9: Creating a compound View layout in code

```
public ClearableEditText(Context context) {
  super(context);

  // Set orientation of layout to vertical
  setOrientation(LinearLayout.VERTICAL);

  // Create the child controls.
  editText = new EditText(getContext());
  clearButton = new Button(getContext());
  clearButton.setText("Clear");

  // Lay them out in the compound control.
  int lHeight = LayoutParams.WRAP_CONTENT;
  int lWidth = LayoutParams.FILL_PARENT;

  addView(editText, new LinearLayout.LayoutParams(lWidth, lHeight));
  addView(clearButton, new LinearLayout.LayoutParams(lWidth, lHeight));

  // Hook up the functionality
  hookupButton();
}
```

Once the View layout has been constructed you can hook up the event handlers for each child control to provide the functionality you need. In this next snippet the hookupButton method is filled in to clear the Edit Text when the Button is pressed.

```
    private void hookupButton() {
      clearButton.setOnClickListener(new Button.OnClickListener() {
        public void onClick(View v) {
          editText.setText("");
        }
      });
    }
```

Creating Custom Views

Creating completely new Views gives you the power to fundamentally shape the way your applications look and feel. By creating your own controls you can create user interfaces that are uniquely suited to your users' needs. To create new controls from a blank canvas you extend either the `View` or `SurfaceView` classes.

The `View` class provides a `Canvas` object with a series of draw methods and `Paint` classes. Use them to create a visual interface with bitmaps and raster graphics. You can then override user events like screen touches or key presses to provide interactivity. In situations in which extremely rapid repaints and 3D graphics aren't required, the `View` base class offers a powerful lightweight solution.

The `SurfaceView` class provides a `Surface` object that supports drawing from a background thread and using `openGL` for 3D graphics. This is an excellent option for graphics-heavy controls that are frequently updated or that display complex graphical information, particularly games and 3D visualizations.

This chapter introduces 2D controls based on the `View` class. To learn more about the `SurfaceView` class and some of the more advanced Canvas paint features available in Android, see Chapter 15.

Creating a New Visual Interface

The base `View` class presents a distinctly empty 100-pixel-by-100-pixel square. To change the size of the control and display a more compelling visual interface, you need to override the `onMeasure` and `onDraw` methods.

Within `onMeasure` the new View will calculate the height and width it will occupy given a set of boundary conditions. The `onDraw` method is where you draw on the Canvas.

Listing 4-10 shows the skeleton code for a new `View` class, which will be examined and developed further in the following sections.

Available for download on Wrox.com

LISTING 4-10: Creating a new View class

```
public class MyView extends View {

    // Constructor required for in-code creation
    public MyView(Context context) {
      super(context);
    }

    // Constructor required for inflation from resource file
    public MyView (Context context, AttributeSet ats, int defaultStyle) {
      super(context, ats, defaultStyle );
    }

    //Constructor required for inflation from resource file
    public MyView (Context context, AttributeSet attrs) {
      super(context, attrs);
    }
```

continues

LISTING 4-10 *(continued)*

```
@Override
protected void onMeasure(int wMeasureSpec, int hMeasureSpec) {
  int measuredHeight = measureHeight(hMeasureSpec);
  int measuredWidth = measureWidth(wMeasureSpec);

  // MUST make this call to setMeasuredDimension
  // or you will cause a runtime exception when
  // the control is laid out.
  setMeasuredDimension(measuredHeight, measuredWidth);
}

private int measureHeight(int measureSpec) {
  int specMode = MeasureSpec.getMode(measureSpec);
  int specSize = MeasureSpec.getSize(measureSpec);

  [ ... Calculate the view height ... ]

  return specSize;
}

private int measureWidth(int measureSpec) {
  int specMode = MeasureSpec.getMode(measureSpec);
  int specSize = MeasureSpec.getSize(measureSpec);

  [ ... Calculate the view width ... ]

  return specSize;
}

@Override
protected void onDraw(Canvas canvas) {
  [ ... Draw your visual interface ... ]
}
}
```

 Note that the onMeasure *method calls* setMeasuredDimension; *you must always call this method within your overridden* onMeasure *method or your control will throw an exception when the parent container attempts to lay it out.*

Drawing Your Control

The onDraw method is where the magic happens. If you're creating a new widget from scratch, it's because you want to create a completely new visual interface. The Canvas parameter in the onDraw method is the surface you'll use to bring your imagination to life.

Android provides a variety of tools to help draw your design on the Canvas using various Paint objects. The Canvas class includes helper methods for drawing primitive 2D objects including circles, lines, rectangles, text, and Drawables (images). It also supports transformations that let you rotate, translate (move), and scale (resize) the Canvas while you draw on it.

When these tools are used in combination with `Drawables` and the `Paint` class (which offer a variety of customizable fills and pens), the complexity and detail that your control can render are limited only by the size of the screen and the power of the processor rendering it.

 One of the most important techniques for writing efficient code in Android is to avoid the repetitive creation and destruction of objects. Any object created in your `onDraw` *method will be created and destroyed every time the screen refreshes. Improve efficiency by making as many of these objects (particularly instances of* `Paint` *and* `Drawable`*) class-scoped and by moving their creation into the constructor.*

Listing 4-11 shows how to override the `onDraw` method to display a simple text string in the center of the control.

LISTING 4-11: Drawing a custom View

```
@Override
protected void onDraw(Canvas canvas) {
    // Get the size of the control based on the last call to onMeasure.
    int height = getMeasuredHeight();
    int width = getMeasuredWidth();

    // Find the center
    int px = width/2;
    int py = height/2;

    // Create the new paint brushes.
    // NOTE: For efficiency this should be done in
    // the views's constructor
    Paint mTextPaint = new Paint(Paint.ANTI_ALIAS_FLAG);
    mTextPaint.setColor(Color.WHITE);

    // Define the string.
    String displayText = "Hello World!";

    // Measure the width of the text string.
    float textWidth = mTextPaint.measureText(displayText);

    // Draw the text string in the center of the control.
    canvas.drawText(displayText, px-textWidth/2, py, mTextPaint);
}
```

So that we don't diverge too far from the current topic, a more detailed look at the techniques available for drawing more complex visuals is included in Chapter 15.

Android does not currently support vector graphics. As a result, changes to any element of your Canvas require that the entire Canvas be repainted; modifying the color of a brush will not change your View's display until the control is invalidated and redrawn. Alternatively, you can use OpenGL to render graphics. For more details, see the discussion on SurfaceView *in Chapter 15.*

Sizing Your Control

Unless you conveniently require a control that always occupies a space 100 pixels square, you will also need to override onMeasure.

The onMeasure method is called when the control's parent is laying out its child controls. It asks the question "How much space will you use?" and passes in two parameters: widthMeasureSpec and heightMeasureSpec. They specify the space available for the control and some metadata describing that space.

Rather than return a result, you pass the View's height and width into the setMeasuredDimension method.

Listing 4-12 shows how to override onMeasure. Note the calls to local method stubs calculateHeight and calculateWidth. They'll be used to decode the widthHeightSpec and heightMeasureSpec values and calculate the preferred height and width values.

LISTING 4-12: Determining View dimensions

```
@Override
protected void onMeasure(int widthMeasureSpec, int heightMeasureSpec) {

    int measuredHeight = measureHeight(heightMeasureSpec);
    int measuredWidth = measureWidth(widthMeasureSpec);

    setMeasuredDimension(measuredHeight, measuredWidth);
}

private int measureHeight(int measureSpec) {
    // Return measured widget height.
}

private int measureWidth(int measureSpec) {
    // Return measured widget width.
}
```

The boundary parameters, widthMeasureSpec and heightMeasureSpec, are passed in as integers for efficiency reasons. Before they can be used, they first need to be decoded using the static getMode and getSize methods from the MeasureSpec class.

```
int specMode = MeasureSpec.getMode(measureSpec);
int specSize = MeasureSpec.getSize(measureSpec);
```

Depending on the *mode* value, the *size* represents either the maximum space available for the control (in the case of AT_MOST), or the exact size that your control will occupy (for EXACTLY). In the case of UNSPECIFIED, your control does not have any reference for what the size represents.

By marking a measurement size as EXACT, the parent is insisting that the View will be placed into an area of the exact size specified. The AT_MOST mode says the parent is asking what size the View would like to occupy, given an upper boundary. In many cases the value you return will be the same.

In either case, you should treat these limits as absolute. In some circumstances it may still be appropriate to return a measurement outside these limits, in which case you can let the parent choose how to deal with the oversized View, using techniques such as clipping and scrolling.

Listing 4-13 shows a typical implementation for handling View measurement.

LISTING 4-13: A typical View measurement implementation

Available for
download on
Wrox.com

```java
@Override
protected void onMeasure(int widthMeasureSpec, int heightMeasureSpec) {
  int measuredHeight = measureHeight(heightMeasureSpec);
  int measuredWidth = measureWidth(widthMeasureSpec);

  setMeasuredDimension(measuredHeight, measuredWidth);
}

private int measureHeight(int measureSpec) {
  int specMode = MeasureSpec.getMode(measureSpec);
  int specSize = MeasureSpec.getSize(measureSpec);

  // Default size if no limits are specified.
  int result = 500;

  if (specMode == MeasureSpec.AT_MOST) {
    // Calculate the ideal size of your
    // control within this maximum size.
    // If your control fills the available
    // space return the outer bound.
    result = specSize;
  } else if (specMode == MeasureSpec.EXACTLY) {
    // If your control can fit within these bounds return that value.
    result = specSize;
  }
  return result;
}

private int measureWidth(int measureSpec) {
  int specMode = MeasureSpec.getMode(measureSpec);
  int specSize = MeasureSpec.getSize(measureSpec);

  // Default size if no limits are specified.
  int result = 500;

  if (specMode == MeasureSpec.AT_MOST) {
```

continues

LISTING 4-13 *(continued)*

```
    // Calculate the ideal size of your control
    // within this maximum size.
    // If your control fills the available space
    // return the outer bound.
    result = specSize;
  } else if (specMode == MeasureSpec.EXACTLY) {
    // If your control can fit within these bounds return that value.
    result = specSize;
  }
  return result;
}
```

Handling User Interaction Events

In order for your new View to be interactive, it will need to respond to user events like key presses, screen touches, and button clicks. Android exposes several virtual event handlers, listed here, that let you react to user input:

➤ onKeyDown   Called when any device key is pressed; includes the D-pad, keyboard, hang-up, call, back, and camera buttons

➤ onKeyUp   Called when a user releases a pressed key

➤ onTrackballEvent   Called when the device's trackball is moved

➤ onTouchEvent   Called when the touchscreen is pressed or released, or when it detects movement

Listing 4-14 shows a skeleton class that overrides each of the user interaction handlers in a View.

LISTING 4-14: Input event handling for Views

```
@Override
public boolean onKeyDown(int keyCode, KeyEvent keyEvent) {
  // Return true if the event was handled.
  return true;
}

@Override
public boolean onKeyUp(int keyCode, KeyEvent keyEvent) {
  // Return true if the event was handled.
  return true;
}

@Override
public boolean onTrackballEvent(MotionEvent event ) {
  // Get the type of action this event represents
  int actionPerformed = event.getAction();
  // Return true if the event was handled.
  return true;
}
```

```
@Override
public boolean onTouchEvent(MotionEvent event) {
  // Get the type of action this event represents
  int actionPerformed = event.getAction();
  // Return true if the event was handled.
  return true;
}
```

Further details on using each of these event handlers, including greater detail on the parameters received by each method and support for multitouch events, are available in Chapter 15.

Creating a Compass View Example

In the following example you'll create a new Compass View by extending the `View` class. This View will display a traditional compass rose to indicate a heading/orientation. When complete, it should appear as in Figure 4-2.

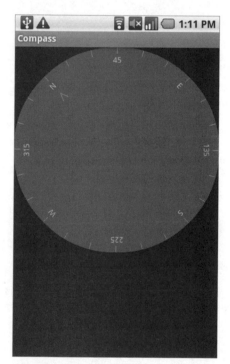

FIGURE 4-2

A compass is an example of a UI control that requires a radically different visual display from the Text Views and Buttons available in the SDK toolbox, making it an excellent candidate for building from scratch.

 In Chapter 14 you'll use this Compass View and the device's built-in accelerometer to display the user's current bearing. Then in Chapter 15 you will learn some advanced techniques for Canvas drawing that will let you dramatically improve its appearance.

1. Create a new `Compass` project that will contain your new Compass View, and create an Activity to display it. Now create a new `CompassView` class that extends `View`. Create constructors that will allow the View to be instantiated either in code or through inflation from a resource layout. Add a new `initCompassView` method that will be used to initialize the control and call it from each constructor.

```
package com.paad.compass;

import android.content.Context;
import android.graphics.*;
import android.graphics.drawable.*;
import android.view.*;
import android.util.AttributeSet;
import android.content.res.Resources;

public class CompassView extends View {
  public CompassView(Context context) {
    super(context);
    initCompassView();
  }

  public CompassView(Context context, AttributeSet attrs) {
    super(context, attrs);
    initCompassView();
  }

  public CompassView(Context context,
                     AttributeSet ats,
                     int defaultStyle) {
    super(context, ats, defaultStyle);
    initCompassView();
  }

  protected void initCompassView() {
    setFocusable(true);
  }
}
```

2. The compass control should always be a perfect circle that takes up as much of the canvas as this restriction allows. Override the `onMeasure` method to calculate the length of the shortest side, and use `setMeasuredDimension` to set the height and width using this value.

```
@Override
protected void onMeasure(int widthMeasureSpec, int heightMeasureSpec) {
  // The compass is a circle that fills as much space as possible.
  // Set the measured dimensions by figuring out the shortest boundary,
  // height or width.
  int measuredWidth = measure(widthMeasureSpec);
  int measuredHeight = measure(heightMeasureSpec);

  int d = Math.min(measuredWidth, measuredHeight);

  setMeasuredDimension(d, d);
}
```

```java
private int measure(int measureSpec) {
  int result = 0;

  // Decode the measurement specifications.
  int specMode = MeasureSpec.getMode(measureSpec);
  int specSize = MeasureSpec.getSize(measureSpec);

  if (specMode == MeasureSpec.UNSPECIFIED) {
    // Return a default size of 200 if no bounds are specified.
    result = 200;
  } else {
    // As you want to fill the available space
    // always return the full available bounds.
    result = specSize;
  }
  return result;
}
```

3. Create two new resource files that store the colors and text strings you'll use to draw the compass.

 3.1. Create the text string resource res/values/strings.xml.

```xml
<?xml version="1.0" encoding="utf-8"?>
<resources>
  <string name="app_name">Compass</string>
  <string name="cardinal_north">N</string>
  <string name="cardinal_east">E</string>
  <string name="cardinal_south">S</string>
  <string name="cardinal_west">W</string>
</resources>
```

 3.2. Create the color resource res/values/colors.xml.

```xml
<?xml version="1.0" encoding="utf-8"?>
<resources>
  <color name="background_color">#F555</color>
  <color name="marker_color">#AFFF</color>
  <color name="text_color">#AFFF</color>
</resources>
```

4. Now return to the CompassView class. Add a new property to store the displayed bearing, and create get and set methods for it.

```java
private float bearing;

public void setBearing(float _bearing) {
  bearing = _bearing;
}
public float getBearing() {
  return bearing;
}
```

5. Next, return to the initCompassView method and get references to each resource created in Step 3. Store the string values as instance variables, and use the color values to create new class-scoped Paint objects. You'll use these objects in the next step to draw the compass face.

```
private Paint markerPaint;
private Paint textPaint;
private Paint circlePaint;
private String northString;
private String eastString;
private String southString;
private String westString;
private int textHeight;

protected void initCompassView() {
  setFocusable(true);

  circlePaint = new Paint(Paint.ANTI_ALIAS_FLAG);
  circlePaint.setColor(r.getColor(R.color.background_color));
  circlePaint.setStrokeWidth(1);
  circlePaint.setStyle(Paint.Style.FILL_AND_STROKE);

  Resources r = this.getResources();
  northString = r.getString(R.string.cardinal_north);
  eastString = r.getString(R.string.cardinal_east);
  southString = r.getString(R.string.cardinal_south);
  westString = r.getString(R.string.cardinal_west);

  textPaint = new Paint(Paint.ANTI_ALIAS_FLAG);
  textPaint.setColor(r.getColor(R.color.text_color));

  textHeight = (int)textPaint.measureText("yY");

  markerPaint = new Paint(Paint.ANTI_ALIAS_FLAG);
  markerPaint.setColor(r.getColor(R.color.marker_color));
}
```

6. The final step is drawing the compass face using the `String` and `Paint` objects you created in Step 5. The following code snippet is presented with only limited commentary. You can find more detail about drawing on the Canvas and using advanced Paint effects in Chapter 15.

   6.1. Start by overriding the `onDraw` method in the `CompassView` class.

   ```
   @Override
   protected void onDraw(Canvas canvas) {
   ```

   6.2. Find the center of the control, and store the length of the smallest side as the compass's radius.

   ```
   int px = getMeasuredWidth() / 2;
   int py = getMeasuredHeight() /2 ;

   int radius = Math.min(px, py);
   ```

   6.3. Draw the outer boundary, and color the background of the compass face using the `drawCircle` method. Use the `circlePaint` object you created in Step 5.

   ```
   // Draw the background
   canvas.drawCircle(px, py, radius, circlePaint);
   ```

   6.4. This compass displays the current heading by rotating the face so that the current direction is always at the top of the device. To achieve this, rotate the canvas in the opposite direction to the current heading.

```
                        // Rotate our perspective so that the 'top' is
                        // facing the current bearing.
                        canvas.save();
                        canvas.rotate(-bearing, px, py);
```

6.5. All that's left is to draw the markings. Rotate the canvas through a full rotation, drawing markings every 15 degrees and the abbreviated direction string every 45 degrees.

```
            int textWidth = (int)textPaint.measureText("W");
            int cardinalX = px-textWidth/2;
            int cardinalY = py-radius+textHeight;

            // Draw the marker every 15 degrees and text every 45.
            for (int i = 0; i < 24; i++) {
              // Draw a marker.
              canvas.drawLine(px, py-radius, px, py-radius+10, markerPaint);

              canvas.save();
              canvas.translate(0, textHeight);

              // Draw the cardinal points
              if (i % 6 == 0) {
                String dirString = "";
                switch (i) {
                  case(0)  : {
                                 dirString = northString;
                                 int arrowY = 2*textHeight;
                                 canvas.drawLine(px, arrowY, px-5, 3*textHeight,
                                               markerPaint);
                                 canvas.drawLine(px, arrowY, px+5, 3*textHeight,
                                               markerPaint);
                                 break;
                             }
                  case(6)  : dirString = eastString; break;
                  case(12) : dirString = southString; break;
                  case(18) : dirString = westString; break;
                }
                canvas.drawText(dirString, cardinalX, cardinalY, textPaint);
              }

              else if (i % 3 == 0) {
                // Draw the text every alternate 45deg
                String angle = String.valueOf(i*15);
                float angleTextWidth = textPaint.measureText(angle);

                int angleTextX = (int)(px-angleTextWidth/2);
                int angleTextY = py-radius+textHeight;
                canvas.drawText(angle, angleTextX, angleTextY, textPaint);
              }
              canvas.restore();

              canvas.rotate(15, px, py);
            }
            canvas.restore();
          }
```

7. To view the compass, modify the main.xml layout resource and replace the `TextView` reference with your new `CompassView`. This process is explained in more detail in the next section.

```xml
<?xml version="1.0" encoding="utf-8"?>
<LinearLayout xmlns:android="http://schemas.android.com/apk/res/android"
  android:orientation="vertical"
  android:layout_width="fill_parent"
  android:layout_height="fill_parent">
  <com.paad.compass.CompassView
    android:id="@+id/compassView"
    android:layout_width="fill_parent"
    android:layout_height="fill_parent"
  />
</LinearLayout>
```

8. Run the Activity, and you should see the `CompassView` displayed. See Chapter 14 to learn how to bind the `CompassView` to the device's compass.

All code snippets in this example are part of the Chapter 4 Compass *project, available for download at Wrox.com.*

Using Custom Controls

Having created your own custom Views, you can use them within code and layouts as you would any other View. Listing 4-15 shows you how to override the `onCreate` method in order to add the `CompassView`, created in the preceding example, to an Activity.

Available for download on Wrox.com

LISTING 4-15: Using a custom View

```java
@Override
public void onCreate(Bundle savedInstanceState) {
  super.onCreate(savedInstanceState);
  CompassView cv = new CompassView(this);
  setContentView(cv);
  cv.setBearing(45);
}
```

To use the same control within a layout resource, specify the fully qualified class name when you create a new node in the layout definition, as shown in the following XML snippet.

```xml
<com.paad.compass.CompassView
  android:id="@+id/compassView"
  android:layout_width="fill_parent"
  android:layout_height="fill_parent"
/>
```

You can inflate the layout and get a reference to the `CompassView` as usual, using the following code:

```java
@Override
public void onCreate(Bundle savedInstanceState) {
  super.onCreate(savedInstanceState);
  setContentView(R.layout.main);
  CompassView cv = (CompassView)this.findViewById(R.id.compassView);
  cv.setBearing(45);
}
```

DRAWABLE RESOURCES

In Chapter 3 you were introduced to the resources framework and shown how to externalize your application resources and include alternative assets for different hardware platforms.

In this section you will be introduced to several new types of Drawables resources — including shapes and transformative and composite Drawables — and be shown how to use these resources to create user interfaces that are independent of screen size and resolution.

All of these resources can be defined and manipulated in code, but in this section we will focus on how to create these Drawables using XML.

 The resources framework, described in Chapter 3, which can be used to define alternative resources for different hardware devices, can be used for all the XML Drawables described in this section.

Shapes, Colors, and Gradients

Android includes a number of simple Drawable resource types that can be defined entirely in XML. These include the `ColorDrawable`, `ShapeDrawable`, and `GradientDrawable` classes. These resources are stored in the `res/drawable` folder, and can then be identified in code by their lowercase XML filenames.

If these Drawables are defined in XML, and you specify their attributes using density-independent pixels, the run time will smoothly scale them. Like vector graphics, these Drawables can be scaled dynamically to display correctly and without scaling artifacts regardless of screen size, resolution, or pixel density. The notable exceptions to this rule are Gradient Drawables, which require a gradient radius defined in pixels.

As you will see later in this chapter, you can use these Drawables in combination with transformative Drawables and composite Drawables. Together, they can result in dynamic, scalable UI elements that require fewer resources and will appear crisp on any screen.

Color Drawable

A `ColorDrawable,` the simplest of the XML-defined Drawables, lets you specify an image asset based on a single solid color. Color Drawables are defined as XML files using the `<color>` tag in the Drawable resources folder. Listing 4-16 shows the XML for a solid red Color Drawable.

LISTING 4-16: A solid red Drawable resource

```xml
<color xmlns:android="http://schemas.android.com/apk/res/android"
    android:color="#FF0000"
/>
```

Shape Drawable

Shape Drawable resources let you define simple primitive shapes by defining their dimensions, background, and stroke/outline using the `<shape>` tag.

Each shape consists of a type (specified via the `shape` attribute), attributes that define the dimensions of that shape, and subnodes to specify padding, stroke (or outline), and background color values.

Android currently supports the following shape types as values for the `shape` attribute:

➤ `oval`   A simple oval shape.

➤ `rectangle`   Also supports a `<corners>` subnode that uses a `radius` attribute to create a rounded rectangle.

➤ `ring`   Supports the `innerRadius` and `thickness` attributes to let you specify, respectively, the inner radius of the ring shape and its thickness. Alternatively, you can use `innerRadiusRatio` and/or `thicknessRatio` to define the ring's inner radius and thickness as a proportion of its width (where an inner radius of a quarter of the width would use the value 4).

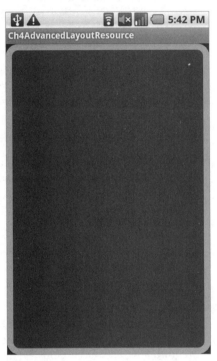

Use the `<stroke>` subnode to specify an outline for your shapes using `width` and `color` attributes.

You can also include a `<padding>` node to offset the positioning of your shape on the canvas.

More usefully, you can include a subnode to specify the background color. The simplest case involves using the `<solid>` node, including the `color` attribute, to define a solid background color.

The following section describes the `GradientDrawable` class and how to specify a gradient fill for your Shape Drawables.

Listing 4-17 shows a rectangular Shape Drawable with a solid fill, rounded edges, 10dp outline, and 10dp of padding around each edge. The result is shown in Figure 4-3.

FIGURE 4-3

LISTING 4-17: A solid red Drawable resource

```xml
<?xml version="1.0" encoding="utf-8"?>
<shape xmlns:android="http://schemas.android.com/apk/res/android"
    android:shape="rectangle">
    <solid
        android:color="#f0600000"/>
    <stroke
        android:width="10dp"
        android:color="#00FF00"/>
    <corners
        android:radius="15dp" />
    <padding
        android:left="10dp"
        android:top="10dp"
```

```
      android:right="10dp"
      android:bottom="10dp"
    />
</shape>
```

Gradient Drawable

A `GradientDrawable` lets you design complex gradient fills. Each gradient defines a smooth transition between two or three colors in a linear, radial, or sweep pattern.

Gradient Drawables are defined using the `<gradient>` tag as a subnode within a Shape Drawable definition (such as those defined above).

Each Gradient Drawable requires at least a `startColor` and `endColor` attribute and supports on optional `middleColor`. Using the `type` attribute you can define your gradient as one of the following:

➤ `linear` The default gradient type, it displays a straight color transition from `startColor` to `endColor` at an angle defined by the `angle` attribute.

➤ `radial` Draws a circular gradient from `startColor` to `endColor` from the outer edge of the shape to the center. It requires a `gradientRadius` attribute that specifies the radius of the gradient transition in pixels. It also optionally supports `centerX` and `centerY` to offset the location of the center of the gradient.

Because the gradient radius is defined in pixels it will not be dynamically scaled for different pixel densities. To minimize banding, you may need to specify different gradient radius values for different screen resolutions.

➤ `sweep` Draws a sweep gradient that transitions from `startColor` to `endColor` along the outer edge of the parent shape (typically a ring).

Listing 4-18 shows the XML for a linear gradient within a rectangle, a radial gradient within an oval, and a sweep gradient within a ring, as shown in Figure 4-4.

Available for download on Wrox.com

LISTING 4-18: Linear, Radial, and Sweep Gradient definitions

```
<!-- Rectangle with Linear Gradient -->
<?xml version="1.0" encoding="utf-8"?>
<shape xmlns:android="http://schemas.android.com/apk/res/android"
  android:shape="rectangle"
  android:useLevel="false">
  <gradient
    android:startColor="#ffffff"
    android:endColor="#ffffff"
    android:centerColor="#000000"
    android:useLevel="false"
    android:type="linear"
    android:angle="45"
  />
</shape>
```

continues

LISTING 4-18 *(continued)*

```xml
<!-- Oval with Radial Gradient -->
<?xml version="1.0" encoding="utf-8"?>
<shape xmlns:android="http://schemas.android.com/apk/res/android"
  android:shape="oval"
  android:useLevel="false">
  <gradient
    android:type="radial"
    android:startColor="#ffffff"
    android:endColor="#ffffff"
    android:centerColor="#000000"
    android:useLevel="false"
    android:gradientRadius="300"
  />
</shape>

<!-- Ring with Sweep Gradient -->
<?xml version="1.0" encoding="utf-8"?>
<shape xmlns:android="http://schemas.android.com/apk/res/android"
  android:shape="ring"
  android:useLevel="false"
  android:innerRadiusRatio="3"
  android:thicknessRatio="8">
  <gradient
    android:startColor="#ffffff"
    android:endColor="#ffffff"
    android:centerColor="#000000"
    android:useLevel="false"
    android:type="sweep"
  />
</shape>
```

Composite Drawables

Use composite Drawables to combine and manipulate other Drawable resources.

Any Drawable resource can be used within the following composite resource definitions, including bitmaps, shapes, and colors. Similarly, these new Drawables can be used within each other and assigned to Views in the same way as all other Drawable assets.

Transformative Drawables

You can scale and rotate existing Drawable resources using the aptly named `ScaleDrawable` and `RotateDrawable` classes. These transformative Drawables are particularly useful for creating progress bars or animating Views.

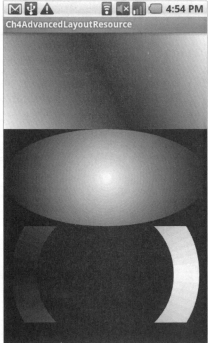

FIGURE 4-4

➤ **ScaleDrawable**   Within the `<scale>` tag, use the `scaleHeight` and `scaleWidth` attributes to define the target height and width relative to the bounding box of the original Drawable. Use the `scaleGravity` attribute to control the anchor point for the scaled image.

➤ **RotateDrawable**   Within the `<rotate>` tag, use `fromDegrees` and `toDegrees` to define the start and end rotation angle around a pivot point. Define the pivot using the `pivotX` and `pivotY` attributes, specifying a percentage of the Drawable's width and height, respectively, using nn% notation.

To apply the scaling and rotation at run time, use the `setLevel` method on the View object hosting the Drawable to move between the start and finish values (0 to 10,000).

When moving through levels, level 0 represents the start angle (or smallest scale result). Level 10, 000 represents the end of the transformation (the finish angle or highest scaling).

Listing 4-19 shows Scale and Rotate Drawable XML definitions, while Listing 4-20 demonstrates how to manipulate them in code after they have been assigned to an Image View.

LISTING 4-19: Resource files for a Rotate Drawable and Scale Drawable

```xml
<!-- Rotation Drawable Resource -->
<?xml version="1.0" encoding="utf-8"?>
<rotate xmlns:android="http://schemas.android.com/apk/res/android"
  android:drawable="@drawable/icon"
  android:fromDegrees="0"
  android:toDegrees="90"
  android:pivotX="50%"
  android:pivotY="50%"
/>

<!-- Scale Drawable Resource -->
<?xml version="1.0" encoding="utf-8"?>
<rotate xmlns:android="http://schemas.android.com/apk/res/android"
  android:drawable="@drawable/icon"
  android:scaleHeight="100%"
  android:scaleWidth="100%"
/>
```

LISTING 4-20: Applying rotation and scale Drawable transformations in code

```java
ImageView rotatingImage = (ImageView)findViewById(R.id.RotatingImageView);
ImageView scalingImage = (ImageView)findViewById(R.id.ScalingImageView);

// Rotate the image 50% of the way to its final orientation.
rotatingImage.setImageLevel(5000);

// Scale the image to 50% of its final size.
scalingImage.setImageLevel(5000);
```

Layer Drawable

A `LayerDrawable` lets you composite several Drawable resources on top of one another. If you define an array of partially transparent Drawables you can stack them on top of one another to create complex combinations of dynamic shapes and transformations.

Similarly, you can use Layer Drawables as the source for the transformative Drawable resources described in the preceding section, or the State List and Level List Drawables that follow.

Listing 4-21 shows a Layer Drawable. These are defined via the `<layer-list>` node tag; within that tag use the `drawable` attribute in each `<item>` subnode to define the Drawables to composite.

Each Drawable will be stacked in index order, with the first item in the array at the bottom of the stack.

LISTING 4-21: A Layer Drawable resource XML definition

```xml
<?xml version="1.0" encoding="utf-8"?>
<layer-list xmlns:android="http://schemas.android.com/apk/res/android">
  <item android:drawable="@drawable/bottomimage"/>
  <item android:drawable="@drawable/image2"/>
  <item android:drawable="@drawable/image3"/>
  <item android:drawable="@drawable/topimage"/>
</layer-list>
```

State List Drawables

A State List Drawable is a composite resource that enables you to specify a different Drawable to display based on the state of the View to which it has been assigned.

Most native Android Views use State List Drawables, including the image used on Buttons and the background used for standard List View items.

To define a State List Drawable, create an XML file that specifies an alternative Drawable resource for each selection state required, as shown in Listing 4-22.

LISTING 4-22: State List Drawable

```xml
<selector xmlns:android="http://schemas.android.com/apk/res/android">
  <item android:state_window_focused="false"
        android:drawable="@drawable/widget_bg_normal"/>
  <item android:state_pressed="true"
        android:drawable="@drawable/widget_bg_pressed"/>
  <item android:state_focused="true"
        android:drawable="@drawable/widget_bg_selected"/>
  <item android:drawable="@drawable/widget_bg_normal"/>
</selector>
```

Level List Drawables

Using a Level List Drawable you can effectively overlay several Drawable resources, specifying an integer index value for each layer, as shown in Listing 4-23.

LISTING 4-23: Level List Drawable resource

```xml
<level-list xmlns:android="http://schemas.android.com/apk/res/android">
    <item android:maxLevel="0"  android:drawable="@drawable/earthquake_0"/>
    <item android:maxLevel="1"  android:drawable="@drawable/earthquake_1"/>
    <item android:maxLevel="2"  android:drawable="@drawable/earthquake_2"/>
    <item android:maxLevel="4"  android:drawable="@drawable/earthquake_4"/>
    <item android:maxLevel="6"  android:drawable="@drawable/earthquake_6"/>
    <item android:maxLevel="8"  android:drawable="@drawable/earthquake_8"/>
    <item android:maxLevel="10" android:drawable="@drawable/earthquake_10"/>
</level-list>
```

To select which image to display in code call `setImageLevel` on the View displaying the Level List Drawable resource, passing in the index of the Drawable you wish to display.

```
imageView.setImageLevel(5);
```

The View will display the image corresponding to the index with an equal or greater value to the one specified. Level List Drawables are particularly useful when creating Widget layouts.

NinePatch Drawable

NinePatch (or stretchable) images are PNG files that mark the parts of an image that can be stretched. NinePatch images must be properly defined PNG files that end in `.9.png`. The resource identifier for NinePatches is the file name without the trailing `.9.png`.

A NinePatch is a variation of a PNG image that uses a one-pixel border to define the area of the image that can be stretched if the image is enlarged. To create a NinePatch, draw single-pixel black lines that represent stretchable areas along the left and top borders of your image. The unmarked sections won't be resized, and the relative size of each of the marked sections will remain the same as the image size changes.

NinePatches are a powerful tool for creating images for the backgrounds of Views or Activities that may have a variable size. For example, Android uses NinePatches to create button borders.

RESOLUTION AND DENSITY INDEPENDENCE

With the first four Android handsets all featuring 3.2" HVGA screens, it was easy for developers to become complacent when designing their user interfaces. For almost a year after the release of the first Android handset, there was only one screen size and pixel density to design for.

The end of 2009 and start of 2010 heralded an explosion in the number of devices running Android, and with a larger variety of handsets came variation in screen sizes and pixel densities.

It's important to create your UIs knowing that your apps will be running on a broad variety of screen resolutions (including HVGA, QVGA, and two flavors of WVGA — 800x480 and 854x480). Similarly, the physical screen sizes have begun to vary beyond 3.2 inches to include the 3.7-inch Nexus One and Motorola Droid, and the 4-inch Sony Ericsson Xperia X10.

With the floodgates now open, you should expect your applications to be running on an even greater variety of hardware — potentially including tablets, netbooks, and consumer electronics.

The following sections will begin by describing the range of screens you need to consider, and how to support them, before summarizing some of the best practices for ensuring your applications are resolution- and density-independent. Finally, you'll learn how to test your applications against a variety of screen hardware without spending a fortune on phones.

The Resource Framework and Resolution Independence

The Android framework provides a number of techniques to enable you to optimize your UI for a variety of screen sizes and pixel densities.

This section describes the resource directory qualifiers you can use to store alternative assets and layouts for different screen configurations, and the manifest elements you can use to limit the screen sizes your application supports.

Resource Qualifiers for Screen Size and Pixel Density

In Chapter 3 you were introduced to the Android resource framework. Using this framework you can create a parallel directory structure to store external resources for different host hardware configurations.

This section summarizes the folder-name qualifiers you can use to include alternative resources for different screen sizes, pixel densities, and aspect ratios.

➤ **Screen size**   The size of the screen relative to a "standard" smartphone (such as the G1 or Droid).

  ➤ `small`   A screen smaller than the standard 3.2"

  ➤ `medium`   Typical smartphone screen size

  ➤ `large`   A screen significantly larger than that of a typical smartphone, such as the screen of a tablet or netbook

➤ **Pixel density**   Refers to the density of pixels on the display. Typically measured in dots per inch (dpi), this is calculated as a function of the physical screen size and resolution.

  ➤ `ldpi`   Used to store low-density resources for screens with pixel density in the range of 100 to 140dpi

  ➤ `mdpi`   Used for medium-density screens with 140 to 180dpi

  ➤ `hdpi`   Used for high-density screens featuring 190 to 250dpi

  ➤ `nodpi`   Used for resources that must not be scaled regardless of the host screen's density

➤ **Aspect ratio**   The screen's aspect ratio is the ratio of its height to its width.

> ➤ `long` Used for screens that are significantly wider in landscape mode than those of standard smartphones (such as the G1)

> ➤ `notlong` Used for screens with a typical smartphone aspect ratio

Each of these qualifiers is independent and can be used independently, or in combination with each other, as shown in Listing 4-24.

Note that these qualifiers can also be used with the other resource folder qualifiers described in Chapter 3.

LISTING 4-24: Sample screen-based resource directory qualifiers

Available for
download on
Wrox.com

```
res/layout-small-long/  // Layouts for small, long screens.
res/layout-large/       // Layouts for large screens.
res/drawable-hdpi/      // Drawables for high density screens.
```

Specifying Supported Screen Sizes

For some applications it may not be possible to optimize your UI to support all possible screen sizes. You can use the `<supports-screens>` manifest element to specify which screens your application can be run on, as shown in Listing 4-25.

LISTING 4-25: Manifest element supporting normal and large screen sizes

Available for
download on
Wrox.com

```
<supports-screens
    android:smallScreens="false"
    android:normalScreens="true"
    android:largeScreens="true"
    android:anyDensity="true"
/>
```

In this context a small screen is any display with resolution smaller than HVGA. A large screen is significantly larger than a smartphone (such as a tablet), while normal screens encompass the majority of smartphone handsets.

The `anyDensity` attribute controls how your application will be scaled when displayed on devices of varying pixel density. If you have taken varying pixel density into account in your UI (and you should have) set this to `true`.

A false value will force Android to use compatibility scaling to attempt to scale your application UI correctly. This will generally result in a UI with degraded image assets that show scaling artifacts.

Applications built with an SDK of API level 4 or higher will default all of these values to `true`.

Best Practices for Resolution Independence

The variety of Android hardware available provides both an exciting opportunity and a potential hazard for application developers.

This section summarizes some of the most common techniques for creating applications that will run effectively on any screen platform.

The most important thing to remember is never make assumptions regarding the screen your application will be running on. Create your layouts and assets for classes of screens (small, normal, and large size with low, medium, and high density) rather than particular screen dimensions or resolutions. By assuming your application will need to be scaled slightly on every device, you can ensure that when it is scaled the UI does not suffer.

The Android Developer site includes some excellent tips for supporting multiple screen types. The section on "Strategies for Legacy Apps" is particularly useful for developers with existing applications looking to support new screen sizes and resolutions. You can find this documentation here: `http://developer.android` `.com/guide/practices/screens_support.html#strategies`

Relative Layouts and Density-Independent Pixels

Wherever possible you should avoid using hard-coded pixel values. This applies to layouts, Drawables and font sizes.

In particular you should avoid the Absolute Layout class, which depends on the specification of pixel-based coordinates for each child View. Instead, use an alternative Layout manager that describes the child Views relative to each other or the screen edges. For most complex UIs the Relative Layout is likely to be the best solution.

Within your layouts you should also avoid specifying View, Drawable, and font sizes using pixel values. Instead, define the height and width of Views using `wrap_content` or `fill_parent` where appropriate, and density-independent pixels (dp) or scale-independent pixels (sp) as required for View and font sizes, respectively.

Density- and scale-independent pixels are means of specifying screen dimensions that will scale to appear the same on hardware using different pixel densities. One density-independent pixel (dp) is equivalent to one pixel on a 160dpi screen. A line specified as 2dp wide will appear as 3 pixels on a display with 240dpi.

Using Scalable Graphics Assets

Earlier in this chapter you were introduced to a number of Drawable resources, most of which can be defined in XML and all of which can be scaled smoothly by the run time, regardless of the screen size or pixel density.

Where possible, use the following Drawable resources rather than fixed bitmap assets:

➤ NinePatches

➤ Shape Drawables

➤ Gradient Drawables

➤ Composite and transformative Drawables such as:

➤ Rotate and Scale Drawables

➤ LevelListDrawables

➤ StateListDrawables

Remember when defining these assets to use density-independent pixels (dp).

Using scalable assets has the advantage of generic support for arbitrary screen sizes and resolutions, with the framework dynamically scaling your assets to produce the best possible image quality.

Provide Optimized Resources for Different Screens

When using Drawable resources that cannot be dynamically scaled well, you should create and include image assets optimized for each pixel density category (low, medium, and high). Application icons are an excellent example of a resource that should be optimized for different pixel densities.

Using the resource framework described earlier in the chapter (and in Chapter 3), you can create annotated Drawable directories to store image assets for each supported density, as shown in the following list:

➤ `res/drawable-ldpi`

➤ `res/drawable-mdpi`

➤ `res/drawable-hdpi`

By creating assets optimized for the pixel density of the host platform you ensure that your UI will be crisp and clear and devoid of artifacts like aliasing and lost pixels — typical side effects of scaling.

Similarly, you should consider creating alternative layout definitions for different screen sizes. A layout optimized for a typical smartphone screen may crop important information on a small device, or appear too sparse when displayed on a large device such as a tablet.

Use the resource framework to annotate the layout resource folder to create specialized layouts for small, normal, and large screens, as shown in the following list:

➤ `res/layout-small`

➤ `res/layout-normal`

➤ `res/layout-large`

Testing, Testing, Testing

With dozens of Android devices of varying screen sizes and pixel densities now available, it's impractical (and in some cases impossible) to physically test your application on every device.

Android Virtual Devices are ideal platforms for testing your application with a number of different screen configurations. Virtual devices also have the advantage of letting you configure alternative platform releases (1.6, 2.0, 2.1, etc.) and hardware configurations (such as keyboards or trackballs).

You learned how to create and use Android Virtual Devices in Chapter 2, so this section will focus on how best to create virtual devices that are representative of different screens.

Emulator Skins

The simplest way to test your application UI is to use the built-in skins. Each skin emulates a known device configuration with a resolution, pixel density, and physical screen size.

As of Android 2.1, the following built-in skins were available for testing:

➤ **QVGA** 320×240, 120dpi, 3.3″

➤ **WQVGA432** 432×240, 120dpi, 3.9″

➤ **HVGA** 480×320, 160dpi, 3.6″

➤ **WVGA800** 800×480, 240dpi, 3.9″

➤ **WVGA854** 854×480, 240dpi, 4.1″

Testing for Custom Resolutions and Screen Sizes

One of the advantages of using an AVD to evaluate devices is the ability to define arbitrary screen resolutions and pixel densities.

Figure 4-5 shows a new AVD for a 1024×768 device with a pixel density of 240dpi.

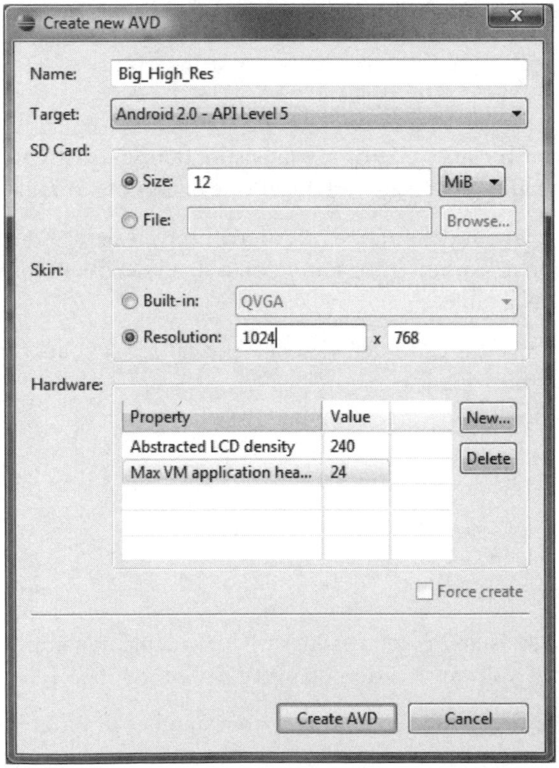

FIGURE 4-5

When you start a new AVD you will be presented with the Launch Options dialog shown in Figure 4-6. If you check the "Scale display to real size" checkbox and specify a screen size for your virtual device, as well as the dpi of your development monitor, the emulator will scale to approximate the physical size and pixel density you specified.

This lets you evaluate your UI against a variety of screen sizes and pixel densities as well as resolutions and skins. This is an ideal way to see how your application will appear on a small, high-resolution phone or a large, low resolution tablet.

FIGURE 4-6

CREATING AND USING MENUS

Menus offer a way to expose application functions without sacrificing valuable screen space. Each Activity can specify its own menu that's displayed when the device's menu button is pressed.

Android also supports context menus that can be assigned to any View. Context menus are normally triggered when a user holds the middle D-pad button, depresses the trackball, or long-presses the touchscreen for around three seconds when the View has focus.

Activity and context menus support submenus, checkboxes, radio buttons, shortcut keys, and icons.

Introducing the Android Menu System

If you've ever tried to navigate a mobile phone menu system using a stylus or trackball, you know that traditional menu systems are awkward to use on mobile devices.

To improve the usability of application menus, Android features a three-stage menu system optimized for small screens:

➤ **The icon menu** This compact menu (shown in Figure 4-7) appears along the bottom of the screen when the menu button is pressed. It displays the icons and text for a limited number of Menu Items (typically six). By convention, menu icons are grayscale images in an embossed style, though this may vary on different devices.

FIGURE 4-7

This icon menu does *not* display checkboxes, radio buttons, or the shortcut keys for Menu Items, so it's generally good practice not to depend on checkboxes or radio buttons in icon Menu Items, as they will not be visible.

If the Activity menu contains more than the maximum number of visible Menu Items, a *More* Menu Item is displayed. When selected, it displays the expanded menu. Pressing the back button closes the icon menu.

➤ **The expanded menu** The expanded menu is triggered when a user selects the *More* Menu Item from the icon menu. The expanded menu (shown in Figure 4-8) displays a scrollable list of *only* the Menu Items that weren't visible in the icon menu. This menu displays full text, shortcut keys, and checkboxes/radio buttons.

It does not, however, display icons. Pressing back from the expanded menu returns you to the icon menu.

FIGURE 4-8

 You cannot force Android to display the expanded menu instead of the icon menu. As a result, special care must be taken with Menu Items that feature checkboxes or radio buttons. The maximum number of icon Menu Items can vary by device, so it's good practice to ensure that their state information is also indicated by an icon or a change in text.

➤ **Submenus** The traditional expanding hierarchical tree can be awkward to navigate using a mouse, so it's no surprise that this metaphor is particularly ill-suited for use on mobile devices. The Android alternative is to display each submenu in a floating window.

For example, when a user selects a submenu such as the creatively labeled *Submenu* shown in Figure 4-8, its items are displayed in a floating menu dialog box, as shown in Figure 4-9.

Note that the name of the submenu is shown in the header bar and that each Menu Item is displayed with its full text, checkbox (if any), and shortcut key. Since Android does not support nested submenus, you can't add a submenu to a submenu (trying will result in an exception).

As with the extended menu, icons are not displayed in the submenu, so it's good practice to avoid assigning icons to submenu items.

Pressing the back button closes the floating window without your having to navigate back to the extended or icon menus.

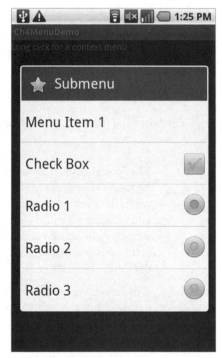

FIGURE 4-9

Defining an Activity Menu

To define a menu for an Activity, override its `onCreateOptionsMenu` handler. This method is triggered the first time an Activity's menu is displayed.

The onCreateOptionsMenu receives a Menu object as a parameter. You can store a reference to, and continue to use, the Menu reference elsewhere in your code until the next time onCreateOptionsMenu is called.

You should always call through to the superclass implementation, as it automatically includes additional system menu options where appropriate.

Use the add method on the Menu object to populate your menu. For each new Menu Item, you must specify the following:

➤ A group value to separate Menu Items for batch processing and ordering.

➤ A unique identifier for each Menu Item. For efficiency reasons, Menu Item selections are generally handled by the onOptionsItemSelected event handler, so this unique identifier is important for determining which Menu Item was pressed. It is convention to declare each menu ID as a private static variable within the Activity class. You can use the Menu.FIRST static constant and simply increment that value for each subsequent item.

➤ An order value that defines the order in which the Menu Items are displayed.

➤ The Menu Item display text, either as a character string or as a string resource.

When you have finished populating the Menu return true.

Listing 4-26 shows how to add a single Menu Item to an Activity Menu.

LISTING 4-26: Adding a Menu Item

Available for
download on
Wrox.com

```
static final private int MENU_ITEM = Menu.FIRST;

@Override
public boolean onCreateOptionsMenu(Menu menu) {
  super.onCreateOptionsMenu(menu);

  // Group ID
  int groupId = 0;
  // Unique menu item identifier. Used for event handling.
  int menuItemId = MENU_ITEM;
  // The order position of the item
  int menuItemOrder = Menu.NONE;
  // Text to be displayed for this menu item.
  int menuItemText = R.string.menu_item;

  // Create the menu item and keep a reference to it.
  MenuItem menuItem = menu.add(groupId, menuItemId,
                               menuItemOrder, menuItemText);

  return true;
}
```

Like the Menu object, each MenuItem returned by add is valid until the next call to onCreateOptionsMenu. Rather than maintaining a reference to each item, you can find a particular Menu Item by passing its ID in to the Menu's findItem method.

Menu Item Options

Android supports most of the traditional Menu Item options you're probably familiar with, including icons, shortcuts, checkboxes, and radio buttons, as listed here:

➤ **Checkboxes and radio buttons** Checkboxes and radio buttons on Menu Items are visible in expanded menus and submenus, as shown in Figure 4-9. To set a Menu Item as a checkbox, use the setCheckable method. The state of that checkbox is controlled via setChecked.

A *radio button group* is a group of items displaying circular buttons, in which only one item can be selected at any given time. Checking one of these items will automatically uncheck any checked item in the same group.

To create a radio button group, assign the same group identifier to each item and then call Menu.setGroupCheckable, passing in that group identifier and setting the exclusive parameter to true.

Checkboxes are not visible in the icon menu, so Menu Items that feature checkboxes should be reserved for submenus and items that appear only in the expanded menu. The following code snippet shows how to add a checkbox and a group of three radio buttons.

```
// Create a new check box item.
menu.add(0, CHECKBOX_ITEM, Menu.NONE, "CheckBox").setCheckable(true);

// Create a radio button group.
menu.add(RB_GROUP, RADIOBUTTON_1, Menu.NONE, "Radiobutton 1");
menu.add(RB_GROUP, RADIOBUTTON_2, Menu.NONE, "Radiobutton 2");
menu.add(RB_GROUP, RADIOBUTTON_3, Menu.NONE,
         "Radiobutton 3").setChecked(true);
menu.setGroupCheckable(RB_GROUP, true, true);
```

➤ **Shortcut keys** You can specify a keyboard shortcut for a Menu Item using the setShortcut method. Each call to setShortcut requires two shortcut keys, one for use with the numeric keypad and a second to support a full keyboard. Neither key is case-sensitive.

```
// Add a shortcut to this menu item, '0' if using the numeric keypad
// or 'b' if using the full keyboard.
menuItem.setShortcut('0', 'b');
```

➤ **Condensed titles** The icon menu does not display shortcuts or checkboxes, so it's often necessary to modify its display text to indicate its state. The setTitleCondensed method lets you specify text to be displayed only in the icon menu.

```
menuItem.setTitleCondensed("Short Title");
```

➤ **Icons** The icon property is a Drawable resource identifier for an icon to be used in the Menu Item. Icons are displayed only in the icon menu; they are not visible in the extended menu or submenus. You can specify any Drawable resource as a menu icon, though by convention menu icons are generally grayscale and use an embossed style.

```
menuItem.setIcon(R.drawable.menu_item_icon);
```

➤ **Menu item click listener** An event handler that will execute when the Menu Item is selected. For efficiency, the use of such an event handler is discouraged; instead, Menu Item selections should be handled by the onOptionsItemSelected handler, as shown later in this section.

```
menuItem.setOnMenuItemClickListener(new OnMenuItemClickListener() {
  public boolean onMenuItemClick(MenuItem _menuItem) {
    [ ... execute click handling, return true if handled ... ]
    return true;
  }
});
```

➤ **Intents** An Intent assigned to a Menu Item is triggered when the clicking of a Menu Item isn't handled by either a `MenuItemClickListener` or the Activity's `onOptionsItemSelected` handler. When the Intent is triggered Android will execute `startActivity`, passing in the specified Intent.

```
menuItem.setIntent(new Intent(this, MyOtherActivity.class));
```

Dynamically Updating Menu Items

By overriding your Activity's `onPrepareOptionsMenu` method you can modify a Menu based on an application's current state immediately before the Menu is displayed. This lets you dynamically disable/enable Menu Items, set visibility, and modify text.

To modify Menu Items dynamically you can either find a reference to them in the `onCreateOptionsMenu` method when they're created, or you can use the `findItem` method on the Menu object, as shown in Listing 4-27, where `onPrepareOptionsMenu` is overridden.

Available for download on Wrox.com

LISTING 4-27: Dynamic menu modification

```
@Override
public boolean onPrepareOptionsMenu(Menu menu) {
  super.onPrepareOptionsMenu(menu);

  MenuItem menuItem = menu.findItem(MENU_ITEM);

  [ ... modify menu items ... ]

  return true;
}
```

Handling Menu Selections

Android handles all of an Activity's Menu Item selections using a single event handler, the `onOptionsItemSelected` method. The Menu Item selected is passed in to this method as the `MenuItem` parameter.

To react to the menu selection, compare the `item.getItemId` value to the Menu Item identifiers you used when populating the Menu, and react accordingly, as shown in Listing 4-28.

Available for download on Wrox.com

LISTING 4-28: Handling Menu Item selections

```
public boolean onOptionsItemSelected(MenuItem item) {
  super.onOptionsItemSelected(item);
```

continues

LISTING 4-28 *(continued)*

```
    // Find which menu item has been selected
    switch (item.getItemId()) {

      // Check for each known menu item
      case (MENU_ITEM):
        [ ... Perform menu handler actions ... ]
        return true;
    }

    // Return false if you have not handled the menu item.
    return false;
  }
```

Submenus and Context Menus

Context menus use the same floating window as the submenus shown in Figure 4-9. While their appearance is the same, the two menu types are populated differently.

Creating Submenus

Submenus are displayed as regular Menu Items that, when selected, reveal more items. Traditionally, submenus are displayed in a hierarchical tree layout. Android uses a different approach to simplify menu navigation for small-screen devices. Rather than a tree structure, selecting a submenu presents a single floating window that displays all of its Menu Items.

You can add submenus using the addSubMenu method. It supports the same parameters as the add method used to add normal Menu Items, enabling you to specify a group, unique identifier, and text string for each submenu. You can also use the setHeaderIcon and setIcon methods to specify an icon to display in the submenu's header bar or icon menu, respectively.

The Menu Items within a submenu support the same options as those assigned to the icon or extended menus. However, unlike traditional systems, Android does not support nested submenus.

The following code snippet shows an extract from an implementation of the onCreateMenuOptions code that adds a submenu to the main menu, sets the header icon, and then adds a submenu Menu Item:

```
SubMenu sub = menu.addSubMenu(0, 0, Menu.NONE, "Submenu");
sub.setHeaderIcon(R.drawable.icon);
sub.setIcon(R.drawable.icon);

MenuItem submenuItem = sub.add(0, 0, Menu.NONE, "Submenu Item");
```

Using Context Menus

Context Menus are contextualized by the currently focused View and are triggered by the user's pressing the trackball, middle D-pad button, or a View for around three seconds.

You define and populate Context Menus much as you define and populate Activity Menus. There are two options available for creating Context Menus for a particular View.

Creating Context Menus

One option is to create a generic `ContextMenu` object for a `View` class by overriding a View's `onCreateContextMenu` handler, as shown here:

```
@Override
public void onCreateContextMenu(ContextMenu menu) {
  super.onCreateContextMenu(menu);
  menu.add("ContextMenuItem1");
}
```

The Context Menu created here will be available within any Activity that includes this `View` class.

The more common alternative is to create Activity-specific Context Menus by overriding the Activity's `onCreateContextMenu` method, and registering the Views that should use it using the `registerForContextMenu` as shown in Listing 4-29.

LISTING 4-29: Assigning a Context Menu to a View

```
@Override
public void onCreate(Bundle savedInstanceState) {
  super.onCreate(savedInstanceState);

  EditText view = new EditText(this);
  setContentView(view);

  registerForContextMenu(view);
}
```

Once a View has been registered, the `onCreateContextMenu` handler will be triggered the first time a Context Menu should be displayed for that View.

Override `onCreateContextMenu` and check which View has triggered the menu creation in order to populate the Context Menu parameter with the appropriate Menu Items, as shown in this extension to Listing 4-29.

```
@Override
public void onCreateContextMenu(ContextMenu menu, View v,
                                ContextMenu.ContextMenuInfo menuInfo) {
  super.onCreateContextMenu(menu, v, menuInfo);

  menu.setHeaderTitle("Context Menu");
  menu.add(0, menu.FIRST, Menu.NONE,
          "Item 1").setIcon(R.drawable.menu_item);
  menu.add(0, menu.FIRST+1, Menu.NONE, "Item 2").setCheckable(true);
  menu.add(0, menu.FIRST+2, Menu.NONE, "Item 3").setShortcut('3', '3');
  SubMenu sub = menu.addSubMenu("Submenu");
  sub.add("Submenu Item");
}
```

As shown in the preceding code, the `ContextMenu` class supports the same `add` method as the `Menu` class, so you can populate a Context Menu in the same way that you populate Activity menus — using the `add` method. This includes using the add method to add submenus to your Context Menus. Note that icons will never be displayed. You can, however, specify the title and icon to display in the Context Menu's header bar.

Android also supports late runtime population of Context Menus via Intent Filters. This mechanism lets you populate a Context Menu by specifying the kind of data presented by the current View, and asking other Android applications if they support any actions for it.

The most common example of this mechanism is the cut/copy/paste Menu Items available on Edit Text controls. Using Intent Filters to populate Context Menus is covered in detail in the next chapter.

Handling Context Menu Selections

Context Menu Item selections are handled much the same as Activity Menu selection. You can attach an Intent or Menu Item Click Listener directly to each Menu Item, or use the preferred technique of overriding the `onContextItemSelected` method on the Activity.

This event handler is triggered whenever a Context Menu Item is selected.

```
@Override
public boolean onContextItemSelected(MenuItem item) {
  super.onContextItemSelected(item);

  [ ... Handle menu item selection ... ]

  return false;
}
```

Defining Menus in XML

Android lets you define your Menu hierarchies as XML resources.

As with layouts and other resources, this gives you the ability to create different Menus for alternative hardware configurations, languages, or locations. For example, you may wish to move some onscreen options to your menu for small displays.

Menu resources are created as XML files in the res/menu folder of your resources directory. Each menu hierarchy must be created as a separate file, for which the lowercase file name becomes the resource identifier.

Create your Menu hierarchy using the `<menu>` tag as the root node and a series of `<item>` tags to specify each Menu Item. Each `item` node supports attributes to specify the Menu Item properties, including the text, icon, shortcut, and checkbox options.

To create a submenu, simply place a new `<menu>` tag as a subnode within an `<item>`.

Listing 4-30 shows how to create the Menu hierarchy described in Listing 4-29 as an XML resource.

LISTING 4-30: Defining a menu in XML

```
<menu xmlns:android="http://schemas.android.com/apk/res/android"
    android:name="Context Menu">
  <item
    android:id="@+id/item01"
```

```
      android:icon="@drawable/menu_item"
      android:title="Item 1">
  </item>
  <item
    android:id="@+id/item02"
    android:checkable="true"
    android:title="Item 2">
  </item>
  <item
    android:id="@+id/item03"
    android:numericShortcut="3"
    android:alphabeticShortcut="3"
    android:title="Item 3">
  </item>
  <item
    android:id="@+id/item04"
    android:title="Submenu">
    <menu>
      <item
        android:id="@+id/item05"
        android:title="Submenu Item">
      </item>
    </menu>
  </item>
</menu>
```

To use your Menu resource, use the `MenuInflator` class within your `onCreateOptionsMenu` or `onCreateContextMenu` event handlers, as shown in Listing 4-31.

LISTING 4-31: Inflating an XML menu resource

```
public void onCreateContextMenu(ContextMenu menu, View v,
                                 ContextMenu.ContextMenuInfo menuInfo) {
  super.onCreateContextMenu(menu, v, menuInfo);
  MenuInflater inflater = getMenuInflater();
  inflater.inflate(R.menu.my_menu, menu);
  menu.setHeaderTitle("Context Menu");
}
```

To-Do List Example Continued

In the following example you'll be adding some simple menu functions to the to-do list application you started in Chapter 2 and continued to improve earlier in this chapter.

You will add the ability to remove to-do items using Context and Activity Menus, and improve the use of screen space by displaying the text entry box only when adding a new item.

1. Start by importing the packages you need to support Menu functionality into the `ToDoList` Activity class.

```
import android.view.Menu;
import android.view.MenuItem;
```

```
import android.view.ContextMenu;
import android.widget.AdapterView;
```

2. Then add private static final variables that define the unique IDs for each Menu Item.

```
static final private int ADD_NEW_TODO = Menu.FIRST;
static final private int REMOVE_TODO = Menu.FIRST + 1;
```

3. Now override the onCreateOptionsMenu method to add two new Menu Items, one to add and the other to remove a to-do item. Specify the appropriate text, and assign icon resources and shortcut keys for each item.

```
@Override
public boolean onCreateOptionsMenu(Menu menu) {
  super.onCreateOptionsMenu(menu);

  // Create and add new menu items.
  MenuItem itemAdd = menu.add(0, ADD_NEW_TODO, Menu.NONE,
                              R.string.add_new);
  MenuItem itemRem = menu.add(0, REMOVE_TODO, Menu.NONE,
                              R.string.remove);

  // Assign icons
  itemAdd.setIcon(R.drawable.add_new_item);
  itemRem.setIcon(R.drawable.remove_item);

  // Allocate shortcuts to each of them.
  itemAdd.setShortcut('0', 'a');
  itemRem.setShortcut('1', 'r');

  return true;
}
```

If you run the Activity, pressing the hardware *menu* button will display the menu as shown in Figure 4-10.

4. Having populated the Activity Menu, create a Context Menu. First, modify onCreate to register the List View to use a Context Menu. Then override onCreateContextMenu to populate the Context Menu with a *remove* item.

```
@Override
  public void onCreate(Bundle savedInstanceState) {

    [ ... existing onCreate method ... ]

  registerForContextMenu(myListView);
}

@Override
public void onCreateContextMenu(ContextMenu menu,
                                View v,
```

FIGURE 4-10

```
                                         ContextMenu.ContextMenuInfo menuInfo) {
      super.onCreateContextMenu(menu, v, menuInfo);

      menu.setHeaderTitle("Selected To Do Item");
      menu.add(0, REMOVE_TODO, Menu.NONE, R.string.remove);
    }
```

5. Now modify the appearance of the Menu based on the application context. Override the `onPrepareOptionsMenu` method; the Menu Item should be customized to show *Cancel* rather than *Delete* if you are currently adding a new to-do item.

```
    private boolean addingNew = false;

    @Override
    public boolean onPrepareOptionsMenu(Menu menu) {
      super.onPrepareOptionsMenu(menu);

      int idx = myListView.getSelectedItemPosition();

      String removeTitle = getString(addingNew ?
                               R.string.cancel : R.string.remove);

      MenuItem removeItem = menu.findItem(REMOVE_TODO);
      removeItem.setTitle(removeTitle);
      removeItem.setVisible(addingNew || idx > -1);

      return true;
    }
```

6. For the code in Step 5 to work you need to increase the scope of the `todoListItems` and `ListView` control beyond the `onCreate` method. Do the same thing for the `ArrayAdapter` and `EditText` to support the *add* and *remove* actions when they're implemented later.

```
    private ArrayList<String> todoItems;
    private ListView myListView;
    private EditText myEditText;
    private ArrayAdapter<String> aa;

    @Override
    public void onCreate(Bundle savedInstanceState) {
      super.onCreate(savedInstanceState);
      setContentView(R.layout.main);

      // Get references to UI widgets
      myListView = (ListView)findViewById(R.id.myListView);
      myEditText = (EditText)findViewById(R.id.myEditText);

      todoItems = new ArrayList<String>();
      int resID = R.layout.todolist_item;
      aa = new ArrayAdapter<String>(this, resID, todoItems);
      myListView.setAdapter(aa);

      myEditText.setOnKeyListener(new OnKeyListener() {
        public boolean onKey(View v, int keyCode, KeyEvent event) {
          if (event.getAction() == KeyEvent.ACTION_DOWN)
```

```
          if (keyCode == KeyEvent.KEYCODE_DPAD_CENTER)
          {
            todoItems.add(0, myEditText.getText().toString());
            myEditText.setText("");
            aa.notifyDataSetChanged();
            return true;
          }
        return false;
      }
  });

  registerForContextMenu(myListView);
}
```

7. Next you need to handle Menu Item clicks. Override the onOptionsItemSelected and onContextItemSelected methods to execute stubs that handle the new Menu Items.

   7.1. Start by overriding onOptionsItemSelected to handle the Activity Menu selections. For the *remove* Menu Item you can use the getSelectedItemPosition method on the List View to find the currently highlighted item.

```
@Override
public boolean onOptionsItemSelected(MenuItem item) {
  super.onOptionsItemSelected(item);

  int index = myListView.getSelectedItemPosition();

  switch (item.getItemId()) {
    case (REMOVE_TODO): {
      if (addingNew) {
        cancelAdd();
      }
      else {
        removeItem(index);
      }
      return true;
    }
    case (ADD_NEW_TODO): {
      addNewItem();
      return true;
    }
  }

  return false;
}
```

   7.2. Next, override onContextItemSelected to handle Context Menu Item selections. Note that you are using the AdapterView-specific implementation of ContextMenuInfo. This includes a reference to the View that triggered the Context Menu and the index of the data it's displaying from the underlying Adapter. Use the latter as the index of the item to remove.

```
@Override
public boolean onContextItemSelected(MenuItem item) {
  super.onContextItemSelected(item);
```

```
            switch (item.getItemId()) {
              case (REMOVE_TODO): {
                AdapterView.AdapterContextMenuInfo menuInfo;
                menuInfo =(AdapterView.AdapterContextMenuInfo)item.getMenuInfo();
                int index = menuInfo.position;

                removeItem(index);
                return true;
              }
            }
            return false;
          }
```

7.3. Create the stubs called in the Menu Item selection handlers you created earlier.

```
private void cancelAdd() {
}

private void addNewItem() {
}

private void removeItem(int _index) {
}
```

8. Now implement each of the stubs to provide the new functionality.

```
private void cancelAdd() {
  addingNew = false;
  myEditText.setVisibility(View.GONE);
}

private void addNewItem() {
  addingNew = true;
  myEditText.setVisibility(View.VISIBLE);
  myEditText.requestFocus();
}

private void removeItem(int _index) {
  todoItems.remove(_index);
  aa.notifyDataSetChanged();
}
```

9. You need to hide the text entry box after you've added a new to-do item. In the onCreate method modify the onKeyListener to call the cancelAdd function after adding a new item.

```
myEditText.setOnKeyListener(new OnKeyListener() {
  public boolean onKey(View v, int keyCode, KeyEvent event) {
    if (event.getAction() == KeyEvent.ACTION_DOWN)
      if (keyCode == KeyEvent.KEYCODE_DPAD_CENTER)
      {
        todoItems.add(0, myEditText.getText().toString());
        myEditText.setText("");
        aa.notifyDataSetChanged();
        cancelAdd();
        return true;
      }
```

```
        return false;
    }
});
```

10. Finally, to ensure a consistent UI, modify the main.xml layout to hide the text entry box until the user chooses to add a new item.

```
<EditText
  android:id="@+id/myEditText"
  android:layout_width="fill_parent"
  android:layout_height="wrap_content"
  android:text=""
  android:visibility="gone"
/>
```

All code snippets in this example are part of the **Chapter 4 Todo List 2** *project, available for download at Wrox.com.*

Running the application should now let you trigger the Activity Menu to add or remove items from the list, and a Context Menu on each item should offer the option of removing it.

SUMMARY

You now know the basics of creating intuitive user interfaces for Android applications. You learned about Views and layouts and were introduced to the Android menu system.

You learned to create Activity screens by positioning Views using layout managers that can be created in code or as resource files. You learned how to extend, group, and create new View-based controls to provide a customized appearance and behavior for your applications.

In this chapter, you:

➤ Were introduced to some of the controls and widgets available as part of the Android SDK.

➤ Learned how to use your custom Views within Activities.

➤ Discovered how to create dynamic Drawable resources in XML.

➤ Learned how to create UIs that are resolution- and pixel-density-independent.

➤ Discovered how to create and use Activity Menus and Context Menus.

➤ Extended the to-do list example to support custom Views and menu-based functions.

➤ Created a new Compass View control from scratch.

Now that we've covered the fundamentals of Android UI design, the next chapter focuses on binding application components using Intents, Broadcast Receivers, and Adapters. You will learn how to start new Activities and broadcast and consume requests for action. Chapter 5 also introduces Internet connectivity and looks at the Dialog class.

5

Intents, Broadcast Receivers, Adapters, and the Internet

WHAT'S IN THIS CHAPTER?

➤ An introduction to Intents

➤ Starting new Activities and sub-Activities using implicit and explicit Intents

➤ Intent filters and intent resolution

➤ Using linkify

➤ Intents, broadcast actions and Broadcast Receivers

➤ Using Adapters to bind data to Views

➤ Using the Internet in Android

➤ How to create and use Dialogs

At first glance the subjects of this chapter might appear to have little in common; in practice they represent the glue that binds applications and their components.

Mobile applications on most platforms run in their own sandboxes. They're isolated from each other, and have strict limitations applied to their interaction with hardware and native components. Android applications are also sandboxed but they can use Intents, Broadcast Receivers, Adapters, Content Providers, and the Internet to interact through those boundaries.

In this chapter you'll look at Intents. Intents are probably the most unique, and important, concept in Android development. You'll learn how to use Intents to broadcast data between applications and application components, and start Activities or Services, both explicitly and using late runtime binding.

Using implicit Intents you'll learn how to request that an action be performed on a piece of data, letting Android determine which application components can best service that request.

Broadcast Intents are used to announce events system-wide. You'll learn how to transmit these broadcasts, and receive them using Broadcast Receivers.

You'll examine Adapters and learn how to use them to bind your presentation layer to data sources, before examining dialog boxes.

Having looked at the mechanisms for transmitting and consuming local data, you'll be introduced to Android's Internet connectivity model and some of the Java techniques for parsing Internet data feeds.

An earthquake-monitoring example will then demonstrate how to tie all these features together. The earthquake monitor will form the basis of an ongoing example that you'll improve and extend in later chapters.

INTRODUCING INTENTS

Intents are used as a message-passing mechanism that works both within your application, and between applications. Intents can be used to:

➤ Declare your intention that an Activity or Service be started to perform an action, usually with (or on) a particular piece of data

➤ Broadcast that an event (or action) has occurred

➤ Explicitly start a particular Service or Activity

You can use Intents to support interaction among any of the application components installed on an Android device, no matter which application they're a part of. This turns your device from a platform containing a collection of independent components into a single interconnected system.

One of the most common uses for Intents is to start new Activities, either *explicitly* (by specifying the class to load) or *implicitly* (by requesting that an action be performed on a piece of data). In the latter case the action need not be performed by an Activity within the calling application.

Intents can also be used to broadcast messages across the system. Any application can register Broadcast Receivers to listen for, and react to, these broadcast Intents. This lets you create event-driven applications based on internal, system, or third-party-application events.

Android broadcasts Intents to announce system events, like changes in Internet connection status or battery charge levels. The native Android applications, such as the phone dialer and SMS manager, simply register components that listen for specific broadcast Intents — such as "incoming phone call" or "SMS message received" — and react accordingly.

Using Intents to propagate actions — even within the same application — is a fundamental Android design principle. It encourages the decoupling of components, to allow the seamless replacement of application elements. It also provides the basis of a simple model for extending an application's functionality.

Using Intents to Launch Activities

The most common use of Intents is to bind your application components. Intents are used to start, and transition between, Activities.

The instructions given in this section refer to starting new Activities, but the same details also apply to Services. Details on starting (and creating) Services are available in Chapter 9.

To open an Activity, call `startActivity`, passing in an `Intent` as shown in the following snippet:

```
startActivity(myIntent);
```

The Intent can either explicitly specify the Activity class to open, or include an action that an Activity must perform. In the latter case the run time will choose an Activity dynamically using a process known as *Intent resolution*.

The `startActivity` method finds and starts the single Activity that best matches your Intent.

When you use `startActivity` your application won't receive any notification when the newly launched Activity finishes. To track feedback from the opened screen use the `startActivityForResult` method described in more detail in the next section.

Explicitly Starting New Activities

You learned in Chapter 2 that applications consist of a number of interrelated screens — Activities — that must be included in the application manifest. To connect them you may want to explicitly specify an Activity to open.

To explicitly select an Activity class to start, create a new Intent, specifying the current application Context and Activity class to launch. Pass this Intent in to `startActivity` as shown in Listing 5-1.

LISTING 5-1: Explicitly starting an Activity

```
Intent intent = new Intent(MyActivity.this, MyOtherActivity.class);
startActivity(intent);
```

After `startActivity` is called, the new Activity (in this example `MyOtherActivity`) will be created and become visible and active, moving to the top of the Activity stack.

Calling `finish` on the new Activity, or pressing the hardware back button, will close it and remove it from the stack. Alternatively, developers can navigate to the previous Activity, or yet another Activity, by calling `startActivity`.

Implicit Intents and Late Runtime Binding

An implicit Intent is a mechanism that lets anonymous application components service action requests. That means you can ask the system to launch an Activity that can perform a given action without knowing which application, or Activity, will do so.

When constructing a new implicit Intent to use with `startActivity`, you nominate an action to perform and, optionally, supply the URI of the data to perform that action on. You can also send additional data to the target Activity by adding extras to the Intent.

When you use this Intent to start an Activity, Android will — at run time — resolve it into the Activity class best suited to performing the required action on the type of data specified. This means you can create projects that use functionality from other applications, without knowing exactly which application you're borrowing functionality from ahead of time.

For example, to let users make calls from your application you could implement a new dialer, or you could use an implicit Intent that requests the action (dialing) be performed on a phone number (represented as a URI), as shown in Listing 5-2.

LISTING 5-2: Implicitly starting an Activity

```
if (somethingWeird && itDontLookGood) {
    Intent intent = new Intent(Intent.ACTION_DIAL, Uri.parse("tel:555-2368"));
    startActivity(intent);
}
```

Android resolves this Intent and starts an Activity that provides the dial action on a telephone number — in this case the dialer Activity.

In circumstances where multiple Activities are capable of performing a given action, the user is presented with a choice. The full process of Intent resolution is described later in this chapter.

Various native applications provide Activities to handle actions performed on specific data. Third-party applications, including your own, can be registered to support new actions, or to provide an alternative provider of native actions. You'll be introduced to some of the native actions, and how to register your own Activities to support them, later in this chapter.

Returning Results from Activities

An Activity started via `startActivity` is independent of its parent and will not provide any feedback when it closes.

Alternatively, you can start an Activity as a sub-Activity that's inherently connected to its parent. A sub-Activity triggers an event handler within its parent Activity when it closes. Sub-Activities are perfect for situations in which one Activity is providing data input (such as a user's selecting an item from a list) for another.

Sub-Activities are really just Activities opened in a different way. As such they must be registered in the application manifest — in fact any manifest-registered Activity can be opened as a sub-Activity including system or third-party application Activities.

Launching Sub-Activities

The `startActivityForResult` method works much like `startActivity`, but with one important difference. As well as the explicit or implicit Intent used to determine which Activity to launch, you also pass in a *request code*. This value will later be used to uniquely identify the sub-Activity that has returned a result.

The skeleton code for launching a sub-Activity is shown in Listing 5-3.

LISTING 5-3: Starting an Activity for a result

```
private static final int SHOW_SUBACTIVITY = 1;

Intent intent = new Intent(this, MyOtherActivity.class);
startActivityForResult(intent, SHOW_SUBACTIVITY);
```

Like regular Activities, sub-Activities can be started implicitly or explicitly. Listing 5-4 uses an implicit Intent to launch a new sub-Activity to pick a contact.

LISTING 5-4: Implicitly starting an Activity for a result

```
private static final int PICK_CONTACT_SUBACTIVITY = 2;

Uri uri = Uri.parse("content://contacts/people");
Intent intent = new Intent(Intent.ACTION_PICK, uri);
startActivityForResult(intent, PICK_CONTACT_SUBACTIVITY);
```

Returning Results

When your sub-Activity is ready to return, call `setResult` before `finish` to return a result to the calling Activity.

The `setResult` method takes two parameters: the result code and the result itself, represented as an Intent.

The result code is the "result" of running the sub-Activity — generally either `Activity.RESULT_OK` or `Activity.RESULT_CANCELED`. In some circumstances you'll want to use your own response codes to handle application specific choices; `setResult` supports any integer value.

The Intent returned as a result often includes a URI to a piece of content (such as the selected contact, phone number, or media file) and a collection of extras used to return additional information.

Listing 5-5 is taken from a sub-Activity's `onCreate` method, and shows how an OK and Cancel button might return different results to the calling Activity.

LISTING 5-5: Creating new Shared Preferences

```
Button okButton = (Button) findViewById(R.id.ok_button);
  okButton.setOnClickListener(new View.OnClickListener() {
  public void onClick(View view) {
    Uri data = Uri.parse("content://horses/" + selected_horse_id);

    Intent result = new Intent(null, data);
    result.putExtra(IS_INPUT_CORRECT, inputCorrect);
    result.putExtra(SELECTED_PISTOL, selectedPistol);
```

continues

LISTING 5-5 *(continued)*

```
        setResult(RESULT_OK, result);
        finish();
    }
});

Button cancelButton = (Button) findViewById(R.id.cancel_button);
cancelButton.setOnClickListener(new View.OnClickListener() {
    public void onClick(View view) {
        setResult(RESULT_CANCELED, null);
        finish();
    }
});
```

If the Activity is closed by the user pressing the hardware back key, or finish is called without a prior call to setResult, the result code will be set to RESULT_CANCELED and the result Intent set to null.

Handling Sub-Activity Results

When a sub-Activity closes, the onActivityResult event handler is fired within the calling Activity. Override this method to handle the results returned by sub-Activities.

The onActivityResult handler receives a number of parameters:

➤ **Request code**   The request code that was used to launch the returning sub-Activity.

➤ **Result code**   The result code set by the sub-Activity to indicate its result. It can be any integer value, but typically will be either Activity.RESULT_OK or Activity.RESULT_CANCELED.

> *If the sub-Activity closes abnormally, or doesn't specify a result code before it closes, the result code is* Activity.RESULT_CANCELED.

➤ **Data**   An Intent used to package returned data. Depending on the purpose of the sub-Activity, it may include a URI that represents a selected piece of content. Alternatively, or additionally, the sub-Activity can return extra information as primitive values using the Intent extras Bundle.

The skeleton code for implementing the onActivityResult event handler within an Activity is shown in Listing 5-6.

LISTING 5-6: Implementing an On Activity Result Handler

```
private static final int SHOW_SUB_ACTIVITY_ONE = 1;
private static final int SHOW_SUB_ACTIVITY_TWO = 2;

@Override
public void onActivityResult(int requestCode,
```

```
                              int resultCode,
                              Intent data) {

       super.onActivityResult(requestCode, resultCode, data);

       switch(requestCode) {
         case (SHOW_SUB_ACTIVITY_ONE) : {
           if (resultCode == Activity.RESULT_OK) {
             Uri horse = data.getData();
             boolean inputCorrect = data.getBooleanExtra(IS_INPUT_CORRECT, false);
             String selectedPistol = data.getStringExtra(SELECTED_PISTOL);
           }
           break;
         }
         case (SHOW_SUB_ACTIVITY_TWO) : {
           if (resultCode == Activity.RESULT_OK) {
             // TODO: Handle OK click.
           }
           break;
         }
       }
     }
```

Native Android Actions

Native Android applications also use Intents to launch Activities and sub-Activities.

The following non-comprehensive list shows some of the native actions available as static string constants in the `Intent` class. When creating implicit Intents you can use these actions, called *Activity Intents*, to start Activities and sub-Activities within your own applications.

 Later you will be introduced to Intent Filters and you'll learn how to register your own Activities as handlers for these actions.

➤ `ACTION_ANSWER` Opens an Activity that handles incoming calls. Currently this is handled by the native in-call screen.

➤ `ACTION_CALL` Brings up a phone dialer and immediately initiates a call using the number supplied in the Intent URI. Generally it's considered better form to use `ACTION_DIAL` if possible.

➤ `ACTION_DELETE` Starts an Activity that lets you delete the data specified at the Intent's data URI.

➤ `ACTION_DIAL` Brings up a dialer application with the number to dial pre-populated from the Intent URI. By default this is handled by the native Android phone dialer. The dialer can normalize most number schemas: for example, `tel:555-1234` and `tel:(212) 555 1212` are both valid numbers.

➤ `ACTION_EDIT` Requests an Activity that can edit the data at the specified Intent URI.

➤ `ACTION_INSERT`   Opens an Activity capable of inserting new items into the Cursor specified in the Intent URI. When called as a sub-Activity it should return a URI to the newly inserted item.

➤ `ACTION_PICK`   Launches a sub-Activity that lets you pick an item from the Content Provider specified by the Intent URI. When closed it should return a URI to the item that was picked. The Activity launched depends on the data being picked: for example, passing `content://contacts/people` will invoke the native contacts list.

➤ `ACTION_SEARCH`   Launches the Activity used for performing a search. Supply the search term as a string in the Intent's extras using the `SearchManager.QUERY` key.

➤ `ACTION_SENDTO`   Launches an Activity to send a message to the contact specified by the Intent URI.

➤ `ACTION_SEND`   Launches an Activity that sends the data specified in the Intent. The recipient contact needs to be selected by the resolved Activity. Use `setType` to set the MIME type of the transmitted data.

The data itself should be stored as an extra by means of the key `EXTRA_TEXT` or `EXTRA_STREAM`, depending on the type. In the case of e-mail, the native Android applications will also accept extras via the `EXTRA_EMAIL`, `EXTRA_CC`, `EXTRA_BCC`, and `EXTRA_SUBJECT` keys. Use the `ACTION_SEND` action only to send data to a remote recipient (not another application on the device).

➤ `ACTION_VIEW`   The most common generic action. View asks that the data supplied in the Intent's URI be viewed in the most reasonable manner. Different applications will handle view requests depending on the URI schema of the data supplied. Natively `http:` addresses will open in the browser, `tel:` addresses will open the dialer to call the number, `geo:` addresses will be displayed in the Google Maps application, and contact content will be displayed in the contact manager.

➤ `ACTION_WEB_SEARCH`   Opens an Activity that performs a web search based on the text supplied in the Intent URI (typically the browser).

> *As well as these Activity actions, Android includes a large number of broadcast actions used to create Intents that are broadcast to announce system events. These broadcast actions are described later in this chapter.*

Using Intent Filters to Service Implicit Intents

If an Intent is a request for an action to be performed on a set of data, how does Android know which application (and component) to use to service the request?

Intent Filters are used to register Activities, Services, and Broadcast Receivers as being capable of performing an action on a particular kind of data. Intent Filters are also used to register Broadcast Receivers as being interested in Intents broadcasting a given action or event.

Using Intent Filters, application components announce that they can respond to action requests from any application installed on the device.

To register an application component as a potential Intent handler, add an `intent-filter` tag to the component's manifest node using the following tags (and associated attributes) within the Intent Filter node:

➤ `action`   Uses the `android:name` attribute to specify the name of the action being serviced. Each Intent Filter must have one (and only one) action tag. Actions should be unique strings that are self-describing. Best practice is to use a naming system based on the Java package naming conventions.

➤ `category`   Uses the `android:name` attribute to specify under which circumstances the action should be serviced. Each Intent Filter tag can include multiple category tags. You can specify your own categories or use the standard values provided by Android and listed here:

   ➤ `ALTERNATIVE`   This category specifies that this action should be available as an alternative to the default action performed on an item of this data type. For example, where the default action for a contact is to view it, the alternative could be to edit it.

   ➤ `SELECTED_ALTERNATIVE`   Similar to the `ALTERNATIVE` category, but where that category will always resolve to a single action using the Intent resolution described below, `SELECTED_ALTERNATIVE` is used when a list of possibilities is required. As you'll see later in this chapter, one of the uses of Intent Filters is to help populate Context Menus dynamically using actions.

   ➤ `BROWSABLE`   Specifies an action available from within the browser. When an Intent is fired from within the browser it will always include the browsable category. If you want your application to respond to actions triggered within the browser (e.g., intercepting links to a particular web site), you must include the browsable category.

   ➤ `DEFAULT`   Set this to make a component the default action for the data type specified in the Intent Filter. This is also necessary for Activities that are launched using an explicit Intent.

   ➤ `GADGET`   By setting the gadget category you specify that this Activity can run embedded inside another Activity.

   ➤ `HOME`   By setting an Intent Filter category as home without specifying an action, you are presenting it as an alternative to the native home screen.

   ➤ `LAUNCHER`   Using this category makes an Activity appear in the application launcher.

➤ `data`   The data tag lets you specify which data types your component can act on; you can include several data tags as appropriate. You can use any combination of the following attributes to specify the data your component supports:

   ➤ `android:host`   Specifies a valid hostname (e.g., `google.com`).

   ➤ `android:mimetype`   Lets you specify the type of data your component is capable of handling. For example, `<type android:value="vnd.android.cursor.dir/*"/>` would match any Android cursor.

   ➤ `android:path`   Specifies valid "path" values for the URI (e.g., `/transport/boats/`).

> ➤ `android:port` Specifies valid ports for the specified host.

> ➤ `android:scheme` Requires a particular scheme (e.g., `content` or `http`).

Listing 5-7 shows an Intent Filter for an Activity that can perform the SHOW_DAMAGE action as either a primary or an alternative action (you'll create earthquake content in the next chapter).

LISTING 5-7: Registering an Activity as an Intent Receiver

```
<activity android:name=".EarthquakeDamageViewer" android:label="View Damage">
  <intent-filter>
    <action android:name="com.paad.earthquake.intent.action.SHOW_DAMAGE"></action>
    <category android:name="android.intent.category.DEFAULT"/>
    <category android:name="android.intent.category.SELECTED_ALTERNATIVE"/>
    <data android:mimeType="vnd.earthquake.cursor.item/*"/>
  </intent-filter>
</activity>
```

How Android Resolves Intent Filters

When you use `startActivity`, the implicit Intent passed in usually resolves to a single Activity. If there are multiple Activities capable of performing the given action on the specified data, the user will be presented with a list of alternatives.

The process of deciding which Activity to start is called *Intent resolution*. The aim of Intent resolution is to find the best Intent Filter match possible by means of the following process:

1. Android puts together a list of all the Intent Filters available from the installed packages.

2. Intent Filters that do not match the action *or* category associated with the Intent being resolved are removed from the list.

 2.1. Action matches are made if the Intent Filter either includes the specified action or has *no* action specified. An Intent Filter will fail the action match check only if it has one or more actions defined, and none of them matches the action specified by the Intent.

 2.2. Category matching is stricter. Intent Filters must include *all* the categories defined in the resolving Intent. An Intent Filter with no categories specified matches only Intents with no categories.

3. Finally, each part of the Intent's data URI is compared to the Intent Filter's `data` tag. If the Intent Filter specifies a scheme, host/authority, path, or MIME type these values are compared to the Intent's URI. Any mismatch will remove the Intent Filter from the list. Specifying no data values in an Intent Filter will result in a match with all Intent data values.

 3.1. The MIME type is the data type of the data being matched. When matching data types you can use wildcards to match subtypes (e.g., `earthquakes/*`). If the Intent Filter specifies a data type it must match the Intent; specifying no data types results in a match with all of them.

 3.2. The scheme is the "protocol" part of the URI — for example, `http:`, `mailto:`, or `tel:`.

3.3. The hostname or *data authority* is the section of the URI between the scheme and the path (e.g., `www.google.com`). For a hostname to match, the Intent Filter's scheme must also pass.

3.4. The data path is what comes after the authority (e.g., `/ig`). A path can match only if the scheme and hostname parts of the data tag also match.

4. When you implicitly start an Activity, if more than one component is resolved from this process all the matching possibilities are offered to the user.

Native Android application components are part of the Intent resolution process in exactly the same way as third-party applications. They do not have a higher priority, and can be completely replaced with new Activities that declare Intent Filters that service the same actions.

Finding and Using the Launch Intent Within an Activity

When an application component is started through an implicit Intent, it needs to find the action it's to perform and the data to perform it on.

Call the `getIntent` method — usually from within the `onCreate` method — to extract the Intent used to start a component, as in Listing 5-8.

LISTING 5-8: Finding the launch Intent in a sub-Activity

```
@Override
public void onCreate(Bundle icicle) {
  super.onCreate(icicle);
  setContentView(R.layout.main);

  Intent intent = getIntent();
}
```

Use the `getData` and `getAction` methods to find the data and action associated with the Intent. Use the type-safe `get<type>Extra` methods to extract additional information stored in its extras Bundle.

```
String action = intent.getAction();
Uri data = intent.getData();
```

Passing on Responsibility

Use the `startNextMatchingActivity` method to pass responsibility for action handling to the next best matching application component, as shown in Listing 5-9.

LISTING 5-9: Passing on Intent Receiver Handling

```
Intent intent = getIntent();
if (isDuringBreak)
  startNextMatchingActivity(intent);
```

This lets you add additional conditions to your components that restrict their use beyond the ability of the Intent Filter–based Intent resolution process.

In some cases your component may wish to perform some processing, or offer the user a choice, before passing the Intent on to an alternative component.

Select a Contact Example

In this example you'll create a new Activity that services ACTION_PICK for contact data. It displays each of the contacts in the contacts database and lets the user select one, before closing and returning the selected contact's URI to the calling Activity.

> *It's worth noting that this example is somewhat contrived. Android already supplies an Intent Filter for picking a contact from a list that can be invoked by means of the* content://contacts/people/ *URI in an implicit Intent. The purpose of this exercise is to demonstrate the form, even if this particular implementation isn't particularly useful.*

1. Create a new ContactPicker project that includes a ContactPicker Activity:

```
package com.paad.contactpicker;

import android.app.Activity;
import android.content.Intent;
import android.database.Cursor;
import android.net.Uri;
import android.os.Bundle;
import android.provider.Contacts.People;
import android.view.View;
import android.widget.AdapterView;
import android.widget.ListView;
import android.widget.SimpleCursorAdapter;
import android.widget.AdapterView.OnItemClickListener;

public class ContactPicker extends Activity {
  @Override
  public void onCreate(Bundle icicle) {
    super.onCreate(icicle);
    setContentView(R.layout.main);
  }
}
```

2. Modify the main.xml layout resource to include a single ListView control. This control will be used to display the contacts.

```
<?xml version="1.0" encoding="utf-8"?>
<LinearLayout xmlns:android="http://schemas.android.com/apk/res/android"
  android:orientation="vertical"
  android:layout_width="fill_parent"
  android:layout_height="fill_parent"
  >
  <ListView android:id="@+id/contactListView"
    android:layout_width="fill_parent"
    android:layout_height="wrap_content"
```

```
  />
</LinearLayout>
```

3. Create a new listitemlayout.xml layout resource that includes a single `TextView`. This will be used to display each contact in the List View.

```xml
<?xml version="1.0" encoding="utf-8"?>
<LinearLayout xmlns:android="http://schemas.android.com/apk/res/android"
  android:orientation="vertical"
  android:layout_width="fill_parent"
  android:layout_height="fill_parent"
  >
  <TextView
    android:id="@+id/itemTextView"
    android:layout_width="fill_parent"
    android:layout_height="wrap_content"
    android:padding="10px"
    android:textSize="16px"
    android:textColor="#FFF"
  />
</LinearLayout>
```

4. Return to the `ContactPicker` Activity. Override the `onCreate` method and extract the data path from the calling Intent:

```java
@Override
public void onCreate(Bundle icicle) {
  super.onCreate(icicle);
  setContentView(R.layout.main);

  Intent intent = getIntent();
  String dataPath = intent.getData().toString();
```

4.1. Create a new data URI for the people stored in the contact list, and bind it to the List View using a `SimpleCursorArrayAdapter`:

> *The* `SimpleCursorArrayAdapter` *lets you assign Cursor data, used by Content Providers, to Views. It's used here without further comment but is examined in detail later in this chapter.*

```java
final Uri data = Uri.parse(dataPath + "people/");
final Cursor c = managedQuery(data, null, null, null);

String[] from = new String[] {People.NAME};
int[]  to = new int[] { R.id.itemTextView };

SimpleCursorAdapter adapter = new SimpleCursorAdapter(this,
                                       R.layout.listitemlayout,
                                       c,
                                       from,
                                       to);
ListView lv = (ListView)findViewById(R.id.contactListView);
lv.setAdapter(adapter);
```

4.2. Add an `onItemClickListener` to the List View. Selecting a contact from the list should return a path to the item to the calling Activity.

```
lv.setOnItemClickListener(new OnItemClickListener() {
  @Override
  public void onItemClick(AdapterView<?> parent, View view, int pos,
                          long id) {
    // Move the cursor to the selected item
    c.moveToPosition(pos);
    // Extract the row id.
    int rowId = c.getInt(c.getColumnIndexOrThrow("_id"));
    // Construct the result URI.
    Uri outURI = Uri.parse(data.toString() + rowId);
    Intent outData = new Intent();
    outData.setData(outURI);
    setResult(Activity.RESULT_OK, outData);
    finish();
  }
});
```

4.3. Close off the `onCreate` method:

```
  }
```

5. Modify the application manifest and replace the `intent-filter` tag of the Activity to add support for the `ACTION_PICK` action on contact data:

```xml
<?xml version="1.0" encoding="utf-8"?>
<manifest xmlns:android="http://schemas.android.com/apk/res/android"
    package="com.paad.contactpicker">
    <application android:icon="@drawable/icon">
        <activity android:name="ContactPicker" android:label="@string/app_name">
            <intent-filter>
              <action android:name="android.intent.action.PICK"></action>
              <category android:name="android.intent.category.DEFAULT"></category>
              <data android:path="contacts" android:scheme="content"></data>
            </intent-filter>
        </activity>
    </application>
</manifest>
```

6. This completes the sub-Activity. To test it, create a new test harness `ContentPickerTester` Activity. Create a new layout resource — `contentpickertester.xml` — that includes a `TextView` to display the selected contact and a `Button` to start the sub-Activity:

```xml
<?xml version="1.0" encoding="utf-8"?>
<LinearLayout xmlns:android="http://schemas.android.com/apk/res/android"
  android:orientation="vertical"
  android:layout_width="fill_parent"
  android:layout_height="fill_parent"
  >
  <TextView
    android:id="@+id/selected_contact_textview"
    android:layout_width="fill_parent"
    android:layout_height="wrap_content"
  />
  <Button
```

```
            android:id="@+id/pick_contact_button"
            android:layout_width="fill_parent"
            android:layout_height="wrap_content"
            android:text="Pick Contact"
      />
  </LinearLayout>
```

7. Override the `onCreate` method of the `ContentPickerTester` to add a click listener to the Button so that it implicitly starts a new sub-Activity by specifying the `ACTION_PICK` and the contact database URI (`content://contacts/`):

```java
package com.paad.contactpicker;

import android.app.Activity;
import android.content.Intent;
import android.database.Cursor;
import android.net.Uri;
import android.os.Bundle;
import android.provider.Contacts.People;
import android.view.View;
import android.view.View.OnClickListener;
import android.widget.Button;
import android.widget.TextView;

public class ContentPickerTester extends Activity {

  public static final int PICK_CONTACT = 1;

  @Override
  public void onCreate(Bundle icicle) {
    super.onCreate(icicle);
    setContentView(R.layout.contentpickertester);

    Button button = (Button)findViewById(R.id.pick_contact_button);

    button.setOnClickListener(new OnClickListener() {
     @Override
     public void onClick(View _view) {
        Intent intent = new Intent(Intent.ACTION_PICK,
                                   Uri.parse("content://contacts/"));
        startActivityForResult(intent, PICK_CONTACT);
     }
    });
  }
}
```

8. When the sub-Activity returns, use the result to populate the Text View with the selected contact's name:

```java
@Override
public void onActivityResult(int reqCode, int resCode, Intent data) {
  super.onActivityResult(reqCode, resCode, data);

  switch(reqCode) {
    case (PICK_CONTACT) : {
```

```
if (resCode == Activity.RESULT_OK) {
  Uri contactData = data.getData();
  Cursor c = managedQuery(contactData, null, null, null);
  c.moveToFirst();
  String name = c.getString(c.getColumnIndexOrThrow(People.NAME));
  TextView tv = (TextView)findViewById(R.id.selected_contact_textview);
  tv.setText(name);
}
break;
    }
  }
}
```

9. With your test harness complete, simply add it to your application manifest. You'll also need to add a READ_CONTACTS permission within a uses-permission tag, to allow the application to access the contacts database.

```xml
<?xml version="1.0" encoding="utf-8"?>
<manifest xmlns:android="http://schemas.android.com/apk/res/android"
    package="com.paad.contactpicker">
    <application android:icon="@drawable/icon">
        <activity android:name=".ContactPicker" android:label="@string/app_name">
          <intent-filter>
            <action android:name="android.intent.action.PICK"></action>
            <category android:name="android.intent.category.DEFAULT"></category>
            <data android:path="contacts" android:scheme="content"></data>
          </intent-filter>
        </activity>
        <activity android:name=".ContentPickerTester"
                  android:label="Contact Picker Test">
          <intent-filter>
            <action android:name="android.intent.action.MAIN" />
            <category android:name="android.intent.category.LAUNCHER" />
          </intent-filter>
        </activity>
    </application>
    <uses-permission android:name="android.permission.READ_CONTACTS"/>
</manifest>
```

All code snippets in this example are part of the Chapter 5 Contact Picker *project, available for download at Wrox.com.*

When your Activity is running, press the button. The contact picker Activity should be shown as in Figure 5-1.

Once you select a contact, the parent Activity should return to the foreground with the selected contact name displayed, as shown in Figure 5-2.

Using Intent Filters for Plug-Ins and Extensibility

You've now learned how to create implicit Intents to launch Activities, but that's only half the story. Android also lets future packages provide new functionality for existing applications, using Intent Filters to populate menus dynamically at run time.

This provides a plug-in model for your Activities that lets them take advantage of future functionality, provided through application components you haven't yet conceived of, without your having to modify or recompile your projects.

The `addIntentOptions` method available from the `Menu` class lets you specify an Intent that describes the data acted upon by the Menu. Android resolves this Intent and returns every action specified in Intent Filters that match the specified data. A new Menu Item is created for each, with the text populated from the matching Intent Filters' labels.

The elegance of this concept is best explained by example. If the data your Activity displays is a list of places, the Menu Items available might include View and "Show directions to." Jump a few years ahead and you've created an application that interfaces with your car, allowing your phone to handle driving. Thanks to the runtime menu generation, when a new Intent Filter — with a `DRIVE_CAR` action — is included within the new Activity's node, Android will automagically add this action as a new Menu Item in your earlier application.

Runtime menu population provides the ability to retrofit functionality when you create new components capable of performing actions on a given type of data. Many of Android's native applications use this functionality, giving you the ability to provide additional actions to native Activities.

Supplying Anonymous Actions to Applications

To use this mechanism to make your Activity's actions available anonymously for existing applications, publish them using `intent-filter` tags within their manifest nodes.

The Intent Filter describes the `action` it performs and the `data` upon which it can be performed. The latter will be used during the Intent resolution process to determine when this action should be available. The `category` tag must be either `ALTERNATIVE` or `SELECTED_ALTERNATIVE` or both. The text used for the Menu Items is specified by the `android:label` attribute.

Listing 5-10 shows an example of an Intent Filter used to advertise an Activity's ability to nuke moon-bases from orbit.

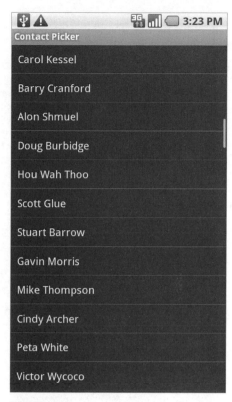

FIGURE 5-1

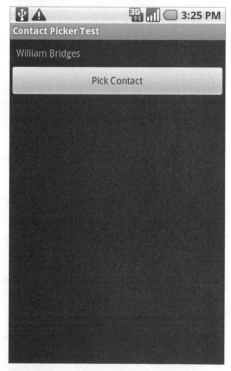

FIGURE 5-2

LISTING 5-10: Advertising-supported Activity actions

```
<activity android:name=".NostromoController">
  <intent-filter
    android:label="Nuke From Orbit">
    <action android:name="com.pad.nostromo.NUKE_FROM_ORBIT" />
    <data android:mimeType="vnd.moonbase.cursor.item/*"/>
    <category android:name="android.intent.category.ALTERNATIVE" />
    <category android:name="android.intent.category.SELECTED_ALTERNATIVE" />
  </intent-filter>
</activity>
```

The Content Provider and other code needed for this example to run aren't provided; in the following sections you'll see how to write the code that adds this action dynamically to another Activity's Menu.

Incorporating Anonymous Actions in Your Activity's Menu

To add Menu Items to your Menus dynamically at run time, use the addIntentOptions method on the Menu object in question: pass in an Intent that specifies the data for which you want to provide actions. Generally this will be handled within your Activities' onCreateOptionsMenu or onCreateContextMenu handlers.

The Intent you create will be used to resolve components with Intent Filters that supply actions for the data you specify. The Intent is being used to find actions, so don't assign it one; it should specify only the data to perform actions on. You should also specify the category of the action, either CATEGORY_ALTERNATIVE or CATEGORY_SELECTED_ALTERNATIVE.

The skeleton code for creating an Intent for menu-action resolution is shown here:

```
Intent intent = new Intent();
intent.setData(MyProvider.CONTENT_URI);
intent.addCategory(Intent.CATEGORY_ALTERNATIVE);
```

Pass this Intent in to addIntentOptions on the Menu you wish to populate, as well as any option flags, the name of the calling class, the menu group to use, and the menu ID values. You can also specify an array of Intents you'd like to use to create additional menu items.

Listing 5-11 gives an idea of how to dynamically populate an Activity menu that would include the "moon-base nuker" action from Listing 5-10.

LISTING 5-11: Dynamic Menu population from advertised actions

```
@Override
public boolean onCreateOptionsMenu(Menu menu) {
  super.onCreateOptionsMenu(menu);

  // Create the intent used to resolve which actions
  // should appear in the menu.
  Intent intent = new Intent();
  intent.setData(MoonBaseProvider.CONTENT_URI);
  intent.addCategory(Intent.CATEGORY_SELECTED_ALTERNATIVE);
```

```
        // Normal menu options to let you set a group and ID
        // values for the menu items you're adding.
        int menuGroup = 0;
        int menuItemId = 0;
        int menuItemOrder = Menu.NONE;

        // Provide the name of the component that's calling
        // the action -- generally the current Activity.
        ComponentName caller = getComponentName();

        // Define intents that should be added first.
        Intent[] specificIntents = null;
        // The menu items created from the previous Intents
        // will populate this array.
        MenuItem[] outSpecificItems = null;

        // Set any optional flags.
        int flags = Menu.FLAG_APPEND_TO_GROUP;

        // Populate the menu
        menu.addIntentOptions(menuGroup,
                              menuItemId,
                              menuItemOrder,
                              caller,
                              specificIntents,
                              intent,
                              flags,
                              outSpecificItems);

        return true;
    }
```

Introducing Linkify

Linkify is a helper class that automagically creates hyperlinks within Text View (and Text View-derived) classes through RegEx pattern matching.

Text that matches a specified RegEx pattern will be converted into a clickable hyperlink that implicitly fires startActivity(new Intent(Intent.ACTION_VIEW, uri)), using the matched text as the target URI.

You can specify any string pattern you want to turn into links; for convenience, the Linkify class provides presets for common content types (like phone numbers and e-mail/web addresses), as described in the following section.

The Native Linkify Link Types

The static Linkify.addLinks method accepts the View to linkify, and a bitmask of one or more of the default content types supported and supplied by the Linkify class: WEB_URLS, EMAIL_ADDRESSES, PHONE_NUMBERS, and ALL.

Listing 5-12 shows how to linkify a Text View to display web and e-mail addresses as hyperlinks. When clicked, they will open the browser and an e-mail application respectively.

LISTING 5-12: Using Linkify in code

```
TextView textView = (TextView)findViewById(R.id.myTextView);
Linkify.addLinks(textView, Linkify.WEB_URLS|Linkify.EMAIL_ADDRESSES);
```

> *Most Android devices have at least two e-mail applications: Gmail and Email. In situations in which multiple Activities are resolved as possible action consumers the user is asked to select his or her preference.*

You can also linkify Views from within a layout resource using the `android:autoLink` attribute. It supports one or more (separated by |) of the following self-describing values: `none`, `web`, `email`, `phone`, and `all`.

Listing 5-13 shows how to add hyperlinks for phone numbers and e-mail addresses:

LISTING 5-13: Using Linkify in XML

```
<TextView
  android:layout_width="fill_parent"
  android:layout_height="fill_parent"
  android:text="@string/linkify_me"
  android:autoLink="phone|email"
/>
```

Creating Custom Link Strings

To define your own linkify strings you create a new RegEx pattern to match the text you want to display as hyperlinks.

As with the native types, you linkify the target View by calling `Linkify.addLinks`, but this time pass in the new RegEx pattern. You can also pass in a prefix that will be prepended to the target URI when a link is clicked.

Listing 5-14 shows a View being linkified to support earthquake data provided by an Android Content Provider (that you will create in Chapter 7). Rather than include the entire schema, the linkify pattern matches any text that starts with "quake" and is followed by a number. The content schema is then prepended to the URI before the Intent is fired.

LISTING 5-14: Creating custom link strings in Linkify

```
int flags = Pattern.CASE_INSENSITIVE;
Pattern p = Pattern.compile("\\bquake[0-9]*\\b", flags);
Linkify.addLinks(myTextView, p,
                 "content://com.paad.earthquake/earthquakes/");
```

Linkify also supports `TransformFilter` and `MatchFilter` interfaces. These offer additional control over the target URI structure and the definition of matching strings, and are used as in the following skeleton code:

```
Linkify.addLinks(myTextView, pattern, prefixWith,
                 new MyMatchFilter(), new MyTransformFilter());
```

Using the Match Filter

Implement the `acceptMatch` method in your Match Filter to add additional conditions to RegEx pattern matches. When a potential match is found `acceptMatch` is triggered, with the match start and end index (along with the full text being searched) passed in as parameters.

Listing 5-15 shows a `MatchFilter` implementation that cancels any match immediately preceded by an exclamation mark.

LISTING 5-15: Using a Linkify Match Filter

```
class MyMatchFilter implements MatchFilter {
  public boolean acceptMatch(CharSequence s, int start, int end) {
    return (start == 0 || s.charAt(start-1) != '!');
  }
}
```

Using the Transform Filter

The Transform Filter gives you more freedom to format your text strings by letting you modify the implicit URI generated by the link text. Decoupling the link text from the target URI gives you more freedom in how you display data strings to your users.

To use the Transform Filter, implement the `transformUrl` method in your Transform Filter. When linkify finds a successful match it calls `transformUrl`, passing in the RegEx pattern used and the default URI string it creates. You can modify the matched string and return the URI as a target suitable to be "viewed" by another Android application.

The `TransformFilter` implementation shown in Listing 5-16 transforms the matched text into a lowercase URI.

LISTING 5-16: Using a Linkify Transform Filter

```
class MyTransformFilter implements TransformFilter {
  public String transformUrl(Matcher match, String url) {
    return url.toLowerCase();
  }
}
```

Using Intents to Broadcast Events

As a system-level message-passing mechanism, Intents are capable of sending structured messages across process boundaries.

So far you've looked at using Intents to start new application components, but they can also be used to broadcast messages anonymously *between* components via the sendBroadcast method. You can implement Broadcast Receivers to listen for, and respond to, these broadcast Intents within your applications.

Broadcast Intents are used to notify listeners of system or application events, extending the event-driven programming model between applications.

Broadcasting Intents helps make your application more open; by broadcasting an event using an Intent you let yourself and third-party developers react to events without having to modify your original application. Within your applications you can listen for broadcast Intents to replace or enhance native (or third-party) applications, or react to system changes and application events.

Android uses broadcast Intents extensively to broadcast system events like battery-charging levels, network connections, and incoming calls.

Broadcasting Events with Intents

Broadcasting Intents is simple. Within your application, construct the Intent you want to broadcast and use the sendBroadcast method to send it.

Set the action, data, and category of your Intent in a way that lets Broadcast Receivers accurately determine their interest. In this scenario the Intent *action* string is used to identify the event being broadcast, so it should be a unique string that identifies the event. By convention, action strings are constructed with the same form as Java package names:

```
public static final String NEW_LIFEFORM_DETECTED =
    "com.paad.action.NEW_LIFEFORM";
```

If you wish to include data within the Intent you can specify a URI using the Intent's data property. You can also include extras to add additional primitive values. Considered in terms of an event-driven paradigm, the extras equate to optional parameters passed into an event handler.

Listing 5-17 shows the basic creation of a broadcast Intent using the action defined previously, with additional event information stored as extras.

Available for download on Wrox.com

LISTING 5-17: Broadcasting an Intent

```
Intent intent = new Intent(NEW_LIFEFORM_DETECTED);
intent.putExtra("lifeformName", lifeformType);
intent.putExtra("longitude", currentLongitude);
intent.putExtra("latitude", currentLatitude);
sendBroadcast(intent);
```

Listening for Broadcasts with Broadcast Receivers

Broadcast Receivers are used to listen for broadcast Intents. For a Broadcast Receiver to be enabled it needs to be registered, either in code or within the application manifest. When registering a Broadcast Receiver you must use an Intent Filter to specify which Intents it is listening for.

To create a new Broadcast Receiver, extend the `BroadcastReceiver` class and override the `onReceive` event handler as shown in Listing 5-18.

LISTING 5-18: Broadcast Receiver skeleton implementation

```
import android.content.BroadcastReceiver;
import android.content.Context;
import android.content.Intent;

public class MyBroadcastReceiver extends BroadcastReceiver {
  @Override
  public void onReceive(Context context, Intent intent) {
    //TODO: React to the Intent received.
  }
}
```

The `onReceive` method will be executed when a broadcast Intent is received that matches the Intent Filter used to register the Receiver. The `onReceive` handler must complete within five seconds or the Force Close dialog will be displayed.

Applications with Broadcast Receivers registered in the manifest don't have to be running when the Intent is broadcast for the receivers to execute. They will be started automatically when a matching Intent is broadcast. This is excellent for resource management as it lets you create event-driven applications that will still respond to broadcast events even after they've been closed or killed.

Typically Broadcast Receivers will update content, launch Services, update Activity UI, or notify the user using the Notification Manager. The five-second execution limit ensures that major processing cannot, and should not, be done within the Broadcast Receiver itself.

Listing 5-19 shows how to implement a Broadcast Receiver. In the following sections you will learn how to register it in code or in your application manifest.

LISTING 5-19: Implementing a Broadcast Receiver

```
public class LifeformDetectedBroadcastReceiver extends BroadcastReceiver {

  public static final String BURN = "com.paad.alien.action.BURN_IT_WITH_FIRE";

  @Override
  public void onReceive(Context context, Intent intent) {
    // Get the lifeform details from the intent.
    Uri data = intent.getData();
    String type = intent.getStringExtra("type");
    double lat = intent.getDoubleExtra("latitude", 0);
    double lng = intent.getDoubleExtra("longitude", 0);
    Location loc = new Location("gps");
    loc.setLatitude(lat);
    loc.setLongitude(lng);
```

continues

LISTING 5-19 *(continued)*

```
      if (type.equals("alien")) {
        Intent startIntent = new Intent(BURN, data);
        startIntent.putExtra("latitude", lat);
        startIntent.putExtra("longitude", lng);

        context.startActivity(startIntent);
      }
    }
  }
```

Registering Broadcast Receivers in Your Application Manifest

To include a Broadcast Receiver in the application manifest, add a `<receiver>` tag within the `application` node, specifying the class name of the Broadcast Receiver to register. The receiver node needs to include an `intent-filter` tag that specifies the action string being listened for, as shown in Listing 5-20.

LISTING 5-20: Registering a Broadcast Reveiver in XML

```
<receiver android:name=".LifeformDetectedBroadcastReceiver">
  <intent-filter>
    <action android:name="com.paad.action.NEW_LIFEFORM"/>
  </intent-filter>
</receiver>
```

Broadcast Receivers registered this way are always active, and will receive broadcast Intents even when the application has been killed or hasn't been started.

Registering Broadcast Receivers in Code

You can also register Broadcast Receivers in code. A receiver registered programmatically will respond to broadcast Intents only when the application component it is registered within is running.

This is typically useful when the Receiver is being used to update UI elements in an Activity. In this case it's good practice to un-register the Broadcast Receiver when the Activity isn't visible (or active).

Listing 5-21 shows how to register a Broadcast Receiver in code using the `IntentFilter` class.

LISTING 5-21: Registering a Broadcast Receiver in code

```
// Create and register the broadcast receiver.
IntentFilter filter = new IntentFilter(NEW_LIFEFORM_DETECTED);
LifeformDetectedBroadcastReceiver r = new LifeformDetectedBroadcastReceiver();
registerReceiver(r, filter);
```

To un-register a Broadcast Receiver use the `unregisterReceiver` method on your application context, passing in a Broadcast Receiver instance as follows:

```
unregisterReceiver(receiver);
```

Further examples can also be found in Chapter 9, where you learn to create your own background Services and use Intents to broadcast events to your Activities.

Broadcasting Sticky and Ordered Intents

When broadcasting an Intent using `sendBroadcast`, your Intent will be received by all registered Broadcast Receivers, but you cannot control the order and they cannot propagate results.

In circumstances where the order in which the Broadcast Receivers receive the Intent is important, or where you require the Receivers to be able to affect the Intent being broadcast, you can use the `sendOrderedBroadcast` method.

```
sendOrderedBroadcast(intent, null);
```

Using this method, your Intent will be delivered to all registered Receivers in order of priority. You can optionally assign your own Broadcast Receiver, which will then receive the Intent after it has been handled (and potentially modified) by all the other registered Broadcast Receivers.

```
sendOrderedBroadcast(intent, null, myBroadcastReceiver, null,
                     Activity.RESULT_OK, null, null);
```

For efficiency reasons, some broadcasts are *sticky*. When you call `registerReceiver` specifying an Intent Filter that matches a sticky broadcast, the return value will be the sticky broadcast Intent. To broadcast a sticky Intent your application must have the `BROADCAST_STICKY` uses-permission.

```
sendStickyBroadcast(intent);
```

To remove a sticky intent call `removeStickyBroadcast`, passing in the sticky Intent to remove.

```
removeStickyBroadcast(intent);
```

Native Android Broadcast Actions

Android broadcasts Intents for many of the system Services. You can use these messages to add functionality to your own projects based on system events such as time-zone changes, data-connection status, incoming SMS messages, or phone calls.

The following list introduces some of the native actions exposed as constants in the Intent class; these actions are used primarily to track device status changes.

➤ `ACTION_BOOT_COMPLETED` Fired once when the device has completed its startup sequence. An application requires the `RECEIVE_BOOT_COMPLETED` permission to receive this broadcast.

➤ `ACTION_CAMERA_BUTTON` Fired when the camera button is clicked.

➤ `ACTION_DATE_CHANGED` and `ACTION_TIME_CHANGED` These actions are broadcast if the date or time on the device is manually changed (as opposed to changing through the inexorable progression of time).

➤ `ACTION_MEDIA_BUTTON` Fired when the media button is clicked.

➤ `ACTION_MEDIA_EJECT` If the user chooses to eject the external storage media, this event is fired first. If your application is reading or writing to the external media storage you should listen for this event in order to save and close any open file handles.

➤ ACTION MEDIA_MOUNTED and ACTION_MEDIA_UNMOUNTED These two events are broadcast whenever new external storage media are successfully added to or removed from the device.

➤ ACTION_NEW_OUTGOING_CALL Broadcast when a new outgoing call is about to be placed. Listen for this broadcast to intercept outgoing calls. The number being dialed is stored in the EXTRA_PHONE_NUMBER extra, while the resultData in the returned Intent will be the number actually dialed. To register a Broadcast Receiver for this action your application must declare the PROCESS_OUTGOING_CALLS uses-permission.

➤ ACTION_SCREEN_OFF and ACTION_SCREEN_ON Broadcast when the screen turns off or on respectively.

➤ ACTION_TIMEZONE_CHANGED This action is broadcast whenever the phone's current time zone changes. The Intent includes a time-zone extra that returns the ID of the new java.util.TimeZone.

A comprehensive list of the broadcast actions used and transmitted natively by Android to notify applications of system state changes is available at http://developer.android.com/reference/android/content/Intent.html

Android also uses broadcast Intents to announce application-specific events like incoming SMS messages. The actions and Intents associated with these events will be discussed in more detail in later chapters when you learn more about the associated Services.

INTRODUCING PENDING INTENTS

The PendingIntent class provides a mechanism for creating Intents that can be fired by another application at a later time.

A Pending Intent is commonly used to package an Intent that will be fired in response to a future event, such as a widget View being clicked or a Notification being selected from the notification panel.

 When used, Pending Intents execute the packaged Intent with the same permissions and identity as if you had executed them yourself, within your own application.

As shown in Listing 5-22, the PendingIntent class offers static methods to construct Pending Intents used to start an Activity, start a Service, or broadcast an Intent.

Available for download on Wrox.com

LISTING 5-22: Creating new Pending Intents

```
// Start an Activity
Intent startActivityIntent = new Intent(this, MyOtherActivity.class);
PendingIntent.getActivity(this, 0, startActivityIntent, 0);

// Broadcast an Intent
Intent broadcastIntent = new Intent(NEW_LIFEFORM_DETECTED);
PendingIntent.getBroadcast(this, 0, broadcastIntent, 0);
```

You'll learn more about using Pending Intents in later chapters when they're used to support other Services such as widgets and Notifications.

INTRODUCING ADAPTERS

Adapters are bridging classes that bind data to Views (such as List Views) used in the user interface. The adapter is responsible for creating the child Views used to represent each item within the parent View, and providing access to the underlying data.

Views that support Adapter binding must extend the `AdapterView` abstract class. It's possible to create your own `AdapterView`-derived controls and to create new Adapter classes to bind them.

Introducing Some Native Adapters

In many cases you won't have to create your own Adapter from scratch. Android supplies a set of Adapters that pump data into native UI controls.

Because Adapters are responsible both for supplying the data and for creating the Views that represent each item, Adapters can radically modify the appearance and functionality of the controls they're bound to.

The following list highlights two of the most useful and versatile native Adapters:

➤ `ArrayAdapter` The Array Adapter uses generics to bind an Adapter View to an array of objects of the specified class. By default the Array Adapter uses the `toString` value of each object in the array to create and populate Text Views. Alternative constructors enable you to use more complex layouts, or you can extend the class to use alternatives to Text Views as shown in the next section.

➤ `SimpleCursorAdapter` The Simple Cursor Adapter attaches Views specified within a layout to the columns of Cursors returned from Content Provider queries. You specify an XML layout definition, and then bind each column to a View within that layout. The adapter will create a new View for each Cursor entry and inflate the layout into it, populating each View within the layout using the Cursor column values.

The following sections will delve into these Adapter classes in more detail. The examples provided bind data to List Views, though the same logic will work just as well for other Adapter View classes such as Spinners and Galleries.

Customizing the Array Adapter

By default the Array Adapter will use the `toString` value of the object array it is binding to populate the Text View available within the specified layout.

In most cases you will need to customize the layout used to represent each View. To do that, you will need to extend `ArrayAdapter` with a type-specific variation, overriding the `getView` method to assign object properties to layout Views as shown in Listing 5-23.

The `getView` method is used to construct, inflate, and populate the View that will be displayed within the parent Adapter View class (e.g., List View) which is being bound to the underlying array using this Adapter.

The `getView` method receives parameters that describe the position of the item to be displayed, the View being updated (or `null`), and the View Group into which this new View will be placed. A call to `getItem` will return the value stored at the specified index in the underlying array.

Return the new populated View instance as a result from this method.

LISTING 5-23: Customizing the Array Adapter

```java
public class MyArrayAdapter extends ArrayAdapter<MyClass> {

    int resource;

    public MyArrayAdapter(Context context,
                          int _resource,
                          List<MyClass> items) {
      super(context, _resource, items);
      resource = _resource;
    }

    @Override
    public View getView(int position, View convertView, ViewGroup parent) {
      LinearLayout newView;

      MyClass classInstance = getItem(position);

      // TODO Retrieve values to display from the
      // classInstance variable.

      // Inflate a new view if this is not an update.
      if (convertView == null) {
        newView = new LinearLayout(getContext());
        String inflater = Context.LAYOUT_INFLATER_SERVICE;
        LayoutInflater vi = (LayoutInflater)getContext().getSystemService(inflater);
        vi.inflate(resource, newView, true);
      } else {
        newView = (LinearLayout)convertView;
      }

      // TODO Retrieve the Views to populate
      // TODO Populate the Views with object property values.

      return newView;
    }
  }
```

Using Adapters for Data Binding

To apply an Adapter to an `AdapterView`-derived class you call the View's `setAdapter` method, passing in an Adapter instance as shown in Listing 5-24.

> **LISTING 5-24: Creating and applying an Adapter**

```
ArrayList<String> myStringArray = new ArrayList<String>();
ArrayAdapter<String> myAdapterInstance;

int layoutID = android.R.layout.simple_list_item_1;
myAdapterInstance = new ArrayAdapter<String>(this, layoutID , myStringArray);

myListView.setAdapter(myAdapterInstance);
```

This snippet shows the most simplistic case, in which the array being bound contains Strings and each List View item is represented by a single Text View.

The first of the following examples demonstrates how to bind an array of complex objects to a List View using a custom layout. The second shows how to use a Simple Cursor Adapter to bind a query result to a custom layout within a List View.

Customizing the To-Do List Array Adapter

This example extends the To-Do List project, storing each item as a `ToDoItem` object that includes the date each item was created.

You will extend `ArrayAdapter` to bind a collection of `ToDoItem` objects to the `ListView` and customize the layout used to display each List View item.

1. Return to the To-Do List project. Create a new `ToDoItem` class that stores the task and its creation date. Override the `toString` method to return a summary of the item data.

```
package com.paad.todolist;

import java.text.SimpleDateFormat;
import java.util.Date;

public class ToDoItem {

  String task;
  Date created;

  public String getTask() {
    return task;
  }

  public Date getCreated() {
    return created;
  }

  public ToDoItem(String _task) {
    this(_task, new Date(java.lang.System.currentTimeMillis()));
  }

  public ToDoItem(String _task, Date _created) {
    task = _task;
```

```
        created = _created;
      }

      @Override
      public String toString() {
        SimpleDateFormat sdf = new SimpleDateFormat("dd/MM/yy");
        String dateString = sdf.format(created);
        return "(" + dateString +  ") " + task;
      }
    }
```

2. Open the ToDoList Activity and modify the ArrayList and ArrayAdapter variable types
    to store ToDoItem objects rather than Strings. You'll then need to modify the onCreate
    method to update the corresponding variable initialization. You'll also need to update the
    onKeyListener handler to support the ToDoItem objects.

```
private ArrayList<ToDoItem> todoItems;
private ListView myListView;
private EditText myEditText;
private ArrayAdapter<ToDoItem> aa;

@Override
public void onCreate(Bundle icicle) {
  super.onCreate(icicle);

  // Inflate your view
  setContentView(R.layout.main);

  // Get references to UI widgets
  myListView = (ListView)findViewById(R.id.myListView);
  myEditText = (EditText)findViewById(R.id.myEditText);

  todoItems = new ArrayList<ToDoItem>();
  int resID = R.layout.todolist_item;
  aa = new ArrayAdapter<ToDoItem>(this, resID, todoItems);
  myListView.setAdapter(aa);

  myEditText.setOnKeyListener(new OnKeyListener() {
    public boolean onKey(View v, int keyCode, KeyEvent event) {
      if (event.getAction() == KeyEvent.ACTION_DOWN)
        if (keyCode == KeyEvent.KEYCODE_DPAD_CENTER) {
          ToDoItem newItem = new ToDoItem(myEditText.getText().toString());
          todoItems.add(0, newItem);
          myEditText.setText("");
          aa.notifyDataSetChanged();
          cancelAdd();
          return true;
        }
      return false;
    }
  });

  registerForContextMenu(myListView);
}
```

3. If you run the Activity it will now display each to-do item as shown in Figure 5-3.

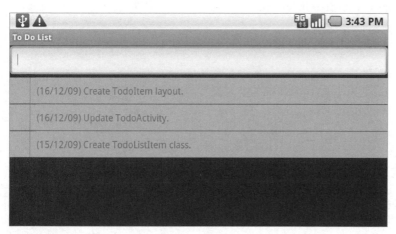

FIGURE 5-3

4. Now you can create a custom layout to display each to-do item.

Start by modifying the custom layout you created in Chapter 4 to include a second `TextView`. It will be used to show the creation date of each to-do item.

```xml
<?xml version="1.0" encoding="utf-8"?>
<RelativeLayout xmlns:android="http://schemas.android.com/apk/res/android"
  android:layout_width="fill_parent"
  android:layout_height="fill_parent"
  android:background="@color/notepad_paper">
  <TextVicw
    android:id="@+id/rowDate"
    android:layout_width="wrap_content"
    android:layout_height="fill_parent"
    android:padding="10dp"
    android:scrollbars="vertical"
    android:fadingEdge="vertical"
    android:textColor="@color/notepad_text"
    android:layout_alignParentRight="true"
  />
  <TextView
    android:id="@+id/row"
    android:layout_width="fill_parent"
    android:layout_height="fill_parent"
    android:padding="10dp"
    android:scrollbars="vertical"
    android:fadingEdge="vertical"
    android:textColor="@color/notepad_text"
    android:layout_alignParentLeft="@+id/rowDate"
  />
</RelativeLayout>
```

5. Create a new class (`ToDoItemAdapter`) that extends an `ArrayAdapter` with a `ToDoItem`-specific variation. Override `getView` to assign the task and date properties in the `ToDoItem` object to the Views in the layout you created in Step 4:

```
import java.text.SimpleDateFormat;
import android.content.Context;
import java.util.*;
import android.view.*;
import android.widget.*;

public class ToDoItemAdapter extends ArrayAdapter<ToDoItem> {

  int resource;

  public ToDoItemAdapter(Context _context,
                         int _resource,
                         List<ToDoItem> _items) {
    super(_context, _resource, _items);
    resource = _resource;
  }

  @Override
  public View getView(int position, View convertView, ViewGroup parent) {
    LinearLayout todoView;

    ToDoItem item = getItem(position);

    String taskString = item.getTask();
    Date createdDate = item.getCreated();
    SimpleDateFormat sdf = new SimpleDateFormat("dd/MM/yy");
    String dateString = sdf.format(createdDate);

    if (convertView == null) {
      todoView = new LinearLayout(getContext());
      String inflater = Context.LAYOUT_INFLATER_SERVICE;
      LayoutInflater vi = (LayoutInflater)getContext().getSystemService(inflater);
      vi.inflate(resource, todoView, true);
    } else {
      todoView = (LinearLayout) convertView;
    }

    TextView dateView = (TextView)todoView.findViewById(R.id.rowDate);
    TextView taskView = (TextView)todoView.findViewById(R.id.row);

    dateView.setText(dateString);
    taskView.setText(taskString);

    return todoView;
  }
}
```

6. Finally, replace the `ArrayAdapter` declaration with a `ToDoItemAdapter`:

```
private ToDoItemAdapter aa;
```

Within `onCreate`, replace the `ArrayAdapter<String>` instantiation with the new `ToDoItemAdapter`:

```
aa = new ToDoItemAdapter(this, resID, todoItems);
```

7. If you run your Activity it should appear as shown in the screenshot in Figure 5-4.

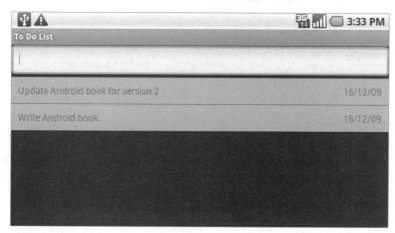

FIGURE 5-4

All code snippets in this example are part of the Chapter 5 Todo List *project, available for download at Wrox.com.*

Using the Simple Cursor Adapter

The `SimpleCursorAdapter` lets you bind a `Cursor` to a List View, using a custom layout definition to define the layout of each row/item, which is populated by a row's column values.

Construct a Simple Cursor Adapter by passing in the current context, a layout resource, a Cursor, and two arrays: one that contains the names of the columns to be used, and a second (equally-sized) array that has resource IDs for the Views to use to display the contents of the corresponding columns.

Listing 5-25 shows how to construct a Simple Cursor Adapter to display contact information.

LISTING 5-25: Creating a Simple Cursor Adapter

```
String uriString = "content://contacts/people/";
Cursor myCursor = managedQuery(Uri.parse(uriString), null, null, null);

String[] fromColumns = new String[] {People.NUMBER, People.NAME};

int[] toLayoutIDs = new int[] { R.id.nameTextView, R.id.numberTextView};

SimpleCursorAdapter myAdapter;
myAdapter = new SimpleCursorAdapter(this,
                                    R.layout.simplecursorlayout,
```

continues

LISTING 5-25 *(continued)*

```
                          myCursor,
                          fromColumns,
                          toLayoutIDs);

     myListView.setAdapter(myAdapter);
```

The Simple Cursor Adapter was used earlier in this chapter in the Contact Picker example. You'll learn more about Content Providers and Cursors in Chapter 7, where you'll also find more Simple Cursor Adapter examples.

USING INTERNET RESOURCES

With Internet connectivity and a WebKit browser, you might well ask if there's any reason to create native Internet-based applications when you could make a web-based version instead.

There are a number of benefits to creating thick- and thin-client native applications rather than relying on entirely web-based solutions:

➤ **Bandwidth**   Static resources like images, layouts, and sounds can be expensive data consumers on devices with limited and often expensive bandwidth restraints. By creating a native application you can limit the bandwidth requirements to updated data only.

➤ **Caching**   Mobile Internet access has not yet reached the point of ubiquity. With a browser-based solution a patchy Internet connection can result in intermittent application availability. A native application can cache data to provide as much functionality as possible without a live connection.

➤ **Native features**   Android devices are more than a simple platform for running a browser: they include location-based services, Notifications, widgets, camera hardware, and accelerometers. By creating a native application you can combine the data available online with the hardware features available on the device to provide a richer user experience.

Modern mobile devices offer a number of alternatives for accessing the Internet. Looked at broadly, Android provides two connection techniques for Internet connectivity. Each is offered transparently to the application layer.

➤ **Mobile Internet**   GPRS, EDGE, and 3G Internet access is available through carriers that offer mobile data plans.

➤ **Wi-Fi**   Wi-Fi receivers and mobile hotspots are becoming increasingly common.

Connecting to an Internet Resource

While the details of working with specific web services won't be covered within this book, it's useful to know the general principles of connecting to the Internet, and getting an input stream from a remote data source.

Before you can access Internet resources, you need to add an `INTERNET uses-permission` node to your application manifest, as shown in the following XML snippet:

```
<uses-permission android:name="android.permission.INTERNET"/>
```

Listing 5-26 shows the basic pattern for opening an Internet data stream.

LISTING 5-26: Opening a data stream

Available for
download on
Wrox.com

```
String myFeed = getString(R.string.my_feed);
try {
  URL url = new URL(myFeed);

  URLConnection connection = url.openConnection();
  HttpURLConnection httpConnection = (HttpURLConnection)connection;

  int responseCode = httpConnection.getResponseCode();
  if (responseCode == HttpURLConnection.HTTP_OK) {
    InputStream in = httpConnection.getInputStream();
    [ ... Process the input stream as required ... ]
  }
}
catch (MalformedURLException e) { }
catch (IOException e) { }
```

Android includes several classes to help you handle network communications. They are available in the `java.net.*` and `android.net.*` packages.

Later in this chapter is a fully worked example that shows how to obtain and process an Internet feed to get a list of earthquakes felt in the last 24 hours.

Chapter 13 features more information on managing specific Internet connections, including information on monitoring connection status and configuring Wi-Fi access point connections.

Using Internet Resources

Android offers several ways to leverage Internet resources.

At one extreme you can use a `WebView` to include a WebKit-based browser View within an Activity. At the other extreme you can use client-side APIs such as Google's GData APIs to interact directly with server processes. Somewhere in between, you can process remote XML feeds to extract and process data using a Java-based XML parser such as `SAX` or the more efficient `XmlPullParser`.

Detailed instructions for parsing XML and interacting with specific web services are outside the scope of this book. That said, the Earthquake example, included later in this chapter, gives a fully worked example of parsing an XML feed using the `SAX` parser.

If you're using Internet resources in your application, remember that your users' data connections are dependent on the communications technology available to them. EDGE and GSM connections are notoriously low-bandwidth, while a Wi-Fi connection may be unreliable in a mobile setting.

Optimize the user experience by limiting the quantity of data being transmitted, and ensure that your application is robust enough to handle network outages and bandwidth limitations.

INTRODUCING DIALOGS

Dialog boxes are a common UI metaphor in desktop, web, and mobile applications. They're used to help users answer questions, make selections, and confirm actions, and to display warning or error messages. Dialog boxes in Android are partially transparent, floating Activities that partially obscure the Activities that launched them.

As in Figure 5-5, they generally obscure the Activities behind them using a blur or dim filter.

There are three ways to implement a dialog in Android:

➤ **Using the Dialog class (or its extensions)**   As well as the general-purpose `AlertDialog` class, Android includes a number of specialist classes that extend `Dialog`. Each is designed to provide specific dialog-box functionality. A Dialog-class-based screen is constructed entirely within its calling Activity, so it doesn't need to be registered in the manifest as its life cycle is controlled entirely by the calling Activity.

➤ **Dialog-themed Activities**   You can apply the dialog theme to a regular Activity to give it the appearance of a standard dialog box.

FIGURE 5-5

➤ **Toasts**   Toasts are special non-modal transient message boxes, often used by Broadcast Receivers and Services to notify users of events occurring in the background. You can learn more about Toasts in Chapter 9.

Introducing the Dialog Classes

To use the base `Dialog` class you create a new instance and set the title and layout, using the `setTitle` and `setContentView` methods as shown in Listing 5-27.

LISTING 5-27: Creating a new dialog using the Dialog class

```
Dialog d = new Dialog(MyActivity.this);

// Have the new window tint and blur the window it
// obscures.
Window window = d.getWindow();
window.setFlags(WindowManager.LayoutParams.FLAG_BLUR_BEHIND,
```

```
                        WindowManager.LayoutParams.FLAG_BLUR_BEHIND);

    // Set the title
    d.setTitle("Dialog Title");
    // Inflate the layout
    d.setContentView(R.layout.dialog_view);

    // Find the TextView used in the layout
    // and set its text value
    TextView text = (TextView)d.findViewById(R.id.dialogTextView);
    text.setText("This is the text in my dialog");
```

Once it's configured to your liking, use the show method to display it.

```
    d.show();
```

The Alert Dialog Class

The AlertDialog class is one of the most versatile Dialog-class implementations. It offers a number of options that let you construct screens for some of the most common dialog-box use cases, including:

➤   Presenting a message to the user offering them one to three options in the form of buttons. This functionality is probably familiar to you if you've done any desktop programming for which the buttons presented are usually a combination of OK, Cancel, Yes, and No.

➤   Offering a list of options in the form of checkboxes or radio buttons.

➤   Providing a text entry box for user input.

To construct the Alert Dialog user interface, create a new AlertDialog.Builder object as follows:

```
    AlertDialog.Builder ad = new AlertDialog.Builder(context);
```

You can then assign values for the title and message to display, and optionally assign values to be used for any buttons, selection items, and text input boxes you wish to display. That includes setting event listeners to handle user interaction.

Listing 5-28 gives an example of a new Alert Dialog used to display a message and offer two button options to continue. Clicking either button will close the Dialog after executing the attached Click Listener.

Available for download on Wrox.com

LISTING 5-28: Configuring an Alert Dialog

```
Context context = MyActivity.this;
String title = "It is Pitch Black";
String message = "You are likely to be eaten by a grue.";
String button1String = "Go Back";
String button2String = "Move Forward";

AlertDialog.Builder ad = new AlertDialog.Builder(context);
ad.setTitle(title);
ad.setMessage(message);
ad.setPositiveButton(button1String,
```

continues

LISTING 5-28 *(continued)*

```
                            new OnClickListener() {
                              public void onClick(DialogInterface dialog, int arg1) {
                                eatenByGrue();
                              }
                            });
        ad.setNegativeButton(button2String,
                            new OnClickListener(){
                              public void onClick(DialogInterface dialog, int arg1) {
                                // do nothing
                              }
                            });
        ad.setCancelable(true);
        ad.setOnCancelListener(new OnCancelListener() {
                                public void onCancel(DialogInterface dialog) {
                                  eatenByGrue();
                                }
                            });
```

To display an Alert Dialog that you've created call show:

```
        ad.show();
```

A better alternative is using your Activity's onCreateDialog and onPrepareDialog handlers to create dialog instances that can persist state. This technique is examined later in this chapter.

Specialist Input Dialogs

One of the major uses of dialog boxes is to provide an interface for user input. Android includes several specialist dialog boxes that encapsulate controls designed to facilitate common user-input requests. They include the following:

➤ CharacterPickerDialog   Lets users select an accented character based on a regular character source.

➤ DatePickerDialog   Lets users select a date from a DatePicker View. The constructor includes a callback listener to alert your calling Activity when the date has been set.

➤ TimePickerDialog   Similar to the Date Picker Dialog, this dialog lets users select a time from a TimePicker View.

➤ ProgressDialog   A dialog that displays a progress bar beneath a message text box. Perfect for keeping the user informed of ongoing progress of a time-consuming operation.

Using Activities as Dialogs

Dialogs offer a simple and lightweight technique for displaying screens, but there will still be times when you need more control over the content and life cycle of your dialog box.

The solution is to implement it as a full Activity. By creating an Activity you lose the lightweight nature of the Dialog class, but you gain the ability to implement any screen you want and full access to the Activity life-cycle event handlers.

The easiest way to make an Activity look like a dialog is to apply the `android:style/Theme.Dialog` theme when you add it to your manifest, as shown in the following XML snippet:

```
<activity android:name="MyDialogActivity"
          android:theme="@android:style/Theme.Dialog">
</activity>
```

This will cause your Activity to behave as a Dialog, floating on top of, and partially obscuring, the Activity beneath it.

Managing and Displaying Dialogs

Rather than creating new instances of a dialog each time it's required, Android provides the `onCreateDialog` and `onPrepareDialog` event handlers within the Activity class to persist and manage dialog-box instances.

By overriding the `onCreateDialog` handler you can specify dialogs that will be created on demand when `showDialog` is used to display a specific dialog. As shown in Listing 5-29, the overridden method includes a switch statement that lets you determine which dialog is required.

LISTING 5-29: Using the On Create Dialog event handler

```
static final private int TIME_DIALOG = 1;

@Override
public Dialog onCreateDialog(int id) {
  switch(id) {
    case (TIME_DIALOG) :
      AlertDialog.Builder timeDialog = new AlertDialog.Builder(this);
      timeDialog.setTitle("The Current Time Is...");
      timeDialog.setMessage("Now");
      return timeDialog.create();
  }
  return null;
}
```

After the initial creation, each time `showDialog` is called it will trigger the `onPrepareDialog` handler. By overriding this method you can modify a dialog each time it is displayed. This lets you contextualize any of the display values, as shown in Listing 5-30 that assigns the current time to the dialog created in Listing 5-29.

LISTING 5-30: Using the On Prepare Dialog event handler

```
@Override
public void onPrepareDialog(int id, Dialog dialog) {
  switch(id) {
    case (TIME_DIALOG) :
      SimpleDateFormat sdf = new SimpleDateFormat("HH:mm:ss");
```

continues

LISTING 5-30 *(continued)*

```
            Date currentTime = new Date(java.lang.System.currentTimeMillis());
            String dateString = sdf.format(currentTime);
            AlertDialog timeDialog = (AlertDialog)dialog;
            timeDialog.setMessage(dateString);

            break;
        }
    }
```

Once you've overridden these methods you can display the dialogs by calling `showDialog` as shown below. Pass in the identifier for the dialog you wish to display, and Android will create (if necessary) and prepare the dialog before displaying it.

```
            showDialog(TIME_DIALOG);
```

As well as providing improved resource use, this technique lets your Activity handle the persistence of state information within Dialogs. Any selection or data input (such as item selection and text entry) will be persisted between displays of each Dialog instance.

CREATING AN EARTHQUAKE VIEWER

In the following example you'll create a tool that uses a USGS earthquake feed to display a list of recent earthquakes.

 You will return to this earthquake application several times, first in Chapters 6 and 7 to save preferences and share the earthquake data with a Content Provider, and again in Chapters 8 and 9 to add mapping support and to move the earthquake updates into a Service.

In this example you'll create a list-based Activity that connects to an earthquake feed and displays the location, magnitude, and time of the earthquakes it contains. You'll use an Alert Dialog to provide a details window that includes a linkified Text View with a link to the USGS web site.

1. Start by creating an Earthquake project featuring an `Earthquake` Activity. Modify the main.xml layout resource to include a List View control — be sure to name it so you can reference it from the Activity code.

```xml
<?xml version="1.0" encoding="utf-8"?>
<LinearLayout xmlns:android="http://schemas.android.com/apk/res/android"
  android:orientation="vertical"
  android:layout_width="fill_parent"
  android:layout_height="fill_parent">
  <ListView
    android:id="@+id/earthquakeListView"
    android:layout_width="fill_parent"
    android:layout_height="wrap_content"
  />
</LinearLayout>
```

2. Create a new public `Quake` class. This class will be used to store the details (date, details, location, magnitude, and link) of each earthquake. Override the `toString` method to provide the string that will be used to represent each quake in the List View.

```
package com.paad.earthquake;

import java.util.Date;
import java.text.SimpleDateFormat;
import android.location.Location;

public class Quake {
  private Date date;
  private String details;
  private Location location;
  private double magnitude;
  private String link;

  public Date getDate() { return date; }
  public String getDetails() { return details; }
  public Location getLocation() { return location; }
  public double getMagnitude() { return magnitude; }
  public String getLink() { return link; }

  public Quake(Date _d, String _det, Location _loc, double _mag, String _link) {
    date = _d;
    details = _det;
    location = _loc;
    magnitude = _mag;
    link = _link;
  }

  @Override
  public String toString() {
    SimpleDateFormat sdf = new SimpleDateFormat("HH.mm");
    String dateString = sdf.format(date);
    return dateString + ": " + magnitude + " " + details;
  }

}
```

3. In the `Earthquake` Activity, override the `onCreate` method to store an `ArrayList` of `Quake` objects and bind that to the `ListView` using an `ArrayAdapter`:

```
package com.paad.earthquake;

import java.io.IOException;
import java.io.InputStream;
import java.net.HttpURLConnection;
import java.net.MalformedURLException;
import java.net.URL;
import java.net.URLConnection;
import java.text.ParseException;
import java.text.SimpleDateFormat;
import java.util.ArrayList;
import java.util.Date;
import java.util.GregorianCalendar;
```

```java
import javax.xml.parsers.DocumentBuilder;
import javax.xml.parsers.DocumentBuilderFactory;
import javax.xml.parsers.ParserConfigurationException;
import org.w3c.dom.Document;
import org.w3c.dom.Element;
import org.w3c.dom.NodeList;
import org.xml.sax.SAXException;
import android.app.Activity;
import android.app.Dialog;
import android.location.Location;
import android.os.Bundle;
import android.view.Menu;
import android.view.View;
import android.view.WindowManager;
import android.view.MenuItem;
import android.widget.AdapterView;
import android.widget.ArrayAdapter;
import android.widget.ListView;
import android.widget.TextView;
import android.widget.AdapterView.OnItemClickListener;

public class Earthquake extends Activity {

  ListView earthquakeListView;
  ArrayAdapter<Quake> aa;

  ArrayList<Quake> earthquakes = new ArrayList<Quake>();

  @Override
  public void onCreate(Bundle icicle) {
    super.onCreate(icicle);
    setContentView(R.layout.main);

    earthquakeListView = (ListView)this.findViewById(R.id.earthquakeListView);

    int layoutID = android.R.layout.simple_list_item_1;
    aa = new ArrayAdapter<Quake>(this, layoutID , earthquakes);
    earthquakeListView.setAdapter(aa);
  }
}
```

4. Next, start processing the earthquake feed. For this example the feed used is the one-day USGS feed for earthquakes with a magnitude greater than 2.5.

 Add the location of your feed as an external string resource. This lets you potentially specify a different feed based on a user's location.

```xml
<?xml version="1.0" encoding="utf-8"?>
<resources>
  <string name="app_name">Earthquake</string>
  <string name="quake_feed">
    http://earthquake.usgs.gov/eqcenter/catalogs/1day-M2.5.xml
  </string>
</resources>
```

5. Before your application can access the Internet it needs to be granted permission for Internet access. Add the `uses-permission` to the manifest:

```
<uses-permission android:name="android.permission.INTERNET"/>
```

6. Returning to the Earthquake Activity, create a new `refreshEarthquakes` method that connects to and parses the earthquake feed. Extract each earthquake and parse the details to obtain the date, magnitude, link, and location. As you finish parsing each earthquake, pass it in to a new `addNewQuake` method.

The earthquake feed XML is parsed here by the SAX parser. Several alternatives exist, including the `XmlPullParser`. An analysis of the alternative XML parsing techniques (and how to use them) is beyond the scope of this book, but it's important to evaluate and compare the options available within your own applications.

```java
private void refreshEarthquakes() {
  // Get the XML
  URL url;
  try {
    String quakeFeed = getString(R.string.quake_feed);
    url = new URL(quakeFeed);

    URLConnection connection;
    connection = url.openConnection();

    HttpURLConnection httpConnection = (HttpURLConnection)connection;
    int responseCode = httpConnection.getResponseCode();

    if (responseCode == HttpURLConnection.HTTP_OK) {
      InputStream in = httpConnection.getInputStream();

      DocumentBuilderFactory dbf = DocumentBuilderFactory.newInstance();
      DocumentBuilder db = dbf.newDocumentBuilder();

      // Parse the earthquake feed.
      Document dom = db.parse(in);
      Element docEle = dom.getDocumentElement();

      // Clear the old earthquakes
      earthquakes.clear();

      // Get a list of each earthquake entry.
      NodeList nl = docEle.getElementsByTagName("entry");
      if (nl != null && nl.getLength() > 0) {
        for (int i = 0 ; i < nl.getLength(); i++) {
          Element entry = (Element)nl.item(i);
          Element title = (Element)entry.getElementsByTagName("title").item(0);
          Element g = (Element)entry.getElementsByTagName("georss:point").item(0);
          Element when = (Element)entry.getElementsByTagName("updated").item(0);
          Element link = (Element)entry.getElementsByTagName("link").item(0);
```

```
              String details = title.getFirstChild().getNodeValue();
              String hostname = "http://earthquake.usgs.gov";
              String linkString = hostname + link.getAttribute("href");

              String point = g.getFirstChild().getNodeValue();
              String dt = when.getFirstChild().getNodeValue();
              SimpleDateFormat sdf = new SimpleDateFormat("yyyy-MM-dd'T'hh:mm:ss'Z'");
              Date qdate = new GregorianCalendar(0,0,0).getTime();
              try {
                qdate = sdf.parse(dt);
              } catch (ParseException e) {
                e.printStackTrace();
              }

              String[] location = point.split(" ");
              Location l = new Location("dummyGPS");
              l.setLatitude(Double.parseDouble(location[0]));
              l.setLongitude(Double.parseDouble(location[1]));

              String magnitudeString = details.split(" ")[1];
              int end = magnitudeString.length()-1;
              double magnitude = Double.parseDouble(magnitudeString.substring(0, end));

              details = details.split(",")[1].trim();

              Quake quake = new Quake(qdate, details, l, magnitude, linkString);

              // Process a newly found earthquake
              addNewQuake(quake);
            }
          }
        }
    } catch (MalformedURLException e) {
      e.printStackTrace();
    } catch (IOException e) {
      e.printStackTrace();
    } catch (ParserConfigurationException e) {
      e.printStackTrace();
    } catch (SAXException e) {
      e.printStackTrace();
    }
    finally {
    }
  }

private void addNewQuake(Quake _quake) {
  // TODO: Add the earthquakes to the array list.
}
```

7. Update the addNewQuake method so that it takes each newly processed quake and adds it to the earthquake Array List. It should also notify the Array Adapter that the underlying data has changed.

```
private void addNewQuake(Quake _quake) {
```

```
   // Add the new quake to our list of earthquakes.
   earthquakes.add(_quake);

   // Notify the array adapter of a change.
   aa.notifyDataSetChanged();
}
```

8. Modify your onCreate method to call refreshEarthquakes on startup:

```
@Override
public void onCreate(Bundle icicle) {
  super.onCreate(icicle);
  setContentView(R.layout.main);

  earthquakeListView = (ListView)this.findViewById(R.id.earthquakeListView);

  int layoutID = android.R.layout.simple_list_item_1;
  aa = new ArrayAdapter<Quake>(this, layoutID , earthquakes);
  earthquakeListView.setAdapter(aa);

  refreshEarthquakes();
}
```

 The Internet lookup is currently happening on the main UI thread. This is bad form, as the application will become unresponsive if the lookup takes longer than a few seconds. In Chapter 9 you'll learn how to move expensive or time-consuming operations like this into a Service and onto a background thread.

9. If you run your project, you should see a List View that features the earthquakes from the last 24 hours with a magnitude greater than 2.5, as shown in the screen shot in Figure 5-6.

10. There are two more steps needed to make this a more useful application. First, create a new Menu Item to let users refresh the earthquake feed on demand.

   10.1. Start by adding a new external string for the menu option:

   ```
   <string name="menu_update">
    Refresh Earthquakes
   </string>
   ```

   10.2. Then override the Activity's onCreate OptionsMenu and onOptionsItem Selected methods to display and handle the *Refresh Earthquakes* Menu Item:

FIGURE 5-6

```
static final private int MENU_UPDATE = Menu.FIRST;

@Override
public boolean onCreateOptionsMenu(Menu menu) {
  super.onCreateOptionsMenu(menu);

  menu.add(0, MENU_UPDATE, Menu.NONE, R.string.menu_update);

  return true;
}

@Override
public boolean onOptionsItemSelected(MenuItem item) {
  super.onOptionsItemSelected(item);

  switch (item.getItemId()) {
    case (MENU_UPDATE): {
      refreshEarthquakes();
      return true;
    }
  }
  return false;
}
```

11. Now add some interaction. Let users find more details by opening a dialog box when they select an earthquake from the list.

11.1. Create a new quake_details.xml layout resource for the dialog box you'll display when an item is clicked:

```xml
<?xml version="1.0" encoding="utf-8"?>
<LinearLayout xmlns:android="http://schemas.android.com/apk/res/android"
  android:orientation="vertical"
  android:layout_width="fill_parent"
  android:layout_height="fill_parent"
  android:padding="10dp">
  <TextView
    android:id="@+id/quakeDetailsTextView"
    android:layout_width="fill_parent"
    android:layout_height="fill_parent"
    android:textSize="14sp"
  />
</LinearLayout>
```

11.2. Then modify your `onCreate` method to add an `ItemClickListener` to the List View that displays a dialog box whenever an earthquake item is clicked:

```java
static final private int QUAKE_DIALOG = 1;
Quake selectedQuake;

@Override
public void onCreate(Bundle icicle) {
  super.onCreate(icicle);
  setContentView(R.layout.main);

  earthquakeListView = (ListView)this.findViewById(R.id.earthquakeListView);
```

```
earthquakeListView.setOnItemClickListener(new OnItemClickListener() {
  @Override
  public void onItemClick(AdapterView _av, View _v, int _index,
    long arg3) {
   selectedQuake = earthquakes.get(_index);
   showDialog(QUAKE_DIALOG);
  }
});

int layoutID = android.R.layout.simple_list_item_1;
aa = new ArrayAdapter<Quake>(this, layoutID , earthquakes);
earthquakeListView.setAdapter(aa);

refreshEarthquakes();
}
```

11.3. Now override the onCreateDialog and onPrepareDialog methods to create and populate the earthquake details dialog box:

```
@Override
public Dialog onCreateDialog(int id) {
  switch(id) {
    case (QUAKE_DIALOG) :
      LayoutInflater li = LayoutInflater.from(this);
      View quakeDetailsView = li.inflate(R.layout.quake_details, null);

      AlertDialog.Builder quakeDialog = new AlertDialog.Builder(this);
      quakeDialog.setTitle("Quake Time");
      quakeDialog.setView(quakeDetailsView);
      return quakeDialog.create();
  }
  return null;
}

@Override
public void onPrepareDialog(int id, Dialog dialog) {
  switch(id) {
    case (QUAKE_DIALOG) :
      SimpleDateFormat sdf = new SimpleDateFormat("dd/MM/yyyy HH:mm:ss");
      String dateString = sdf.format(selectedQuake.getDate());
      String quakeText = "Magnitude " + selectedQuake.getMagnitude() +
                         "\n" + selectedQuake.getDetails()  + "\n" +
                         selectedQuake.getLink();

      AlertDialog quakeDialog = (AlertDialog)dialog;
      quakeDialog.setTitle(dateString);
      TextView tv = (TextView)quakeDialog.findViewById
         (R.id.quakeDetailsTextView);
      tv.setText(quakeText);

      break;
  }
}
```

11.4. The final step is to linkify the dialog to make the link to the USGS a hyperlink. Adjust the dialog box's XML layout resource definition to include an `autolink` attribute:

```xml
<?xml version="1.0" encoding="utf-8"?>
<LinearLayout xmlns:android="http://schemas.android.com/apk/res/android"
  android:orientation="vertical"
  android:layout_width="fill_parent"
  android:layout_height="fill_parent"
  android:padding="10dp">
  <TextView
    android:id="@+id/quakeDetailsTextView"
    android:layout_width="fill_parent"
    android:layout_height="fill_parent"
    android:textSize="14sp"
    android:autoLink="all"
  />
</LinearLayout>
```

All code snippets in this example are part of the Chapter 5 Earthquake *project, available for download at Wrox.com.*

Launch your application again. When you click a particular earthquake a dialog will appear, partially obscuring the list, as shown in Figure 5-7.

SUMMARY

The focus of this chapter has been on binding your application components.

Intents provide a versatile messaging system that lets you pass intentions between your application and others, to perform actions and signal events. You learned how to use implicit and explicit Intents to start new Activities, and how to populate an Activity menu dynamically through runtime resolution of Activity Intent Filters.

You were introduced to broadcast Intents, and saw how they can be used to send messages throughout the device, particularly to support an event-driven model based on system- and application-specific events.

You learned how to use sub-Activities to pass data between Activities, and how to use Dialogs to display information and facilitate user input.

Adapters were introduced and used to bind underlying data to visual components. In particular you saw how to use an Array Adapter and Simple Cursor Adapter to bind a List View to Array Lists and Cursors.

FIGURE 5-7

Finally, you learned the basics behind connecting to the Internet and using remote feeds as data sources for your native client applications.

You also learned:

➤ To use linkify to add implicit Intents to Text Views at run time.

➤ Which native Android actions are available for you to extend, replace, or embrace.

➤ How to use Intent Filters to let your own Activities become handlers for completing action requests from your own or other applications.

➤ How to listen for broadcast Intents using Broadcast Receivers.

➤ How to use an Activity as a dialog box.

In the next chapter you will learn how to persist information within your applications. Android provides a number of mechanisms for saving application data, including files, simple preferences, and fully featured relational databases (using the SQLite database library). Chapter 6 will focus on using Preferences and saving Activity state, while Chapter 7 will examine Content Providers and SQLite databases.

Files, Saving State, and Preferences

WHAT'S IN THIS CHAPTER?

➤ Persisting simple application data

➤ Saving Activity instance data between sessions

➤ Creating Preference Screens and managing application preferences

➤ Saving and loading files and managing the local file system

➤ Including static files as external resources

In this chapter you'll be introduced to two of the simplest but most versatile data persistence techniques in Android — Shared Preferences and local files.

Saving and loading data are essential for most applications. At a minimum, an Activity should save its user interface (UI) state each time it moves into the background. This ensures that the same UI state is presented when the Activity returns to the foreground, even if the process has been killed and restarted before that happens.

It's also likely that you'll need to save user application preferences and UI selections or data entry. Android's nondeterministic Activity and application lifetimes make persisting UI state and application data between sessions particularly important. Android offers several alternatives for saving application data, each optimized to fulfill a particular need.

Shared Preferences are a simple, lightweight key/value pair mechanism for saving primitive application data, most commonly a user's application preferences. Android also provides access to the local file system, through both specialized methods and the normal `Java.IO` classes.

SAVING SIMPLE APPLICATION DATA

The data-persistence techniques in Android provide options for balancing speed, efficiency, and robustness.

➤ **Shared Preferences**   When storing UI state, user preferences, or application settings, you want a lightweight mechanism to store a known set of values. Shared Preferences let you save groups of key/value pairs of primitive data as named preferences.

➤ **Saved Application State**   Activities include specialized event handlers to record the current UI state when your application is moved to the background.

➤ **Files**   It's not pretty, but sometimes writing to and reading from files is the only way to go. Android lets you create and load files on the device's internal or external media.

There are two lightweight techniques for saving simple application data for Android applications — Shared Preferences and a pair of event handlers used for saving Activity instance details. Both mechanisms use a name/value pair (NVP) mechanism to store simple primitive values.

Using the SharedPreferences class you can create named maps of key/value pairs within your application that can be shared among application components running in the same application context.

Shared Preferences support the primitive types Boolean, string, float, long, and integer, making them an ideal means of quickly storing default values, class instance variables, the current UI state, and user preferences. They are most commonly used to persist data across user sessions and to share settings among application components.

Activities also offer the onSaveInstanceState handler. It's designed specifically to persist UI state when the Activity becomes eligible for termination by a resource-hungry run time.

The handler works like the Shared Preference mechanism. It offers a Bundle parameter that represents a key/value map of primitive types that can be used to save the Activity's instance values. This Bundle is then made available as a parameter passed in to the onCreate and onRestoreInstanceState method handlers.

This UI state Bundle should be used to record the values needed for an Activity to present an identical UI when it's displayed after an unexpected close.

CREATING AND SAVING PREFERENCES

To create or modify a Shared Preference, call getSharedPreferences on the application Context, passing in the name of the Shared Preference to change. Shared Preferences are shared across an application's components, but aren't available to other applications.

To modify a Shared Preference use the SharedPreferences.Editor class. Get the Editor object by calling edit on the Shared Preferences object you want to change. To save edits call commit on the Editor, as shown in Listing 6-1.

LISTING 6-1: Creating new Shared Preferences

```
    // Retrieve an editor to modify the shared preferences.
    SharedPreferences.Editor editor = mySharedPreferences.edit();

    // Store new primitive types in the shared preferences object.
    editor.putBoolean("isTrue", true);
    editor.putFloat("lastFloat", 1f);
    editor.putInt("wholeNumber", 2);
    editor.putLong("aNumber", 31);
    editor.putString("textEntryValue", "Not Empty");

    // Commit the changes.
    editor.commit();
  }
```

RETRIEVING SHARED PREFERENCES

Accessing Shared Preferences, like editing and saving them, is done using the getSharedPreferences method. Pass in the name of the Shared Preference you want to access, and use the type-safe get<type> methods to extract saved values.

Each getter takes a key and a default value (used when no value has yet been saved for that key), as shown in the Listing 6-2.

LISTING 6-2: Retreiving saved Shared Preferences

```
public static String MY_PREFS = "MY_PREFS";
public void loadPreferences() {
  // Get the stored preferences
  int mode = Activity.MODE_PRIVATE;
  SharedPreferences mySharedPreferences = getSharedPreferences(MY_PREFS, mode);

  // Retrieve the saved values.
  boolean isTrue = mySharedPreferences.getBoolean("isTrue", false);
  float lastFloat = mySharedPreferences.getFloat("lastFloat", 0f);
  int wholeNumber = mySharedPreferences.getInt("wholeNumber", 1);
  long aNumber = mySharedPreferences.getLong("aNumber", 0);
  String stringPreference = mySharedPreferences.getString("textEntryValue", "");
}
```

CREATING A SETTINGS ACTIVITY FOR THE EARTHQUAKE VIEWER

In Chapter 5 you created an earthquake monitor that showed a list of recent earthquakes based on an RSS feed.

In the following example you'll build an Activity to set application preferences for this earthquake viewer. It will let users configure settings for a more personalized experience. You'll provide the option to toggle automatic updates, control the frequency of updates, and filter the minimum earthquake magnitude displayed.

 Later in this chapter you'll replace this Activity with a standard settings screen.

1. Open the Earthquake project you created in Chapter 5.

Add new string resources for the labels displayed in the preferences screen. Also add a string for the new Menu Item that will let users access this Activity:

```xml
<?xml version="1.0" encoding="utf-8"?>
<resources>
  <string name="app_name">Earthquake</string>
  <string name="quake_feed">
    http://earthquake.usgs.gov/eqcenter/catalogs/1day-M2.5.xml
  </string>
  <string name="menu_update">Refresh Earthquakes</string>
  <string name="auto_update_prompt">Auto Update?</string>
  <string name="update_freq_prompt">Update Frequency</string>
  <string name="min_quake_mag_prompt">Minimum Quake Magnitude</string>
  <string name="menu_preferences">Preferences</string>
</resources>
```

2. Create a new preferences.xml layout resource for the `Preferences` Activity. Include a checkbox for indicating the "automatic update" toggle, and spinners to select the update rate and magnitude filter:

```xml
<LinearLayout xmlns:android="http://schemas.android.com/apk/res/android"
  android:orientation="vertical"
  android:layout_width="fill_parent"
  android:layout_height="fill_parent">
  <TextView
    android:layout_width="fill_parent"
    android:layout_height="wrap_content"
    android:text="@string/auto_update_prompt"
  />
  <CheckBox android:id="@+id/checkbox_auto_update"
    android:layout_width="fill_parent"
    android:layout_height="wrap_content"
  />
  <TextView
    android:layout_width="fill_parent"
    android:layout_height="wrap_content"
    android:text="@string/update_freq_prompt"
  />
  <Spinner android:id="@+id/spinner_update_freq"
    android:layout_width="fill_parent"
    android:layout_height="wrap_content"
    android:drawSelectorOnTop="true"
  />
  <TextView
    android:layout_width="fill_parent"
```

```
    android:layout_height="wrap_content"
    android:text="@string/min_quake_mag_prompt"
  />
  <Spinner android:id="@+id/spinner_quake_mag"
    android:layout_width="fill_parent"
    android:layout_height="wrap_content"
    android:drawSelectorOnTop="true"
  />
  <LinearLayout
    android:orientation="horizontal"
    android:layout_width="fill_parent"
    android:layout_height="wrap_content">
    <Button android:id="@+id/okButton"
      android:layout_width="wrap_content"
      android:layout_height="wrap_content"
      android:text="@android:string/ok"
    />
    <Button android:id="@+id/cancelButton"
      android:layout_width="wrap_content"
      android:layout_height="wrap_content"
      android:text="@android:string/cancel"
    />
  </LinearLayout>
</LinearLayout>
```

3. Create four array resources in a new res/values/arrays.xml file. They will provide the values to use for the update frequency and minimum magnitude spinners:

```xml
<?xml version="1.0" encoding="utf-8"?>
<resources>
  <string-array name="update_freq_options">
    <item>Every Minute</item>
    <item>5 minutes</item>
    <item>10 minutes</item>
    <item>15 minutes</item>
    <item>Every Hour</item>
  </string-array>

  <array name="magnitude">
    <item>3</item>
    <item>5</item>
    <item>6</item>
    <item>7</item>
    <item>8</item>
  </array>

  <string-array name="magnitude_options">
    <item>3</item>
    <item>5</item>
    <item>6</item>
    <item>7</item>
    <item>8</item>
  </string-array>

  <array name="update_freq_values">
    <item>1</item>
```

```
      <item>5</item>
      <item>10</item>
      <item>15</item>
      <item>60</item>
    </array>
</resources>
```

4. Create the `Preferences` Activity.

Override `onCreate` to inflate the layout you created in Step 2, and get references to the checkbox and both the spinner controls. Then make a call to the `populateSpinners` stub:

```java
package com.paad.earthquake;

import android.app.Activity;
import android.content.SharedPreferences;
import android.content.SharedPreferences.Editor;
import android.os.Bundle;
import android.view.View;
import android.widget.ArrayAdapter;
import android.widget.Button;
import android.widget.CheckBox;
import android.widget.Spinner;

public class Preferences extends Activity {

  CheckBox autoUpdate;
  Spinner updateFreqSpinner;
  Spinner magnitudeSpinner;

  @Override
  public void onCreate(Bundle savedInstanceState) {
    super.onCreate(savedInstanceState);
    setContentView(R.layout.preferences);

    updateFreqSpinner = (Spinner)findViewById(R.id.spinner_update_freq);
    magnitudeSpinner = (Spinner)findViewById(R.id.spinner_quake_mag);
    autoUpdate = (CheckBox)findViewById(R.id.checkbox_auto_update);

    populateSpinners();
  }

  private void populateSpinners() {
  }
}
```

5. Fill in the `populateSpinners` method, using Array Adapters to bind each spinner to its corresponding array:

```java
private void populateSpinners() {
  // Populate the update frequency spinner
  ArrayAdapter<CharSequence> fAdapter;
  fAdapter = ArrayAdapter.createFromResource(this, R.array.update_freq_options,
                                    android.R.layout.simple_spinner_item);
  int spinner_dd_item = android.R.layout.simple_spinner_dropdown_item;
  fAdapter.setDropDownViewResource(spinner_dd_item);
  updateFreqSpinner.setAdapter(fAdapter);
```

```
// Populate the minimum magnitude spinner
ArrayAdapter<CharSequence> mAdapter;
mAdapter = ArrayAdapter.createFromResource(this,
  R.array.magnitude_options,
  android.R.layout.simple_spinner_item);
mAdapter.setDropDownViewResource(spinner_dd_item);
magnitudeSpinner.setAdapter(mAdapter);
}
```

6. Add public static string values that you'll use to identify the Shared Preference keys you'll use to store each preference value. Update the onCreate method to retrieve the named preference and call updateUIFromPreferences. The updateUIFromPreferences method uses the get<type> methods on the Shared Preference object to retrieve each preference value and apply it to the current UI.

Use the default application Shared Preference object to save your settings values:

```
public static final String PREF_AUTO_UPDATE = "PREF_AUTO_UPDATE";
public static final String PREF_MIN_MAG = "PREF_MIN_MAG";
public static final String PREF_UPDATE_FREQ = "PREF_UPDATE_FREQ";

SharedPreferences prefs;

@Override
public void onCreate(Bundle savedInstanceState) {
  super.onCreate(savedInstanceState);
  setContentView(R.layout.preferences);

  updateFreqSpinner = (Spinner)findViewById(R.id.spinner_update_freq);
  magnitudeSpinner = (Spinner)findViewById(R.id.spinner_quake_mag);
  autoUpdate = (CheckBox)findViewById(R.id.checkbox_auto_update);

  populateSpinners();

  Context context = getApplicationContext();
  prefs = PreferenceManager.getDefaultSharedPreferences(context);
  updateUIFromPreferences();
}

private void updateUIFromPreferences() {
  boolean autoUpChecked = prefs.getBoolean(PREF_AUTO_UPDATE, false);
  int updateFreqIndex = prefs.getInt(PREF_UPDATE_FREQ, 2);
  int minMagIndex = prefs.getInt(PREF_MIN_MAG, 0);

  updateFreqSpinner.setSelection(updateFreqIndex);
  magnitudeSpinner.setSelection(minMagIndex);
  autoUpdate.setChecked(autoUpChecked);
}
```

7. Still in the onCreate method, add event handlers for the OK and Cancel buttons. Cancel should close the Activity, while OK should call savePreferences first:

```
@Override
public void onCreate(Bundle savedInstanceState) {
  super.onCreate(savedInstanceState);
  setContentView(R.layout.preferences);
```

```
    updateFreqSpinner - (Spinner)findViewById(R.id.spinner_update_freq);
    magnitudeSpinner = (Spinner)findViewById(R.id.spinner_quake_mag);
    autoUpdate = (CheckBox)findViewById(R.id.checkbox_auto_update);

    populateSpinners();

    Context context = getApplicationContext();
    prefs = PreferenceManager.getDefaultSharedPreferences(context);
    updateUIFromPreferences();

    Button okButton = (Button) findViewById(R.id.okButton);
    okButton.setOnClickListener(new View.OnClickListener() {

      public void onClick(View view) {
        savePreferences();
        Preferences.this.setResult(RESULT_OK);
        finish();
      }
    });

    Button cancelButton = (Button) findViewById(R.id.cancelButton);
    cancelButton.setOnClickListener(new View.OnClickListener() {

      public void onClick(View view) {
        Preferences.this.setResult(RESULT_CANCELED);
        finish();
      }
    });
  }

  private void savePreferences() {
  }
```

8. Fill in the `savePreferences` method to record the current preferences, based on the UI selections, to the Shared Preference object:

```
  private void savePreferences() {
    int updateIndex = updateFreqSpinner.getSelectedItemPosition();
    int minMagIndex = magnitudeSpinner.getSelectedItemPosition();
    boolean autoUpdateChecked = autoUpdate.isChecked();

    Editor editor = prefs.edit();
    editor.putBoolean(PREF_AUTO_UPDATE, autoUpdateChecked);
    editor.putInt(PREF_UPDATE_FREQ, updateIndex);
    editor.putInt(PREF_MIN_MAG, minMagIndex);
    editor.commit();
  }
```

9. That completes the `Preferences` Activity. Make it accessible in the application by adding it to the manifest:

```
<activity android:name=".Preferences"
          android:label="Earthquake Preferences">
</activity>
```

10. Now return to the Earthquake Activity, and add support for the new Shared Preferences file and a Menu Item to display the Preferences Activity. Start by adding the new Menu Item. Extend the onCreateOptionsMenu method to include a new item that opens the Preferences Activity:

```
static final private int MENU_PREFERENCES = Menu.FIRST+1;

@Override
public boolean onCreateOptionsMenu(Menu menu) {
  super.onCreateOptionsMenu(menu);

  menu.add(0, MENU_UPDATE, Menu.NONE, R.string.menu_update);
  menu.add(0, MENU_PREFERENCES, Menu.NONE, R.string.menu_preferences);

  return true;
}
```

11. Modify the onOptionsItemSelected method to display the Preferences Activity when the new Menu Item is selected. Create an explicit Intent and pass it in to the startActivityForResult method. This will launch the Preferences screen and alert the Earthquake class when the preferences are saved through the onActivityResult handler:

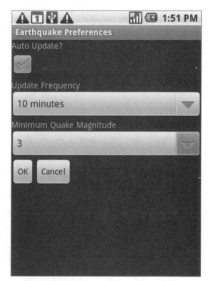

FIGURE 6-1

```
private static final int SHOW_PREFERENCES = 1;

public boolean onOptionsItemSelected(MenuItem item){

  super.onOptionsItemSelected(item);

  switch (item.getItemId()) {
    case (MENU_UPDATE): {
      refreshEarthquakes();
      return true;
    }
    case (MENU_PREFERENCES): {
      Intent i = new Intent(this, Preferences.class);
      startActivityForResult(i, SHOW_PREFERENCES);
      return true;
    }
  }
  return false;
}
```

12. Launch your application and select Preferences from the Activity menu. The Preferences Activity should be displayed as shown in Figure 6-1.

13. All that's left is to apply the preferences to the earthquake functionality. Implementing the automatic updates will be left until Chapter 9, when you'll learn to use Services and background threads. For now you can put the framework in place and apply the magnitude filter.

Start by creating a new `updateFromPreferences` method that reads the Shared Preference values and creates instance variables for each of them:

```
int minimumMagnitude = 0;
boolean autoUpdate = false;
int updateFreq = 0;

private void updateFromPreferences() {
  Context context = getApplicationContext();
  SharedPreferences prefs =
    PreferenceManager.getDefaultSharedPreferences(context);

  int minMagIndex = prefs.getInt(Preferences.PREF_MIN_MAG, 0);
  if (minMagIndex < 0)
    minMagIndex = 0;

  int freqIndex = prefs.getInt(Preferences.PREF_UPDATE_FREQ, 0);
  if (freqIndex < 0)
    freqIndex = 0;

  autoUpdate = prefs.getBoolean(Preferences.PREF_AUTO_UPDATE, false);

  Resources r = getResources();
  // Get the option values from the arrays.
  int[] minMagValues = r.getIntArray(R.array.magnitude);
  int[] freqValues = r.getIntArray(R.array.update_freq_values);

  // Convert the values to ints.
  minimumMagnitude = minMagValues[minMagIndex];
  updateFreq = freqValues[freqIndex];
}
```

14. Apply the magnitude filter by updating the `addNewQuake` method to check a new earthquake's magnitude before adding it to the list:

```
private void addNewQuake(Quake _quake) {
  if (_quake.getMagnitude() > minimumMagnitude) {
    // Add the new quake to our list of earthquakes.
    earthquakes.add(_quake);

    // Notify the array adapter of a change.
    aa.notifyDataSetChanged();
  }
}
```

15. Override the `onActivityResult` handler to call `updateFromPreferences` and refresh the earthquakes whenever the `Preferences` Activity saves changes:

```
@Override
public void onActivityResult(int requestCode, int resultCode, Intent data) {
  super.onActivityResult(requestCode, resultCode, data);

  if (requestCode == SHOW_PREFERENCES)
    if (resultCode == Activity.RESULT_OK) {
      updateFromPreferences();
```

```
        refreshEarthquakes();
      }
    }
```

16. Finally, call `updateFromPreferences` in `onCreate` (before the call to `refreshEarthquakes`) to ensure the preferences are applied when the Activity starts:

```java
@Override
public void onCreate(Bundle savedInstanceState) {
  super.onCreate(savedInstanceState);
  setContentView(R.layout.main);

  earthquakeListView = (ListView)this.findViewById(R.id.earthquakeListView);

  earthquakeListView.setOnItemClickListener(new OnItemClickListener() {

    @Override
    public void onItemClick(AdapterView _av, View _v, int _index, long arg3) {
      selectedQuake = earthquakes.get(_index);
      showDialog(QUAKE_DIALOG);
    }
  });

  int layoutID = android.R.layout.simple_list_item_1;
  aa = new ArrayAdapter<Quake>(this, layoutID , earthquakes);
  earthquakeListView.setAdapter(aa);

  updateFromPreferences();
  refreshEarthquakes();
}
```

All code snippets in this example are part of the **Chapter 6 Earthquake** *project, available for download at Wrox.com.*

INTRODUCING THE PREFERENCE ACTIVITY AND PREFERENCES FRAMEWORK

Android offers an XML-driven framework to create system-style preference screens for your applications. By using this framework you can ensure that the preference Activities in your applications are consistent with those used in both native and other third-party applications.

This has two distinct advantages:

➤ Users will be familiar with the layout and use of your application settings screen.

➤ You can integrate settings screens from other applications (including system settings such as location settings) into your application's settings screens.

The Preference Activity framework consists of three parts:

➤ **Preference Screen Layout** An XML file that defines the hierarchy displayed in your Preference Activity. It specifies the controls to display, the values to allow, and the Shared Preference keys to use for each UI control.

➤ **Preference Activity** An extension of `PreferenceActivity` that will be used to host your application preference screens.

➤ **Shared Preference Change Listener** An implementation of the `onSharedPreferenceChangeListener` class used to listen for changes to Shared Preferences.

The Activity Preference framework is a powerful tool for creating fully customizable dynamic preference screens. The full range of possibilities available through this framework is beyond the scope of this book; however, the following sections will introduce it and demonstrate how to create and use each of the components described above.

Defining a Preference Screen Layout in XML

The most important part of the Preference Activity is the XML layout. Unlike in the standard UI layout, preference definitions are stored in the `res/xml` resources folder.

While conceptually they are similar to the UI layout resources described in Chapter 4, Preference Screen layouts use a specialized set of controls designed specifically to create preference screens like those used for system settings. These native preference controls are described in the next section.

Each preference layout is defined as a hierarchy, beginning with a single `PreferenceScreen` element:

```xml
<?xml version="1.0" encoding="utf-8"?>
<PreferenceScreen
  xmlns:android="http://schemas.android.com/apk/res/android">
</PreferenceScreen>
```

You can include additional Preference Screen elements, each of which will be represented as a selectable element that will display a new screen if clicked.

Within each Preference Screen you can include any combination of `PreferenceCategory` and `Preference<control>` elements. Preference Category elements, shown in the following snippet, are used to break each Preference Screen into subcategories using a title bar separator:

```xml
<PreferenceCategory
  android:title="My Preference Category"/>
</PreferenceCategory>
```

Figure 6-2 shows the SIM card lock, passwords, and credential storage Preference Categories used in the "Location & security" Preference Screen.

All that remains is to add the preference controls that will be used to set the application preferences. While the specific attributes available for each preference control vary, each of them includes at least the following four:

➤ `android:key` The Shared Preference key the selected value will be recorded against.

FIGURE 6-2

➤   `android:title`   The text displayed to represent the preference.

➤   `android:summary`   The longer text description displayed in a smaller font below the title text.

➤   `android:defaultValue`   The default value that will be displayed (and selected) if no preference value has been assigned to this preference key.

Listing 6-3 shows a sample Preference Screen that includes a Preference Category and CheckBox Preference.

LISTING 6-3: A simple Shared Preferences screen

```xml
<?xml version="1.0" encoding="utf-8"?>
<PreferenceScreen
  xmlns:android="http://schemas.android.com/apk/res/android">
  <PreferenceCategory
    android:title="My Preference Category"/>
    <CheckBoxPreference
      android:key="PREF_CHECK_BOX"
      android:title="Check Box Preference"
      android:summary="Check Box Preference Description"
      android:defaultValue="true"
    />
  </PreferenceCategory>
</PreferenceScreen>
```

This Preference Screen will appear as shown in Figure 6-3.

Native Preference Controls

Android includes several preference controls to build your Preference Screens:

➤   `CheckBoxPreference`   A standard preference checkbox control. Used to set preferences to true or false.

➤   `EditTextPreference`   Allows users to enter a string value as a preference. Selecting the preference text will display a text entry dialog.

➤   `ListPreference`   The preference equivalent of a spinner. Selecting this preference will display a dialog box containing a list of values from which to select. You can specify different arrays to contain the display text and selection values.

➤   `RingtonePreference`   A specialized List Preference that presents the list of available ringtones for user selection. This is particularly useful when you're constructing a screen to configure notification settings.

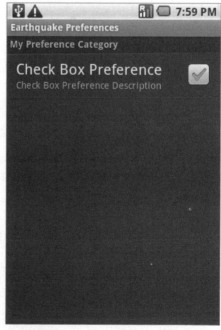

FIGURE 6-3

Each of these preference controls can be used to construct your Preference Screen hierarchy. Alternatively, you can create your own specialized preference controls by extending the `Preference` class (or any of these subclasses).

You can find further details on the Android documentation at: `http://developer.android.com/reference/android/preference/Preference.html`

Using Intents to Import System Preference Screens

As well as your own Preference Screens, preference hierarchies can include Preference Screens from other applications — including system Preference Screens.

You can invoke any Activity within your Preference Screen using an Intent. If you add an Intent node within any Preference Screen element, the system will interpret this as a request to call `startActivity` using the specified action.

This is particularly useful for including links to relevant system Preference Screens within your own application settings. The following XML snippet adds a link to the system display settings:

```
<PreferenceScreen
  android:title="Intent preference"
  android:summary="System preference imported using an intent">
  <intent android:action="android.settings.DISPLAY_SETTINGS "/>
</PreferenceScreen>
```

The `android.provider.Settings` class includes a number of `android.settings.*` constants that can be used to invoke the system settings screens.

To make your own Preference Screens available for invocation using this technique, simply add an Intent Filter to the manifest entry for the host Preference Activity (described in detail in the following section):

```
<activity android:name=".UserPreferences" android:label="Earthquake Preferences">
  <intent-filter>
    <action android:name="com.paad.myapp.ACTION_USER_PREFERENCE" />
  </intent-filter>
</activity>
```

Introducing the Preference Activity

The `PreferenceActivity` class is used to host the preference hierarchy defined using the preferences XML file. To create a new Preference Activity, extend the `PreferenceActivity` class as follows:

```
public class MyPreferenceActivity extends PreferenceActivity {
}
```

To inflate the preferences, override the `onCreate` handler and call `addPreferencesFromResource`, as shown in the following snippet:

```
@Override
public void onCreate(Bundle savedInstanceState) {
  super.onCreate(savedInstanceState);
  addPreferencesFromResource(R.xml.preferences);
}
```

Like all Activities, the Preference Activity must be included in the application manifest:

```
<activity android:name=".MyPreferenceActivity"
          android:label="My Preferences">
</activity>
```

This is all that's required for a simple Preference Activity implementation. To display the application settings hosted in this Activity, open it by calling startActivity or startActivityForResult:

```
Intent i = new Intent(this, MyPreferenceActivity.class);
startActivityForResult(i, SHOW_PREFERENCES);
```

Finding and Using Preference Screen Shared Preferences

The Shared Preference values recorded for the options presented in a Preference Activity are stored against the application Context. This lets any application component, including Activities, Services, and Broadcast Receivers, access the values, as shown in the following snippet:

```
Context context = getApplicationContext();
SharedPreferences prefs = PreferenceManager.getDefaultSharedPreferences(context);
// TODO Retrieve values using get<type> methods.
```

Introducing Shared Preference Change Listeners

The onSharedPreferenceChangeListener is a useful class that can be implemented to invoke a callback whenever a particular Shared Preference value is added, removed, or modified.

This is particularly useful for Activities and Services that use the Shared Preference framework to set application preferences. Using this handler your application components can listen for changes to user preferences and update their UIs or behavior as required.

Register Shared Preference Change Listeners using the Shared Preference you want to monitor. The implementation of the Shared Preference Change Listener is shown in Listing 6-4.

LISTING 6-4: On Shared Preference Change Listener skeleton implementation

Available for
download on
Wrox.com

```
public class MyActivity extends Activity implements
  OnSharedPreferenceChangeListener {

  @Override
  public void onCreate(Bundle SavedInstanceState) {
    // Register this OnSharedPreferenceChangeListener
    Context context = getApplicationContext();
    SharedPreferences prefs =
      PreferenceManager.getDefaultSharedPreferences(context);
    prefs.registerOnSharedPreferenceChangeListener(this);
  }

  public void onSharedPreferenceChanged(SharedPreferences prefs, String key) {
    // TODO Check the shared preference and key parameters and change UI or
    // behavior as appropriate.
  }
}
```

CREATING A STANDARD PREFERENCE ACTIVITY FOR THE EARTHQUAKE VIEWER

Previously in this chapter you created a custom Activity to let users modify the application settings for the earthquake viewer. In this example you'll replace this custom Activity with the standard application settings framework described in the previous section.

1. Start by creating a new XML resource folder at res/xml. Within it create a new userpreferences.xml file. This file will define the settings UI for your earthquake application settings. Use the same controls and data sources as in the previous Activity, but this time create them using the standard application settings framework.

Be sure to use the preference keys you defined earlier.

```xml
<?xml version="1.0" encoding="utf-8"?>
<PreferenceScreen
  xmlns:android="http://schemas.android.com/apk/res/android">
  <CheckBoxPreference
    android:key="PREF_AUTO_UPDATE"
    android:title="Auto refresh"
    android:summary="Select to turn on automatic updating"
    android:defaultValue="true"
  />
  <ListPreference
   android:key="PREF_UPDATE_FREQ"
   android:title="Refresh frequency"
   android:summary="Frequency at which to refresh earthquake list"
   android:entries="@array/update_freq_options"
   android:entryValues="@array/update_freq_values"
   android:dialogTitle="Refresh frequency"
   android:defaultValue="60"
  />
  <ListPreference
    android:key="PREF_MIN_MAG"
    android:title="Minimum magnitude"
    android:summary="Select the minimum magnitude earthquake to report"
    android:entries="@array/magnitude_options"
    android:entryValues="@array/magnitude"
    android:dialogTitle="Magnitude"
    android:defaultValue="3"
  />
</PreferenceScreen>
```

2. Open the Preference Activity and modify its inheritance to extend `PreferenceActivity`:

```
public class UserPreferences extends PreferenceActivity
```

3. The Preference Activity will handle the controls used in the UI, so you can remove the variables used to store the checkbox and spinner objects. You can also remove the `populateSpinners`, `updateUIFromPreferences`, and `savePreferences` methods.

4. Now update `onCreate`. Remove all the references to the UI controls and the OK and Cancel buttons. Instead of using these, inflate the preferences UI file you created in Step 1:

```
@Override
public void onCreate(Bundle savedInstanceState) {
  super.onCreate(savedInstanceState);
  addPreferencesFromResource(R.xml.preferences);
}
```

5. If you run your application now, and select the Preferences menu item, your new "native" settings screen should be visible, as shown in Figure 6-4.

All code snippets in this example are part of the Chapter 6 Earth-quake Part 2 *project, available for download at Wrox.com.*

SAVING ACTIVITY STATE

If you want to save Activity information that doesn't need to be shared with other components (e.g., class instance variables), you can call `Activity.getPreferences()` without specifying a Shared Preferences name. Access to the returned Shared Preferences map is restricted to the calling Activity; each Activity supports a single unnamed Shared Preferences object.

Listing 6-5 shows how to use the Activity's private Shared Preference.

FIGURE 6-4

LISTING 6-5: Saving Activity state

Available for download on Wrox.com

```java
protected void saveActivityPreferences(){
    // Create or retrieve the activity preference object.
    SharedPreferences activityPreferences = getPreferences(Activity.MODE_PRIVATE);

    // Retrieve an editor to modify the shared preferences.
    SharedPreferences.Editor editor = activityPreferences.edit();

    // Retrieve the View
    TextView myTextView = (TextView)findViewById(R.id.myTextView);

    // Store new primitive types in the shared preferences object.
    editor.putString("currentTextValue", myTextView.getText().toString());

    // Commit changes.
    editor.commit();
}
```

Saving and Restoring Instance State

To save Activity instance variables, Android offers a specialized variation of Shared Preferences.

By overriding an Activity's onSaveInstanceState event handler, you can use its Bundle parameter to save UI instance values. Store values using the same get and put methods as shown for Shared Preferences, before passing the modified Bundle into the superclass's handler, as shown in Listing 6-6.

LISTING 6-6: Saving Activity instance state

```
private static final String TEXTVIEW_STATE_KEY = "TEXTVIEW_STATE_KEY";

@Override
public void onSaveInstanceState(Bundle saveInstanceState) {
  // Retrieve the View
  TextView myTextView = (TextView)findViewById(R.id.myTextView);

  // Save its state
  saveInstanceState.putString(TEXTVIEW_STATE_KEY, myTextView.getText().toString());
  super.onSaveInstanceState(saveInstanceState);
}
```

This handler will be triggered whenever an Activity completes its active lifecycle, but only when it's not being explicitly finished (with a call to finish). As a result, it's used to ensure a consistent Activity state between active life cycles of a single user session.

The saved Bundle is passed in to the onRestoreInstanceState and onCreate methods if the application is forced to restart during a session. Listing 6-7 shows how to extract values from the Bundle and use them to update the Activity instance state.

LISTING 6-7: Restoring Activity instance state

```
@Override
public void onCreate(Bundle savedInstanceState) {
  super.onCreate(savedInstanceState);
  setContentView(R.layout.main);

  TextView myTextView = (TextView)findViewById(R.id.myTextView);

  String text = "";
  if (savedInstanceState != null && savedInstanceState.containsKey(TEXTVIEW_STATE_KEY))

    text = savedInstanceState.getString(TEXTVIEW_STATE_KEY);

  myTextView.setText(text);
}
```

 It's important to remember that onSaveInstanceState *is called only when an Activity becomes inactive, and* not *when it is being closed by a call to finish or by the user's pressing the back button.*

Saving the To-Do List Activity State

Currently, each time the To-Do List example application is restarted, all the to-do items are lost and any text entered into the text entry box is cleared. In this example you'll start to save the application state of the To-Do List application across sessions.

The instance state in the ToDoList Activity consists of three variables:

➤ Is a new item being added?

➤ What text exists in the new item entry textbox?

➤ What is the currently selected item?

Using the Activity's default Shared Preference you can store each of these values and update the UI when the Activity is restarted.

> *Later in this chapter you'll learn how to use the SQLite database to persist the to-do items as well. This example is a first step that shows how to ensure a seamless experience by saving Activity instance details.*

1. Start by adding static string variables to use as preference keys:

```
private static final String TEXT_ENTRY_KEY = "TEXT_ENTRY_KEY";
private static final String ADDING_ITEM_KEY = "ADDING_ITEM_KEY";
private static final String SELECTED_INDEX_KEY = "SELECTED_INDEX_KEY";
```

2. Next, override the onPause method. Get the Activity's private Shared Preference object and its Editor object.

Using the keys you created in Step 1, store the instance values according to whether a new item is being added, and also store any text in the "new item" edit box:

```
@Override
protected void onPause(){
  super.onPause();

  // Get the activity preferences object.
  SharedPreferences uiState = getPreferences(0);
  // Get the preferences editor.
  SharedPreferences.Editor editor = uiState.edit();

  // Add the UI state preference values.
  editor.putString(TEXT_ENTRY_KEY, myEditText.getText().toString());
  editor.putBoolean(ADDING_ITEM_KEY, addingNew);
  // Commit the preferences.
  editor.commit();
}
```

3. Write a `restoreUIState` method that applies the instance values you recorded in the previous step when the application restarts. Modify the `onCreate` method to add a call to the `restoreUIState` method at the very end:

```
@Override
public void onCreate(Bundle savedInstanceState) {
  [ ... existing onCreate logic ... ]
  restoreUIState();
}

private void restoreUIState() {
  // Get the activity preferences object.
  SharedPreferences settings = getPreferences(Activity.MODE_PRIVATE);

  // Read the UI state values, specifying default values.
  String text = settings.getString(TEXT_ENTRY_KEY, "");
  Boolean adding = settings.getBoolean(ADDING_ITEM_KEY, false);

  // Restore the UI to the previous state.
  if (adding) {
    addNewItem();
    myEditText.setText(text);
  }
}
```

4. Record the index of the selected item using the `onSaveInstanceState`/`onRestoreInstanceState` mechanism. It's then saved and applied only if the application is killed without the user's explicit instruction:

```
@Override
public void onSaveInstanceState(Bundle savedInstanceState) {
  savedInstanceState.putInt(SELECTED_INDEX_KEY, myListView.getSelectedItemPosition());

  super.onSaveInstanceState(saveInstanceState);
}

@Override
public void onRestoreInstanceState(Bundle savedInstanceState) {
  int pos = -1;

  if (savedInstanceState != null)
    if (savedInstanceState.containsKey(SELECTED_INDEX_KEY))
      pos = savedInstanceState.getInt(SELECTED_INDEX_KEY, -1);

  myListView.setSelection(pos);
}
```

All code snippets in this example are part of the **Chapter 6 Todo List** *project, available for download at Wrox.com.*

When you run the To-Do List application you should now see the UI state persisted across sessions. That said, the application still won't persist the To-Do List items — you'll add this essential piece of functionality in the next chapter.

SAVING AND LOADING FILES

It's good practice to use Shared Preferences or a database to store your application data, but there are still times when you'll want to use files directly rather than rely on Android's managed mechanisms.

As well as the standard Java I/O classes and methods, Android offers `openFileInput` and `openFileOuput` to simplify reading and writing streams from and to local files, as shown in Listing 6-8.

LISTING 6-8: Saving and loading files

```
String FILE_NAME = "tempfile.tmp";

// Create a new output file stream that's private to this application.
FileOutputStream fos = openFileOutput(FILE_NAME, Context.MODE_PRIVATE);
// Create a new file input stream.
FileInputStream fis = openFileInput(FILE_NAME);
```

These methods support only those files in the current application folder; specifying path separators will cause an exception to be thrown.

If the file name you specify when creating a `FileOutputStream` does not exist, Android will create it for you. The default behavior for existing files is to overwrite them; to append an existing file, specify the mode as `Context.MODE_APPEND`.

By default, files created using the `openFileOutput` method are private to the calling application — a different application will be denied access. The standard way to share a file between applications is to use a Content Provider. Alternatively, you can specify either `Context.MODE_WORLD_READABLE` or `Context.MODE_WORLD_WRITEABLE` when creating the output file, to make it available in other applications, as shown in the following snippet:

```
String OUTPUT_FILE = "publicCopy.txt";
FileOutputStream fos = openFileOutput(OUTPUT_FILE, Context.MODE_WORLD_WRITEABLE);
```

INCLUDING STATIC FILES AS RESOURCES

If your application requires external file resources, you can include them in your distribution package by placing them in the `res/raw` folder of your project hierarchy.

To access these read-only file resources, call the `openRawResource` method from your application's `Resource` object to receive an `InputStream` based on the specified file. Pass in the file name (without extension) as the variable name from the `R.raw` class, as shown in the following skeleton code:

```
Resources myResources = getResources();
InputStream myFile = myResources.openRawResource(R.raw.myfilename);
```

Adding raw files to your resources hierarchy is an excellent alternative for large, preexisting data sources (such as dictionaries) for which it's not desirable (or even possible) to convert them into Android databases.

Android's resource mechanism lets you specify alternative resource files for different languages, locations, and hardware configurations. You could, for example, create an application that loads a different dictionary resource based on the user's language settings.

FILE MANAGEMENT TOOLS

Android supplies some basic file management tools to help you deal with the file system. Many of these utilities are located within the standard `java.io.File` package.

Complete coverage of Java file management utilities is beyond the scope of this book, but Android does supply some specialized utilities for file management that are available from the application Context.

➤   `deleteFile`   Enables you to remove files created by the current application.

➤   `fileList`   Returns a string array that includes all the files created by the current application.

These methods are particularly useful for cleaning up temporary files left behind if your application crashes or is killed unexpectedly.

SUMMARY

In this chapter you learned how to persist simple data within your applications and how to manage files and preferences.

After learning how to save the Activity instance data between sessions using the save and restore instance state handlers, you were introduced to Shared Preferences and the system Preference Screen framework. You used them to save instance values and user preferences that can be used across your application components.

Along the way you also learned to:

➤   Save and load files directly to and from the underlying file system.

➤   Include static files as external project resources.

In the next chapter you will learn how to persist more complex and structured information within your applications. As well as the techniques described in this chapter, Android provides fully featured relational databases (using the SQLite database library) that can be shared among applications by means of Content Providers. Both SQLite and Content Providers will be explored in the next chapter.

7

Databases and Content Providers

In this chapter you'll be introduced to the SQLite library, and you'll look at how to use Content Providers to share and use structured data within and between applications.

SQLite offers a powerful SQL database library that provides a robust persistence layer over which you have total control.

Content Providers offer a generic interface to any data source by decoupling the data storage layer from the application layer.

By default, access to a database is restricted to the application that created it. Content Providers offer a standard interface your applications can use to share data with and consume data from other applications — including many of the native data stores.

INTRODUCING ANDROID DATABASES

Structured data persistence in Android is provided through the following mechanisms:

➤ **SQLite Databases**   When managed, structured data is the best approach, Android offers the SQLite relational database library. Every application can create its own databases over which it has complete control.

➤ **Content Providers** Content Providers offer a generic, well-defined interface for using and sharing data.

Introducing SQLite Databases

Using SQLite you can create independent relational databases for your applications. Use them to store and manage complex, structured application data.

Android databases are stored in the `/data/data/<package_name>/databases` folder on your device (or emulator). By default all databases are private, accessible only by the application that created them.

Database design is a big topic that deserves more thorough coverage than is possible within this book. It is worth highlighting that standard database best practices still apply in Android. In particular, when you're creating databases for resource-constrained devices (such as mobile phones), it's important to normalize your data to reduce redundancy.

Introducing Content Providers

Content Providers provide an interface for publishing and consuming data, based around a simple URI addressing model using the `content://` schema. They let you decouple the application layer from the data layer, making your applications data-source agnostic by hiding the underlying data source.

Shared Content Providers can be queried for results, existing records updated or deleted, and new records added. Any application with the appropriate permissions can add, remove, or update data from any other application — including from the native Android databases.

Many native databases are available as Content Providers, accessible by third-party applications, including the phone's contact manager, media store, and other native databases as described later in this chapter.

By publishing your own data sources as Content Providers, you make it possible for you (and other developers) to incorporate and extend your data in new applications.

INTRODUCING SQLite

SQLite is a well regarded relational database management system (RDBMS). It is:

➤ Open-source

➤ Standards-compliant

➤ Lightweight

➤ Single-tier

It has been implemented as a compact C library that's included as part of the Android software stack.

By being implemented as a library, rather than running as a separate ongoing process, each SQLite database is an integrated part of the application that created it. This reduces external dependencies, minimizes latency, and simplifies transaction locking and synchronization.

SQLite has a reputation for being extremely reliable and is the database system of choice for many consumer electronic devices, including several MP3 players, the iPhone, and the iPod Touch.

Lightweight and powerful, SQLite differs from many conventional database engines by loosely typing each column, meaning that column values are not required to conform to a single type. Instead, each value is typed individually for each row. As a result, type checking isn't necessary when assigning or extracting values from each column within a row.

For more comprehensive coverage of SQLite, including its particular strengths and limitations, check out the official site at `http://www.sqlite.org/`

CURSORS AND CONTENT VALUES

`ContentValues` are used to insert new rows into tables. Each Content Values object represents a single table row as a map of column names to values.

Queries in Android are returned as `Cursor` objects. Rather than extracting and returning a copy of the result values, Cursors are pointers to the result set within the underlying data. Cursors provide a managed way of controlling your position (row) in the result set of a database query.

The Cursor class includes a number of navigation functions including, but not limited to, the following:

- ➤ `moveToFirst` Moves the cursor to the first row in the query result
- ➤ `moveToNext` Moves the cursor to the next row
- ➤ `moveToPrevious` Moves the cursor to the previous row
- ➤ `getCount` Returns the number of rows in the result set
- ➤ `getColumnIndexOrThrow` Returns the index for the column with the specified name (throwing an exception if no column exists with that name)
- ➤ `getColumnName` Returns the name of the specified column index
- ➤ `getColumnNames` Returns a string array of all the column names in the current Cursor
- ➤ `moveToPosition` Moves the Cursor to the specified row
- ➤ `getPosition` Returns the current Cursor position

Android provides a convenient mechanism for simplifying the management of Cursors within your Activities. The `startManagingCursor` method integrates the Cursor's lifetime into the calling Activity's. When you've finished with the Cursor, call `stopManagingCursor` to do just that.

Later in this chapter you'll learn how to query a database and how to extract specific row/column values from the resulting Cursors.

WORKING WITH SQLite DATABASES

It's good practice to create a helper class to simplify your database interactions.

The following section shows you how to create a database adapter class for your database. This abstraction layer encapsulates your database interactions. It will provide intuitive, strongly typed methods for adding, removing, and updating items. A database adapter should also handle queries and expose methods for creating, opening, and closing the database.

It can also be used as a convenient location to publish static database constants, including table and column names.

Listing 7-1 shows the skeleton code for a standard database adapter class. It includes an extension of the SQLiteOpenHelper class (discussed in more detail in the following section), used to simplify opening, creating, and upgrading the database.

LISTING 7-1: Skeleton code for a standard database adapter implementation

```
import android.content.Context;
import android.database.*;
import android.database.sqlite.*;
import android.database.sqlite.SQLiteDatabase.CursorFactory;
import android.util.Log;

public class MyDBAdapter {
  private static final String DATABASE_NAME = "myDatabase.db";
  private static final String DATABASE_TABLE = "mainTable";
  private static final int DATABASE_VERSION = 1;

  // The index (key) column name for use in where clauses.
  public static final String KEY_ID="_id";

  // The name and column index of each column in your database.
  public static final String KEY_NAME="name";
  public static final int NAME_COLUMN = 1;
  // TODO: Create public field for each column in your table.

  // SQL Statement to create a new database.
  private static final String DATABASE_CREATE = "create table " +
    DATABASE_TABLE + " (" + KEY_ID +
    " integer primary key autoincrement, " +
    KEY_NAME + " text not null);";

  // Variable to hold the database instance
  private SQLiteDatabase db;
  // Context of the application using the database.
  private final Context context;
  // Database open/upgrade helper
  private myDbHelper dbHelper;

  public MyDBAdapter(Context _context) {
    context = _context;
    dbHelper = new myDbHelper(context, DATABASE_NAME, null, DATABASE_VERSION);
  }

  public MyDBAdapter open() throws SQLException {
    db = dbHelper.getWritableDatabase();
    return this;
  }
```

```java
public void close() {
    db.close();
}

public int insertEntry(MyObject _myObject) {
  // TODO: Create a new ContentValues to represent my row
  // and insert it into the database.
  return index;
}

public boolean removeEntry(long _rowIndex) {
  return db.delete(DATABASE_TABLE, KEY_ID + "=" + _rowIndex, null) > 0;
}

public Cursor getAllEntries () {
  return db.query(DATABASE_TABLE, new String[] {KEY_ID, KEY_NAME},
                  null, null, null, null, null);
}

public MyObject getEntry(long _rowIndex) {
  // TODO: Return a cursor to a row from the database and
  // use the values to populate an instance of MyObject
  return objectInstance;
}

public boolean updateEntry(long _rowIndex, MyObject _myObject) {
  // TODO: Create a new ContentValues based on the new object
  // and use it to update a row in the database.
  return true;
}

private static class myDbHelper extends SQLiteOpenHelper {

  public myDbHelper(Context context, String name,
                    CursorFactory factory, int version) {
    super(context, name, factory, version);
  }

  // Called when no database exists in disk and the helper class needs
  // to create a new one.
  @Override
  public void onCreate(SQLiteDatabase _db) {
    _db.execSQL(DATABASE_CREATE);
  }

  // Called when there is a database version mismatch meaning that the version
  // of the database on disk needs to be upgraded to the current version.
  @Override
  public void onUpgrade(SQLiteDatabase _db, int _oldVersion, int _newVersion) {
    // Log the version upgrade.
    Log.w("TaskDBAdapter", "Upgrading from version " +
                           _oldVersion + " to " +
                           _newVersion + ", which will destroy all old data");
```

continues

LISTING 7-1 *(continued)*

```
            // Upgrade the existing database to conform to the new version. Multiple
            // previous versions can be handled by comparing _oldVersion and _newVersion
            // values.

            // The simplest case is to drop the old table and create a new one.
            _db.execSQL("DROP TABLE IF EXISTS " + DATABASE_TABLE);
            // Create a new one.
            onCreate(_db);
        }
    }
}
```

Introducing the SQLiteOpenHelper

`SQLiteOpenHelper` is an abstract class used to implement the best practice pattern for creating, opening, and upgrading databases. By implementing an SQLite Open Helper you hide the logic used to decide if a database needs to be created or upgraded before it's opened.

Listing 7-1 showed how to extend the `SQLiteOpenHelper` class by overriding the constructor, `onCreate`, and `onUpgrade` methods to handle the creation of a new database and upgrading to a new version, respectively.

 In the previous example `onUpgrade` *simply drops the existing table and replaces it with the new definition. In practice, a better solution is to migrate existing data into the new table.*

To use an implementation of the helper class, create a new instance, passing in the context, database name, and current version, and a `CursorFactory` (if you're using one).

Call `getReadableDatabase` or `getWritableDatabase` to open and return a readable/writable instance of the underlying database.

A call to `getWritableDatabase` can fail because of disk space or permission issues, so it's good practice to provide fallback to the `getReadableDatabase` method, as shown in Listing 7-2.

LISTING 7-2: Using the SQLiteOpenHelper to access a database

```
dbHelper = new myDbHelper(context, DATABASE_NAME, null, DATABASE_VERSION);

SQLiteDatabase db;
try {
  db = dbHelper.getWritableDatabase();
}
catch (SQLiteException ex){
  db = dbHelper.getReadableDatabase();
}
```

Behind the scenes, if the database doesn't exist the helper executes its `onCreate` handler. If the database version has changed, the `onUpgrade` handler will fire. In either case the `get<read/writ>ableDatabase` call will return the existing, newly created, or upgraded database, as appropriate.

Opening and Creating Databases without SQLiteHelper

You can create and open databases without using the SQLite Helper by using the `openOrCreateData base` method from the application Context.

Setting up a database is a two-step process. First call `openOrCreateDatabase` to create the new database. Then call `execSQL` on the resulting database instance to run the SQL commands that will create your tables and their relationships. The general process is shown in Listing 7-3.

Available for download on Wrox.com

LISTING 7-3: Creating a new database

```
private static final String DATABASE_NAME = "myDatabase.db";
private static final String DATABASE_TABLE = "mainTable";

private static final String DATABASE_CREATE =
  "create table " + DATABASE_TABLE + " ( _id integer primary key autoincrement," +
  "column_one text not null);";

SQLiteDatabase myDatabase;

private void createDatabase() {
  myDatabase = openOrCreateDatabase(DATABASE_NAME, Context.MODE_PRIVATE, null);
  myDatabase.execSQL(DATABASE_CREATE);
}
```

Android Database Design Considerations

There are several considerations specific to Android that you should keep in mind when designing your database.

➤   Files (such as bitmaps or audio files) are not usually stored within database tables. Use a string to store a path to the file, preferably a fully qualified URI.

➤   While not strictly a requirement, it's strongly recommended that all tables include an auto-increment key field as a unique index field for each row. If you plan to share your table using a Content Provider, a unique ID field is mandatory.

Querying a Database

Each database query is returned as a `Cursor`. This lets Android manage resources more efficiently by retrieving and releasing row and column values on demand.

To execute a query on a database use the `query` method, passing in:

➤   An optional Boolean that specifies if the result set should contain only unique values.

➤   The name of the table to query.

➤ A projection, as an array of strings, that lists the columns to include in the result set.

➤ A "where" clause that defines the rows to be returned. You can include ? wildcards that will be replaced by the values passed in through the selection argument parameter.

➤ An array of selection argument strings that will replace the ?'s in the *where* clause.

➤ A "group by" clause that defines how the resulting rows will be grouped.

➤ A "having" filter that defines which row groups to include if you specified a *group by* clause.

➤ A string that describes the order of the returned rows.

➤ An optional string that defines a limit for the number of returned rows.

Listing 7-4 shows snippets for returning some, and all, of the rows in a particular table.

LISTING 7-4: Querying a database

```java
// Return all rows for columns one and three, no duplicates
String[] result_columns = new String[] {KEY_ID, KEY_COL1, KEY_COL3};

Cursor allRows = myDatabase.query(true, DATABASE_TABLE, result_columns,
                                  null, null, null, null, null, null);

// Return all columns for rows where column 3 equals a set value
// and the rows are ordered by column 5.
String where = KEY_COL3 + "=" + requiredValue;
String order = KEY_COL5;
Cursor myResult = myDatabase.query(DATABASE_TABLE, null, where,
                                   null, null, null, order);
```

Extracting Results from a Cursor

To extract values from a result Cursor, first use the `moveTo<location>` methods described earlier to position the cursor at the correct row of the result Cursor.

Then use the type safe `get<type>` methods (passing in a column index) to return the value stored at the current row for the specified column, as shown in the following snippet.

```java
String columnValue = myResult.getString(columnIndex);
```

Database implementations should publish static constants that provide the column names and/or indexes using easily recognizable variable names based on the column names. These static constants are generally exposed within the database adapter.

Listing 7-5 shows how to iterate over a result Cursor, extracting and summing a column of float values.

LISTING 7-5: Extracting values from a Cursor

```
int GOLD_HOARDED_COLUMN = 2;
Cursor myGold = myDatabase.query("GoldHoards", null, null, null, null, null, null);
float totalHoard = 0f;

// Make sure there is at least one row.
if (myGold.moveToFirst()) {
  // Iterate over each cursor.
  do {
    float hoard = myGold.getFloat(GOLD_HOARDED_COLUMN);
    totalHoard += hoard;
  } while(myGold.moveToNext());
}

float averageHoard = totalHoard / myGold.getCount();
```

Because SQLite database columns are loosely typed, you can cast individual values into valid types as required. For example, values stored as floats can be read back as strings.

Adding, Updating, and Removing Rows

The SQLiteDatabase class exposes insert, delete, and update methods that encapsulate the SQL statements required to perform these actions. Additionally, the execSQL method lets you execute any valid SQL on your database tables should you want to execute these (or any other) operations manually.

Any time you modify the underlying database values, you should call refreshQuery on each Cursor that has a view on the affected table.

Inserting New Rows

To create a new row, construct a ContentValues object and use its put methods to provide a value for each column. Insert the new row by passing the Content Values object into the insert method called on the target database — along with the table name — as shown in Listing 7-6.

LISTING 7-6: Inserting new rows into a database

```
// Create a new row of values to insert.
ContentValues newValues = new ContentValues();

// Assign values for each row.
newValues.put(COLUMN_NAME, newValue);
[ ... Repeat for each column ... ]

// Insert the row into your table
myDatabase.insert(DATABASE_TABLE, null, newValues);
```

Updating a Row

Updating rows is also done with Content Values.

Create a new `ContentValues` object, using the `put` methods to assign new values to each column you want to update. Call `update` on the database, passing in the table name, the updated Content Values object, and a where clause that specifies the row(s) to update as shown in Listing 7-7.

LISTING 7-7: Updating a database row

```
// Define the updated row content.
ContentValues updatedValues = new ContentValues();

// Assign values for each row.
newValues.put(COLUMN_NAME, newValue);
[ ... Repeat for each column ... ]

String where = KEY_ID + "=" + rowId;

// Update the row with the specified index with the new values.
myDatabase.update(DATABASE_TABLE, newValues, where, null);
```

Deleting Rows

To delete a row simply call `delete` on a database, specifying the table name and a *where* clause that returns the rows you want to delete as shown in Listing 7-8.

LISTING 7-8: Deleting a database row

```
myDatabase.delete(DATABASE_TABLE, KEY_ID + "=" + rowId, null);
```

Saving Your To-Do List

In Chapter 6 you enhanced the To-Do List example to persist the Activity's UI state across sessions. That was only half the job; in the following example you'll create a database to save the to-do items.

1. Start by creating a new `ToDoDBAdapter` class. It will be used to manage your database interactions. Create private variables to store the `SQLiteDatabase` object and the Context of the calling application. Add a constructor that takes an application Context, and create static class variables for the name and version of the database, as well as a name for the to-do item table.

    ```
    package com.paad.todolist;

    import android.content.ContentValues;
    import android.content.Context;
    import android.database.Cursor;
    import android.database.SQLException;
    import android.database.sqlite.SQLiteException;
    ```

```
import android.database.sqlite.SQLiteDatabase;
import android.database.sqlite.SQLiteOpenHelper;
import android.util.Log;

public class ToDoDBAdapter {
  private static final String DATABASE_NAME = "todoList.db";
  private static final String DATABASE_TABLE = "todoItems";
  private static final int DATABASE_VERSION = 1;

  private SQLiteDatabase db;
  private final Context context;

  public ToDoDBAdapter(Context _context) {
      this.context = _context;
  }
}
```

2. Create public convenience variables that define the column names: this will make it easier to find the correct columns when extracting values from query result Cursors.

```
public static final String KEY_ID = "_id";
public static final String KEY_TASK = "task";
public static final String KEY_CREATION_DATE = "creation_date";
```

3. Create a new taskDBOpenHelper class within the ToDoDBAdapter that extends SQLiteOpen-Helper. It will be used to simplify version management of your database. Within it, overwrite the onCreate and onUpgrade methods to handle the database creation and upgrade logic.

```
private static class toDoDBOpenHelper extends SQLiteOpenHelper {

  public toDoDBOpenHelper(Context context, String name,
                          CursorFactory factory, int version) {
    super(context, name, factory, version);
  }

  // SQL Statement to create a new database.
  private static final String DATABASE_CREATE = "create table " +
    DATABASE_TABLE + " (" + KEY_ID + " integer primary key autoincrement, " +
    KEY_TASK + " text not null, " + KEY_CREATION_DATE + " long);";

  @Override
  public void onCreate(SQLiteDatabase _db) {
    _db.execSQL(DATABASE_CREATE);
  }

  @Override
  public void onUpgrade(SQLiteDatabase _db, int _oldVersion, int _newVersion) {
    Log.w("TaskDBAdapter", "Upgrading from version " +
                          _oldVersion + " to " +
                          _newVersion + ", which will destroy all old data");

    // Drop the old table.
    _db.execSQL("DROP TABLE IF EXISTS " + DATABASE_TABLE);
    // Create a new one.
    onCreate(_db);
  }
}
```

4. Within the `ToDoDBAdapter` class, add a private variable to store an instance of the `toDoDBOpenHelper` class you just created, and assign it within the constructor.

```
private toDoDBOpenHelper dbHelper;

public ToDoDBAdapter(Context _context) {
  this.context = _context;
  dbHelper = new toDoDBOpenHelper(context, DATABASE_NAME,
                                  null, DATABASE_VERSION);
}
```

5. Still in the adapter class, create `open` and `close` methods that encapsulate the open and close logic for your database. Start with a close method that simply calls close on the database object.

```
public void close() {
  db.close();
}
```

6. The `open` method should use the `toDoDBOpenHelper` class. Call `getWritableDatabase` to let the helper handle database creation and version checking. Wrap the call to try to provide a readable database if a writable instance can't be opened.

```
public void open() throws SQLiteException {
  try {
    db = dbHelper.getWritableDatabase();
  } catch (SQLiteException ex) {
    db = dbHelper.getReadableDatabase();
  }
}
```

7. Add strongly typed methods for adding, removing, and updating items.

```
// Insert a new task
public long insertTask(ToDoItem _task) {
  // Create a new row of values to insert.
  ContentValues newTaskValues = new ContentValues();
  // Assign values for each row.
  newTaskValues.put(KEY_TASK, _task.getTask());
  newTaskValues.put(KEY_CREATION_DATE, _task.getCreated().getTime());
  // Insert the row.
  return db.insert(DATABASE_TABLE, null, newTaskValues);
}

// Remove a task based on its index
public boolean removeTask(long _rowIndex) {
  return db.delete(DATABASE_TABLE, KEY_ID + "=" + _rowIndex, null) > 0;
}

// Update a task
public boolean updateTask(long _rowIndex, String _task) {
  ContentValues newValue = new ContentValues();
  newValue.put(KEY_TASK, _task);
  return db.update(DATABASE_TABLE, newValue, KEY_ID + "=" + _rowIndex, null) > 0;
}
```

8. Now add helper methods to handle queries. Write three methods — one to return all the items, another to return a particular row as a Cursor, and finally one that returns a strongly typed `ToDoItem`.

```
public Cursor getAllToDoItemsCursor() {
  return db.query(DATABASE_TABLE,
                  new String[] { KEY_ID, KEY_TASK, KEY_CREATION_DATE},
                  null, null, null, null, null);
}

public Cursor setCursorToToDoItem(long _rowIndex) throws SQLException {
  Cursor result = db.query(true, DATABASE_TABLE,
                           new String[] {KEY_ID, KEY_TASK},
                           KEY_ID + "=" + _rowIndex, null, null, null,
                           null, null);
  if ((result.getCount() == 0) || !result.moveToFirst()) {
    throw new SQLException("No to do items found for row: " + _rowIndex);
  }
  return result;
}

public ToDoItem getToDoItem(long _rowIndex) throws SQLException {
  Cursor cursor = db.query(true, DATABASE_TABLE,
                           new String[] {KEY_ID, KEY_TASK},
                           KEY_ID + "=" + _rowIndex, null, null, null,
                           null, null);
  if ((cursor.getCount() == 0) || !cursor.moveToFirst()) {
    throw new SQLException("No to do item found for row: " + _rowIndex);
  }

  String task = cursor.getString(TASK_COLUMN);
  long created = cursor.getLong(CREATION_DATE_COLUMN);

  ToDoItem result = new ToDoItem(task, new Date(created));
  return result;
}
```

9. That completes the database helper class. Return the `ToDoList` Activity and update it to persist the to-do list array. Start by updating the Activity's `onCreate` method to create an instance of the `toDoDBAdapter` and open a connection to the database. Also include a call to the `populateTodoList` method stub.

```
ToDoDBAdapter toDoDBAdapter;

public void onCreate(Bundle icicle) {
  [ ... existing onCreate logic ... ]

  toDoDBAdapter = new ToDoDBAdapter(this);

  // Open or create the database
  toDoDBAdapter.open();

  populateTodoList();
}

private void populateTodoList() { }
```

10. Create a new instance variable to store a Cursor over all the to-do items in the database. Update the populateTodoList method to use the toDoDBAdapter instance to query the database, and call startManagingCursor to let the Activity manage the Cursor. It should also make a call to updateArray, a method that will be used to repopulate the to-do list array using the Cursor.

```
Cursor toDoListCursor;

private void populateTodoList() {
  // Get all the todo list items from the database.
  toDoListCursor = toDoDBAdapter. getAllToDoItemsCursor();
  startManagingCursor(toDoListCursor);

  // Update the array.
  updateArray();
}

private void updateArray() { }
```

11. Now implement the updateArray method to update the current to-do list array. Call requery on the result Cursor to ensure it's fully up to date, then clear the array and iterate over the result set. When the update is complete call notifyDataSetChanged on the Array Adapter.

```
private void updateArray() {
  toDoListCursor.requery();

  todoItems.clear();

  if (toDoListCursor.moveToFirst())
    do {
      String task = toDoListCursor.getString(ToDoDBAdapter.TASK_COLUMN);
      long created = toDoListCursor.getLong(ToDoDBAdapter.CREATION_DATE_COLUMN);

      ToDoItem newItem = new ToDoItem(task, new Date(created));
      todoItems.add(0, newItem);
    } while(toDoListCursor.moveToNext());

  aa.notifyDataSetChanged();
}
```

12. To join the pieces together, modify the OnKeyListener assigned to the text entry box in the onCreate method, and update the removeItem method. Both should now use the toDoDBAdapter to add and remove items from the database rather than modifying the to-do list array directly.

> **12.1.** Start with the OnKeyListener, insert the new item into the database, and refresh the array.
> ```
> public void onCreate(Bundle icicle) {
>   super.onCreate(icicle);
>   setContentView(R.layout.main);
>
>   myListView = (ListView)findViewById(R.id.myListView);
>   myEditText = (EditText)findViewById(R.id.myEditText);
> ```

```
                      todoItems = new ArrayList<ToDoItem>();
                      int resID = R.layout.todolist_item;
                      aa = new ToDoItemAdapter(this, resID, todoItems);
                      myListView.setAdapter(aa);

                      myEditText.setOnKeyListener(new OnKeyListener() {
                        public boolean onKey(View v, int keyCode, KeyEvent event) {
                          if (event.getAction() == KeyEvent.ACTION_DOWN)
                            if (keyCode == KeyEvent.KEYCODE_DPAD_CENTER) {
                              ToDoItem newItem = new ToDoItem(myEditText.getText().toString());
                              toDoDBAdapter.insertTask(newItem);
                              updateArray();
                              myEditText.setText("");
                              aa.notifyDataSetChanged();
                              cancelAdd();
                              return true;
                            }
                          return false;
                        }
                      });

                      registerForContextMenu(myListView);
                      restoreUIState();

                      toDoDBAdapter = new ToDoDBAdapter(this);

                      // Open or create the database
                      toDoDBAdapter.open();

                      populateTodoList();
                    }
```

12.2. Then modify the `removeItem` method to remove the item from the database and refresh the array list.

```
              private void removeItem(int _index) {
                // Items are added to the listview in reverse order, so invert the index.
                toDoDBAdapter.removeTask(todoItems.size()-_index);
                updateArray();
              }
```

13. As a final step, override the `onDestroy` method of your activity to close your database connection.

```
@Override
public void onDestroy() {
  super.onDestroy();

  // Close the database
  toDoDBAdapter.close();
}
```

All code snippets in this example are part of the Chapter 7 Todo List *project, available for download at Wrox.com.*

Your to-do items will now be saved between sessions. As a further enhancement you could change the Array Adapter to a Simple Cursor Adapter and have the List View update dynamically with changes to the database.

Because you're using a private database your tasks are not available to other applications. To provide access to your tasks in other applications, expose them using a Content Provider. You'll do exactly that next.

CREATING A NEW CONTENT PROVIDER

To create a new Content Provider, extend the abstract `ContentProvider` class. Override the `onCreate` method to create (and initialize) the underlying data source you're planning to publish with this provider. Sample skeleton code for a new Content Provider is shown in Listing 7-9.

LISTING 7-9: Creating a new Content Provider

```
import android.content.*;
import android.database.Cursor;
import android.net.Uri;
import android.database.SQLException;

public class MyProvider extends ContentProvider {

  @Override
  public boolean onCreate() {
    // TODO Construct the underlying database.
    return true;
  }
}
```

You should expose a public static `CONTENT_URI` property that returns the full URI of this provider. A Content Provider URI must be unique to the provider, so it's good practice to base the URI path on your package name. The general form for defining a Content Provider's URI is:

```
content://com.<CompanyName>.provider.<ApplicationName>/<DataPath>
```

For example:

```
content://com.paad.provider.myapp/elements
```

Content URIs can represent either of two forms. The previous URI represents a request for all values of that type (in this case all elements).

A trailing `/<rownumber>`, as shown in the following code, represents a request for a single record (in this case the fifth element).

```
content://com.paad.provider.myapp/elements/5
```

It's good practice to support access to your provider for both of these forms.

The simplest way to do this is to use a `UriMatcher`. Create and configure a Uri Matcher to parse URIs and determine their forms. This is particularly useful when you're processing Content Resolver requests. Listing 7-10 shows the skeleton code for this pattern.

LISTING 7-10: Using the UriMatcher to handle single or multiple query requests

```java
public class MyProvider extends ContentProvider {

  private static final String myURI = "content://com.paad.provider.myapp/items";
  public static final Uri CONTENT_URI = Uri.parse(myURI);

  @Override
  public boolean onCreate() {
    // TODO: Construct the underlying database.
    return true;
  }

  // Create the constants used to differentiate between the different URI
  // requests.
  private static final int ALLROWS = 1;
  private static final int SINGLE_ROW = 2;

  private static final UriMatcher uriMatcher;

  // Populate the UriMatcher object, where a URI ending in 'items' will
  // correspond to a request for all items, and 'items/[rowID]'
  // represents a single row.
  static {
    uriMatcher = new UriMatcher(UriMatcher.NO_MATCH);
    uriMatcher.addURI("com.paad.provider.myApp", "items", ALLROWS);
    uriMatcher.addURI("com.paad.provider.myApp", "items/#", SINGLE_ROW);
  }
}
```

You can use the same technique to expose alternative URIs for different subsets of data, or different tables within your database, using the same Content Provider.

It's also good practice to expose the name of each of the columns available in your provider, to simplify extracting data from a query-result Cursor.

Exposing Access to the Data Source

Expose queries and transactions on your Content Provider by implementing the delete, insert, update, and query methods.

These methods are the interface used by the Content Resolver to access the underlying data. They allow applications to share data across application boundaries without having to publish different interfaces for each data source.

The most common scenario is to use a Content Provider to expose a private SQLite database, but within these methods you can access any source of data (including files or application instance variables).

Listing 7-11 shows the skeleton code for implementing queries and transactions within a Content Provider. Notice that the UriMatcher object is used to refine the transaction and query requests.

LISTING 7-11: Implementing queries and transactions within a Content Provider

```java
@Override
public Cursor query(Uri uri,
                    String[] projection,
                    String selection,
                    String[] selectionArgs,
                    String sort) {

  // If this is a row query, limit the result set to the passed in row.
  switch (uriMatcher.match(uri)) {
    case SINGLE_ROW :
      // TODO: Modify selection based on row id, where:
      // rowNumber = uri.getPathSegments().get(1));
  }
  return null;
}

@Override
public Uri insert(Uri _uri, ContentValues _initialValues) {
  long rowID = [ ... Add a new item ... ]

  // Return a URI to the newly added item.
  if (rowID > 0) {
    return ContentUris.withAppendedId(CONTENT_URI, rowID);
  }
  throw new SQLException("Failed to add new item into " + _uri);
}

@Override
public int delete(Uri uri, String where, String[] whereArgs) {
  switch (uriMatcher.match(uri)) {
    case ALLROWS:
    case SINGLE_ROW:
    default: throw new IllegalArgumentException("Unsupported URI:" + uri);
  }
}

@Override
public int update(Uri uri, ContentValues values, String where, String[]
whereArgs) {
  switch (uriMatcher.match(uri)) {
    case ALLROWS:
    case SINGLE_ROW:
    default: throw new IllegalArgumentException("Unsupported URI:" + uri);
  }
}
```

The final step in creating a Content Provider is defining the MIME type that identifies the data the provider returns.

Override the `getType` method to return a String that uniquely describes your data type. The type returned should include two forms, one for a single entry and another for all the entries, following these forms:

➤ **Single item** `vnd.<companyname>.cursor.item/<contenttype>`

➤ **All items** `vnd.<companyName>.cursor.dir/<contenttype>`

Listing 7-12 shows how to override the `getType` method to return the correct MIME type based on the URI passed in.

LISTING 7-12: Returning a Content Provider MIME type

```
@Override
public String getType(Uri _uri) {
  switch (uriMatcher.match(_uri)) {
    case ALLROWS: return "vnd.paad.cursor.dir/myprovidercontent";
    case SINGLE_ROW: return "vnd.paad.cursor.item/myprovidercontent";
    default: throw new IllegalArgumentException("Unsupported URI: " + _uri);
  }
}
```

Registering Your Provider

Once you have completed your Content Provider, it must be added to the application manifest.

Use the `authorities` tag to specify its base URI, as shown in the following XML snippet.

```
<provider android:name="MyProvider"
          android:authorities="com.paad.provider.myapp"/>
```

USING CONTENT PROVIDERS

The following sections introduce the `ContentResolver` class, and how to use it to query and transact with a Content Provider.

Introducing Content Resolvers

Each application Context includes a `ContentResolver instance`, accessible using the `getContentResolver` method.

```
ContentResolver cr = getContentResolver();
```

The Content Resolver includes a number of methods to modify and query Content Providers. Each method accepts a URI that specifies the Content Provider to interact with.

A Content Provider's URI is its *authority* as defined by its manifest node. An authority URI is an arbitrary string, so most Content Providers include a public `CONTENT_URI` property to publish that authority.

Content Providers usually expose two forms of URI, one for requests against all data, and another that specifies only a single row. The form for the latter appends /<rowID> to the general CONTENT_URI.

Querying for Content

Content Provider queries take a form very similar to that of database queries. Query results are returned as Cursors over a result set, like databases, in the same way as described previously in this chapter.

You can extract values from the result Cursor using the same techniques described within the database section on "Extracting Results from a Cursor."

Using the query method on the ContentResolver object, pass in:

➤ The URI of the Content Provider data you want to query.

➤ A projection that lists the columns you want to include in the result set.

➤ A *where* clause that defines the rows to be returned. You can include ? wildcards that will be replaced by the values passed into the selection argument parameter.

➤ An array of selection argument strings that will replace the ?s in the *where* clause.

➤ A string that describes the order of the returned rows.

Listing 7-13 shows how to use a Content Resolver to apply a query to a Content Provider:

LISTING 7-13: Querying a Content Provider with a Content Resolver

```
ContentResolver cr = getContentResolver();
// Return all rows
Cursor allRows = cr.query(MyProvider.CONTENT_URI, null, null, null, null);
// Return all columns for rows where column 3 equals a set value
// and the rows are ordered by column 5.
String where = KEY_COL3 + "=" + requiredValue;
String order = KEY_COL5;
Cursor someRows = cr.query(MyProvider.CONTENT_URI,
                          null, where, null, order);
```

You'll see more examples of querying for content later in this chapter when the native Android Content Providers are introduced.

Adding, Updating, and Deleting Content

To perform transactions on Content Providers, use the delete, update, and insert methods on the ContentResolver object.

Inserts

The Content Resolver offers two methods for inserting new records into your Content Provider — insert and bulkInsert. Both methods accept the URI of the item-type you're adding; where the former takes a single new ContentValues object, the latter takes an array.

The simple `insert` method will return a URI to the newly added record, while `bulkInsert` returns the number of successfully added rows.

Listing 7-14 shows how to use the `insert` and `bulkInsert` methods.

LISTING 7-14: Inserting new rows into a Content Provider

```
// Get the Content Resolver
ContentResolver cr = getContentResolver();

// Create a new row of values to insert.
ContentValues newValues = new ContentValues();

// Assign values for each row.
newValues.put(COLUMN_NAME, newValue);
[ ... Repeat for each column ... ]

Uri myRowUri = cr.insert(MyProvider.CONTENT_URI, newValues);

// Create a new row of values to insert.
ContentValues[] valueArray = new ContentValues[5];

// TODO: Create an array of new rows
int count = cr.bulkInsert(MyProvider.CONTENT_URI, valueArray);
```

Deletes

To delete a single record, call delete on the Content Resolver, passing in the URI of the row you want to remove. Alternatively, you can specify a *where* clause to remove multiple rows. Both techniques are shown in Listing 7-15.

LISTING 7-15: Deleting records from a Content Provider

```
ContentResolver cr = getContentResolver();

// Remove a specific row.
cr.delete(myRowUri, null, null);
// Remove the first five rows.
String where = "_id < 5";
cr.delete(MyProvider.CONTENT_URI, where, null);
```

Updates

Content Provider row updates are made with the Content Resolver `update` method. The `update` method takes the URI of the target Content Provider, a `ContentValues` object that maps column names to updated values, and a *where* clause that indicates which rows to update.

When the update is executed, every row matched by the *where* clause is updated using the specified Content Values, and the number of successful updates is returned as shown in Listing 7-16.

LISTING 7-16: Updating records in a Content Provider

```
// Create a new row of values to insert.
ContentValues newValues = new ContentValues();

// Create a replacement map, specifying which columns you want to
// update, and what values to assign to each of them.
newValues.put(COLUMN_NAME, newValue);

// Apply to the first 5 rows.
String where = "_id < 5";

getContentResolver().update(MyProvider.CONTENT_URI, newValues, where, null);
```

Accessing Files in Content Providers

Content Providers represent files as fully qualified URIs rather than as raw file blobs. To insert a file into a Content Provider, or access a saved file, use the Content Resolvers openOutputStream or openInputStream methods respectively. The process for storing a file is shown in Listing 7-17.

LISTING 7-17: Adding files to Content Providers

```
// Insert a new row into your provider, returning its unique URI.
Uri uri = getContentResolver().insert(MyProvider.CONTENT_URI, newValues);

try {
  // Open an output stream using the new row's URI.
  OutputStream outStream = getContentResolver().openOutputStream(uri);
  // Compress your bitmap and save it into your provider.
  sourceBitmap.compress(Bitmap.CompressFormat.JPEG, 50, outStream);
}
catch (FileNotFoundException e) { }
```

CREATING AND USING AN EARTHQUAKE CONTENT PROVIDER

Having created an application that features a list of earthquakes, you have an excellent opportunity to share this information with other applications.

By exposing this data through a Content Provider you make it possible for yourself, and others, to create new applications based on earthquake data without having to duplicate network traffic and the associated XML parsing.

Creating the Content Provider

1. First open the Earthquake project and create a new EarthquakeProvider class that extends ContentProvider. Include stubs to override the onCreate, getType, query, insert, delete, and update methods.

```java
package com.paad.earthquake;

import android.content.*;
import android.database.Cursor;
import android.database.SQLException;
import android.database.sqlite.SQLiteOpenHelper;
import android.database.sqlite.SQLiteDatabase;
import android.database.sqlite.SQLiteQueryBuilder;
import android.net.Uri;
import android.text.TextUtils;
import android.util.Log;

public class EarthquakeProvider extends ContentProvider {

  @Override
  public boolean onCreate() {
  }

  @Override
  public String getType(Uri url) {
  }

  @Override
  public Cursor query(Uri url, String[] projection, String selection,
                      String[] selectionArgs, String sort) {
  }

  @Override
  public Uri insert(Uri _url, ContentValues _initialValues) {
  }

  @Override
  public int delete(Uri url, String where, String[] whereArgs) {
  }

  @Override
  public int update(Uri url, ContentValues values,
                    String where, String[]wArgs) {
  }
}
```

2. Publish the URI for this provider. This URI will be used to access this Content Provider from within other application components via the `ContentResolver`.

```java
public static final Uri CONTENT_URI =
  Uri.parse("content://com.paad.provider.earthquake/earthquakes");
```

3. Create the database that will be used to store the earthquakes. Within the `EarthquakeProvider` create a new `SQLiteDatabase` instance and expose public variables that describe the column names and indexes. Include an extension of `SQLiteOpenHelper` to manage database creation and version control.

```java
// The underlying database
private SQLiteDatabase earthquakeDB;
```

```
private static final String TAG = "EarthquakeProvider";
private static final String DATABASE NAME = "earthquakes.db";
private static final int DATABASE_VERSION = 1;
private static final String EARTHQUAKE_TABLE = "earthquakes";

// Column Names
public static final String KEY_ID = "_id";
public static final String KEY_DATE = "date";
public static final String KEY_DETAILS = "details";
public static final String KEY_LOCATION_LAT = "latitude";
public static final String KEY_LOCATION_LNG = "longitude";
public static final String KEY_MAGNITUDE = "magnitude";
public static final String KEY_LINK = "link";

// Column indexes
public static final int DATE_COLUMN = 1;
public static final int DETAILS_COLUMN = 2;
public static final int LONGITUDE_COLUMN = 3;
public static final int LATITUDE_COLUMN = 4;
public static final int MAGNITUDE_COLUMN = 5;
public static final int LINK_COLUMN = 6;

// Helper class for opening, creating, and managing database version control
private static class earthquakeDatabaseHelper extends SQLiteOpenHelper {
  private static final String DATABASE_CREATE =
    "create table " + EARTHQUAKE_TABLE + " ("
    + KEY_ID + " integer primary key autoincrement, "
    + KEY_DATE + " INTEGER, "
    + KEY_DETAILS + " TEXT, "
    + KEY_LOCATION_LAT + " FLOAT, "
    + KEY_LOCATION_LNG + " FLOAT, "
    + KEY_MAGNITUDE + " FLOAT), "
    + KEY_LINK + " TEXT);";

  public earthquakeDatabaseHelper(Context context, String name,
                                  CursorFactory factory, int version) {
    super(context, name, factory, version);
  }

  @Override
  public void onCreate(SQLiteDatabase db) {
    db.execSQL(DATABASE_CREATE);
  }

  @Override
  public void onUpgrade(SQLiteDatabase db, int oldVersion, int newVersion) {
    Log.w(TAG, "Upgrading database from version " + oldVersion + " to "
               + newVersion + ", which will destroy all old data");

    db.execSQL("DROP TABLE IF EXISTS " + EARTHQUAKE_TABLE);
    onCreate(db);
  }
}
```

4. Create a `UriMatcher` to handle requests using different URIs. Include support for queries and transactions over the entire dataset (`QUAKES`) and a single record matching a quake index value (`QUAKE_ID`).

```
// Create the constants used to differentiate between the different URI
// requests.
private static final int QUAKES = 1;
private static final int QUAKE_ID = 2;

private static final UriMatcher uriMatcher;

// Allocate the UriMatcher object, where a URI ending in 'earthquakes' will
// correspond to a request for all earthquakes, and 'earthquakes' with a
// trailing '/[rowID]' will represent a single earthquake row.
static {
  uriMatcher = new UriMatcher(UriMatcher.NO_MATCH);
  uriMatcher.addURI("com.paad.provider.Earthquake", "earthquakes", QUAKES);
  uriMatcher.addURI("com.paad.provider.Earthquake", "earthquakes/#", QUAKE_ID);
}
```

5. Override the getType method to return a string for each of the URI structures supported.

```
@Override
public String getType(Uri uri) {
  switch (uriMatcher.match(uri)) {
    case QUAKES: return "vnd.android.cursor.dir/vnd.paad.earthquake";
    case QUAKE_ID: return "vnd.android.cursor.item/vnd.paad.earthquake";
    default: throw new IllegalArgumentException("Unsupported URI: " + uri);
  }
}
```

6. Override the provider's onCreate handler to create a new instance of the database helper class, and open a connection to the database.

```
@Override
public boolean onCreate() {
  Context context = getContext();

  earthquakeDatabaseHelper dbHelper = new earthquakeDatabaseHelper(context,
    DATABASE_NAME, null, DATABASE_VERSION);
  earthquakeDB = dbHelper.getWritableDatabase();
  return (earthquakeDB == null) ? false : true;
}
```

7. Implement the query and transaction stubs. Start with the query method, which should decode the request being made based on the URI (either all content or a single row), and apply the selection, projection, and sort-order criteria parameters to the database before returning a result Cursor.

```
@Override
public Cursor query(Uri uri,
                    String[] projection,
                    String selection,
                    String[] selectionArgs,
                    String sort) {

  SQLiteQueryBuilder qb = new SQLiteQueryBuilder();

  qb.setTables(EARTHQUAKE_TABLE);
```

```
  // If this is a row query, limit the result set to the passed in row.
  switch (uriMatcher.match(uri)) {
    case QUAKE_ID: qb.appendWhere(KEY_ID + "=" + uri.getPathSegments().get(1));
                   break;
    default      : break;
  }

  // If no sort order is specified sort by date / time
  String orderBy;
  if (TextUtils.isEmpty(sort)) {
    orderBy = KEY_DATE;
  } else {
    orderBy = sort;
  }

  // Apply the query to the underlying database.
  Cursor c = qb.query(earthquakeDB,
                      projection,
                      selection, selectionArgs,
                      null, null,
                      orderBy);

  // Register the contexts ContentResolver to be notified if
  // the cursor result set changes.
  c.setNotificationUri(getContext().getContentResolver(), uri);

  // Return a cursor to the query result.
  return c;
}
```

8. Now implement methods for inserting, deleting, and updating content. In this case the process is an exercise in mapping Content Provider transaction requests to their database equivalents.

```
@Override
public Uri insert(Uri _uri, ContentValues _initialValues) {
  // Insert the new row, will return the row number if
  // successful.
  long rowID = earthquakeDB.insert(EARTHQUAKE_TABLE, "quake", _initialValues);

  // Return a URI to the newly inserted row on success.
  if (rowID > 0) {
    Uri uri = ContentUris.withAppendedId(CONTENT_URI, rowID);
    getContext().getContentResolver().notifyChange(uri, null);
    return uri;
  }
  throw new SQLException("Failed to insert row into " + _uri);
}

@Override
public int delete(Uri uri, String where, String[] whereArgs) {
  int count;
```

```
switch (uriMatcher.match(uri)) {
  case QUAKES:
    count = earthquakeDB.delete(EARTHQUAKE_TABLE, where, whereArgs);
    break;

  case QUAKE_ID:
    String segment = uri.getPathSegments().get(1);
    count = earthquakeDB.delete(EARTHQUAKE_TABLE, KEY_ID + "="
                              + segment
                              + (!TextUtils.isEmpty(where) ? " AND ("
                              + where + ')' : ""), whereArgs);
    break;

  default: throw new IllegalArgumentException("Unsupported URI: " + uri);
}

getContext().getContentResolver().notifyChange(uri, null);
return count;
}

@Override
public int update(Uri uri, ContentValues values, String where, String[]
whereArgs) {
  int count;
  switch (uriMatcher.match(uri)) {
    case QUAKES: count = earthquakeDB.update(EARTHQUAKE_TABLE, values,
                                            where, whereArgs);
            break;

    case QUAKE_ID: String segment = uri.getPathSegments().get(1);
                count = earthquakeDB.update(EARTHQUAKE_TABLE, values, KEY_ID
                          + "=" + segment
                          + (!TextUtils.isEmpty(where) ? " AND ("
                          + where + ')' : ""), whereArgs);
                break;

    default: throw new IllegalArgumentException("Unknown URI " + uri);
  }

  getContext().getContentResolver().notifyChange(uri, null);
  return count;
}
```

9. With the Content Provider complete, register it in the manifest by creating a new <provider> node within the application tag.

```
<provider android:name=".EarthquakeProvider"
        android:authorities="com.paad.provider.earthquake" />
```

All code snippets in this example are part of the **Chapter 7 Todo List 2** *project, available for download at Wrox.com.*

Using the Provider

You can now update the Earthquake Activity to use the Earthquake Provider to store quakes and use them to populate the List View.

1. Within the `Earthquake` Activity, update the `addNewQuake` method. It should use the application's Content Resolver to insert each new Earthquake into the provider. Move the existing array control logic into a separate `addQuakeToArray` method.

```java
private void addNewQuake(Quake _quake) {
  ContentResolver cr = getContentResolver();
  // Construct a where clause to make sure we don't already have this
  // earthquake in the provider.
  String w = EarthquakeProvider.KEY_DATE + " = " + _quake.getDate().getTime();

  // If the earthquake is new, insert it into the provider.
  if (cr.query(EarthquakeProvider.CONTENT_URI, null, w, null, null).getCount()==0){
    ContentValues values = new ContentValues();

    values.put(EarthquakeProvider.KEY_DATE, _quake.getDate().getTime());
    values.put(EarthquakeProvider.KEY_DETAILS, _quake.getDetails());

    double lat = _quake.getLocation().getLatitude();
    double lng = _quake.getLocation().getLongitude();
    values.put(EarthquakeProvider.KEY_LOCATION_LAT, lat);
    values.put(EarthquakeProvider.KEY_LOCATION_LNG, lng);
    values.put(EarthquakeProvider.KEY_LINK, _quake.getLink());
    values.put(EarthquakeProvider.KEY_MAGNITUDE, _quake.getMagnitude());

    cr.insert(EarthquakeProvider.CONTENT_URI, values);
    earthquakes.add(_quake);

    addQuakeToArray(_quake);
  }
}

private void addQuakeToArray(Quake _quake) {
  if (_quake.getMagnitude() > minimumMagnitude) {
    // Add the new quake to our list of earthquakes.
    earthquakes.add(_quake);

    // Notify the array adapter of a change.
    aa.notifyDataSetChanged();
  }
}
```

2. Create a new `loadQuakesFromProvider` method that loads all the earthquakes from the Earthquake Provider, and inserts them into the Array List using the `addQuakeToArray` method created in Step 1.

```java
private void loadQuakesFromProvider() {
  // Clear the existing earthquake array
  earthquakes.clear();

  ContentResolver cr = getContentResolver();
```

```java
      // Return all the saved earthquakes
      Cursor c = cr.query(EarthquakeProvider.CONTENT_URI, null, null, null, null);

      if (c.moveToFirst())
        {
          do {
            // Extract the quake details.
            Long datems = c.getLong(EarthquakeProvider.DATE_COLUMN);
            String details = c.getString(EarthquakeProvider.DETAILS_COLUMN);
            Float lat = c.getFloat(EarthquakeProvider.LATITUDE_COLUMN);
            Float lng = c.getFloat(EarthquakeProvider.LONGITUDE_COLUMN);
            Double mag = c.getDouble(EarthquakeProvider.MAGNITUDE_COLUMN);
            String link = c.getString(EarthquakeProvider.LINK_COLUMN);

            Location location = new Location("dummy");
            location.setLongitude(lng);
            location.setLatitude(lat);

            Date date = new Date(datems);

            Quake q = new Quake(date, details, location, mag, link);
            addQuakeToArray(q);
          } while(c.moveToNext());
        }
    }
```

3. Call `loadQuakesFromProvider` from `onCreate` to initialize the earthquake List View at start-up.

```java
@Override
public void onCreate(Bundle icicle) {
  super.onCreate(icicle);
  setContentView(R.layout.main);

  earthquakeListView = (ListView)this.findViewById(R.id.earthquakeListView);

  earthquakeListView.setOnItemClickListener(new OnItemClickListener() {

    @Override
    public void onItemClick(AdapterView _av, View _v, int _index, long arg3) {
      selectedQuake = earthquakes.get(_index);
      showDialog(QUAKE_DIALOG);
    }
  });

  int layoutID = android.R.layout.simple_list_item_1;
  aa = new ArrayAdapter<Quake>(this, layoutID , earthquakes);
  earthquakeListView.setAdapter(aa);

  loadQuakesFromProvider();

  updateFromPreferences();
  refreshEarthquakes();
}
```

4. Finally, make a change to the refreshEarthquakes method so that it loads the saved earthquakes from the provider after clearing the array, but before adding any new quakes received.

```
private void refreshEarthquakes() {
  [ ... exiting refreshEarthquakes method ... ]

  // Clear the old earthquakes
  earthquakes.clear();
  loadQuakesFromProvider();

  [ ... exiting refreshEarthquakes method ... ]
}
```

All code snippets in this example are part of the Chapter 7 Todo List 3 *project, available for download at Wrox.com.*

NATIVE ANDROID CONTENT PROVIDERS

Android exposes several native databases using Content Providers.

You can access these Content Providers directly using the techniques described earlier in this chapter. Alternatively, the android.provider package includes classes that can simplify access to many of the most useful providers, including:

➤ Browser   Use the browser Content Provider to read or modify bookmarks, browser history, or web searches.

➤ CallLog   View or update the call history, including both incoming and outgoing calls, together with missed calls and call details like caller ID and call durations.

➤ ContactsContract   Use the Contacts Contract provider to retrieve, modify, or store your contacts' details. This Content Provider replaces the Contact Content Provider.

➤ MediaStore   The Media Store provides centralized, managed access to the multimedia on your device, including audio, video, and images. You can store your own multimedia within the media store and make it globally available, as shown in Chapter 11.

➤ Settings   You can access the device's preferences using the Settings provider. You can view most system settings and modify some of them. More usefully, the android.provider.Settings class includes a collection of Intent actions that can be used to open the appropriate settings screen to let users modify their own settings.

➤ UserDictionary   Access (or add to) the user defined words added to the dictionary for use in IME predictive text input.

You should use these native Content Providers wherever possible to ensure your application integrates seamlessly with other native and third-party applications.

While a detailed description of how to use each of these helpers is beyond the scope of this chapter, the following sections describe how to use the Media Store and Contacts Contract Content Provider.

Using the Media Store Provider

The Android Media Store is a managed repository of audio, video, and image files.

Whenever you add a new multimedia file to the file system, it should also be added to the Media Store. This will expose it to other applications, including the default media player. Chapter 11 shows you how to use the Content Scanner to add new media to the Media Store.

To access media from the Media Store, query the image, video, or audio Content Providers using the techniques described earlier within this chapter. The MediaStore class includes Audio, Video, and Images subclasses, which in turn contain subclasses that are used to provide the column names and content URIs for each media provider.

The Media Store segregates media kept on the internal and external volumes of the host device. Each of the Media Store subclasses provides a URI for either the internally or externally stored media using the forms:

➤   MediaStore.<mediatype>.Media.EXTERNAL_CONTENT_URI

➤   MediaStore.<mediatype>.Media.INTERNAL_CONTENT_URI

Listing 7-18 shows a simple code snippet used to find the song title and album name for each piece of audio stored on the external volume.

Available for download on Wrox.com

LISTING 7-18: Accessing the Media Store Content Provider

```
// Get a cursor over every piece of audio on the external volume.
Cursor cursor =
getContentResolver().query(MediaStore.Audio.Media.EXTERNAL_CONTENT_URI,
                           null, null, null, null);

// Let the activity manage the cursor lifecycle.
startManagingCursor(cursor);

// Use the convenience properties to get the index of the columns
int albumIdx = cursor.getColumnIndexOrThrow(MediaStore.Audio.Media.ALBUM);
int titleIdx = cursor. getColumnIndexOrThrow(MediaStore.Audio.Media.TITLE);

String[] result = new String[cursor.getCount()];
if (cursor.moveToFirst())
  do {
    // Extract the song title.
    String title = cursor.getString(titleIdx);
    // Extract the album name.
    String album = cursor.getString(albumIdx);

    result[cursor.getPosition()] = title + " (" + album + ")";
  } while(cursor.moveToNext());
```

In Chapter 11 you'll learn how to play audio and video resources stored in the Media Store by specifying the URI of a particular multi media item.

Using the Contacts Provider

Access to the contact manager is particularly useful on a communications device. Android does the right thing by exposing all the information available from the contacts database to any application granted the READ_CONTACTS permission.

Android 2.0 (API level 5) introduced the ContactsContract class, which superceded the Contacts class that had previously been used to store and manage the contacts stored on the device.

The new contact Content Provider extends the scope of contacts management in Android by providing an extensible database of contact-related information. This allows users to specify multiple sources for their contact information. More importantly for us, it allows developers to arbitrarily extend the data stored against each contact, or even become an alternative provider for contacts and contact details.

Introducing the Contacts Contract Content Provider

The Contacts Contract Content Provider is an extensible database of contact-related information.

Rather than using a single well-defined table of contact detail columns, the Contacts Contract provider uses a three-tier data model to store data, associate it with a contact, and aggregate it to a single person using the following ContactsContract subclasses:

➤ Data   In the underlying table, each row defines a set of personal data (e.g., phone numbers, e-mail addresses, etc.), separated by MIME type. While there is a predefined set of common column names for each personal data-type (available, along with the appropriate MIME types from subclasses within ContactsContract.CommonDataKinds), this table can be used to store any value.

Importantly, the *kind* of data stored in a particular row is determined by the MIME type specified for that row. A series of generic columns is used to store up to 15 different pieces of data varying by data type.

When adding new data to the Data table, you specify a Raw Contact to which a set of data will be associated.

➤ RawContacts   From Android 2.0 onwards, users can specify multiple contact accounts (e.g., Gmail, Facebook, etc.). Each row in the Raw Contacts table defines an account to which a set of Data values is associated.

➤ Contacts   The Contacts table aggregates rows from Raw Contacts that all describe the same person.

Typically you will use the Data table to add, delete, or modify data stored against an existing contact account, the Raw Contacts table to create and manage accounts, and both the Contact and Data tables to query the database and extract contact details.

Reading Contact Details

You can use the Content Resolver to query any of the three Contact Contracts tables described above using the CONTENT_URI static constant available from each class. Each class includes a number of static properties that describe the column names included in the underlying tables.

In order to access any contact details you need to include the READ_CONTACTS uses-permission in your application manifest:

```
<uses-permission android:name="android.permission.READ_CONTACTS"/>
```

Listing 7-19 queries the Contacts table for a Cursor to every person in the address book, creating an array of strings that holds each contact's name and unique ID.

LISTING 7-19: Accessing the contact Content Provider

Available for download on Wrox.com

```
// Get a cursor over every aggregated contact.
Cursor cursor =
getContentResolver().query(ContactsContract.Contacts.CONTENT_URI,
                           null, null, null, null);

// Let the activity manage the cursor lifecycle.
startManagingCursor(cursor);

// Use the convenience properties to get the index of the columns
int nameIdx =
cursor.getColumnIndexOrThrow(ContactsContract.Contacts.DISPLAY_NAME);
int idIdx = cursor. getColumnIndexOrThrow(ContactsContract.Contacts._ID);

String[] result = new String[cursor.getCount()];
if (cursor.moveToFirst())
  do {
    // Extract the name.
    String name = cursor.getString(nameIdx);
    // Extract the phone number.
    String id = cursor.getString(idIdx);

    result[cursor.getPosition()] = name + " (" + id + ")";
  } while(cursor.moveToNext());

stopManagingCursor(cursor);
```

The ContactsContract.Data Content Provider is used to store all the contact details — such as addresses, phone numbers, and e-mail addresses — making it the best approach when searching for one of these details.

The Data table is also used for finding details for a given contact. In most cases, you will likely be querying for contact details based on a full or partial contact name.

To simplify this lookup, Android provides the ContactsContract.Contacts.CONTENT_FILTER_URI query URI. Append the full or partial name to lookup as an additional path segment to the URI. To extract the associated contact details, find the _ID value from the returned Cursor and use it to create a query on the Data table.

The content of each column with a row in the Data table depends on the MIME type specified for that row. As a result, any query on the Data table must filter the rows by MIME-type in order to meaningfully extract data.

Listing 7-20 shows how to use the contact-detail column names available in the `CommonDataKinds` subclasses to extract the display name and mobile phone number from the Data table for a particular contact.

LISTING 7-20: Finding contact details after finding a contact

```
// Find a contact using a partial name match
Uri lookupUri =
Uri.withAppendedPath(ContactsContract.Contacts.CONTENT_FILTER_URI, "kristy");

Cursor idCursor = getContentResolver().query(lookupUri, null, null, null,
                                              null);

String id = null;
if (idCursor.moveToFirst()) {
  int idIdx = idCursor.getColumnIndexOrThrow(ContactsContract.Contacts._ID);
  id = idCursor.getString(idIdx);
}
idCursor.close();

if (id != null) {
  // Return all the contact details of type PHONE for the contact we found
  String where = ContactsContract.Data.CONTACT_ID + " = " + id + " AND " +
                 ContactsContract.Data.MIMETYPE + " = '" +
                 ContactsContract.CommonDataKinds.Phone.CONTENT_ITEM_TYPE +
                 "'";

Cursor dataCursor =
 getContentResolver().query(ContactsContract.Data.CONTENT_URI,
 null, where, null, null);

  // Use the convenience properties to get the index of the columns
  int nameIdx =
dataCursor.getColumnIndexOrThrow(ContactsContract.Data.DISPLAY_NAME);
  int phoneIdx =

dataCursor.getColumnIndexOrThrow(ContactsContract.CommonDataKinds.Phone.NUMBER)
;

  String[] result = new String[dataCursor.getCount()];
  if (dataCursor.moveToFirst())
    do {
      // Extract the name.
      String name = dataCursor.getString(nameIdx);
      // Extract the phone number.
      String number = dataCursor.getString(phoneIdx);

      result[dataCursor.getPosition()] = name + " (" + number + ")";
    } while(dataCursor.moveToNext());
  dataCursor.close();
}
```

The Contacts sub-class also offers a phone number lookup URI to help find a contact associated with a particular phone number. This query is highly optimized to return fast results for incoming caller-ID notification.

Use `ContactsContract.PhoneLookup.CONTENT_FILTER_URI`, appending the number to find as an additional path segment, as shown in Listing 7-21.

LISTING 7-21: Performing a caller-ID lookup

```
String incomingNumber = "5551234";

Uri lookupUri =
Uri.withAppendedPath(ContactsContract.PhoneLookup.CONTENT_FILTER_URI,
                     incomingNumber);

Cursor idCursor = getContentResolver().query(lookupUri, null, null, null,
                                             null);

if (idCursor.moveToFirst()) {
  int nameIdx =
    idCursor.getColumnIndexOrThrow(ContactsContract.Contacts.DISPLAY_NAME);
  String caller = idCursor.getString(nameIdx);
  Toast.makeText(getApplicationContext(), caller, Toast.LENGTH_LONG).show();
}
idCursor.close();
```

In addition to the static contact details described above, the `ContactsContract.StatusUpdates` table contains social status updates and instant messenger availability. Using this table you can look up or modify the status, and presence, of any contact who has an associated social networking and/or instant messaging account.

Modifying and Augmenting Contact Details

As well as querying the contacts database, you can use these Content Providers to modify, delete, or insert contact records after adding the `WRITE_CONTACTS` uses-permission to your application manifest.

The extensible nature of the Contacts Contract provider allows you to add arbitrary Data table rows to any account stored as a Raw Contact. In practice it is poor form to extend a third-party account with custom data as it will be unable to synchronize your custom data with its online server.

Better practice is to create your own syncing contact adapter that will be aggregated with the other third-party account details.

The process for creating your own syncing contact account adapter is beyond the scope of this book. However, in general terms, by creating a record in the Raw Contacts provider it's possible for you to create a contacts account type for your own custom data.

You can add new records into the contacts Data provider that are associated with your custom contact account. Once added, your custom contact data will be aggregated with the details provided by native and other third-party contact information adapters and made available when developers query the Contacts Content Provider as described in the previous section.

SUMMARY

In this chapter you learned how to add a robust persistence layer to your applications and access native and third-party Content Providers.

Android provides a fully featured SQLite RDBMS to all applications. This small, efficient, and robust database library lets you create relational databases to persist application data. Using Content Providers, you learned how to share private data, particularly databases, across application boundaries.

All database and Content Provider queries are returned as Cursors; you learned how to perform queries and extract data from the resulting Cursor objects.

Along the way you also learned to:

➤   Create new SQLite databases

➤   Interact with databases to insert, update, and delete rows

➤   Use the native Content Providers included with Android to access and manage native data like media and contacts

Now that you have a solid foundation in the fundamentals of Android development, the remainder of this book will investigate some of the more interesting optional Android features.

Starting in the next chapter you'll be introduced to the geographic APIs. Android offers a rich suite of geographical functionality, including location-based services (such as GPS) and forward and reverse geocoding, as well as a fully integrated Google maps implementation. Using Google maps you can create map-based Activities that feature annotations to develop native map-mashups.

8

Maps, Geocoding, and Location-Based Services

WHAT'S IN THIS CHAPTER?

➤ Forward and reverse geocoding

➤ Creating interactive maps with Map Views and Map Activities

➤ Creating and adding Overlays to maps

➤ Finding your location with location-based services

➤ Using proximity alerts

One of the defining features of mobile phones is their portability, so it's not surprising that some of the most enticing Android features are the services that let you find, contextualize, and map physical locations.

You can create map-based Activities using Google Maps as a user interface element. You have full access to the map, which enables you to control display settings, alter the zoom level, and pan the display. Using Overlays you can annotate maps and handle user input to provide map-contextualized information and functionality.

Also covered in this chapter are the *location-based services* (LBS), the services that let you find the device's current location. They include technologies like GPS and Google's cell-based location technology. You can specify which location-sensing technology to use explicitly by name, or implicitly by defining a set of criteria in terms of accuracy, cost, and other requirements.

Maps and location-based services use latitude and longitude to pinpoint geographic locations, but your users are more likely to think in terms of an address. Android provides a Geocoder that supports forward and reverse geocoding. Using the Geocoder you can convert back and forth between latitude/longitude values and real-world addresses.

Used together, the mapping, geocoding, and location-based services provide a powerful toolkit for incorporating your phone's native mobility into your mobile applications.

USING LOCATION-BASED SERVICES

Location-based services is an umbrella term used to describe the different technologies used to find a device's current location. The two main LBS elements are:

➤ **Location Manager**   Provides hooks to the location-based services

➤ **Location Providers**   Each of these represents a different location-finding technology used to determine the device's current location

Using the Location Manager, you can:

➤ Obtain your current location

➤ Track movement

➤ Set proximity alerts for detecting movement into and out of a specified area

➤ Find available Location Providers

CONFIGURING THE EMULATOR TO TEST LOCATION-BASED SERVICES

Location-based services are dependent on device hardware to find the current location. When you are developing and testing with the emulator your hardware is virtualized, and you're likely to stay in pretty much the same location.

To compensate, Android includes hooks that let you emulate Location Providers for testing location-based applications. In this section you'll learn how to mock the position of the supported GPS provider.

> *If you're planning on doing location-based application development and are using the Android Emulator, this section will show you how to create an environment that simulates real hardware and location changes. For the remainder of this chapter it will be assumed that you have used the examples in this section to update the location for the* GPS_PROVIDER *within the emulator, or that you are using a physical device.*

UPDATING LOCATIONS IN EMULATOR LOCATION PROVIDERS

Use the Location Controls available from the DDMS perspective in Eclipse (shown in Figure 8-1) to push location changes directly into the emulator's GPS Location Provider.

Figure 8-1 shows the Manual and KML tabs. Using the Manual tab you can specify particular latitude/longitude pairs. Alternatively, the KML and GPX tabs let you load KML (Keyhole Markup Language) and GPX (GPS Exchange Format) files, respectively. Once these are loaded you can jump to particular waypoints (locations) or play back each location sequentially.

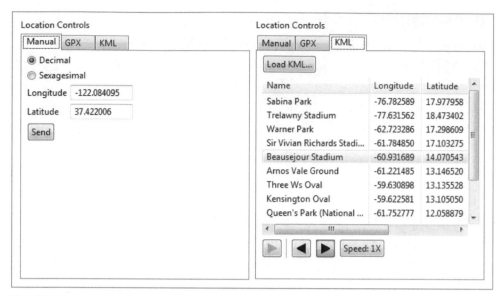

FIGURE 8-1

Most GPS systems record track-files using GPX, while KML is used extensively online to define geographic information. You can handwrite your own KML file or generate one by using Google Earth to find directions between two locations.

All location changes applied using the DDMS Location Controls will be applied to the GPS receiver, which must be enabled and active.

Note that the GPS values returned by `getLastKnownLocation` *will not change unless at least one application has requested location updates.*

SELECTING A LOCATION PROVIDER

Depending on the device, there may be several technologies that Android can use to determine the current location. Each technology, or Location Provider, will offer different capabilities, including differences in power consumption, monetary cost, accuracy, and the ability to determine altitude, speed, or heading information.

To get an instance of a specific provider, call `getProvider`, passing in the name:

```
String providerName = LocationManager.GPS_PROVIDER;
LocationProvider gpsProvider;
gpsProvider = locationManager.getProvider(providerName);
```

This is generally useful only for determining the abilities of a particular provider. Most Location Manager methods require only a provider name to perform location-based services.

Finding the Available Providers

The `LocationManager` class includes static string constants that return the provider name for the two most common Location Providers:

➤   `LocationManager.GPS_PROVIDER`

➤   `LocationManager.NETWORK_PROVIDER`

To get a list of names for all the providers available on the device, call `getProviders`, using a Boolean to indicate if you want all, or only the enabled, providers to be returned:

```
boolean enabledOnly = true;
List<String> providers = locationManager.getProviders(enabledOnly);
```

Finding Location Providers Using Criteria

In most scenarios it's unlikely that you will want to explicitly choose the Location Provider to use. More commonly, you'll specify the requirements that a provider must meet and let Android determine the best technology to use.

Use the `Criteria` class to dictate the requirements of a provider in terms of accuracy (fine or coarse), power use (low, medium, high), financial cost, and the ability to return values for altitude, speed, and bearing.

Listing 8-1 specifies Criteria requiring coarse accuracy, low power consumption, and no need for altitude, bearing, or speed. The provider is permitted to have an associated cost.

Available for download on Wrox.com

LISTING 8-1: Specifying Location Provider Criteria

```
Criteria criteria = new Criteria();
criteria.setAccuracy(Criteria.ACCURACY_COARSE);
criteria.setPowerRequirement(Criteria.POWER_LOW);
criteria.setAltitudeRequired(false);
criteria.setBearingRequired(false);
criteria.setSpeedRequired(false);
criteria.setCostAllowed(true);
```

Having defined the required Criteria, you can use `getBestProvider` to return the best matching Location Provider or `getProviders` to return all the possible matches. The following snippet demonstrates the use of `getBestProvider` to return the best provider for your criteria where the Boolean lets you restrict the result to a currently enabled provider:

```
String bestProvider = locationManager.getBestProvider(criteria, true);
```

If more than one Location Provider matches your criteria, the one with the greatest accuracy is returned. If no Location Providers meet your requirements the criteria are loosened, in the following order, until a provider is found:

➤   Power use

➤   Accuracy

➤   Ability to return bearing, speed, and altitude

The criterion for allowing a device with monetary cost is never implicitly relaxed. If no provider is found, null is returned.

To see a list of names for all the providers that match your criteria you can use getProviders. It accepts a Criteria object and returns a filtered String list of all available Location Providers that match them. As with the getBestProvider call, if no matching providers are found, this call returns null.

```
List<String> matchingProviders = locationManager.getProviders(criteria,
                                                              false);
```

FINDING YOUR LOCATION

The purpose of location-based services is to find the physical location of the device.

Access to the location-based services is handled by the Location Manager system Service. To access the Location Manager, request an instance of the LOCATION_SERVICE using the getSystemService method, as shown in the following snippet:

```
String serviceString = Context.LOCATION_SERVICE;
LocationManager locationManager;
locationManager = (LocationManager)getSystemService(serviceString);
```

Before you can use the Location Manager you need to add one or more uses-permission tags to your manifest to support access to the LBS hardware.

The following snippet shows the *fine* and *coarse* permissions. An application that has been granted fine permission will have coarse permission granted implicitly.

```
<uses-permission android:name="android.permission.ACCESS_FINE_LOCATION"/>
<uses-permission android:name="android.permission.ACCESS_COARSE_LOCATION"/>
```

The GPS provider requires fine permission, while the Network (Cell ID/Wi-Fi) provider requires only coarse.

You can find the last location fix determined by a particular Location Provider using the getLastKnownLocation method, passing in the name of the Location Provider. The following example finds the last location fix taken by the GPS provider:

```
String provider = LocationManager.GPS_PROVIDER;
Location location = locationManager.getLastKnownLocation(provider);
```

Note that getLastKnownLocation *does not ask the Location Provider to update the current position. If the device has not recently updated the current position, this value may not exist or be out of date.*

The Location object returned includes all the position information available from the provider that supplied it. This can include latitude, longitude, bearing, altitude, speed, and the time the location fix was taken. All these properties are available via get methods on the Location object. In some instances additional details will be included in the extras Bundle.

'Where Am I?' Example

The following example — Where Am I? — features a new Activity that finds the device's current location using the GPS Location Provider. You will expand on this example throughout the chapter as you learn new geographic functionality.

 This example assumes that you have enabled the GPS_PROVIDER *Location Provider using the techniques shown previously in this chapter, or that you're running it on a device that supports GPS and has that hardware enabled.*

1. Create a new Where Am I? project with a WhereAmI Activity. This example uses the GPS provider (either mock or real), so modify the manifest file to include the `<uses-permission>` tags for ACCESS_FINE_LOCATION and INTERNET.

```
<?xml version="1.0" encoding="utf-8"?>
<manifest xmlns:android="http://schemas.android.com/apk/res/android"
          package="com.paad.whereami">
  <application
    android:icon="@drawable/icon">
    <activity
      android:name=".WhereAmI"
      android:label="@string/app_name">
      <intent-filter>
        <action android:name="android.intent.action.MAIN" />
        <category android:name="android.intent.category.LAUNCHER" />
      </intent-filter>
    </activity>
  </application>
  <uses-permission
    android:name="android.permission.ACCESS_FINE_LOCATION"
  />
</manifest>
```

2. Modify the main.xml layout resource to include an android:ID attribute for the TextView control so that you can access it from within the Activity.

```
<?xml version="1.0" encoding="utf-8"?>
<LinearLayout
  xmlns:android="http://schemas.android.com/apk/res/android"
  android:orientation="vertical"
  android:layout_width="fill_parent"
  android:layout_height="fill_parent">
  <TextView
    android:id="@+id/myLocationText"
    android:layout_width="fill_parent"
    android:layout_height="wrap_content"
    android:text="@string/hello"
  />
```

```
        <uses permission
            android:name="android.permission.INTERNET
        />
    </LinearLayout>
```

3. Override the `onCreate` method of the `WhereAmI` Activity to get a reference to the Location Manager. Call `getLastKnownLocation` to get the last location fix value, and pass it in to the `updateWithNewLocation` method stub.

```java
package com.paad.whereami;

import android.app.Activity;
import android.content.Context;
import android.location.Location;
import android.location.LocationManager;
import android.os.Bundle;
import android.widget.TextView;

public class WhereAmI extends Activity {
  @Override
  public void onCreate(Bundle savedInstanceState) {
    super.onCreate(savedInstanceState);
    setContentView(R.layout.main);

    LocationManager locationManager;
    String context = Context.LOCATION_SERVICE;
    locationManager = (LocationManager)getSystemService(context);

    String provider = LocationManager.GPS_PROVIDER;
    Location location =
      locationManager.getLastKnownLocation(provider);

    updateWithNewLocation(location);
  }

  private void updateWithNewLocation(Location location) {}
}
```

4. Fill in the `updateWithNewLocation` method to display the passed-in Location in the Text View by extracting the latitude and longitude values.

```java
private void updateWithNewLocation(Location location) {
  String latLongString;
  TextView myLocationText;
  myLocationText = (TextView)findViewById(R.id.myLocationText);
  if (location != null) {
    double lat = location.getLatitude();
    double lng = location.getLongitude();
    latLongString = "Lat:" + lat + "\nLong:" + lng;
  } else {
    latLongString = "No location found";
  }
  myLocationText.setText("Your Current Position is:\n" +
                         latLongString);
}
```

All code snippets in this example are part of the Chapter 8 Where Am I? *project, available for download at Wrox.com.*

5. When running, your Activity should look like Figure 8-2.

FIGURE 8-2

Tracking Movement

Most location-sensitive applications will need to be reactive to user movement. Simply polling the Location Manager will not force it to get new updates from the Location Providers.

Use the `requestLocationUpdates` method to get updates whenever the current location changes, using a `LocationListener`. Location Listeners also contain hooks for changes in a provider's status and availability.

The `requestLocationUpdates` method accepts either a specific Location Provider name or a set of Criteria to determine the provider to use.

To optimize efficiency and minimize cost and power use, you can also specify the minimum time and the minimum distance between location change updates.

Listing 8-2 shows the skeleton code for requesting regular updates based on a minimum time and distance.

LISTING 8-2: Requesting location updates

```java
String provider = LocationManager.GPS_PROVIDER;

int t = 5000; // milliseconds
int distance = 5; // meters

LocationListener myLocationListener = new LocationListener() {

  public void onLocationChanged(Location location) {
    // Update application based on new location.
  }

  public void onProviderDisabled(String provider){
    // Update application if provider disabled.
  }

  public void onProviderEnabled(String provider){
    // Update application if provider enabled.
  }

  public void onStatusChanged(String provider, int status,
                              Bundle extras){
    // Update application if provider hardware status changed.
  }
};

locationManager.requestLocationUpdates(provider, t, distance,
                                       myLocationListener);
```

When the minimum time and distance values are exceeded, the attached Location Listener will execute its `onLocationChanged` event.

You can request multiple location updates pointing to different Location Listeners and using different minimum thresholds. A common design pattern is to create a single listener for your application that broadcasts Intents to notify other components of location changes. This centralizes your listeners and ensures that the Location Provider hardware is used as efficiently as possible.

To stop location updates, call removeUpdates, as shown in the following code. Pass in the Location Listener instance you no longer want to have triggered.

```
locationManager.removeUpdates(myLocationListener);
```

Most GPS hardware incurs significant power cost. To minimize this you should disable updates whenever possible in your application, especially when your application isn't visible and location changes are being used to update an Activity's user interface. You can improve performance further by making the minimum time between updates as long as possible.

Privacy is also a factor when your application tracks the user location. Ensure that your application is using the device location data in a way that respects the user's privacy by:

➤ Only tracking location when necessary for your application

➤ Notifying users of when you are tracking their locations, and how that location information is being used and stored

➤ Allowing users to disable location updates, and respecting the system settings for LBS preferences.

Updating Your Location in 'Where Am I?'

In the following example, the Where Am I? project is enhanced to track your current location by listening for location changes. Updates are restricted to one every two seconds, and only when movement of more than 10 meters has been detected.

Rather than explicitly selecting the GPS provider, in this example you'll create a set of Criteria and let Android choose the best provider available.

1. Start by opening the WhereAmI Activity in the Where Am I? project. Update the onCreate method to find the best Location Provider that features high accuracy and draws as little power as possible.

```
@Override
public void onCreate(Bundle savedInstanceState) {
  super.onCreate(savedInstanceState);
  setContentView(R.layout.main);

  LocationManager locationManager;
  String context = Context.LOCATION_SERVICE;
  locationManager = (LocationManager)getSystemService(context);

  Criteria criteria = new Criteria();
  criteria.setAccuracy(Criteria.ACCURACY_FINE);
```

```
    criteria.setAltitudeRequired(false);
    criteria.setBearingRequired(false);
    criteria.setCostAllowed(true);
    criteria.setPowerRequirement(Criteria.POWER_LOW);
    String provider = locationManager.getBestProvider(criteria, true);

    Location location = locationManager.getLastKnownLocation(provider);
    updateWithNewLocation(location);
  }
```

2.   Create a new `LocationListener` instance variable that fires the existing `updateWithNew`
`Location` method whenever a location change is detected.

```
private final LocationListener locationListener = new LocationListener() {
  public void onLocationChanged(Location location) {
    updateWithNewLocation(location);
  }

  public void onProviderDisabled(String provider){
    updateWithNewLocation(null);
  }

  public void onProviderEnabled(String provider){ }
  public void onStatusChanged(String provider, int status,
                              Bundle extras){ }
};
```

3.   Return to `onCreate` and execute `requestLocationUpdates`, passing in the new Location Listener object. It should listen for location changes every two seconds but fire only when it
detects movement of more than 10 meters.

```
@Override
public void onCreate(Bundle savedInstanceState) {
  super.onCreate(savedInstanceState);
  setContentView(R.layout.main);

  LocationManager locationManager;
  String context = Context.LOCATION_SERVICE;
  locationManager = (LocationManager)getSystemService(context);

  Criteria criteria = new Criteria();
  criteria.setAccuracy(Criteria.ACCURACY_FINE);
  criteria.setAltitudeRequired(false);
  criteria.setBearingRequired(false);
  criteria.setCostAllowed(true);
  criteria.setPowerRequirement(Criteria.POWER_LOW);
  String provider = locationManager.getBestProvider(criteria, true);

  Location location =
    locationManager.getLastKnownLocation(provider);
  updateWithNewLocation(location);

  locationManager.requestLocationUpdates(provider, 2000, 10,
                                         locationListener);
}
```

If you run the application and start changing the device location, you will see the Text View update accordingly.

All code snippets in this example are part of the Chapter 8 Where Am I? *project, available for download at Wrox.com.*

USING PROXIMITY ALERTS

It's often useful to have your applications react when a user moves toward, or away from, a specific location. Proximity alerts let your applications set triggers that are fired when a user moves within or beyond a set distance from a geographic location.

 Internally, Android may use different Location Providers depending on how close you are to the outside edge of your target area. This allows the power use and cost to be minimized when the alert is unlikely to be fired based on your distance from the target area interface.

To set a proximity alert for a given coverage area, select the center point (using longitude and latitude values), a radius around that point, and an expiry time-out for the alert. The alert will fire if the device crosses over that boundary, both when it moves from outside to within the radius, and when it moves from inside to beyond it.

When triggered, proximity alerts fire Intents, most commonly broadcast Intents. To specify the Intent to fire, you use a `PendingIntent`, a class that wraps an Intent in a kind of method pointer, as shown in the following code snippet:

```
Intent intent = new Intent(MY_ACTION);
PendingIntent pendingIntent = PendingIntent.getBroadcast(this, -1, intent, 0);
```

The following example sets a proximity alert that never expires and that is triggered when the device moves within 10 meters of its target:

```
private static String TREASURE_PROXIMITY_ALERT = "com.paad.treasurealert";

private void setProximityAlert() {
  String locService = Context.LOCATION_SERVICE;
  LocationManager locationManager;
  locationManager = (LocationManager)getSystemService(locService);

  double lat = 73.147536;
  double lng = 0.510638;
  float radius = 100f; // meters
  long expiration = -1; // do not expire

  Intent intent = new Intent(TREASURE_PROXIMITY_ALERT);
```

```
PendingIntent proximityIntent = PendingIntent.getBroadcast(this, -1,
                                                           intent,
                                                           0);

locationManager.addProximityAlert(lat, lng, radius,
                                  expiration,
                                  proximityIntent);
}
```

When the Location Manager detects that you have crossed the radius boundary — that is, you have moved either from outside to within or from inside to beyond the specified proximity radius — the packaged Intent will be fired with an `extra` keyed as `LocationManager.KEY_PROXIMITY_ENTERING` set to `true` or `false` accordingly.

To handle proximity alerts you need to create a `BroadcastReceiver`, such as the one shown in Listing 8-3.

LISTING 8-3: Creating a proximity alert Broadcast Receiver

```
public class ProximityIntentReceiver extends BroadcastReceiver {

  @Override
  public void onReceive (Context context, Intent intent) {
    String key = LocationManager.KEY_PROXIMITY_ENTERING;

    Boolean entering = intent.getBooleanExtra(key, false);
    [ ...  perform proximity alert actions ...  ]
  }

}
```

To start listening for proximity alerts, register your receiver:

```
IntentFilter filter = new IntentFilter(TREASURE_PROXIMITY_ALERT);
registerReceiver(new ProximityIntentReceiver(), filter);
```

USING THE GEOCODER

Geocoding lets you translate between street addresses and longitude/latitude map coordinates. This can give you a recognizable context for the locations and coordinates used in location-based services and map-based Activities.

The geocoding lookups are done on the server, so your applications will require you to include an Internet uses-permission in your manifest, as shown here:

```
<uses-permission android:name="android.permission.INTERNET"/>
```

The `Geocoder` class provides access to two geocoding functions:

➤ **Forward geocoding** Finds the latitude and longitude of an address

➤ **Reverse geocoding** Finds the street address for a given latitude and longitude

The results from these calls are contextualized by means of a locale (used to define your usual location and language). The following snippet shows how you set the locale when creating your Geocoder. If you don't specify a locale, it will assume your device's default.

```
Geocoder geocoder = new Geocoder(getApplicationContext(),
                                 Locale.getDefault());
```

Both geocoding functions return a list of Address objects. Each list can contain several possible results, up to a limit you specify when making the call.

Each Address object is populated with as much detail as the Geocoder was able to resolve. This can include the latitude, longitude, phone number, and increasingly granular address details from country to street and house number.

Geocoder lookups are performed synchronously, so they will block the calling thread. For slow data connections, this can lead to a Force Close dialog. In most cases it's good form to move these lookups into a Service or background thread, as demonstrated in Chapter 9.

For clarity and brevity, the calls made in the code samples within this chapter are made on the main application thread.

Reverse Geocoding

Reverse geocoding returns street addresses for physical locations, specified by latitude/longitude pairs. It provides a recognizable context for the locations returned by location-based services.

To perform a reverse lookup, you pass the target latitude and longitude to a Geocoder's getFromLocation method. It will return a list of possible matching addresses. If the Geocoder could not resolve any addresses for the specified coordinate, it will return null.

Listing 8-4 shows how to reverse-geocode your last known location.

LISTING 8-4: Reverse-geocoding your last known location

```
location =
  locationManager.getLastKnownLocation(LocationManager.GPS_PROVIDER);

double latitude = location.getLatitude();
double longitude = location.getLongitude();
List<Address> addresses = null;

Geocoder gc = new Geocoder(this, Locale.getDefault());
try {
  addresses = gc.getFromLocation(latitude, longitude, 10);
} catch (IOException e) {}
```

The accuracy and granularity of reverse lookups are entirely dependent on the quality of data in the geocoding database; as a result, the quality of the results may vary widely between different countries and locales.

Forward Geocoding

Forward geocoding (or just geocoding) determines map coordinates for a given location.

> *What constitutes a valid location varies depending on the locale (geographic area) within which you're searching. Generally, it will include regular street addresses of varying granularity (from country to street name and number), postcodes, train stations, landmarks, and hospitals. As a general guide, valid search terms will be similar to the addresses and locations you can enter into the Google Maps search bar.*

To do a forward-geocoding lookup, call `getFromLocationName` on a Geocoder instance. Pass in the location you want the coordinates for and the maximum number of results to return:

```
List<Address> result = geocoder.getFromLocationName(aStreetAddress, maxResults);
```

The returned list of Addresses can include multiple possible matches for the named location. Each address result will include latitude and longitude and any additional address information available for those coordinates. This is useful to confirm that the correct location was resolved, as well as for providing location specifics in searches for landmarks.

> *As with reverse geocoding, if no matches are found, `null` will be returned. The availability, accuracy, and granularity of geocoding results will depend entirely on the database available for the area you're searching.*

When you're doing forward lookups, the Locale object specified during the creation of the Geocoder object is particularly important. The Locale provides the geographical context for interpreting your search requests, as the same location names can exist in multiple areas. Where possible, consider selecting a regional Locale to help avoid place-name ambiguity.

Additionally, try to use as many address details as possible, as shown in Listing 8-5.

LISTING 8-5: Geocoding an address

```
Geocoder fwdGeocoder = new Geocoder(this, Locale.US);
String streetAddress = "160 Riverside Drive, New York, New York";

List<Address> locations = null;
try {
  locations = fwdGeocoder.getFromLocationName(streetAddress, 10);
} catch (IOException e) {}
```

For even more specific results, use the `getFromLocationName` overload, which lets you restrict your search to within a geographical bounding box.

```
List<Address> locations = null;
try {
  locations = fwdGeocoder.getFromLocationName(streetAddress, 10,
                                              n, e, s, w);
} catch (IOException e) {}
```

This overload is particularly useful in conjunction with a Map View, as you can restrict the search to within the visible map.

Geocoding 'Where Am I?'

Using the Geocoder you can determine the street address at your current location. In this example you'll further extend the Where Am I? project to include and update the current street address whenever the device moves.

Start by modifying the manifest to include the Internet uses-permission:

```
<uses-permission android:name="android.permission.INTERNET"/>
```

Then open the `WhereAmI` Activity. Modify the `updateWithNewLocation` method to instantiate a new Geocoder object, and call the `getFromLocation` method, passing in the newly received location and limiting the results to a single address.

Extract each line in the street address, as well as the locality, postcode, and country, and append this information to an existing Text View string.

```
private void updateWithNewLocation(Location location) {
  String latLongString;
  TextView myLocationText;
  myLocationText = (TextView)findViewById(R.id.myLocationText);

  String addressString = "No address found";

  if (location != null) {
    double lat = location.getLatitude();
    double lng = location.getLongitude();
    latLongString = "Lat:" + lat + "\nLong:" + lng;

    double latitude = location.getLatitude();
    double longitude = location.getLongitude();
    Geocoder gc = new Geocoder(this, Locale.getDefault());
    try {
      List<Address> addresses = gc.getFromLocation(latitude, longitude, 1);
      StringBuilder sb = new StringBuilder();
      if (addresses.size() > 0) {
        Address address = addresses.get(0);

        for (int i = 0; i < address.getMaxAddressLineIndex(); i++)
          sb.append(address.getAddressLine(i)).append("\n");

        sb.append(address.getLocality()).append("\n");
        sb.append(address.getPostalCode()).append("\n");
```

```
            sb.append(address.getCountryName());
        }
        addressString = sb.toString();
    } catch (IOException e) {}
} else {
    latLongString = "No location found";
}
myLocationText.setText("Your Current Position is:\n" +
                        latLongString + "\n" + addressString);
}
```

All code snippets in this example are part of the **Chapter 8 Where Am I?** *project, available for download at Wrox.com.*

If you run the example now, it should appear as shown in Figure 8-3.

FIGURE 8-3

CREATING MAP-BASED ACTIVITIES

The `MapView` provides an ideal user interface option for presenting geographical data.

One of the most intuitive ways of providing context for a physical location or address is to display it on a map. Using a `MapView`, you can create Activities that feature an interactive map.

Map Views support annotation using Overlays and by pinning Views to geographical locations. Map Views offer full programmatic control of the map display, letting you control the zoom, location, and display modes — including the option to display satellite, street, and traffic views.

In the following sections you'll see how to use Overlays and the `MapController` to create dynamic map-based Activities. Unlike online mashups, your map Activities will run natively on the device, enabling you to leverage its hardware and mobility to provide a more customized and personal user experience.

Introducing Map View and Map Activity

This section introduces several classes used to support Android maps:

➤ `MapView` is the Map View control.

➤ `MapActivity` is the base class you extend to create a new Activity that can include a Map View. The `MapActivity` class handles the application life cycle and background service management required for displaying maps. As a result you can use Map Views only within `MapActivity`-derived Activities.

➤ `Overlay` is the class used to annotate your maps. Using Overlays, you can use a Canvas to draw onto any number of layers that are displayed on top of a Map View.

➤ `MapController` is used to control the map, enabling you to set the center location and zoom levels.

➤ `MyLocationOverlay` is a special Overlay that can be used to display the current position and orientation of the device.

➤ `ItemizedOverlays` and `OverlayItems` are used together to let you create a layer of map markers, displayed using Drawables and associated text.

Getting Your Maps API Key

In order to use a Map View in your application you must first obtain an API key from the Android developer web site at `http://code.google.com/android/maps-api-signup.html`.

Without an API key the Map View will not download the tiles used to display the map.

To obtain a key you need to specify the MD5 fingerprint of the certificate used to sign your application. Generally, you will sign your application using two certificates — a default debug certificate and a production certificate. The following sections explain how to obtain the MD5 fingerprint of each signing certificate used for your application.

Getting Your Development/Debugging MD5 Fingerprint

If you are using Eclipse with the ADT plug-in to debug your applications, they will be signed with the default debug certificate. To view map tiles while debugging you will need to obtain a Maps API key registered via the MD5 fingerprint of the debug certificate.

You can find the location of your keystore in the Default Debug Keystore textbox after selecting Windows ➪ Preferences ➪ Android ➪ build. Typically the debug keystore is stored in the following platform-specific locations:

➤ **Windows Vista**   \users\<username>\.android\debug.keystore

➤ **Windows XP**   \Documents and Settings\<username>\.android\debug.keystore

➤ **Linux or Mac**   ~/.android/debug.keystore

 Each computer you use for development will have a different debug certificate and MD5 value. If you want to debug and develop map applications across multiple computers you will need to generate and use multiple API keys.

To find the MD5 fingerprint of your debug certificate use the keytool command from your Java installation, as shown here:

```
keytool -list -alias androiddebugkey -keystore <keystore_location>.keystore
-storepass android -keypass android
```

Getting your Production/Release MD5 Fingerprint

Before you compile and sign your application for release, you will need to obtain a map API key using the MD5 fingerprint for your release certificate.

Find the MD5 fingerprint using the keytool command and specifying the -list parameter and the keystore and alias you will use to sign your release application.

```
keytool -list -alias my-android-alias -keystore my-android-keystore
```

You will be prompted for your keystore and alias passwords before the MD5 fingerprint is returned.

Creating a Map-Based Activity

To use maps in your applications you need to extend MapActivity. The layout for the new class must then include a MapView to display a Google Maps interface element. The Android maps library is not a standard Android package; as an optional API, it must be explicitly included in the application manifest before it can be used. Add the library to your manifest using a uses-library tag within the application node, as shown in the following XML snippet:

```
<uses-library android:name="com.google.android.maps"/>
```

The maps package as described here is not part of the standard Android open-source project. It is provided within the Android SDK by Google and is available on most Android devices. However, be aware that because it is a nonstandard package, an Android device may not feature this particular library.

Google Maps downloads the map tiles on demand; as a result, it implicitly requires permission to use the Internet. To see map tiles in your Map View you need to add a <uses-permission> tag to your application manifest for INTERNET, as shown here:

```
<uses-permission android:name="android.permission.INTERNET"/>
```

Once you've added the library and configured your permission, you're ready to create your new map-based Activity.

MapView controls can be used only within an Activity that extends MapActivity. Override the onCreate method to lay out the screen that includes a MapView, and override isRouteDisplayed to return true if the Activity will be displaying routing information (such as traffic directions).

Listing 8-6 shows the framework for creating a new map-based Activity.

LISTING 8-6: A skeleton Map Activity

```
import com.google.android.maps.MapActivity;
import com.google.android.maps.MapController;
import com.google.android.maps.MapView;
import android.os.Bundle;
```

```
public class MyMapActivity extends MapActivity {
  private MapView mapView;

  private MapController mapController;

  @Override
  public void onCreate(Bundle savedInstanceState) {
    super.onCreate(savedInstanceState);
    setContentView(R.layout.map_layout);
    mapView = (MapView)findViewById(R.id.map_view);
  }

  @Override
  protected boolean isRouteDisplayed() {
    // IMPORTANT: This method must return true if your Activity
    // is displaying driving directions. Otherwise return false.
    return false;
  }
}
```

The corresponding layout file used to include the MapView is shown in Listing 8-7. Note that you need to include your map API key (as described earlier in this chapter) to use a Map View in your application.

LISTING 8-7: A Map Activity layout resource

```xml
<?xml version="1.0" encoding="utf-8"?>
<LinearLayout
  xmlns:android="http://schemas.android.com/apk/res/android"
  android:orientation="vertical"
  android:layout_width="fill_parent"
  android:layout_height="fill_parent">
  <com.google.android.maps.MapView
    android:id="@+id/map_view"
    android:layout_width="fill_parent"
    android:layout_height="fill_parent"
    android:enabled="true"
    android:clickable="true"
    android:apiKey="mymapapikey"
  />
</LinearLayout>
```

Figure 8-4 shows an example of a basic map-based Activity.

 *Android currently supports only **one** MapActivity and **one** MapView per application.*

Configuring and Using Map Views

The MapView class displays the Google map; it includes several options for specifying how the map is displayed.

By default the Map View will show the standard street map, as shown in Figure 8-4. In addition, you can choose to display a satellite view, StreetView, and expected traffic, as shown in the following code snippet:

```
mapView.setSatellite(true);
mapView.setStreetView(true);
mapView.setTraffic(true);
```

You can also query the Map View to find the current and maximum available zoom levels, as well as the center point and currently visible longitude and latitude span (in decimal degrees). The latter (shown in the following snippet) is particularly useful for performing geographically limited Geocoder lookups:

```
int maxZoom = mapView.getMaxZoomLevel();
GeoPoint center = mapView.getMapCenter();
int latSpan = mapView.getLatitudeSpan();
int longSpan = mapView.getLongitudeSpan();
```

You can also optionally display the standard map zoom controls using the setBuiltInZoomControls method.

```
mapView.setBuiltInZoomControls(true);
```

Using the Map Controller

Use the Map Controller to pan and zoom a MapView. You can get a reference to a MapView's controller using getController.

FIGURE 8-4

```
MapController mapController = myMapView.getController();
```

Map locations in the Android mapping classes are represented by GeoPoint objects, which contain latitude and longitude measured in microdegrees. To convert degrees to microdegrees, multiply by 1E6 (1,000,000).

Before you can use the latitude and longitude values stored in the Location objects returned by location-based services, you'll need to convert them to microdegrees and store them as GeoPoints.

```
Double lat = 37.422006*1E6;
Double lng = -122.084095*1E6;
GeoPoint point = new GeoPoint(lat.intValue(), lng.intValue());
```

Re-center and zoom the Map View using the setCenter and setZoom methods available on the Map View's MapController.

```
mapController.setCenter(point);
mapController.setZoom(1);
```

When you are using setZoom, 1 represents the widest (or most distant) zoom and 21 the tightest (nearest) view.

The actual zoom level available for a specific location depends on the resolution of Google's maps and imagery for that area. You can also use `zoomIn` and `zoomOut` to change the zoom level by one step.

The `setCenter` method will "jump" to a new location; to show a smooth transition, use `animateTo`.

```
mapController.animateTo(point);
```

Mapping 'Where Am I?'

In the following code example the Where Am I? project is extended again. This time you'll add mapping functionality by transforming it into a Map Activity. As the device location changes, the map will automatically re-center on the new position.

1. Start by adding the `<uses-permission>` tag for Internet access to the application manifest. Also import the Android maps library within the `application` tag.

```
<?xml version="1.0" encoding="utf-8"?>
<manifest xmlns:android="http://schemas.android.com/apk/res/android"
          package="com.paad.whereami">
  <application
    android:icon="@drawable/icon">
    <uses-library android:name="com.google.android.maps"/>
    <activity
      android:name=".WhereAmI"
      android:label="@string/app_name">
      <intent-filter>
        <action android:name="android.intent.action.MAIN" />
        <category android:name="android.intent.category.LAUNCHER" />
      </intent-filter>
    </activity>
  </application>
  <uses-permission android:name="android.permission.INTERNET"/>
  <uses-permission
android:name="android.permission.ACCESS_FINE_LOCATION"/>
</manifest>
```

2. Change the inheritance of `WhereAmI` to descend from `MapActivity` instead of `Activity`. You'll also need to include an override for the `isRouteDisplayed` method. Because this Activity won't show routing directions, you can return `false`.

```
public class WhereAmI extends MapActivity {
  @Override
  protected boolean isRouteDisplayed() {
    return false;
  }
  [ ...  existing Activity code ...  ]
}
```

3. Modify the main.xml layout resource to include a `MapView` using the fully qualified class name. You will need to obtain a maps API key to include within the `android:apikey` attribute of the `com.android.MapView` node.

```
<?xml version="1.0" encoding="utf-8"?>
<LinearLayout
```

```
  xmlns:android="http://schemas.android.com/apk/res/android"
  android:orientation="vertical"
  android:layout_width="fill_parent"
  android:layout_height="fill_parent">
  <TextView
    android:id="@+id/myLocationText"
    android:layout_width="fill_parent"
    android:layout_height="wrap_content"
    android:text="@string/hello"
  />
  <com.google.android.maps.MapView
    android:id="@+id/myMapView"
    android:layout_width="fill_parent"
    android:layout_height="fill_parent"
    android:enabled="true"
    android:clickable="true"
    android:apiKey="myMapKey"
  />
</LinearLayout>
```

FIGURE 8-5

4. Running the application now should display the original geolocation text with a `MapView` beneath it, as shown in Figure 8-5.

5. Configure the Map View and store a reference to its `MapController` as an instance variable. Set up the Map View display options to show the satellite and `StreetView` and zoom in for a closer look.

```
MapController mapController;

@Override
public void onCreate(Bundle savedInstance
State) {
  super.onCreate(savedInstanceState);
  setContentView(R.layout.main);

  // Get a reference to the MapView
  MapView myMapView = (MapView)findViewById(R.id.myMapView);
  // Get the Map View's controller
  mapController = myMapView.getController();

  // Configure the map display options
  myMapView.setSatellite(true);
  myMapView.setStreetView(true);
  myMapView.displayZoomControls(false);

  // Zoom in
  mapController.setZoom(17);

  LocationManager locationManager;
  String context = Context.LOCATION_SERVICE;
  locationManager = (LocationManager)getSystemService(context);

  Criteria criteria = new Criteria();
```

```
        criteria.setAccuracy(Criteria.ACCURACY_FINE);
        criteria.setAltitudeRequired(false);
        criteria.setBearingRequired(false);
        criteria.setCostAllowed(true);
        criteria.setPowerRequirement(Criteria.POWER_LOW);
        String provider = locationManager.getBestProvider(criteria, true);

        Location location =
          locationManager.getLastKnownLocation(provider);

        updateWithNewLocation(location);

        locationManager.requestLocationUpdates(provider, 2000, 10,
                                                locationListener);
      }
```

6. The final step is to modify the `updateWithNewLocation` method to re-center the map on the current location using the Map Controller.

```
    private void updateWithNewLocation(Location location) {
      String latLongString;
      TextView myLocationText;
      myLocationText = (TextView)findViewById(R.id.myLocationText);
      String addressString = "No address found";

      if (location != null) {
        // Update the map location.
        Double geoLat = location.getLatitude()*1E6;
        Double geoLng = location.getLongitude()*1E6;
        GeoPoint point = new GeoPoint(geoLat.intValue(),
                                      geoLng.intValue());

        mapController.animateTo(point);

        double lat = location.getLatitude();
        double lng = location.getLongitude();
        latLongString = "Lat:" + lat + "\nLong:" + lng;

        double latitude = location.getLatitude();
        double longitude = location.getLongitude();

        Geocoder gc = new Geocoder(this, Locale.getDefault());
        try {
          List<Address> addresses = gc.getFromLocation(latitude, longitude, 1);
          StringBuilder sb = new StringBuilder();
          if (addresses.size() > 0) {
            Address address = addresses.get(0);

            for (int i = 0; i < address.getMaxAddressLineIndex(); i++)
              sb.append(address.getAddressLine(i)).append("\n");

            sb.append(address.getLocality()).append("\n");
            sb.append(address.getPostalCode()).append("\n");
            sb.append(address.getCountryName());
          }
```

```
            addressString = sb.toString();
          } catch (IOException e) {}
        } else {
          latLongString = "No location found";
        }
        myLocationText.setText("Your Current Position is:\n" +
                                latLongString + "\n" + addressString);
    }
```

All code snippets in this example are part of the Chapter 8 Where Am I? *project, available for download at Wrox.com.*

Creating and Using Overlays

Overlays enable you to add annotations and click handling to `MapViews`. Each Overlay lets you draw 2D primitives, including text, lines, images, and shapes, directly onto a canvas, which is then overlaid onto a Map View.

You can add several Overlays onto a single map. All the Overlays assigned to a Map View are added as layers, with newer layers potentially obscuring older ones. User clicks are passed through the stack until they are either handled by an Overlay or registered as clicks on the Map View itself.

Creating New Overlays

Each Overlay is a canvas with a transparent background that is layered onto a Map View and used to handle map touch events.

To add a new Overlay create a new class that extends `Overlay`. Override the `draw` method to draw the annotations you want to add, and override `onTap` to react to user clicks (generally made when the user taps an annotation added by this Overlay).

Listing 8-8 shows the framework for creating a new Overlay that can draw annotations and handle user clicks.

LISTING 8-8: Creating a new Overlay

```
import android.graphics.Canvas;
import com.google.android.maps.MapView;
import com.google.android.maps.Overlay;

public class MyOverlay extends Overlay {
  @Override
  public void draw(Canvas canvas, MapView mapView, boolean shadow) {
    if (shadow == false) {
      [ ...  Draw annotations on main map layer ...  ]
    }
    else {
      [ ...  Draw annotations on the shadow layer ...  ]
    }
  }

  @Override
  public boolean onTap(GeoPoint point, MapView mapView) {
```

```
      // Return true if screen tap is handled by this overlay
      return false;
    }
  }
```

Introducing Projections

The canvas used to draw Overlay annotations is a standard Canvas that represents the visible display surface. To add annotations based on physical locations, you need to convert between geographical points and screen coordinates.

The Projection class lets you translate between latitude/longitude coordinates (stored as GeoPoints) and x/y screen pixel coordinates (stored as Points).

A map's Projection may change between subsequent calls to draw, so it's good practice to get a new instance each time. Get a Map View's Projection by calling getProjection.

```
      Projection projection = mapView.getProjection();
```

Use the fromPixel and toPixel methods to translate from GeoPoints to Points and vice versa.

For performance reasons, you can best use the toPixel Projection method by passing a Point object to be populated (rather than relying on the return value), as shown in Listing 8-9.

LISTING 8-9: Using map projections

```
Point myPoint = new Point();
// To screen coordinates
projection.toPixels(geoPoint, myPoint);
// To GeoPoint location coordinates
projection.fromPixels(myPoint.x, myPoint.y);
```

Drawing on the Overlay Canvas

You handle Canvas drawing for Overlays by overriding the Overlay's draw handler.

The passed-in Canvas is the surface on which you draw your annotations, using the same techniques introduced in Chapter 4 for creating custom user interfaces for Views. The Canvas object includes the methods for drawing 2D primitives on your map (including lines, text, shapes, ellipses, images, etc.). Use Paint objects to define the style and color.

Listing 8-10 uses a Projection to draw text and an ellipse at a given location.

LISTING 8-10: A simple Map Overlay

```
@Override
public void draw(Canvas canvas, MapView mapView, boolean shadow) {
    Projection projection = mapView.getProjection();

    Double lat = -31.960906*1E6;
```

continues

LISTING 8-10 *(continued)*

```
Double lng = 115.844822*1E6;
GeoPoint geoPoint = new GeoPoint(lat.intValue(), lng.intValue());

if (shadow == false) {
  Point myPoint = new Point();
  projection.toPixels(geoPoint, myPoint);

  // Create and setup your paint brush
  Paint paint = new Paint();
  paint.setARGB(250, 255, 0, 0);
  paint.setAntiAlias(true);
  paint.setFakeBoldText(true);

  // Create the circle
  int rad = 5;
  RectF oval = new RectF(myPoint.x-rad, myPoint.y-rad,
                         myPoint.x+rad, myPoint.y+rad);

  // Draw on the canvas
  canvas.drawOval(oval, paint);
  canvas.drawText("Red Circle", myPoint.x+rad, myPoint.y, paint);
  }
}
```

 For more advanced drawing features see Chapter 11, where gradients, strokes, and filters are introduced.

Handling Map Tap Events

To handle map taps (user clicks), override the `onTap` event handler within the Overlay extension class.

The `onTap` handler receives two parameters:

➤   A `GeoPoint` that contains the latitude/longitude of the map location tapped

➤   The `MapView` that was tapped to trigger this event

When you are overriding `onTap`, the method should return `true` if it has handled a particular tap and `false` to let another Overlay handle it, as shown in Listing 8-11.

LISTING 8-11: Handling map-tap events

```
@Override
public boolean onTap(GeoPoint point, MapView mapView) {
  // Perform hit test to see if this overlay is handling the click
  if ([ ...  perform hit test ...  ]) {
    [ ...  execute on tap functionality ...  ]
    return true;
  }
```

```
        // If not handled return false
        return false;
    }
```

Adding and Removing Overlays

Each `MapView` contains a list of Overlays currently displayed. You can get a reference to this list by calling `getOverlays`, as shown in the following snippet:

```
List<Overlay> overlays = mapView.getOverlays();
```

Adding and removing items from the list is thread-safe and synchronized, so you can modify and query the list safely. You should still iterate over the list within a synchronization block synchronized on the List.

To add an Overlay onto a Map View, create a new instance of the Overlay and add it to the list, as shown in the following snippet.

```
List<Overlay> overlays = mapView.getOverlays();
MyOverlay myOverlay = new MyOverlay();
overlays.add(myOverlay);
mapView.postInvalidate();
```

The added Overlay will be displayed the next time the Map View is redrawn, so it's usually a good practice to call `postInvalidate` after you modify the list to update the changes on the map display.

Annotating 'Where Am I?'

This final modification to "Where Am I?" creates and adds a new Overlay that displays a white circle at the device's current position.

1. Start by creating a new `MyPositionOverlay` Overlay class in the Where Am I? project.

```
package com.paad.whereami;

import android.graphics.Canvas;
import android.graphics.Paint;
import android.graphics.Point;
import android.graphics.RectF;
import android.location.Location;
import com.google.android.maps.GeoPoint;
import com.google.android.maps.MapView;
import com.google.android.maps.Overlay;
import com.google.android.maps.Projection;

public class MyPositionOverlay extends Overlay {

  @Override
  public void draw(Canvas canvas, MapView mapView, boolean shadow) {
  }

  @Override
  public boolean onTap(GeoPoint point, MapView mapView) {
```

```
      return false;
    }
}
```

2. Create a new instance variable to store the current Location, and add setter and getter methods for it.

```
Location location;

public Location getLocation() {
  return location;
}
public void setLocation(Location location) {
  this.location = location;
}
```

3. Override the `draw` method to add a small white circle at the current location.

```
private final int mRadius = 5;

@Override
public void draw(Canvas canvas, MapView mapView, boolean shadow) {
  Projection projection = mapView.getProjection();

  if (shadow == false) {
    // Get the current location
    Double latitude = location.getLatitude()*1E6;
    Double longitude = location.getLongitude()*1E6;
    GeoPoint geoPoint;
    geoPoint = new
      GeoPoint(latitude.intValue(),longitude.intValue());

    // Convert the location to screen pixels
    Point point = new Point();
    projection.toPixels(geoPoint, point);

    RectF oval = new RectF(point.x - mRadius, point.y - mRadius,
                           point.x + mRadius, point.y + mRadius);

    // Setup the paint
    Paint paint = new Paint();
    paint.setARGB(250, 255, 255, 255);
    paint.setAntiAlias(true);
    paint.setFakeBoldText(true);

    Paint backPaint = new Paint();
    backPaint.setARGB(175, 50, 50, 50);
    backPaint.setAntiAlias(true);

    RectF backRect = new RectF(point.x + 2 + mRadius,
                               point.y - 3*mRadius,
                               point.x + 65, point.y + mRadius);

    // Draw the marker
    canvas.drawOval(oval, paint);
    canvas.drawRoundRect(backRect, 5, 5, backPaint);
    canvas.drawText("Here I Am",
```

```
                            point.x + 2*mRadius, point.y,
                            paint);
      }
      super.draw(canvas, mapView, shadow);
}
```

4. Now open the `WhereAmI` Activity class, and add the `MyPositionOverlay` to the `MapView`.

Start by adding a new instance variable to store the `MyPositionOverlay`, then override `onCreate` to create a new instance of the class, and add it to the `MapView`'s Overlay list.

```
MyPositionOverlay positionOverlay;

@Override
public void onCreate(Bundle savedInstanceState) {
  super.onCreate(savedInstanceState);
  setContentView(R.layout.main);

  MapView myMapView = (MapView)findViewById(R.id.myMapView);
  mapController = myMapView.getController();

  myMapView.setSatellite(true);
  myMapView.setStreetView(true);
  myMapView.displayZoomControls(false);

  mapController.setZoom(17);

  // Add the MyPositionOverlay
  positionOverlay = new MyPositionOverlay();
  List<Overlay> overlays = myMapView.getOverlays();
  overlays.add(positionOverlay);

  LocationManager locationManager;
  String context = Context.LOCATION_SERVICE;
  locationManager = (LocationManager)getSystemService(context);

  Criteria criteria = new Criteria();
  criteria.setAccuracy(Criteria.ACCURACY_FINE);
  criteria.setAltitudeRequired(false);
  criteria.setBearingRequired(false);
  criteria.setCostAllowed(true);
  criteria.setPowerRequirement(Criteria.POWER_LOW);
  String provider = locationManager.getBestProvider(criteria, true);

  Location location = locationManager.getLastKnownLocation(provider);

  updateWithNewLocation(location);

  locationManager.requestLocationUpdates(provider, 2000, 10,
                                         locationListener);
}
```

5. Finally, update the `updateWithNewLocation` method to pass the new location to the Overlay.

```
private void updateWithNewLocation(Location location) {
  String latLongString;
  TextView myLocationText;
```

```
myLocationText = (TextView)findViewById(R.id.myLocationText);
String addressString = "No address found";

if (location != null) {
  // Update my location marker
  positionOverlay.setLocation(location);

  // Update the map location.
  Double geoLat = location.getLatitude()*1E6;
  Double geoLng = location.getLongitude()*1E6;
  GeoPoint point = new GeoPoint(geoLat.intValue(),
                                geoLng.intValue());

  mapController.animateTo(point);

  double lat = location.getLatitude();
  double lng = location.getLongitude();
  latLongString = "Lat:" + lat + "\nLong:" + lng;

  double latitude = location.getLatitude();
  double longitude = location.getLongitude();

  Geocoder gc = new Geocoder(this, Locale.getDefault());
  try {
    List<Address> addresses = gc.getFromLocation(latitude,
                                                 longitude, 1);
    StringBuilder sb = new StringBuilder();
    if (addresses.size() > 0) {
      Address address = addresses.get(0);

      for (int i = 0; i < address.getMaxAddressLineIndex(); i++)
        sb.append(address.getAddressLine(i)).append("\n");

      sb.append(address.getLocality()).append("\n");
      sb.append(address.getPostalCode()).append("\n");
      sb.append(address.getCountryName());
    }
    addressString = sb.toString();
  } catch (IOException e) {}
} else {
  latLongString = "No location found";
}
myLocationText.setText("Your Current Position is:\n" +
                       latLongString + "\n" + addressString);
}
```

All code snippets in this example are part of the Chapter 8 Where Am I? *project, available for download at Wrox.com.*

When run, your application will display your current device location with a white circle and supporting text, as shown in Figure 8-6.

It's worth noting that this is not the preferred technique for displaying your current location on a map. This functionality is implemented natively by Android through the MyLocationOverlay *class. If you want to display and follow your current location, you should consider using (or extending) this class, as shown in the next section, instead of implementing it manually as shown here.*

Introducing My Location Overlay

The MyLocationOverlay class is a special Overlay designed to show your current location and orientation on a MapView.

To use My Location Overlay you need to create a new instance, passing in the application Context and target Map View, and add it to the MapView's Overlay list, as shown here:

```
List<Overlay> overlays =
  mapView.getOverlays();
MyLocationOverlay myLocationOverlay =
  new MyLocationOverlay(this, mapView);
overlays.add(myLocationOverlay);
```

You can use My Location Overlay to display both your current location (represented as a flashing blue marker) and your current orientation (shown as a compass on the map display).

The following snippet shows how to enable both the compass and marker; in this instance the Map View's MapController is also passed in, allowing the Overlay to automatically scroll the map if the marker moves offscreen.

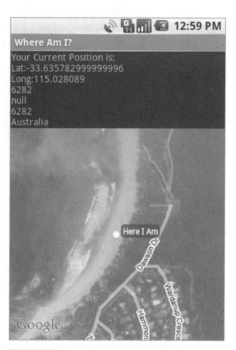

FIGURE 8-6

```
myLocationOverlay.enableCompass();
myLocationOverlay.enableMyLocation(mapView.getMapController());
```

Introducing Itemized Overlays and Overlay Items

OverlayItems are used to supply simple maker functionality to your Map Views via the ItemizedOverlay class.

ItemizedOverlays provide a convenient shortcut for adding markers to a map, letting you assign a marker image and associated text to a particular geographical position. The ItemizedOverlay instance handles the drawing, placement, click handling, focus control, and layout optimization of each OverlayItem marker for you.

To add an `ItemizedOverlay` marker layer to your map, start by creating a new class that extends `ItemizedOverlay<OverlayItem>`, as shown in Listing 8-12.

 `ItemizedOverlay` *is a generic class that lets you create extensions based on any* `OverlayItem`-*derived subclass.*

Within the constructor you need to call through to the superclass after defining the bounds for your default marker. You must then call `populate` to trigger the creation of each `OverlayItem`; `populate` must be called whenever the data used to create the items changes.

Within the implementation, override `size` to return the number of markers to display and `createItem` to create a new item based on the index of each marker.

LISTING 8-12: Creating a new Itemized Overlay

```java
import android.graphics.drawable.Drawable;
import com.google.android.maps.GeoPoint;
import com.google.android.maps.ItemizedOverlay;
import com.google.android.maps.OverlayItem;

public class MyItemizedOverlay extends ItemizedOverlay<OverlayItem> {

  public MyItemizedOverlay(Drawable defaultMarker) {
    super(boundCenterBottom(defaultMarker));
    populate();
  }

  @Override
  protected OverlayItem createItem(int index) {
    switch (index) {
      case 1:
        Double lat = 37.422006*1E6;
        Double lng = -122.084095*1E6;
        GeoPoint point = new GeoPoint(lat.intValue(), lng.intValue());

        OverlayItem oi;
        oi = new OverlayItem(point, "Marker", "Marker Text");
        return oi;
    }
    return null;
  }

  @Override
  public int size() {
    // Return the number of markers in the collection
    return 1;
  }
}
```

To add an `ItemizedOverlay` implementation to your map, create a new instance (passing in the Drawable marker image to use for each marker) and add it to the map's Overlay list.

```
List<Overlay> overlays = mapView.getOverlays();
MyItemizedOverlay markers = new
  MyItemizedOverlay(r.getDrawable(R.drawable.marker));
overlays.add(markers);
```

> *Note that the map markers placed by the Itemized Overlay use state to indicate if they are selected. Use the* `StateListDrawable` *described in Chapter 4 to indicate when a marker has been selected.*

In Listing 8-12, the list of Overlay items is static and defined in code. More typically your Overlay items will be a dynamic ArrayList to which you will want to add and remove items at run time.

Listing 8-13 shows the skeleton class for a dynamic Itemized Overlay implementation, backed by an ArrayList, and supporting the addition and removal of items at run time.

LISTING 8-13: Skeleton code for a dynamic Itemized Overlay

```
public class MyDynamicItemizedOverlay extends ItemizedOverlay<OverlayItem>
{
  private ArrayList<OverlayItem> items;

  public MyDynamicItemizedOverlay(Drawable defaultMarker) {
    super(boundCenterBottom(defaultMarker));
    items = new ArrayList<OverlayItem>();
    populate();
  }

  public void addNewItem(GeoPoint location, String markerText,
                         String snippet) {
    items.add(new OverlayItem(location, markerText, snippet));
    populate();
  }

  public void removeItem(int index) {
    items.remove(index);
    populate();
  }

  @Override
  protected OverlayItem createItem(int index) {
    return itcms.get(index);
  }
```

continues

LISTING 8-13 *(continued)*

```
  @Override
  public int size() {
    return items.size();
  }
}
```

Pinning Views to the Map and Map Positions

You can pin any View-derived object to a Map View (including layouts and other View Groups), attaching it to either a screen position or a geographical map location.

In the latter case, the View will move to follow its pinned position on the map, effectively acting as an interactive map marker. As a more resource-intensive solution, this is usually reserved for supplying the detail "balloons" often displayed on mashups to provide further detail when a marker is clicked.

You implement both pinning mechanisms by calling `addView` on the `MapView`, usually from the `onCreate` or `onRestore` methods within the `MapActivity` containing it. Pass in the View you want to pin and the layout parameters to use.

The `MapView.LayoutParams` parameters you pass in to `addView` determine how, and where, the View is added to the map.

To add a new View to the map relative to the screen, specify a new `MapView.LayoutParams`, including arguments that set the height and width of the View, the x/y screen coordinates to pin to, and the alignment to use for positioning, as shown in Listing 8-14.

LISTING 8-14: Pinning a View to a map

```
int y = 10;
int x = 10;

EditText editText1 = new EditText(getApplicationContext());
editText1.setText("Screen Pinned");

MapView.LayoutParams screenLP;
screenLP = new MapView.LayoutParams(MapView.LayoutParams.WRAP_CONTENT,
                                    MapView.LayoutParams.WRAP_CONTENT,
                                    x, y,
                                    MapView.LayoutParams.TOP_LEFT);
mapView.addView(editText1, screenLP);
```

To pin a View relative to a physical map location, pass four parameters when constructing the new Map View `LayoutParams`, representing the height, width, GeoPoint to pin to, and layout alignment as shown in Listing 8-15.

LISTING 8-15: Pinning a View to a geographical location

```
Double lat = 37.422134*1E6;
Double lng = -122.084069*1E6;
GeoPoint geoPoint = new GeoPoint(lat.intValue(), lng.intValue());
```

```
MapView.LayoutParams geoLP;
geoLP = new MapView.LayoutParams(MapView.LayoutParams.WRAP_CONTENT,
                                 MapView.LayoutParams.WRAP_CONTENT,
                                 geoPoint,
                                 MapView.LayoutParams.TOP_LEFT);

EditText editText2 = new EditText(getApplicationContext());
editText2.setText("Location Pinned");

mapView.addView(editText2, geoLP);
```

Panning the map will leave the first TextView stationary in the upper left corner, while the second TextView will move to remain pinned to a particular position on the map.

To remove a View from a Map View, call removeView, passing in the View instance you wish to remove, as shown here.

```
mapView.removeView(editText2);
```

MAPPING EARTHQUAKES EXAMPLE

The following step-by-step guide demonstrates how to build a map-based Activity for the Earthquake project you started in Chapter 5. The new MapActivity will display a map of recent earthquakes using techniques you learned within this chapter.

1. Create a new earthquake_map.xml layout resource that includes a MapView, being sure to include an android:id attribute and an android:apiKey attribute that contains your Android Maps API key.

```xml
<?xml version="1.0" encoding="utf-8"?>
<LinearLayout
  xmlns:android="http://schemas.android.com/apk/res/android"
  android:orientation="vertical"
  android:layout_width="fill_parent"
  android:layout_height="fill_parent">
  <com.google.android.maps.MapView
    android:id="@+id/map_view"
    android:layout_width="fill_parent"
    android:layout_height="fill_parent"
    android:enabled="true"
    android:clickable="true"
    android:apiKey="myapikey"
  />
</LinearLayout>
```

2. Create a new EarthquakeMap Activity that inherits from MapActivity. Use setContentView within onCreate to inflate the earthquake_map resource you created in Step 1.

```java
package com.paad.earthquake;

import android.os.Bundle;
import com.google.android.maps.MapActivity;
```

```java
public class EarthquakeMap extends MapActivity {
  @Override
  public void onCreate(Bundle savedInstanceState) {
    super.onCreate(savedInstanceState);
    setContentView(R.layout.earthquake_map);
  }

  @Override
  protected boolean isRouteDisplayed() {
    return false;
  }
}
```

3. Update the application manifest to include your new `EarthquakeMap` Activity and import the map library.

```xml
<?xml version="1.0" encoding="utf-8"?>
<manifest xmlns:android="http://schemas.android.com/apk/res/android"
  package="com.paad.earthquake">
  <application android:icon="@drawable/icon">
    <activity
      android:name=".Earthquake"
      android:label="@string/app_name">
      <intent-filter>
        <action android:name="android.intent.action.MAIN" />
        <category android:name="android.intent.category.LAUNCHER" />
      </intent-filter>
    </activity>
    <activity android:name=".Preferences"
            android:label="Earthquake Preferences"/>
    <activity android:name=".EarthquakeMap"
            android:label="View Earthquakes"/>
    <provider android:name=".EarthquakeProvider"
            android:authorities="com.paad.provider.earthquake" />
    <uses-library android:name="com.google.android.maps"/>
  </application>
  <uses-permission android:name="android.permission.INTERNET"/>
</manifest>
```

4. Add a new menu option to the `Earthquake` Activity to display the `EarthquakeMap` Activity.

4.1. Start by adding a new string to the strings.xml resource for the menu text.

```xml
<?xml version="1.0" encoding="autf-8"?>
<resources>
  <string name="app_name">Earthquake</string>
  <string name="quake_feed">
    http://earthquake.usgs.gov/eqcenter/catalogs/1day-M2.5.xml
  </string>
  <string name="menu_update">Refresh Earthquakes</string>
  <string name="auto_update_prompt">Auto Update?</string>
  <string name="update_freq_prompt">Update Frequency</string>
  <string name="min_quake_mag_prompt">
    Minimum Quake Magnitude
  </string>
  <string name="menu_preferences">Preferences</string>
  <string name="menu_earthquake_map">Earthquake Map</string>
</resources>
```

4.2. Then add a new menu identifier before modifying the `onCreateOptionsMenu` handler to add the new Menu Item. It should use the text defined in Step 4.1, and when selected it should fire an Intent to explicitly start the `EarthquakeMap` Activity.

```
static final private int MENU_EARTHQUAKE_MAP = Menu.FIRST+2;

@Override
public boolean onCreateOptionsMenu(Menu menu) {
  super.onCreateOptionsMenu(menu);

  menu.add(0, MENU_UPDATE, Menu.NONE, R.string.menu_update);
  menu.add(0, MENU_PREFERENCES, Menu.NONE,
           R.string.menu_preferences);
  Intent startMap = new Intent(this, EarthquakeMap.class);
  menu.add(0, MENU_EARTHQUAKE_MAP,
           Menu.NONE,
           R.string.menu_earthquake_map).setIntent(startMap);
  return true;
}
```

5. Now create a new `EarthquakeOverlay` class that extends `Overlay`. It will draw the position and magnitude of each earthquake on the Map View.

```
package com.paad.earthquake;

import java.util.ArrayList;
import android.database.Cursor;
import android.database.DataSetObserver;
import android.graphics.Canvas;
import android.graphics.Paint;
import android.graphics.Point;
import android.graphics.RectF;
import com.google.android.maps.GeoPoint;
import com.google.android.maps.MapView;
import com.google.android.maps.Overlay;
import com.google.android.maps.Projection;

public class EarthquakeOverlay extends Overlay {
  @Override
  public void draw(Canvas canvas, MapView mapView, boolean shadow) {
    Projection projection = mapView.getProjection();

    if (shadow == false) {
     // TODO: Draw earthquakes
    }
  }
}
```

5.1. Add a new constructor that accepts a `Cursor` to the current earthquake data, and store that Cursor as an instance variable.

```
Cursor earthquakes;

public EarthquakeOverlay(Cursor cursor, ContentResolver resolver) {
  super();

  earthquakes = cursor;
}
```

5.2. Create a new `refreshQuakeLocations` method that iterates over the results Cursor and extracts the location of each earthquake, extracting the latitude and longitude before storing each coordinate in a List of `GeoPoints`.

```
ArrayList<GeoPoint> quakeLocations;

private void refreshQuakeLocations() {
  if (earthquakes.moveToFirst())
    do {
      Double lat =
        earthquakes.getFloat(EarthquakeProvider.LATITUDE_COLUMN) * 1E6;
      Double lng =
        earthquakes.getFloat(EarthquakeProvider.LONGITUDE_COLUMN) * 1E6;

      GeoPoint geoPoint = new GeoPoint(lng.intValue(),
                                       lat.intValue());
      quakeLocations.add(geoPoint);

    } while(earthquakes.moveToNext());
}
```

5.3. Call `refreshQuakeLocations` from the Overlay's constructor. Also register a `DataSetObserver` on the results Cursor that refreshes the Earthquake Location list if a change in the Earthquake Cursor is detected.

```
public EarthquakeOverlay(Cursor cursor) {
  super();
  earthquakes = cursor;

  quakeLocations = new ArrayList<GeoPoint>();
  refreshQuakeLocations();
  earthquakes.registerDataSetObserver(new DataSetObserver() {
    @Override
    public void onChanged() {
      refreshQuakeLocations();
    }
  });
}
```

5.4. Complete the `EarthquakeOverlay` by overriding the `draw` method to iterate over the list of `GeoPoints`, drawing a marker at each earthquake location. In this example a simple red circle is drawn, but you could easily modify it to include additional information, such as by adjusting the size of each circle based on the magnitude of the quake.

```
int rad = 5;

@Override
public void draw(Canvas canvas, MapView mapView, boolean shadow) {
  Projection projection = mapView.getProjection();

  // Create and setup your paint brush
  Paint paint = new Paint();
  paint.setARGB(250, 255, 0, 0);
  paint.setAntiAlias(true);
  paint.setFakeBoldText(true);
```

```
      if (shadow == false) {
        for (GeoPoint point : quakeLocations) {
          Point myPoint = new Point();
          projection.toPixels(point, myPoint);

          RectF oval = new RectF(myPoint.x-rad, myPoint.y-rad,
                                 myPoint.x+rad, myPoint.y+rad);

          canvas.drawOval(oval, paint);
        }
      }
    }
```

6. Return to the `EarthquakeMap` class. Within the `onCreate` method, create a Cursor that returns the earthquakes you want to display on the map. Use this Cursor to create a new `EarthquakeOverlay` before adding the new instance to the Map View's list of Overlays.

```
Cursor earthquakeCursor;

@Override
  public void onCreate(Bundle savedInstanceState) {
    super.onCreate(savedInstanceState);
    setContentView(R.layout.earthquake_map);

    String earthquakeURI = EarthquakeProvider.CONTENT_URI;
    earthquakeCursor = getContentResolver().query(earthquakeURI,
                                          null, null, null,
                                          null);

    MapView earthquakeMap = (MapView)findViewById(R.id.map_view);
    EarthquakeOverlay eo = new EarthquakeOverlay(earthquakeCursor);
    earthquakeMap.getOverlays().add(eo);
}
```

7. Finally, override `onResume` to call `requery` on the Earthquake result set whenever this Activity becomes visible. Also, override `onPause` and `onDestroy` to optimize use of the Cursor resources.

```
@Override
public void onResume() {
  earthquakeCursor.requery();
  super.onResume();
}

@Override
public void onPause() {
  earthquakeCursor.deactivate();
  super.onPause();
}

@Override
public void onDestroy() {
  earthquakeCursor.close();
  super.onDestroy();
}
```

8. If you run the application and select Earthquake Map from the main menu, your application should appear as shown in Figure 8-7.

All code snippets in this example are part of the Chapter 8 Earthquake *project, available for download at Wrox.com.*

SUMMARY

Location-based services, the Geocoder, and MapViews are available to create intuitive, location-aware applications that feature geographical information.

This chapter introduced the Geocoder and showed how to perform forward and reverse geocoding lookups to translate between map coordinates and street addresses. You were introduced to location-based services, used to find the current geographical position of a device. You also used them to track movement and create proximity alerts.

Then you created interactive map applications. Using Overlays and Views you annotated `MapViews` with 2D graphics, as well as markers in the form of `OverlayItems` and Views (including View Groups and layouts).

In Chapter 9 you'll learn how to work from the background. You'll be introduced to the Service component and learn how to move processing onto background threads. To interact with the user while hidden from view, you'll use Toasts to display transient messages and the Notification Manager to ring, vibrate, and flash the phone.

FIGURE 8-7

Working in the Background

Android offers the `Service` class to create application components specifically to handle operations and functionality that should run invisibly, without a user interface.

Android accords Services a higher priority than inactive Activities, so they're less likely to be killed when the system requires resources. In fact, should the run time prematurely terminate a Service that's been started, it can be configured to restart as soon as sufficient resources become available. In extreme cases, the termination of a Service — such as an interruption in music playback — will noticeably affect the user experience, and in these cases a Service's priority can be raised to the equivalent of a foreground Activity.

By using Services, you can ensure that your applications continue to run and respond to events, even when they're not in active use.

Services run without a dedicated GUI, but, like Activities and Broadcast Receivers, they still execute in the main thread of the application's process. To help keep your applications responsive, you'll learn to move time-consuming processes (like network lookups) into background threads using the `Thread` and `AsyncTask` classes.

Android offers several techniques for applications to communicate with users without an Activity. You'll learn how to use Notifications and Toasts to alert and update users without interrupting the active application.

Toasts are a transient, non-modal dialog-box mechanism used to display information to users without stealing focus from the active application. You'll learn to display Toasts from any application component to send unobtrusive on-screen messages to your users.

Where Toasts are silent and transient, *Notifications* represent a more robust mechanism for alerting users. In many cases, when the user isn't actively using the mobile phone it sits silent and unwatched in a pocket or on a desk until it rings, vibrates, or flashes. Should a user miss these alerts, status bar icons are used to indicate that an event has occurred. All these attention-grabbing antics are available to your Android application through Notifications.

Alarms provide a mechanism for firing Intents at set times, outside the control of your application life cycle. You'll learn to use Alarms to start Services, open Activities, or broadcast Intents based on either the clock time or the time elapsed since device boot. An Alarm will fire even after its owner application has been closed, and can (if required) wake a device from sleep.

INTRODUCING SERVICES

Unlike Activities, which present a rich graphical interface to users, Services run in the background — updating your Content Providers, firing Intents, and triggering Notifications. They are the perfect means of performing ongoing or regular processing and of handling events even when your application's Activities are invisible or inactive, or have been closed.

Services are started, stopped, and controlled from other application components, including other Services, Activities, and Broadcast Receivers. If your application performs actions that don't depend directly on user input, Services may be the answer.

Started Services always have higher priority than inactive or invisible Activities, making them less likely to be terminated by the run time's resource management. The only reason Android will stop a Service prematurely is to provide additional resources for a foreground component (usually an Activity). When that happens, your Service will be restarted automatically when resources become available.

If your Service is interacting directly with the user (for example, by playing music) it may be necessary to increase its priority to that of a foreground Activity. This will ensure that your Service isn't terminated except in extreme circumstances, but reduces the run time's ability to manage its resources, potentially degrading the overall user experience.

Applications that update regularly but only rarely or intermittently need user interaction are good candidates for implementation as Services. MP3 players and sports-score monitors are examples of applications that should continue to run and update without a visible Activity.

Further examples can be found within the software stack itself: Android implements several Services, including the Location Manager, Media Controller, and Notification Manager.

Creating and Controlling Services

In the following sections you'll learn how to create a new Service, and how to start and stop it using Intents and the startService method. Later you'll learn how to bind a Service to an Activity to provide a richer communications interface.

Creating a Service

To define a Service, create a new class that extends Service. You'll need to override onBind and onCreate, as shown in Listing 9-1.

LISTING 9-1: A skeleton Service class

```java
import android.app.Service;
import android.content.Intent;
import android.os.IBinder;

public class MyService extends Service {

  @Override
  public void onCreate() {
    // TODO: Actions to perform when service is created.
  }

  @Override
  public IBinder onBind(Intent intent) {
    // TODO: Replace with service binding implementation.
    return null;
  }
}
```

In most cases you'll also want to override onStartCommand. This is called whenever the Service is started with a call to startService, so it may be executed several times within a Service's lifetime. You should ensure that your Service accounts for this.

The onStartCommand handler replaces the onStart event that was used prior to Android 2.0. By contrast, it enables you to tell the system how to handle restarts if the Service is killed by the system prior to an explicit call to stopService or stopSelf.

The following snippet extends Listing 9-1 to show the skeleton code for overriding the onStartCommand handler. Note that it returns a value that controls how the system will respond if the Service is restarted after being killed by the run time.

```java
@Override
public int onStartCommand(Intent intent, int flags, int startId) {
  // TODO Launch a background thread to do processing.
  return Service.START_STICKY;
}
```

Services are launched on the main Application thread, meaning that any processing done in the onStartCommand handler will happen on the main GUI thread. The standard pattern for implementing a Service is to create and run a new thread from onStartCommand to perform the processing in the background and stop the Service when it's complete (you will be shown how to create and manage background threads later in this chapter).

This pattern lets onStartCommand complete quickly, and lets you control the restart behavior using one of the following Service constants:

➤ START_STICKY   Describes the standard behavior, which is similar to the way in which onStart was implemented prior to Android 2.0. If you return this value, onStartCommand will be called any time your Service restarts after being terminated by the run time. Note that on a restart the Intent parameter passed in to onStartCommand will be null.

This mode is typically used for Services that handle their own states, and that are explicitly started and stopped as required (via startService and stopService). This includes Services that play music or handle other ongoing background tasks.

➤ START_NOT_STICKY   This mode is used for Services that are started to process specific actions or commands. Typically they will use stopSelf to terminate once that command has been completed.

Following termination by the run time, Services set to this mode will restart only if there are pending start calls. If no startService calls have been made since the Service was terminated, the Service will be stopped without a call being made to onStartCommand.

This mode is ideal for Services that handle specific requests, particularly regular processing such as updates or network polling. Rather than restarting the Service during a period of resource contention, it's often more prudent to let the Service stop and retry at the next scheduled interval.

➤ START_REDELIVER_INTENT   In some circumstances you will want to ensure that the commands you have requested from your Service are completed.

This mode is a combination of the first two — if the Service is terminated by the run time, it will restart only if there are pending start calls *or* the process was killed prior to its calling stopSelf.

In the latter case, a call to onStartCommand will be made, passing in the initial Intent whose processing did not properly complete.

Note that each mode requires you to explicitly stop your Service, through stopService or stopSelf respectively, when your processing has completed. Both of these methods are discussed in more detail later in this chapter.

Prior to Android SDK 2.0 (SDK API level 5) the Service class triggered the onStart *event handler to let you perform actions when the Service started. Implementing the* onStart *handler is now the equivalent of overriding* onStartCommand *and returning the* START_STICKY *flag.*

The restart mode you specify in your onStartCommand return value will affect the parameter values passed in to subsequent calls.

Initially the Intent will be the parameter you passed in to `startService` to start your Service. After system-based restarts it will be either null, in the case of `START_STICKY` mode, or the original Intent, if the mode is set to `START_REDELIVER_INTENT`.

The `flag` parameter can be used to discover how the Service was started. In particular you can use the code snippet shown in Listing 9-2 to determine if either of the following cases is true:

➤ `START_FLAG_REDELIVERY` Indicates that the Intent parameter is a redelivery caused by the system run time's having terminated the Service before it was explicitly stopped by a call to `stopSelf`.

➤ `START_FLAG_RETRY` Indicates that the Service has been restarted after an abnormal termination. Passed in when the Service was previously set to `START_STICKY`.

LISTING 9-2: Determining the cause of a system start

Available for
download on
Wrox.com

```
@Override
public int onStartCommand(Intent intent, int flags, int startId) {
    if ((flags & START_FLAG_RETRY) == 0) {
        // TODO If it's a restart, do something.
    }
    else {
        // TODO Alternative background process.
    }
    return Service.START_STICKY;
}
```

Registering a Service in the Manifest

Once you've constructed a new Service, you have to register it in the application manifest.

Do this by including a `<service>` tag within the `application` node. Use the `requires-permission` attribute to require a uses-permission for other applications to access this Service.

The following is the `service` tag you'd add for the skeleton Service you created earlier:

```
<service android:enabled="true" android:name=".MyService"/>
```

Self-Terminating a Service

Once your Service has completed the actions or processing it was started for, you should make a call to `stopSelf`, either without a parameter to force a stop, or by passing in a `startId` value to insure processing has been completed for each instance of `startService` called so far, as shown in the following snippet:

```
stopSelf(startId);
```

By explicitly stopping the Service when your processing is complete, you allow the system to recover the resources otherwise required to keep it running. Due to the high priority of Services they are not commonly killed by the run time, so self-termination can significantly improve the resource footprint of your application.

Starting, Controlling, and Interacting with a Service

To start a Service, call `startService`; you can either use an action to implicitly start a Service with the appropriate Intent Receiver registered, or you can explicitly specify the Service using its class. If the Service requires permissions that your application does not have, the call to `startService` will throw a `SecurityException`.

In both cases you can pass values in to the Service's `onStart` handler by adding extras to the Intent, as shown in Listing 9-3, which demonstrates both techniques available for starting a Service.

LISTING 9-3: Starting a Service

```
// Implicitly start a Service
Intent myIntent = new Intent(MyService.ORDER_PIZZA);
myIntent.putExtra("TOPPING", "Margherita");
startService(myIntent);

// Explicitly start a Service
startService(new Intent(this, MyService.class));
```

To use this example you would need to include a `MY_ACTION` constant in the `MyService` class and use an Intent Filter to register the Service as a provider of `MY_ACTION`.

To stop a Service use `stopService`, passing an Intent that defines the Service to stop. Listing 9-4 first starts and then stops a Service both explicitly and by using the component name returned from a call to `startService`.

LISTING 9-4: Stopping a Service

```
ComponentName service = startService(new Intent(this, BaseballWatch.class));
// Stop a service using the service name.
stopService(new Intent(this, service.getClass()));
// Stop a service explicitly.
try {
  Class serviceClass = Class.forName(service.getClassName());
  stopService(new Intent(this, serviceClass));
} catch (ClassNotFoundException e) {}
```

If `startService` is called on a Service that's already running, the Service's `onStartCommand` handler will be executed again. Calls to `startService` do not nest, so a single call to `stopService` will terminate it no matter how many times `startService` has been called.

An Earthquake Monitoring Service Example

In this chapter you'll modify the Earthquake example you started in Chapter 5 (and continued to enhance in Chapters 6, 7, and 8). In this example you'll move the earthquake updating and processing functionality into a separate Service component.

Later in this chapter you'll build additional functionality within this Service, starting by moving the network lookup and XML parsing to a background thread. Later you'll use Toasts and Notifications to alert users of new earthquakes.

1. Start by creating a new `EarthquakeService` that extends `Service`.

```
package com.paad.earthquake;

import android.app.Service;
import android.content.Intent;
import android.os.IBinder;
import java.util.Timer;
import java.util.TimerTask;

public class EarthquakeService extends Service {
  @Override
  public void onCreate() {
    // TODO: Initialize variables, get references to GUI objects
  }

  @Override
  public IBinder onBind(Intent intent) {
    return null;
  }
}
```

2. Add this new Service to the manifest by adding a new `service` tag within the `application` node.

```
<service android:enabled="true" android:name=".EarthquakeService"/>
```

3. Move the `refreshEarthquakes` and `addNewQuake` methods out of the `Earthquake` Activity and into the `EarthquakeService`.

You'll need to remove the calls to `addQuakeToArray` and `loadQuakesFromProvider` (leave both of these methods in the Earthquake Activity because they're still required). In the `EarthquakeService` also remove all references to the earthquakes ArrayList.

```
private void addNewQuake(Quake _quake) {
  ContentResolver cr = getContentResolver();
  // Construct a where clause to make sure we don't already have
  // this earthquake in the provider.
  String w = EarthquakeProvider.KEY_DATE + " = " +
             _quake.getDate().getTime();

  // If the earthquake is new, insert it into the provider.
  Cursor c = cr.query(EarthquakeProvider.CONTENT_URI,
                      null, w, null, null);
  if (c.getCount()==0){
    ContentValues values = new ContentValues();

    values.put(EarthquakeProvider.KEY_DATE,
    _quake.getDate().getTime());
    values.put(EarthquakeProvider.KEY_DETAILS, _quake.getDetails());
```

```
      double lat = _quake.getLocation().getLatitude();
      double lng = _quake.getLocation().getLongitude();
      values.put(EarthquakeProvider.KEY_LOCATION_LAT, lat);
      values.put(EarthquakeProvider.KEY_LOCATION_LNG, lng);
      values.put(EarthquakeProvider.KEY_LINK, _quake.getLink());
      values.put(EarthquakeProvider.KEY_MAGNITUDE, _quake.getMagnitude());

      cr.insert(EarthquakeProvider.CONTENT_URI, values);
    }
    c.close();
}

private void refreshEarthquakes() {
  // Get the XML
  URL url;
  try {
    String quakeFeed = getString(R.string.quake_feed);
    url = new URL(quakeFeed);

    URLConnection connection;
    connection = url.openConnection();

    HttpURLConnection httpConnection =
      (HttpURLConnection)connection;
    int responseCode = httpConnection.getResponseCode();

    if (responseCode == HttpURLConnection.HTTP_OK) {
      InputStream in = httpConnection.getInputStream();

      DocumentBuilderFactory dbf =
        DocumentBuilderFactory.newInstance();
      DocumentBuilder db = dbf.newDocumentBuilder();

      // Parse the earthquake feed.
      Document dom = db.parse(in);
      Element docEle = dom.getDocumentElement();

      // Get a list of each earthquake entry.
      NodeList nl = docEle.getElementsByTagName("entry");
      if (nl != null && nl.getLength() > 0) {
        for (int i = 0 ; i < nl.getLength(); i++) {
          Element entry = (Element)nl.item(i);
          Element title;
          title =
            (Element)entry.getElementsByTagName("title").item(0);
          Element g =
            (Element)entry.getElementsByTagName("georss:point").item(0);
          Element when =
            (Element)entry.getElementsByTagName("updated").item(0);
          Element link =
            (Element)entry.getElementsByTagName("link").item(0);

          String details = title.getFirstChild().getNodeValue();
```

```
                String hostname = "http://earthquake.usgs.gov";
                String linkString = hostname + link.getAttribute("href");

                String point = g.getFirstChild().getNodeValue();
                String dt = when.getFirstChild().getNodeValue();
                SimpleDateFormat sdf;
                sdf = new SimpleDateFormat("yyyy-MM-dd'T'hh:mm:ss'Z'");
                Date qdate = new GregorianCalendar(0,0,0).getTime();
                try {
                  qdate = sdf.parse(dt);
                } catch (ParseException e) {
                  e.printStackTrace();
                }

                String[] location = point.split(" ");
                Location l = new Location("parsed");
                l.setLatitude(Double.parseDouble(location[0]));
                l.setLongitude(Double.parseDouble(location[1]));

                String magnitudeString = details.split(" ")[1];
                int end =  magnitudeString.length()-1;
                double magnitude =
                  Double.parseDouble(magnitudeString.substring(0, end));

                details = details.split(",")[1].trim();

                Quake quake = new Quake(qdate, details, l, magnitude,
                                        linkString);

                // Process a newly found earthquake
                addNewQuake(quake);
              }
            }
          }
        } catch (MalformedURLException e) {
          e.printStackTrace();
        } catch (IOException e) {
          e.printStackTrace();
        } catch (ParserConfigurationException e) {
          e.printStackTrace();
        } catch (SAXException e) {
          e.printStackTrace();
        }
        finally {
        }
      }
```

4. Within the Earthquake Activity, create a new `refreshEarthquakes` method. It should explicitly start the `EarthquakeService`.

```
private void refreshEarthquakes() {
  startService(new Intent(this, EarthquakeService.class));
}
```

5. Return to the `EarthquakeService`. Override the `onStartCommand` and `onCreate` methods to support a new Timer that will be used to update the earthquake list. `onStartCommand` should return `START_STICKY` because we are using a timer to trigger multiple refreshes. This is generally poor form; the Timer behavior should be moved to a background thread and triggered by Alarms. You'll learn how to do both of these things later in this chapter.

Use the `SharedPreference` object created in Chapter 6 to determine if the earthquakes should be regularly updated.

```java
private Timer updateTimer;
private float minimumMagnitude;

@Override
public int onStartCommand(Intent intent, int flags, int startId) {
  // Retrieve the shared preferences
  SharedPreferences prefs =
    getSharedPreferences(Preferences.USER_PREFERENCE,
                         Activity.MODE_PRIVATE);

  int minMagIndex = prefs.getInt(Preferences.PREF_MIN_MAG, 0);
  if (minMagIndex < 0)
    minMagIndex = 0;

  int freqIndex = prefs.getInt(Preferences.PREF_UPDATE_FREQ, 0);
  if (freqIndex < 0)
    freqIndex = 0;

  boolean autoUpdate =
    prefs.getBoolean(Preferences.PREF_AUTO_UPDATE, false);

  Resources r = getResources();
  int[] minMagValues = r.getIntArray(R.array.magnitude);
  int[] freqValues = r.getIntArray(R.array.update_freq_values);

  minimumMagnitude = minMagValues[minMagIndex];
  int updateFreq = freqValues[freqIndex];

  updateTimer.cancel();
  if (autoUpdate) {
    updateTimer = new Timer("earthquakeUpdates");
    updateTimer.scheduleAtFixedRate(doRefresh, 0,
      updateFreq*60*1000);
  }
  else
    refreshEarthquakes();

  return Service.START_STICKY;
};

private TimerTask doRefresh = new TimerTask() {
  public void run() {
```

```
      refreshEarthquakes();
    }
  };

  @Override
  public void onCreate() {
    updateTimer = new Timer("earthquakeUpdates");
  }
```

6.   The `EarthquakeService` will now update the earthquake Provider each time it is asked to refresh, as well as on an automated schedule (if one is specified). The updates are not yet passed back to the Earthquake Activity's List View or the Earthquake Map Activity.

    To alert those components, and any other applications interested in earthquake data, modify the `EarthquakeService` to broadcast a new Intent whenever a new earthquake is added.

    6.1.   Modify the `addNewQuake` method to call a new `announceNewQuake` method.

```
public static final String NEW_EARTHQUAKE_FOUND = "New_Earthquake_Found";

private void addNewQuake(Quake _quake) {
  ContentResolver cr = getContentResolver();
  // Construct a where clause to make sure we don't already have
  // this earthquake in the provider.
  String w = EarthquakeProvider.KEY_DATE +
              " = " + _quake.getDate().getTime();

  // If the earthquake is new, insert it into the provider.
  Cursor c = cr.query(EarthquakeProvider.CONTENT_URI,
                      null, w, null, null);
  if (c.getCount()==0){
    ContentValues values = new ContentValues();

    values.put(EarthquakeProvider.KEY_DATE, _quake.getDate().getTime());
    values.put(EarthquakeProvider.KEY_DETAILS, _quake.getDetails());

    double lat = _quake.getLocation().getLatitude();
    double lng = _quake.getLocation().getLongitude();
    values.put(EarthquakeProvider.KEY_LOCATION_LAT, lat);
    values.put(EarthquakeProvider.KEY_LOCATION_LNG, lng);
    values.put(EarthquakeProvider.KEY_LINK, _quake.getLink());
    values.put(EarthquakeProvider.KEY_MAGNITUDE,
                _quake.getMagnitude());

    cr.insert(EarthquakeProvider.CONTENT_URI, values);
    announceNewQuake(_quake);
  }
  c.close();
}

private void announceNewQuake(Quake quake) {
}
```

6.2. Within `announceNewQuake`, broadcast a new Intent whenever a new earthquake is found.

```
private void announceNewQuake(Quake quake) {
    Intent intent = new Intent(NEW_EARTHQUAKE_FOUND);
    intent.putExtra("date", quake.getDate().getTime());
    intent.putExtra("details", quake.getDetails());
    intent.putExtra("longitude", quake.getLocation().getLongitude());
    intent.putExtra("latitude", quake.getLocation().getLatitude());
    intent.putExtra("magnitude", quake.getMagnitude());

    sendBroadcast(intent);
}
```

7. That completes the `EarthquakeService` implementation. You still need to modify the two Activity components to listen for the Service Intent broadcasts and refresh their displays accordingly.

7.1. Within the Earthquake Activity, create a new internal `EarthquakeReceiver` class that extends `BroadcastReceiver`. Override the `onReceive` method to call `loadFromProviders` to update the earthquake array and refresh the list.

```
public class EarthquakeReceiver extends BroadcastReceiver {
    @Override
    public void onReceive(Context context, Intent intent) {
        loadQuakesFromProvider();
    }
}
```

7.2. Override the `onResume` method to register the new Receiver and update the List View contents when the Activity becomes active. Override `onPause` to unregister it when the Activity moves out of the foreground.

```
EarthquakeReceiver receiver;

@Override
public void onResume() {
    IntentFilter filter;
    filter = new IntentFilter(EarthquakeService.NEW_EARTHQUAKE_FOUND);
    receiver = new EarthquakeReceiver();
    registerReceiver(receiver, filter);

    loadQuakesFromProvider();
    super.onResume();
}

@Override
public void onPause() {
    unregisterReceiver(receiver);
    super.onPause();
}
```

7.3. Do the same for the `EarthquakeMap` Activity, this time calling `requery` on the result Cursor before invalidating the Map View whenever the Intent is received.

```
EarthquakeReceiver receiver;

@Override
```

```
public void onResume() {
  earthquakeCursor.requery();

  IntentFilter filter;
  filter = new IntentFilter(EarthquakeService.NEW_EARTHQUAKE_FOUND);
  receiver = new EarthquakeReceiver();
  registerReceiver(receiver, filter);

  super.onResume();
}

@Override
public void onPause() {
  earthquakeCursor.deactivate();
  super.onPause();
}

public class EarthquakeReceiver extends BroadcastReceiver {
  @Override
  public void onReceive(Context context, Intent intent) {
    earthquakeCursor.requery();
    MapView earthquakeMap = (MapView)findViewById(R.id.map_view);
    earthquakeMap.invalidate();
  }
}
```

All code snippets in this example are part of the Chapter 9 Earthquake *project, available for download at Wrox.com.*

Now when the Earthquake Activity is launched it will start the Earthquake Service. This Service will then continue to run, updating the earthquake Content Provider in the background, even after the Activity is suspended or closed.

 You'll continue to upgrade and enhance the Earthquake Service throughout the chapter, first using Toasts and later using Notifications and Alarms.

At this stage the earthquake processing is done in a Service, but it's still being executed on the main GUI thread. Later in this chapter you'll learn how to move time-consuming operations onto background threads to improve performance and avoid "Force Close" messages.

Similarly, the Service is constantly running, taking up valuable resources. Later sections will explain how to replace the Timer with Alarms.

Binding Activities to Services

When an Activity is bound to a Service, it maintains a reference to the Service instance itself, enabling you to make method calls on the running Service as you would on any other instantiated class.

Binding is available for Activities that would benefit from a more detailed interface with a Service. To support binding for a Service, implement the onBind method, as shown in Listing 9-5.

LISTING 9-5: Implementing binding on a Service

```java
private final IBinder binder = new MyBinder();

@Override
public IBinder onBind(Intent intent) {
  return binder;
}

public class MyBinder extends Binder {
  MyService getService() {
    return MyService.this;
  }
}
```

The connection between the Service and Activity is represented as a ServiceConnection.
You'll need to implement a new ServiceConnection, overriding the onServiceConnected and
onServiceDisconnected methods to get a reference to the Service instance once a connection has been
established, as shown in Listing 9-6.

LISTING 9-6: Binding to a Service

```java
// Reference to the service
private MyService serviceBinder;

// Handles the connection between the service and activity
private ServiceConnection mConnection = new ServiceConnection() {
  public void onServiceConnected(ComponentName className, IBinder service) {
    // Called when the connection is made.
    serviceBinder = ((MyService.MyBinder)service).getService();
  }

  public void onServiceDisconnected(ComponentName className) {
    // Received when the service unexpectedly disconnects.
    serviceBinder = null;
  }
};
```

To perform the binding, call bindService, passing in an Intent (either explicit or implicit) that selects
the Service to bind to and an instance of your new ServiceConnection implementation, as shown in
this extension of Listing 9-6:

```java
@Override
public void onCreate(Bundle savedInstanceState) {
  super.onCreate(savedInstanceState);

  // Bind to the service
  Intent bindIntent = new Intent(MyActivity.this, MyService.class);
  bindService(bindIntent, mConnection, Context.BIND_AUTO_CREATE);
}
```

Once the Service has been bound, all of its public methods and properties are available through the `serviceBinder` object obtained from the `onServiceConnected` handler.

Android applications do not (normally) share memory, but in some cases your application may want to interact with (and bind to) Services running in different application processes.

You can communicate with a Service running in a different process using broadcast Intents or through the extras Bundle in the Intent used to start the Service. If you need a more tightly coupled connection you can make a Service available for binding across application boundaries using AIDL. AIDL defines the Service's interface in terms of OS level primitives, allowing Android to transmit objects across process boundaries. AIDL definitions are covered in Chapter 15.

Prioritizing Background Services

As you learned in Chapter 3, Android uses a dynamic approach to manage resources that can result in your applications, Activities, and Services being terminated by the run time with little or no warning.

When calculating which applications and application components should be killed, Android assigns running Services the second-highest priority. Only active, foreground Activities are considered a higher priority in terms of system resources.

In extreme cases, in which your Service is interacting directly with the user, it may be appropriate to lift its priority to the equivalent of a foreground Activity's. You do this by setting your Service to run in the foreground using the `startForeground` method.

It is expected that Services running in the foreground will be interacting directly with the user (for example, by playing music). Because of this, the user should always be aware of a foreground Service. To ensure this, calls to `startForeground` must specify an ongoing Notification (described in more detail later in this chapter), as shown in Listing 9-7. This notification will continue for at least as long as the Service is running in the foreground.

By moving your Service to the foreground you effectively make it impossible for the run time to kill in order to free resources. Having multiple unkillable Services running simultaneously can make it extremely difficult for the system to recover from resource-starved situations.

Use this technique only if it is necessary in order for your Service to function properly, and even then keep the Service in the foreground only as long as absolutely necessary.

LISTING 9-7: Moving a Service to the foreground

```
int NOTIFICATION_ID = 1;

Intent intent = new Intent(this, MyActivity.class);
PendingIntent pi = PendingIntent.getActivity(this, 1, intent, 0));
```

continues

LISTING 9-7 *(continued)*

```
Notification notification = new Notification(R.drawable.icon,
  "Running in the Foreground", System.currentTimeMillis());
notification.setLatestEventInfo(this, "Title", "Text", pi);

notification.flags = notification.flags |
                     Notification.FLAG_ONGOING_EVENT;

startForeground(NOTIFICATION_ID, notification);
```

Listing 9-7 uses setLatestEventInfo to update the notification using the default status window layout. Later in this chapter you'll learn how to specify a custom layout for your Notification. Using this technique you can provide more details of your ongoing Service to users.

Once your Service no longer requires foreground priority you can move it back to the background, and optionally remove the ongoing notification using the stopForeground method, as shown in Listing 9-8. The Notification will be canceled automatically if your Service stops or is terminated.

LISTING 9-8: Moving a Service back to the background

```
// Move to the background and remove the Notification
stopForeground(true);
```

Prior to Android 2.0 it was possible to set a Service to the foreground using the setForeground *method. This method has now been deprecated and will result in a no-op, effectively doing nothing.*

USING BACKGROUND THREADS

To ensure that your applications remain responsive, it's good practice to move all slow, time-consuming operations off the main application thread and onto a child thread.

All Android application components — including Activities, Services, and Broadcast Receivers — start on the main application thread. As a result, time-consuming processing in any component will block all other components including Services and the visible Activity.

Android offers two alternatives for backgrounding your processing. The AsyncTask class lets you define an operation to be performed in the background, then provides event handlers you can use to monitor progress and post the results on the GUI thread.

Alternatively, you can implement your own Threads and use the Handler class to synchronize with the GUI thread before updating the UI. Both techniques are described in this section.

Using background threads is vital for avoiding the "Force Close" dialog box described in Chapter 2. In Android, Activities that don't respond to an input event (such as a key press) within five seconds, and Broadcast Receivers that don't complete their `onReceive` handlers within 10 seconds, are considered unresponsive.

Not only do you want to avoid this scenario, you don't want to even get close. Use background threads for all time-consuming processing, including file operations, network lookups, database transactions, and complex calculations.

Using AsyncTask to Run Asynchronous Tasks

The `AsyncTask` class offers a simple, convenient mechanism for moving your time-consuming operations onto a background thread. It offers the convenience of event handlers synchronized with the GUI thread to let you update Views and other UI elements to report progress or publish results when your task is complete.

AsyncTask handles all of the thread creation, management, and synchronization, enabling you to create an asynchronous task consisting of processing to be done in the background and a UI update to be performed when processing is complete.

Creating a new Asynchronous Task

To create a new asynchronous task you need to extend `AsyncTask`, as shown in the skeleton code of Listing 9-9. Your implementation should specify the classes used for input parameters on the `execute` method, the progress-reporting values, and the result values in the following format:

```
AsyncTask<[Input Parameter Type], [Progress Report Type], [Result Type]>
```

If you don't need or want to take input parameters, update progress, or report a final result, simply specify `Void` for any or all of the types required.

LISTING 9-9: Skeleton AsyncTask implementation using a string parameter and integer progress and result values

```java
private class MyAsyncTask extends AsyncTask<String, Integer, Integer> {
  @Override
  protected void onProgressUpdate(Integer... progress) {
    // [... Update progress bar, Notification, or other UI element ...]
  }

  @Override
  protected void onPostExecute(Integer... result) {
    // [... Report results via UI update, Dialog, or notification ...]
  }

  @Override
  protected Integer doInBackground(String... parameter) {
    int myProgress = 0;
```

continues

LISTING 9-9 *(continued)*

```
        // [... Perform background processing task, update myProgress ...]
        PublishProgress(myProgress)
        // [... Continue performing background processing task ...]

        // Return the value to be passed to onPostExecute
        return result;
    }
}
```

As shown in Listing 9-9, your subclass should implement the following event handlers:

➤ `doInBackground` Takes a set of parameters of the type defined in your class implementation. This method will be executed on the background thread, so it must not attempt to interact with UI objects.

Place your long-running code here, using the `publishProgress` method to allow `onProgressUpdate` to post progress updates to the UI.

When your background task is complete, return the final result for the `onPostExecute` handler to report it to the UI.

➤ `onProgressUpdate` Override this handler to post interim updates to the UI thread. This handler receives the set of parameters passed in to `publishProgress` from within `doInBackground`.

This handler is synchronized with the GUI thread when executed, so you can safely modify UI elements.

➤ `onPostExecute` When `doInBackground` has completed, the return value from that method is passed in to this event handler.

Use this handler to update the UI once your asynchronous task has completed. This handler is synchronized with the GUI thread when executed, so you can safely modify UI elements.

Running an Asynchronous Task

Once you've implemented your asynchronous task, execute it by creating a new instance and calling `execute`, as shown in Listing 9-10. You can pass in a number of parameters, each of the type specified in your implementation.

LISTING 9-10: Executing an asynchronous task

```
new MyAsyncTask().execute("inputString1", "inputString2");
```

 Each `AsyncTask` *instance can be executed only once. If you attempt to call* `execute` *a second time an exception will be thrown.*

Moving the Earthquake Service to a Background Thread Using AsyncTask

The following example shows how to move the network lookup and XML processing done in the EarthquakeService onto a background thread using an AsyncTask.

1. Create a new AsyncTask implementation, EarthquakeLookupTask, specifying Void for the input parameters and result variable types, and Quake for the progress reporting. Include stubs that override doInBackground, onProgressUpdate, and onPostExecute.

```
private class EarthquakeLookupTask extends AsyncTask<Void, Quake,
Void> {
  @Override
  protected Void doInBackground(Void... params) {
    return null;
  }

  @Override
  protected void onProgressUpdate(Quake... values) {
    super.onProgressUpdate(values);
  }

  @Override
  protected void onPostExecute(Void result) {
    super.onPostExecute(result);
  }
}
```

2. Move all the existing code from the refreshEarthquakes method into the new doInBackground handler. Add a new call to publishProgress, passing in the most recently parsed Quake, each time a new quake is processed. When the parsing is complete, return null.

```
@Override
protected Void doInBackground(Void... params) {
  [ ... existing XML parsing ... ]

  // Process a newly found earthquake
  addNewQuake(quake);
  publishProgress(quake);

  [ ... existing exception handling ... ]

  return null;
}
```

3. Update the now-empty refreshEarthquakes method. It should create and execute a new EarthquakeLookupTask. First check to see if another asynchronous task has already begun. To avoid stacking refresh requests you should begin an update only if one is not already in progress.

```
EarthquakeLookupTask lastLookup = null;

private void refreshEarthquakes() {
  if (lastLookup == null ||
      lastLookup.getStatus().equals(AsyncTask.Status.FINISHED)) {
    lastLookup = new EarthquakeLookupTask();
    lastLookup.execute((Void[])null);
  }
}
```

All code snippets in this example are part of the Chapter 9 Earthquake 2 *project, available for download at Wrox.com.*

Manual Thread Creation and GUI Thread Synchronization

While using `AsyncTask` is a useful shortcut, there are times when you will want to create and manage your own threads to perform background processing.

In this section you will learn how to create and start new Thread objects, and how to synchronize with the GUI thread before updating the UI.

Creating a New Thread

You can create and manage child threads using Android's `Handler` class and the threading classes available within `java.lang.Thread`. Listing 9-11 shows the simple skeleton code for moving processing onto a child thread.

LISTING 9-11: Moving processing to a background Thread

```
// This method is called on the main GUI thread.
private void mainProcessing() {
  // This moves the time consuming operation to a child thread.
  Thread thread = new Thread(null, doBackgroundThreadProcessing,
                             "Background");
  thread.start();
}

// Runnable that executes the background processing method.
private Runnable doBackgroundThreadProcessing = new Runnable() {
  public void run() {
    backgroundThreadProcessing();
  }
};

// Method which does some processing in the background.
private void backgroundThreadProcessing() {
  [ ... Time consuming operations ... ]
}
```

Using the Handler for Performing GUI Operations

Whenever you're using background threads in a GUI environment it's important to synchronize child threads with the main application (GUI) thread before creating or modifying graphical elements.

Within your application components, Notifications and Intents are always received and handled on the GUI thread. In all other cases, operations that explicitly interact with objects created on the GUI thread (such as Views) or that display messages (like Toasts) must be invoked on the main thread.

If you are running within an Activity, you can also use the runOnUiThread method, which lets you force a method to execute on the same thread as the Activity UI, as shown in Listing 9-12.

Available for download on Wrox.com

LISTING 9-12: Synchronizing with the Activity's GUI thread

```
runOnUiThread(new Runnable() {
  public void run() {
    // TODO Update a View.
  }
});
```

In other circumstances (such as Toasts and Notifications) you can use the Handler class to post methods onto the thread in which the Handler was created.

Using the Handler class you can post updates to the user interface from a background thread using the Post method. Listing 9-13 shows the outline for using the Handler to update the GUI thread.

Available for download on Wrox.com

LISTING 9-13: Using a Handler to synchronize with the GUI thread

```
// Initialize a handler on the main thread.
private Handler handler = new Handler();

private void mainProcessing() {
  Thread thread = new Thread(null, doBackgroundThreadProcessing,
                             "Background");
  thread.start();
}

private Runnable doBackgroundThreadProcessing = new Runnable() {
  public void run() {
    backgroundThreadProcessing();
  }
};

// Method which does some processing in the background.
private void backgroundThreadProcessing() {
  [ ... Time consuming operations ... ]
  handler.post(doUpdateGUI);
}

// Runnable that executes the update GUI method.
private Runnable doUpdateGUI = new Runnable() {
  public void run() {
    updateGUI();
  }
};
```

continues

LISTING 9-13 *(continued)*

```
private void updateGUI() {
  [ ... Open a dialog or modify a GUI element ... ]
}
```

The `Handler` class also lets you delay posts or execute them
at a specific time, using the `postDelayed` and `postAtTime`
methods respectively.

LET'S MAKE A TOAST

Toasts are transient Dialog boxes that remain visible for only
a few seconds before fading out. Toasts don't steal focus and
are non-modal, so they don't interrupt the active application.

Toasts are perfect for informing your users of events without forcing them to open an Activity or read a Notification.
They provide an ideal mechanism for alerting users to events
occurring in background Services without interrupting foreground applications.

The `Toast` class includes a static `makeText` method that
creates a standard Toast display window. Pass the application Context, the text message to display, and the length
of time to display it (`LENGTH_SHORT` or `LENGTH_LONG`) in to the
`makeText` method to construct a new Toast. Once a Toast
has been created, display it by calling `show`, as shown in
Listing 9-14.

FIGURE 9-1

LISTING 9-14: Displaying a Toast

```
Context context = getApplicationContext();
String msg = "To health and happiness!";
int duration = Toast.LENGTH_SHORT;

Toast toast = Toast.makeText(context, msg, duration);
toast.show();
```

Figure 9-1 shows a Toast. It will remain on screen for around two seconds before fading out. The
application behind it remains fully responsive and interactive while the Toast is visible.

Customizing Toasts

The standard Toast text message window is often sufficient, but in many situations you'll want to
customize its appearance and screen position. You can modify a Toast by setting its display position
and assigning it alternative Views or layouts.

Listing 9-15 shows how to align a Toast to the bottom of the screen using the `setGravity` method.

LISTING 9-15: Customizing a Toast

```
Context context = getApplicationContext();
String msg = "To the bride and groom!";
int duration = Toast.LENGTH_SHORT;
Toast toast = Toast.makeText(context, msg, duration);
int offsetX = 0;
int offsetY = 0;

toast.setGravity(Gravity.BOTTOM, offsetX, offsetY);
toast.show();
```

When a text message just isn't going to get the job done, you can specify a custom View or layout to use a more complex, or more visual, display. Using `setView` on a Toast object, you can specify any View (including a layout) to display using the transient message window mechanism.

For example, Listing 9-16 assigns a layout, containing the `CompassView` widget from Chapter 4 along with a `TextView`, to be displayed as a Toast.

LISTING 9-16: Using Views to customize Toasts

```
Context context = getApplicationContext();
String msg = "Cheers!";
int duration = Toast.LENGTH_LONG;
Toast toast = Toast.makeText(context, msg, duration);
toast.setGravity(Gravity.TOP, 0, 0);

LinearLayout ll = new LinearLayout(context);
ll.setOrientation(LinearLayout.VERTICAL);

TextView myTextView = new TextView(context);
CompassView cv = new CompassView(context);

myTextView.setText(msg);

int lHeight = LinearLayout.LayoutParams.FILL_PARENT;
int lWidth = LinearLayout.LayoutParams.WRAP_CONTENT;

ll.addView(cv, new LinearLayout.LayoutParams(lHeight, lWidth));
ll.addView(myTextView, new LinearLayout.LayoutParams(lHeight, lWidth));

ll.setPadding(40, 50, 0, 50);

toast.setView(ll);
toast.show();
```

The resulting Toast will appear as shown in Figure 9-2.

FIGURE 9-2

Using Toasts in Worker Threads

As GUI components, Toasts must be opened on the GUI thread or risk throwing a cross-thread exception. In Listing 9-17 a Handler is used to ensure that the Toast is opened on the GUI thread.

LISTING 9-17: Opening a Toast on the GUI thread

```
private void mainProcessing() {
    Thread thread = new Thread(null, doBackgroundThreadProcessing,
                               "Background");
    thread.start();
}

private Runnable doBackgroundThreadProcessing = new Runnable() {
    public void run() {
        backgroundThreadProcessing();
    }
};

private void backgroundThreadProcessing() {
```

```
    handler.post(doUpdateGUI);
}

// Runnable that executes the update GUI method.
private Runnable doUpdateGUI = new Runnable() {
  public void run() {
    Context context = getApplicationContext();
    String msg = "To open mobile development!";
    int duration = Toast.LENGTH_SHORT;
    Toast.makeText(context, msg, duration).show();
  }
};
```

INTRODUCING NOTIFICATIONS

Your applications can use Notifications to alert users without using an Activity. Notifications are handled by the Notification Manager, and currently have the ability to:

➤ Create new status bar icons

➤ Display additional information (and launch an Intent) in the extended status bar window

➤ Flash the lights/LEDs

➤ Vibrate the phone

➤ Sound audible alerts (ringtones, Media Store audio)

Using Notifications is the preferred way for invisible application components (Broadcast Receivers, Services, and inactive Activities) to alert users that events have occurred that may require attention. They are also used to indicate ongoing background Services — particularly Services that have been set to foreground priority.

As a user interface metaphor, Notifications are particularly well suited to mobile devices. It's likely that your users will have their phones with them at all times but quite unlikely that they will be paying attention to them, or your application, at any given time. Generally users will have several applications open in the background, and they won't be paying attention to any of them.

In this environment it's important that your applications be able to alert users when specific events occur that require their attention.

Notifications can be persisted through insistent repetition, being marked ongoing, or simply by displaying an icon on the status bar. Status bar icons can be updated regularly or expanded to show additional information using the expanded status bar window shown in Figure 9-3.

FIGURE 9-3

To display the expanded status bar view, click a status bar icon and drag it toward the bottom of the screen. To "lock" it in place, ensure that you release your drag only after the window covers the entire screen. To hide it, simply drag it back upward.

Introducing the Notification Manager

The *Notification Manager* is a system Service used to handle Notifications. Get a reference to it using the `getSystemService` method, as shown in Listing 9-18.

LISTING 9-18: Using the Notification Manager

```
String svcName = Context.NOTIFICATION_SERVICE;

NotificationManager notificationManager;
notificationManager = (NotificationManager)getSystemService(svcName);
```

Using the Notification Manager you can trigger new Notifications, modify existing ones, or remove those that are no longer required.

Creating Notifications

Android offers a number of ways to convey information to users using Notifications.

1. The status bar icon

2. The extended notification status drawer

3. Additional phone effects such as sound and vibration

This section will examine the first two while later in this chapter you'll learn how to enhance Notifications using various properties on the Notification object to flash the device LEDs, vibrate the phone, and play audio.

Creating a Notification and Configuring the Status Bar Icon

Start by creating a new Notification object, passing in the icon to display in the status bar, along with the status bar ticker text and the time of this Notification, as shown in Listing 9-19.

LISTING 9-19: Creating a Notification

```
// Choose a drawable to display as the status bar icon
int icon = R.drawable.icon;
// Text to display in the status bar when the notification is launched
String tickerText = "Notification";
// The extended status bar orders notification in time order
long when = System.currentTimeMillis();

Notification notification = new Notification(icon, tickerText, when);
```

The ticker text will scroll along the status bar when the Notification is fired.

You can also set the Notification object's `number` property to display the number of events a status bar icon represents. Setting this value to a number greater than 1, as shown in the following line of code, overlays the values as a small number over the status bar icon:

```
notification.number++;
```

As with all changes to a Notification, you will need to re-trigger it to apply the change. To remove the number overlay, set the `number` value to `0` or `-1`.

Configuring the Extended Status Notification Display

You can configure the appearance of the Notification within the extended status window in two ways:

1. Use the `setLatestEventInfo` method to update the details displayed in the standard extended status Notification display.

2. Set the `contentView` and `contentIntent` properties to assign a custom UI for the extended status display using a Remote View.

The simplest technique is to use the `setLatestEventInfo` method to populate the default status window layout. The standard extended status window layout shows the icon and time defined in the constructor, along with a title and a details string, as shown in Figure 9-4.

Notifications often represent a request for action or attention, so you can specify a `PendingIntent` that will be fired if a user clicks the Notification item. In most cases that Intent should open your application and navigate to the Activity that provides context for the notification (e.g., showing an unread SMS or e-mail message).

FIGURE 9-4

Listing 9-20 uses `setLatestEventInfo` to set Notification values.

LISTING 9-20: Setting Notification values

```
Context context = getApplicationContext();
// Text to display in the extended status window
String expandedText = "Extended status text";
// Title for the expanded status
String expandedTitle = "Notification Title";
// Intent to launch an activity when the extended text is clicked
Intent intent = new Intent(this, MyActivity.class);
PendingIntent launchIntent = PendingIntent.getActivity(context, 0, intent, 0);

notification.setLatestEventInfo(context,
                                expandedTitle,
                                expandedText,
                                launchIntent);
```

It's good form to use one Notification icon to represent multiple instances of the same event (e.g., receiving multiple SMS messages). To do this, update the values set by `setLatestEventInfo` to reflect the most recent message (or a summary of multiple messages) and re-trigger the Notification to update the display values.

If the details available in the standard extended view are insufficient (or unsuitable) for your Notification, you can create your own layout and assign it to your Notification using a Remote View. Figure 9-5 shows the custom layout defined, assigned, and modified in Listings 9-21, 9-22, and 9-23, respectively.

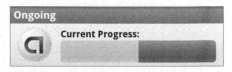

FIGURE 9-5

Listing 9-21 defines a custom layout that includes an icon, Text View, and progress bar.

LISTING 9-21: Creating a custom layout for the Notification status window

```xml
<?xml version="1.0" encoding="utf-8"?>
<RelativeLayout
    xmlns:android="http://schemas.android.com/apk/res/android"
    android:padding="5dp"
    android:layout_width="fill_parent"
    android:layout_height="fill_parent">
    <ImageView
        android:id="@+id/status_icon"
        android:layout_width="wrap_content"
        android:layout_height="fill_parent"
        android:layout_alignParentLeft="true"
    />
    <RelativeLayout
        android:layout_width="fill_parent"
        android:layout_height="fill_parent"
        android:paddingLeft="10px"
        android:layout_toRightOf="@id/status_icon">
        <TextView
            android:id="@+id/status_text"
            android:layout_width="fill_parent"
            android:layout_height="wrap_content"
            android:layout_alignParentTop="true"
            android:textColor="#000"
            android:textSize="14sp"
            android:textStyle="bold"
        />
        <ProgressBar
            android:id="@+id/status_progress"
            android:layout_width="fill_parent"
            android:layout_height="wrap_content"
            android:layout_below="@id/status_text"
            android:progressDrawable="@android:drawable/progress_horizontal"
            android:indeterminate="false"
            android:indeterminateOnly="false"
        />
    </RelativeLayout>
</RelativeLayout>
```

To assign your custom layout to the Notification, create a new RemoteView object and assign it to the contentView property. You will also need to assign a Pending Intent to the contentIntent property, as shown in Listing 9-22, in which a custom content View is assigned to an ongoing Notification.

LISTING 9-22: Applying a custom layout to the Notification status window

```
Notification notification = new Notification(R.drawable.icon,
                                     "Custom Content",
                                     System.currentTimeMillis());
notification.flags = notification.flags | Notification.FLAG_ONGOING_EVENT;

notification.contentView = new RemoteViews(this.getPackageName(),
  R.layout.my_status_window_layout);

Intent intent = new Intent(this, MyActivity.class);
PendingIntent.getActivity(this, 0, intent, 0));
notification.contentIntent = pendingIntent;
```

Note that when you manually set the contentView *property you must also set the* contentIntent *or an exception will be thrown when the notification is triggered.*

Remote Views are a mechanism that enables you to embed and control a layout embedded within a separate application, most commonly when creating home screen widgets. There are strict limits on the Views you can use when creating a layout to be used for a Remote View. These are covered in some detail in the next chapter.

To modify the properties and appearance of the Views used in your status window layout, use the set* methods on the Remote View object, as shown in Listing 9-23, which modifies each of the Views used in the layout defined in Listing 9-21.

LISTING 9-23: Customizing your extended notification window layout

```
notification.contentView.setImageViewResource(R.id.status_icon,
                                     R.drawable.icon);
notification.contentView.setTextViewText(R.id.status_text,
                                     "Current Progress:");
notification.contentView.setProgressBar(R.id.status_progress,
                                     100, 50, false);
```

This technique is particularly useful when used with ongoing events (such as in progress downloads or playing media) to convey details on progress. You'll learn more about ongoing Notifications later in this chapter.

Triggering Notifications

To fire a Notification, pass it in to the notify method on the NotificationManager along with an integer reference ID, as shown in Listing 9-24.

LISTING 9-24: Triggering a Notification

```
int notificationRef = 1;
notificationManager.notify(notificationRef, notification);
```

To update a Notification that's already been fired, re-trigger it using the Notification Manager, passing the `notify` method the same reference ID. You can pass in either the same Notification object or an entirely new one. As long as the ID values are the same, the new Notification will be used to replace the status icon and extended status window details.

You also use the reference ID to cancel Notifications by calling the `cancel` method on the Notification Manager, as shown here:

```
notificationManager.cancel(notificationRef);
```

Canceling a Notification removes its status bar icon and clears it from the extended status window.

Adding Notifications and Toasts to the Earthquake Monitor

In the following example, the `EarthquakeService` is enhanced to trigger a Notification for each new earthquake. As well as displaying a status bar icon, the expanded Notification view will display the magnitude and location of the latest quake, and selecting it will open the Earthquake Activity.

1. Within the `EarthquakeService`, start by creating a new `Notification` instance variable to store the Notification object used to control the status bar icon and extended status window item details.

```
private Notification newEarthquakeNotification;
public static final int NOTIFICATION_ID = 1;
```

2. Extend the `onCreate` method to create this Notification object.

```
@Override
public void onCreate() {
  updateTimer = new Timer("earthquakeUpdates");

  int icon = R.drawable.icon;
  String tickerText = "New Earthquake Detected";
  long when = System.currentTimeMillis();

  newEarthquakeNotification= new Notification(icon,
                                              tickerText,
                                              when);
}
```

3. Now return to the `EarthquakeLookupTask` implementation. Expand the `onProgressUpdate` stub to trigger the Notification after each new earthquake is added to the Content Provider. Before initiating the Notification, update the extended details using `setLatestEventInfo`. Also create and display a new Toast to announce each new quake.

```
@Override
protected void onProgressUpdate(Quake... values) {
  String svcName = Context.NOTIFICATION_SERVICE;
  NotificationManager notificationManager =
    (NotificationManager)getSystemService(svcName);
```

```
Context context = getApplicationContext();
String expandedText = values[0].getDate().toString();
String expandedTitle = "M:" + values[0].getMagnitude() + " " +
                       values[0].getDetails();
Intent startActivityIntent = new Intent(EarthquakeService.this,
                                         Earthquake.class);
PendingIntent launchIntent =
  PendingIntent.getActivity(context, 0, startActivityIntent, 0);

newEarthquakeNotification.setLatestEventInfo(context,
                                             expandedTitle,
                                             expandedText,
                                             launchIntent);
newEarthquakeNotification.when =
  java.lang.System.currentTimeMillis();

notificationManager.notify(NOTIFICATION_ID,
                           newEarthquakeNotification);

Toast.makeText(context, expandedTitle, Toast.LENGTH_SHORT).show();
}
```

4. The final step is to clear and disable Notifications within the two Activity classes. This is done to dismiss the status icon when the application is active.

   4.1. Starting with the Earthquake Activity, modify the `onCreate` method to get a reference to the Notification Manager.

   ```
   NotificationManager notificationManager;

   @Override
   public void onCreate(Bundle savedInstanceState) {
     [ ... existing onCreate ... ]

     String svcName = Context.NOTIFICATION_SERVICE;
     notificationManager =
       (NotificationManager)getSystemService(svcName);
   }
   ```

   4.2. Modify the `onReceive` method of the `EarthquakeReceiver`. As this is registered only (so it will execute only) when the Activity is active, you can safely cancel all earthquake Notifications here as soon as they're triggered.

   ```
   @Override
   public void onReceive(Context context, Intent intent) {
     loadQuakesFromProvider();

     notificationManager.cancel(EarthquakeService.NOTIFICATION_ID);
   }
   ```

   4.3. Next, extend the `onResume` method to cancel the Notification when the Activity becomes active.

   ```
   @Override
   public void onResume() {
     notificationManager.cancel(EarthquakeService.NOTIFICATION_ID);

     IntentFilter filter;
     filter = new IntentFilter(EarthquakeService.NEW_EARTHQUAKE_FOUND);
   ```

```
    receiver = new EarthquakeReceiver();
    registerReceiver(receiver, filter);
    super.onResume();
  }
```

4.4. Repeat the same process with the `EarthquakeMap` Activity.

```
  NotificationManager notificationManager;

  @Override
  public void onCreate(Bundle savedInstanceState) {
    super.onCreate(savedInstanceState);
    setContentView(R.layout.earthquake_map);

    ContentResolver cr = getContentResolver();
    earthquakeCursor = cr.query(EarthquakeProvider.CONTENT_URI,
                                null, null, null, null);

    MapView earthquakeMap = (MapView)findViewById(R.id.map_view);
    earthquakeMap.getOverlays().add(new
      EarthquakeOverlay(earthquakeCursor));

    String svcName = Context.NOTIFICATION_SERVICE;
    notificationManager = (NotificationManager)getSystemService(svcName);
  }

  @Override
  public void onResume() {
    notificationManager.cancel(EarthquakeService.NOTIFICATION_ID);

    earthquakeCursor.requery();

    IntentFilter filter;
    filter = new IntentFilter(EarthquakeService.NEW_EARTHQUAKE_FOUND);
    receiver = new EarthquakeReceiver();
    registerReceiver(receiver, filter);

    super.onResume();
  }

  public class EarthquakeReceiver extends BroadcastReceiver {
    @Override
    public void onReceive(Context context, Intent intent) {
      notificationManager.cancel(EarthquakeService.NOTIFICATION_ID);

      earthquakeCursor.requery();
      MapView earthquakeMap = (MapView)findViewById(R.id.map_view);
      earthquakeMap.invalidate();
    }
  }
```

All code snippets in this example are part of the **Chapter 9 Earthquake 3** *project, available for download at Wrox.com.*

Advanced Notification Techniques

In the following sections you'll learn to enhance Notifications to provide additional alerting through hardware, particularly by making the device ring, flash, and vibrate.

As each enhancement is described, you will be provided with a code snippet that can be added to the Earthquake example to provide user feedback on the severity of each earthquake as it's detected.

 To use the Notification techniques described here without also displaying the status bar icon, simply cancel the Notification directly after triggering it. This stops the icon from displaying but doesn't interrupt the other effects.

Using the Defaults

The simplest and most consistent way to add sound, light, and vibration to your Notifications is to use the current user default settings. Using the `defaults` property you can combine:

➤ `Notification.DEFAULT_LIGHTS`

➤ `Notification.DEFAULT_SOUND`

➤ `Notification.DEFAULT_VIBRATE`

The following code snippet assigns the default sound and vibration settings to a Notification:

```
notification.defaults = Notification.DEFAULT_SOUND |
                        Notification.DEFAULT_VIBRATE;
```

If you want to use all the default values you can use the `Notification.DEFAULT_ALL` constant.

Making Sounds

Using an audio alert to notify the user of a device event (like incoming calls) is a technique that predates the mobile, and has stood the test of time. Most native phone events, from incoming calls to new messages and low battery, are announced by audible ringtones.

Android lets you play any audio file on the phone as a Notification by assigning a location URI to the `sound` property, as shown in the following snippet:

`notification.sound = ringURI;`

To use your own custom audio, push the file onto your device, or include it as a raw resource, as described in Chapter 11.

The following snippet can be added to the `announceNewQuake` method within the Earthquake Service from the earlier example. It adds an audio component to the earthquake Notification, ringing the default notification ringtone if a significant earthquake (one with a magnitude greater than 6) occurs.

```
if (quake.getMagnitude() > 6) {
  Uri ringURI =
    RingtoneManager.getDefaultUri(RingtoneManager.TYPE_NOTIFICATION);
  newEarthquakeNotification.sound = ringURI;
}
```

Vibrating the Phone

You can use the phone's vibration function to execute a vibration pattern specific to your Notification. Android lets you control the pattern of a vibration; you can use vibration to convey information as well as to get the user's attention.

To set a vibration pattern, assign an array of longs to the Notification's vibrate property. Construct the array so that values representing the length of time (in milliseconds) to vibrate alternate with values representing the length of time to pause.

Before you can use vibration in your application, you need to be granted permission. Add a uses-permission to your application to request access to the device vibration using the following code snippet:

```
<uses-permission android:name="android.permission.VIBRATE"/>
```

The following example shows how to modify a Notification to vibrate in a repeating pattern of one second on and one second off, for five seconds total.

```
long[] vibrate = new long[] { 1000, 1000, 1000, 1000, 1000 };
notification.vibrate = vibrate;
```

You can take advantage of this fine-grained control to pass information to your users. In the following update to the announceNewQuake method, the phone is set to vibrate in a pattern based on the power of the quake. Earthquakes are measured on an exponential scale, so you'll use the same scale when creating the vibration pattern.

For a barely perceptible magnitude 1 quake the phone will vibrate for a fraction of a second; for one of magnitude 10, an earthquake that would split the earth in two, your users will have a head start on the Apocalypse when their devices vibrate for a full 20 seconds. Most significant quakes fall between 3 and 7 on the Richter scale, or a more reasonable 200-millisecond-to-four-second range of vibration duration.

```
double vibrateLength = 100*Math.exp(0.53*quake.getMagnitude());
long[] vibrate = new long[] {100, 100, (long)vibrateLength };
newEarthquakeNotification.vibrate = vibrate;
```

The current Android Emulator does not visually or audibly indicate that the device is vibrating.

Flashing the Lights

Notifications also include properties to configure the color and flash frequency of the device's LED.

Each device may have different limitations with regard to control over the LED. Where the color you specify is not available, as close an approximation as possible will be used. When using LEDs to convey information to the user keep this limitation in mind and avoid making it the only way such information is made available.

The ledARGB property can be used to set the LED's color, while the ledOffMS and ledOnMS properties let you set the frequency and pattern of the flashing LED. You can turn the LED on by setting the ledOnMS property to 1 and the ledOffMS property to 0, or turn it off by setting both properties to 0.

Once you have configured the LED settings you must also add the FLAG_SHOW_LIGHTS flag to the Notification's flags property.

The following code snippet shows how to turn on the red device LED:

```
notification.ledARGB = Color.RED;
notification.ledOffMS = 0;
notification.ledOnMS = 1;
notification.flags = notification.flags | Notification.FLAG_SHOW_LIGHTS;
```

Controlling the color and flash frequency gives you another opportunity to pass additional information to users.

In the earthquake-monitoring example you can help your users perceive the nuances of an exponential scale by also using the device's LED to help convey the magnitude. In the following snippet the color of the LED depends on the size of the quake, and the frequency of the flashing is inversely related to the power of the quake:

```
int color;
if (quake.getMagnitude() < 5.4)
  color = Color.GREEN;
else if (quake.getMagnitude() < 6)
  color = Color.YELLOW;
else
  color = Color.RED;

newEarthquakeNotification.ledARGB = color;
newEarthquakeNotification.ledOffMS = (int)vibrateLength;
newEarthquakeNotification.ledOnMS = (int)vibrateLength;
newEarthquakeNotification.flags = newEarthquakeNotification.flags |
                          Notification.FLAG_SHOW_LIGHTS;
```

 The current Android Emulator does not visually illustrate the LEDs.

Ongoing and Insistent Notifications

You can configure Notifications as ongoing and/or insistent by setting the FLAG_INSISTENT and FLAG_ONGOING_EVENT flags.

Notifications flagged as ongoing, as in the following snippet, are used to represent events that are currently in progress (such as a download in progress or music playing in the background). An ongoing Notification is a requirement for a foreground Service, as described earlier in this chapter.

```
notification.flags = notification.flags |
  Notification.FLAG_ONGOING_EVENT;
```

Ongoing events are separated from regular Notifications within the extended Notification drawer, as shown in Figure 9-6.

Insistent Notifications repeat their audio, vibration, and light settings continuously until canceled. These Notifications are typically used for events that require immediate and timely attention — such as an incoming call or the ringing of an alarm clock.

The following code snippet shows how to set a Notification as insistent:

```
notification.flags = notification.flags |
    Notification.FLAG_INSISTENT;
```

USING ALARMS

Alarms are an application-independent means of firing Intents at predetermined times and intervals.

Alarms are set outside the scope of your applications, so they can be used to trigger application events or actions even after your application has been closed. They can be particularly powerful in combination with Broadcast Receivers, enabling you to set Alarms that fire broadcast Intents, start Services, or even open Activities, without the applications' needing to be open or running until they're required.

As such, Alarms are an extremely effective means of reducing your application's resource requirements, particularly when running in the background, by enabling you to stop Services and eliminate timers while maintaining the ability to perform scheduled actions.

For example, you can use Alarms to implement an alarm clock application, perform regular network lookups, or schedule time-consuming or cost-bound operations at "off-peak" times.

FIGURE 9-6

 For timing operations that occur only during the lifetime of your applications, using the Handler *class in combination with Timers and Threads is a better approach than using Alarms, as this allows Android better control over system resources. Alarms provide a mechanism to reduce the lifetime of your applications by moving scheduled events out of their control.*

Alarms in Android remain active while the device is in sleep mode and can optionally be set to wake the device; however, all Alarms are canceled whenever the device is rebooted.

Alarm operations are handled through the AlarmManager, a system Service accessed via getSystemService, as shown here:

```
AlarmManager alarms =
    (AlarmManager)getSystemService(Context.ALARM_SERVICE);
```

To create a new one-shot Alarm, use the set method and specify an alarm type, a trigger time, and a Pending Intent to fire when the Alarm triggers. If the trigger time you specify for the Alarm occurs in the past, the Alarm will be triggered immediately.

There are four alarm types available. Your selection will determine if the time value passed in the set method represents a specific time or an elapsed wait:

➤ RTC_WAKEUP   Wake the device from sleep to fire the Pending Intent at the clock time specified.

➤ RTC   Fire the Pending Intent at the time specified, but do not wake the device.

➤ ELAPSED_REALTIME   Fire the Pending Intent based on the amount of time elapsed since the device was booted, but do not wake the device. The elapsed time includes any period of time the device was asleep. Note that the time elapsed is calculated based on when the device was last booted.

➤ ELAPSED_REALTIME_WAKEUP   After a specified length of time has passed since device boot, wake the device from sleep and fire the Pending Intent.

The Alarm-creation process is shown in Listing 9-25.

LISTING 9-25: Creating an Alarm

Available for download on Wrox.com

```
int alarmType = AlarmManager.ELAPSED_REALTIME_WAKEUP;
long timeOrLengthofWait = 10000;
String ALARM_ACTION = "ALARM_ACTION";
Intent intentToFire = new Intent(ALARM_ACTION);
PendingIntent pendingIntent = PendingIntent.getBroadcast(this, 0,
    intentToFire, 0);

alarms.set(alarmType, timeOrLengthofWait, pendingIntent);
```

When the Alarm goes off, the Pending Intent you specified will be broadcast. Setting a second Alarm using the same Pending Intent replaces the preexisting Alarm.

To cancel an Alarm, call cancel on the Alarm Manager, passing in the Pending Intent you no longer wish to trigger, as shown in the following snippet:

```
alarms.cancel(pendingIntent);
```

In Listing 9-26, two Alarms are set and the first one is subsequently canceled. The first is explicitly set to a specific time and will wake up the device in order to fire. The second is set to fire 30 minutes after the device is started, but will not wake the device if it's sleeping.

LISTING 9-26: Setting and canceling an Alarm

Available for download on Wrox.com

```
AlarmManager alarms =
(AlarmManager)getSystemService(Context.ALARM_SERVICE);

String MY_RTC_ALARM = "MY_RTC_ALARM";
String ALARM_ACTION = "MY_ELAPSED_ALARM";

PendingIntent rtcIntent =
  PendingIntent.getBroadcast(this, 0,
                      new Intent(MY_RTC_ALARM), 1);
```

continues

LISTING 9-26 *(continued)*

```
PendingIntent elapsedIntent =
  PendingIntent.getBroadcast(this, 0,
                             new Intent(ALARM_ACTION), 1);

// Wakeup and fire intent in 5 hours.
Date t = new Date();
t.setTime(java.lang.System.currentTimeMillis() + 60*1000*5);
alarms.set(AlarmManager.RTC_WAKEUP, t.getTime(), rtcIntent);

// Fire intent in 30 mins if already awake.
alarms.set(AlarmManager.ELAPSED_REALTIME, 30*60*1000, elapsedIntent);

// Cancel the first alarm.
alarms.cancel(rtcIntent);
```

Setting Repeating Alarms

The Alarm Manager lets you set repeating alarms for situations requiring regularly scheduled events. Repeating alarms work in exactly the same way as the one-shot alarms described earlier, but will continue to trigger at a specified interval until canceled.

Because alarms are set outside your Application context they are perfect for scheduling regular updates or data lookups so that they don't require a Service to be constantly running in the background.

To set a repeating alarm, use the setRepeating or setInexactRepeating method on the Alarm Manager, as shown in Listing 9-27. Both support an alarm type, an initial trigger time, and a Pending Intent to fire when the alarm triggers (as described in the previous section).

Use setRepeating when you need fine-grained control over the exact interval of your repeating alarm. The interval value passed in to this method lets you specify an exact interval for your alarm, down to the millisecond.

The setInexactRepeating method is a powerful technique for reducing the battery drain associated with waking the device on a regular schedule to perform updates. Rather than specifying an exact interval, this method accepts one of the following Alarm Manager constants:

➤ INTERVAL_FIFTEEN_MINUTES

➤ INTERVAL_HALF_HOUR

➤ INTERVAL_HOUR

➤ INTERVAL_HALF_DAY

➤ INTERVAL_DAY

At run time Android will synchronize multiple inexact repeating alarms and trigger them simultaneously. This prevents each application from separately waking the device in a similar but non-overlapping period to perform an update or poll a network data source. By synchronizing these alarms the system is able to limit the impact of regularly repeating events on battery resources.

LISTING 9-27: Setting repeating alarms

```
// Fire an intent exactly every hour if already awake.
alarms.setRepeating(AlarmManager.ELAPSED_REALTIME_WAKEUP,
                    60*60*1000, 60*60*1000, elapsedIntent);

// Wakeup and fire an alarm about every hour
alarms.setInexactRepeating(AlarmManager.ELAPSED_REALTIME_WAKEUP,
                           60*60*1000, AlarmManager.INTERVAL_DAY,
                           elapsedIntent);
```

> *The battery impact of setting regularly repeating alarms can be significant. It is good practice to limit your alarm frequency to the slowest acceptable rate, wake the device only if necessary, and use the inexact repeating alarm whenever possible.*

Using Repeating Alarms to Update Earthquakes

In this final modification to the Earthquake example you'll use Alarms to replace the Timer currently used to schedule Earthquake network refreshes.

One of the most significant advantages of this approach is that it allows the Service to stop itself when it has completed a refresh, freeing significant system resources.

1. Start by creating a new `EarthquakeAlarmReceiver` class that extends `BroadcastReceiver`.

```
package com.paad.earthquake;

import android.content.BroadcastReceiver;
import android.content.Context;
import android.content.Intent;

public class EarthquakeAlarmReceiver extends BroadcastReceiver {

}
```

2. Override the `onReceive` method to explicitly start the `EarthquakeService`.

```
@Override
public void onReceive(Context context, Intent intent) {
  Intent startIntent = new Intent(context, EarthquakeService.class);
  context.startService(startIntent);
}
```

3. Create a new public static String to define the action that will be used to trigger the Broadcast Receiver.

```
public static final String ACTION_REFRESH_EARTHQUAKE_ALARM =
  "com.paad.earthquake.ACTION_REFRESH_EARTHQUAKE_ALARM";
```

4. Add the new `EarthquakeAlarmReceiver` to the manifest, including an `<intent-filter>` tag that listens for the action defined in Step 3.

```
<receiver android:name=".EarthquakeAlarmReceiver">
  <intent-filter>
    <action
android:name="com.paad.earthquake.ACTION_REFRESH_EARTHQUAKE_ALARM"
    />
  </intent-filter>
</receiver>
```

5. Within the EarthquakeService, update the `onCreate` method to get a reference to the `AlarmManager`, and create a new `PendingIntent` that will be fired when the Alarm goes off. You can also remove the `timerTask` initialization.

```
AlarmManager alarms;
PendingIntent alarmIntent;

@Override
public void onCreate() {
  int icon = R.drawable.icon;
  String tickerText = "New Earthquake Detected";
  long when = System.currentTimeMillis();

  newEarthquakeNotification =
    new Notification(icon, tickerText, when);

  alarms = (AlarmManager)getSystemService(Context.ALARM_SERVICE);

  String ALARM_ACTION;
  ALARM_ACTION =
  EarthquakeAlarmReceiver.ACTION_REFRESH_EARTHQUAKE_ALARM;
  Intent intentToFire = new Intent(ALARM_ACTION);
  alarmIntent =
    PendingIntent.getBroadcast(this, 0, intentToFire, 0);
}
```

6. Modify the `onStartCommand` method to set a repeating Alarm rather than use a Timer to schedule the refreshes (if automated updates are enabled). Setting a new Intent with the same action will automatically cancel any previous Alarms.

Take this opportunity to modify the return result. Rather than setting the Service to sticky, return `Service.START_NOT_STICKY`. In Step 7 you will stop the Service when the background refresh is complete; the use of alarms guarantees that another refresh will occur at the specified update frequency, so there's no need for the system to restart the Service if it is killed mid-refresh.

```
@Override
public int onStartCommand(Intent intent, int flags, int startId) {
  SharedPreferences prefs =
    getSharedPreferences(Preferences.USER_PREFERENCE,
    Activity.MODE_PRIVATE);

  int minMagIndex = prefs.getInt(Preferences.PREF_MIN_MAG, 0);
  if (minMagIndex < 0)
    minMagIndex = 0;
```

```
int freqIndex = prefs.getInt(Preferences.PREF_UPDATE_FREQ, 0);
if (freqIndex < 0)
  freqIndex = 0;

boolean autoUpdate =
  prefs.getBoolean(Preferences.PREF_AUTO_UPDATE, false);

Resources r = getResources();
int[] minMagValues = r.getIntArray(R.array.magnitude);
int[] freqValues = r.getIntArray(R.array.update_freq_values);

minimumMagnitude = minMagValues[minMagIndex];
int updateFreq = freqValues[freqIndex];

if (autoUpdate) {
  int alarmType = AlarmManager.ELAPSED_REALTIME_WAKEUP;
  long timeToRefresh = SystemClock.elapsedRealtime() +
                       updateFreq*60*1000;
  alarms.setRepeating(alarmType, timeToRefresh,
                      updateFreq*60*1000, alarmIntent);
}
else
  alarms.cancel(alarmIntent);

refreshEarthquakes();

return Service.START_NOT_STICKY;
};
```

7. In the `EarthquakeLookupTask`, fill in the `onPostExecute` stub to call `stopSelf` when the background refresh has completed. Because the asynchronous lookup task is called only from within `onStartCommand`, and only if not already running, this ensures the Service is never prematurely terminated.

```
@Override
protected void onPostExecute(Void result) {
  stopSelf();
}
```

8. Remove the `updateTimer` instance variable and the Timer Task instance `doRefresh`.

All code snippets in this example are part of the **Chapter 9 Earthquake 4** *project, available for download at Wrox.com.*

SUMMARY

Background Services are one of the most compelling reasons to develop applications on the Android platform, but using them introduces several complexities to your applications. In this chapter you learned how to use these invisible application components to perform processing while your applications are running in the background.

You were introduced to Toasts, transient message boxes that let you display information to users without stealing focus or interrupting their workflow.

You used the Notification Manager to send alerts to your users from within Services and Activities, using customized LEDs, vibration patterns, and audio files to convey detailed event information. You learned how (and when) to create ongoing Notifications and how to customize their extended status window Layouts.

Using Alarms, you were able to schedule one-off and repeating events that broadcast Intents or started Services.

This chapter also demonstrated how to:

➤   Bind a Service to an Activity to make use of a more detailed, structured interface than the simple Intent extras.

➤   Ensure that your applications remain responsive by moving time-consuming processing like network lookups onto worker threads using `AsyncTask`.

➤   Use handlers to synchronize child threads with the main application GUI when performing operations using visual controls and Toasts.

In Chapter 10 you'll learn how to integrate your application into the home screen. Starting with creating dynamic, interactive home screen widgets you'll move on to creating Live Folders and Live Wallpapers. Finally you'll be introduced to the Quick Search Box, and learn how to surface your application's search results to the home screen search widget.

10

Invading the Phone-Top

WHAT'S IN THIS CHAPTER?

➤ Creating home screen Widgets

➤ Implementing Live Folders

➤ Adding search to your applications

➤ Surfacing search results to the Quick Search Box

➤ Creating Live Wallpaper

Widgets, Live Folders, Live Wallpaper, and the Quick Search Box let you own a piece of the user's home screen, providing either a window to your application or a stand-alone source of information directly on the home screen. They're an exciting innovation for users and developers, providing the following:

➤ Users get instant access to interesting information without needing to open an application.

➤ Developers get an entry point to their applications directly from the home screen.

A useful widget, Live Folder, or dynamic wallpaper decreases the chance that an application will be uninstalled, and increases the likelihood of its being used.

With such power comes responsibility. Widgets run constantly as subprocesses of the home-screen process. You need to be particularly careful when creating widgets to ensure they remain responsive and don't drain system resources.

This chapter demonstrates how to create and use App Widgets, Live Folders, and Live Wallpaper detailing what they are, how to use them, and some techniques for incorporating interactivity into these application components.

It also describes how to integrate the Android search frame-work into your application and surface search results to the Quick Search Box.

INTRODUCING HOME-SCREEN WIDGETS

Widgets, more properly `AppWidgets`, are visual application components that can be added to other applications. The most notable example is the default Android home screen, where users can add widgets to their phone-top, though any application you create can become an `AppHost` and support third-party widgets if you desire.

Widgets enable your application to own a piece of interactive screen real estate, and an entry point, directly on the user's home screen. A good App Widget provides useful, concise, and timely information with a minimal resource cost.

Widgets can be either stand-alone applications (such as the native clock) or compact but highly visible components of larger applications — such as the calendar and media player widgets.

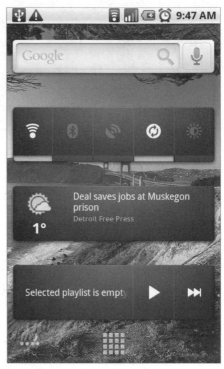

FIGURE 10-1

Figure 10-1 shows four of the standard home-screen widgets available on Android devices: the search box, power control, news and weather, and media player.

 To add a widget to the home screen, long-press a piece of empty space and select Widgets. You will be presented with a list of available widgets. Once you've added one you can move it by long-pressing it and dragging it around the screen. Remove widgets by dragging them into the garbage can icon at the bottom of the screen.

Widgets embedded into the home screen are hosted within the home screen's process. They will wake the device based on their update rates to ensure each widget is up to date when it is visible. As a developer, you need to take extra care when creating your widgets to ensure that the update rate is as low as possible, and that the code executed within the update method is lightweight.

The following sections show how to create widgets and describe some best practices for performing updates and adding interaction.

CREATING APP WIDGETS

App Widgets are implemented as `IntentReceivers`. They use `RemoteViews` to update a view hierarchy hosted within another application process; in most cases that host process is the home screen.

To create a widget for your application you need to create three components:

1. A layout resource that defines the UI for the widget
2. An XML definition file that describes the metadata associated with the widget
3. An Intent Receiver that defines and controls the widget

You can create as many widgets as you want for a single application, or have an application that consists of a single widget. Each widget can use the same size, layout, refresh rate, and update logic, or they can all use different ones. In many cases it can be useful to offer multiple versions of your widgets in different sizes.

Creating the Widget Layout

The first step in creating your widget is to design and implement its user interface.

Construct your widget's UI as you would other visual components in Android, as described in Chapter 4. Best practice is to define your widget layout using XML as an external layout resource, but it's also possible to lay out your UI programmatically within the Intent Receiver's `onCreate` method.

Widget Design Guidelines

Widgets are often displayed alongside both native and third-party widgets, so it's important that yours conform to design standards. This is particularly important because widgets are most often used on the home screen.

There are widget UI design guidelines for controlling both layout size and visual styling. The former is rigidly enforced while the latter is a guide only; both are summarized in the following sections. Additional detail can also be found on the Android Developers Widget Design Guidelines site at `http://developer.android.com/guide/practices/ui_guidelines/widget_design.html`

Widget Layout Sizes

The default Android home screen is divided into a four-by-four grid of cells, each a minimum of 74×74 device-independent pixels (dp). To select the height and width of your widget, start by calculating the number of cells you wish to use. The total pixels required will be 74 times the cell count minus two pixels for padding, as shown in the following formula:

```
Minimum size in dp = (Cell count * 74dp) - 2dp
```

Where your minimum dimensions don't match the exact dimensions of the home screen cells, your widget's size will be rounded up to fill all the cells.

Widget dimensions are specified in the widget settings file, as described later in this chapter.

Widget Visual Styling

The visual styling of your widget, your application's presence on the home screen, is very important. You should ensure that its style is consistent with that of your application, as well as with those of the other home-screen components.

It's beyond the scope of this book to describe the widget style promoted by Google in detail, but note the description available at the widget UI guidelines link given earlier. Google's description includes the image resources used to create the native Android widgets shipped with Google Experience devices.

App Widgets fully support transparent backgrounds and allow the use of NinePatches and partially transparent PNG-drawable resources.

Supported Widget Views and Layouts

Because of security and performance considerations there are several restrictions on the layouts and Views available to you when you're constructing your widget UI.

In general, the following Views are unavailable for App Widget layouts and will result in a null pointer error (NPE) if used:

➤ All custom Views

➤ Descendents of the allowed Views

➤ `EditText`

Currently, the layouts available are limited to:

➤ `FrameLayout`

➤ `LinearLayout`

➤ `RelativeLayout`

The Views they contain are restricted to:

➤ `AnalogClock`

➤ `Button`

➤ `Chronometer`

➤ `ImageButton`

➤ `ImageView`

➤ `ProgressBar`

➤ `TextView`

The Text Views and Image Views are particularly useful. Later in this chapter you'll see how to use the Image View in conjunction with the `SelectionStateDrawable` resource to create interactive widgets with little or no code.

Listing 10-1 shows a sample layout resource used to define the UI of an App Widget.

LISTING 10-1: App Widget XML layout resource

```xml
<?xml version="1.0" encoding="utf-8"?>
<LinearLayout
    xmlns:android="http://schemas.android.com/apk/res/android"
    android:orientation="horizontal"
    android:layout_width="fill_parent"
    android:layout_height="fill_parent"
    android:padding="10sp">
```

```
  <ImageView
    android:id="@+id/widget_image"
    android:layout_width="wrap_content"
    android:layout_height="wrap_content"
    android:src="@drawable/icon"
  />
  <TextView
    android:id="@+id/widget_text"
    android:layout_width="fill_parent"
    android:layout_height="fill_parent"
    android:text="Text Goes Here"
  />
</LinearLayout>
```

Defining Your Widget Settings

Widget definition resources are stored as XML in the res/xml folder of your project. The appwidget-provider tag lets you describe the widget metadata that defines the size, layout, and update rate for your widget using the following attributes:

➤ initialLayout   The layout resource to use in constructing the widget's user interface.

➤ minWidth / minHeight   Respectively, the minimum width and minimum height of the widget, as described in the previous section.

➤ label   The title used by your widget in the widget-picker.

➤ updatePeriodMillis   The minimum period between widget updates in milliseconds. Android will wake the device to update your widget at this rate, so you should specify at least an hour. Ideally your widget shouldn't use this update technique more than once or twice daily. More details on this and other update techniques are provided later in this chapter.

➤ configure   You can optionally specify a fully qualified Activity to be launched when your widget is added to the home screen. This Activity can be used to specify widget settings and user preferences. Using a configuration Activity is described later in this chapter.

Listing 10-2 shows the widget resource file for a two-cell-by-two-cell widget that updates once every hour and uses the layout resource defined in the previous section.

LISTING 10-2: App Widget Provider definition

Available for
download on
Wrox.com

```
<?xml version="1.0" encoding="utf-8"?>
<appwidget-provider
  xmlns:android="http://schemas.android.com/apk/res/android"
  android:initialLayout="@layout/my_widget_layout"
  android:minWidth="146dp"
  android:minHeight="146dp"
  android:label="My App Widget"
  android:updatePeriodMillis="3600000"
/>
```

Creating Your Widget Intent Receiver and Adding It to the Application Manifest

Widgets are implemented as Intent Receivers with Intent Filters that catch broadcast Intents, which request widget updates using the `AppWidget.ACTION_APPWIDGET_UPDATE`, `DELETED`, `ENABLED`, and `DISABLED` actions. You can create your widget by extending the `IntentReceiver` class directly and interpreting those broadcast Intents by overriding the `onReceive` method.

The `AppWidgetProvider` class provides a simplified alternative by encapsulating the Intent processing and presenting you with event handlers for the update, delete, enable, and disable events.

Listing 10-3 shows a simple widget implementation that extends `AppWidgetProvider` and overrides the `onUpdate` method:

LISTING 10-3: App Widget implementation

```java
import android.appwidget.AppWidgetManager;
import android.appwidget.AppWidgetProvider;
import android.content.Context;

public class MyAppWidget extends AppWidgetProvider {
  @Override
  public void onUpdate(Context context,
                       AppWidgetManager appWidgetManager,
                       int[] appWidgetIds) {
    // TODO Update the Widget UI.
  }
}
```

Widgets are added to the application manifest much like other Intent Receivers. However, to specify an Intent Receiver as an App Widget you need to add two additional tags to its manifest node (Listing 10-4).

➤ An Intent Filter for the `android.appwidget.action.APPWIDGET_UPDATE` action

➤ A reference to the metadata XML resource that describes your widget

LISTING 10-4: App Widget manifest node

```xml
<receiver android:name=".MyAppWidget" android:label="My App Widget">
  <intent-filter>
    <action android:name="android.appwidget.action.APPWIDGET_UPDATE" />
  </intent-filter>
  <meta-data
    android:name="android.appwidget.provider"
    android:resource="@xml/my_app_widget_info"
  />
</receiver>
```

Introducing Remote Views and the App Widget Manager

The RemoteViews class is used to describe and manipulate a View hierarchy that's hosted within another application process. This lets you change a property, or run a method, on a View running as part of another application.

For example, the Views within App Widgets are hosted within a separate process (generally the home screen), so Remote Views can be used to modify the widget UI from the Intent Receiver running within your application.

The AppWidgetManager is used to update App Widgets and provide details related to them.

Using Remote Views with the App Widget Manager, you can modify the appearance of the Views supported by the App Widget framework. Among other things, you can change the visibility, text, or image values, and add click listeners.

This section describes how to create new Remote Views from within and without the onUpdate method of an App Widget Provider. It also demonstrates how to use Remote Views to update widget UI and add interactivity to your widgets.

Creating Remote Views and Using the App Widget Manager to Apply Them

To create a new Remote Views object you must pass the name of the calling application package, and the layout resource you plan to manipulate, into the constructor, as shown in Listing 10-5. Later in this section you'll learn how to use this Remote Views object to update the Views and layout of your widget.

LISTING 10-5: Using Remote Views

```
RemoteViews views = new RemoteViews(context.getPackageName(),
                            R.layout.my_remote_layout);
```

To use Remote Views on widgets, call the static getInstance method to return an instance of the App Widget Manager and use it to find identifiers for each instance of a particular widget class, as in this continuation of Listing 10-5:

```
// Get the App Widget Manager.
AppWidgetManager appWidgetManager = AppWidgetManager.getInstance(context);
// Retrieve the identifiers for each instance of your chosen widget.
ComponentName thisWidget = new ComponentName(context, MyAppWidget.class);
int[] appWidgetIds = appWidgetManager.getAppWidgetIds(thisWidget);
```

When you've finished making changes to a Remote Views object, apply those modifications to one or more widgets by calling the updateAppWidget method on the App Widget Manager, passing in either an individual widget ID or an array of identifiers:

```
appWidgetManager.updateAppWidget(appWidgetIds, views);
```

The standard pattern used to update widget UI is to iterate over the widget ID array as shown in Listing 10-6. This enables you to apply different UI values to each widget based on its configuration settings or UI requirements.

LISTING 10-6: A standard pattern for updating Widget UI

```
final int N = appWidgetIds.length;
// Iterate through each widget, creating a RemoteViews object and
// applying the modified RemoteViews to each widget.
for (int i = 0; i < N; i++) {
  int appWidgetId = appWidgetIds[i];
  // Create a Remove View
  RemoteViews views = new RemoteViews(context.getPackageName(),
                                      R.layout.my_widget_layout);

  // TODO Update the widget UI using the views object.

  // Notify the App Widget Manager to update the widget using
  // the modified remote view.
  appWidgetManager.updateAppWidget(appWidgetId, views);
}
```

Using a Remote View within the App Widget Provider's onUpdate Handler

The App Widget Provider simplifies your widget interactions by passing the App Widget Manager, and an array of matching App Widget IDs, as parameters into the onUpdate handler.

You can then follow the same pattern as shown above, without the need to obtain a reference to the App Widget Manager or find the identifier values for the affected widgets first as shown in Listing 10-7.

LISTING 10-7: Using a Remote View within the App Widget Provider's onUpdate Handler

```
@Override
public void onUpdate(Context context,
                     AppWidgetManager appWidgetManager,
                     int[] appWidgetIds) {
  final int N = appWidgetIds.length;
  for (int i = 0; i < N; i++) {
    int appWidgetId = appWidgetIds[i];
    // Create a Remove View
    RemoteViews views = new RemoteViews(context.getPackageName(),
                                        R.layout.my_widget_layout);
    // TODO Update the UI.

    // Notify the App Widget Manager to update the widget using
    // the modified remote view.
    appWidgetManager.updateAppWidget(appWidgetId, views);
  }
}
```

Using Remote Views to Modify UI

Remote Views expose a variety of methods designed to provide access to the properties and methods available on Views in order for you to change their appearance.

The most versatile of these is a series of methods that lets you execute a target method name on a remotely hosted View. These methods support the passing of single-value parameters. Supported method signatures include a parameter for each primitive type, including Boolean, integer, and float, plus strings, bitmaps, and URI parameters.

Listing 10-8 shows examples of some of the method signatures supported.

LISTING 10-8: Using a Remote View to modify App Widget UI

Available for
download on
Wrox.com

```
// Set the image level for an ImageView.
views.setInt(R.id.widget_image_view, "setImageLevel", 2);
// Show the cursor of a TextView.
views.setBoolean(R.id.widget_text_view, "setCursorVisible", true);
// Assign a bitmap to an ImageButton.
views.setBitmap(R.id.widget_image_button, "setImageBitmap", myBitmap);
```

Remote Views also include a set of View-specific methods to set values applicable to a particular View class, including Text Views, Image Views, Progress Bars, and Chronometers.

Listing 10-9 shows examples of some of these specialist methods:

LISTING 10-9: Modifying View properties within an App Widget Remote View

Available for
download on
Wrox.com

```
// Update a Text View
views.setTextViewText(R.id.widget_text_view, "Updated Text");
views.setTextColor(R.id.widget_text_view, Color.BLUE);
// Update an Image View
views.setImageViewBitmap(R.id.widget_image_view, myBitmap);
// Update a Progress Bar
views.setProgressBar(R.id.widget_progressbar, 100, 50, false);
// Update a Chronometer
views.setChronometer(.id.widget_chronometer,
SystemClock.elapsedRealtime(), null, true);
```

You can also set the visibility of any View hosted within Remote Views by calling `setViewVisibility`, as shown here:

```
views.setViewVisibility(R.id.widget_text_view, View.VISIBLE);
```

As described in the previous section, once you've made changes to a Remote Views object you must use the App Widget Manager to apply those changes to a particular widget, as shown here:

```
appWidgetManager.updateAppWidget(appWidgetId, views);
```

Making Your Widgets Interactive

You can also add interactivity to your widgets using Remote Views, but reactions to user input are tightly restricted.

Because they run within the home-screen process, the widgets themselves inherit its permissions. As a result of these security implications widget interactivity is carefully controlled.

Widget interaction is generally limited to two possibilities:

➤ Adding a click listener to one or more views within the layout

➤ Changing the UI based on selection changes

It's notable that there is no supported technique for entering text directly into an App Widget.

If you need text input from your widget, best practice is to add a click listener that displays an Activity to accept the user data when a portion of the widget is clicked.

One popular alternative is to use Image Views designed to look like Edit Text controls. By means of Selection State Drawables they can appear to gain focus. When the Image View is clicked, a partially transparent Activity is launched to accept the user input.

Using a Click Listener

The most powerful technique for adding interactivity to your widget is through the use of the `setOnClickPendingIntent` method on a Remote Views object.

This lets you specify a Pending Intent that will be fired when the user clicks on the specified widget View. Pending Intents (described in more detail in Chapter 5) can contain Intents used to start Activities or Services or broadcast Intents.

Listing 10-10 demonstrates a broadcast Intent assigned to a Text View element within a widget layout:

LISTING 10-10: Adding a Click Listener to an App Widget

```
Intent intent = new Intent("com.paad.ACTION_WIDGET_CLICK");
PendingIntent pendingIntent = PendingIntent.getBroadcast(this, 0, intent, 0);
views.setOnClickPendingIntent(R.id.my_text_view, pendingIntent);
```

Using this technique you can add click handlers to one or more of the Views used within your widget, which means you can add support for multiple actions.

For example, the standard media player widget assigns different broadcast Intents to several buttons, providing playback control through the play, pause, and next buttons.

Changing Image Views Based on Selection Focus

Image Views are one of the most flexible types of View available for your widget UI, providing support for some basic user interactivity within your widgets.

Using a `SelectionStateDrawable` resource (described in Chapter 3) you can create a Drawable resource that displays a different image based on the selection state of the View it is assigned to. By using a Selection State Drawable in your widget design, you can create a dynamic UI that highlights the user selection as he or she navigates though the widget's controls.

The XML snippet in Listing 10-11 shows a sample Selection State Drawable resource.

Available for download on Wrox.com

LISTING 10-11: A Selection State Drawable resource for an App Widget

```xml
<selector xmlns:android="http://schemas.android.com/apk/res/android">
  <item android:state_window_focused="false"
        android:drawable="@drawable/widget_bg_normal"/>
  <item android:state_focused="true"
        android:drawable="@drawable/widget_bg_selected"/>
  <item android:state_pressed="true"
        android:drawable="@drawable/widget_bg_pressed"/>
  <item android:drawable="@drawable/widget_bg_normal"/>
</selector>
```

The Drawable resources referenced should be stored, along with the selection state xml file, in the application's res/drawable folder. You can then use the Selection State Drawable directly as the source for an Image View, or as the background image for any widget View.

Refreshing Your Widgets

Widgets are most commonly displayed on the home screen, so it's important that they're always kept relevant and up to date. It's just as important to balance that relevance with your widget's impact on system resources — particularly battery life.

The following sections describe several techniques for managing your widget refresh intervals.

Using the Minimum Update Rate

The simplest, but potentially most resource-intensive, technique is to set the minimum update rate for a widget in the XML definition file, as shown in Listing 10-12, where the widget is updated once every hour:

Available for download on Wrox.com

LISTING 10-12: Setting the App Widget minimum update rate

```xml
<?xml version="1.0" encoding="utf-8"?>
<appwidget-provider
  xmlns:android="http://schemas.android.com/apk/res/android"
  android:initialLayout="@layout/my_widget_layout"
  android:minWidth="146dp"
  android:minHeight="146dp"
  android:label="My App Widget"
  android:updatePeriodMillis="3600000"
/>
```

Setting this value will cause the device to broadcast an Intent requesting an update of your widget at the rate specified.

> *The host device will wake up to complete these updates, meaning they are completed even when the device is on standby. This has the potential to be a significant resource drain, so it's very important to consider the implications of your update rate.*

This technique should be used to define the absolute minimum rate at which your widget must be updated to remain useful. Generally the minimum expected update rate should be at least an hour, ideally not more than once or twice a day.

If your device requires more frequent updates, consider using one of the techniques described in the following sections to dynamically perform updates using either an event/Intent-driven model or a more efficient scheduled model using Alarms.

Listening for Intents

As widgets are implemented as Intent Receivers you can trigger updates and UI refreshes by registering Intent Filters for additional actions.

This is a dynamic approach to refreshing your widget that uses a more efficient event model rather than the potentially battery-draining method of specifying a short minimum refresh rate.

The XML snippet in Listing 10-13 assigns a new Intent Filter to the manifest entry of the widget defined earlier:

LISTING 10-13: Listening for Intent broacasts within App Widgets

```xml
<receiver android:name=".MyAppWidget" android:label="My App Widget">
  <intent-filter>
    <action android:name="android.appwidget.action.APPWIDGET_UPDATE" />
  </intent-filter>
  <intent-filter>
    <action android:name="com.paad.chapter9.FORCE_WIDGET_UPDATE" />
  </intent-filter>
  <meta-data
    android:name="android.appwidget.provider"
    android:resource="@xml/my_app_widget_info"
  />
</receiver>
```

By updating the widget's `onReceive` method handler as shown in Listing 10-14, you can listen for this new Intent and use it to update your widget.

LISTING 10-14: Updating App Widgets based on broadcast Intents

```
public static String FORCE_WIDGET_UPDATE =
"com.paad.chapter9.FORCE_WIDGET_UPDATE";

@Override
public void onReceive(Context context, Intent intent) {
  super.onReceive(context, intent);

  if (FORCE_WIDGET_UPDATE.equals(intent.getAction())) {
    // TODO Update widget UI.
  }
}
```

To trigger an update of your widget at any point in your application, you can broadcast an Intent using this action:

```
context.sendBroadcast(new Intent(FORCE_WIDGET_UPDATE));
```

This technique is particularly useful for reacting to system, user, or application events — like a data refresh, or a user action such as clicking buttons on the widget itself. You can also register for system event broadcasts such as changes to network connectivity, battery level, or screen brightness.

Using Alarms

Alarms provide a middle-ground alternative to the polling and Intent-based techniques described so far.

Alarms, covered in detail in Chapter 9, provide a flexible way to schedule regular events within your application. Using alarms you can poll at regular intervals, using an Intent to trigger your updates.

Using Alarms to refresh your widgets is similar to using the Intent-driven model described earlier. Add a new Intent Filter to the manifest entry for your widget and override its onReceive method to identify the Intent that triggered it. Within your application, use the Alarm Manager to create an Alarm that fires an Intent with the registered action.

Alarms have an advantage over the minimum refresh rate, thanks to their flexibility.

Like the widgets' refresh rate, Alarms also have the ability to wake the device when they fire — making it equally important to take care to minimize battery use.

Alternatively, by using the RTC or ELAPSED_REALTIME modes when constructing your alarm, you can configure it to trigger after a minimum interval has elapsed, but only after the device has awakened:

```
alarmManager.setRepeating(AlarmManager.ELAPSED_REALTIME,
                          AlarmManager.INTERVAL_HOUR,
                          AlarmManager.INTERVAL_HOUR,
                          pi);
```

Using this technique will ensure your widget is up to date when visible, without draining the battery unnecessarily to update the widget when the screen is off.

If your widget does need to be updated even when the device is on standby, you can optimize this process with the inexact repeating option, shown here:

```
String alarmService = Context.ALARM_SERVICE;
AlarmManager alarmManager = (AlarmManager)getSystemService(alarmService);

Intent intent = new Intent(MyAppWidget.FORCE_WIDGET_UPDATE);
PendingIntent pi = PendingIntent.getBroadcast(this,
                                              0,
                                              intent,
                                              0);

alarmManager.setInexactRepeating(AlarmManager.ELAPSED_REALTIME_WAKEUP,
                                 AlarmManager.INTERVAL_HALF_DAY,
                                 AlarmManager.INTERVAL_HALF_DAY,
                                 pi);
```

As described in Chapter 9, the inexact repeating Alarm will optimize the alarm triggers by phase-shifting all the alarms scheduled to occur at similar times. This ensures the device is only awakened once, rather than several times within a few minutes.

Creating and Using a Widget Configuration Activity

In some cases an App Widget will be significantly more useful if the user is given the opportunity to customize the data it displays and how the data is displayed. This is particularly important given that multiple instances of the same widget can be added to the home screen.

An App Widget configuration Activity is an Activity that is launched immediately when a widget is added to the home screen. It can be any Activity within your application, provided it has an Intent Filter for the APPWIDGET_CONFIGURE action, as shown here:

```
<activity android:name=". MyWidgetConfigurationActivity">
  <intent-filter>
    <action android:name="android.apwidget.action.APPWIDGET_CONFIGURE"/>
  </intent-filter>
</activity>
```

It must also return a result Intent that includes an extra that describes the App Widget ID of the widget it is configuring using the EXTRA_APPWIDGET_ID constant. This extra is included in the Intent that launches the Activity.

```
Intent result = new Intent();
result.putExtra(AppWidgetManager.EXTRA_APPWIDGET_ID, appWidgetId);
setResult(RESULT_OK, result);
finish();
```

To assign a completed configuration Activity to a widget you must add it to the widget settings file using the configure tag. The activity must be specified by its fully qualified package name, as shown here:

```
<?xml version="1.0" encoding="utf-8"?>
<appwidget-provider
  xmlns:android="http://schemas.android.com/apk/res/android"
  android:initialLayout="@layout/my_widget_layout"
  android:minWidth="146dp"
  android:minHeight="146dp"
  android:label="My App Widget"
  android:updatePeriodMillis="3600000"
  android:configure="com.paad.chapter9.MyWidgetConfigurationActivity"
/>
```

CREATING AN EARTHQUAKE WIDGET

The following instructions show you how to create a new home-screen widget to display details for the latest earthquake detected. The UI for this widget is simple to the point of being inane; this is a side effect of keeping the example as concise as possible. Note that it does not conform to the widget style guidelines.

Once completed and added to the home screen, your widget will appear as in Figure 10-2.

Using a combination of the update techniques described above, this widget listens for broadcast Intents that announce an update has been performed and sets the minimum update rate to ensure it is updated once per day regardless.

The following code extends the Earthquake application last seen in Chapter 8:

FIGURE 10-2

1. Start by creating the layout for the widget UI as an XML resource. Use a Linear Layout to configure Text Views that display the quake magnitude and location:

```
<LinearLayout
  xmlns:android="http://schemas.android.com/apk/res/android"
  android:orientation="horizontal"
  android:layout_width="fill_parent"
  android:layout_height="fill_parent"
  android:background="#F111"
  android:padding="5sp">
  <TextView
    android:id="@+id/widget_magnitude"
    android:layout_width="wrap_content"
```

```
      android:layout_height="fill_parent"
      android:textSize="24sp"
      android:padding="3dp"
    />
    <TextView
      android:id="@+id/widget_details"
      android:layout_width="fill_parent"
      android:layout_height="fill_parent"
      android:textSize="14sp"
      android:padding="3dp"
    />
</LinearLayout>
```

2. Create a stub for a new `EarthquakeWidget` class that extends `AppWidgetProvider`. You'll return to this class to update your widget with the latest quake details.

```
package com.paad.earthquake;

import android.widget.RemoteViews;
import android.appwidget.AppWidgetManager;
import android.appwidget.AppWidgetProvider;
import android.content.ComponentName;
import android.content.Context;
import android.content.Intent;
import android.database.Cursor;

public class EarthquakeWidget extends AppWidgetProvider {
}
```

3. Create a new widget definition file, `quake_widget_info.xml`, and place it in the res/xml folder. Set the minimum update rate to 24 hours and set the widget dimensions to two cells wide and one cell high — 146dp×74dp. Use the widget layout you created in Step 1 for the initial layout.

```
<?xml version="1.0" encoding="utf-8"?>
<appwidget-provider
  xmlns:android="http://schemas.android.com/apk/res/android"
  android:initialLayout="@layout/quake_widget"
  android:minWidth="146dp"
  android:minHeight="74dp"
  android:label="Last Earthquake"
  android:updatePeriodMillis="86400000"
/>
```

4. Add your widget to the application manifest, including a reference to the widget definition resource you created in Step 3, and registering an Intent Filter for the App Widget update action.

```
<receiver android:name="EarthquakeWidget" android:label="Last Earthquake">
  <intent-filter>
    <action android:name="android.appwidget.action.APPWIDGET_UPDATE" />
  </intent-filter>
```

```
<meta-data
  android:name="android.appwidget.provider"
  android:resource="@xml/earthquake_widget_info"
/>
</receiver>
```

Your widget is now configured and will be available to add to the home screen. You now need to update the EarthquakeWidget class from Step 2 to update the widget to display the details of the latest quake.

5. Start by creating two new updateQuake methods within the Earthquake Widget class:

5.1. The first should take an App Widget Manager and an array of widget IDs as well as the context. Later you'll extend this second stub to update the widget appearance using Remote Views.

```
public void updateQuake(Context context,
                        AppWidgetManager appWidgetManager,
                        int[] appWidgetIds) {

}
```

5.2. The second method stub should take only the context, using that to obtain an instance of the AppWidgetManager. Then use the App Widget Manager to find the widget IDs of the active Earthquake widgets, passing both into the method you created in Step 5.1.

```
public void updateQuake(Context context) {
  ComponentName thisWidget = new ComponentName(context,
                                               EarthquakeWidget.class);
  AppWidgetManager appWidgetManager =
    AppWidgetManager.getInstance(context);
  int[] appWidgetIds = appWidgetManager.getAppWidgetIds(thisWidget);
  updateQuake(context, appWidgetManager, appWidgetIds);
}
```

5.3. Within the updateQuake stub from Step 5.1, use the Earthquake Content Provider created in Chapter 6 to retrieve the newest quake and extract its magnitude and location:

```
public void updateQuake(Context context,
                        AppWidgetManager appWidgetManager,
                        int[] appWidgetIds) {

  Cursor lastEarthquake;
  ContentResolver cr = context.getContentResolver();
  lastEarthquake = cr.query(EarthquakeProvider.CONTENT_URI,
                            null, null, null, null);

  String magnitude = "--";
  String details = "-- None --";

  if (lastEarthquake != null) {
    try {
      if (lastEarthquake.moveToFirst()) {
```

```
        magnitude =
lastEarthquake.getString(EarthquakeProvider.MAGNITUDE_COLUMN);
        details =
lastEarthquake.getString(EarthquakeProvider.DETAILS_COLUMN);
      }
    }
    finally {
      lastEarthquake.close();
    }
  }
}
```

5.4. Create a new `RemoteViews` object to set the text displayed by the widget's Text View elements to show the magnitude and location of the last quake:

```
public void updateQuake(Context context,
                        AppWidgetManager appWidgetManager,
                        int[] appWidgetIds) {

  Cursor lastEarthquake;
  ContentResolver cr = context.getContentResolver();
  lastEarthquake = cr.query(EarthquakeProvider.CONTENT_URI,
                            null, null, null, null);

  String magnitude = "--";
  String details = "-- None --";

  if (lastEarthquake != null) {
    try {
      if (lastEarthquake.moveToFirst()) {
        magnitude =
lastEarthquake.getString(EarthquakeProvider.MAGNITUDE_COLUMN);
        details =
lastEarthquake.getString(EarthquakeProvider.DETAILS_COLUMN);
      }
    }
    finally {
      lastEarthquake.close();
    }
  }

  final int N = appWidgetIds.length;
  for (int i = 0; i < N; i++) {
    int appWidgetId = appWidgetIds[i];
    RemoteViews views = new RemoteViews(context.getPackageName(),
                                        R.layout.quake_widget);
    views.setTextViewText(R.id.widget_magnitude, magnitude);
    views.setTextViewText(R.id.widget_details, details);
    appWidgetManager.updateAppWidget(appWidgetId, views);
  }
}
```

6. Override the onUpdate handler to call updateQuake:

```
@Override
public void onUpdate(Context context,
                     AppWidgetManager appWidgetManager,
                     int[] appWidgetIds) {
  updateQuake(context, appWidgetManager, appWidgetIds);
}
```

Your widget is now ready to be used, and will update with new earthquake details when added to the home screen and once every 24 hours thereafter.

7. Now enhance the widget to update whenever the Earthquake Service you created in Chapter 8 has refreshed the earthquake database:

7.1. Start by updating the doRefreshEarthquakes method in the EarthquakeService to broadcast an Intent when it has completed.

```
public static String QUAKES_REFRESHED =
  "com.paad.earthquake.QUAKES_REFRESHED";
public void doRefreshEarthquakes() {
  [ ... Existing doRefreshEarthquakes code ... ]
  sendBroadcast(new Intent(QUAKES_REFRESHED));
}
```

7.2. Override the onReceive method in the EarthquakeWidget class, but be sure to call through to the superclass to ensure that the standard widget event handlers are still triggered:

```
@Override
public void onReceive(Context context, Intent intent){
  super.onReceive(context, intent);
}
```

7.3. Add a check for the QUAKES_REFRESHED action you broadcast in Step 7.1, and call updateQuakes when it's received:

```
@Override
public void onReceive(Context context, Intent intent){
  super.onReceive(context, intent);

  if (intent.getAction().equals(EarthquakeService.QUAKES_REFRESHED))
    updateQuake(context);
}
```

7.4. Finally, add an Intent Filter for this Intent action to the widget's manifest entry:

```
<receiver android:name="EarthquakeWidget" android:label="Last
Earthquake">
  <intent-filter>
    <action android:name="android.appwidget.action.APPWIDGET_UPDATE" />
  </intent-filter>
  <intent-filter>
```

```
    <action android:name="com.paad.earthquake.QUAKES_REFRESHED" />
  </intent-filter>
  <meta-data
    android:name="android.appwidget.provider"
    android:resource="@xml/earthquake_widget_info"
  />
</receiver>
```

Your widget will now update once per day, and every time the Earthquake Service performs a lookup.

To enhance the Earthquake Widget, consider how you could use Layered Drawables within an Image View to indicate the magnitude of the earthquake being shown. Figure 10-3 shows one possibility.

INTRODUCING LIVE FOLDERS

Live Folders are a unique and powerful means by which your applications can expose data from their Content Providers directly on the home screen. They provide dynamic shortcuts to information stored in your application.

When added, a Live Folder is represented on the home screen as a shortcut icon. Selecting the icon will open the Live Folder, as shown in Figure 10-4. This figure shows a Live Folder open on an Android home screen, in this case the starred contacts list.

FIGURE 10-3

 To add a Live Folder to the home screen, long-press a piece of empty space and select Folders. You will be presented with a list of available Live Folders; click one to select and add. Once it is added, click to open the Live Folder, and long-press to move the shortcut.

Creating Live Folders

Live Folders are a combination of two things: a Content Provider that returns the data required to populate a Live Folder in a standard format, and an Activity that returns an Intent used to generate the Live Folder.

To create a new Live Folder you need to define:

➤ An Activity responsible for creating and configuring the Live Folder by generating and returning a specially formatted Intent

➤ A Content Provider that provides the items to be displayed using the correct column names

Each Live Folder item can display up to three pieces of information: an icon, a title, and a description.

Live Folder Content Providers

Any Content Provider can provide the data displayed within a Live Folder. Live Folders use a standard set of column names:

➤ `LiveFolders._ID` A unique identifier used to indicate which item was selected if a user clicks the Live Folder list.

➤ `LiveFolders.NAME` The primary text, displayed in a large font. This is the only required column.

➤ `LiveFolders.DESCRIPTION` A longer descriptive field in a smaller font, displayed beneath the name column.

➤ `LiveFolders.IMAGE` An image displayed at the left of each item.

When displayed, a Live Folder will use these column names to extract data from your Content Provider for display.

Rather than renaming your Content Provider to suit the requirements of Live Folders, you should apply a projection that maps the required column names to columns used within your existing Content Provider, as shown in Listing 10-15.

FIGURE 10-4

LISTING 10-15: Creating a projection to support a Live Folder

Available for
download on
Wrox.com

```
final HashMap<String, String> liveFolderProjection =
  new HashMap<String, String>();
liveFolderProjection.put(LiveFolders._ID,
                         KEY_ID + " AS " +
                         LiveFolders._ID);
liveFolderProjection.put(LiveFolders.NAME,
                         KEY_NAME_COLUMN + " AS " +
                         LiveFolders.NAME);
liveFolderProjection.put(LiveFolders.DESCRIPTION,
                         KEY_DESCRIPTION_COLUMN + " AS " +
                         LiveFolders.DESCRIPTION);
liveFolderProjection.put(LiveFolders.IMAGE,
                         KEY_IMAGE_COLUMN + " AS " +
                         LiveFolders.IMAGE);

SQLiteQueryBuilder qb = new SQLiteQueryBuilder();
qb.setTables(MY_TABLES);
qb.setProjectionMap(LIVE_FOLDER_PROJECTION);
```

Only the ID and name columns are required; the image and description columns can be used or left unmapped as required.

Live Folder Activity

The Live Folder itself is created with an Intent returned as a result from an Activity. The Intent's data property indicates the URI of the Content Provider supplying the data (with the appropriate projection applied), while a series of extras are used to configure settings such as the display mode, icon, and folder name.

Listing 10-16 shows the overridden onCreate method of an Activity used to create a Live Folder.

The Live Folder definition Intent is constructed and set as the Activity result, before the Activity is closed with a call to finish.

LISTING 10-16: Live Folder creation Activity

```java
@Override
public void onCreate(Bundle savedInstanceState) {
  super.onCreate(savedInstanceState);
  String action = getIntent().getAction();
  if (LiveFolders.ACTION_CREATE_LIVE_FOLDER.equals(action)) {
    Intent intent = new Intent();
    intent.setData(EarthquakeProvider.LIVE_FOLDER_URI);
    intent.putExtra(LiveFolders.EXTRA_LIVE_FOLDER_BASE_INTENT,
                    new Intent(Intent.ACTION_VIEW,
                               EarthquakeProvider.CONTENT_URI));
    intent.putExtra(LiveFolders.EXTRA_LIVE_FOLDER_DISPLAY_MODE,
                    LiveFolders.DISPLAY_MODE_LIST);
    intent.putExtra(LiveFolders.EXTRA_LIVE_FOLDER_ICON,
                    Intent.ShortcutIconResource.fromContext(context,
                                                    R.drawable.icon));
    intent.putExtra(LiveFolders.EXTRA_LIVE_FOLDER_NAME, "Earthquakes");
    setResult(RESULT_OK, createLiveFolderIntent(this));
  }
  else
    setResult(RESULT_CANCELED);
  finish();
}
```

As well as the standard configuration values you can add a LiveFolders.EXTRA_LIVE_FOLDER_BASE_INTENT extra to specify a base Intent to fire when a Live Folder item is selected.

When an item is chosen the Live Folder will call showActivity, passing in an Intent that has the data parameter set to the Live Folder's base URI with the selected item's _id value appended.

When adding your Live Folder Activity to the application manifest you need to include an Intent Filter for the CREATE_LIVE_FOLDER action, as shown in Listing 10-17.

LISTING 10-17: Adding the Live Folder Intent Filter

```xml
<activity android:name=".MyLiveFolder "
          android:label="My Live Folder">
  <intent-filter>
    <action android:name="android.intent.action.CREATE_LIVE_FOLDER"/>
  </intent-filter>
</activity>
```

Creating an Earthquake Live Folder

In the following example you'll extend the Earthquake application again, this time to include a Live Folder that displays the magnitude and location of each quake.

1. Start by modifying the `EarthquakeProvider` class. Create a new static URI definition that will be used to return the Live Folder items.

```
public static final Uri LIVE_FOLDER_URI =
  Uri.parse("content://com.paad.provider.earthquake/live_folder");
```

2. Modify the `uriMatcher` object and `getType` method to check for this new URI request.

```
private static final int LIVE_FOLDER = 3;

static {
 uriMatcher = new UriMatcher(UriMatcher.NO_MATCH);
 uriMatcher.addURI("com.paad.provider.Earthquake", "earthquakes", QUAKES);
 uriMatcher.addURI("com.paad.provider.Earthquake", "earthquakes/#", QUAKE_ID);
 uriMatcher.addURI("com.paad.provider.Earthquake", "live_folder", LIVE_FOLDER);
}

@Override
public String getType(Uri uri) {
  switch (uriMatcher.match(uri)) {
    case QUAKES|LIVE_FOLDER :
      return "vnd.android.cursor.dir/vnd.paad.earthquake";
    case QUAKE_ID: return "vnd.android.cursor.item/vnd.paad.earthquake";
    default: throw new IllegalArgumentException("Unsupported URI: " + uri);
  }
}
```

3. Create a new hash map that defines a projection suitable for a Live Folder. It should return the magnitude and location details as the description and name columns respectively.

```
static final HashMap<String, String> LIVE_FOLDER_PROJECTION;
static {
  LIVE_FOLDER_PROJECTION = new HashMap<String, String>();
  LIVE_FOLDER_PROJECTION.put(LiveFolders._ID,
                             KEY_ID + " AS " + LiveFolders._ID);
  LIVE_FOLDER_PROJECTION.put(LiveFolders.NAME,
                             KEY_DETAILS + " AS " + LiveFolders.NAME);
  LIVE_FOLDER_PROJECTION.put(LiveFolders.DESCRIPTION,
                             KEY_DATE + " AS " + LiveFolders.DESCRIPTION);
}
```

4. Update the `query` method to apply the projection map from Step 4 to the returned earthquake query for Live Folder requests.

```
@Override
public Cursor query(Uri uri,
                    String[] projection,
                    String selection,
                    String[] selectionArgs,
                    String sort) {
```

```
SQLiteQueryBuilder qb = new SQLiteQueryBuilder();
qb.setTables(EARTHQUAKE_TABLE);

switch (uriMatcher.match(uri)) {
  case QUAKE_ID :
    qb.appendWhere(KEY_ID + "=" + uri.getPathSegments().get(1));
    break;
  case LIVE_FOLDER : qb.setProjectionMap(LIVE_FOLDER_PROJECTION);
                     break;
  default : break;
}
[ ... existing query method ... ]
}
```

5. Create a new `EarthquakeLiveFolders` class that contains a static `EarthquakeLiveFolder`
Activity.

```
package com.paad.earthquake;

import android.app.Activity;
import android.content.Context;
import android.content.Intent;
import android.os.Bundle;
import android.provider.LiveFolders;

public class EarthquakeLiveFolders extends Activity {
  public static class EarthquakeLiveFolder extends Activity {
  }
}
```

6. Add a new method that builds the Intent used to create the Live Folder. It should use the
query URI you created in Step 1, set the display mode to list, and define the icon and title
string to use. Also set the base Intent Intent to the individual item query from the Earthquake
Provider:

```
private static Intent createLiveFolderIntent(Context context) {
  Intent intent = new Intent();
  intent.setData(EarthquakeProvider.LIVE_FOLDER_URI);
  intent.putExtra(LiveFolders.EXTRA_LIVE_FOLDER_BASE_INTENT,
                  new Intent(Intent.ACTION_VIEW,
                             EarthquakeProvider.CONTENT_URI));
  intent.putExtra(LiveFolders.EXTRA_LIVE_FOLDER_DISPLAY_MODE,
                  LiveFolders.DISPLAY_MODE_LIST);
  intent.putExtra(LiveFolders.EXTRA_LIVE_FOLDER_ICON,
                  Intent.ShortcutIconResource.fromContext(context,
                                                          R.drawable.icon));
  intent.putExtra(LiveFolders.EXTRA_LIVE_FOLDER_NAME, "Earthquakes");
  return intent;
}
```

7. Override the `onCreate` method of the `EarthquakeLiveFolder` class to return the Intent
defined in Step 6:

```
@Override
public void onCreate(Bundle savedInstanceState) {
  super.onCreate(savedInstanceState);
```

```
      String action = getIntent().getAction();
      if (LiveFolders.ACTION_CREATE_LIVE_FOLDER.equals(action))
        setResult(RESULT_OK, createLiveFolderIntent(this));
      else
        setResult(RESULT_CANCELED);
      finish();
    }
```

8. Add the `EarthquakeLiveFolder` Activity to the application manifest, including an Intent Filter for the action `android.intent.action.CREATE_LIVE_FOLDER`:

```xml
<activity android:name=".EarthquakeLiveFolders$EarthquakeLiveFolder"
          android:label="All Earthquakes">
  <intent-filter>
    <action android:name="android.intent.action.CREATE_LIVE_FOLDER"/>
  </intent-filter>
</activity>
```

Figure 10-5 shows the earthquake Live Folder open on the home screen.

You could expand this example by using the Earthquake Map Activity to display a specific quake when it's selected from the list.

Start by adding an Intent Filter to the Earthquake Map Activity that listens for View actions on earthquake Content Provider data described by the Intent created in Step 6. Then improve the Activity to retrieve the location of the selected quake and center the map to that point.

FIGURE 10-5

ADDING SEARCH TO YOUR APPLICATIONS AND THE QUICK SEARCH BOX

With applications featuring large back-end databases and storing large volumes of data, the ability to search for information within an application is an increasingly important feature.

Android includes a framework to simplify searching within your Content Providers and surfacing the results using a consistent framework. This section explains how to add search functionality to your application using this search framework.

Adding Search to Your Application

Most Android devices feature a hardware *search* key. Using this framework you can expose your application-specific search functionality whenever a user presses the search button. The search box will dynamically display search results as the user types a query.

Creating a Search Activity

To enable application search, you must create an Activity that will be used to initiate and display the search.

The first step is to create a new searchable metadata XML resource in the res/xml folder. This file, shown in Listing 10-18, specifies the authority of the Content Provider you will be performing the search on, and the action to fire if a suggested search result is clicked.

LISTING 10-18: Defining application search metadata

```xml
<searchable xmlns:android="http://schemas.android.com/apk/res/android"
  android:label="@string/app_name"
  android:searchSuggestAuthority="myauthority"
  android:searchSuggestIntentAction="android.intent.action.VIEW">
</searchable>
```

Next, you will need to create an Activity that will be used to display the search results. In many cases this will be a simple List View-based Activity, but it can use any user interface you require. As shown in Listing 10-19, include a `<meta-data>` tag that includes a `name` attribute that specifies `android.app.searchable` and a `resource` attribute that specifies the XML resource you created in Listing 10-18.

You must also include an Intent Filter registered for the `android.intent.action.SEARCH` action and the `DEFAULT` category.

LISTING 10-19: Registering a search results Activity

```xml
<activity android:name=".EarthquakeSearch" android:label="Earthquake Search">
  <intent-filter>
    <action android:name="android.intent.action.SEARCH" />
    <category android:name="android.intent.category.DEFAULT" />
  </intent-filter>
  <meta-data
    android:name="android.app.searchable"
    android:resource="@xml/searchable"
  />
</activity>
```

The search query that caused this search result Activity to be displayed will be returned within the calling Intent using the `SearchMananger.USER_QUERY` extra as shown in the following:

```java
String searchTerm = getIntent().getStringExtra(SearchManager.USER_QUERY);
```

It's good practice to use the same search results form for your entire application. To set an Activity as the default search results provider for an application you need to add a new `<meta-data>` tag to the `<application>` manifest node as shown in Listing 10-20.

Set the `name` attribute to `android.app.default_searchable` and specify your search Activity using the `value` attribute.

LISTING 10-20: Setting a default search result Activity for an application

```
<meta-data
  android:name="android.app.default_searchable"
  android:value=".EarthquakeSearch"
/>
```

Responding to Search Queries from a Content Provider

The search Activity described in the previous section can be used to initiate a search and display the results for an application. In order for it to have data to display you need to create (or modify) a Content Provider to handle search queries and return results.

To support the Android search framework you need to support specific query path URI values. Listing 10-21 shows a URI Matcher that compares a requested URI to the known search query path values.

LISTING 10-21: Detecting search requests in Content Providers

```
private static int SEARCH = 1;

static {
  uriMatcher = new UriMatcher(UriMatcher.NO_MATCH);
  uriMatcher.addURI("com.paad.provider.earthquake", "earthquakes", QUAKES);
  uriMatcher.addURI("com.paad.provider.earthquake", "earthquakes/#", QUAKE_ID);
  uriMatcher.addURI("com.paad.provider.earthquake",
    SearchManager.SUGGEST_URI_PATH_QUERY, SEARCH);
  uriMatcher.addURI("com.paad.provider.earthquake",
    SearchManager.SUGGEST_URI_PATH_QUERY + "/*", SEARCH);
  uriMatcher.addURI("com.paad.provider.earthquake",
    SearchManager.SUGGEST_URI_PATH_SHORTCUT, SEARCH);
  uriMatcher.addURI("com.paad.provider.earthquake",
    SearchManager.SUGGEST_URI_PATH_SHORTCUT + "/*", SEARCH);
}
```

Use a similar URI Matcher pattern within your Content Provider to return the appropriate MIME type for search queries as shown in Listing 10-22. Search results should be returned as SearchManager.SUGGEST_MIME_TYPE in order to support live search suggestions.

LISTING 10-22: Returning the correct MIME type for search results

```
@Override
public String getType(Uri uri) {
  switch (uriMatcher.match(uri)) {
    case QUAKES  : return "vnd.android.cursor.dir/vnd.paad.earthquake";
    case QUAKE_ID: return "vnd.android.cursor.item/vnd.paad.earthquake";
    case SEARCH  : return SearchManager.SUGGEST_MIME_TYPE;
    default: throw new IllegalArgumentException("Unsupported URI: " + uri);
  }
}
```

The URI Matcher can also be used within the `query` method. If an incoming search query is detected, find the search term by examining the last segment of the query URI.

```
uri.getPathSegments().get(1);
```

To return search results that can be displayed using the Android search framework you will need to create and apply a projection that assigns your column names to those supplied and supported by the Search Manager. The Search Manager class includes a number of static constants of the form `SUGGEST_COLUMN_*` that can be used in the projection.

There are two required columns, `SUGGEST_COLUMN_TEXT_1` which displays the search result text and `id_`, which indicates the unique row ID.

Listing 10-23 shows the skeleton code for creating and applying a projection within a query that returns a Cursor suitable for search results.

LISTING 10-23: Returning search results from a query

```java
private static final HashMap<String, String> SEARCH_PROJECTION_MAP;
static {
  SEARCH_PROJECTION_MAP = new HashMap<String, String>();
  SEARCH_PROJECTION_MAP.put(SearchManager.SUGGEST_COLUMN_TEXT_1,
                            KEY_SEARCH_COLUMN + " AS " +
                            SearchManager.SUGGEST_COLUMN_TEXT_1);
  SEARCH_PROJECTION_MAP.put("_id", KEY_ID + " AS " + "_id");
}

@Override
public Cursor query(Uri uri, String[] projection, String selection, String[]
                    selectionArgs, String sort) {
  SQLiteQueryBuilder qb = new SQLiteQueryBuilder();
  qb.setTables(MY_TABLE);

  switch (uriMatcher.match(uri)) {
    case SINGLE_ID:
      qb.appendWhere(KEY_ID + "=" + uri.getPathSegments().get(1));
      break;
    case SEARCH    : qb.appendWhere(KEY_SEARCH_COLUMN + " LIKE \"%" +
                                    uri.getPathSegments().get(1) + "%\"");
                     qb.setProjectionMap(SEARCH_PROJECTION_MAP);
                     break;
    default        : break;
  }

  Cursor c = qb.query(MyDB,
                      projection,
                      selection, selectionArgs,
                      null, null, orderBy);

  return c;
}
```

Surfacing Search Results to the Quick Search Box

Android 1.6 (API Level 4) introduced the ability to serve your application search results through the universal Quick Search Box widget.

The Quick Search Box is positioned prominently on the home screen, and the user can launch it at any time by pressing the hardware search key. By surfacing search results from your application through this mechanism you provide users with an additional access point to your application through live search results.

To serve your search results to the Quick Search Box, you must first implement search functionality within your application as described in the previous section.

To make your results available globally, modify the searchable.xml file that describes the application search metadata and add two new attributes as shown in Listing 10-24:

➤   `searchSettingsDescription`   Used to describe your search results in the Settings menu.

➤   `includeInGlobalSearch`   Set this to true to surface these results to the quick search box.

LISTING 10-24: Adding your search result to the Quick Search Box

```xml
<searchable xmlns:android="http://schemas.android.com/apk/res/android"
    android:label="@string/app_name"
    android:searchSettingsDescription="@string/app_name"
    android:includeInGlobalSearch="true"
    android:searchSuggestAuthority="com.paad.provider.earthquake"
    android:searchSuggestIntentAction="android.intent.action.VIEW">
</searchable>
```

Note that your search results will not automatically be surfaced directly to the Quick Search Box. To avoid the possibility of misuse, adding new search providers requires users to opt-in.

To add new Quick Search Box search providers, use the system settings. Navigate to Settings ➪ Search ➪ Searchable Items and tick the check boxes alongside each provider you wish to enable.

> *Because result surfacing in the Quick Search Box is strictly opt-in, you should consider notifying your users that this additional functionality is available.*

Adding Search to the Earthquake Example

In the following example you'll add search functionality to the Earthquake project, and make sure results are available from the home-screen Quick Search Box.

1.   Start by adding two new string resources to the strings.xml file in the res/values folder. One will be the name used to identify the earthquake search results; the other will be a description of what they represent.

```xml
<string name="search_label">Earthquakes</string>
<string name="search_description">Earthquake locations</string>
```

2. Next, create a new XML resources folder, res/xml. Create a new searchable.xml file which will define the metadata for your Earthquake search results provider. Specify the strings from Step 1 as the label and description values. Specify the Earthquake Content Provider's authority and set the `includeInGlobalSearch` attribute to true.

```
<searchable xmlns:android="http://schemas.android.com/apk/res/android"
  android:label="@string/app_name"
  android:searchSettingsDescription="@string/app_name"
  android:includeInGlobalSearch="true"
  android:searchSuggestAuthority="com.paad.provider.earthquake"
  android:searchSuggestIntentAction="android.intent.action.VIEW">
</searchable>
```

3. Open the Earthquake Content Provider. Start by adding a new SEARCH_URI static constant that you can use to execute a search within the application.

```
public static final Uri SEARCH_URI =
  Uri.parse("content://com.paad.provider.earthquake/" +
            SearchManager.SUGGEST_URI_PATH_QUERY);
```

4. Now create a new Projection that will be used to supply search results.

```
private static final HashMap<String, String> SEARCH_PROJECTION_MAP;
static {
  SEARCH_PROJECTION_MAP = new HashMap<String, String>();
  SEARCH_PROJECTION_MAP.put(SearchManager.SUGGEST_COLUMN_TEXT_1, KEY_DETAILS +
    " AS " + SearchManager.SUGGEST_COLUMN_TEXT_1);
  SEARCH_PROJECTION_MAP.put("_id", KEY_ID +
    " AS " + "_id");
}
```

5. Now modify the UriMatcher to include search queries.

```
private static int SEARCH = 3;

static {
  uriMatcher = new UriMatcher(UriMatcher.NO_MATCH);
  uriMatcher.addURI("com.paad.provider.earthquake", "earthquakes", QUAKES);
  uriMatcher.addURI("com.paad.provider.earthquake", "earthquakes/#", QUAKE_ID);
  uriMatcher.addURI("com.paad.provider.earthquake",
    SearchManager.SUGGEST_URI_PATH_QUERY, SEARCH);
  uriMatcher.addURI("com.paad.provider.earthquake",
    SearchManager.SUGGEST_URI_PATH_QUERY + "/*", SEARCH);
  uriMatcher.addURI("com.paad.provider.earthquake",
    SearchManager.SUGGEST_URI_PATH_SHORTCUT, SEARCH);
  uriMatcher.addURI("com.paad.provider.earthquake",
    SearchManager.SUGGEST_URI_PATH_SHORTCUT + "/*", SEARCH);
}
```

6. Modify the getType method to return the appropriate MIME type for search results.

```
@Override
public String getType(Uri uri) {
  switch (uriMatcher.match(uri)) {
```

```
case QUAKES  : return "vnd.android.cursor.dir/vnd.paad.earthquake";
case QUAKE_ID: return "vnd.android.cursor.item/vnd.paad.earthquake";
case SEARCH  : return SearchManager.SUGGEST_MIME_TYPE;
default: throw new IllegalArgumentException("Unsupported URI: " + uri);
    }
  }
```

7. The final change to the Content Provider is to modify the `query` method to apply the search term and return the result query using the Projection you created in Step 4. This will allow the Quick Search Box search suggestions, and your search Activity, to display the results.

```
@Override
public Cursor query(Uri uri, String[] projection, String selection, String[]
                    selectionArgs, String sort) {
  SQLiteQueryBuilder qb = new SQLiteQueryBuilder();
  qb.setTables(EARTHQUAKE_TABLE);

  // If this is a row query, limit the result set to the passed in row.
  switch (uriMatcher.match(uri)) {
    case QUAKE_ID: qb.appendWhere(KEY_ID + "=" + uri.getPathSegments().get(1));
                   break;
    case SEARCH  : qb.appendWhere(KEY_DETAILS + " LIKE \"%" +
                                    uri.getPathSegments().get(1) + "%\"");
                   qb.setProjectionMap(SEARCH_PROJECTION_MAP);
                   break;
    default      : break;
  }

  [ ... existing query method ... ]
}
```

8. Now create a new Activity that will be used to display the search results. For these purposes, create a simple `EarthquakeSearch` Activity that extends `ListActivity`. EarthquakeSearch will only be displayed as a result of a search query, so extract the user query from the search Intent that launched the application and use it to query the Earthquake Content Provider. Create a Simple Cursor Adapter to bind the search results cursor to the Activity's List View.

```
import android.app.ListActivity;
import android.app.SearchManager;
import android.database.Cursor;
import android.net.Uri;
import android.os.Bundle;
import android.widget.SimpleCursorAdapter;

public class EarthquakeSearch extends ListActivity {
  @Override
  public void onCreate(Bundle savedInstanceState) {
    super.onCreate(savedInstanceState);

    String searchTerm = getIntent().getStringExtra(SearchManager.USER_QUERY);
    String searchQuery = Uri.withAppendedPath(EarthquakeProvider.SEARCH_URI,
                                              searchTerm);
```

```
Cursor c = getContentResolver().query(searchQuery, null, null, null, null);
startManagingCursor(c);

String[] from = new String[] {SearchManager.SUGGEST_COLUMN_TEXT_1};
int[] to = new int[] {android.R.id.text1};
SimpleCursorAdapter searchResults = new SimpleCursorAdapter(this,
  android.R.layout.simple_list_item_1, c, from, to);
  setListAdapter(searchResults);
  }
}
```

9. Open the application Manifest and add the new EarthquakeSearch Activity. Make sure you add an Intent Filter for the SEARCH action in the DEFAULT category. You will also need to add a `<meta-data>` tag that specifies the searchable XML resource you created in Step 2.

```xml
<activity android:name=".EarthquakeSearch" android:label="Earthquake Search">
  <intent-filter>
    <action android:name="android.intent.action.SEARCH" />
    <category android:name="android.intent.category.DEFAULT" />
  </intent-filter>
  <meta-data
    android:name="android.app.searchable"
    android:resource="@xml/searchable"
  />
</activity>
```

10. The final step is to add a new `<meta-data>` tag to the `<application>` node in the manifest that describes the EarthquakeSearch Activity as the default search provider for the application.

```xml
<application android:icon="@drawable/icon">
  <meta-data
    android:name="android.app.default_searchable"
    android:value=".EarthquakeSearch"
  />
  [ ... existing application node ... ]
</application>
```

All code snippets in this example are part of the Chapter 10 Earthquake *project, available for download at Wrox.com.*

If you run this application, pressing the hardware search key in any of the Activities will provide a search box that returns suggestions and search results as you type. To have your results available in the home screen Quick Search Box, you will need to go to Settings ➪ Search ➪ Searchable Items and tick the "Earthquake" item.

CREATING LIVE WALLPAPER

Live Wallpaper is a new way to add an application component to the home screen introduced in Android 2.1 (API level 7). Live Wallpaper lets you create dynamic, interactive home-screen backgrounds, providing you with an exciting new alternative for displaying information to your users directly on the home screen.

Live Wallpaper uses a Surface to render a dynamic display and listens for screen touch events to let users interact with the display.

To create a new Live Wallpaper you need three components:

➤ A Live Wallpaper XML resource

➤ A Wallpaper Service implementation

➤ A Wallpaper Engine implementation (returned through the Wallpaper Service)

Creating a Live Wallpaper Definition Resource

The Live Wallpaper resource definition is an XML file stored in the res/xml folder. Use attributes within the `<wallpaper>` tag to define the author name, wallpaper description, and thumbnail to display in the Live Wallpaper gallery at run time. You can also use the `settingsActivity` tag to specify an Activity to launch to configure the wallpaper's settings.

Listing 10-25 shows a sample Live Wallpaper resource.

LISTING 10-25: Sample Live Wallpaper resource definition

```xml
<wallpaper xmlns:android="http://schemas.android.com/apk/res/android"
    android:author="@string/author"
    android:description="@string/description"
    android:thumbnail="@drawable/wallpapericon"
/>
```

Note that you must use references to existing string resources for the author and description attribute values. String literals are not valid.

Creating a Wallpaper Service

Extend the `WallpaperService` class to create a wrapper Service that instantiates a Wallpaper Service Engine class.

All the drawing and interaction for Live Wallpaper is handled in the Wallpaper Service Engine class described later in this chapter. Override the `onCreateEngine` handler to return a new instance of your custom Wallpaper Service Engine as shown in Listing 10-26.

LISTING 10-26: A Live Wallpaper Service

```java
public class MyWallpaperService extends WallpaperService {
    @Override
    public Engine onCreateEngine() {
        return new MyWallpaperServiceEngine();
    }
}
```

Once you've created it, add your Live Wallpaper Service to your application manifest using the `<service>` tag. A Live Wallpaper must also include an Intent Filter to listen for the android.service.wallpaper.WallpaperService action, and a <meta-data> node that specifies the android.service.wallpaper as the name attribute, and associates it with the resource file described in the previous section using a resource attribute.

Your Live Wallpaper Service must also require the android.permission.BIND_WALLPAPER permission using the android.permission attribute. Listing 10-27 shows how to add the Live Wallpaper from Listing 10-26 to the manifest.

LISTING 10-27: Adding a Live Wallpaper Service to the manifest

```
<service android:name=".MyWallpaperService"
    android.permission="android.permission.BIND_WALLPAPER">
    <intent-filter>
      <action android:name="android.service.wallpaper.WallpaperService" />
    </intent-filter>
    <meta-data
      android:name="android.service.wallpaper"
      android:resource="@xml/wallpaper"
    />
</service>
```

Creating a Wallpaper Service Engine

The WallpaperService.Engine class is where you create the Live Wallpaper itself.

The Wallpaper Service Engine encapsulates a Surface which is used to display the wallpaper and handle touch events. A Surface is a specialized drawing canvas that supports updates from background threads, making it ideal for creating smooth, dynamic, and interactive graphics. Both the Surface View, and handling touch events, are covered in more detail in Chapter 15.

To implement your own Wallpaper Service engine, extend the WallpaperService.Engine class. Before you can start drawing on the Surface, you must wait for it to complete initialization, indicated by the onSurfaceCreated event handler.

The Wallpaper Service Engine also includes an onTouchEvent callback to provide user-interactivity with the wallpaper, and the onOffsetsChanged handler to notify you that the parent Activity (usually the home screen) has been offset (panned).

Listing 10-28 shows the skeleton code for a Wallpaper Service Engine implementation. Refer to Chapter 15 for more details on how to draw on a Surface and use the onTouchEvent handler and Motion Events.

LISTING 10-28: Wallpaper Service Engine skeleton code

```
public class MyWallpaperServiceEngine extends WallpaperService.Engine {
  @Override
  public void onCreate(SurfaceHolder surfaceHolder) {
    super.onCreate(surfaceHolder);
    // TODO Handle initialization.
  }
```

```
@Override
public void onOffsetsChanged(float xOffset, float yOffset,
                            float xOffsetStep, float yOffsetStep,
                            int xPixelOffset, int yPixelOffset) {
  super.onOffsetsChanged(xOffset, yOffset, xOffsetStep, yOffsetStep,
                         xPixelOffset, yPixelOffset);
  // TODO Handle homescreen offset events.
}

@Override
public void onTouchEvent(MotionEvent event) {
  super.onTouchEvent(event);
  // TODO Handle touch and motion events.
}

@Override
public void onSurfaceCreated(SurfaceHolder holder) {
  super.onSurfaceCreated(holder);
  // TODO Surface has been created, run the Thread that will
  // update the display.
}
}
```

SUMMARY

In this chapter you learned how to create App Widgets and Live Folders for your application.

In particular you saw how to do the following:

➤ Implement widgets and add them to your applications.

➤ Control the update rate of your widgets by setting the minimum refresh rate or using Intents and Alarms.

➤ Update the UI of your widgets using Remote Views.

➤ Add interactivity to your widgets.

➤ Create and register a Live Folder for your application's Content Provider.

➤ Add a projection to your Content Provider to provide a Live Folder schema.

➤ Create and use Live Wallpaper.

➤ Add search to your application and surface search results to the Quick Search Box.

In the following chapter you will explore the audiovisual APIs available in Android. You'll take a look at multimedia playback and recording using the microphone and camera.

11

Audio, Video, and Using the Camera

WHAT'S IN THIS CHAPTER?

- ➤ Playing audio and video with the Media Player
- ➤ Packaging audio as an application resource
- ➤ Using the Video View for video playback
- ➤ Recording audio and video with the Media Recorder
- ➤ Recording video and taking pictures using Intents
- ➤ Previewing recorded video and displaying live camera streams
- ➤ Taking pictures and controlling the camera
- ➤ Reading and modifying image EXIF data
- ➤ Adding media to the Media Store
- ➤ Manipulating raw audio
- ➤ Using speech recognition

The only modern technology that can compete with mobile phones for ubiquity is the portable digital media player. As a result, the multimedia capabilities of mobile devices are a significant consideration for many consumers.

Android's open platform and provider-agnostic philosophy ensures that it offers a multimedia API capable of playing and recording a wide range of image, audio, and video formats, both locally and streamed.

The Camera API and OpenCORE multimedia platform expose these capabilities to your applications, providing comprehensive multimedia functionality.

In this chapter you'll learn how to play and record multimedia content including audio, video, and still images, as well as use the camera to capture images and preview and record live video.

You'll also learn how to manipulate raw audio files using the Audio Track and Audio Record classes, add newly recorded media files to the Media Store, and make use of speech recognition to add voice input to your applications.

PLAYING AUDIO AND VIDEO

Android includes a comprehensive `Media Player` to simplify the playback of audio and video. This section describes how to use it to control and manipulate media playback within your applications.

Android 2.1 (API level 7) supports the following multimedia formats for playback as part of the base framework. Note that some devices may support playback of additional file formats:

Audio

- ➤ AAC LC/LTP
- ➤ HE-AACv1 (AAC+)
- ➤ HE-AACv2 (Enhanced AAC+)
- ➤ AMR-NB
- ➤ AMR-WB
- ➤ MP3
- ➤ MIDI
- ➤ Ogg Vorbis
- ➤ PCM / WAVE

Video

- ➤ H.263
- ➤ H.264 AVC
- ➤ MPEG-4 SP

Introducing the Media Player

Multimedia playback in Android is handled by the `MediaPlayer` class. You can play media stored in application resources, local files, Content Providers, or streamed from a network URL. In each case, the file format and type of multimedia being played is abstracted from you as a developer.

The Media Player's management of audio and video files and streams is handled as a state machine. In the most simplistic terms, transitions through the state machine can be described as follows:

- ➤ Initialize the Media Player with media to play.
- ➤ Prepare the Media Player for playback.

➤ Start the playback.

➤ Pause or stop the playback prior to its completing.

➤ Playback complete.

A more detailed and thorough description of the Media Player state machine is provided at the Android developer site at `http://developer.android.com/reference/android/media/MediaPlayer .html#StateDiagram`

To play a media resource you need to create a new `MediaPlayer` instance, initialize it with a media source, and prepare it for playback.

The following section describes how to initialize and prepare the Media Player. After that, you'll learn to control the playback to start, pause, stop, or seek the prepared media.

In each case, once you've finished playback, call `release` on your Media Player object to free the associated resources:

```
mediaPlayer.release();
```

Android supports a limited number of simultaneous Media Player objects; not releasing them can cause runtime exceptions when the system runs out of resources.

Preparing Audio for Playback

There are a number of ways you can play audio content through the Media Player. You can include it as an application resource, play it from local files or Content Providers, or stream it from a remote URL.

Packaging Audio as an Application Resource

You can include audio files in your application package by adding them to the res/raw folder of your resources hierarchy.

Raw resources are not compressed or manipulated in any way when packaged into your application, making them an ideal way to store pre-compressed files such as audio content.

To access a raw resource simply use the lowercase filename without an extension, as shown in Listing 11-1.

Initializing Audio Content for Playback

To play back audio content using the Media Player, you need to create a new Media Player object and set the data source of the audio in question.

To play back audio using the Media Player, you can use the static `create` method, passing in the application Context and one of the following (as shown in Listing 11-1):

➤ A resource identifier

➤ A URI to a local file using the `file://` schema

➤ A URI to an online audio resource as a URL

➤ A URI to a local Content Provider row

Note that the Media Player object returned by the `create` methods have already had `prepare` called. It's important that you do not call it again.

LISTING 11-1: Initializing audio content for playback

```
Context appContext = getApplicationContext();

MediaPlayer resourcePlayer = MediaPlayer.create(appContext,
  R.raw.my_audio);
MediaPlayer filePlayer = MediaPlayer.create(appContext,
  Uri.parse("file:///sdcard/localfile.mp3"));
MediaPlayer urlPlayer = MediaPlayer.create(appContext,
  Uri.parse("http://site.com/audio/audio.mp3"));
MediaPlayer contentPlayer = MediaPlayer.create(appContext,
  Settings.System.DEFAULT_RINGTONE_URI);
```

Alternatively, you can use the `setDataSource` method on an existing Media Player instance. This method accepts a file path, Content Provider URI, streaming media URL path, or File Descriptor.

When using the `setDataSource` method it is vital that you call `prepare` on the Media Player before you begin playback, as shown in Listing 11-2.

LISTING 11-2: Using setDataSource and prepare to initialize audio playback

```
MediaPlayer mediaPlayer = new MediaPlayer();
mediaPlayer.setDataSource("/sdcard/test.3gp");
mediaPlayer.prepare();
```

 If you're passing a URL to an online media file, the file must be capable of progressive download using the RTSP or HTTP protocols.

Preparing for Video Playback

Playback of video content is slightly more involved than audio. To show a video, you must specify a display surface on which to show it. The following sections describe two alternatives for the playback of video content.

The first, using the Video View control, encapsulates the creation of a display surface and allocation and preparation of video content within a Media Player.

The second technique allows you to specify your own display surface and manipulate the underlying Media Player instance directly.

Playing Video Using the Video View

The simplest way to play back video is to use the VideoView control. The Video View includes a Surface on which the video is displayed and encapsulates and manages a Media Player to manage the video playback.

The Video View supports the playback of local or streaming video as supported by the Media Player component.

Video Views conveniently encapsulate the initialization of the Media Player. To assign a video to play, simply call setVideoPath or setVideoUri to specify the path to a local file, or the URI of a Content Provider or remote video stream:

```
streamingVideoView.setVideoUri("http://www.mysite.com/videos/myvideo.3gp");
localVideoView.setVideoPath("/sdcard/test2.3gp");
```

Once initialized, you can control playback using the start, stopPlayback, pause, and seekTo methods. The Video View also includes the setKeepScreenOn method to apply a screen Wake Lock that will prevent the screen from being dimmed while playback is in progress.

Listing 11-3 shows the simple skeleton code used to assign a video to a Video View and control playback.

LISTING 11-3: Video playback using a Video View

```
VideoView videoView = (VideoView)findViewById(R.id.surface);
videoView.setKeepScreenOn(true);
videoView.setVideoPath("/sdcard/test2.3gp");
if (videoView.canSeekForward())
  videoView.seekTo(videoView.getDuration()/2);
videoView.start();
[ ... do something ... ]
videoView.stopPlayback();
```

Setting up a Surface for Video Playback

The first step to using the Media Player to view video content is to prepare a Surface onto which the video will be displayed. The Media Player requires a SurfaceHolder object for displaying video content, assigned using the setDisplay method.

> *If you do not assign a Surface Holder for your Media Player the video component will not be shown.*

To include a Surface Holder in your UI layout you use the SurfaceView control as shown in the sample layout XML in Listing 11-4.

LISTING 11-4: Sample layout including a Surface View

```xml
<?xml version="1.0" encoding="utf-8"?>
<LinearLayout xmlns:android="http://schemas.android.com/apk/res/android"
  android:orientation="vertical"
  android:layout_width="fill_parent"
  android:layout_height="fill_parent">
  <SurfaceView
    android:id="@+id/surface"
    android:layout_width="wrap_content"
    android:layout_height="wrap_content"
    android:layout_gravity="center">
  </SurfaceView>
</LinearLayout>
```

The Surface View is a wrapper around the Surface Holder object, which in turn is a wrapper around the Surface that is used to support visual updates from background threads.

The Surface View will be examined in more detail in Chapter 15, but Listing 11-5 shows the skeleton code used to initialize a Surface View within your Activity, and assign it as a display target for your Media Player.

Note that you must implement the `SurfaceHolder.Callback` interface. Surface Holders are created asynchronously, so you must wait until the `surfaceCreated` handler has been fired before assigning the returned Surface Holder object to the Media Player.

LISTING 11-5: Initializing and assigning a Surface View to a Media Player

```java
public class MyActivity extends Activity implements SurfaceHolder.Callback
{
  private MediaPlayer mediaPlayer;

  @Override
  public void onCreate(Bundle savedInstanceState) {
    super.onCreate(savedInstanceState);
    setContentView(R.layout.main);
    mediaPlayer = new MediaPlayer();

    SurfaceView surface = (SurfaceView)findViewById(R.id.surface);
    SurfaceHolder holder = surface.getHolder();
    holder.addCallback(this);
    holder.setType(SurfaceHolder.SURFACE_TYPE_PUSH_BUFFERS);
    holder.setFixedSize(400, 300);
  }

  public void surfaceCreated(SurfaceHolder holder) {
    try {
      mediaPlayer.setDisplay(holder);
    } catch (IllegalArgumentException e) {
      Log.d("MEDIA_PLAYER", e.getMessage());
```

```
      } catch (IllegalStateException e) {
        Log.d("MEDIA_PLAYER", e.getMessage());
      } catch (IOException e) {
        Log.d("MEDIA_PLAYER", e.getMessage());
      }
    }

    public void surfaceDestroyed(SurfaceHolder holder) {
      mediaPlayer.release();
    }

    public void surfaceChanged(SurfaceHolder holder,
                               int format, int width, int height) { }
  }
```

Initializing Video Content for Playback

Once you have created and assigned the Surface Holder to your Media Player, use the `setDataSource` method to specify the path, URL, or Content Provider URI of the video resource to play.

As with audio playback, if you're passing a URL to an online media file, the file must be capable of progressive download using the RTSP or HTTP protocols.

Once you've selected your media source, call `prepare` to initialize the Media Player in preparation for playback as shown in Listing 11-6.

LISTING 11-6: Initializing video for playback using the Media Player

```
public void surfaceCreated(SurfaceHolder holder) {
  try {
    mediaPlayer.setDisplay(holder);
    mediaPlayer.setDataSource("/sdcard/test2.3gp");
    mediaPlayer.prepare();
    mediaPlayer.start();
  } catch (IllegalArgumentException e) {
    Log.d("MEDIA_PLAYER", e.getMessage());
  } catch (IllegalStateException e) {
    Log.d("MEDIA_PLAYER", e.getMessage());
  } catch (IOException e) {
    Log.d("MEDIA_PLAYER", e.getMessage());
  }
}
```

 Unlike audio resources, Android doesn't yet support the playback of video resources included in the application package. Similarly, you cannot use the `create` *static methods as shortcuts to creating your Media Player objects, nor can you use a URI to point to a local file using the* `file://` *schema.*

Controlling Playback

Once a Media Player is prepared, call `start` to begin playback of the associated media:

```
mediaPlayer.start();
```

Use the `stop` and `pause` methods to stop or pause playback.

The Media Player also provides the `getDuration` method to find the length of the media being played, and `getCurrentPosition` to find the playback position. Use `seekTo` to jump to a specific position in the media as shown in Listing 11-7.

LISTING 11-7: Controlling playback

```
mediaPlayer.start();

int pos = mediaPlayer.getCurrentPosition();
int duration = mediaPlayer.getDuration();

mediaPlayer.seekTo(pos + (duration-pos)/10);

[ ...  wait for a duration ...  ]

mediaPlayer.stop();
```

Managing Media Playback Output

The Media Player provides methods to control the volume of the output, manage the screen lock during playback, and set the looping status.

It is not currently possible to play audio into a phone conversation; the Media Player always plays audio using the standard output device — the speaker or connected Bluetooth headset.

Use the `isLooping` and `setLooping` methods to specify if the media being played should loop when it completes.

```
if (!mediaPlayer.isLooping())
  mediaPlayer.setLooping(true);
```

To enable a Wake Lock that will keep the screen on during video playback use the `setScreenOnWhile Playing` method. This is preferred to setting manual Wake Lock as it doesn't require an additional permission. Wake Locks are described in more detail in Chapter 15.

```
mediaPlayer.setScreenOnWhilePlaying(true);
```

You can control the volume for each channel during playback using the `setVolume` method. It takes a scalar float value between 0 and 1 for both the left and right channels (where 0 is silent and 1 is maximum volume).

```
mediaPlayer.setVolume(1f, 0.5f);
```

When playing video resources, you can use getFrame *to take a Bitmap screen grab of video media at the specified frame.*

RECORDING AUDIO AND VIDEO

Android offers two alternatives for recording audio and video within your application.

The simplest technique is to use Intents to launch the video camera app. This option lets you specify the output location and video recording quality, while letting the native video recording application handle the user experience and error handling.

In cases where you want to replace the native app, or simply need more fine-grained control over the video capture UI or recording settings, you can use the Media Recorder class.

Using Intents to Record Video

The easiest way to initiate video recording is using the ACTION_VIDEO_CAPTURE Media Store static constant in an Intent passed to startActivityForResult.

```
startActivityForResult(new Intent(MediaStore.ACTION_VIDEO_CAPTURE),
                       RECORD_VIDEO);
```

This will launch the native video camera Activity, allowing users to start, stop, review, and retake their video, and preventing you from having to rewrite the entire video camera application.

The video capture action supports two optional extras, available as static constants from the MediaStore class:

➤ EXTRA_OUTPUT   By default, the video recorded by the video capture action will be stored in the default Media Store. If you want to record it elsewhere, you can specify an alternative URI using this extra.

➤ EXTRA_VIDEO_QUALITY   The video record action allows you to specify an image quality using an integer value. There are currently two possible values: 0 for low (MMS) quality videos or 1 for high (full resolution) videos. By default, the high resolution mode will be used.

Listing 11-8 shows how to use the video capture action to record a new video in high quality to either a specified URI or the default media store.

LISTING 11-8: Recording video using an Intent

 Available for download on Wrox.com

```
private static int RECORD_VIDEO = 1;
private static int HIGH_VIDEO_QUALITY = 1;
private static int MMS_VIDEO_QUALITY = 0;
```

continues

LISTING 11-8 *(continued)*

```
private void recordVideo(Uri outputpath) {
  Intent intent = new Intent(MediaStore.ACTION_VIDEO_CAPTURE);

  if (outputpath != null)
    intent.putExtra(MediaStore.EXTRA_OUTPUT, output);
  intent.putExtra(MediaStore.EXTRA_VIDEO_QUALITY, HIGH_VIDEO_QUALITY);

  startActivityForResult(intent, RECORD_VIDEO);
}

@Override
protected void onActivityResult(int requestCode,
                                int resultCode, Intent data) {
  if (requestCode == RECORD_VIDEO) {
    Uri recordedVideo = data.getData();
    // TODO Do something with the recorded video
  }
}
```

Using the Media Recorder

Multimedia recording is handled by the aptly named `MediaRecorder` class. You can use it to record audio and/or video files that can be used in your own applications, or added to the Media Store.

To record audio or video, create a new Media Recorder object.

```
MediaRecorder mediaRecorder = new MediaRecorder();
```

Before you can record any media in Android, your application needs the `RECORD_AUDIO` and / or `RECORD_VIDEO` permissions. Add `uses-permission` tags for each of them, as required, in your application manifest.

```
<uses-permission android:name="android.permission.RECORD_AUDIO"/>
<uses-permission android:name="android.permission.RECORD_VIDEO"/>
```

The Media Recorder lets you specify the audio and video source, the output file format, and the audio and video encoders to use when recording your file.

Much like the Media Player, the Media Recorder manages recording as a state machine. That means that the order in which you configure and manage the Media Recorder is important.

In the simplest terms, the transitions through the state machine can be described as follows:

➤ Create a new Media Recorder.

➤ Assign it the input sources to record from.

➤ Define the output format.

➤ Specify the audio and video encoder, frame rate, and output size.

➤ Select an output file.

➤ Prepare for recording.

> ➤ Record.

> ➤ End recording.

A more detailed and thorough description of the Media Recorder state machine is provided at the Android developer site at `http://developer.android.com/reference/android/media/MediaRecorder.html`

Once you've finished recording your media, call `release` on your Media Recorder object to free the associated resources.

```
mediaRecorder.release();
```

Configuring and Controlling Video Recording

As described in the state model above, before recording you must specify the input sources, output format, audio and video encoder, and an output file — in that order.

The `setAudioSource` and `setVideoSource` methods let you specify a `MediaRecorder.AudioSource` or `MediaRecorder.VideoSource` static constant that define the audio and video source, respectively.

Once you've selected your input sources, select the output format using the `setOutputFormat` method to specify a `MediaRecorder.OutputFormat` constant.

Use the `set[audio/video]Encoder` methods to specify an audio or video encoder constant from the `MediaRecorder.[Audio/Video]Encoder` class. Take this opportunity to set the frame rate or video output size if desired.

Finally, assign a file to store the recorded media using the `setOutputFile` method before calling `prepare`.

Listing 11-9 shows how to configure a Media Recorder to record audio and video from the microphone and camera using the default format and encoder to a file on the SD card.

LISTING 11-9: Configuring the Media Recorder

Available for
download on
Wrox.com

```java
MediaRecorder mediaRecorder = new MediaRecorder();

// Configure the input sources
mediaRecorder.setAudioSource(MediaRecorder.AudioSource.MIC);
mediaRecorder.setVideoSource(MediaRecorder.VideoSource.CAMERA);

// Set the output format
mediaRecorder.setOutputFormat(MediaRecorder.OutputFormat.DEFAULT);

// Specify the audio and video encoding
mediaRecorder.setAudioEncoder(MediaRecorder.AudioEncoder.DEFAULT);
mediaRecorder.setVideoEncoder(MediaRecorder.VideoEncoder.DEFAULT);

// Specify the output file
mediaRecorder.setOutputFile("/sdcard/myoutputfile.mp4");

// Prepare to record
mediaRecorder.prepare();
```

To begin recording, call the `start` method, as shown in this extension to Listing 11-9.

```
mediaRecorder.start();
```

 The `setOutputFile` *method must be called before* `prepare` *and after* `setOutputFormat` *or it will throw an Illegal State Exception.*

When you're finished, call `stop` to end the playback, followed by `release` to free the Media Recorder resources.

```
mediaRecorder.stop();
mediaRecorder.release();
```

Previewing Video Recording

When recording video, it's generally considered good practice to display a preview of the incoming video feed in real time. Using the `setPreviewDisplay` method, you can assign a `Surface` to display the video stream in real-time.

This works in much the same way as described earlier in this chapter when playing video using the Media Player.

Start by creating a new Activity that includes a `SurfaceView` control as part of the UI, and which implements the `SurfaceHolder.Callback` interface.

Once the Surface Holder has been created, assign it to the Media Recorder using the `setPreviewDisplay` method as shown in Listing 11-10.

The live video preview stream will begin displaying as soon as you make a call to `prepare`.

LISTING 11-10: Previewing video recording

```
public class MyActivity extends Activity implements SurfaceHolder.Callback
{
  private MediaRecorder mediaRecorder;

  @Override
  public void onCreate(Bundle savedInstanceState) {
    super.onCreate(savedInstanceState);
    setContentView(R.layout.main);

    SurfaceView surface = (SurfaceView)findViewById(R.id.surface);
    SurfaceHolder holder = surface.getHolder();
    holder.addCallback(this);
    holder.setType(SurfaceHolder.SURFACE_TYPE_PUSH_BUFFERS);
    holder.setFixedSize(400, 300);
  }
```

```java
public void surfaceCreated(SurfaceHolder holder) {
  if (mediaRecorder == null) {
    try {
      mediaRecorder.setAudioSource(MediaRecorder.AudioSource.MIC);
      mediaRecorder.setVideoSource(MediaRecorder.VideoSource.CAMERA);

      mediaRecorder.setOutputFormat(MediaRecorder.OutputFormat.DEFAULT);

      mediaRecorder.setAudioEncoder(MediaRecorder.AudioEncoder.DEFAULT);
      mediaRecorder.setVideoEncoder(MediaRecorder.VideoEncoder.DEFAULT);
      mediaRecorder.setOutputFile("/sdcard/myoutputfile.mp4");

      mediaRecorder.setPreviewDisplay(holder.getSurface());
      mediaRecorder.prepare();
    } catch (IllegalArgumentException e) {
      Log.d("MEDIA_PLAYER", e.getMessage());
    } catch (IllegalStateException e) {
      Log.d("MEDIA_PLAYER", e.getMessage());
    } catch (IOException e) {
      Log.d("MEDIA_PLAYER", e.getMessage());
    }
  }
}

public void surfaceDestroyed(SurfaceHolder holder) {
  mediaRecorder.release();
}

public void surfaceChanged(SurfaceHolder holder,
                           int format, int width, int height) { }
}
```

USING THE CAMERA AND TAKING PICTURES

The popularity of digital cameras (particularly within phone handsets) has caused their prices to drop just as their size has shrunk dramatically. It's now becoming difficult to even find a mobile phone without a camera, and Android devices are certainly no exception.

The G1 was released in 2008 with a 3.2-megapixel camera. Today several devices feature 5-megapixel cameras, with one model sporting an 8.1-megapixel sensor.

The following sections will demonstrate the mechanisms you can use to control the camera and take photos within your applications.

Using Intents to Take Pictures

The easiest way to take a picture using the device camera is using the ACTION_IMAGE_CAPTURE Media Store static constant in an Intent passed to startActivityForResult.

```java
startActivityForResult(new Intent(MediaStore.ACTION_IMAGE_CAPTURE),
                       TAKE_PICTURE);
```

This will launch the camera Activity, allowing users to modify the image settings manually, and preventing you from having to rewrite the entire camera application.

The image capture action supports two modes, thumbnail and full image.

➤ **Thumbnail** By default, the picture taken by the image capture action will return a thumbnail Bitmap in the data extra within the Intent parameter returned in onActivityResult. As shown in Listing 11-11, call getParcelableExtra specifying the extra name data on the Intent parameter to return the thumbnail as a Bitmap.

➤ **Full image** If you specify an output URI using a MediaStore.EXTRA_OUTPUT extra in the launch Intent, the full-size image taken by the camera will be saved to the specified location. In this case no thumbnail will be returned in the Activity result callback and the result Intent data will be null.

Listing 11-11 shows how to use the image capture action to capture either a thumbnail or full image using an Intent.

LISTING 11-11: Taking a picture using an Intent

```java
private static int TAKE_PICTURE = 1;
private Uri outputFileUri;

private void getThumbailPicture() {
  Intent intent = new Intent(MediaStore.ACTION_IMAGE_CAPTURE);
  startActivityForResult(intent, TAKE_PICTURE);
}

private void saveFullImage() {
  Intent intent = new Intent(MediaStore.ACTION_IMAGE_CAPTURE);
  File file = new File(Environment.getExternalStorageDirectory(),
                       "test.jpg");
  outputFileUri = Uri.fromFile(file);
  intent.putExtra(MediaStore.EXTRA_OUTPUT, outputFileUri);
  startActivityForResult(intent, TAKE_PICTURE);
}

@Override
protected void onActivityResult(int requestCode,
                                int resultCode, Intent data) {
  if (requestCode == TAKE_PICTURE) {
    Uri imageUri = null;

    // Check if the result includes a thumbnail Bitmap
    if (data != null) {
      if (data.hasExtra("data")) {
        Bitmap thumbnail = data.getParcelableExtra("data");
        // TODO Do something with the thumbnail
      }
    }
    else {
```

```
        // TODO Do something with the full image stored
        // in outputFileUri
      }
    }
  }
```

Once you have taken the picture, you can either add it to the Media Store as shown later in this chapter, or process it for use within your application before removing it.

Controlling the Camera and Taking Pictures

To access the camera hardware directly, you need to add the CAMERA permission to your application manifest.

```
<uses-permission android:name="android.permission.CAMERA"/>
```

Use the Camera class to adjust camera settings, specify image preferences, and take pictures.

To access the Camera Service, use the static open method on the Camera class. When your application has finished with the Camera, remember to relinquish your hold on it by calling release, as shown in the simple pattern shown in the Listing 11-12.

LISTING 11-12: Using the Camera

```
Camera camera = Camera.open();
[ ...  Do things with the camera ...  ]
camera.release();
```

The Camera.open method will turn on and initialize the Camera. At this point it is ready for you to modify settings, configure the preview surface, and take pictures, as shown in the following sections.

Controlling and Monitoring Camera Settings and Image Options

The camera settings are stored using a Camera.Parameters object, accessible by calling the getParameters method on the Camera object.

In order to modify the camera settings, use the set* methods on the Parameters object before calling the Camera's setParameters method and passing in the modified Parameters object.

LISTING 11-13: Reading and modifying camera settings

```
Camera.Parameters parameters = camera.getParameters();
[ ...  make changes ...  ]
camera.setParameters(parameters);
```

Android 2.0 (API level 5) introduced a wide range of Camera Parameters, each with a setter and getter including:

➤ `[get/set]SceneMode` Takes or returns a `SCENE_MODE_*` static string constant from the Camera Parameters class. Each scene mode describes a particular scene type (party, beach, sunset, etc.).

➤ `[get/set]FlashMode` Takes or returns a `FLASH_MODE_*` static string constant. Lets you specify the flash mode as on, off, red-eye reduction, or flashlight mode.

➤ `[get/set]WhiteBalance` Takes or returns a `WHITE_BALANCE_*` static string constant to describe the white balance of the scene being photographed.

➤ `[get/set]ColorEffect` Takes or returns a `EFFECT_*` static string constant to modify how the image is presented. Available color effects include sepia tone or black and white.

➤ `[get/set]FocusMode` Takes or returns a `FOCUS_MODE_*` static string constant to specify how the camera autofocus should attempt to focus the camera.

 Most of the parameters described above are useful primarily if you are replacing the native camera application. That said, they can also be useful for customizing the way the camera preview is displayed, allowing you to customize the live camera stream for augmented reality applications.

Camera Parameters can also be used to read or specify size, quality, and format parameters for the image, thumbnail, and camera preview. The following list explains how to set some of these values:

➤ **JPEG and thumbnail quality** Use the `setJpegQuality` and `setJpegThumbnailQuality` methods, passing in an integer value between 0 and 100, where 100 is the best quality.

➤ **Image, preview, and thumbnail size** Use `setPictureSize`, `setPreviewSize`, `setJpegThumbnailSize` to specify a height and width for the image, preview, and thumbnail respectively.

➤ **Image and preview pixel format** Use `setPictureFormat` and `setPreviewFormat` to set the image format using a static constant from the `PixelFormat` class.

➤ **Preview frame rate** Use `setPreviewFrameRate` to specify the preview frame rate in fps (frames per second).

Each device may potentially support a different subset of these parameter values. The Camera Parameters class also includes a range of `getSupported*` methods to find valid options to display to the user, or confirm that a desired parameter value is supported before assigning the value in code, as shown in Listing 11-14.

Checking for supported parameter values is particularly important when selecting valid preview or image sizes as each device's camera will potentially support a different subset.

LISTING 11-14: Confirming supported camera settings

```
Camera.Parameters parameters = camera.getParameters();
List<String> colorEffects = parameters.getSupportedColorEffects();
if (colorEffects.contains(Camera.Parameters.EFFECT_SEPIA))
  parameters.setColorEffect(Camera.Parameters.EFFECT_SEPIA);
camera.setParameters(parameters);
```

Monitoring Auto Focus

If the host Camera supports auto focus, and it is enabled, you can monitor the success of the auto focus operation by adding an `AutoFocusCallback` to the Camera object.

Listing 11-15 shows how to create and assign a simple Auto Focus Callback to a Camera object. The `onAutoFocus` event handler receives a Camera parameter when auto focus status has changed, and a success Boolean parameter indicating if the auto focus has been achieved.

LISTING 11-15: Monitoring auto focus

```
camera.autoFocus(new AutoFocusCallback() {
  public void onAutoFocus(boolean success, Camera camera) {
    // TODO Do something on Auto-Focus success
  }
});
```

Using the Camera Preview

Access to the camera's streaming video means that you can incorporate live video into your applications.

Some of the most exciting Android applications use this functionality as the basis for implementing augmented reality (the process of overlaying dynamic contextual data — such as details for landmarks or points of interest — on top of a live camera feed).

Much like the Media Player and Media Recorder classes, the camera preview is displayed onto a `SurfaceHolder`. To view the live camera stream within your application, you must include a Surface View within your UI. Implement a `SurfaceHolder.Callback` to listen for the construction of a valid surface, before passing it in to the `setPreviewDisplay` method of your Camera object.

A call to `startPreview` will begin the streaming and `stopPreview` will end it, as shown in Listing 11-16.

LISTING 11-16: Previewing real-time camera stream

```
public class MyActivity extends Activity implements SurfaceHolder.Callback {
  private Camera camera;

  @Override
  public void onCreate(Bundle savedInstanceState) {
```

continues

LISTING 11-16 *(continued)*

```
      super.onCreate(savedInstanceState);
      setContentView(R.layout.main);

      SurfaceView surface = (SurfaceView)findViewById(R.id.surface);
      SurfaceHolder holder = surface.getHolder();
      holder.addCallback(this);
      holder.setType(SurfaceHolder.SURFACE_TYPE_PUSH_BUFFERS);
      holder.setFixedSize(400, 300);
    }

    public void surfaceCreated(SurfaceHolder holder) {
      if (mediaRecorder == null) {
        try {
          camera = camera.open();
          camera.setPreviewDisplay(holder);
          camera.startPreview();
          [ ...  Draw on the Surface ... ]
        } catch (IOException e) {
          Log.d("CAMERA", e.getMessage());
        }
      }
    }

    public void surfaceDestroyed(SurfaceHolder holder) {
      camera.stopPreview();
      camera.release();
    }
  }
```

You'll learn more about Surfaces in Chapter 15, although the Android SDK includes an excellent example of using a SurfaceView to display the camera preview in real time.

You can also assign a PreviewCallback to be fired for each preview frame, allowing you to manipulate or display each preview frame individually.

Call the setPreviewCallback method on the Camera object, passing in a new PreviewCallback implementation overriding the onPreviewFrame method as shown in Listing 11-17.

LISTING 11-17: Assigning a preview frame callback

```
camera.setPreviewCallback(new PreviewCallback() {
  public void onPreviewFrame(byte[] _data, Camera _camera) {
    // TODO Do something with the preview image.
  }
});
```

Each frame will be received by the onPreviewFrame event with the image passed in through the byte array.

Taking a Picture

Take a picture by calling takePicture on a Camera object and passing in a ShutterCallback and two PictureCallback implementations (one for the RAW and one for JPEG-encoded images).

Each picture callback will receive a byte array representing the image in the appropriate format, while the shutter callback is triggered immediately after the shutter is closed.

Listing 11-18 shows the skeleton code for taking a picture and saving the JPEG image to the SD card.

LISTING 11-18: Taking a picture

```java
private void takePicture() {
    camera.takePicture(shutterCallback, rawCallback, jpegCallback);
}

ShutterCallback shutterCallback = new ShutterCallback() {
    public void onShutter() {
        // TODO Do something when the shutter closes.
    }
};

PictureCallback rawCallback = new PictureCallback() {
    public void onPictureTaken(byte[] data, Camera camera) {
        // TODO Do something with the image RAW data.
    }
};

PictureCallback jpegCallback = new PictureCallback() {
    public void onPictureTaken(byte[] data, Camera camera) {
        // Save the image JPEG data to the SD card
        FileOutputStream outStream = null;
        try {
            outStream = new FileOutputStream("/sdcard/test.jpg");
            outStream.write(data);
            outStream.close();
        } catch (FileNotFoundException e) {
            Log.d("CAMERA", e.getMessage());
        } catch (IOException e) {
            Log.d("CAMERA", e.getMessage());
        }
    }
};
```

Reading and Writing JPEG EXIF Image Details

The ExifInterface class provides mechanisms for you to read and modify the EXIF (Exchangeable Image File Format) data stored within a JPEG file. Create a new ExifInterface instance by passing the full filename in to the constructor.

```java
ExifInterface exif = new ExifInterface(filename);
```

EXIF data is used to store a wide range of metadata on photographs, including date and time, camera settings (such as make and model), and image settings (such as aperture and shutter speed), as well as image descriptions and locations.

To read an EXIF attribute, call getAttribute on the ExifInterface object, passing in the name of the attribute to read. The Exifinterface class includes a number of static TAG_* constants that can be used to access common EXIF metadata. To modify an EXIF attribute, use setAttribute, passing in the name of the attribute to read and the value to set it to.

Listing 11-19 shows how to read the location coordinates and camera model from a file stored on the SD card, before modifying the camera manufacturer details.

LISTING 11-19: Reading and modifying EXIF data

```java
File file = new File(Environment.getExternalStorageDirectory(),
                     "test.jpg");
try {
  ExifInterface exif = new ExifInterface(file.getCanonicalPath());
  // Read the camera model and location attributes
  String model = exif.getAttribute(ExifInterface.TAG_MODEL);
  float[] latLng = new float[2];
  exif.getLatLong(latLng);
  // Set the camera make
  exif.setAttribute(ExifInterface.TAG_MAKE, "My Phone");
} catch (IOException e) {
  Log.d("EXIF", e.getMessage());
}
```

ADDING NEW MEDIA TO THE MEDIA STORE

By default, media files created by your application will be unavailable to other applications. As a result, it's good practice to insert it into the Media Store to make it available to other applications.

Android provides two alternatives for inserting media into the Media Store, either using the Media Scanner to interpret your file and insert it automatically, or manually inserting a new record in the appropriate Content Provider.

Using the Media Scanner

If you have recorded new media of any kind, the MediaScannerConnection class provides a simple way for you to add it to the Media Store without needing to construct the full record for the Media Store Content Provider.

Before you can use the scanFile method to initiate a content scan on your file, you must call connect and wait for the connection to the Media Scanner to complete.

This call is asynchronous, so you will need to implement a MediaScannerConnectionClient to notify you when the connection has been made. You can use this same class to notify you when the scan is complete, at which point you can disconnect your Media Scanner Connection.

This sounds more complex than it is. Listing 11-20 shows the skeleton code for creating a new `MediaScannerConnectionClient` that defines a `MediaScannerConnection` which is used to add a new file to the Media Store.

LISTING 11-20: Adding files to the Media Store using the Media Scanner

```java
MediaScannerConnectionClient mediaScannerClient = new
MediaScannerConnectionClient() {
  private MediaScannerConnection msc = null;

  {
    msc = new MediaScannerConnection(getApplicationContext(), this);
    msc.connect();
  }

  public void onMediaScannerConnected() {
    msc.scanFile("/sdcard/test1.jpg", null);
  }

  public void onScanCompleted(String path, Uri uri) {
    msc.disconnect();
  }
};
```

Inserting Media into the Media Store

Rather than relying on the Media Scanner you can add new media to the Media Store by creating a new `ContentValues` object and inserting it into the appropriate Media Store Content Provider yourself.

The metadata you specify here can include the title, time stamp, and geocoding information for your new media file, as shown in the code snippet below:

```java
ContentValues content = new ContentValues(3);
content.put(Audio.AudioColumns.TITLE, "TheSoundandtheFury");
content.put(Audio.AudioColumns.DATE_ADDED,
            System.currentTimeMillis() / 1000);
content.put(Audio.Media.MIME_TYPE, "audio/amr");
```

You must also specify the absolute path of the media file being added.

```java
content.put(MediaStore.Audio.Media.DATA, "/sdcard/myoutputfile.mp4");
```

Get access to the application's `ContentResolver`, and use it to insert this new row into the Media Store as shown in the following code snippet.

```java
ContentResolver resolver = getContentResolver();
Uri uri = resolver.insert(MediaStore.Video.Media.EXTERNAL_CONTENT_URI,
                          content);
```

Once the media file has been inserted into the Media Store you should announce its availability using a broadcast Intent as shown below.

```java
sendBroadcast(new Intent(Intent.ACTION_MEDIA_SCANNER_SCAN_FILE, uri));
```

RAW AUDIO MANIPULATION

The `AudioTrack` and `AudioRecord` classes let you record audio directly from the audio input hardware of the device, and stream PCM audio buffers directly to the audio hardware for playback.

Using the Audio Track streaming mode you can process incoming audio and playback in near real time, letting you manipulate incoming or outgoing audio and perform signal processing on raw audio on the device.

While a detailed account of raw audio processing and manipulation is beyond the scope of this book, the following sections offer an introduction to recording and playing back raw PCM data.

Recording Sound with Audio Record

Use the `AudioRecord` class to record audio directly from the hardware buffers. Create a new Audio Record object, specifying the source, frequency, channel configuration, audio encoding, and buffer size.

```
int bufferSize = AudioRecord.getMinBufferSize(frequency,
                                              channelConfiguration,
                                              audioEncoding);

AudioRecord audioRecord = new AudioRecord(MediaRecorder.AudioSource.MIC,
                                          frequency, channelConfiguration,
                                          audioEncoding, bufferSize);
```

For privacy reasons, Android requires that the `RECORD_AUDIO` manifest permission be included in your manifest.

```
<uses-permission android:name="android.permission.RECORD_AUDIO"/>
```

The frequency, audio encoding, and channel configuration values will affect the size and quality of the recorded audio. Note that none of this meta-data is associated with the recorded files.

When your Audio Record object is initialized, run the `startRecording` method to begin asynchronous recording, and use the `read` method to add raw audio data into the recording buffer:

```
audioRecord.startRecording();
while (isRecording) {
  [ ...  populate the buffer ...  ]
  int bufferReadResult = audioRecord.read(buffer, 0, bufferSize);
}
```

Listing 11-21 records raw audio from the microphone to a file stored on the SD card. The next section will show you how to use an Audio Track to play this audio.

LISTING 11-21: Recording raw audio with Audio Record

```
int frequency = 11025;
int channelConfiguration = AudioFormat.CHANNEL_CONFIGURATION_MONO;
int audioEncoding = AudioFormat.ENCODING_PCM_16BIT;
File file = new File(Environment.getExternalStorageDirectory(), "raw.pcm");
```

```
// Create the new file.
try {
  file.createNewFile();
} catch (IOException e) {}

try {
  OutputStream os = new FileOutputStream(file);
  BufferedOutputStream bos = new BufferedOutputStream(os);
  DataOutputStream dos = new DataOutputStream(bos);

  int bufferSize = AudioRecord.getMinBufferSize(frequency,
                                                channelConfiguration,
                                                audioEncoding);
  short[] buffer = new short[bufferSize];

  // Create a new AudioRecord object to record the audio.
  AudioRecord audioRecord = new AudioRecord(MediaRecorder.AudioSource.MIC,
                                            frequency,
                                            channelConfiguration,
                                            audioEncoding, bufferSize);
  audioRecord.startRecording();

  while (isRecording) {
    int bufferReadResult = audioRecord.read(buffer, 0, bufferSize);
    for (int i = 0; i < bufferReadResult; i++)
      dos.writeShort(buffer[i]);
  }

  audioRecord.stop();
  dos.close();
} catch (Throwable t) {}
```

Playing Sound with Audio Track

Use the AudioTrack class to play raw audio directly into the hardware buffers. Create a new Audio Track object, specifying the streaming mode, frequency, channel configuration, and the audio encoding type and length of the audio to play back.

```
AudioTrack audioTrack = new AudioTrack(AudioManager.STREAM_MUSIC,
                                       frequency,
                                       channelConfiguration,
                                       audioEncoding,
                                       audioLength,
                                       AudioTrack.MODE_STREAM);
```

Because this is raw audio, there is no meta-data associated with the recorded files, so it's important to correctly set the audio data properties to the same values as those used when recording the file.

When your Audio Track is initialized, run the play method to begin asynchronous playback, and use the write method to add raw audio data into the playback buffer.

```
audioTrack.play();
audioTrack.write(audio, 0, audioLength);
```

You can write audio into the Audio Track buffer either before `play` has been called or after. In the former case, playback will commence as soon as `play` is called, while in the latter playback will begin as soon as you write data to the Audio Track buffer.

Listing 11-22 plays back the raw audio recorded in Listing 11-21, but does so at double speed by halving the expected frequency of the audio file.

LISTING 11-22: Playing raw audio with Audio Track

```
int frequency = 11025/2;
int channelConfiguration = AudioFormat.CHANNEL_CONFIGURATION_MONO;
int audioEncoding = AudioFormat.ENCODING_PCM_16BIT;
File file = new File(Environment.getExternalStorageDirectory(), "raw.pcm");

// Short array to store audio track (16 bit so 2 bytes per short)
int audioLength = (int)(file.length()/2);
short[] audio = new short[audioLength];

try {
  InputStream is = new FileInputStream(file);
  BufferedInputStream bis = new BufferedInputStream(is);
  DataInputStream dis = new DataInputStream(bis);

  int i = 0;
  while (dis.available() > 0) {
    audio[audioLength] = dis.readShort();
    i++;
  }

  // Close the input streams.
  dis.close();

  // Create and play a new AudioTrack object
  AudioTrack audioTrack = new AudioTrack(AudioManager.STREAM_MUSIC,
                                         frequency,
                                         channelConfiguration,
                                         audioEncoding,
                                         audioLength,
                                         AudioTrack.MODE_STREAM);
  audioTrack.play();
  audioTrack.write(audio, 0, audioLength);
} catch (Throwable t) {}
```

SPEECH RECOGNITION

Since Android 1.5 (API level 3), Android has supported voice input and speech recognition using the `RecognizerIntent` class.

This API lets you accept voice input into your application using the standard voice input dialog shown in Figure 11-1.

Voice recognition is initiated by calling `startNewActivity ForResult`, and passing in an Intent specifying the `RecognizerIntent.ACTION_RECOGNIZE_SPEECH` action constant.

The launch Intent must include the `RecognizerIntent .EXTRA_LANGUAGE_MODEL` extra to specify the language model used to parse the input audio. This can be either `LANGUAGE_MODEL_FREE_FORM` or `LANGUAGE_MODEL_WEB_SEARCH`; both are available as static constants from the `RecognizerIntent` class.

You can also specify a number of optional extras to control the language, potential result count, and display prompt using the following Recognizer Intent constants:

➤ `EXTRA_PROMPT` Specify a string that will be displayed in the voice input dialog (shown in Figure 11-1) to prompt the user to speak.

➤ `EXTRA_MAXRESULTS` Use an integer value to limit the number of potential recognition results returned.

➤ `EXTRA_LANGUAGE` Specify a language constant from the `Locale` class to specify an input language other than the device default. You can find the current default by calling the static `getDefault` method on the `Locale` class.

FIGURE 11-1

 The engine that handles the speech recognition may not be capable of understanding spoken input from all the languages available from the `Locale` *class.*

Not all devices will include support for speech recognition. In such cases it is generally possible to download the voice recognition library from the Android Market.

Listing 11-23 shows how to initiate voice recognition in English, returning one result, and using a custom prompt.

LISTING 11-23: Initiating a speech recognition request

```
Intent intent = new Intent(RecognizerIntent.ACTION_RECOGNIZE_SPEECH)
// Specify free form input
intent.putExtra(RecognizerIntent.EXTRA_LANGUAGE_MODEL,
                RecognizerIntent.LANGUAGE_MODEL_FREE_FORM);
intent.putExtra(RecognizerIntent.EXTRA_PROMPT,
```

continues

LISTING 11-23 *(continued)*

```
                        "or forever hold your peace");
    intent.putExtra(RecognizerIntent.EXTRA_MAX_RESULTS, 1);
    intent.putExtra(RecognizerIntent.EXTRA_LANGUAGE, Locale.ENGLISH);
    startActivityForResult(intent, VOICE_RECOGNITION);
```

When the user has completed his or her voice input, the resulting audio will be analyzed and processed by the speech recognition engine. The results will then be returned through the `onActivityResult` handler as an Array List of strings in the `EXTRA_RESULTS` extra as shown in Listing 11-24.

Each string returned in the Array List represents a potential match for the spoken input.

LISTING 11-24: Finding the results of a speech recognition request

```
@Override
protected void onActivityResult(int requestCode,
                                int resultCode,
                                Intent data) {
  if (requestCode == VOICE VOICE_RECOGNITION && resultCode == RESULT_OK) {
    ArrayList<String> results;
    results = data.getStringArrayListExtra(RecognizerIntent.EXTRA_RESULTS);
    // TODO Do something with the recognized voice strings
  }
  super.onActivityResult(requestCode, resultCode, data);
}
```

SUMMARY

In this chapter you learned how to play, record, and capture multimedia within your application.

Beginning with the Media Player, you learned how to play back audio and video from local files, application resources, and online streaming sites. You were introduced to the Video View and learned how to create and use Surface Views to play back video content, provide video recording preview, and display a live camera feed.

You learned how to use Intents to leverage the native applications to record video and take pictures, as well as use the Media Recorder and Camera classes to implement your own still and moving image capture solutions.

You were also shown how to read and modify Exif image data, add new media to the Media Store, and manipulate raw audio.

Finally, you were introduced to the voice and speech recognition libraries, and learned how to use them to add voice input to your applications.

In the next chapter you'll explore the low-level communication APIs available on the Android platform.

You'll learn to use Android's telephony APIs to monitor mobile connectivity, calls, and SMS activity. You'll also learn to use the telephony and SMS APIs to initiate outgoing calls and send and receive SMS messages from within your application.

12

Telephony and SMS

WHAT'S IN THIS CHAPTER?

➤ Initiating phone calls

➤ Reading the phone, network, data connectivity, and SIM states

➤ Monitoring changes to the phone, network, data connectivity, and SIM states

➤ Using Intents to send SMS and MMS messages

➤ Using the SMS Manager to send SMS Messages

➤ Handling incoming SMS messages

In this chapter, you'll learn to use Android's telephony APIs to monitor mobile voice and data connections as well as incoming and outgoing calls, and to send and receive SMS (short messaging service) messages.

You'll take a look at the communication hardware by examining the telephony package for monitoring phone state and phone calls, as well as initiating calls and monitoring incoming call details.

Android also offers full access to SMS functionality, letting you send and receive SMS messages from within your applications. Using the Android APIs, you can create your own SMS client application to replace the native clients available as part of the software stack. Alternatively, you can incorporate the messaging functionality within your own applications to create social applications using SMS as the transport layer.

At the end of this chapter, you'll use the SMS Manager in a detailed project that involves creating an emergency SMS responder. In emergency situations, the responder will let users quickly, or automatically, respond to people asking after their safety.

TELEPHONY

The Android telephony APIs let your applications access the underlying telephone hardware stack, making it possible to create your own dialer — or integrate call handling and phone state monitoring into your applications.

> *Because of security concerns, the current Android SDK does not allow you to create your own "in call" Activity — the screen that is displayed when an incoming call is received or an outgoing call has been placed.*

The following sections focus on how to monitor and control phone, service, and cell events in your applications to augment and manage the native phone-handling functionality. If you wish, you can use the same techniques to implement a replacement dialer application.

Launching the Dialer to Initiate Phone Calls

Best practice is to use Intents to launch a dialer application to initiate new phone calls. Use an Intent action to start a dialer activity; you should specify the number to dial using the `tel:` schema as the data component of the Intent.

Use the `Intent.ACTION_DIAL` Activity action to launch a dialer rather than dial the number immediately. This action starts a dialer Activity, passing in the specified number but allowing the dialer application to manage the call initialization (the default dialer asks the user to explicitly initiate the call). This action doesn't require any permissions and is the standard way applications should initiate calls.

Listing 12-1 shows the basic technique for dialing a number.

LISTING 12-1: Dialing a number

```
Intent intent = new Intent(Intent.ACTION_DIAL, Uri.parse("tel:1234567"));
startActivity(intent);
```

By using an Intent to announce your intention to dial a number, your application can remain decoupled from the dialer implementation used to initiate the call. For example, if you were to replace the existing dialer with a hybrid that allows IP-based telephony, using Intents to dial a number from your other applications would let you leverage this new dialer functionality.

Replacing the Native Dialer

Replacing the native dialer application involves two steps:

1. Intercepting Intents that are currently serviced by the native dialer.
2. Initiating, and optionally managing, outgoing calls.

The native dialer application currently responds to Intent actions corresponding to a user's pressing the hardware call button, asking to view data using the tel: schema, or making a request to dial a number using the tel: schema.

To intercept these requests include <intent-filter> tags on your new Activity that listens for the following actions:

➤ Intent.ACTION_CALL_BUTTON This action is broadcast when the device's hardware call button is pressed. Create an Intent Filter listening for this action as a default action.

➤ Intent.ACTION_DIAL The Intent action described in the previous section, this Intent is used by applications which want to launch the dialer to make a phone call. The Intent Filter used to capture this action should be both default and browsable (to support dial requests from the browser), and must specify the tel: schema to replace existing dialer functionality (though it can support additional schemes).

➤ Intent.ACTION_VIEW The view action is used by applications wanting to view a piece of data. Ensure that the Intent Filter specifies the tel: schema to allow your new Activity to be used to view telephone numbers.

The following manifest snippet shows an Activity with Intent Filters that will capture each of these actions.

```
<activity
  android:name=".MyDialerActivity"
  android:label="@string/app_name">
  <intent-filter>
    <action android:name="android.intent.action.CALL_BUTTON" />
    <category android:name="android.intent.category.DEFAULT" />
  </intent-filter>
  <intent-filter>
    <action android:name="android.intent.action.VIEW" />
    <action android:name="android.intent.action.DIAL" />
    <category android:name="android.intent.category.DEFAULT" />
    <category android:name="android.intent.category.BROWSABLE" />
    <data android:scheme="tel" />
  </intent-filter>
</activity>
```

Once your application has been started, it is up to you to allow users to enter or modify the number to call and initiate the outgoing call.

The simplest technique is to use the existing telephony stack. In this case you can use the Intent.ACTION_CALL action to initiate a call using the standard in-call Activity and letting the system handle the dialing, connection, and voice handling. Your application must have the CALL_PHONE uses-permission to broadcast this action.

Alternatively, you can completely replace the outgoing telephony stack by implementing your own dialing and voice handling framework. This is the perfect alternative if you are implementing a VOIP (voice over IP) application. Note that the implementation of an alternative telephony platform is beyond the scope of this book.

Note also that you can intercept these Intents to modify or block outgoing calls as an alternative to completely replacing the dialer screen.

Accessing Phone and Network Properties and Status

Access to the telephony APIs is managed by the Telephony Manager, accessible using the `getSystemService` method as shown in Listing 12-2.

LISTING 12-2: Accessing the Telephony Manager

```
String srvcName = Context.TELEPHONY_SERVICE;
TelephonyManager telephonyManager = (TelephonyManager)getSystemService(srvcName);
```

The Telephony Manager provides direct access to many of the phone properties, including device, network, SIM, and data state details.

Reading Phone Device Details

Using the Telephony Manager you can obtain the phone type (GSM or CDMA), unique ID (IMEI or MEID), software version, and number. Note that, except for the phone type, reading each of these properties requires that the `READ_PHONE_STATE` uses-permission be included in the application manifest.

```
<uses-permission android:name="android.permission.READ_PHONE_STATE"/>
```

Listing 12-3 shows how to extract each of these details.

LISTING 12-3: Reading phone details

```
int phoneType = telephonyManager.getPhoneType();
switch (phoneType) {
  case (TelephonyManager.PHONE_TYPE_CDMA): break;
  case (TelephonyManager.PHONE_TYPE_GSM) : break;
  case (TelephonyManager.PHONE_TYPE_NONE): break;
  default: break;
}

// -- These require READ_PHONE_STATE uses-permission --
// Read the IMEI for GSM or MEID for CDMA
String deviceId = telephonyManager.getDeviceId();
// Read the software version on the phone (note -- not the SDK version)
String softwareVersion = telephonyManager.getDeviceSoftwareVersion();
// Get the phone's number
String phoneNumber = telephonyManager.getLine1Number();
```

Reading Data Connection and Transfer State

Using the `getDataState` and `getDataActivity` methods you can find the current data connection state and transfer activity respectively as shown in Listing 12-4.

Generally it will be more useful to detect changes in the data connection or transfer status. You'll learn how to monitor both later in this chapter.

LISTING 12-4: Reading phone data connection and transfer state

```
int dataActivity = telephonyManager.getDataActivity();
int dataState = telephonyManager.getDataState();

switch (dataActivity) {
  case TelephonyManager.DATA_ACTIVITY_IN : break;
  case TelephonyManager.DATA_ACTIVITY_OUT : break;
  case TelephonyManager.DATA_ACTIVITY_INOUT : break;
  case TelephonyManager.DATA_ACTIVITY_NONE : break;
}

switch (dataState) {
  case TelephonyManager.DATA_CONNECTED : break;
  case TelephonyManager.DATA_CONNECTING : break;
  case TelephonyManager.DATA_DISCONNECTED : break;
  case TelephonyManager.DATA_SUSPENDED : break;
}
```

Reading Network Details

When you are connected to a network, you can use the Telephony Manager to read the mobile country and network code (MCC+MNC), the country ISO code, and the type of network you're connected to. These commands will only work when you are connected to a mobile network, and can be unreliable if it is a CDMA network. Use the getPhoneType method as described above to determine which network type you are connected to.

Listing 12-5 shows how to extract the network details, as well as showing a list of the network connection types currently supported.

LISTING 12-5: Reading network details

```
// Get connected network country ISO code
String networkCountry = telephonyManager.getNetworkCountryIso();
// Get the connected network operator ID (MCC + MNC)
String networkOperatorId = telephonyManager.getNetworkOperator();
// Get the connected network operator name
String networkName = telephonyManager.getNetworkOperatorName();
// Get the type of network you are connected to
int networkType = telephonyManager.getNetworkType();
switch (networkType) {
  case (TelephonyManager.NETWORK_TYPE_1xRTT)   : [ ...  do something ... ]
                                                 break;
  case (TelephonyManager.NETWORK_TYPE_CDMA)    : [ ...  do something ... ]
                                                 break;
  case (TelephonyManager.NETWORK_TYPE_EDGE)    : [ ...  do something ... ]
                                                 break;
  case (TelephonyManager.NETWORK_TYPE_EVDO_0)  : [ ...  do something ... ]
                                                 break;
```

continues

LISTING 12-5 (*continued*)

```
    case (TelephonyManager.NETWORK_TYPE_EVDO_A)  : [ ...  do something ... ]
                                                   break;
    case (TelephonyManager.NETWORK_TYPE_GPRS)    : [ ...  do something ... ]
                                                   break;
    case (TelephonyManager.NETWORK_TYPE_HSDPA)   : [ ...  do something ... ]
                                                   break;
    case (TelephonyManager.NETWORK_TYPE_HSPA)    : [ ...  do something ... ]
                                                   break;
    case (TelephonyManager.NETWORK_TYPE_HSUPA)   : [ ...  do something ... ]
                                                   break;
    case (TelephonyManager.NETWORK_TYPE_UMTS)    : [ ...  do something ... ]
                                                   break;
    case (TelephonyManager.NETWORK_TYPE_UNKNOWN) : [ ...  do something ... ]
                                                   break;
    default: break;
}
```

Reading SIM Details

If your application is running on a GSM device it will have a SIM. You can query the SIM details from the Telephony Manager to obtain the ISO country code, operator name, and operator MCC (mobile country code) and MNC (mobile network code) for the SIM installed in the current device. These details can be useful if you need to provide specialized functionality for a particular carrier.

You can also obtain the serial number for the current SIM if you include the READ_PHONE_STATE uses-permission in your application manifest.

Before you can use any of these methods you must ensure that the SIM is in a ready state. You can determine this using the getSimState method as shown in Listing 12-6.

LISTING 12-6: Reading SIM details

```
int simState = telephonyManager.getSimState();
switch (simState) {
  case (TelephonyManager.SIM_STATE_ABSENT): break;
  case (TelephonyManager.SIM_STATE_NETWORK_LOCKED): break;
  case (TelephonyManager.SIM_STATE_PIN_REQUIRED): break;
  case (TelephonyManager.SIM_STATE_PUK_REQUIRED): break;
  case (TelephonyManager.SIM_STATE_UNKNOWN): break;
  case (TelephonyManager.SIM_STATE_READY): {
    // Get the SIM country ISO code
    String simCountry = telephonyManager.getSimCountryIso();
    // Get the operator code of the active SIM (MCC + MNC)
    String simOperatorCode = telephonyManager.getSimOperator();
    // Get the name of the SIM operator
    String simOperatorName = telephonyManager.getSimOperatorName();
    // -- Requires READ_PHONE_STATE uses-permission --
    // Get the SIM's serial number
    String simSerial = telephonyManager.getSimSerialNumber();
```

```
        break;
    }
    default: break;
}
```

Monitoring Changes in Phone State, Phone Activity, and Data Connections

The Android telephony API lets you monitor phone state, retrieve incoming phone numbers, and observe changes to data connections, signal strength, and network connectivity.

In order to monitor and manage phone state, your application must specify the READ_PHONE_STATE uses-permission in its manifest using the following XML code snippet:

```
<uses-permission android:name="android.permission.READ_PHONE_STATE"/>
```

Changes to the phone state are monitored using the PhoneStateListener class. Extend the Phone State Listener to listen for, and respond to, phone state change events including call state (ringing, off hook, etc.), cell location changes, voice-mail and call-forwarding status, phone service changes, and changes in mobile signal strength.

To react to phone state change events, create a new Phone State Listener implementation, and override the event handlers of the events you want to react to. Each handler receives parameters that indicate the new phone state, such as the current cell location, call state, or signal strength.

Listing 12-7 highlights the available state change handlers in a skeleton Phone State Listener implementation.

LISTING 12-7: Phone State Listener skeleton class

Available for download on Wrox.com

```
PhoneStateListener phoneStateListener = new PhoneStateListener() {
    public void onCallForwardingIndicatorChanged(boolean cfi) {}
    public void onCallStateChanged(int state, String incomingNumber) {}
    public void onCellLocationChanged(CellLocation location) {}
    public void onDataActivity(int direction) {}
    public void onDataConnectionStateChanged(int state) {}
    public void onMessageWaitingIndicatorChanged(boolean mwi) {}
    public void onServiceStateChanged(ServiceState serviceState) {}
    public void onSignalStrengthChanged(int asu) {}
};
```

Once you've created your own Phone State Listener, register it with the Telephony Manager using a bitmask to indicate the events you want to listen for, as shown in Listing 12-8.

LISTING 12-8: Registering a Phone State Listener

Available for download on Wrox.com

```
telephonyManager.listen(phoneStateListener,
                  PhoneStateListener.LISTEN_CALL_FORWARDING_INDICATOR |
```

continues

LISTING 12-8 *(continued)*

```
                        PhoneStateListener.LISTEN_CALL_STATE |
                        PhoneStateListener.LISTEN_CELL_LOCATION |
                        PhoneStateListener.LISTEN_DATA_ACTIVITY |
                        PhoneStateListener.LISTEN_DATA_CONNECTION_STATE |
                        PhoneStateListener.LISTEN_MESSAGE_WAITING_INDICATOR |
                        PhoneStateListener.LISTEN_SERVICE_STATE |
                        PhoneStateListener.LISTEN_SIGNAL_STRENGTH);
```

To unregister a listener, call `listen` and pass in `PhoneStateListener.LISTEN_NONE` as the bit field parameter, as shown below:

```
    telephonyManager.listen(phoneStateListener,
                            PhoneStateListener.LISTEN_NONE);
```

Monitoring Incoming Phone Calls

One of the most popular reasons for monitoring phone state is to detect, and react to, incoming phone calls.

To do so, override the `onCallStateChanged` method in a Phone State Listener implementation, and register it as shown in Listing 12-9 to receive notifications when the call state changes.

LISTING 12-9: Monitoring phone calls

```
PhoneStateListener callStateListener = new PhoneStateListener() {
  public void onCallStateChanged(int state, String incomingNumber) {
    // TODO React to incoming call.
  }
};

telephonyManager.listen(callStateListener,
                        PhoneStateListener.LISTEN_CALL_STATE);
```

The `onCallStateChanged` handler receives the phone number associated with incoming calls, and the state parameter represents the current call state as one of the following three values:

➤ `TelephonyManager.CALL_STATE_IDLE`   When the phone is neither ringing nor in a call

➤ `TelephonyManager.CALL_STATE_RINGING`   When the phone is ringing

➤ `TelephonyManager.CALL_STATE_OFFHOOK`   When the phone is currently in a call

Tracking Cell Location Changes

You can get notifications whenever the current cell location changes by overriding `onCellLocationChanged` on a Phone State Listener implementation. Before you can register to listen for cell location changes, you need to add the `ACCESS_COARSE_LOCATION` permission to your application manifest.

```
        <uses-permission android:name="android.permission.ACCESS_COARSE_LOCATION"/>
```

The `onCellLocationChanged` handler receives a `CellLocation` object that includes methods for extracting the cell ID (`getCid`) and the current LAC (`getLac`).

Listing 12-10 shows how to implement a Phone State Listener to monitor cell location changes, displaying a Toast that includes the new location's cell ID.

LISTING 12-10: Tracking cell changes

```
PhoneStateListener cellLocationListener = new PhoneStateListener() {
  public void onCellLocationChanged(CellLocation location) {
    GsmCellLocation gsmLocation = (GsmCellLocation)location;
    Toast.makeText(getApplicationContext(),
                   String.valueOf(gsmLocation.getCid()),
                   Toast.LENGTH_LONG).show();
  }
};
telephonyManager.listen(cellLocationListener,
                        PhoneStateListener.LISTEN_CELL_LOCATION);
```

Tracking Service Changes

The onServiceStateChanged handler tracks the service details for the device's cell service. Use the ServiceState parameter to find details of the current service state.

The getState method on the Service State object returns the current service state as one of the following ServiceState constants:

➤ STATE_IN_SERVICE   Normal phone service is available.

➤ STATE_EMERGENCY_ONLY   Phone service is available but only for emergency calls.

➤ STATE_OUT_OF_SERVICE   No cell phone service is currently available.

➤ STATE_POWER_OFF   The phone radio is turned off (usually when airplane mode is enabled).

A series of getOperator* methods is available to retrieve details on the operator supplying the cell phone service, while getRoaming tells you if the device is currently using a roaming profile.

Listing 12-11 shows how to register for service state changes and displays a Toast showing the operator name of the current phone service.

LISTING 12-11: Monitoring service state changes

```
PhoneStateListener serviceStateListener = new PhoneStateListener() {
  public void onServiceStateChanged(ServiceState serviceState) {
    if (serviceState.getState() == ServiceState.STATE_IN_SERVICE) {
      String toastText = serviceState.getOperatorAlphaLong();
      Toast.makeText(getApplicationContext(), toastText, Toast.LENGTH_SHORT);
    }
  }
};

telephonyManager.listen(serviceStateListener,
                        PhoneStateListener.LISTEN_SERVICE_STATE);
```

Monitoring Data Connectivity and Activity

As well as voice and service details, you can also use a Phone State Listener to monitor changes in mobile data connectivity and mobile data transfer.

The Phone State Listener includes two event handlers for monitoring the device data connection. Override `onDataActivity` to track data transfer activity, and `onDataConnectionStateChanged` to request notifications for data connection state changes.

Listing 12-12 shows both handlers overridden, with switch statements demonstrating each of the possible values for the `state` and data-flow `direction` parameters passed in to each event.

Available for download on Wrox.com

LISTING 12-12: Monitoring data connections and transfers

```
PhoneStateListener dataStateListener = new PhoneStateListener() {
  public void onDataActivity(int direction) {
    switch (direction) {
      case TelephonyManager.DATA_ACTIVITY_IN : break;
      case TelephonyManager.DATA_ACTIVITY_OUT : break;
      case TelephonyManager.DATA_ACTIVITY_INOUT : break;
      case TelephonyManager.DATA_ACTIVITY_NONE : break;
    }
  }

  public void onDataConnectionStateChanged(int state) {
    switch (state) {
      case TelephonyManager.DATA_CONNECTED : break;
      case TelephonyManager.DATA_CONNECTING : break;
      case TelephonyManager.DATA_DISCONNECTED : break;
      case TelephonyManager.DATA_SUSPENDED : break;
    }
  }
};

telephonyManager.listen(dataStateListener,
                  PhoneStateListener.LISTEN_DATA_ACTIVITY |
                  PhoneStateListener.LISTEN_DATA_CONNECTION_STATE);
```

INTRODUCING SMS AND MMS

If you own a mobile phone that's less than two decades old, chances are you're familiar with SMS messaging. SMS (short messaging service) is now one of the most-used features on mobile phones, with many people favoring it over making phone calls.

SMS technology is designed to send short text messages between mobile phones. It provides support for sending both text messages (designed to be read by people) and data messages (meant to be consumed by applications). More recently MMS (multimedia messaging service) messages have allowed users to send and receive messages that include multimedia attachments such as photos, videos, and audio.

Because SMS and MMS are mature mobile technologies, there's a lot of information out there that describes the technical details of how an SMS or MMS message is constructed and transmitted over the air. Rather than rehash that information here, the following sections focus on the practicalities of sending and receiving text, data, and multimedia messages from within Android applications.

Using SMS and MMS in Your Application

Android provides full SMS functionality from within your applications through the SMSManager. Using the SMS Manager, you can replace the native SMS application to send text messages, react to incoming texts, or use SMS as a data transport layer.

At this time, the Android API does not include simple support for creating MMS messages from within your applications, though you can use the SEND and SEND_TO actions in Intents to send both SMS and MMS messages using a messaging application installed on the device.

This chapter will demonstrate how to use both the SMS Manager and Intents to send messages from within your applications.

SMS message delivery is not timely. Compared to using an IP or socket-based transport, using SMS to pass data messages between applications is slow, possibly expensive, and can suffer from high latency. As a result SMS is not really suitable for anything that requires real-time responsiveness.

That said, the widespread adoption and resiliency of SMS networks make it a particularly good tool for delivering content to non-Android users and reducing the dependency on third-party servers.

Sending SMS and MMS from Your Application Using Intents and the Native Client

In many circumstances you may find it easier to pass on the responsibility for sending SMS and MMS messages to another application, rather than implementing a full SMS client within your app.

To do so, call startActivity using an Intent with the Intent.ACTION_SENDTO action. Specify a target number using sms: schema notation as the Intent data. Include the message you want to send within the Intent payload using an sms_body extra, as shown in Listing 12-13.

LISTING 12-13: Sending an SMS message using Intents

```
Intent smsIntent = new Intent(Intent.ACTION_SENDTO,
                              Uri.parse("sms:55512345"));
smsIntent.putExtra("sms_body", "Press send to send me");
startActivity(smsIntent);
```

You can also attach files (effectively creating an MMS message) to your messages. Add an Intent.EXTRA_STREAM with the URI of the resource to attach, and set the Intent type to the mime-type of the attached resource.

Note that the native MMS application doesn't include an Intent Receiver for ACTION_SENDTO with a type set. Instead, you will need to use ACTION_SEND and include the target phone number as an address extra, as shown in Listing 12-14.

LISTING 12-14: Sending an MMS message with an attached image

```
// Get the URI of a piece of media to attach.
Uri attached_Uri = Uri.parse("content://media/external/images/media/1");

// Create a new MMS intent
Intent mmsIntent = new Intent(Intent.ACTION_SEND, attached_Uri);
mmsIntent.putExtra("sms_body", "Please see the attached image");
mmsIntent.putExtra("address", "07912355432");
mmsIntent.putExtra(Intent.EXTRA_STREAM, attached_Uri);
mmsIntent.setType("image/png");
startActivity(mmsIntent);
```

When running the MMS example shown in Listing 12-14, users are likely to be prompted to select one of a number of applications capable of fulfilling the send request, including the Gmail, e-mail, and SMS applications.

Sending SMS Messages Manually

SMS messaging in Android is handled by the SmsManager. You can get a reference to the SMS Manager using the static method SmsManager.getDefault, as shown in the following snippet.

```
SmsManager smsManager = SmsManager.getDefault();
```

Prior to Android 1.6 (SDK level 4) the SmsManager and SmsMessage classes were provided by the android.telephony.gsm package. These have now been deprecated and the SMS classes moved to android.telephony to ensure generic support for GSM and CDMA devices.

To send SMS messages, your applications must specify the SEND_SMS uses-permission. To request this permission, add it to the manifest as shown below:

```
<uses-permission android:name="android.permission.SEND_SMS"/>
```

Sending Text Messages

To send a text message, use sendTextMessage from the SMS Manager, passing in the address (phone number) of your recipient and the text message you want to send, as shown in Listing 12-15.

LISTING 12-15: Sending an SMS message

```
String sendTo = "5551234";
String myMessage = "Android supports programmatic SMS messaging!";

smsManager.sendTextMessage(sendTo, null, myMessage, null, null);
```

The second parameter can be used to specify the SMS service center to use; if you enter null as shown in Listing 12-15 the default service center will be used for your carrier.

The final two parameters let you specify Intents to track the transmission and successful delivery of your messages.

To react to these Intents, create and register Broadcast Receivers as shown in the next section.

> *The Android debugging bridge supports sending SMS messages among multiple emulator instances. To send an SMS from one emulator to another, specify the port number of the target emulator as the "to" address when sending a new message.*
>
> *Android will automatically route your message to the target emulator instance, where it'll be handled as a normal SMS.*

Tracking and Confirming SMS Message Delivery

To track the transmission and delivery success of your outgoing SMS messages, implement and register Broadcast Receivers that listen for the actions you specify when creating the Pending Intents you pass in to the `sendTextMessage` method.

The first Pending Intent parameter, `sentIntent`, is fired when the message either is successfully sent or fails to send. The result code for the Broadcast Receiver that receives this Intent will be one of the following:

➤ `Activity.RESULT_OK` To indicate a successful transmission

➤ `SmsManager.RESULT_ERROR_GENERIC_FAILURE` To indicate a nonspecific failure

➤ `SmsManager.RESULT_ERROR_RADIO_OFF` When the phone radio is turned off

➤ `SmsManager.RESULT_ERROR_NULL_PDU` To indicate a PDU (protocol description unit) failure

The second Pending Intent parameter, `deliveryIntent`, is fired only after the destination recipient receives your SMS message.

Listing 12-16 shows a typical pattern for sending an SMS and monitoring the success of its transmission and delivery.

LISTING 12-16: SMS delivery monitoring pattern

```
String SENT_SMS_ACTION = "SENT_SMS_ACTION";
String DELIVERED_SMS_ACTION = "DELIVERED_SMS_ACTION";

// Create the sentIntent parameter
Intent sentIntent = new Intent(SENT_SMS_ACTION);
PendingIntent sentPI = PendingIntent.getBroadcast(getApplicationContext(),
                                                  0,
```

continues

LISTING 12-16 *(continued)*

```
                                                        sentIntent,
                                                        0);

    // Create the deliveryIntent parameter
    Intent deliveryIntent = new Intent(DELIVERED_SMS_ACTION);
    PendingIntent deliverPI =
      PendingIntent.getBroadcast(getApplicationContext(),
                                 0,
                                 deliveryIntent,
                                 0);

    // Register the Broadcast Receivers
    registerReceiver(new BroadcastReceiver() {
                @Override
                public void onReceive(Context _context, Intent _intent)
                {
                  switch (getResultCode()) {
                    case Activity.RESULT_OK:
                      [ ...  send success actions ...  ]; break;
                    case SmsManager.RESULT_ERROR_GENERIC_FAILURE:
                      [ ...  generic failure actions ...  ]; break;
                    case SmsManager.RESULT_ERROR_RADIO_OFF:
                      [ ...  radio off failure actions ...  ]; break;
                    case SmsManager.RESULT_ERROR_NULL_PDU:
                      [ ...  null PDU failure actions ...  ]; break;
                  }
                }
              },
              new IntentFilter(SENT_SMS_ACTION));

    registerReceiver(new BroadcastReceiver() {
                @Override
                public void onReceive(Context _context, Intent _intent)
                {
                  [ ...  SMS delivered actions ...  ]
                }
              },
              new IntentFilter(DELIVERED_SMS_ACTION));

    // Send the message
    smsManager.sendTextMessage(sendTo, null, myMessage, sentPI, deliverPI);
```

Conforming to the Maximum SMS Message Size

SMS text messages are normally limited to 160 characters, so longer messages need to be broken into a series of smaller parts. The SMS Manager includes the divideMessage method, which accepts a string as an input and breaks it into an Array List of messages, wherein each is less than the maximum allowable size.

You can then use the sendMultipartTextMessage method on the SMS Manager to transmit the array of messages, as shown in Listing 12-17.

The `sentIntent` and `deliveryIntent` parameters in the `sendMultipartTextMessage` method are Array Lists that can be used to specify different Pending Intents to fire for each message part.

LISTING 12-17: Sending long messages in multiple parts

```
ArrayList<String> messageArray = smsManager.divideMessage(myMessage);
ArrayList<PendingIntent> sentIntents = new ArrayList<PendingIntent>();
for (int i = 0; i < messageArray.size(); i++)
  sentIntents.add(sentPI);

smsManager.sendMultipartTextMessage(sendTo,
                                    null,
                                    messageArray,
                                    sentIntents, null);
```

Sending Data Messages

You can send binary data via SMS using the `sendDataMessage` method on an SMS Manager. The `sendDataMessage` method works much like `sendTextMessage`, but includes additional parameters for the destination port and an array of bytes that constitutes the data you want to send.

Listing 12-18 shows the basic structure of sending a data message.

LISTING 12-18: Sending SMS data messages

```
Intent sentIntent = new Intent(SENT_SMS_ACTION);
PendingIntent sentPI = PendingIntent.getBroadcast(getApplicationContext(),
                                                  0, sentIntent, 0);

short destinationPort = 80;
byte[] data = [ ...  your data ...  ];
smsManager.sendDataMessage(sendTo, null, destinationPort,
                           data, sentPI, null);
```

Listening for Incoming SMS Messages

When a new SMS message is received by the device, a new broadcast Intent is fired with the `android.provider.Telephony.SMS_RECEIVED` action. Note that this is a string literal, the SDK currently doesn't include a reference to this string, so you must specify it explicitly when using it in your applications.

The SMS received action string is hidden (therefore unsupported). As such it is subject to change at any future platform release. As always, be very cautious when using unsupported platform features as they are subject to change in future platform releases.

For an application to listen for SMS Intent broadcasts, it needs to specify the `RECEIVE_SMS` manifest permission. Request this permission by adding a `<uses-permission>` tag to the application manifest, as shown in the following snippet:

```
<uses-permission
 android:name="android.permission.RECEIVE_SMS"
/>
```

The SMS broadcast Intent includes the incoming SMS details. To extract the array of `SmsMessage` objects packaged within the SMS broadcast Intent bundle, use the `pdu` extras key to extract an array of SMS PDUs (protocol description units — used to encapsulate an SMS message and its metadata), each of which represents an SMS message. To convert each PDU byte array into an SMS Message object, call `SmsMessage.createFromPdu`, passing in each byte array as shown in Listing 12-19.

LISTING 12-19: Extracting SMS messages from Incoming SMS Intent broadcasts

```
Bundle bundle = intent.getExtras();
if (bundle != null) {
  Object[] pdus = (Object[]) bundle.get("pdus");
  SmsMessage[] messages = new SmsMessage[pdus.length];
  for (int i = 0; i < pdus.length; i++)
    messages[i] = SmsMessage.createFromPdu((byte[]) pdus[i]);
}
```

Each `SmsMessage` contains the SMS message details, including the originating address (phone number), time stamp, and the message body.

Listing 12-20 shows a Broadcast Receiver implementation whose `onReceive` handler checks incoming SMS texts that start with the string `@echo`, and then sends the same text back to the number that sent it.

LISTING 12-20: Listening for incoming SMS messages

```
public class IncomingSMSReceiver extends BroadcastReceiver {
  private static final String queryString = "@echo";
  private static final String SMS_RECEIVED =
    "android.provider.Telephony.SMS_RECEIVED";

  public void onReceive(Context _context, Intent _intent) {
    if (_intent.getAction().equals(SMS_RECEIVED)) {
      SmsManager sms = SmsManager.getDefault();

      Bundle bundle = _intent.getExtras();
      if (bundle != null) {
        Object[] pdus = (Object[]) bundle.get("pdus");
        SmsMessage[] messages = new SmsMessage[pdus.length];
        for (int i = 0; i < pdus.length; i++)
          messages[i] = SmsMessage.createFromPdu((byte[]) pdus[i]);

        for (SmsMessage message : messages) {
          String msg = message.getMessageBody();
```

```
          String to = message.getOriginatingAddress();

          if (msg.toLowerCase().startsWith(queryString)) {
            String out = msg.substring(queryString.length());
            sms.sendTextMessage(to, null, out, null, null);
          }
        }
      }
    }
  }
}
```

To listen for incoming messages, register the Broadcast Receiver from Listing 12-20 using an Intent Filter that listens for the `android.provider.Telephony.SMS_RECEIVED` action String, as shown in Listing 12-21.

LISTING 12-21: Registering an SMS listener receiver

Available for download on Wrox.com

```
final String SMS_RECEIVED = "android.provider.Telephony.SMS_RECEIVED";
IntentFilter filter = new IntentFilter(SMS_RECEIVED);
BroadcastReceiver receiver = new IncomingSMSReceiver();
registerReceiver(receiver, filter);
```

Simulating Incoming SMS Messages in the Emulator

There are two techniques available for simulating incoming SMS messages in the emulator. The first was described previously in this section; you can send an SMS message from one emulator to another by using its port number as its phone number.

Alternatively, you can use the Android debug tools introduced in Chapter 2 to simulate incoming SMS messages from arbitrary numbers, as shown in Figure 12-1.

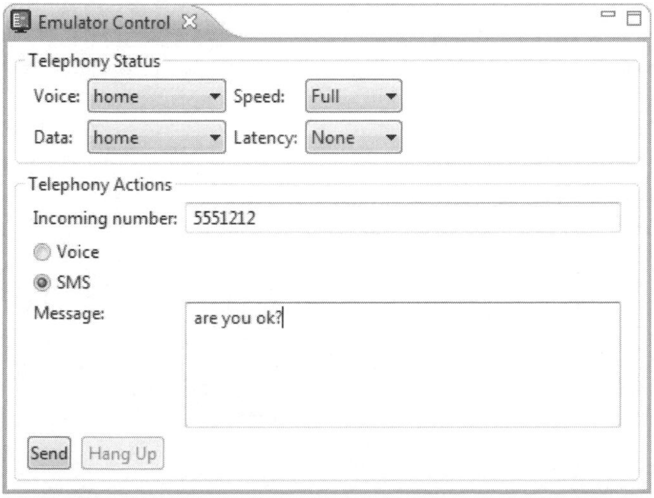

FIGURE 12-1

Handling Data SMS Messages

Data messages are received in the same way as normal SMS text messages and are extracted in the same way as shown in the preceding section.

To extract the data transmitted within a data SMS, use the `getUserData` method, as shown in the following snippet.

```
byte[] data = msg.getUserData();
```

The `getUserData` method returns a byte array of the data included in the message.

Emergency Responder SMS Example

In this example, you'll create an SMS application that turns an Android phone into an emergency response beacon.

Once finished, the next time you're in unfortunate proximity to an alien invasion or find yourself in a robot-uprising scenario, you can set your phone to automatically respond to your friends' and family members' pleas for a status update with a friendly message (or a desperate cry for help).

To make things easier for your would-be saviors, you'll use location-based services to tell your rescuers exactly where to find you. The robustness of SMS network infrastructure makes SMS an excellent option for applications like this for which reliability and accessibility are critical.

1. Start by creating a new `EmergencyResponder` project that features an `EmergencyResponder` Activity.

```
package com.paad.emergencyresponder;

import java.io.IOException;
import java.util.ArrayList;
import java.util.Locale;
import java.util.concurrent.locks.ReentrantLock;
import java.util.List;
import android.app.Activity;
import android.app.PendingIntent;
import android.content.Context;
import android.content.Intent;
import android.content.IntentFilter;

import android.content.BroadcastReceiver;
import android.content.SharedPreferences;
import android.location.Address;
import android.location.Geocoder;
import android.location.Location;
import android.location.LocationManager;

import android.os.Bundle;
import android.telephony.SmsManager;
import android.telephony.SmsMessage;
import android.view.View;
import android.view.View.OnClickListener;
import android.widget.ArrayAdapter;
```

```
import android.widget.Button;
import android.widget.CheckBox;
import android.widget.ListView;

public class EmergencyResponder extends Activity {

  @Override
  public void onCreate(Bundle savedInstanceState) {
    super.onCreate(savedInstanceState);
    setContentView(R.layout.main);
  }
}
```

2. Add permissions for finding your location as well as sending and receiving incoming SMS messages to the project manifest.

```
<?xml version="1.0" encoding="utf-8"?>
<manifest xmlns:android="http://schemas.android.com/apk/res/android"
  package="com.paad.emergencyresponder">
  <application
    android:icon="@drawable/icon"
    android:label="@string/app_name">
    <activity
      android:name=".EmergencyResponder"
      android:label="@string/app_name">
      <intent-filter>
        <action android:name="android.intent.action.MAIN" />
        <category android:name="android.intent.category.LAUNCHER" />
      </intent-filter>
    </activity>
  </application>
  <uses-permission android:name="android.permission.RECEIVE_SMS"/>
  <uses-permission android:name="android.permission.SEND_SMS"/>
  <uses-permission
    android:name="android.permission.ACCESS_FINE_LOCATION"
  />
</manifest>
```

3. Modify the main.xml layout resource. Include a ListView to display the list of people requesting a status update, and a series of buttons for sending response SMS messages. Use external resource references to fill in the button text; you'll create them in Step 4.

```
<?xml version="1.0" encoding="utf-8"?>
<RelativeLayout
  xmlns:android="http://schemas.android.com/apk/res/android"
  android:layout_width="fill_parent"
  android:layout_height="fill_parent">
  <TextView
    android:id="@+id/labelRequestList"
    android:layout_width="fill_parent"
    android:layout_height="wrap_content"
    android:text="These people want to know if you're ok"
    android:layout_alignParentTop="true"
  />
  <LinearLayout
    android:id="@+id/buttonLayout"
```

```
            xmlns:android="http://schemas.android.com/apk/res/android"
            android:orientation="vertical"
            android:layout_width="fill_parent"
            android:layout_height="wrap_content"
            android:padding="5px"
            android:layout_alignParentBottom="true">
            <CheckBox
              android:id="@+id/checkboxSendLocation"
              android:layout_width="fill_parent"
              android:layout_height="wrap_content"
              android:text="Include Location in Reply"/>
            <Button
              android:id="@+id/okButton"
              android:layout_width="fill_parent"
              android:layout_height="wrap_content"
              android:text="@string/respondAllClearButtonText"/>
            <Button
              android:id="@+id/notOkButton"
              android:layout_width="fill_parent"
              android:layout_height="wrap_content"
              android:text="@string/respondMaydayButtonText"/>
            <Button
              android:id="@+id/autoResponder"
              android:layout_width="fill_parent"
              android:layout_height="wrap_content"
              android:text="Setup Auto Responder"/>
          </LinearLayout>
          <ListView
            android:id="@+id/myListView"
            android:layout_width="fill_parent"
            android:layout_height="fill_parent"
            android:layout_below="@id/labelRequestList"
            android:layout_above="@id/buttonLayout"/>
        </RelativeLayout>
```

4. Update the external strings.xml resource to include the text for each button and default response messages to use when responding, including "I'm safe" or "I'm in danger" messages. You should also define the incoming message text to use when your phone detects requests for status responses.

```
        <?xml version="1.0" encoding="utf-8"?>
        <resources>
          <string name="app_name">Emergency Responder</string>
          <string name="respondAllClearButtonText">I am Safe and Well
          </string>
          <string name="respondMaydayButtonText">MAYDAY! MAYDAY! MAYDAY!
          </string>
          <string name="respondAllClearText">I am safe and well. Worry not!
          </string>
          <string name="respondMaydayText">Tell my mother I love her.
          </string>
          <string name="querystring">are you ok?</string>
        </resources>
```

5. At this point, the GUI will be complete, so starting the application should show you the screen in Figure 12-2.

6. Create a new Array List of Strings within the EmergencyResponder Activity to store the phone numbers of the incoming requests for your status. Bind the Array List to the List View, using an Array Adapter in the Activity's onCreate method, and create a new ReentrantLock object to ensure thread safe handling of the Array List.

Take the opportunity to get a reference to the checkbox and to add Click Listeners for each of the response buttons. Each button should call the respond method, while the Setup Auto Responder button should call the startAutoResponder stub.

FIGURE 12-2

```java
ReentrantLock lock;
CheckBox locationCheckBox;
ArrayList<String> requesters;
ArrayAdapter<String> aa;

@Override
public void onCreate(Bundle savedInstanceState){
  super.onCreate(savedInstanceState);
  setContentView(R.layout.main);

  lock = new ReentrantLock();
  requesters = new ArrayList<String>();
  wireUpControls();
}

private void wireUpControls() {
  locationCheckBox = (CheckBox)findViewById(R.id.checkboxSendLocation);
  ListView myListView = (ListView)findViewById(R.id.myListView);

  int layoutID = android.R.layout.simple_list_item_1;
  aa = new ArrayAdapter<String>(this, layoutID, requesters);
  myListView.setAdapter(aa);

  Button okButton = (Button)findViewById(R.id.okButton);
  okButton.setOnClickListener(new OnClickListener() {
    public void onClick(View arg0) {
      respond(true, locationCheckBox.isChecked());
    }
  });

  Button notOkButton = (Button)findViewById(R.id.notOkButton);
  notOkButton.setOnClickListener(new OnClickListener() {
    public void onClick(View arg0) {
```

```
      respond(false, locationCheckBox.isChecked());
    }
  });

  Button autoResponderButton =
    (Button)findViewById(R.id.autoResponder);
  autoResponderButton.setOnClickListener(new OnClickListener() {
    public void onClick(View arg0) {
      startAutoResponder();
    }
  });
}

public void respond(boolean _ok, boolean _includeLocation) {}
private void startAutoResponder() {}
```

7. Next, implement a Broadcast Receiver that will listen for incoming SMS messages.

   7.1. Start by creating a new static string variable to store the incoming SMS message intent action.

   ```
   public static final String SMS_RECEIVED =
     "android.provider.Telephony.SMS_RECEIVED";
   ```

   7.2. Then create a new Broadcast Receiver as a variable in the EmergencyResponder Activity. The receiver should listen for incoming SMS messages and call the requestReceived method when it sees SMS messages containing the "are you safe" String you defined as an external resource in Step 4.

   ```
   BroadcastReceiver emergencyResponseRequestReceiver =
     new BroadcastReceiver() {
       @Override
       public void onReceive(Context _context, Intent _intent) {
         if (_intent.getAction().equals(SMS_RECEIVED)) {
           String queryString = getString(R.string.querystring);

           Bundle bundle = _intent.getExtras();
           if (bundle != null) {
             Object[] pdus = (Object[]) bundle.get("pdus");
             SmsMessage[] messages = new SmsMessage[pdus.length];
             for (int i = 0; i < pdus.length; i++)
               messages[i] =
                 SmsMessage.createFromPdu((byte[]) pdus[i]);

             for (SmsMessage message : messages) {
               if (message.getMessageBody().toLowerCase().contains
                 (queryString))
                 requestReceived(message.getOriginatingAddress());
             }
           }
         }
       }
     };

   public void requestReceived(String _from) {}
   ```

8. Update the `onCreate` method of the Emergency Responder Activity to register the Broadcast Receiver created in Step 7.

```
@Override
public void onCreate(Bundle savedInstanceState) {
  super.onCreate(savedInstanceState);
  setContentView(R.layout.main);

  lock = new ReentrantLock();
  requesters = new ArrayList<String>();
  wireUpControls();

  IntentFilter filter = new IntentFilter(SMS_RECEIVED);
  registerReceiver(emergencyResponseRequestReceiver, filter);
}
```

9. Update the `requestReceived` method stub so that it adds the originating number of each status request's SMS to the "requesters" Array List.

```
public void requestReceived(String _from) {
  if (!requesters.contains(_from)) {
    lock.lock();
    requesters.add(_from);
    aa.notifyDataSetChanged();
    lock.unlock();
  }
}
```

10. The Emergency Responder Activity should now be listening for status request SMS messages and adding them to the List View as they arrive. Start the application and send SMS messages to the device or emulator on which it's running. Once they've arrived they should be displayed as shown in Figure 12-3.

11. Now update the Activity to let users respond to these status requests.

Start by completing the `respond` method stub you created in Step 6. It should iterate over the Array List of status requesters and send a new SMS message to each. The SMS message text should be

FIGURE 12-3

based on the response strings you defined as resources in Step 4. Fire the SMS using an overloaded `respond` method that you'll complete in the next step.

```
public void respond(boolean _ok, boolean _includeLocation) {
  String okString = getString(R.string.respondAllClearText);
  String notOkString = getString(R.string.respondMaydayText);
```

```
String outString = _ok ? okString : notOkString;

ArrayList<String> requestersCopy =
  (ArrayList<String>)requesters.clone();

for (String to : requestersCopy)
  respond(to, outString, _includeLocation);
}

private void respond(String _to, String _response,
                     boolean _includeLocation) {}
```

12. Update the `respond` method that handles the sending of each response SMS.

Start by removing each potential recipient from the "requesters" Array List before sending the SMS. If you are responding with your current location, use the Location Manager to find it before sending a second SMS with your current position as raw longitude/latitude points and a geocoded address.

```
public void respond(String _to, String _response,
                    boolean _includeLocation) {
  // Remove the target from the list of people we
  // need to respond to.
  lock.lock();
  requesters.remove(_to);
  aa.notifyDataSetChanged();
  lock.unlock();

  SmsManager sms = SmsManager.getDefault();

  // Send the message
  sms.sendTextMessage(_to, null, _response, null, null);

  StringBuilder sb = new StringBuilder();

  // Find the current location and send it
  // as SMS messages if required.
  if (_includeLocation) {
    String ls = Context.LOCATION_SERVICE;
    LocationManager lm = (LocationManager)getSystemService(ls);
    Location l =
      lm.getLastKnownLocation(LocationManager.GPS_PROVIDER);

    sb.append("I'm @:\n");
    sb.append(l.toString() + "\n");

    List<Address> addresses;
    Geocoder g = new Geocoder(getApplicationContext(),
                              Locale.getDefault());
    try {
      addresses = g.getFromLocation(l.getLatitude(),
                                    l.getLongitude(), 1);
      if (addresses != null) {
```

```
      Address currentAddress = addresses.get(0);
      if (currentAddress.getMaxAddressLineIndex() > 0) {
        for (int i = 0;
             i < currentAddress.getMaxAddressLineIndex();
             i++)
        {
          sb.append(currentAddress.getAddressLine(i));
          sb.append("\n");
        }
      }
      else {
        if (currentAddress.getPostalCode() != null)
          sb.append(currentAddress.getPostalCode());
      }
    }
  } catch (IOException e) {}

  ArrayList<String> locationMsgs =
    sms.divideMessage(sb.toString());
  for (String locationMsg : locationMsgs)
    sms.sendTextMessage(_to, null, locationMsg, null, null);
  }
}
```

13. In emergencies, it's important that messages get through. Improve the robustness of the application by including auto-retry functionality. Monitor the success of your SMS transmissions so that you can rebroadcast a message if it doesn't successfully send.

   13.1. Start by creating a new public static String in the Emergency Responder Activity to be used as a local "SMS Sent" action.

```
public static final String SENT_SMS =
  "com.paad.emergencyresponder.SMS_SENT";
```

   13.2. Update the respond method to include a new PendingIntent that broadcasts the action created in the previous step when the SMS transmission has completed. The packaged Intent should include the intended recipient's number as an extra.

```
public void respond(String _to, String _response,
                    boolean _includeLocation) {
  // Remove the target from the list of people we
  // need to respond to.
  lock.lock();
  requesters.remove(_to);
  aa.notifyDataSetChanged();
  lock.unlock();

  SmsManager sms = SmsManager.getDefault();

  Intent intent = new Intent(SENT_SMS);
  intent.putExtra("recipient", _to);

  PendingIntent sent =
    PendingIntent.getBroadcast(getApplicationContext(),
                               0, intent, 0);
```

```
// Send the message
sms.sendTextMessage(_to, null, _response, sent, null);

StringBuilder sb = new StringBuilder();

if (_includeLocation) {
  [ ...  existing respond method that finds the location ...  ]
  ArrayList<String> locationMsgs =
    sms.divideMessage(sb.toString());
  for (String locationMsg : locationMsgs)
    sms.sendTextMessage(_to, null, locationMsg, sentIntent, null);
}
}
```

13.3. Then implement a new Broadcast Receiver to listen for this broadcast Intent. Override its `onReceive` handler to confirm that the SMS was successfully delivered; if it wasn't, then put the intended recipient back onto the requester Array List.

```
private BroadcastReceiver attemptedDeliveryReceiver = new
BroadcastReceiver() {
  @Override
  public void onReceive(Context _context, Intent _intent) {
    if (_intent.getAction().equals(SENT_SMS)) {
      if (getResultCode() != Activity.RESULT_OK) {
        String recipient = _intent.getStringExtra("recipient");
        requestReceived(recipient);
      }
    }
  }
};
```

13.4. Finally, register the new Broadcast Receiver by extending the `onCreate` method of the Emergency Responder Activity.

```
@Override
public void onCreate(Bundle savedInstanceState) {
  super.onCreate(savedInstanceState);
  setContentView(R.layout.main);

  lock = new ReentrantLock();
  requesters = new ArrayList<String>();
  wireUpControls();

  IntentFilter filter = new IntentFilter(SMS_RECEIVED);
  registerReceiver(emergencyResponseRequestReceiver, filter);

  IntentFilter attemptedDeliveryfilter = new IntentFilter(SENT_SMS);
  registerReceiver(attemptedDeliveryReceiver,
                   attemptedDeliveryfilter);
}
```

All code snippets in this example are part of the Chapter 12 Emergency Responder *project, available for download at Wrox.com.*

This example has been simplified to focus on the SMS-based functionality it is attempting to demonstrate. Keen-eyed observers should have noticed at least two areas where it could be improved:

1. The Broadcast Receiver created and registered in Steps 7 and 8 would be better registered within the manifest to allow the application to respond to incoming SMS messages even when it isn't running.

2. The parsing of the incoming SMS messages performed by the Broadcast Receiver in Steps 7 and 9 should be moved into a Service, and executed on a background thread. Similarly, Step 13, sending the response SMS messages, would be better executed on a background thread within a Service.

The implementation of these improvements is left as an exercise for the reader based on the techniques you learned in Chapter 9.

Automating the Emergency Responder

In the following example, you'll fill in the code behind the Setup Auto Responder button added in the previous example, to let the Emergency Responder automatically respond to status update requests.

1. Start by creating a new autoresponder.xml layout resource that will be used to lay out the automatic response configuration window. Include an EditText for entering a status message to send, a Spinner for choosing the auto-response expiry time, and a CheckBox to let users decide whether they want to include their location in the automated responses.

```xml
<?xml version="1.0" encoding="utf-8"?>
<LinearLayout
  xmlns:android="http://schemas.android.com/apk/res/android"
  android:orientation="vertical"
  android:layout_width="fill_parent"
  android:layout_height="fill_parent">
  <TextView
    android:layout_width="fill_parent"
    android:layout_height="wrap_content"
    android:text="Respond With"/>
  <EditText
    android:id="@+id/responseText"
    android:layout_width="fill_parent"
    android:layout_height="wrap_content"/>
  <CheckBox
    android:id="@+id/checkboxLocation"
    android:layout_width="fill_parent"
    android:layout_height="wrap_content"
    android:text="Transmit Location"/>
  <TextView
    android:layout_width="fill_parent"
    android:layout_height="wrap_content"
    android:text="Auto Respond For"/>
  <Spinner
    android:id="@+id/spinnerRespondFor"
    android:layout_width="fill_parent"
```

```
        android:layout_height="wrap_content"
        android:drawSelectorOnTop="true"/>
    <LinearLayout
      xmlns:android="http://schemas.android.com/apk/res/android"
      android:orientation="horizontal"
      android:layout_width="fill_parent"
      android:layout_height="wrap_content">
      <Button
        android:id="@+id/okButton"
        android:layout_width="wrap_content"
        android:layout_height="wrap_content"
        android:text="Enable"/>
      <Button
        android:id="@+id/cancelButton"
        android:layout_width="wrap_content"
        android:layout_height="wrap_content"
        android:text="Disable"/>
    </LinearLayout>
  </LinearLayout>
```

2. Update the application's string.xml resource to define a name for an application
`SharedPreference` and strings to use for each of its keys.

```
<?xml version="1.0" encoding="utf-8"?>
<resources>
  <string name="app_name">Emergency Responder</string>
  <string name="respondAllClearButtonText">I am Safe and Well
  </string>
  <string name="respondMaydayButtonText">MAYDAY! MAYDAY! MAYDAY!
  </string>
  <string name="respondAllClearText">I am safe and well. Worry not!
  </string>
  <string name="respondMaydayText">Tell my mother I love her.
  </string>
  <string name="querystring">"are you ok?"</string>

  <string
    name="user_preferences">com.paad.emergencyresponder.preferences
  </string>
  <string name="includeLocationPref">PREF_INCLUDE_LOC</string>
  <string name="responseTextPref">PREF_RESPONSE_TEXT</string>
  <string name="autoRespondPref">PREF_AUTO_RESPOND</string>
  <string name="respondForPref">PREF_RESPOND_FOR</string>
</resources>
```

3. Then create a new arrays.xml resource, and create arrays to use for populating the Spinner.

```
<resources>
  <string-array name="respondForDisplayItems">
    <item>- Disabled -</item>
    <item>Next 5 minutes</item>
    <item>Next 15 minutes</item>
    <item>Next 30 minutes</item>
    <item>Next hour</item>
    <item>Next 2 hours</item>
```

```
    <item>Next 8 hours</item>
  </string-array>

  <array name="respondForValues">
    <item>0</item>
    <item>5</item>
    <item>15</item>
    <item>30</item>
    <item>60</item>
    <item>120</item>
    <item>480</item>
  </array>
</resources>
```

4. Now create a new `AutoResponder` Activity, populating it with the layout you created in Step 1.

```
package com.paad.emergencyresponder;

import android.app.Activity;
import android.app.AlarmManager;
import android.app.PendingIntent;
import android.content.res.Resources;
import android.content.Context;
import android.content.Intent;
import android.content.IntentFilter;
import android.content.BroadcastReceiver;
import android.content.SharedPreferences;
import android.content.SharedPreferences.Editor;
import android.os.Bundle;
import android.view.View;
import android.widget.ArrayAdapter;
import android.widget.Button;
import android.widget.CheckBox;
import android.widget.EditText;
import android.widget.Spinner;

public class AutoResponder extends Activity {
  @Override
  public void onCreate(Bundle savedInstanceState) {
      super.onCreate(savedInstanceState);
      setContentView(R.layout.autoresponder);
  }
}
```

5. Update `onCreate` further to get references to each of the controls in the layout and wire up the Spinner using the arrays defined in Step 3. Create two new stub methods, `savePreferences` and `updateUIFromPreferences`, that will be updated to save the auto-responder settings to a named `SharedPreference` and apply the saved `SharedPreferences` to the current UI, respectively.

```
Spinner respondForSpinner;
CheckBox locationCheckbox;
EditText responseTextBox;
```

```
@Override
public void onCreate(Bundle savedInstanceState) {
  super.onCreate(savedInstanceState);
  setContentView(R.layout.autoresponder);
```

5.1.   Start by getting references to each View.

```
respondForSpinner = (Spinner)findViewById(R.id.spinnerRespondFor);
locationCheckbox = (CheckBox)findViewById(R.id.checkboxLocation);
responseTextBox = (EditText)findViewById(R.id.responseText);
```

5.2.   Populate the Spinner to let users select the auto-responder expiry time.

```
ArrayAdapter<CharSequence> adapter =
  ArrayAdapter.createFromResource(this,
    R.array.respondForDisplayItems,
    android.R.layout.simple_spinner_item);

adapter.setDropDownViewResource(
  android.R.layout.simple_spinner_dropdown_item);
respondForSpinner.setAdapter(adapter);
```

5.3.   Now wire up the OK and Cancel buttons to let users save or cancel setting changes.

```
Button okButton = (Button) findViewById(R.id.okButton);
okButton.setOnClickListener(new View.OnClickListener() {
  public void onClick(View view) {
    savePreferences();
    setResult(RESULT_OK, null);
    finish();
  }
});

Button cancelButton = (Button) findViewById(R.id.cancelButton);
cancelButton.setOnClickListener(new View.OnClickListener() {
  public void onClick(View view) {
    respondForSpinner.setSelection(-1);
    savePreferences();
    setResult(RESULT_CANCELED, null);
    finish();
  }
});
```

5.4.   Finally, make sure that when the Activity starts, it updates the GUI to represent the current settings.

```
// Load the saved preferences and update the UI
updateUIFromPreferences();
```

5.5.   Close off the onCreate method, and add the updateUIFromPreferences and savePreferences stubs.

```
  }

private void updateUIFromPreferences() {}
private void savePreferences() {}
```

6.   Next, complete the two stub methods from Step 5. Start with updateUIFromPreferences; it should read the current saved AutoResponder preferences and apply them to the UI.

```
private void updateUIFromPreferences() {
  // Get the saves settings
  String preferenceName = getString(R.string.user_preferences);
  SharedPreferences sp = getSharedPreferences(preferenceName, 0);

  String autoResponsePref = getString(R.string.autoRespondPref);
  String responseTextPref = getString(R.string.responseTextPref);
  String autoLocPref = getString(R.string.includeLocationPref);
  String respondForPref = getString(R.string.respondForPref);

  boolean autoRespond = sp.getBoolean(autoResponsePref, false);
  String respondText = sp.getString(responseTextPref, "");
  boolean includeLoc = sp.getBoolean(includeLocPref, false);
  int respondForIndex = sp.getInt(respondForPref, 0);

  // Apply the saved settings to the UI
  if (autoRespond)
    respondForSpinner.setSelection(respondForIndex);
  else
    respondForSpinner.setSelection(0);

  locationCheckbox.setChecked(includeLoc);
  responseTextBox.setText(respondText);
}
```

7. Complete the `savePreferences` stub to save the current UI settings to a Shared Preferences file.

```
private void savePreferences() {
  // Get the current settings from the UI
  boolean autoRespond =
    respondForSpinner.getSelectedItemPosition() > 0;
  int respondForIndex = respondForSpinner.getSelectedItemPosition();
  boolean includeLoc = locationCheckbox.isChecked();
  String respondText = responseTextBox.getText().toString();

  // Save them to the Shared Preference file
  String preferenceName = getString(R.string.user_preferences);
  SharedPreferences sp = getSharedPreferences(preferenceName, 0);

  Editor editor = sp.edit();
  editor.putBoolean(getString(R.string.autoRespondPref),
                    autoRespond);
  editor.putString(getString(R.string.responseTextPref),
                             respondText);
  editor.putBoolean(getString(R.string.includeLocationPref),
                             includeLoc );
  editor.putInt(getString(R.string.respondForPref),respondForIndex);
  editor.commit();

  // Set the alarm to turn off the autoresponder
  setAlarm(respondForIndex);
}

private void setAlarm(int respondForIndex) {}
```

8. The `setAlarm` stub from Step 7 is used to create a new Alarm that fires an Intent that should result in the AutoResponder's being disabled.

You'll need to create a new `Alarm` object and a `BroadcastReceiver` that listens for it before disabling the auto-responder accordingly.

8.1. Start by creating the action String that will represent the Alarm Intent.

```
public static final String alarmAction =
  "com.paad.emergencyresponder.AUTO_RESPONSE_EXPIRED";
```

8.2. Then create a new Broadcast Receiver instance that listens for an Intent that includes the action specified in Step 8.1. When this Intent is received, it should modify the auto-responder settings to disable the automatic response.

```
private BroadcastReceiver stopAutoResponderReceiver = new
BroadcastReceiver() {
  @Override
  public void onReceive(Context context, Intent intent) {
    if (intent.getAction().equals(alarmAction)) {
      String preferenceName = getString(R.string.user_preferences);
      SharedPreferences sp = getSharedPreferences(preferenceName,0);

      Editor editor = sp.edit();
      editor.putBoolean(getString(R.string.autoRespondPref), false);
      editor.commit();
    }
  }
};
```

8.3. Finally, complete the `setAlarm` method. It should cancel the existing alarm if the auto-responder is turned off; otherwise, it should update the alarm with the latest expiry time.

```
PendingIntent intentToFire;

private void setAlarm(int respondForIndex) {
  // Create the alarm and register the alarm intent receiver.

  AlarmManager alarms =
    (AlarmManager)getSystemService(ALARM_SERVICE);

  if (intentToFire == null) {
    Intent intent = new Intent(alarmAction);
    intentToFire =
      PendingIntent.getBroadcast(getApplicationContext(),
                                 0,intent,0);

    IntentFilter filter = new IntentFilter(alarmAction);

    registerReceiver(stopAutoResponderReceiver, filter);
  }

  if (respondForIndex < 1)
    // If "disabled" is selected, cancel the alarm.
    alarms.cancel(intentToFire);
```

```
            else {
              // Otherwise find the length of time represented
              // by the selection and and set the alarm to
              // trigger after that time has passed.
              Resources r = getResources();
              int[] respondForValues =
                r.getIntArray(R.array.respondForValues);
              int respondFor = respondForValues [respondForIndex];

              long t = System.currentTimeMillis();
              t = t + respondFor*1000*60;

              // Set the alarm.
              alarms.set(AlarmManager.RTC_WAKEUP, t, intentToFire);
            }
          }
```

9. That completes the AutoResponder, but before you can use it, you'll need to add it to your application manifest.

```
<?xml version="1.0" encoding="utf-8"?>
<manifest
  xmlns:android="http://schemas.android.com/apk/res/android"
  package="com.paad.emergencyresponder">
  <application
    android:icon="@drawable/icon"
    android:label="@string/app_name">
    <activity
      android:name=".EmergencyResponder"
      android:label="@string/app_name">
      <intent-filter>
        <action android:name="android.intent.action.MAIN" />
        <category android:name="android.intent.category.LAUNCHER" />
      </intent-filter>
    </activity>
    <activity
      android:name=".AutoResponder"
      android:label="Auto Responder Setup"/>
  </application>
  <uses-permission android:name="android.permission.ACCESS_GPS"/>
  <uses-permission
android:name="android.permission.ACCESS_LOCATION"/>
  <uses-permission android:name="android.permission.RECEIVE_SMS"/>
  <uses-permission android:name="android.permission.SEND_SMS"/>
</manifest>
```

10. To enable the auto-responder, return to the Emergency Responder Activity and update the startAutoResponder method stub that you created in the previous example. It should open the AutoResponder Activity you just created.

```
private void startAutoResponder() {
  startActivityForResult(new Intent(EmergencyResponder.this,
                                    AutoResponder.class), 0);
}
```

11. If you start your project, you should now be able to bring up the Auto Responder Setup window to set the auto-response settings. It should appear as shown in Figure 12-4.

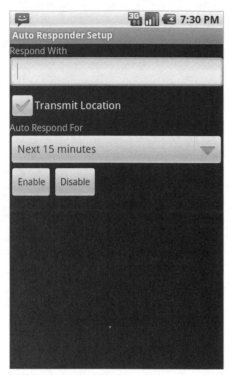

FIGURE 12-4

12. The final step is to update the `requestReceived` method in the Emergency Responder Activity to check if the auto-responder has been enabled.

If it has, the `requestReceived` method should automatically execute the `respond` method, using the message and location settings defined in the application's Shared Preferences.

```
public void requestReceived(String _from) {
  if (!requesters.contains(_from)) {
    lock.lock();
    requesters.add(_from);
    aa.notifyDataSetChanged();
    lock.unlock();

    // Check for auto-responder
    String preferenceName = getString(R.string.user_preferences);
    SharedPreferences prefs = getSharedPreferences(preferenceName,
                                                    0);
```

```
   String autoRespondPref = getString(R.string.autoRespondPref)
   boolean autoRespond = prefs.getBoolean(autoRespondPref, false);

   if (autoRespond) {
     String responseTextPref =
       getString(R.string.responseTextPref);
     String includeLocationPref =
       getString(R.string.includeLocationPref);

     String respondText = prefs.getString(responseTextPref, "");
     boolean includeLoc = prefs.getBoolean(includeLocationPref,
                                           false);

     respond(_from, respondText, includeLoc);
   }
  }
 }
```

All code snippets in this example are part of the Chapter 12 Emergency Responder 2 *project, available for download at Wrox.com.*

You should now have a fully functional interactive and automated emergency responder.

SUMMARY

The telephony stack is one of the fundamental technologies available on mobile phones. While not all Android devices will necessarily provide telephony APIs, those that do are particularly versatile platforms for person-to-person communication.

Using the telephony APIs you learned how to initiate calls directly and through the dialer. You also discovered how to read and monitor phone, network, data, and SIM states.

Android lets you use SMS to create applications that exchange data between devices and send and receive text messages for your users.

You also learned how to use Intents to allow the SMS applications already available on the phone to send SMS and MMS messages on your behalf.

Chapter 13 explores access to other device communication technologies. You'll investigate network management using Wi-Fi and explore the functionality available through the Bluetooth APIs.

13

Bluetooth, Networks, and Wi-Fi

In this chapter you'll continue to explore Android's low-level communications APIs by examining the Bluetooth, network, and Wi-Fi packages.

Android offers APIs to manage and monitor your Bluetooth device settings, to control discoverability, to discover nearby Bluetooth devices, and to use Bluetooth as a proximity-based peer-to-peer transport layer for your applications.

A full network and Wi-Fi package is also available. Using these APIs you can scan for hotspots, create and modify Wi-Fi configuration settings, monitor your Internet connectivity, and control and monitor Internet settings and preferences.

USING BLUETOOTH

In this section you'll learn how to interact with the local Bluetooth device and communicate with remote devices on nearby phones.

Using Bluetooth you can search for, and connect to, other devices within range. By initiating a communications link using Bluetooth Sockets you can then transmit and receive streams of data between devices from within your applications.

The Bluetooth libraries have been available in Android only since Android version 2.0 (SDK API level 5). It's also important to remember that not all Android devices will necessarily include Bluetooth hardware.

Bluetooth is a communications protocol designed for short-range, low-bandwidth peer-to-peer communications. As of Android 2.1, only encrypted communication is supported, meaning you can only form connections between paired devices. In Android, Bluetooth devices and connections are handled by the following classes:

➤ `BluetoothAdapter` The Bluetooth Adapter represents the local Bluetooth device — that is, the Android device on which your application is running.

➤ `BluetoothDevice` Each remote device with which you wish to communicate is represented as a `BluetoothDevice`.

➤ `BluetoothSocket` Call `createRfcommSocketToServiceRecord` on a remote Bluetooth Device object to create a Bluetooth Socket that will let you make a connection request to the remote device, and then initiate communications.

➤ `BluetoothServerSocket` By creating a Bluetooth Server Socket (using the `listenUsingRfcommWithServiceRecord` method) on your local Bluetooth Adapter, you can listen for incoming connection requests from Bluetooth Sockets on remote devices.

Accessing the Local Bluetooth Device Adapter

The local Bluetooth device is controlled via the `BluetoothAdapter` class.

To access the default Bluetooth adapter on the host device call `getDefaultAdapter`, as shown in Listing 13-1. It is possible that some Android devices will feature multiple Bluetooth adapters, though it is currently only possible to access the default device.

LISTING 13-1: Accessing the default Bluetooth Adapter

```
BluetoothAdapter bluetooth = BluetoothAdapter.getDefaultAdapter();
```

To read any of the local Bluetooth Adapter properties, initiate discovery, or find bonded devices you will need to include the `BLUETOOTH` manifest permission. In order to modify any of the local device properties the `BLUETOOTH_ADMIN` uses-permission is also required.

```
<uses-permission android:name="android.permission.BLUETOOTH"/>
<uses-permission android:name="android.permission.BLUETOOTH_ADMIN"/>
```

Managing Bluetooth Properties and State

The Bluetooth Adapter offers methods for reading and setting properties of the local Bluetooth hardware.

 The Bluetooth Adapter properties can be read and changed only if the Bluetooth adapter is currently turned on (that is, if its device state is enabled). If the device is off, these methods will return `null`.

If the Bluetooth Adapter is turned on, and you have included the BLUETOOTH permission in your manifest, you can access the Bluetooth Adapter's *friendly name* (an arbitrary string that users can set and then use to identify a particular device) and hardware address, as shown in Listing 13-2.

Use the isEnabled method, as shown in Listing 13-2, to confirm the device is enabled before accessing these properties.

LISTING 13-2: Reading Bluetooth Adapter properties

```
BluetoothAdapter bluetooth = BluetoothAdapter.getDefaultAdapter();

String toastText;
if (bluetooth.isEnabled()) {
  String address = bluetooth.getAddress();
  String name = bluetooth.getName();
  toastText = name + " : " + address;
}
else
  toastText = "Bluetooth is not enabled";

Toast.makeText(this, toastText, Toast.LENGTH_LONG).show();
```

If you also have the BLUETOOTH_ADMIN permission you can change the friendly name of the Bluetooth Adapter using the setName method:

```
bluetooth.setName("Blackfang");
```

To find a more detailed description of the current Bluetooth Adapter state, use the getState method, which will return one of the following BluetoothAdapter constants:

➤ STATE_TURNING_ON

➤ STATE_ON

➤ STATE_TURNING_OFF

➤ STATE_OFF

By default the Bluetooth adapter will be turned off. In order to conserve battery life and optimize security, most users will keep Bluetooth disabled unless it's in use.

To enable the Bluetooth Adapter you can start a system sub-Activity using the `ACTION_REQUEST_ENABLE` Bluetooth Adapter static constant as a `startActivityForResult` action string:

```
String enableBT = BluetoothAdapter.ACTION_REQUEST_ENABLE;
startActivityForResult(new Intent(enableBT), 0);
```

The sub-Activity is shown in Figure 13-1. It prompts the user to turn on Bluetooth and asks for confirmation. If the user agrees, the sub-Activity will close and return to the calling Activity once the Bluetooth Adapter has turned on (or has encountered an error). If the user selects no, the sub-Activity will close and return immediately. Use the result code parameter returned in the `onActivityResult` handler to determine the success of this operation.

FIGURE 13-1

 It is also possible to turn the Bluetooth Adapter on and off directly, using the enable *and* disable *methods, if you include the* BLUETOOTH_ADMIN *permission in your manifest.*

Note that this should be done only when absolutely necessary and that the user should always be notified if you are manually changing the Bluetooth Adapter status on the user's behalf. In most cases you should use the Intent mechanism described earlier.

Enabling and disabling the Bluetooth Adapter are somewhat time-consuming, asynchronous operations. Rather than polling the Bluetooth Adapter, your application should register a Broadcast Receiver that listens for ACTION_STATE_CHANGED. The broadcast Intent will include two extras, EXTRA_STATE and EXTRA_PREVIOUS_STATE, which indicate the current and previous Bluetooth Adapter states, respectively.

Listing 13-3 shows how to use an Intent to prompt the user to enable Bluetooth and a Broadcast Receiver to track changes in the Bluetooth Adapter status.

Available for download on Wrox.com

LISTING 13-3: Enabling Bluetooth and tracking the adapter state

```java
BluetoothAdapter bluetooth = BluetoothAdapter.getDefaultAdapter();

BroadcastReceiver bluetoothState = new BroadcastReceiver() {
  @Override
  public void onReceive(Context context, Intent intent) {
    String prevStateExtra = BluetoothAdapter.EXTRA_PREVIOUS_STATE;
    String stateExtra = BluetoothAdapter.EXTRA_STATE;
    int state = intent.getIntExtra(stateExtra, -1);
    int previousState = intent.getIntExtra(prevStateExtra, -1);

    String tt = "";
    switch (state) {
      case (BluetoothAdapter.STATE_TURNING_ON) : {
        tt = "Bluetooth turning on"; break;
      }
      case (BluetoothAdapter.STATE_ON) : {
        tt = "Bluetooth on";
        unregisterReceiver(this);
        break;
      }
      case (BluetoothAdapter.STATE_TURNING_OFF) : {
        tt = "Bluetooth turning off"; break;
      }
      case (BluetoothAdapter.STATE_OFF) : {
        tt = "Bluetooth off"; break;
      }
      default: break;
    }

    Toast.makeText(this, tt, Toast.LENGTH_LONG).show();
  }
};

if (!bluetooth.isEnabled()) {
  String actionStateChanged = BluetoothAdapter.ACTION_STATE_CHANGED;
  String actionRequestEnable = BluetoothAdapter.ACTION_REQUEST_ENABLE;
  registerReceiver(bluetoothState,
                   new IntentFilter(actionStateChanged));
  startActivityForResult(new Intent(actionRequestEnable), 0);
}
```

Being Discoverable and Remote Device Discovery

The process of two devices finding each other in order to connect is called *discovery*. Before you can establish a Bluetooth Socket for communications, the local Bluetooth Adapter must bond with the remote device. Before two devices can bond and connect, they first need to discover each other.

 While the Bluetooth protocol supports ad-hoc connections for data transfer, this mechanism is not currently available in Android. Android Bluetooth communication is currently supported only between bonded devices.

Managing Device Discoverability

In order for remote Android Devices to find your local Bluetooth Adapter during a discovery scan, you need to ensure that it is discoverable.

The Bluetooth Adapter's discoverability is indicated by its scan mode. You can find the adapter's scan mode by calling `getScanMode` on the `BluetoothAdapter` object. It will return one of the following `BluetoothAdapter` constants:

> ➤ `SCAN_MODE_CONNECTABLE_DISCOVERABLE` Inquiry scan and page scan are both enabled, meaning that the device is discoverable from any Bluetooth device performing a discovery scan.

> ➤ `SCAN_MODE_CONNECTABLE` Page Scan is enabled but inquiry scan is not. This means that devices that have previously connected and bonded to the local device can find it during discovery, but new devices can't.

> ➤ `SCAN_MODE_NONE` Discoverability is turned off. No remote devices can find the local adapter during discovery.

FIGURE 13-2

For privacy reasons, Android devices will default to having discoverability disabled. To turn on discovery you need to obtain explicit permission from the user; you do this by starting a new Activity using the `ACTION_REQUEST_DISCOVERABLE` action:

```
String aDiscoverable = BluetoothAdapter.ACTION_REQUEST_DISCOVERABLE;
startActivityForResult(new Intent(aDiscoverable),
                       DISCOVERY_REQUEST);
```

By default discoverability will be enabled for two minutes. You can modify this setting by adding an `EXTRA_DISCOVERABLE_DURATION` extra to the launch Intent, specifying the number of seconds you want discoverability to last.

When the Intent is broadcast the user will be prompted by the dialog shown in Figure 13-2 to turn discoverability on for the specified duration.

To learn if the user has allowed or rejected your discovery request, override the `onActivityResult` handler, as shown in Listing 13-4. The returned `resultCode` parameter indicates the duration of discoverability, or a negative number if the user has rejected your request.

LISTING 13-4: Monitoring discoverability modes

```
@Override
protected void onActivityResult(int requestCode,
                                int resultCode, Intent data) {
  if (requestCode == DISCOVERY_REQUEST) {
    boolean isDiscoverable = resultCode > 0;
    int discoverableDuration = resultCode;
  }
}
```

Alternatively you can monitor changes in discoverability by receiving the `ACTION_SCAN_MODE_CHANGED` broadcast action, as shown in Listing 13-5. The broadcast Intent includes the current and previous scan modes as extras.

LISTING 13-5: Monitoring discoverability modes

```
registerReceiver(new BroadcastReceiver() {
  @Override
  public void onReceive(Context context, Intent intent) {
    String prevScanMode = BluetoothAdapter.EXTRA_PREVIOUS_SCAN_MODE;
    String scanMode = BluetoothAdapter.EXTRA_SCAN_MODE;
    int scanMode = intent.getIntExtra(scanMode, -1);

    int prevMode = intent.getIntExtra(prevScanMode, -1);
  }
},
new IntentFilter(BluetoothAdapter.ACTION_SCAN_MODE_CHANGED));
```

Discovering Remote Devices

In this section you'll now learn how to initiate discovery from your local adapter to find discoverable devices nearby.

The discovery process can take some time to complete (up to 12 seconds). During this time, performance of your Bluetooth Adapter communications will be seriously degraded. Use the techniques in this section to check and monitor the discovery status of the Bluetooth Adapter, and avoid doing high-bandwidth operations (including connecting to a new remote Bluetooth Device) while discovery is in progress.

You can check to see if the local Bluetooth Adapter is already performing a discovery scan using the `isDiscovering` method.

To initiate the discovery process call `startDiscovery` on the Bluetooth Adapter. To cancel a discovery in progress call `cancelDiscovery`.

```
bluetooth.startDiscovery();
bluetooth.cancelDiscovery();
```

The discovery process is asynchronous. Android uses broadcast Intents to notify you of the start and end of discovery as well as remote devices discovered during the scan.

You can monitor changes in the discovery process by creating Broadcast Receivers to listen for the `ACTION_DISCOVERY_STARTED` and `ACTION_DISCOVERY_FINISHED` broadcast Intents, as shown in Listing 13-6.

LISTING 13-6: Monitoring discovery

```java
BroadcastReceiver discoveryMonitor = new BroadcastReceiver() {

    String dStarted = BluetoothAdapter.ACTION_DISCOVERY_STARTED;
    String dFinished = BluetoothAdapter.ACTION_DISCOVERY_FINISHED;

    @Override
    public void onReceive(Context context, Intent intent) {
      if (dStarted.equals(intent.getAction())) {
        // Discovery has started.
        Toast.makeText(getApplicationContext(),
                   "Discovery Started ... ", Toast.LENGTH_SHORT).show();
      }
      else if (dFinished.equals(intent.getAction())) {
        // Discovery has completed.
        Toast.makeText(getApplicationContext(),
                   "Discovery Completed ... ", Toast.LENGTH_SHORT).show();
      }
    }
};
registerReceiver(discoveryMonitor,
                 new IntentFilter(dStarted));
registerReceiver(discoveryMonitor,
                 new IntentFilter(dFinished));
```

Discovered Bluetooth Devices are returned via broadcast Intents by means of the `ACTION_FOUND` broadcast action.

As shown in Listing 13-7, each broadcast Intent includes the name of the remote device in an extra indexed as `BluetoothDevice.EXTRA_NAME`, and an immutable representation of the remote Bluetooth device as a `BluetoothDevice` parcelable object stored under the `BluetoothDevice.EXTRA_DEVICE` extra.

LISTING 13-7: Discovering remote Bluetooth Devices

```java
BroadcastReceiver discoveryResult = new BroadcastReceiver() {
  @Override
  public void onReceive(Context context, Intent intent) {
    String remoteDeviceName =
      intent.getStringExtra(BluetoothDevice.EXTRA_NAME);
```

```
       BluetoothDevice remoteDevice;
       remoteDevice = intent.getParcelableExtra(BluetoothDevice.EXTRA_DEVICE);

       Toast.makeText(getApplicationContext(),
                   "Discovered: " + remoteDeviceName,
                   Toast.LENGTH_SHORT).show();

       // TODO Do something with the remote Bluetooth Device.
     }
   };
   registerReceiver(discoveryResult,
               new IntentFilter(BluetoothDevice.ACTION_FOUND));

   if (!bluetooth.isDiscovering())
     bluetooth.startDiscovery();
```

The `BluetoothDevice` object returned through the discovery broadcast represents the remote Bluetooth Device discovered. In the following sections it will be used to create a connection, bond, and ultimately transfer data between the local Bluetooth Adapter and the remote Bluetooth Device.

Bluetooth Communications

The Bluetooth communications APIs are wrappers around RFCOMM, the Bluetooth radio frequency communications protocol. RFCOMM supports RS232 serial communication over the Logical Link Control and Adaptation Protocol (L2CAP) layer.

In practice, this alphabet soup provides a mechanism for opening communication sockets between two paired Bluetooth devices.

Before your application can communicate between devices they must be paired (bonded). At the time of writing (Android API level 7) there is no way to manually initiate pairing between the local Bluetooth Adapter and a remote Bluetooth Device.

If two devices are to be paired the user will need to explicitly allow this, either through the Bluetooth Settings screen or when prompted by your application when you attempt to connect a Bluetooth Socket between two unpaired devices.

You can establish an RFCOMM communication channel for bidirectional communications using the following classes.

➤   `BluetoothServerSocket`   Used to establish a listening socket for initiating a link between devices. To establish a handshake, one device acts as a server to listen for, and accept, incoming connection requests.

➤   `BluetoothSocket`   Used in creating a new client socket to connect to a listening Bluetooth Server Socket, and returned by the Server Socket once a connection is established. Once the connection is made, Bluetooth Sockets are used on both the server and client sides to transfer data streams.

When creating an application that uses Bluetooth as a peer-to-peer transport layer, you'll need to implement both a Bluetooth Server Socket to listen for connections and a Bluetooth Socket to initiate a new channel and handle communications.

Once connected, the Socket Server returns a Bluetooth Socket that's subsequently used by the server device to send and receive data. This server-side Bluetooth Socket is used in exactly the same way as the client socket. The designations of *server* and *client* are relevant only to how the connection is established. They don't affect how data flows once that connection is made.

Opening a Bluetooth Server Socket Listener

A Bluetooth Server Socket is used to listen for incoming Bluetooth Socket connection requests from remote Bluetooth Devices. In order for two Bluetooth devices to be connected, one must act as a server (listening for and accepting incoming requests) and the other as a client (initiating the request to connect to the server).

Once the two are connected, the communications between the server and host device are handled through a Bluetooth Socket at both ends.

To listen for incoming connection requests call the `listenUsingRfcommWithServiceRecord` method on your Bluetooth Adapter, passing in both a string "name" to identify your server and a UUID (universally unique identifier). This will return a `BluetoothServerSocket` object. Note that the client Bluetooth Socket that connects to this listener will need to know the UUID in order to connect.

To start listening for connections call `accept` on this Server Socket, optionally passing in a timeout duration. The Server Socket will now block until a remote Bluetooth Socket client with a matching UUID attempts to connect. If a connection request is made from a remote device that is not yet paired with the local adapter, the user will be prompted to accept a pairing request before the accept call returns. This prompt is made via a notification, as shown in Figure 13-3.

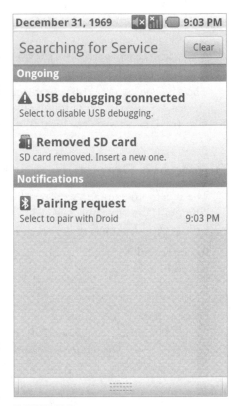

FIGURE 13-3

If an incoming connection request is successful, `accept` will return a Bluetooth Socket connected to the client device. You can use this socket to transfer data, as shown later in this section.

 Note that `accept` is a blocking operation, so it's best practice to listen for incoming connection requests on a background thread rather than block the UI thread until a connection has been made.

It's also important to note that your Bluetooth Adapter must be discoverable for remote Bluetooth Devices to connect to it. Listing 13-8 shows some typical skeleton code that uses the `ACTION_REQUEST_DISCOVERABLE` broadcast to request that the device be made discoverable, before listening for incoming connection requests for the returned discoverability duration.

LISTING 13-8: Listening for Bluetooth Socket connection requests

```
startActivityForResult(new
  Intent(BluetoothAdapter.ACTION_REQUEST_DISCOVERABLE),
        DISCOVERY_REQUEST);

@Override
protected void onActivityResult(int requestCode,
                                int resultCode, Intent data) {
  if (requestCode == DISCOVERY_REQUEST) {
    boolean isDiscoverable = resultCode > 0;
    int discoverableDuration = resultCode;
    if (isDiscoverable) {
      UUID uuid = UUID.fromString("a60f35f0-b93a-11de-8a39-08002009c666");
      String name = "bluetoothserver";

      final BluetoothServerSocket btserver =
        bluetooth.listenUsingRfcommWithServiceRecord(name, uuid);

      Thread acceptThread = new Thread(new Runnable() {
        public void run() {
          try {
            // Block until client connection established.
            BluetoothSocket serverSocket = btserver.accept();
            // TODO Transfer data using the server socket
          } catch (IOException e) {
            Log.d("BLUETOOTH", e.getMessage());
          }
        }
      });
      acceptThread.start();
    }
  }
}
```

Selecting Remote Bluetooth Devices for Communications

The BluetoothSocket class is used on the client device to initiate a communications channel from within your application to a listening Bluetooth Server Socket.

You create client-side Bluetooth Sockets by calling createRfcommSocketToServiceRecord on a BluetoothDevice object. That object represents the target remote server device. It should have a Bluetooth Server Socket listening for connection requests (as described in the previous section).

There are a number of ways to obtain a reference to a remote Bluetooth Device, and some important caveats regarding the devices with which you can create a communications link.

Bluetooth Device Connection Requirements

In order for a Bluetooth Socket to establish a connection to a remote Bluetooth Device, the following conditions must be true:

➤ The remote device must be discoverable.

➤ The remote device must accept connections using a Bluetooth Server Socket.

➤ The local and remote devices must be paired (or bonded). If the devices are not paired, the user will be prompted to pair them when you initiate the connection request.

Finding a Bluetooth Device to Connect To

Each Bluetooth Device object represents a remote device. These objects are used to obtain remote device properties and to initiate Bluetooth Socket connections. There are several ways for you to obtain a `BluetoothDevice` object in code.

In each case you should check to ensure that the device you intend to connect to is discoverable, and (optionally) determine whether you are bonded to it. If you can't discover the remote device, you should prompt the user to enable discoverability on it.

You learned one technique for finding discoverable Bluetooth Devices earlier in this section using the `startDiscovery` method and monitoring `ACTION_FOUND` broadcasts. You learned that each received broadcast includes a `BluetoothDevice.EXTRA_DEVICE` extra that contains the discovered Bluetooth Device.

You can also use the `getRemoteDevice` method on your local Bluetooth Adapter, specifying the hardware address of the remote Bluetooth Device you want to connect to.

```
BluetoothDevice device = bluetooth.getRemoteDevice("01:23:77:35:2F:AA");
```

To find the set of currently paired devices call `getBondedDevices` on the local Bluetooth Adapter. You can query the returned set to find out if a target Bluetooth Device is paired with the local adapter.

```
Set<BluetoothDevice> bondedDevices = bluetooth.getBondedDevices();
if (bondedDevices.contains(remoteDevice))
    // TODO Target device is bonded / paired with the local device.
```

Listing 13-9 shows a typical implementation pattern that checks a given Bluetooth Device for discoverability and pairing.

LISTING 13-9: Checking remote devices for discoverability and pairing

```
final BluetoothDevice device =
bluetooth.getRemoteDevice("01:23:77:35:2F:AA");
final Set<BluetoothDevice> bondedDevices = bluetooth.getBondedDevices();

BroadcastReceiver discoveryResult = new BroadcastReceiver() {
@Override
public void onReceive(Context context, Intent intent) {
  BluetoothDevice remoteDevice =
    intent.getParcelableExtra(BluetoothDevice.EXTRA_DEVICE);

    if ((remoteDevice.equals(device) &&
        (bondedDevices.contains(remoteDevice)) {
      // TODO Target device is paired and discoverable
    }
};
registerReceiver(discoveryResult,
                new IntentFilter(BluetoothDevice.ACTION_FOUND));
```

```
if (!bluetooth.isDiscovering())
    bluetooth.startDiscovery();
```

Opening a Client Bluetooth Socket Connection

To initiate a communications channel to a remote device, create a Bluetooth Socket from the `BluetoothDevice` object that represents it.

To create a new connection call `createRfcommSocketToServiceRecord` on the Bluetooth Device to connect to, passing in the UUID of the Bluetooth Server Socket accepting requests.

If you attempt to connect to a Bluetooth Device that has not yet been paired (bonded) with the host device, you will be prompted to accept the pairing before the `connect` call completes, as shown in Figure 13-4.

The user must accept the pairing request on both the host and remote devices for the connection to be established.

The returned Bluetooth Socket can then be used to initiate the connection with a call to `connect`, as shown in Listing 13-10.

FIGURE 13-4

 Note that connect *is a blocking operation, so it's best practice to initiate connection requests on a background thread rather than block the UI thread until a connection has been made.*

Available for download on Wrox.com

LISTING 13-10: Connecting to a remote Bluetooth server

```
Try{
    BluetoothDevice device = bluetooth.getRemoteDevice("00:23:76:35:2F:AA");
    BluetoothSocket clientSocket =
        device.createRfcommSocketToServiceRecord(uuid);
    clientSocket.connect();
    // TODO Transfer data using the Bluetooth Socket
} catch (IOException e) {
    Log.d("BLUETOOTH", e.getMessage());
}
```

Transmitting Data Using Bluetooth Sockets

Once a connection has been established, you will have a Bluetooth Socket on both the client and the server devices. From this point onward there is no significant distinction between them: you can send and receive data using the Bluetooth Socket on both devices.

Data transfer across Bluetooth Sockets is handled via standard Java `InputStream` and `OutputStream` objects, which you can obtain from a Bluetooth Socket using the appropriately named `getInputStream` and `getOutputStream` methods, respectively.

Listing 13-11 shows two simple skeleton methods, the first used to send a string to a remote device using an Output Stream, and the second to listen for incoming strings using an Input Stream. The same technique can be used to transfer any streamable data.

LISTING 13-11: Sending and receiving strings using Bluetooth Sockets

```
private void sendMessage(String message){
  OutputStream outStream;
  try {
    outStream = socket.getOutputStream();

    // Add a stop character.
    byte[] byteArray = (message + " ").getBytes();
    byteArray[byteArray.length - 1] = 0;

    outStream.write(byteArray);
  } catch (IOException e) { }
}

private String listenForMessage()
  String result = "";
  int bufferSize = 1024;
  byte[] buffer = new byte[bufferSize];

  try {
    InputStream instream = socket.getInputStream();
    int bytesRead = -1;

    while (true) {
      bytesRead = instream.read(buffer);
      if (bytesRead != -1) {
        while ((bytesRead == bufferSize) && (buffer[bufferSize-1] != 0)){
          message = message + new String(buffer, 0, bytesRead);
          bytesRead = instream.read(buffer);
        }
        message = message + new String(buffer, 0, bytesRead - 1);
        return result;
      }
    }
  }
```

```
    } catch (IOException e) {}

  return result;
}
```

Bluetooth Data Transfer Example

The following example uses the Android Bluetooth APIs to construct a simple peer-to-peer messaging system that works between two paired Bluetooth devices.

Unfortunately the Android emulator can't currently be used to test Bluetooth functionality. In order to test this application you will need to have two physical devices.

1. Start by creating a new `BluetoothTexting` project featuring a `BluetoothTexting` Activity. Modify the manifest to include `BLUETOOTH` and `BLUETOOTH_ADMIN` permissions.

```xml
<?xml version="1.0" encoding="utf-8"?>
<manifest xmlns:android="http://schemas.android.com/apk/res/android"
  package="com.paad.chapter13_bluetoothtexting"
  android:versionCode="1"
  android:versionName="1.0">
  <application
    android:icon="@drawable/icon"
    android:label="@string/app_name">
    <activity
      android:name=".BluetoothTexting"
      android:label="@string/app_name">
      <intent-filter>
        <action android:name="android.intent.action.MAIN" />
        <category android:name="android.intent.category.LAUNCHER" />
      </intent-filter>
    </activity>
  </application>
  <uses-sdk android:minSdkVersion="5" />
  <uses-permission android:name="android.permission.BLUETOOTH"/>
  <uses-permission android:name="android.permission.BLUETOOTH_ADMIN"/>
</manifest>
```

2. Modify the main.xml layout resource. It should contain a `ListView` that will display the discovered Bluetooth devices above two buttons — one to start the Server Socket listener, and another to initiate a connection to a listening server.

Also include Text View and Edit Text controls to use for reading and writing messages across the connection.

```xml
<?xml version="1.0" encoding="utf-8"?>
<RelativeLayout
  xmlns:android="http://schemas.android.com/apk/res/android"
  android:orientation="vertical"
  android:layout_width="fill_parent"
  android:layout_height="fill_parent">
```

```xml
  <EditText
    android:id="@+id/text_message"
    android:layout_width="fill_parent"
    android:layout_height="wrap_content"
    android:layout_alignParentBottom="true"
    android:enabled="false"
  />
  <Button
    android:id="@+id/button_search"
    android:text="Search for listener"
    android:layout_width="fill_parent"
    android:layout_height="wrap_content"
    android:layout_above="@id/text_message"
  />
  <Button
    android:id="@+id/button_listen"
    android:text="Listen for connection"
    android:layout_width="fill_parent"
    android:layout_height="wrap_content"
    android:layout_above="@id/button_search"
  />
  <ListView
    android:id="@+id/list_discovered"
    android:layout_width="fill_parent"
    android:layout_height="fill_parent"
    android:layout_above="@id/button_listen"
    android:layout_alignParentTop="true"
  />
  <TextView
    android:id="@+id/text_messages"
    android:layout_width="fill_parent"
    android:layout_height="fill_parent"
    android:layout_above="@id/button_listen"
    android:layout_alignParentTop="true"
    android:visibility="gone"
  />
</RelativeLayout>
```

3. Override the `onCreate` method of the `BluetoothTexting` Activity. Make calls to a collection of stub methods that will be used to access the Bluetooth device and wire up the UI controls.

```java
import java.io.IOException;
import java.io.InputStream;
import java.io.OutputStream;
import java.util.ArrayList;
import java.util.UUID;
import android.app.Activity;
import android.bluetooth.BluetoothAdapter;
import android.bluetooth.BluetoothDevice;
import android.bluetooth.BluetoothServerSocket;
import android.bluetooth.BluetoothSocket;
import android.content.BroadcastReceiver;
import android.content.Context;
import android.content.Intent;
import android.content.IntentFilter;
```

```
import android.os.AsyncTask;
import android.os.Bundle;
import android.os.Handler;
import android.util.Log;
import android.view.KeyEvent;
import android.view.View;
import android.view.View.OnClickListener;
import android.view.View.OnKeyListener;
import android.widget.AdapterView;
import android.widget.ArrayAdapter;
import android.widget.Button;
import android.widget.EditText;
import android.widget.ListView;
import android.widget.TextView;
import android.widget.AdapterView.OnItemClickListener;

public class BluetoothTexting extends Activity {

  @Override
  public void onCreate(Bundle savedInstanceState) {
    super.onCreate(savedInstanceState);
    setContentView(R.layout.main);

    // Get the Bluetooth Adapter
    configureBluetooth();

    // Setup the ListView of discovered devices
    setupListView();

    // Setup search button
    setupSearchButton();

    // Setup listen button
    setupListenButton();
  }

  private void configureBluetooth() {}
  private void setupListenButton() {}
  private void setupListView() {}
  private void setupSearchButton() {}
}
```

4. Fill in the `configureBluetooth` stub to get access to the local Bluetooth Adapter and store it in a field variable. Take this opportunity to create a field variable for a Bluetooth Socket. This will be used to store either the server or client communications socket once a channel has been established. You should also define a UUID to identify your application when connections are being established.

```
private BluetoothAdapter bluetooth;
private BluetoothSocket socket;
private UUID uuid = UUID.fromString("a60f35f0-b93a-11de-8a39-08002009c666");

private void configureBluetooth() {
  bluetooth = BluetoothAdapter.getDefaultAdapter();
}
```

5. Create a new `switchUI` method. It will be called once a connection is established to enable the Views used for reading and writing messages.

```java
private void switchUI() {
  final TextView messageText = (TextView)findViewById(R.id.text_messages);
  final EditText textEntry = (EditText)findViewById(R.id.text_message);

  messageText.setVisibility(View.VISIBLE);
  list.setVisibility(View.GONE);
  textEntry.setEnabled(true);
}
```

6. Create the server listener by filling in the `setupListenButton` stub. The Listen button should prompt the user to enable discovery. When the discovery window returns, open a Bluetooth Server Socket to listen for connection requests for the discovery duration. Once a connection has been made, make a call to the `switchUI` method you created in Step 5.

```java
private static int DISCOVERY_REQUEST = 1;

private void setupListenButton() {
  Button listenButton = (Button)findViewById(R.id.button_listen);
  listenButton.setOnClickListener(new OnClickListener() {
    public void onClick(View view) {
      intent disc;
      disc = new Intent(BluetoothAdapter.ACTION_REQUEST_DISCOVERABLE);
      startActivityForResult(disc, DISCOVERY_REQUEST);
    }
  });
}

@Override
protected void onActivityResult(int requestCode, int resultCode, Intent
data) {
  if (requestCode == DISCOVERY_REQUEST) {
    boolean isDiscoverable = resultCode > 0;
    if (isDiscoverable) {
      String name = "bluetoothserver";
      try {
        final BluetoothServerSocket btserver =
          bluetooth.listenUsingRfcommWithServiceRecord(name, uuid);

        AsyncTask<Integer, Void, BluetoothSocket> acceptThread =
          new AsyncTask<Integer, Void, BluetoothSocket>() {

          @Override
          protected BluetoothSocket doInBackground(Integer ...   params) {
            try {
              socket = btserver.accept(params[0]*1000);
              return socket;
            } catch (IOException e) {
              Log.d("BLUETOOTH", e.getMessage());
            }
```

```
          return null;
        }
        @Override
        protected void onPostExecute(BluetoothSocket result) {
          if (result != null)
            switchUI();
        }
      };
      acceptThread.execute(resultCode);
    } catch (IOException e) {
      Log.d("BLUETOOTH", e.getMessage());
    }
  }
 }
}
```

7. Now create the client-side connection code. By performing discovery and displaying each of the possible devices, this code will provide a means for the client device to search for the listening server.

   7.1. Start by creating a field variable to store an Array List of discovered Bluetooth Devices.
   ```
   private ArrayList<BluetoothDevice> foundDevices;
   ```

   7.2. Fill in the setupListView stub. Create a new Array Adapter that binds the List View to the found devices array.
   ```
   private ArrayAdapter<BluetoothDevice> aa;
   private ListView list;

   private void setupListView() {
     aa = new ArrayAdapter<BluetoothDevice>(this,
                 android.R.layout.simple_list_item_1,
                 foundDevices);
     list = (ListView)findViewById(R.id.list_discovered);
     list.setAdapter(aa);
   }
   ```

   7.3. Create a new Broadcast Receiver that listens for Bluetooth Device discovery broadcasts, adds each discovered device to the array of found devices created in Step 7-1, and notifies the Array Adapter created in Step 7-2.
   ```
   BroadcastReceiver discoveryResult = new BroadcastReceiver() {
     @Override
     public void onReceive(Context context, Intent intent) {
       BluetoothDevice remoteDevice;
       remoteDevice = intent.getParcelableExtra(BluetoothDevice.EXTRA_DEVICE);
       if (bluetooth.getBondedDevices().contains(remoteDevice)) {
         foundDevices.add(remoteDevice);
         aa.notifyDataSetChanged();
       }
     }
   };
   ```

7.4. Complete the `setupSearchButton` stub to register the Broadcast Receiver from the previous step and initiate a discovery session.

```
private void setupSearchButton() {
  Button searchButton = (Button)findViewById(R.id.button_search);

  searchButton.setOnClickListener(new OnClickListener() {
    public void onClick(View view) {
      registerReceiver(discoveryResult,
                       new IntentFilter(BluetoothDevice.ACTION_FOUND));

      if (!bluetooth.isDiscovering()) {
        foundDevices.clear();
        bluetooth.startDiscovery();
      }
    }
  });
}
```

8. The final step to completing the connection-handling code is to extend the `setupListView` method from Step 7b. Extend this method to include an `onItemClickListener` that will attempt to asynchronously initiate a client-side connection with the selected remote Bluetooth Device. If it is successful, keep a reference to the socket it creates and make a call to the `switchUI` method created in Step 5.

```
private void setupListView() {
  aa = new ArrayAdapter<BluetoothDevice>(this,
              android.R.layout.simple_list_item_1,
              foundDevices);
  list = (ListView)findViewById(R.id.list_discovered);
  list.setAdapter(aa);

  list.setOnItemClickListener(new OnItemClickListener() {
    public void onItemClick(AdapterView<?> arg0, View view,
                            int index, long arg3) {
      AsyncTask<Integer, Void, Void> connectTask =
        new AsyncTask<Integer, Void, Void>() {
          @Override
          protected Void doInBackground(Integer ...  params) {
            try {
              BluetoothDevice device = foundDevices.get(params[0]);
              socket = device.createRfcommSocketToServiceRecord(uuid);
              socket.connect();
            } catch (IOException e) {
              Log.d("BLUETOOTH_CLIENT", e.getMessage());
            }
            return null;
          }

          @Override
          protected void onPostExecute(Void result) {
```

```
                      switchViews();
                    }
                  };
                connectTask.execute(index);
              }
            });
          }
```

9. If you run the application on two devices, you can click the "Listen for connection" button on one device, and the "Search for listener" button on the other. The List View should then be populated with all the bonded devices within range, as shown in Figure 13-5.

    If you select the other Android device running this application from that list, a connection will be established between the two devices. The following steps will use this communications channel to send simple text messages between the devices.

10. Start by extending the switchUI method. Add a new key listener to the text-entry Edit Text to listen for a D-pad click. When one is detected, read its contents and send them across the Bluetooth communications socket.

FIGURE 13-5

```
private void switchUI() {
  final TextView messageText = (TextView)findViewById(R.id.text_messages);
  final EditText textEntry = (EditText)findViewById(R.id.text_message);

  messageText.setVisibility(View.VISIBLE);
  list.setVisibility(View.GONE);
  textEntry.setEnabled(true);

  textEntry.setOnKeyListener(new OnKeyListener() {
    public boolean onKey(View view, int keyCode, KeyEvent keyEvent) {
      if ((keyEvent.getAction() == KeyEvent.ACTION_DOWN) &&
          (keyCode == KeyEvent.KEYCODE_DPAD_CENTER)) {
        sendMessage(socket, textEntry.getText().toString());
        textEntry.setText("");
        return true;
      }
      return false;
    }
  });
}

private void sendMessage(BluetoothSocket socket, String msg) {
```

```
OutputStream outStream;
try {
  outStream = socket.getOutputStream();
  byte[] byteString = (msg + " ").getBytes();
  stringAsBytes[byteString.length − 1] = 0;
  outStream.write(byteString);
} catch (IOException e) {
  Log.d("BLUETOOTH_COMMS", e.getMessage());
}
}
```

11. In order to receive messages you will need to create an asynchronous listener that monitors the Bluetooth Socket for incoming messages.

11.1. Start by creating a new `MessagePoster` class that implements Runnable. It should accept two parameters, a Text View and a message string. The received message should be inserted into the Text View parameter. This class will be used to post incoming messages to the UI from a background thread.

```
private class MessagePoster implements Runnable {
  private TextView textView;
  private String message;

  public MessagePoster(TextView textView, String message) {
    this.textView = textView;
    this.message = message;
  }

  public void run() {
    textView.setText(message);
  }
}
```

11.2. Now create a new `BluetoothSocketListener` that implements `Runnable`. It should take a Bluetooth Socket to listen to, a Text View to post incoming messages to, and a Handler to synchronize when posting updates.

When a new message is received, use the `MessagePoster` Runnable you created in the previous step to post the new message in the Text View.

```
private class BluetoothSocketListener implements Runnable {

  private BluetoothSocket socket;
  private TextView textView;
  private Handler handler;

  public BluetoothSocketListener(BluetoothSocket socket,
                                  Handler handler, TextView textView) {
    this.socket = socket;
    this.textView = textView;
    this.handler = handler;
  }
```

```
            public void run() {
              int bufferSize = 1024;
              byte[] buffer = new byte[bufferSize];
              try {
                InputStream instream = socket.getInputStream();
                int bytesRead = -1;
                String message = "";
                while (true) {
                  message = "";
                  bytesRead = instream.read(buffer);
                  if (bytesRead != -1) {
                    while ((bytesRead==bufferSize)&&(buffer[bufferSize-1] != 0)) {
                      message = message + new String(buffer, 0, bytesRead);
                      bytesRead = instream.read(buffer);
                    }
                    message = message + new String(buffer, 0, bytesRead - 1);

                    handler.post(new MessagePoster(textView, message));

                    socket.getInputStream();
                  }
                }
              } catch (IOException e) {
                Log.d("BLUETOOTH_COMMS", e.getMessage());
              }
            }
          }
```

11.3. Finally, make one more addition to the swichUI method, this time creating and starting the new BluetoothSocketListener you created in the previous step.

```
        private Handler handler = new Handler();

        private void switchUI() {
          final TextView messageText = (TextView)findViewById(R.id.text_messages);
          final EditText textEntry = (EditText)findViewById(R.id.text_message);

          messageText.setVisibility(View.VISIBLE);
          list.setVisibility(View.GONE);
          textEntry.setEnabled(true);

          textEntry.setOnKeyListener(new OnKeyListener() {
            public boolean onKey(View view, int keyCode, KeyEvent keyEvent) {
              if ((keyEvent.getAction() == KeyEvent.ACTION_DOWN) &&
                  (keyCode == KeyEvent.KEYCODE_DPAD_CENTER)) {
                sendMessage(socket, textEntry.getText().toString());
                textEntry.setText("");
                return true;
              }
              return false;
            }
          });
```

```
BluetoothSocketListener bsl = new BluetoothSocketListener(socket,
                                     handler, messageText);
Thread messageListener = new Thread(bsr);
messageListener.start();
}
```

All code snippets in this example are part of the Chapter 13 Bluetooth Texting *project, available for download at Wrox.com.*

If you run the application now, you should be able to configure one device to listen for a connection, use a second device to connect to it — and then, once connected, send simple text messages between the devices.

Note that this example has been kept as simple as possible to highlight the Bluetooth functionality being described. A better implementation would move all the connection state and logic code into a Service, as well as unregistering Broadcast Receivers once discovery and pairing had been completed.

MANAGING NETWORK CONNECTIVITY

The incredible growth of Internet services and the ubiquity of mobile devices have made mobile Internet access an increasingly prevalent feature on mobile phones.

With the speed, reliability, and cost of Internet connectivity dependent on the network technology being used (Wi-Fi, GPRS, 3G), letting your applications know and manage these connections can help to ensure they run efficiently and responsively.

Android broadcasts Intents that describe changes in network connectivity and offers APIs that provide control over network settings and connections.

Just as importantly, users can specify their connectivity preferences — particularly in the case of allowing background data transfers.

Android networking is principally handled via the `ConnectivityManager`, a Service that lets you monitor the connectivity state, set your preferred network connection, and manage connectivity failover.

Later you'll learn how to use the `WifiManager` to monitor and control the device's Wi-Fi connectivity specifically. The Wi-Fi Manager lets you create new Wi-Fi configurations, monitor and modify the existing Wi-Fi network settings, manage the active connection, and perform access point scans.

Introducing the Connectivity Manager

The `ConnectivityManager` represents the Network Connectivity Service. It's used to monitor the state of network connections, configure failover settings, and control the network radios.

To access the Connectivity Manager, use `getSystemService`, passing in `Context.CONNECTIVITY_SERVICE` as the service name, as shown in Listing 13-12.

LISTING 13-12: Accessing the Connectivity Manager

```
String service =
Context.CONNECTIVITY_SERVICE;ConnectivityManager connectivity =
   (ConnectivityManager)getSystemService(service);
```

To use the Connectivity Manager, your application needs read and write network state access permissions. Add each to your manifest, as shown here:

```
<uses-permission android:name="android.permission.ACCESS_NETWORK_STATE"/>
<uses-permission android:name="android.permission.CHANGE_NETWORK_STATE"/>
```

Reading User Preferences for Background Data Transfer

One of the most important pieces of information available via the Connectivity Manager is the user's preference for background data transfers.

Users can elect to enable or disable background data transfers through the Settings ➪ Accounts & sync settings ➪ Background data setting, as shown in Figure 13-6.

FIGURE 13-6

This value is enforced at the application level, meaning that you are responsible for reading the value and adhering to the user's preference for allowing background data transfers.

To obtain the background data setting, call the `getBackgroundDataSetting` method on the Connectivity Manager object:

```
boolean backgroundEnabled = connectivity.getBackgroundDataSetting();
```

If the background data setting is disabled, your application should transfer data only when it is active and in the foreground. By turning this value off, the user explicitly requests that your application not transfer data when it is not visible and in the foreground.

If your application requires background data transfer to function, it's best practice to notify users of this requirement and offer to take them to the settings page to alter their preference.

If the user does change the background data preference, the system will send a broadcast Intent with the `ConnectivityManager.ACTION_BACKGROUND_DATA_SETTING_CHANGED` action.

To monitor changes in the background data setting, create and register a new Broadcast Receiver that listens for this broadcast Intent, as shown in Listing 13-13.

LISTING 13-13: Accessing the Connectivity Manager

```
registerReceiver(
  new BroadcastReceiver() {
    @Override
    public void onReceive(Context context, Intent intent) {
      // Do something when the background data setting changes.
    },
  new IntentFilter(ConnectivityManager.ACTION_BACKGROUND_DATA_SETTING_CHANGED));
```

 While your applications are not forced to obey the user's preference for background data transfers, not doing so is likely to earn vocal criticism from users who installed your application and were rewarded with a significant mobile data bill.

Monitoring Network Details

The Connectivity Manager provides a high-level view of the available network connections. Using the `getActiveNetworkInfo` or `getNetworkInfo` methods, as shown in Listing 13-14, returns `NetworkInfo` objects that include details on the currently active network or on an inactive network of the type specified.

Use the returned `NetworkInfo` details to find the connection status, network type, and detailed state information of the returned network.

LISTING 13-14: Accessing network information

```
// Get the active network information.
NetworkInfo activeNetwork = connectivity.getActiveNetworkInfo();
int networkType = networkInfo.getType();
switch (networkType) {
  case (ConnectivityManager.TYPE_MOBILE) : break;
  case (ConnectivityManager.TYPE_WIFI) : break;
  default: break;
}

// Get the mobile network information.
int network = ConnectivityManager.TYPE_MOBILE;
NetworkInfo mobileNetwork = connectivity.getNetworkInfo(network);
```

```
NetworkInfo.State state = mobileNetwork.getState();
NetworkInfo.DetailedState detailedState = mobileNetwork.getDetailedState();
```

Finding and Configuring Network Preferences and Controlling Hardware Radios

The Connectivity Manager can also be used to control network hardware and configure failover preferences.

Android will attempt to connect to the preferred network whenever an authorized application requests an Internet connection. You can find the current, and set the preferred, network using the `getNetworkPreference` and `setNetworkPreference` methods, respectively, as shown in the following code snippet:

```
int networkPreference = connectivity.getNetworkPreference();
connectivity.setNetworkPreference(NetworkPreference.PREFER_WIFI);
```

If the preferred connection is unavailable, or connectivity on this network is lost, Android will automatically attempt to connect to the secondary network.

You can control the availability of the network types using the `setRadio` method. This method lets you set the state of the radio associated with a particular network (Wi-Fi, mobile, etc.). For example, in the following code snippet the Wi-Fi radio is turned off and the mobile radio is turned on:

```
connectivity.setRadio(NetworkType.WIFI, false);
connectivity.setRadio(NetworkType.MOBILE, true);
```

Monitoring Network Connectivity

One of the most useful functions of the Connectivity Manager is to notify applications of changes in network connectivity.

To monitor network connectivity create your own Broadcast Receiver implementation that listens for `ConnectivityManager.CONNECTIVITY_ACTION` broadcast Intents. Such Intents include several extras that provide additional details on the change to the connectivity state. You can access each extra using one of the static constants available from the `ConnectivityManager` class:

➤ `EXTRA_IS_FAILOVER` A Boolean that returns `true` if the current connection is the result of a failover from a preferred network.

➤ `EXTRA_NO_CONNECTIVITY` A Boolean that returns `true` if the device is not connected to any network.

➤ `EXTRA_REASON` If the associated broadcast represents a connection failure, this string value includes a description of why the connection attempt failed.

➤ `EXTRA_NETWORK_INFO` Returns a `NetworkInfo` object containing more fine-grained details about the network associated with the current connectivity event.

➤ `EXTRA_OTHER_NETWORK_INFO` After a network disconnection this value will return a `NetworkInfo` object populated with the details for the possible failover network connection.

➤ `EXTRA_EXTRA_INFO` Contains additional network-specific extra connection details.

MANAGING YOUR WI-FI

The WifiManager represents the Android Wi-Fi Connectivity Service. It can be used to configure Wi-Fi network connections, manage the current Wi-Fi connection, scan for access points, and monitor changes in Wi-Fi connectivity.

As with the Connectivity Manager, you access the Wi-Fi Manager using the getSystemService method, passing in the Context.WIFI_SERVICE constant, as shown in Listing 13-15.

LISTING 13-15: Accessing the Wi-Fi Manager

```
String service = Context.WIFI_SERVICE;
WifiManager wifi = (WifiManager)getSystemService(service);
```

To use the Wi-Fi Manager your application must have uses-permissions for accessing and changing the Wi-Fi state included in its manifest.

```
<uses-permission android:name="android.permission.ACCESS_WIFI_STATE"/>
<uses-permission android:name="android.permission.CHANGE_WIFI_STATE"/>
```

You can use the Wi-Fi Manager to enable or disable your Wi-Fi hardware using the setWifiEnabled method, or request the current Wi-Fi state using the getWifiState or isWifiEnabled methods, as shown in Listing 13-16.

LISTING 13-16: Monitoring and changing Wi-Fi state

```
if (!wifi.isWifiEnabled())
  if (wifi.getWifiState() != WifiManager.WIFI_STATE_ENABLING)
    wifi.setWifiEnabled(true);
```

The following sections begin with tracking the current Wi-Fi connection status and monitoring changes in signal strength. Later you'll also learn how to scan for and connect to specific access points.

These functions are likely to be sufficient for most application developers, but the WifiManager does also provide low-level access to the Wi-Fi network configurations. You have full control over each Wi-Fi configuration setting, which enables you to completely replace the native Wi-Fi management application if required. Later in this section you'll get a brief introduction to the APIs used to create, delete, and modify network configurations.

Monitoring Wi-Fi Connectivity

The Wi-Fi Manager broadcasts Intents whenever the connectivity status of the Wi-Fi network changes, using an action from one of the following constants defined in the WifiManager class:

➤ WIFI_STATE_CHANGED_ACTION   Indicates that the Wi-Fi hardware status has changed, moving between enabling, enabled, disabling, disabled, and unknown. It includes two extra values keyed on EXTRA_WIFI_STATE and EXTRA_PREVIOUS_STATE that provide the new and previous Wi-Fi states, respectively.

➤ SUPPLICANT_CONNECTION_CHANGE_ACTION This Intent is broadcast whenever the connection state with the active supplicant (access point) changes. It is fired when a new connection is established or an existing connection is lost, using the EXTRA_NEW_STATE Boolean extra, which returns true in the former case.

➤ NETWORK_STATE_CHANGED_ACTION Fired whenever the Wi-Fi connectivity state changes. This Intent includes two extras — the first EXTRA_NETWORK_INFO includes a NetworkInfo object that details the current network state, while the second EXTRA_BSSID includes the BSSID of the access point you're connected to.

➤ RSSI_CHANGED_ACTION You can monitor the current signal strength of the connected Wi-Fi network by listening for the RSSI_CHANGED_ACTION Intent. This Broadcast Intent includes an integer extra, EXTRA_NEW_RSSI, that holds the current signal strength. To use this signal strength you should use the calculateSignalLevel static method on the Wi-Fi Manager to convert it to an integer value on a scale you specify.

Monitoring Active Connection Details

Once an active network connection has been established, use the getConnectionInfo method on the Wi-Fi Manager to find information on the active connection's status. The returned WifiInfo object includes the SSID, BSSID, Mac address, and IP address of the current access point, as well as the current link speed and signal strength.

Listing 13-17 queries the active Wi-Fi connection.

Available for download on Wrox.com

LISTING 13-17: Querying the active network connection

```
WifiInfo info = wifi.getConnectionInfo();
if (info.getBSSID() != null) {
  int strength = WifiManager.calculateSignalLevel(info.getRssi(), 5);
  int speed = info.getLinkSpeed();
  String units = WifiInfo.LINK_SPEED_UNITS;
  String ssid = info.getSSID();

  String cSummary = String.format("Connected to %s at %s%s. Strength %s/5",
                                  ssid, speed, units, strength);
}
```

Scanning for Hotspots

You can also use the Wi-Fi Manager to conduct access point scans using the startScan method.

An Intent with the SCAN_RESULTS_AVAILABLE_ACTION action will be broadcast to asynchronously announce that the scan is complete and results are available.

Call getScanResults to get those results as a list of ScanResult objects.

Each Scan Result includes the details retrieved for each access point detected, including link speed, signal strength, SSID, and the authentication techniques supported.

Listing 13-18 shows how to initiate a scan for access points that displays a Toast indicating the total number of access points found and the name of the access point with the strongest signal.

LISTING 13-18: Querying the active network connection

```
// Register a broadcast receiver that listens for scan results.
registerReceiver(new BroadcastReceiver() {
  @Override
  public void onReceive(Context context, Intent intent) {
    List<ScanResult> results = wifi.getScanResults();
    ScanResult bestSignal = null;
    for (ScanResult result : results) {
      if (bestSignal == null ||
          WifiManager.compareSignalLevel(bestSignal.level,result.level)<0)
        bestSignal = result;
    }

    String toastText = String.format("%s networks found. %s is
                                      the strongest.",
                                      results.size(), bestSignal.SSID);

    Toast.makeText(getApplicationContext(), toastText, Toast.LENGTH_LONG);
  }
}, new IntentFilter(WifiManager.SCAN_RESULTS_AVAILABLE_ACTION));

// Initiate a scan.
wifi.startScan();
```

Managing Wi-Fi Configurations

You can use the Wi-Fi Manager to manage the configured network settings and control which networks to connect to. Once connected, you can interrogate the active network connection to get additional details of its configuration and settings.

Get a list of the current network configurations using `getConfiguredNetworks`. The list of `WifiConfiguration` objects returned includes the network ID, SSID, and other details for each configuration.

To use a particular network configuration, use the `enableNetwork` method, passing in the network ID to use and specifying `true` for the `disableAllOthers` parameter, as shown in Listing 13-19.

LISTING 13-19: Activating a network connection

```
// Get a list of available configurations
List<WifiConfiguration> configurations = wifi.getConfiguredNetworks();
// Get the network ID for the first one.
if (configurations.size() > 0) {
  int netID = configurations.get(0).networkId;
  // Enable that network.
  boolean disableAllOthers = true;
  wifi.enableNetwork(netID, disableAllOtherstrue);
}
```

Creating Wi-Fi Network Configurations

To connect to a Wi-Fi network you need to create and register a configuration. Normally, your users would do this using the native Wi-Fi configuration settings, but there's no reason you can't expose the same functionality within your own applications, or for that matter replace the native Wi-Fi configuration Activity entirely.

Network configurations are stored as `WifiConfiguration` objects. The following is a non-exhaustive list of some of the public fields available for each Wi-Fi configuration:

- ➤ `BSSID`   The BSSID for an access point
- ➤ `SSID`   The SSID for a particular network
- ➤ `networkId`   A unique identifier used to identify this network configuration on the current device
- ➤ `priority`   The network configuration's priority to use when ordering the list of potential access points to connect to
- ➤ `status`   The current status of this network connection, which will be one of the following: `WifiConfiguration.Status.ENABLED`, `WifiConfiguration.Status.DISABLED`, or `WifiConfiguration.Status.CURRENT`

The configuration object also contains the supported authentication techniques, as well as the keys used previously to authenticate with this access point.

The `addNetwork` method lets you specify a new configuration to add to the current list; similarly, `updateNetwork` lets you update a network configuration by passing in a `WifiConfiguration` that's sparsely populated with a network ID and the values you want to change.

You can also use `removeNetwork`, passing in a network ID, to remove a configuration.

To persist any changes made to the network configurations, you must call `saveConfiguration`.

SUMMARY

In this chapter you learned how to monitor and control some of the low-level communication hardware services available on Android devices.

The chapter included an introduction to Bluetooth management and communications mechanisms, a look at how to monitor and control Internet and network connectivity settings, and an introduction to the Wi-Fi manager — used to monitor and control the device's Wi-Fi connectivity and configurations.

In the next chapter you'll learn how to interact with the Sensor Manager to provide your applications access to the physical world. You will learn how to access the hardware sensors — particularly the compass and accelerometer — and how to monitor and interpret these sensors' values.

14

Sensors

WHAT'S IN THIS CHAPTER?

➤ Using the Sensor Manager

➤ The available sensor-types

➤ Monitoring sensors and interpreting sensor values

➤ Using the compass, accelerometer, and orientation sensors

➤ Remapping your orientation reference frame

➤ Controlling device vibration

Modern mobile phones are much more than simple communications devices with a connection to the Internet. With microphones, cameras, accelerometers, compasses, temperature gauges, and brightness detectors, smartphones have become extra-sensory devices, able to augment your own perceptions.

Later chapters will explore use of the camera and microphone; in this chapter you will explore the environmental sensors potentially available on Android devices.

Sensors that detect physical and environmental properties offer an exciting innovation for enhancing the user experience of mobile applications. The incorporation of electronic compasses, gravity sensors, brightness gauges, and proximity sensors in modern devices provides an array of new possibilities for interacting with devices, such as augmented reality and physical movement-based input.

In this chapter you'll be introduced to the sensors available in Android and how to use the Sensor Manager to monitor them. You'll take a closer look at the accelerometer and orientation sensors and use them to determine changes in the device orientation and acceleration. This is particularly useful for creating motion-based user interfaces, letting you add new dimensions to your location-based applications.

You'll also learn how to control device vibration to use force feedback in your applications.

USING SENSORS AND THE SENSOR MANAGER

The Sensor Manager is used to manage the sensor hardware available on Android devices. Use `getSystemService` to return a reference to the Sensor Manager Service, as shown in the following snippet:

```
String service_name = Context.SENSOR_SERVICE;
SensorManager sensorManager = (SensorManager)getSystemService(service_name);
```

Introducing Sensors

Like location-based Services, Android abstracts the sensor implementations of each device. The `Sensor` class is used to describe the properties of each hardware sensor, including its type, name, manufacturer, and details on its accuracy and range.

The Sensor class includes a set of constants used to describe what type of hardware sensor is being represented by a Sensor object. These constants take the form of `Sensor.TYPE_<TYPE>`. The following section describes each supported sensor-type, after which you'll learn how to find and use those sensors.

Supported Android Sensors

The following is a list of the sensor-types currently available; note that the hardware on the host device determines which of these sensors are actually available to your application.

➤ `Sensor.TYPE_ACCELEROMETER`   A three-axis accelerometer sensor that returns the current acceleration along three axes in m/s^2. The accelerometer is explored in greater detail later in this chapter.

➤ `Sensor.TYPE_GYROSCOPE`   A gyroscopic sensor that returns the current device orientation on three axes in degrees.

➤ `Sensor.TYPE_LIGHT`   An ambient light sensor that returns a single value describing the ambient illumination in lux. A light sensor is commonly used to dynamically control the screen brightness.

➤ `Sensor.TYPE_MAGNETIC_FIELD`   A magnetic field sensor that finds the current magnetic field in microteslas along three axes.

➤ `Sensor.TYPE_ORIENTATION`   An orientation sensor that returns the device orientation on three axes in degrees. The orientation sensor is explored in greater detail later in this chapter.

➤ `Sensor.TYPE_PRESSURE`   A pressure sensor that returns a single value, the current pressure exerted on the device in kilopascals.

➤ `Sensor.TYPE_PROXIMITY`   A proximity sensor that indicates the distance between the device and the target object in meters. How a target object is selected, and the distances supported, will depend on the hardware implementation of the proximity detector. A typical use for the proximity sensor is to detect when the device is being held up against the user's ear and to automatically adjust screen brightness or initiate a voice command.

➤   Sensor.TYPE_TEMPERATURE   A thermometer that returns temperature in degrees Celsius. The temperature returned may be the ambient room temperature, device battery temperature, or remote sensor temperature, depending on the hardware implementation.

Finding Sensors

An Android device can include multiple implementations of a particular sensor-type. To find the default Sensor implementation for a particular type use the Sensor Manager's getDefaultSensor method, passing in the sensor-type required from the constants described in the previous section.

The following snippet returns the default gyroscope. If no default Sensor exists for the given type, the method returns null.

```
Sensor defaultGyroscope = sensorManager.getDefaultSensor(Sensor.TYPE_GYROSCOPE);
```

Alternatively, use getSensorList to return a list of all the available Sensors of a given type, as shown in the following code, which returns all the available pressure sensor objects:

```
List<Sensor> pressureSensors = sensorManager.getSensorList(Sensor.TYPE_PRESSURE);
```

To find every Sensor available on the host platform use getSensorList, passing in Sensor.TYPE_ALL, as shown here:

```
List<Sensor> allSensors = sensorManager.getSensorList(Sensor.TYPE_ALL);
```

This technique lets you determine which Sensors, and sensor-types, are available on the host platform.

Using Sensors

Listing 14-1 shows the standard pattern for monitoring hardware sensor results. Later sections will take a closer look at orientation and acceleration Sensor implementations in particular.

Implement a SensorEventListener. Use the onSensorChanged method to monitor Sensor values and onAccuracyChanged to react to changes in a Sensor's accuracy.

LISTING 14-1: Sensor Event Listener skeleton code

```
final SensorEventListener mySensorEventListener = new SensorEventListener() {
  public void onSensorChanged(SensorEvent sensorEvent) {
    // TODO Monitor Sensor changes.
  }

  public void onAccuracyChanged(Sensor sensor, int accuracy) {
    // TODO React to a change in Sensor accuracy.
  }
};
```

The SensorEvent parameter in the onSensorChanged method includes four properties used to describe a Sensor event:

➤   sensor   The Sensor object that triggered the event.

➤   accuracy   The accuracy of the Sensor when the event occurred (low, medium, high, or unreliable, as described in the next list).

➤ `values` A float array that contains the new value(s) detected. The next section explains the values returned for each sensor-type.

➤ `timestamp` The time (in nanoseconds) at which the Sensor event occurred.

You can monitor changes in the accuracy of a Sensor separately, using the `onAccuracyChanged` method. In both handlers the `accuracy` value represents feedback from the monitored Sensor's accuracy, using one of the following constants:

➤ `SensorManager.SENSOR_STATUS_ACCURACY_LOW` Indicates that the Sensor is reporting with low accuracy and needs to be calibrated

➤ `SensorManager.SENSOR_STATUS_ACCURACY_MEDIUM` Indicates that the Sensor data is of average accuracy, and that calibration might improve the readings

➤ `SensorManager.SENSOR_STATUS_ACCURACY_HIGH` Indicates that the Sensor is reporting with the highest possible accuracy

➤ `SensorManager.SENSOR_STATUS_UNRELIABLE` Indicates that the Sensor data is unreliable, meaning that either calibration is required or readings are not currently possible

To receive Sensor events, register your Sensor Event Listener with the Sensor Manager. Specify the Sensor object to observe, and the rate at which you want to receive updates. The following example registers a Sensor Event Listener for the default proximity Sensor at the normal update rate:

```
Sensor sensor = sensorManager.getDefaultSensor(Sensor.TYPE_PROXIMITY);
sensorManager.registerListener(mySensorEventListener,
                               sensor,
                               SensorManager.SENSOR_DELAY_NORMAL);
```

The Sensor Manager includes the following constants (shown in descending order of responsiveness) to let you select a suitable update rate:

➤ `SensorManager.SENSOR_DELAY_FASTEST` Specifies the fastest possible Sensor update rate

➤ `SensorManager.SENSOR_DELAY_GAME` Selects an update rate suitable for use in controlling games

➤ `SensorManager.SENSOR_DELAY_NORMAL` Specifies the default update rate

➤ `SensorManager.SENSOR_DELAY_UI` Specifies a rate suitable for updating UI features

The rate you select is not binding; the Sensor Manager may return results faster or slower than you specify, though it will tend to be faster. To minimize the associated resource cost of using the Sensor in your application you should try to select the slowest suitable rate.

It's also important to unregister your Sensor Event Listeners when your application no longer needs to receive updates:

```
sensorManager.unregisterListener(mySensorEventListener);
```

It's good practice to register and unregister your Sensor Event Listener in the `onResume` and `onPause` methods of your Activities to ensure they're being used only when the Activity is active.

INTERPRETING SENSOR VALUES

The length and composition of the values returned in the `onSensorChanged` event vary depending on the Sensor being monitored.

The details are summarized in Table 14-1. Further details on the use of the accelerometer, orientation, and magnetic field Sensors can be found in the following sections.

 The Android documentation describes the values returned by each sensor-type with some additional commentary at `http://developer.android.com/reference/android/hardware/Sensor.html`

TABLE 14-1: Sensor Return Values

SENSOR-TYPE	VALUE COUNT	VALUE COMPOSITION	COMMENTARY
TYPE_ACCELEROMETER	3	value[0] : Lateral value[1] : Longitudinal value[2] : Vertical	Acceleration along three axes in m/s². The Sensor Manager includes a set of gravity constants of the form `SensorManager.GRAVITY_*`
TYPE_GYROSCOPE	3	value[0] : Azimuth value[1] : Pitch value[2] : Roll	Device orientation in degrees along three axes.
TYPE_ LIGHT	1	value[0] : Illumination	Measured in lux. The Sensor Manager includes a set of constants representing different standard illuminations of the form `SensorManager.LIGHT_*`
TYPE_MAGNETIC_FIELD	3	value[0] : Lateral value[1] : Longitudinal value[2] : Vertical	Ambient magnetic field measured in microteslas (µT).
TYPE_ORIENTATION	3	value[0] : Azimuth value[1] : Roll value[2] : Pitch	Device orientation in degrees along three axes.
TYPE_PRESSURE	1	value[0] : Pressure	Measured in kilopascals (KP).
TYPE_PROXIMITY	1	value[0] : Distance	Measured in meters.
TYPE_TEMPERATURE	1	value[0] : Temperature	Measured in degrees Celsius.

USING THE COMPASS, ACCELEROMETER, AND ORIENTATION SENSORS

Using movement and orientation within applications is possible thanks to the inclusion of orientation and accelerometer sensors in many modern devices.

In recent years these sensors have become increasingly common, having found their way into game controllers like the Nintendo Wii and mobile smartphone handsets like the Apple iPhone, Palm Pre, and many Android devices.

Accelerometers and compasses are used to provide functionality based on device direction, orientation, and movement. A recent trend is to use this functionality to provide input mechanisms other than the traditional touchscreen, trackball, and keyboard.

The availability of compass and accelerometer Sensors depends on the hardware on which your application runs. When available, they are exposed through the Sensor Manager, allowing you to do the following:

➤ Determine the current device orientation

➤ Monitor and track changes in orientation

➤ Know which direction the user is facing

➤ Monitor acceleration — changes in movement rate — in any direction: vertically, laterally, or longitudinally

This opens some intriguing possibilities for your applications. By monitoring orientation, direction, and movement, you can:

➤ Use the compass and accelerometer to determine your speed and direction. Use these with a map, camera, and location-based services to create augmented reality interfaces that overlay location-based data over the real-time camera feed.

➤ Create user interfaces that adjust dynamically to suit the orientation of your device. Android already alters the native screen orientation when the device is rotated from portrait to landscape or vice versa.

➤ Monitor for rapid acceleration to detect if a device has been dropped or thrown.

➤ Measure movement or vibration. For example you could create an application that lets you lock your device; if any movement is detected while it's locked it could send an alert SMS that includes the current location.

➤ Create user interface controls that use physical gestures and movement as input.

You should always check for the availability of any required Sensors and make sure your applications fail gracefully if they are missing.

Introducing Accelerometers

Accelerometers, as their name suggests, are used to measure acceleration. They are also sometimes referred to as gravity sensors.

Accelerometers are also known as gravity sensors because of their inability to differentiate between acceleration caused by movement and gravity. As a result, an accelerometer detecting acceleration on the z-axis (up/down) will read -9.8m/s² when it's at rest (this value is available as the `SensorManager.STANDARD_GRAVITY` *constant).*

Acceleration is defined as the rate of change of velocity, so accelerometers measure how quickly the speed of the device is changing in a given direction. Using an accelerometer you can detect movement and, more usefully, the rate of change of the speed of that movement.

 It's important to note that accelerometers do not *measure velocity, so you can't measure speed directly based on a single accelerometer reading. Instead you need to measure changes in acceleration over time.*

Generally you'll be interested in acceleration changes relative to a rest state, or rapid movement (signified by rapid changes in acceleration) such as gestures used for user input. In the former case you'll often need to calibrate the device to calculate the initial orientation and acceleration to take those effects into account for future results.

Detecting Acceleration Changes

Acceleration can be measured along three directional axes: left-right (lateral), forward-backward (longitudinal), and up-down (vertical). The Sensor Manager reports accelerometer Sensor changes along all three axes.

The values passed in through the `values` property of the Sensor Event Listener's Sensor Event parameter represent lateral, longitudinal, and vertical acceleration, in that order.

Figure 14-1 illustrates the mapping of the three directional acceleration axes in relation to the device at rest. The Sensor Manager considers the device "at rest" when it is sitting face up on a flat surface in portrait orientation.

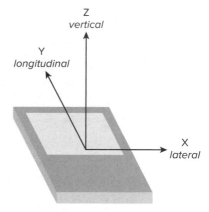

FIGURE 14-1

> **x-axis (lateral)** Sideways (left or right) acceleration, for which positive values represent movement toward the right side of the device, and negative values indicate movement to the left. For example, positive x-axis acceleration would be detected on a device flat on its back, facing up, and in portrait orientation being moved along a surface to your right.

> **y-axis (longitudinal)** Forward or backward acceleration, for which forward acceleration is represented by a positive value. In the same configuration as described for lateral movement, you would create positive longitudinal acceleration by moving the device in the direction of the top of the device.

➤ **z-axis (vertical)** Upward or downward acceleration, for which positive represents upward movement such as the device being lifted. While at rest the vertical accelerometer will register -9.8m/s^2 as a result of gravity.

As described earlier, you monitor changes in acceleration using a Sensor Event Listener. Register an implementation of `SensorEventListener` with the Sensor Manager, using a Sensor object of type `Sensor.TYPE_ACCELEROMETER` to request accelerometer updates. Listing 14-2 registers the default accelerometer using the normal update rate.

LISTING 14-2: Listening to changes to the default accelerometer

```
SensorManager sm = (SensorManager)getSystemService(Context.SENSOR_SERVICE);
int sensorType = Sensor.TYPE_ACCELEROMETER;
sm.registerListener(mySensorEventListener,
                    sm.getDefaultSensor(sensorType),
                    SensorManager.SENSOR_DELAY_NORMAL);
```

Your Sensor Listener should implement the `onSensorChanged` method that will be fired when acceleration in any direction is measured.

The `onSensorChanged` method receives a `SensorEvent` that includes a `float` array containing the acceleration measured along all three axes. Based on a rest state of the device sitting flat on its back in portrait orientation, the first element represents lateral, the second longitudinal, and the final vertical acceleration, as shown in the following extension to Listing 14-2.

```
final SensorEventListener mySensorEventListener = new SensorEventListener() {
  public void onSensorChanged(SensorEvent sensorEvent) {
    if (sensorEvent.sensor.getType() == Sensor.TYPE_ACCELEROMETER) {
      float xAxis_lateralA = sensorEvent.values[0];
      float yAxis_longitudinalA = sensorEvent.values[1];
      float zAxis_verticalA = sensorEvent.values[2];
      // TODO apply the acceleration changes to your application.
    }
  }
};
```

Creating a G-Forceometer

You can create a simple tool to measure g-force by summing the acceleration in all three directions and comparing it to the value in free fall. In the following example you'll create a simple device to measure g-force using the accelerometers to determine the current force being exerted on the device.

Thanks to gravity the force exerted on the device at rest is 9.8m/s^2 toward the center of the Earth. In this example you'll negate the force of gravity by accounting for it using the `SensorManager.STANDARD_GRAVITY` constant.

1. Start by creating a new Forceometer project with a `Forceometer` Activity. Modify the main.xml layout resource to display two centered lines of large, bold text that will be used to display the current g-force and maximum observed g-force:

```xml
<?xml version="1.0" encoding="utf-8"?>
<LinearLayout xmlns:android="http://schemas.android.com/apk/res/android"
  android:orientation="vertical"
  android:layout_width="fill_parent"
  android:layout_height="fill_parent">
  <TextView android:id="@+id/acceleration"
    android:gravity="center"
    android:layout_width="fill_parent"
    android:layout_height="wrap_content"
    android:textStyle="bold"
    android:textSize="32sp"
    android:text="CENTER"
    android:editable="false"
    android:singleLine="true"
    android:layout_margin="10px"/>
  />
  <TextView android:id="@+id/maxAcceleration"
    android:gravity="center"
    android:layout_width="fill_parent"
    android:layout_height="wrap_content"
    android:textStyle="bold"
    android:textSize="40sp"
    android:text="CENTER"
    android:editable="false"
    android:singleLine="true"
    android:layout_margin="10px"/>
  />
</LinearLayout>
```

2. Within the `Forceometer` Activity, create instance variables to store references to both `TextView` Views and the `SensorManager`. Also create variables to record the last and maximum detected acceleration values:

```java
SensorManager sensorManager;
TextView accelerationTextView;
TextView maxAccelerationTextView;
float currentAcceleration = 0;
float maxAcceleration = 0;
```

3. Create a new `SensorEventListener` implementation that sums the acceleration detected along each axis and negates the acceleration caused by gravity. It should update the current and maximum acceleration whenever a change in acceleration is detected:

```java
private final SensorEventListener sensorEventListener = new SensorEventListener() {
  double calibration = SensorManager.STANDARD_GRAVITY;

  public void onAccuracyChanged(Sensor sensor, int accuracy) { }

  public void onSensorChanged(SensorEvent event) {
    double x = event.values[0];
    double y = event.values[1];
    double z = event.values[2];

    double a = Math.round(Math.sqrt(Math.pow(x, 2) +
                                    Math.pow(y, 2) +
```

```
                                      Math.pow(z, 2)));
       currentAcceleration = Math.abs((float)(a-calibration));

       if (currentAcceleration > maxAcceleration)
         maxAcceleration = currentAcceleration;
    }
};
```

4. Update the `onCreate` method to register your new Listener for accelerometer updates using the `SensorManager`. Take the opportunity to get a reference to the two Text Views:

```
@Override
public void onCreate(Bundle savedInstanceState) {
  super.onCreate(savedInstanceState);
  setContentView(R.layout.main);

  accelerationTextView = (TextView)findViewById(R.id.acceleration);
  maxAccelerationTextView = (TextView)findViewById(R.id.maxAcceleration);
  sensorManager = (SensorManager)getSystemService(Context.SENSOR_SERVICE);

  Sensor accelerometer = sensorManager.getDefaultSensor(Sensor.TYPE_ACCELEROMETER);
  sensorManager.registerListener(sensorEventListener,
                                 accelerometer,
                                 SensorManager.SENSOR_DELAY_FASTEST);
}
```

5. The accelerometers can be very sensitive, so updating the Text Views for every detected acceleration change can be very expensive. Instead, create a new `updateGUI` method that synchronizes with the GUI thread based on a Timer before updating the Text Views:

```
private void updateGUI() {
  runOnUiThread(new Runnable() {
    public void run() {
      String currentG = currentAcceleration/SensorManager.STANDARD_GRAVITY
                        + "Gs";
      accelerationTextView.setText(currentG);
      accelerationTextView.invalidate();
      String maxG = maxAcceleration/SensorManager.STANDARD_GRAVITY + "Gs";
      maxAccelerationTextView.setText(maxG);
      maxAccelerationTextView.invalidate();
    }
  });
};
```

6. Finally, update the `onCreate` method to start a timer that's used to update the GUI every 100ms:

```
@Override
public void onCreate(Bundle savedInstanceState) {
  super.onCreate(savedInstanceState);
  setContentView(R.layout.main);
  accelerationTextView = (TextView)findViewById(R.id.acceleration);
  maxAccelerationTextView = (TextView)findViewById(R.id.maxAcceleration);
  sensorManager = (SensorManager)getSystemService(Context.SENSOR_SERVICE);
```

```
Sensor accelerometer =
  sensorManager.getDefaultSensor(Sensor.TYPE_ACCELEROMETER);
sensorManager.registerListener(sensorEventListener,
                               accelerometer,
                               SensorManager.SENSOR_DELAY_FASTEST);

Timer updateTimer = new Timer("gForceUpdate");
updateTimer.scheduleAtFixedRate(new TimerTask() {
  public void run() {
    updateGUI();
  }
}, 0, 100);
}
```

All code snippets in this example are part of the Chapter 14 G-Forceometer *project, available for download at Wrox.com.*

Once you're finished you'll want to test this out. Ideally you can do that in an F16 while Maverick performs high-g maneuvers over the Atlantic. That's been known to end badly, so failing that you can experiment with running or driving in the safety of your neighborhood.

Given that keeping constant watch on your handset while driving, cycling, or flying is also likely to end poorly, you might consider some further enhancements before you take it out for a spin.

Consider incorporating vibration or media player functionality to shake or beep with an intensity proportional to your current force, or simply log changes as they happen for later review.

Determining Your Orientation

The orientation Sensor is a combination of the magnetic field Sensors, which function as an electronic compass, and accelerometers, which determine the pitch and roll.

If you've done a bit of trigonometry you've got the skills required to calculate the device orientation based on the accelerometer and magnetic field values along all three axes. If you enjoyed trig as much as I did you'll be happy to learn that Android does these calculations for you.

In fact, Android provides two alternatives for determining the device orientation. You can query the orientation Sensor directly or derive the orientation using the accelerometers and magnetic field Sensors. The latter option is slower, but offers the advantages of increased accuracy and the ability to modify the reference frame when determining your orientation. The following sections demonstrate both techniques.

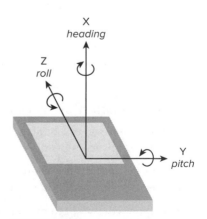

Using the standard reference frame, the device orientation is reported along three dimensions, as illustrated in Figure 14-2. As when using the accelerometers, the device is considered at rest faceup on a flat surface.

➤ **x-axis (azimuth)** The azimuth (also heading or yaw) is the direction the device is facing around the x-axis, where 0/360 degrees is north, 90 east, 180 south, and 270 west.

FIGURE 14-2

➤ **y-axis (pitch)** Pitch represents the angle of the device around the y-axis. The tilt angle returned shows 0 when the device is flat on its back, -90 when it is standing upright (top of device pointing at the ceiling), 90 when it's upside down, and 180/-180 when it's facedown.

➤ **z-axis (roll)** The roll represents the device's sideways tilt between -90 and 90 degrees on the z-axis. Zero is the device flat on its back, -90 is the screen facing left, and 90 is the screen facing right.

Determining Orientation Using the Orientation Sensor

The simplest way to monitor device orientation is by using a dedicated orientation Sensor. Create and register a Sensor Event Listener with the Sensor Manager, using the default orientation Sensor, as shown in Listing 14-3.

LISTING 14-3: Determining orientation using the orientation Sensor

```
SensorManager sm = (SensorManager)getSystemService(Context.SENSOR_SERVICE);
int sensorType = Sensor.TYPE_ORIENTATION;
sm.registerListener(myOrientationListener,
                    sm.getDefaultSensor(sensorType),
                    SensorManager.SENSOR_DELAY_NORMAL);
```

When the device orientation changes, the `onSensorChanged` method in your `SensorEventListener` implementation is fired. The `SensorEvent` parameter includes a `values` float array that provides the device's orientation along three axes.

The first element of the values array is the azimuth (heading), the second pitch, and the third roll.

```
final SensorEventListener myOrientationListener = new SensorEventListener() {
  public void onSensorChanged(SensorEvent sensorEvent) {
    if (sensorEvent.sensor.getType() == Sensor.TYPE_ORIENTATION) {
      float headingAngle = sensorEvent.values[0];
      float pitchAngle =  sensorEvent.values[1];
      float rollAngle = sensorEvent.values[2];

      // TODO Apply the orientation changes to your application.
    }
  }

  public void onAccuracyChanged(Sensor sensor, int accuracy) {}
};
```

Calculating Orientation Using the Accelerometer and Magnetic Field Sensors

The best approach for finding the device orientation is to calculate it from the accelerometer and magnetic field Sensor results directly.

This technique enables you to change the orientation reference frame to remap the x-, y-, and z-axes to suit the device orientation you expect during use.

This approach uses both the accelerometer and magnetic field Sensors, so you need to create and register two Sensor Event Listeners. Within the `onSensorChanged` methods for each Sensor Event Listener, record the `values` array property received in two separate field variables, as shown in Listing 14-4.

LISTING 14-4: Finding orientation using the accelerometer and magnetic field Sensors

```java
float[] accelerometerValues;
float[] magneticFieldValues;

final SensorEventListener myAccelerometerListener = new SensorEventListener() {
  public void onSensorChanged(SensorEvent sensorEvent) {
    if (sensorEvent.sensor.getType() == Sensor.TYPE_ACCELEROMETER)
      accelerometerValues = sensorEvent.values;
  }

  public void onAccuracyChanged(Sensor sensor, int accuracy) {}
};

final SensorEventListener myMagneticFieldListener = new SensorEventListener() {
  public void onSensorChanged(SensorEvent sensorEvent) {
    if (sensorEvent.sensor.getType() == Sensor.TYPE_MAGNETIC_FIELD)
      magneticFieldValues = sensorEvent.values;
  }

  public void onAccuracyChanged(Sensor sensor, int accuracy) {}
};
```

Register both with the Sensor Manager, as shown in the following code extending Listing 14-4; this snippet uses the default hardware and UI update rate for both Sensors:

```java
SensorManager sm = (SensorManager)getSystemService(Context.SENSOR_SERVICE);
Sensor aSensor = sm.getDefaultSensor(Sensor.TYPE_ACCELEROMETER);
Sensor mfSensor = sm.getDefaultSensor(Sensor.TYPE_MAGNETIC_FIELD);

sm.registerListener(myAccelerometerListener,
                    aSensor,
                    SensorManager.SENSOR_DELAY_UI);

sm.registerListener(myMagneticFieldListener,
                    mfSensor,
                    SensorManager.SENSOR_DELAY_UI);
```

To calculate the current orientation from these Sensor values you use the getRotationMatrix and getOrientation methods from the Sensor Manager, as follows. Note that getOrientation returns radians rather than degrees.

```java
float[] values = new float[3];
float[] R = new float[9];
SensorManager.getRotationMatrix(R, null,
                                accelerometerValues,
                                magneticFieldValues);
SensorManager.getOrientation(R, values);

// Convert from radians to degrees.
values[0] = (float) Math.toDegrees(values[0]);
values[1] = (float) Math.toDegrees(values[1]);
values[2] = (float) Math.toDegrees(values[2]);
```

Remapping the Orientation Reference Frame

To measure device orientation using a reference frame other than the default described earlier, use the `remapCoordinateSystem` method from the Sensor Manager.

Earlier in this chapter the standard reference frame was described as the device being faceup on a flat surface. This method lets you remap the coordinate system used to calculate your orientation, for example by specifying the device to be at rest when mounted vertically.

The `remapCoordinateSystem` method accepts four parameters:

➤ The initial rotation matrix, found using `getRotationMatrix`, as described earlier

➤ A variable used to store the output (transformed) rotation matrix

➤ The remapped x-axis

➤ The remapped y-axis

Two final parameters are used to specify the new reference frame. The values used specify the new x- and y-axes relative to the default frame. The Sensor Manager provides a set of constants to let you specify the axis values: `AXIS_X`, `AXIS_Y`, `AXIS_Z`, `AXIS_MINUS_X`, `AXIS_MINUS_Y`, and `AXIS_MINUS_Z`.

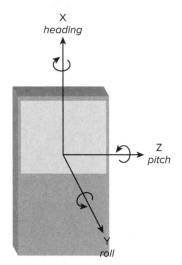

Listing 14-5 shows how to remap the reference frame so that a device is at rest when mounted vertically — held in portrait mode with its screen facing the user — as shown in Figure 14-3.

FIGURE 14-3

LISTING 14-5: Remapping the orientation reference frame

```
SensorManager.getRotationMatrix(R, null, aValues, mValues);

float[] outR = new float[9];
SensorManager.remapCoordinateSystem(R,
                                    SensorManager.AXIS_X,
                                    SensorManager.AXIS_Z,
                                    outR);
SensorManager.getOrientation(outR, values);

// Convert from radians to degrees.
values[0] = (float) Math.toDegrees(values[0]);
values[1] = (float) Math.toDegrees(values[1]);
values[2] = (float) Math.toDegrees(values[2]);
```

Creating a Compass and Artificial Horizon

In Chapter 4 you created a simple `CompassView` to experiment with owner-drawn controls. In this example you'll extend the functionality of the Compass View to display the device pitch and roll, before using it to display the device orientation.

1. Open the Compass project you created in Chapter 4. You will be making changes to the `CompassView` as well as the `Compass` Activity used to display it. To ensure that the view and controller remain as decoupled as possible, the `CompassView` won't be linked to the Sensors directly; instead it will be updated by the Activity. Start by adding field variables and get/set methods for pitch and roll to the `CompassView`.

```
float pitch = 0;
float roll = 0;

public float getPitch() {
  return pitch;
}
public void setPitch(float pitch) {
  this.pitch = pitch;
}

public float getRoll() {
  return roll;
}
public void setRoll(float roll) {
  this.roll = roll;
}
```

2. Update the `onDraw` method to include two circles that will be used to indicate the pitch and roll values.

```
@Override
protected void onDraw(Canvas canvas) {

  [ ... Existing onDraw method ... ]
```

2.1. Create a new circle that's half filled and rotates in line with the sideways tilt (roll).

```
RectF rollOval = new RectF((mMeasuredWidth/3)-mMeasuredWidth/7,
                           (mMeasuredHeight/2)-mMeasuredWidth/7,
                           (mMeasuredWidth/3)+mMeasuredWidth/7,
                           (mMeasuredHeight/2)+mMeasuredWidth/7
                          );
markerPaint.setStyle(Paint.Style.STROKE);
canvas.drawOval(rollOval, markerPaint);
markerPaint.setStyle(Paint.Style.FILL);
canvas.save();
canvas.rotate(roll, mMeasuredWidth/3, mMeasuredHeight/2);
canvas.drawArc(rollOval, 0, 180, false, markerPaint);

canvas.restore();
```

2.2. Create a new circle that starts half filled and varies between full and empty based on the forward angle (pitch):

```
RectF pitchOval = new RectF((2*mMeasuredWidth/3)-mMeasuredWidth/7,
                            (mMeasuredHeight/2)-mMeasuredWidth/7,
                            (2*mMeasuredWidth/3)+mMeasuredWidth/7,
                            (mMeasuredHeight/2)+mMeasuredWidth/7
                           );
```

```
    markerPaint.setStyle(Paint.Style.STROKE);
    canvas.drawOval(pitchOval, markerPaint);
    markerPaint.setStyle(Paint.Style.FILL);
    canvas.drawArc(pitchOval, 0-pitch/2, 180+(pitch), false, markerPaint);
    markerPaint.setStyle(Paint.Style.STROKE);
  }
```

3. That completes the changes to the `CompassView`. If you run the application now it should appear as shown in Figure 14-4.

4. Now update the `Compass` Activity. Use the Sensor Manager to listen for orientation changes using the magnetic field and accelerometer Sensors. Start by adding local field variables to store the last magnetic field and accelerometer values, as well as references to the `CompassView` and `SensorManager`.

```
float[] aValues = new float[3];
float[] mValues = new float[3];
CompassView compassView;
SensorManager sensorManager;
```

5. Create a new `updateOrientation` method that uses new heading, pitch, and roll values to update the `CompassView`.

FIGURE 14-4

```
private void updateOrientation(float[] values) {
  if (compassView!= null) {
    compassView.setBearing(values[0]);
    compassView.setPitch(values[1]);
    compassView.setRoll(-values[2]);
    compassView.invalidate();
  }
}
```

6. Update the `onCreate` method to get references to the `CompassView` and `SensorManager`, and initialize the heading, pitch, and roll.

```
@Override
public void onCreate(Bundle savedInstanceState) {
  super.onCreate(savedInstanceState);
  setContentView(R.layout.main);

  compassView = (CompassView)this.findViewById(R.id.compassView);
  sensorManager = (SensorManager)getSystemService(Context.SENSOR_SERVICE);
  updateOrientation(new float[] {0, 0, 0});
}
```

7. Create a new `calculateOrientation` method to evaluate the device orientation using the last recorded accelerometer and magnetic field values.

```
private float[] calculateOrientation() {
  float[] values = new float[3];
  float[] R = new float[9];

  SensorManager.getRotationMatrix(R, null, aValues, mValues);
  SensorManager.getOrientation(R, values);

  // Convert from Radians to Degrees.
  values[0] = (float) Math.toDegrees(values[0]);
  values[1] = (float) Math.toDegrees(values[1]);
  values[2] = (float) Math.toDegrees(values[2]);

  return values;
}
```

8. Implement a `SensorEventListener` as a field variable. Within `onSensorChanged` it should check for the calling Sensor's type and update the last accelerometer or magnetic field values as appropriate before making a call to `updateOrientation` using the `calculateOrientation` method.

```
private final SensorEventListener sensorEventListener = new SensorEventListener() {

  public void onSensorChanged(SensorEvent event) {
    if (event.sensor.getType() == Sensor.TYPE_ACCELEROMETER)
      aValues = event.values;
    if (event.sensor.getType() == Sensor.TYPE_MAGNETIC_FIELD)
      mValues = event.values;

    updateOrientation(calculateOrientation());
  }

  public void onAccuracyChanged(Sensor sensor, int accuracy) {}
};
```

9. Now override `onResume` and `onStop` to register and unregister the `SensorEventListener` when the Activity becomes visible and hidden, respectively.

```
@Override
protected void onResume()
{
  super.onResume();

  Sensor accelerometer = sensorManager.getDefaultSensor(Sensor.TYPE_ACCELEROMETER);
  Sensor magField = sensorManager.getDefaultSensor(Sensor.TYPE_MAGNETIC_FIELD);

  sensorManager.registerListener(sensorEventListener,
                                 accelerometer,
                                 SensorManager.SENSOR_DELAY_FASTEST);
  sensorManager.registerListener(sensorEventListener,
```

```
                                                  magField,
                                                  SensorManager.SENSOR_DELAY_FASTEST);
    }

    @Override
    protected void onStop()
    {
      sensorManager.unregisterListener(sensorEventListener);
      super.onStop();
    }
```

If you run the application now you should see the three face dials update dynamically when the orientation of the device changes.

10. An artificial horizon is more useful if it's mounted vertically. Modify the reference frame of the artificial horizon to match this orientation by updating `calculateOrientation` to remap the coordinate system.

```
    private float[] calculateOrientation() {
      float[] values = new float[3];
      float[] R = new float[9];
      float[] outR = new float[9];

      SensorManager.getRotationMatrix(R, null, aValues, mValues);
      SensorManager.remapCoordinateSystem(R,
                                          SensorManager.AXIS_X,
                                          SensorManager.AXIS_Z,
                                          outR);

      SensorManager.getOrientation(outR, values);

      // Convert from Radians to Degrees.
      values[0] = (float) Math.toDegrees(values[0]);
      values[1] = (float) Math.toDegrees(values[1]);
      values[2] = (float) Math.toDegrees(values[2]);

      return values;
    }
```

All code snippets in this example are part of the **Chapter 14 Artificial Horizon** *project, available for download at Wrox.com.*

CONTROLLING DEVICE VIBRATION

In Chapter 9 you learned how to create Notifications that can use vibration to enrich event feedback. In some circumstances you may want to vibrate the device independently of Notifications. Vibrating the device is an excellent way to provide haptic user feedback, and is particularly popular as a feedback mechanism for games.

To control device vibration, your applications needs the VIBRATE permission. Add this to your application manifest using the following XML snippet:

```
    <uses-permission android:name="android.permission.VIBRATE"/>
```

Device vibration is controlled through the `Vibrator` Service, accessible via the `getSystemService` method, as shown in Listing 14-6.

LISTING 14-6: Controlling device vibration

```
String vibratorService = Context.VIBRATOR_SERVICE;
Vibrator vibrator = (Vibrator)getSystemService(vibratorService);
```

Call `vibrate` to start device vibration; you can pass in either a vibration duration or a pattern of alternating vibration/pause sequences along with an optional index parameter that will repeat the pattern starting at the index specified. Both techniques are demonstrated in the following extension to Listing 14-6:

```
long[] pattern = {1000,  2000, 4000, 8000, 16000 };
vibrator.vibrate(pattern, 0); // Execute vibration pattern.
vibrator.vibrate(1000); // Vibrate for 1 second.
```

To cancel vibration call `cancel`; exiting your application will automatically cancel any vibration it has initiated.

SUMMARY

In this chapter you learned how to use the Sensor Manager to let your application respond to the physical environment. You were introduced to the Sensors available on the Android platform and learned how to listen for Sensor Events using the Sensor Event Listener and how to interpret those results.

Then you took a more detailed look at the accelerometer, orientation, and magnetic field detection hardware, using these Sensors to determine the device's orientation and acceleration. In the process you created a g-forceometer and an artificial horizon.

You also learned:

➤   Which Sensors are available to Android applications

➤   How to remap the reference frame when determining a device's orientation

➤   The composition and meaning of the Sensor Event values returned by each sensor

➤   How to use device vibration to provide physical feedback for application events

In the final chapter, you'll be introduced to some of the advanced Android features. You'll learn more about security, how to use AIDL to facilitate interprocess communication, and using Wake Locks. You'll be introduced to Android's TTS library and learn about Android's User Interface and graphics capabilities by exploring animations and advanced Canvas drawing techniques. Finally, you'll be introduced to the SurfaceView and touch-screen input functionality.

15

Advanced Android Development

WHAT'S IN THIS CHAPTER?

- ➤ Android security using Permissions
- ➤ Using Wake Locks
- ➤ The Text to Speech libraries
- ➤ Interprocess communication (IPC) using AIDL and Parcelables
- ➤ Creating frame-by-frame and tweened animations
- ➤ Advanced Canvas drawing
- ➤ Using the Surface View
- ➤ Listening for key presses, screen touches, and trackball movement

In this chapter, you'll be returning to some of the possibilities touched on in previous chapters and exploring some of the topics that deserve more attention.

In the first seven chapters, you learned the fundamentals of creating mobile applications for Android devices. In Chapters 8 through 14, you were introduced to some of the more powerful and some optional APIs, including location-based services, maps, Bluetooth, and hardware monitoring and control.

This chapter starts by taking a closer look at security, in particular, how Permissions work and how to use them to secure your own applications.

Next you'll examine Wake Locks and the text to speech libraries before looking at the Android Interface Definition Language (AIDL). You'll use AIDL to create rich application interfaces that support full object-based interprocess communication (IPC) between Android applications running in different processes.

You'll then take a closer look at the rich toolkit available for creating user interfaces for your Activities. Starting with animations, you'll learn how to apply tweened animations to Views and View Groups, and construct frame-by-frame cell-based animations.

Next is an in-depth examination of the possibilities available with Android's raster graphics engine. You'll be introduced to the drawing primitives available before learning some of the more advanced possibilities available with Paint. Using transparency, creating gradient Shaders, and incorporating bitmap brushes are then covered, before you are introduced to mask and color filters, as well as Path Effects and the possibilities of using different transfer modes.

You'll then delve a little deeper into the design and execution of more complex user interface Views, learning how to create three-dimensional and high frame-rate interactive controls using the Surface View, and how to use the touch screen, trackball, and device keys to create intuitive input possibilities for your UIs.

PARANOID ANDROID

Much of Android's security is native to the underlying Linux kernel. Resources are sandboxed to their owner applications, making them inaccessible from others. Android provides broadcast Intents, Services, and Content Providers to let you relax these strict process boundaries, using the permission mechanism to maintain application-level security.

You've already used the permission system to request access to native system services — notably the location-based services and contacts Content Provider — for your applications using the `<uses-permission>` manifest tag.

The following sections provide a more detailed look at the security available. For a comprehensive view, the Android documentation provides an excellent resource that describes the security features in depth at `developer.android.com/guide/topics/security/security.html`

Linux Kernel Security

Each Android package has a unique Linux user ID assigned to it during installation. This has the effect of sandboxing the process and the resources it creates, so that it can't affect (or be affected by) other applications.

Because of this kernel-level security, you need to take additional steps to communicate between applications. Enter Content Providers, broadcast Intents, and AIDL interfaces. Each of these mechanisms opens a tunnel through which information can flow between applications. Android permissions act as border guards at either end to control the traffic allowed through.

Introducing Permissions

Permissions are an application-level security mechanism that lets you restrict access to application components. Permissions are used to prevent malicious applications from corrupting data, gaining access to sensitive information, or making excessive (or unauthorized) use of hardware resources or external communication channels.

As you've learned in earlier chapters, many of Android's native components have permission requirements. The native permission strings used by native Android Activities and Services can be found as static constants in the `android.Manifest.permission` class.

To use permission-protected components, you need to add `<uses-permission>` tags to application manifests, specifying the permission string that each application requires.

When an application package is installed, the permissions requested in its manifest are analyzed and granted (or denied) by checks with trusted authorities and user feedback.

Unlike many existing mobile platforms, all Android permission checks are done at installation. Once an application is installed, the user will not be prompted to reevaluate those permissions.

Declaring and Enforcing Permissions

Before you can assign a permission to an application component, you need to define it within your manifest using the `<permission>` tag as shown in the Listing 15-1.

LISTING 15-1: Declaring a new permission

```
<permission
    android:name="com.paad.DETONATE_DEVICE"
    android:protectionLevel="dangerous"
    android:label="Self Destruct"
    android:description="@string/detonate_description">
</permission>
```

Within the permission tag, you can specify the level of access that the permission will permit (`normal`, `dangerous`, `signature`, `signatureOrSystem`), a label, and an external resource containing the description that explains the risks of granting this permission.

To include permission requirements for your own application components, use the `permission` attribute in the application manifest. Permission constraints can be enforced throughout your application, most usefully at application interface boundaries, for example:

➤ **Activities**   Add a permission to limit the ability of other applications to launch an Activity.

➤ **Broadcast Receivers**   Control which applications can send broadcast Intents to your Receiver.

➤ **Content Providers**   Limit read access and write operations on Content Providers.

➤ **Services**   Limit the ability of other applications to start, or bind to, a Service.

In each case, you can add a `permission` attribute to the application component in the manifest, specifying a required permission string to access each component. Listing 15-2 shows a manifest excerpt that requires the permission defined in Listing 15-1 to start an Activity.

LISTING 15-2: Enforcing a permission requirement for an Activity

```
<activity
    android:name=".MyActivity"
    android:label="@string/app_name"
    android:permission="com.paad.DETONATE_DEVICE">
</activity>
```

Content Providers let you set `readPermission` and `writePermission` attributes to offer a more granular control over read/write access.

Enforcing Permissions for Broadcast Intents

As well as requiring permissions for Intents to be received by your Broadcast Receivers, you can also attach a permission requirement to each Intent you broadcast.

When calling `sendIntent`, you can supply a permission string required by Broadcast Receivers before they can receive the Intent. This process is shown here:

```
sendBroadcast(myIntent, REQUIRED_PERMISSION);
```

USING WAKE LOCKS

In order to prolong battery life, over time Android devices will first dim, then turn off the screen, before turning off the CPU. `WakeLocks` are a Power Manager system Service feature, available to your applications to control the power state of the host device.

Wake Locks can be used to keep the CPU running, prevent the screen from dimming, prevent the screen from turning off, and prevent the keyboard backlight from turning off.

 Creating and holding Wake Locks can have a dramatic influence on the battery drain associated with your application. It's good practice to use Wake Locks only when strictly necessary, for as short a time as needed, and to release them as soon as possible.

Screen Wake Locks are typically used to prevent the screen from dimming during applications that are likely to involve little user interaction while users observe the screen (e.g., playing videos).

CPU Wake Locks are used to prevent the device from going to sleep until an action is performed. This is most commonly the case for Services started within Intent Receivers, which may receive Intents while the device is asleep. It's worth noting that in this case the system will hold a CPU Wake Lock throughout the `onReceive` handler of the Broadcast Receiver.

 If you start a Service, or broadcast an Intent within the `onReceive` *handler of a Broadcast Receiver, it is possible that the Wake Lock it holds will be released before your Service has started. To ensure the Service is executed you will need to put a separate Wake Lock policy in place.*

To create a Wake Lock, call `newWakeLock` on the Power Manager, specifying one of the following Wake Lock types:

➤ `FULL_WAKE_LOCK`   Keeps the screen at full brightness, the keyboard backlight illuminated, and the CPU running.

➤ `SCREEN_BRIGHT_WAKE_LOCK`   Keeps the screen at full brightness, and the CPU running.

➤ `SCREEN_DIM_WAKE_LOCK` Keeps the screen on (but lets it dim) and the CPU running.

➤ `PARTIAL_WAKE_LOCK` Keeps the CPU running.

```
PowerManager pm = (PowerManager)getSystemService(Context.POWER_SERVICE);
WakeLock wakeLock = pm.newWakeLock(PowerManager.PARTIAL_WAKE_LOCK,
                                   "MyWakeLock");
```

Once you have created it, acquire the Wake Lock by calling `acquire`. You can optionally specify a timeout to ensure the maximum duration the Wake Lock will be held for. When the action for which you're holding the Wake Lock completes, call `release` to let the system manage the power state.

Listing 15-3 shows the typical use pattern for creating, acquiring, and releasing a Wake Lock.

LISTING 15-3: Using a Wake Lock

```
PowerManager pm = (PowerManager)getSystemService(Context.POWER_SERVICE);
WakeLock wakeLock = pm.newWakeLock(PowerManager.PARTIAL_WAKE_LOCK,
                                   "MyWakeLock");
wakeLock.acquire();
[ ... Do things requiring the CPU stay active ... ]
wakeLock.release();
```

INTRODUCING ANDROID TEXT TO SPEECH

Android 1.6 (SDK API level 4) introduced the text to speech (TTS) engine. You can use this API to produce speech synthesis from within your applications, allowing them to "talk" to your users.

Due to storage space constraints on some Android devices, the language packs are not always preinstalled on each device. Before using the TTS engine, it's good practice to confirm the language packs are installed.

Start a new Activity for a result using the `ACTION_CHECK_TTS_DATA` action from the `TextToSpeech.Engine` class to check for the TTS libraries.

```
Intent intent = new Intent(TextToSpeech.Engine.ACTION_CHECK_TTS_DATA);
startActivityForResult(intent, TTS_DATA_CHECK);
```

The `onActivityResult` handler will receive `CHECK_VOICE_DATA_PASS` if the voice data has been installed successfully.

If the voice data is not currently available, start a new Activity using the `ACTION_INSTALL_TTS_DATA` action from the TTS Engine class to initiate its installation.

Once you've confirmed the voice data is available, you need to create and initialize a new `TextToSpeech` instance. Note that you cannot use the new Text To Speech object until initialization is complete. Pass an `OnInitListener` into the constructor (as shown in Listing 15-4) that will be fired when the TTS engine has been initialized.

LISTING 15-4: Initializing Text to Speech

```
boolean ttsIsInit = false;
TextToSpeech tts = null;

tts = new TextToSpeech(this, new OnInitListener() {
        public void onInit(int status) {
          if (status == TextToSpeech.SUCCESS) {
            ttsIsInit = true;
            // TODO Speak!
          }
        }
      });
```

When Text To Speech has been initialized you can use the `speak` method to synthesize voice using the default device audio output.

```
tts.speak("Hello, Android", TextToSpeech.QUEUE_ADD, null);
```

The `speak` method lets you specify a parameter to either add the new voice output to the existing queue, or flush the queue and start speaking straight away.

You can affect the way the voice output sounds using the `setPitch` and `setSpeechRate` methods. Each accepts a float parameter that modifies the pitch and speed, respectively, of the voice output.

More importantly, you can change the pronunciation of your voice output using the `setLanguage` method. This method takes a Locale value to specify the country and language of the text being spoken. This will affect the way the text is spoken to ensure the correct language and pronunciation models are used.

When you have finished speaking, use `stop` to halt voice output and `shutdown` to free the TTS resources.

Listing 15-5 determines whether the TTS voice library is installed, initializes a new TTS engine, and uses it to speak in UK English.

LISTING 15-5: Using Text to Speech

```
private static int TTS_DATA_CHECK = 1;

private TextToSpeech tts = null;
private boolean ttsIsInit = false;

private void initTextToSpeech() {
  Intent intent = new Intent(Engine.ACTION_CHECK_TTS_DATA);
  startActivityForResult(intent, TTS_DATA_CHECK);
}

protected void onActivityResult(int requestCode,
                                int resultCode, Intent data) {
  if (requestCode == TTS_DATA_CHECK) {
    if (resultCode == Engine.CHECK_VOICE_DATA_PASS) {
```

```java
        tts = new TextToSpeech(this, new OnInitListener() {
         public void onInit(int status) {
           if (status == TextToSpeech.SUCCESS) {
             ttsIsInit = true;
             if (tts.isLanguageAvailable(Locale.UK) >= 0)
               tts.setLanguage(Locale.UK);
             tts.setPitch(0.8f);
             tts.setSpeechRate(1.1f);
             speak();
           }
          }
         });
       } else {
         Intent installVoice = new Intent(Engine.ACTION_INSTALL_TTS_DATA);
         startActivity(installIntent);
       }
      }
    }

    private void speak() {
      if (tts != null && ttsIsInit) {
        tts.speak("Hello, Android", TextToSpeech.QUEUE_ADD, null);
      }
    }

    @Override
    public void onDestroy() {
      if (tts != null) {
        tts.stop();
        tts.shutdown();
      }
      super.onDestroy();
    }
```

USING AIDL TO SUPPORT IPC FOR SERVICES

One of the more interesting possibilities of Services is the idea of running independent background processes to supply processing, data lookup, or other useful functionality to multiple independent applications.

In Chapter 9, you learned how to create Services for your applications. Here, you'll learn how to use the Android Interface Definition Language (AIDL) to support rich interprocess communication (IPC) between Services and application components. This will give your Services the ability to support multiple applications across process boundaries.

To pass objects between processes, you need to deconstruct them into OS-level primitives that the underlying operating system can then marshal across application boundaries.

AIDL is used to simplify the code that lets your processes exchange objects. It's similar to interfaces like COM or Corba in that it lets you create public methods within your Services that can accept and return object parameters and return values between processes.

Implementing an AIDL Interface

AIDL supports the following data types:

➤   Java language primitives (`int`, `boolean`, `float`, `char`, etc.).

➤   `String` and `CharSequence` values.

➤   `List` (including generic) objects, where each element is a supported type. The receiving class will always receive the List object instantiated as an `ArrayList`.

➤   `Map` (not including generic) objects, when every key and element is of a supported type. The receiving class will always receive the `Map` object instantiated as a `HashMap`.

➤   AIDL-generated interfaces (covered later). An `import` statement is always needed for these.

➤   Classes that implement the `Parcelable` interface (covered next). An `import` statement is always needed for these.

The following sections demonstrate how to make your application classes AIDL-compatible by implementing the `Parcelable` interface, before creating an AIDL interface definition and implementing it within your Service.

Passing Class Objects as Parcelables

For non-native objects to be passed between processes, they must implement the `Parcelable` interface. This lets you decompose your objects into primitive types stored within a `Parcel` that can be marshaled across process boundaries.

Implement the `writeToParcel` method to decompose your class object, then implement the public static `Creator` field (which implements a new `Parcelable.Creator` class), which will create a new object based on an incoming Parcel.

Listing 15-6 shows a basic example of using the `Parcelable` interface for the `Quake` class you've been using in the ongoing Earthquake example.

LISTING 15-6: Making the Quake class a Parcelable

```java
package com.paad.earthquake;

import java.util.Date;
import android.location.Location;
import android.os.Parcel;
import android.os.Parcelable;

public class Quake implements Parcelable {
  private Date date;
  private String details;
  private Location location;
  private double magnitude;
  private String link;
```

```java
    public Date getDate() { return date; }
    public String getDetails() { return details; }
    public Location getLocation() { return location; }
    public double getMagnitude() { return magnitude; }
    public String getLink() { return link; }

    public Quake(Date _d, String _det, Location _loc,
                 double _mag, String _link) {
      date = _d;
      details = _det;
      location = _loc;
      magnitude = _mag;
      link = _link;
    }

    @Override
    public String toString(){
      SimpleDateFormat sdf = new SimpleDateFormat("HH.mm");
      String dateString = sdf.format(date);
      return dateString + ":" + magnitude + " " + details;
    }

    private Quake(Parcel in) {
      date.setTime(in.readLong());
      details = in.readString();
      magnitude = in.readDouble();
      Location location = new Location("generated");
      location.setLatitude(in.readDouble());
      location.setLongitude(in.readDouble());
      link= in.readString();
    }

    public void writeToParcel(Parcel out, int flags) {
      out.writeLong(date.getTime());
      out.writeString(details);
      out.writeDouble(magnitude);
      out.writeDouble(location.getLatitude());
      out.writeDouble(location.getLongitude());
      out.writeString(link);
    }

    public static final Parcelable.Creator<Quake> CREATOR =
      new Parcelable.Creator<Quake>() {
        public Quake createFromParcel(Parcel in) {
          return new Quake(in);
        }

        public Quake[] newArray(int size) {
         return new Quake[size];
        }
      };

    public int describeContents() {
      return 0;
    }
}
```

Now that you've got a Parcelable class, you need to create an AIDL definition to make it available when defining your Service's AIDL interface.

Listing 15-7 shows the contents of the Quake.aidl file you need to create for the `Quake` Parcelable defined in the preceding listing.

LISTING 15-7: The Quake class AIDL definition

```
package com.paad.earthquake;

parcelable Quake;
```

Remember that when you're passing class objects between processes, the client process must understand the definition of the object being passed.

Creating the AIDL Service Definition

In this section, you will be defining a new AIDL interface definition for a Service you'd like to use across processes.

Start by creating a new `.aidl` file within your project. This will define the methods and fields to include in an interface that your Service will implement.

The syntax for creating AIDL definitions is similar to that used for standard Java interface definitions.

Start by specifying a fully qualified package name, then `import` all the packages required. Unlike normal Java interfaces, AIDL definitions need to import packages for any class or interface that isn't a native Java type even if it's defined in the same project.

Define a new `interface`, adding the properties and methods you want to make available.

Methods can take zero or more parameters and return void or a supported type. If you define a method that takes one or more parameters, you need to use a directional tag to indicate if the parameter is a value or reference type using the `in`, `out`, and `inout` keywords.

 Where possible, you should limit the direction of each parameter, as marshaling parameters is an expensive operation.

Listing 15-8 shows a basic AIDL definition in the IEarthquakeService.aidl file.

LISTING 15-8: An Earthquake Service AIDL Interface definition

```
package com.paad.earthquake;

import com.paad.earthquake.Quake;

interface IEarthquakeService {
```

```
    List<Quake> getEarthquakes();

    void refreshEarthquakes();
}
```

Implementing and Exposing the IPC Interface

If you're using the ADT plug-in, saving the AIDL file will automatically code-generate a Java `Interface` file. This interface will include an inner `Stub` class that implements the interface as an abstract class.

Have your Service extend the `Stub` and implement the functionality required. Typically, you'll do this using a private field variable within the Service whose functionality you'll be exposing.

Listing 15-9 shows an implementation of the `IEarthquakeService` AIDL definition created in Listing 15-8.

LISTING 15-9: Implementing the AIDL Interface definition within a Service

Available for download on Wrox.com

```java
IBinder myEarthquakeServiceStub = new IEarthquakeService.Stub() {
  public void refreshEarthquakes() throws RemoteException {
    EarthquakeService.this.refreshEarthquakes();
  }

  public List<Quake> getEarthquakes() throws RemoteException {
    ArrayList<Quake> result = new ArrayList<Quake>();

    ContentResolver cr = EarthquakeService.this.getContentResolver();
    Cursor c = cr.query(EarthquakeProvider.CONTENT_URI,
                        null, null, null, null);
    if (c.moveToFirst())
      do {
        Double lat = c.getDouble(EarthquakeProvider.LATITUDE_COLUMN);
        Double lng = c.getDouble(EarthquakeProvider.LONGITUDE_COLUMN);
        Location location = new Location("dummy");
        location.setLatitude(lat);
        location.setLongitude(lng);

        String details = c.getString(EarthquakeProvider.DETAILS_COLUMN);
        String link =  c.getString(EarthquakeProvider.LINK_COLUMN);

        double magnitude =
          c.getDouble(EarthquakeProvider.MAGNITUDE_COLUMN);

        long datems =  c.getLong(EarthquakeProvider.DATE_COLUMN);
        Date date = new Date(datems);

        result.add(new Quake(date, details, location, magnitude, link));
      } while(c.moveToNext());
    return result;
  }
};
```

When implementing these methods, be aware of the following:

➤ All exceptions will remain local to the implementing process; they will not be propagated to the calling application.

➤ All IPC calls are synchronous. If you know that the process is likely to be time-consuming, you should consider wrapping the synchronous call in an asynchronous wrapper or moving the processing on the receiver side onto a background thread.

With the functionality implemented, you need to expose this interface to client applications. Expose the IPC-enabled Service interface by overriding the onBind method within your Service implementation to return an instance of the interface.

Listing 15-10 demonstrates the onBind implementation for the EarthquakeService.

LISTING 15-10: Exposing an AIDL Interface implementation to Service clients

```
@Override
public IBinder onBind(Intent intent) {
    return myEarthquakeServiceStub;
}
```

To use the IPC Service from within an Activity, you must bind it as shown in Listing 15-11, taken from the Earthquake Activity.

LISTING 15-11: Using an IPC Service method

```
IEarthquakeService earthquakeService = null;

private void bindService() {
    bindService(new Intent(IEarthquakeService.class.getName()),
                serviceConnection, Context.BIND_AUTO_CREATE);
}

private ServiceConnection serviceConnection = new ServiceConnection() {
    public void onServiceConnected(ComponentName className,
                                   IBinder service) {
        earthquakeService = IEarthquakeService.Stub.asInterface(service);
    }

    public void onServiceDisconnected(ComponentName className) {
        earthquakeService = null;
    }
};
```

USING INTERNET SERVICES

Software as a service, or *cloud computing*, is becoming increasingly popular as companies try to reduce the cost overheads associated with installation, upgrades, and maintenance of deployed software. The result is a range of rich Internet services with which you can build thin mobile applications that enrich online services with the personalization available from your mobile.

The idea of using a middle tier to reduce client-side load is not a novel one, and happily there are many Internet-based options to supply your applications with the level of service you need.

The sheer volume of Internet services available makes it impossible to list them all here (let alone look at them in any detail), but the following list shows some of the more mature and interesting Internet services currently available.

➤ **Google's gData Services** As well as the native Google applications, Google offers web APIs for access to their calendar, spreadsheet, Blogger, and Picasaweb platforms. These APIs collectively make use of Google's standardized gData framework, a form of read/write XML data communication.

➤ **Yahoo! Pipes** Yahoo! Pipes offers a graphical web-based approach to XML feed manipulation. Using pipes, you can filter, aggregate, analyze, and otherwise manipulate XML feeds and output them in a variety of formats to be consumed by your applications.

➤ **Google App Engine** Using the Google App Engine, you can create cloud-hosted web services that shift complex processing away from your mobile client. Doing so reduces the load on your system resources but comes at the price of Internet-connection dependency.

➤ **Amazon Web Services** Amazon offers a range of cloud-based services, including a rich API for accessing its media database of books, CDs, and DVDs. Amazon also offers a distributed storage solution (S3) and Elastic Compute Cloud (EC2).

BUILDING RICH USER INTERFACES

Mobile phone user interfaces have improved dramatically in recent years, thanks not least of all to the iPhone's innovative take on mobile UI.

In this section, you'll learn how to use more advanced UI visual effects like Shaders, translucency, animations, touch screens with multiple touch, and OpenGL to add a level of polish to your Activities and Views.

Working with Animations

In Chapter 3, you learned how to define animations as external resources. Now, you get the opportunity to put them to use.

Android offers two kinds of animation:

➤ **Frame-by-Frame Animations** Traditional cell-based animations in which a different Drawable is displayed in each frame. Frame-by-frame animations are displayed within a View, using its Canvas as a projection screen.

➤ **Tweened Animations** Tweened animations are applied to Views, letting you define a series of changes in position, size, rotation, and opacity that animate the View contents.

 Both animation types are restricted to the original bounds of the View they're applied to. Rotations, translations, and scaling transformations that extend beyond the original boundaries of the View will result in the contents being clipped.

Introducing Tweened Animations

Tweened animations offer a simple way to provide depth, movement, or feedback to your users at a minimal resource cost.

Using animations to apply a set of orientation, scale, position, and opacity changes is much less resource-intensive than manually redrawing the Canvas to achieve similar effects, not to mention far simpler to implement.

Tweened animations are commonly used to:

➤ Transition between Activities.

➤ Transition between layouts within an Activity.

➤ Transition between different content displayed within the same View.

➤ Provide user feedback such as:

    ➤ Indicating progress.

    ➤ "Shaking" an input box to indicate an incorrect or invalid data entry.

Creating Tweened Animations

Tweened animations are created using the `Animation` class. The following list explains the animation types available.

➤ `AlphaAnimation` Lets you animate a change in the View's transparency (opacity or alpha blending).

➤ `RotateAnimation` Lets you spin the selected View canvas in the XY plane.

➤ `ScaleAnimation` Allows you to zoom in to or out from the selected View.

➤ `TranslateAnimation` Lets you move the selected View around the screen (although it will only be drawn within its original bounds).

Android offers the `AnimationSet` class to group and configure animations to be run as a set. You can define the start time and duration of each animation used within a set to control the timing and order of the animation sequence.

> *It's important to set the start offset and duration for each child animation, or they will all start and complete at the same time.*

Listings 15-12 and 15-13 demonstrate how to create the same animation sequence in code or as an external resource.

LISTING 15-12: Creating a tweened animation in code

Available for download on Wrox.com

```
// Create the AnimationSet
AnimationSet myAnimation = new AnimationSet(true);
```

```
// Create a rotate animation.
RotateAnimation rotate = new RotateAnimation(0, 360,
  RotateAnimation.RELATIVE_TO_SELF, 0.5f,
  RotateAnimation.RELATIVE_TO_SELF, 0.5f);
rotate.setFillAfter(true);
rotate.setDuration(1000);

// Create a scale animation
ScaleAnimation scale = new ScaleAnimation(1, 0,
                                          1, 0,
                                          ScaleAnimation.RELATIVE_TO_SELF,
                                          0.5f,
                                          ScaleAnimation.RELATIVE_TO_SELF,
                                          0.5f);
scale.setFillAfter(true);
scale.setDuration(500);
scale.setStartOffset(500);

// Create an alpha animation
AlphaAnimation alpha = new AlphaAnimation(1, 0);
scale.setFillAfter(true);
scale.setDuration(500);
scale.setStartOffset(500);

// Add each animation to the set
myAnimation.addAnimation(rotate);
myAnimation.addAnimation(scale);
myAnimation.addAnimation(alpha);
```

The code snippet in Listing 15-12 above implements the same animation sequence shown in the XML snippet in Listing 15-13 below.

LISTING 15-13: Defining a tweened animation in XML

```
<?xml version="1.0" encoding="utf-8"?>
<set
  xmlns:android="http://schemas.android.com/apk/res/android"
  android:shareInterpolator="true">
  <rotate
    android:fromDegrees="0"
    android:toDegrees="360"
    android:pivotX="50%"
    android:pivotY="50%"
    android:startOffset="0"
    android:duration="1000" />
  <scale
    android:fromXScale="1.0"
    android:toXScale="0.0"
    android:fromYScale="1.0"
    android:toYScale="0.0"
    android:pivotX="50%"
```

continues

LISTING 15-13 *(continued)*

```
      android:pivotY="50%"
      android:startOffset="500"
      android:duration="500" />
  <alpha
    android:fromAlpha="1.0"
    android:toAlpha="0.0"
    android:startOffset="500"
    android:duration="500" />
</set>
```

As you can see, it's generally both easier and more intuitive to create your animation sequences using an external animation resource.

Applying Tweened Animations

Animations can be applied to any View by calling its startAnimation method and passing in the Animation or Animation Set to apply.

Animation sequences will run once and then stop, unless you modify this behavior using the setRepeatMode and setRepeatCount methods on the Animation or Animation Set. You can force an animation to loop or repeat in reverse by setting the repeat mode of RESTART or REVERSE respectively. Setting the repeat count controls the number of times the animation will repeat.

Listing 15-14 shows an Animation that repeats indefinitely.

LISTING 15-14: Applying an Animation that loops continuously

```
myAnimation.setRepeatMode(Animation.RESTART);
myAnimation.setRepeatCount(Animation.INFINITE);
myView.startAnimation(myAnimation);
```

Using Animation Listeners

The AnimationListener lets you create an event handler that's fired when an animation begins or ends. This lets you perform actions before or after an animation has completed, such as changing the View contents or chaining multiple animations.

Call setAnimationListener on an Animation object, and pass in a new implementation of AnimationListener, overriding onAnimationEnd, onAnimationStart, and onAnimationRepeat as required.

Listing 15-15 shows the basic implementation of an Animation Listener.

LISTING 15-15: Creating an Animation Listener

```
myAnimation.setAnimationListener(new AnimationListener() {
  public void onAnimationEnd(Animation _animation) {
    // TODO Do something after animation is complete.
  }
```

```
    public void onAnimationRepeat(Animation _animation) {
      // TODO Do something when the animation repeats.
    }

    public void onAnimationStart(Animation _animation) {
      // TODO Do something when the animation starts.
    }
});
```

Animated Sliding User Interface Example

In this example, you'll create a new Activity that uses an Animation to smoothly change the content of the user interface based on the direction pressed on the D-pad.

1. Start by creating a new `ContentSlider` project featuring a `ContentSlider` Activity.

```
package com.paad.contentslider;

import android.app.Activity;
import android.view.KeyEvent;
import android.os.Bundle;
import android.view.animation.Animation;
import android.view.animation.Animation.AnimationListener;
import android.view.animation.AnimationUtils;
import android.widget.TextView;

public class ContentSlider extends Activity {
  @Override
  public void onCreate(Bundle savedInstanceState) {
    super.onCreate(savedInstanceState);
    setContentView(R.layout.main);
  }
}
```

2. Next, modify the main.xml layout resource. It should contain a single `TextView` with the text bold, centered, and relatively large.

```
<?xml version="1.0" encoding="utf-8"?>
<LinearLayout
  xmlns:android="http://schemas.android.com/apk/res/android"
  android:orientation="vertical"
  android:layout_width="fill_parent"
  android:layout_height="fill_parent">
  <TextView
    android:id="@+id/myTextView"
    android:layout_width="fill_parent"
    android:layout_height="fill_parent"
    android:gravity="center"
    android:textStyle="bold"
    android:textSize="30sp"
    android:text="CENTER"
    android:editable="false"
    android:singleLine="true"
    android:layout_margin="10dp"
  />
</LinearLayout>
```

3. Then create a series of animations that slide the current View out-of, and the next View into, the frame for each direction: left, right, up, and down. Each animation should have its own file.

3.1. Create `slide_bottom_in.xml`.

```xml
<set xmlns:android="http://schemas.android.com/apk/res/android"
    android:interpolator="@android:anim/accelerate_interpolator">
  <translate
    android:fromYDelta="-100%p"
    android:toYDelta="0"
    android:duration="700"
  />
</set>
```

3.2. Create `slide_bottom_out.xml`.

```xml
<set xmlns:android="http://schemas.android.com/apk/res/android"
    android:interpolator="@android:anim/accelerate_interpolator">
  <translate
    android:fromYDelta="0"
    android:toYDelta="100%p"
    android:duration="700"
  />
</set>
```

3.3. Create `slide_top_in.xml`.

```xml
<set xmlns:android="http://schemas.android.com/apk/res/android"
    android:interpolator="@android:anim/accelerate_interpolator">
  <translate
    android:fromYDelta="100%p"
    android:toYDelta="0"
    android:duration="700"
  />
</set>
```

3.4. Create `slide_top_out.xml`.

```xml
<set xmlns:android="http://schemas.android.com/apk/res/android"
    android:interpolator="@android:anim/accelerate_interpolator">
  <translate
    android:fromYDelta="0"
    android:toYDelta="-100%p"
    android:duration="700"
  />
</set>
```

3.5. Create `slide_left_in.xml`.

```xml
<set xmlns:android="http://schemas.android.com/apk/res/android"
    android:interpolator="@android:anim/accelerate_interpolator">
  <translate
    android:fromXDelta="100%p"
    android:toXDelta="0"
    android:duration="700"
  />
</set>
```

3.6. Create `slide_left_out.xml`.

```xml
<set xmlns:android="http://schemas.android.com/apk/res/android"
    android:interpolator="@android:anim/accelerate_interpolator">
  <translate
    android:fromXDelta="0"
    android:toXDelta="-100%p"
    android:duration="700"
  />
</set>
```

3.7. Create `slide_right_in.xml`.

```xml
<set xmlns:android="http://schemas.android.com/apk/res/android"
    android:interpolator="@android:anim/accelerate_interpolator">
  <translate
    android:fromXDelta="-100%p"
    android:toXDelta="0"
    android:duration="700"
  />
</set>
```

3.8. Create `slide_right_out.xml`.

```xml
<set xmlns:android="http://schemas.android.com/apk/res/android"
    android:interpolator="@android:anim/accelerate_interpolator">
  <translate
    android:fromXDelta="0"
    android:toXDelta="100%p"
    android:duration="700"
  />
</set>
```

4. Return to the `ContentSlider` Activity and get references to the Text View and each of the animations you created in Step 3.

```java
Animation slideInLeft;
Animation slideOutLeft;
Animation slideInRight;
Animation slideOutRight;
Animation slideInTop;
Animation slideOutTop;
Animation slideInBottom;
Animation slideOutBottom;
TextView myTextView;

@Override
public void onCreate(Bundle savedInstanceState) {
  super.onCreate(savedInstanceState);
  setContentView(R.layout.main);

  slideInLeft = AnimationUtils.loadAnimation(this,
    R.anim.slide_left_in);
  slideOutLeft = AnimationUtils.loadAnimation(this,
    R.anim.slide_left_out);
  slideInRight = AnimationUtils.loadAnimation(this,
    R.anim.slide_right_in);
```

```
slideOutRight = AnimationUtils.loadAnimation(this,
  R.anim.slide_right_out);
slideInTop = AnimationUtils.loadAnimation(this,
  R.anim.slide_top_in);
slideOutTop = AnimationUtils.loadAnimation(this,
  R.anim.slide_top_out);
slideInBottom = AnimationUtils.loadAnimation(this,
  R.anim.slide_bottom_in);
slideOutBottom = AnimationUtils.loadAnimation(this,
  R.anim.slide_bottom_out);

myTextView = (TextView)findViewById(R.id.myTextView);
}
```

Each screen transition consists of two animations chained together: sliding out the old text before sliding in the new text. Rather than create multiple Views, you can change the value of the View once it's "off screen" before sliding it back in from the opposite side.

5. Create a new method that applies a slide-out animation and waits for it to complete before modifying the text and initiating the slide-in animation.

```
private void applyAnimation(Animation _out,
                            Animation _in,
                            String _newText) {
  final String text = _newText;
  final Animation in = _in;

  // Ensure the text stays out of screen when the slide-out
  // animation has completed.
  _out.setFillAfter(true);

  // Create a listener to wait for the slide-out
  // animation to complete.
  _out.setAnimationListener(new AnimationListener() {
    public void onAnimationEnd(Animation _animation) {
      // Change the text
      myTextView.setText(text);
      // Slide it back in to view
      myTextView.startAnimation(in);
    }

    public void onAnimationRepeat(Animation _animation) {}
    public void onAnimationStart(Animation _animation) {}
  });

  // Apply the slide-out animation
  myTextView.startAnimation(_out);
}
```

6. The text displayed can represent nine positions. To keep track of the current location, create an enum for each position and an instance variable to track it.

```
TextPosition textPosition = TextPosition.Center;
enum TextPosition { UpperLeft, Top, UpperRight,
                    Left, Center, Right,
                    LowerLeft, Bottom, LowerRight };
```

7. Create a new method `movePosition` that takes the current position, and the direction to move, and calculates the new position. It should then execute the appropriate animation sequence created in Step 5.

```
private void movePosition(TextPosition _current,
                          TextPosition _directionPressed) {
  Animation in;
  Animation out;
  TextPosition newPosition;

  if (_directionPressed == TextPosition.Left){
    in = slideInLeft;
    out = slideOutLeft;
  }
  else if (_directionPressed == TextPosition.Right){
    in = slideInRight;
    out = slideOutRight;
  }
  else if (_directionPressed == TextPosition.Top){
    in = slideInTop;
    out = slideOutTop;
  }
  else {
    in = slideInBottom;
    out = slideOutBottom;
  }

  int newPosValue = _current.ordinal();
  int currentValue = _current.ordinal();

  // To simulate the effect of 'tilting' the device moving in one
  // direction should make text for the opposite direction appear.
  // Ie. Tilting right should make left appear.
  if (_directionPressed == TextPosition.Bottom)
    newPosValue = currentValue - 3;
  else if (_directionPressed == TextPosition.Top)
    newPosValue = currentValue + 3;
  else if (_directionPressed == TextPosition.Right) {
    if (currentValue % 3 != 0)
      newPosValue = currentValue - 1;
  }
  else if (_directionPressed == TextPosition.Left) {
    if ((currentValue+1) % 3 != 0)
      newPosValue = currentValue + 1;
  }

  if (newPosValue != currentValue &&
      newPosValue > -1 &&
      newPosValue < 9){
    newPosition = TextPosition.values()[newPosValue];

    applyAnimation(in, out, newPosition.toString());
    textPosition = newPosition;
  }
}
```

8.   Wire up the D-pad by overriding the Activity's `onKeyDown` handler to listen for key presses and trigger `movePosition` accordingly.

```
@Override
public boolean onKeyDown(int _keyCode, KeyEvent _event) {
  if (super.onKeyDown(_keyCode, _event))
    return true;

  if (_event.getAction() == KeyEvent.ACTION_DOWN){
    switch (_keyCode) {
      case (KeyEvent.KEYCODE_DPAD_LEFT):
        movePosition(textPosition, TextPosition.Left); return true;
      case (KeyEvent.KEYCODE_DPAD_RIGHT):
        movePosition(textPosition, TextPosition.Right); return true;
      case (KeyEvent.KEYCODE_DPAD_UP):
        movePosition(textPosition, TextPosition.Top); return true;
      case (KeyEvent.KEYCODE_DPAD_DOWN):
        movePosition(textPosition, TextPosition.Bottom);
        return true;
    }
  }
  return false;
}
```

All code snippets in this example are part of the Chapter 15 Animated Slider *project, available for download at Wrox.com.*

Running the application now will show a screen displaying "Center"; pressing any of the four directions will slide out this text and display the appropriate new position.

 As an extra step, you could wire up the accelerometer sensor rather than relying on pressing the D-pad.

Animating Layouts and View Groups

A `LayoutAnimation` is used to animate View Groups, applying a single Animation (or Animation Set) to each child View in a predetermined sequence.

Use a `LayoutAnimationController` to specify an Animation (or Animation Set) that's applied to each child View in a View Group. Each View it contains will have the same animation applied, but you can use the Layout Animation Controller to specify the order and start time for each View.

Android includes two `LayoutAnimationController` classes.

➤   `LayoutAnimationController`   Lets you select the start offset of each View (in milliseconds) and the order (`forward`, `reverse`, and `random`) to apply the animation to each child View.

➤   `GridLayoutAnimationController`   Is a derived class that lets you assign the animation sequence of the child Views using grid row and column references.

Creating Layout Animations

To create a new Layout Animation, start by defining the Animation to apply to each child View. Then create a new `LayoutAnimation`, either in code or as an external animation resource, that references the animation to apply and defines the order and timing in which to apply it.

Listing 15-16 show the definition of a simple Animation stored as popin.xml in the res/anim folder, and a Layout Animation definition stored as popinlayout.xml.

The Layout Animation applies a simple "pop-in" animation randomly to each child View of any View Group it's assigned to.

LISTING 15-16: Creating a Layout Animation

res/anim/popin.xml

```xml
<set xmlns:android="http://schemas.android.com/apk/res/android"
     android:interpolator="@android:anim/accelerate_interpolator">
  <scale
    android:fromXScale="0.0" android:toXScale="1.0"
    android:fromYScale="0.0" android:toYScale="1.0"
    android:pivotX="50%"
    android:pivotY="50%"
    android:duration="400"
  />
</set>
```

res/anim/popinlayout.xml

```xml
<layoutAnimation
  xmlns:android="http://schemas.android.com/apk/res/android"
  android:delay="0.5"
  android:animationOrder="random"
  android:animation="@anim/popin"
/>
```

Using Layout Animations

Once you've defined a Layout Animation, you can apply it to a View Group either in code or in the layout XML resource. In XML this is done using the `android:layoutAnimation` tag in the layout definition:

```xml
android:layoutAnimation="@anim/popinlayout"
```

To set a Layout Animation in code, call `setLayoutAnimation` on the View Group, passing in a reference to the `LayoutAnimation` object you want to apply.

In each case, the Layout Animation will execute once, when the View Group is first laid out. You can force it to execute again by calling `scheduleLayoutAnimation` on the `ViewGroup` object. The animation will then be executed the next time the View Group is laid out.

Layout Animations also support Animation Listeners.

In Listing 15-17, a View Group's animation is re-run with a listener attached to trigger additional actions once it's complete.

LISTING 15-17: Applying a Layout Animation and Animation Listener

```
aViewGroup.setLayoutAnimationListener(new AnimationListener() {
  public void onAnimationEnd(Animation _animation) {
    // TODO: Actions on animation complete.
  }
  public void onAnimationRepeat(Animation _animation) {}
  public void onAnimationStart(Animation _animation) {}
});

aViewGroup.scheduleLayoutAnimation();
```

Creating and Using Frame-by-Frame Animations

Frame-by-frame animations are akin to traditional cel-based cartoons in which an image is chosen for each frame. Where tweened animations use the target View to supply the content of the animation, frame-by-frame animations let you specify a series of `Drawable` objects that are used as the background to a View.

The `AnimationDrawable` class is used to create a new frame-by-frame animation presented as a `Drawable` resource. You can define your Animation Drawable resource as an external resource in your project's res/drawable folder using XML.

Use the `<animation-list>` tag to group a collection of `<item>` nodes, each of which uses a `drawable` attribute to define an image to display, and a `duration` attribute to specify the time (in milliseconds) to display it.

Listing 15-18 shows how to create a simple animation that displays a rocket taking off (rocket images not included). The file is stored as res/drawable/animated_rocket.xml.

LISTING 15-18: Creating a frame-by-frame animation in XML

```
<animation-list
  xmlns:android="http://schemas.android.com/apk/res/android"
  android:oneshot="false">
  <item android:drawable="@drawable/rocket1" android:duration="500" />
  <item android:drawable="@drawable/rocket2" android:duration="500" />
  <item android:drawable="@drawable/rocket3" android:duration="500" />
</animation-list>
```

To display your animation, set it as the background to a View using the `setBackgroundResource` method.

```
ImageView image = (ImageView)findViewById(R.id.my_animation_frame);
image.setBackgroundResource(R.drawable.animated_rocket);
```

Alternatively, use the `setBackgroundDrawable` to use a Drawable instance instead of a resource reference. Run the animation calling its `start` method.

```
AnimationDrawable animation = (AnimationDrawable)image.getBackground();
animation.start();
```

Advanced Canvas Drawing

You were introduced to the `Canvas` class in Chapter 4, where you learned how to create your own Views. The Canvas was also used in Chapter 8 to annotate Overlays for `MapViews`.

The concept of the canvas is a common metaphor used in graphics programming and generally consists of three basic drawing components:

➤ `Canvas`   Supplies the draw methods that paint drawing primitives onto the underlying bitmap.

➤ `Paint`   Also referred to as a "brush," `Paint` lets you specify how a primitive is drawn on the bitmap.

➤ `Bitmap`   Is the surface being drawn on.

Most of the advanced techniques described in this chapter involve variations and modifications to the `Paint` object that let you add depth and texture to otherwise flat raster drawings.

The Android drawing API supports translucency, gradient fills, rounded rectangles, and anti-aliasing. Unfortunately, owing to resource limitations, it does not yet support vector graphics; instead, it uses traditional raster-style repaints.

The result of this raster approach is improved efficiency, but changing a `Paint` object will not affect primitives that have already been drawn; it will affect only new elements.

 If you've got a Windows development background, the two-dimensional (2D) drawing capabilities of Android are roughly equivalent to those available in GDI+.

What Can You Draw?

The `Canvas` class wraps up the bitmap that's used as a surface for your artistic endeavors; it also exposes the `draw*` methods used to implement your designs.

Without going into detail about each of the `draw` methods, the following list provides a taste of the primitives available:

➤ `drawARGB/drawRGB/drawColor`   Fill the canvas with a single color.

➤ `drawArc`   Draws an arc between two angles within an area bounded by a rectangle.

➤ `drawBitmap`   Draws a bitmap on the Canvas. You can alter the appearance of the target bitmap by specifying a target size or using a matrix to transform it.

➤ `drawBitmapMesh`   Draws a bitmap using a mesh that lets you manipulate the appearance of the target by moving points within it.

➤ `drawCircle`   Draws a circle of a specified radius centered on a given point.

➤ `drawLine(s)`   Draws a line (or series of lines) between two points.

➤ `drawOval`   Draws an oval bounded by the rectangle specified.

➤ `drawPaint`   Fills the entire Canvas with the specified Paint.

➤ `drawPath`   Draws the specified Path. A `Path` object is often used to hold a collection of drawing primitives within a single object.

➤ `drawPicture`   Draws a `Picture` object within the specified rectangle.

➤ `drawPosText`   Draws a text string specifying the offset of each character.

➤ `drawRect`   Draws a rectangle.

➤ `drawRoundRect`   Draws a rectangle with rounded edges.

➤ `drawText`   Draws a text string on the Canvas. The text font, size, color, and rendering properties are all set in the `Paint` object used to render the text.

➤ `drawTextOnPath`   Draws text that follows along a specified path.

➤ `drawVertices`   Draws a series of tri-patches specified as a series of vertex points.

Each of these drawing methods lets you specify a `Paint` object to render it. In the following sections, you'll learn how to create and modify Paint objects to get the most out of your drawing.

Getting the Most from Your Paint

The `Paint` class represents a paint brush and palette. It lets you choose how to render the primitives you draw onto the Canvas using the draw methods described in the previous section. By modifying the `Paint` object, you can control the color, style, font, and special effects used when drawing.

Most simply, `setColor` lets you select the color of a Paint while the style of a `Paint` object (controlled using `setStyle`) lets you decide if you want to draw only the outline of a drawing object (STROKE), just the filled portion (FILL), or both (STROKE_AND_FILL).

Beyond these simple controls, the `Paint` class also supports transparency and can also be modified with a variety of Shaders, filters, and effects to provide a rich palette of complex paints and brushes.

The Android SDK includes several excellent projects that demonstrate most of the features available in the `Paint` class. They are available in the graphics subfolder of the API demos at:

```
[sdk root folder]\samples\ApiDemos\src\com\android\samples\graphics
```

In the following sections, you'll learn what some of these features are and how to use them. These sections outline what can be achieved (such as gradients and edge embossing) without exhaustively listing all possible alternatives.

Using Translucency

All colors in Android include an opacity component (alpha channel).

You define an alpha value for a color when you create it using the `argb` or `parseColor` methods:

```
// Make color red and 50% transparent
int opacity = 127;
int intColor = Color.argb(opacity, 255, 0, 0);
int parsedColor = Color.parseColor("#7FFF0000");
```

Alternatively, you can set the opacity of an existing Paint object using the setAlpha method:

```
// Make color 50% transparent
int opacity = 127;
myPaint.setAlpha(opacity);
```

Creating a paint color that's not 100 percent opaque means that any primitive drawn with it will be partially transparent — making whatever is drawn beneath it partially visible.

You can use transparency effects in any class or method that uses colors including Paint colors, Shaders, and Mask Filters.

Introducing Shaders

Extensions of the Shader class let you create Paints that fill drawn objects with more than a single solid color.

The most common use of Shaders is to define gradient fills; gradients are an excellent way to add depth and texture to 2D drawings. Android includes three gradient Shaders as well as a Bitmap Shader and a Compose Shader.

Trying to describe painting techniques seems inherently futile, so have a look at Figure 15-1 to get an idea of how each of the Shaders works. Represented from left to right are LinearGradient, RadialGradient, and SweepGradient.

Not included in the image in Figure 15-1 is the ComposeShader, which lets you create a composite of multiple Shaders and the BitmapShader that lets you create a paint brush based on a bitmap image.

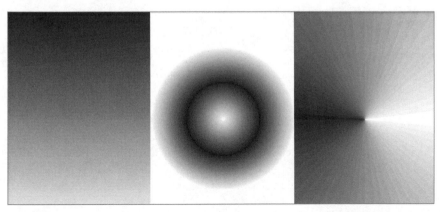

FIGURE 15-1

To use a Shader when drawing, apply it to a Paint using the setShader method:

```
Paint shaderPaint = new Paint();
shaderPaint.setShader(myLinearGradient);
```

Anything you draw with this Paint will be filled with the Shader you specified rather than the paint color.

Defining Gradient Shaders

As shown in the previous section, using gradient Shaders lets you fill drawings with an interpolated color range; you can define the gradient in two ways. The first is a simple transition between two colors, as shown in the LinearGradientShader in the Listing 15-19.

LISTING 15-19: Creating a Linear Gradient Shader

```
int colorFrom = Color.BLACK;
int colorTo = Color.WHITE;

LinearGradient linearGradientShader = new LinearGradient(x1, y1, x2, y2,
                                                         colorFrom,
                                                         colorTo,
                                                         TileMode.CLAMP);
```

The second alternative is to specify a more complex series of colors distributed at set proportions, as shown in Listing 15-20.

LISTING 15-20: Creating a Radial Gradient Shader

```
int[] gradientColors = new int[3];
gradientColors[0] = Color.GREEN;
gradientColors[1] = Color.YELLOW;
gradientColors[2] = Color.RED;

float[] gradientPositions = new float[3];
gradientPositions[0] = 0.0f;
gradientPositions[1] = 0.5f;
gradientPositions[2] = 1.0f;

RadialGradient radialGradientShader = new RadialGradient(centerX, centerY,
                                                         radius,
                                                         gradientColors,
                                                         gradientPositions,
                                                         TileMode.CLAMP);
```

Each of the gradient Shaders (linear, radial, and sweep) lets you define the gradient fill using either of these techniques.

Using Shader Tile Modes

The brush sizes of the gradient Shaders are defined using explicit bounding rectangles or center points and radius lengths; the Bitmap Shader implies a brush size through its bitmap size.

If the area defined by your Shader brush is smaller than the area being filled, the `TileMode` determines how the remaining area will be covered.

➤ CLAMP   Uses the edge colors of the Shader to fill the extra space

➤ MIRROR   Flips the Shader image horizontally and vertically so that each image seams with the last

➤ REPEAT   Repeats the Shader image horizontally and vertically, but doesn't flip it

Using Mask Filters

The `MaskFilter` classes let you assign edge effects to your Paint.

Extensions to `MaskFilter` apply transformations to the alpha-channel of a Paint along its outer edge. Android includes the following Mask Filters:

➤ BlurMaskFilter   Specifies a blur style and radius to feather the edges of your Paint

➤ EmbossMaskFilter   Specifies the direction of the light source and ambient light level to add an embossing effect

To apply a Mask Filter, use the `setMaskFilter` method, passing in a `MaskFilter` object. Listing 15-21 applies an `EmbossMaskFilter` to an existing Paint.

LISTING 15-21: Applying an Emboss Mask Filter to a Paint

```java
// Set the direction of the light source
float[] direction = new float[]{ 1, 1, 1 };
// Set the ambient light level
float light = 0.4f;
// Choose a level of specularity to apply
float specular = 6;
// Apply a level of blur to apply to the mask
float blur = 3.5f;
EmbossMaskFilter emboss = new EmbossMaskFilter(direction, light,
                                               specular, blur);

// Apply the mask
myPaint.setMaskFilter(emboss);
```

The `FingerPaint` API demo included in the SDK is an excellent example of how to use `MaskFilters`. It demonstrates the effect of both the emboss and blur filters.

Using Color Filters

Where Mask Filters are transformations of the alpha-channel of a Paint, a `ColorFilter` applies a transformation to each of the RGB channels. All `ColorFilter`-derived classes ignore the alpha-channel when performing their transformations.

Android includes three Color Filters:

➤ ColorMatrixColorFilter   Lets you specify a 4 x 5 ColorMatrix to apply to a Paint. Color Matrixes are commonly used to perform image processing programmatically and are useful as they support chaining transformations using matrix multiplication.

➤ `LightingColorFilter` Multiplies the RGB channels by the first color before adding the second. The result of each transformation will be clamped between 0 and 255.

➤ `PorterDuffColorFilter` Lets you use any one of the 16 Porter-Duff rules for digital image compositing to apply a specified color to the Paint.

Apply `ColorFilters` using the `setColorFilter` method:

```
myPaint.setColorFilter(new LightingColorFilter(Color.BLUE, Color.RED));
```

There is an excellent example of using a Color Filter and Color Matrixes in the `ColorMatrixSample` API example.

Using Path Effects

The effects so far have affected the way the Paint *fills* a drawing; Path Effects are used to control how its outline (or stroke) is drawn.

Path Effects are particularly useful for drawing Path primitives, but they can be applied to any Paint to affect the way the stroke is drawn.

Using Path Effects, you can change the appearance of a shape's corners and control the appearance of the outline. Android includes several Path Effects including:

➤ `CornerPathEffect` Lets you smooth sharp corners in the shape of a primitive by replacing them with rounded corners.

➤ `DashPathEffect` Rather than drawing a solid outline, you can use the `DashPathEffect` to create an outline of broken lines (dashes/dots). You can specify any repeating pattern of solid/empty line segments.

➤ `DiscretePathEffect` Similar to the `DashPathEffect`, but with added randomness. Specifies the length of each segment and a degree of deviation from the original path to use when drawing it.

➤ `PathDashPathEffect` This effect lets you define a new shape (path) to use as a stamp to outline the original path.

The following effects let you combine multiple Path Effects to a single Paint.

➤ `SumPathEffect` Adds two effects to a path in sequence, such that each effect is applied to the original path and the two results are combined.

➤ `ComposePathEffect` Applies first one effect and then applies the second effect to the result of the first.

Path Effects that modify the shape of the object being drawn will change the area of the affected shape. This ensures that any fill effects being applied to the same shape are drawn within the new bounds.

Path Effects are applied to `Paint` objects using the `setPathEffect` method.

```
borderPaint.setPathEffect(new CornerPathEffect(5));
```

The Path Effects API sample gives an excellent guide to how to apply each of these effects.

Changing the Xfermode

Change a Paint's `Xfermode` to affect the way it paints new colors on top of what's already on the Canvas.

Under normal circumstances, painting on top of an existing drawing will layer the new shape on top. If the new Paint is fully opaque, it will totally obscure the paint underneath; if it's partially transparent, it will tint the colors underneath.

The following `Xfermode` subclasses let you change this behavior:

➤   `AvoidXfermode`   Specifies a color and tolerance to force your Paint to avoid drawing over (or only draw over) it.

➤   `PixelXorXfermode`   Applies a simple pixel XOR operation when covering existing colors.

➤   `PorterDuffXfermode`   This is a very powerful transfer mode with which you can use any of the 16 Porter-Duff rules for image composition to control how the paint interacts with the existing canvas image.

To apply transfer modes, use the `setXferMode` method:

```
AvoidXfermode avoid = new AvoidXfermode(Color.BLUE, 10,
                                        AvoidXfermode.Mode.AVOID);
borderPen.setXfermode(avoid);
```

Improving Paint Quality with Anti-Aliasing

When you create a new `Paint` object, you can pass in several flags that affect the way the Paint will be rendered. One of the most interesting is the `ANTI_ALIAS_FLAG`, which ensures that diagonal lines drawn with this paint are anti-aliased to give a smooth appearance (at the cost of performance).

Anti-aliasing is particularly important when drawing text, as anti-aliased text can be significantly easier to read. To create even smoother text effects, you can apply the `SUBPIXEL_TEXT_FLAG`, which will apply subpixel anti-aliasing.

You can also set both of these flags manually using the `setSubpixelText` and `setAntiAlias` methods:

```
myPaint.setSubpixelText(true);
myPaint.setAntiAlias(true);
```

Canvas Drawing Best Practice

2D owner-draw operations tend to be expensive in terms of processor use; inefficient drawing routines can block the GUI thread and have a detrimental effect on application responsiveness. This is particularly true in a resource-constrained environment with a single, limited processor.

You need to be aware of the resource drain and CPU-cycle cost of your `onDraw` methods, to ensure you don't end up with an attractive application that's completely unresponsive.

A lot of techniques exist to help minimize the resource drain associated with owner-drawn controls. Rather than focus on general principles, I'll describe some Android specific considerations for ensuring that you can create activities that look good and remain interactive (note that this list is not exhaustive):

➤ **Consider size and orientation**   When you're designing your Views and Overlays, be sure to consider (and test!) how they will look at different resolutions, pixel densities, and sizes.

➤ **Create static objects once**   Object creation and garbage collection are particularly expensive. Where possible, create drawing objects like `Paint` objects, Paths, and Shaders once, rather than recreating them each time the View is invalidated.

➤ **Remember `onDraw` is expensive**   Performing the `onDraw` method is an expensive process that forces Android to perform several image composition and bitmap construction operations. Many of the following points suggest ways to modify the appearance of your Canvas without having to redraw it:

  ➤ **Use Canvas transforms**   Use Canvas transforms like `rotate` and `translate` to simplify complex relational positioning of elements on your canvas. For example, rather than positioning and rotating each text element around a clock face, simply rotate the canvas 22.5 degrees, and draw the text in the same place.

  ➤ **Use Animations**   Consider using Animations to perform pre-set transformations of your View rather than manually redrawing it. Scale, rotation, and translation Animations can be performed on any View within an Activity and provide a resource-efficient way to provide zoom, rotate, or shake effects.

  ➤ **Consider using Bitmaps, 9 Patches, and Drawable resources**   If your Views feature static backgrounds, you should consider using a Drawable like a bitmap, scalable NinePatch, or static XML Drawable rather than dynamically creating it.

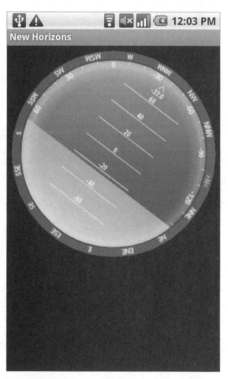

Advanced Compass Face Example

In Chapter 4, you created a simple compass UI. In Chapter 14 you returned to it, extending it to display the pitch and roll using the accelerometer hardware.

The UI of the View used in those examples was kept simple to keep the code in those chapters as clear as possible.

In the following example, you'll make some significant changes to the Compass View's `onDraw` method to change it from a simple, flat compass into a dynamic artificial horizon, as shown in Figure 15-2.

As the previous image is limited to black and white, you'll need to create the control in order to see the full effect.

FIGURE 15-2

1. Start by modifying the colors.xml resource file to include color values for the border gradient, the glass compass shading, the sky, and the ground. Also update the colors used for the border and the face markings.

```xml
<?xml version="1.0" encoding="utf-8"?>
<resources>
  <color name="text_color">#FFFF</color>
  <color name="background_color">#F000</color>
  <color name="marker_color">#FFFF</color>
  <color name="shadow_color">#7AAA</color>
  <color name="outer_border">#FF444444</color>
  <color name="inner_border_one">#FF323232</color>
  <color name="inner_border_two">#FF414141</color>
  <color name="inner_border">#FFFFFFFF</color>
  <color name="horizon_sky_from">#FFA52A2A</color>
  <color name="horizon_sky_to">#FFFFC125</color>
  <color name="horizon_ground_from">#FF5F9EA0</color>
  <color name="horizon_ground_to">#FF00008B</color>
</resources>
```

2. The Paint and Shader objects used for the sky and ground in the artificial horizon are created based on the size of the current View, so they're not static like the Paint objects you created in Chapter 4. Instead of creating Paint objects, construct the gradient arrays and colors they use.

```java
int[] borderGradientColors;
float[] borderGradientPositions;

int[] glassGradientColors;
float[] glassGradientPositions;

int skyHorizonColorFrom;
int skyHorizonColorTo;
int groundHorizonColorFrom;
int groundHorizonColorTo;
```

3. Update the Compass View's initCompassView method to initialize the variables created in Step 2 using the resources from Step 1. The existing method code can be left largely intact, with some changes to the textPaint, circlePaint, and markerPaint variables, as highlighted in the following code:

```java
protected void initCompassView() {
  setFocusable(true);
  // Get external resources
  Resources r = this.getResources();

  circlePaint = new Paint(Paint.ANTI_ALIAS_FLAG);
  circlePaint.setColor(R.color.background_color);
  circlePaint.setStrokeWidth(1);
  circlePaint.setStyle(Paint.Style.STROKE);

  northString = r.getString(R.string.cardinal_north);
  eastString = r.getString(R.string.cardinal_east);
  southString = r.getString(R.string.cardinal_south);
```

```
westString = r.getString(R.string.cardinal_west);

textPaint = new Paint(Paint.ANTI_ALIAS_FLAG);
textPaint.setColor(r.getColor(R.color.text_color));
textPaint.setFakeBoldText(true);
textPaint.setSubpixelText(true);
textPaint.setTextAlign(Align.LEFT);

textHeight = (int)textPaint.measureText("yY");

markerPaint = new Paint(Paint.ANTI_ALIAS_FLAG);
markerPaint.setColor(r.getColor(R.color.marker_color));
markerPaint.setAlpha(200);
markerPaint.setStrokeWidth(1);
markerPaint.setStyle(Paint.Style.STROKE);
markerPaint.setShadowLayer(2, 1, 1, r.getColor(R.color.shadow_color));
```

3.1.   Create the color and position arrays that will be used by a radial Shader to paint the outer border.

```
borderGradientColors = new int[4];
borderGradientPositions = new float[4];

borderGradientColors[3] = r.getColor(R.color.outer_border);
borderGradientColors[2] = r.getColor(R.color.inner_border_one);
borderGradientColors[1] = r.getColor(R.color.inner_border_two);
borderGradientColors[0] = r.getColor(R.color.inner_border);
borderGradientPositions[3] = 0.0f;
borderGradientPositions[2] = 1-0.03f;
borderGradientPositions[1] = 1-0.06f;
borderGradientPositions[0] = 1.0f;
```

3.2.   Now create the radial gradient color and position arrays that will be used to create the semitransparent "glass dome" that sits on top of the View to give it the illusion of depth.

```
glassGradientColors = new int[5];
glassGradientPositions = new float[5];

int glassColor = 245;
glassGradientColors[4] = Color.argb(65, glassColor,
                                    glassColor, glassColor);
glassGradientColors[3] = Color.argb(100, glassColor,
                                    glassColor, glassColor);
glassGradientColors[2] = Color.argb(50, glassColor,
                                    glassColor, glassColor);
glassGradientColors[1] = Color.argb(0, glassColor,
                                    glassColor, glassColor);
glassGradientColors[0] = Color.argb(0, glassColor,
                                    glassColor, glassColor);
glassGradientPositions[4] = 1-0.0f;
glassGradientPositions[3] = 1-0.06f;
glassGradientPositions[2] = 1-0.10f;
glassGradientPositions[1] = 1-0.20f;
glassGradientPositions[0] = 1-1.0f;
```

3.3. Finally, get the colors you'll use to create the linear gradients that will represent the sky and the ground in the artificial horizon.

```
skyHorizonColorFrom = r.getColor(R.color.horizon_sky_from);
skyHorizonColorTo = r.getColor(R.color.horizon_sky_to);

groundHorizonColorFrom = r.getColor(R.color.horizon_ground_from);
groundHorizonColorTo = r.getColor(R.color.horizon_ground_to);
}
```

4. Before you start drawing the face, create a new `enum` that stores each of the cardinal directions.

```
private enum CompassDirection { N, NNE, NE, ENE,
                                E, ESE, SE, SSE,
                                S, SSW, SW, WSW,
                                W, WNW, NW, NNW }
```

Now you need to completely replace the existing `onDraw` method. You'll start by figuring out some size-based values including the center of the View, the radius of the circular control, and the rectangles that will enclose the outer (heading) and inner (tilt and roll) face elements.

```
@Override
protected void onDraw(Canvas canvas) {
```

1. Calculate the width of the outer (heading) ring based on the size of the font used to draw the heading values.

```
float ringWidth = textHeight + 4;
```

2. Then calculate the height and width of the View, and use those values to establish the radius of the inner and outer face dials, as well as create the bounding boxes for each face.

```
int height = getMeasuredHeight();
int width =getMeasuredWidth();

int px = width/2;
int py = height/2;
Point center = new Point(px, py);

int radius = Math.min(px, py)-2;

RectF boundingBox = new RectF(center.x - radius,
                              center.y - radius,
                              center.x + radius,
                              center.y + radius);

RectF innerBoundingBox = new RectF(center.x - radius + ringWidth,
                                   center.y - radius + ringWidth,
                                   center.x + radius - ringWidth,
                                   center.y + radius - ringWidth);

float innerRadius = innerBoundingBox.height()/2;
```

3. With the dimensions of the View established, it's time to start drawing the faces.

Start from the bottom layer at the outside, and work your way in and up, starting with the outer face (heading). Create a new `RadialGradient` Shader using the colors and positions you defined in Step 3.2 of the previous code sample, and assign that Shader to a new Paint before using it to draw a circle.

```
RadialGradient borderGradient = new RadialGradient(px, py, radius,
  borderGradientColors, borderGradientPositions, TileMode.CLAMP);

Paint pgb = new Paint();
pgb.setShader(borderGradient);

Path outerRingPath = new Path();
outerRingPath.addOval(boundingBox, Direction.CW);

canvas.drawPath(outerRingPath, pgb);
```

4. Next you need to draw the artificial horizon. You do this by dividing the circular face into two sections, one representing the sky and the other the ground. The proportion of each section depends on the current pitch.

    Start by creating the `Shader` and `Paint` objects that will be used to draw the sky and earth.

```
LinearGradient skyShader = new LinearGradient(center.x,
  innerBoundingBox.top, center.x, innerBoundingBox.bottom,
  skyHorizonColorFrom, skyHorizonColorTo, TileMode.CLAMP);

Paint skyPaint = new Paint();
skyPaint.setShader(skyShader);

LinearGradient groundShader = new LinearGradient(center.x,
  innerBoundingBox.top, center.x, innerBoundingBox.bottom,
  groundHorizonColorFrom, groundHorizonColorTo, TileMode.CLAMP);

Paint groundPaint = new Paint();
groundPaint.setShader(groundShader);
```

5. Now normalize the pitch and roll values to clamp them within ±90 degrees and ±180 degrees, respectively.

```
float tiltDegree = pitch;
while (tiltDegree > 90 || tiltDegree < -90)
{
  if (tiltDegree > 90) tiltDegree = -90 + (tiltDegree - 90);
    if (tiltDegree < -90) tiltDegree = 90 - (tiltDegree + 90);
}

float rollDegree = roll;
while (rollDegree > 180 || rollDegree < -180)
{
  if (rollDegree > 180) rollDegree = -180 + (rollDegree - 180);
   if (rollDegree < -180) rollDegree = 180 - (rollDegree + 180);
}
```

6. Create paths that will fill each segment of the circle (ground and sky). The proportion of each segment should be related to the clamped pitch.

```
Path skyPath = new Path();
skyPath.addArc(innerBoundingBox,
               -tiltDegree,
               (180 + (2 * tiltDegree)));
```

7. Spin the canvas around the center in the opposite direction to the current roll, and draw the sky and ground paths using the Paints you created in Step 4.

```
canvas.rotate(-rollDegree, px, py);
canvas.drawOval(innerBoundingBox, groundPaint);
canvas.drawPath(skyPath, skyPaint);
canvas.drawPath(skyPath, markerPaint);
```

8. Next is the face marking. Start by calculating the start and end points for the horizontal horizon markings.

```
int markWidth = radius / 3;
int startX = center.x - markWidth;
int endX = center.x + markWidth;
```

9. To make the horizon values easier to read, you should ensure that the pitch scale always starts at the current value. The following code calculates the position of the interface between the ground and sky on the horizon face:

```
double h = innerRadius*Math.cos(Math.toRadians(90-tiltDegree));
double justTiltY = center.y - h;
```

10. Find the number of pixels representing each degree of tilt.

```
float pxPerDegree = (innerBoundingBox.height()/2)/45f;
```

11. Now iterate over 180 degrees, centered on the current tilt value, to give a sliding scale of possible pitch.

```
for (int i = 90; i >= -90; i -= 10)
{
  double ypos = justTiltY + i*pxPerDegree;

  // Only display the scale within the inner face.
  if ((ypos < (innerBoundingBox.top + textHeight)) ||
      (ypos > innerBoundingBox.bottom - textHeight))
    continue;

  // Draw a line and the tilt angle for each scale increment.
  canvas.drawLine(startX, (float)ypos,
                  endX, (float)ypos,
                  markerPaint);
  int displayPos = (int)(tiltDegree - i);
  String displayString = String.valueOf(displayPos);
  float stringSizeWidth = textPaint.measureText(displayString);
  canvas.drawText(displayString,
                  (int)(center.x-stringSizeWidth/2),
                  (int)(ypos)+1,
                  textPaint);
}
```

12. Now draw a thicker line at the earth/sky interface. Change the stroke thickness of the `markerPaint` object before drawing the line (then set it back to the previous value).

```
markerPaint.setStrokeWidth(2);
canvas.drawLine(center.x - radius / 2,
                (float)justTiltY,
                center.x + radius / 2,
                (float)justTiltY,
                markerPaint);
markerPaint.setStrokeWidth(1);
```

13. To make it easier to read the exact roll, you should draw an arrow and display a text string that shows the value.

Create a new `Path`, and use the `moveTo`/`lineTo` methods to construct an open arrow that points straight up. Draw the path and a text string that shows the current roll.

```
// Draw the arrow
Path rollArrow = new Path();
rollArrow.moveTo(center.x - 3, (int)innerBoundingBox.top + 14);
rollArrow.lineTo(center.x, (int)innerBoundingBox.top + 10);
rollArrow.moveTo(center.x + 3, innerBoundingBox.top + 14);
rollArrow.lineTo(center.x, innerBoundingBox.top + 10);
canvas.drawPath(rollArrow, markerPaint);
// Draw the string
String rollText = String.valueOf(rollDegree);
double rollTextWidth = textPaint.measureText(rollText);
canvas.drawText(rollText,
                (float)(center.x - rollTextWidth / 2),
                innerBoundingBox.top + textHeight + 2,
                textPaint);
```

14. Spin the canvas back to upright so that you can draw the rest of the face markings.

```
canvas.restore();
```

15. Draw the roll dial markings by rotating the canvas 10 degrees at a time to draw either a mark or a value. When you've completed the face, restore the canvas to its upright position.

```
canvas.save();
canvas.rotate(180, center.x, center.y);
for (int i = -180; i < 180; i += 10)
{
  // Show a numeric value every 30 degrees
  if (i % 30 == 0) {
    String rollString = String.valueOf(i*-1);
    float rollStringWidth = textPaint.measureText(rollString);
    PointF rollStringCenter =
      new PointF(center.x-rollStringWidth/2,
                 innerBoundingBox.top+1+textHeight);
    canvas.drawText(rollString,
                    rollStringCenter.x, rollStringCenter.y,
                    textPaint);
  }
  // Otherwise draw a marker line
```

```
    else {
      canvas.drawLine(center.x, (int)innerBoundingBox.top,
                      center.x, (int)innerBoundingBox.top + 5,
                      markerPaint);
    }

    canvas.rotate(10, center.x, center.y);
  }
canvas.restore();
```

16. The final step in creating the face is drawing the heading markers around the outside edge.

```
canvas.save();
canvas.rotate(-1*(bearing), px, py);

double increment = 22.5;

for (double i = 0; i < 360; i += increment) {
  CompassDirection cd = CompassDirection.values()
                            [(int)(i / 22.5)];
  String headString = cd.toString();

  float headStringWidth = textPaint.measureText(headString);
  PointF headStringCenter =
    new PointF(center.x - headStringWidth / 2,
               boundingBox.top + 1 + textHeight);

  if (i % increment == 0)
    canvas.drawText(headString,
                    headStringCenter.x, headStringCenter.y,
                    textPaint);
  else
    canvas.drawLine(center.x, (int)boundingBox.top,
                    center.x, (int)boundingBox.top + 3,
                    markerPaint);

  canvas.rotate((int)increment, center.x, center.y);
}
canvas.restore();
```

17. With the face complete, you get to add some finishing touches.

Start by adding a "glass dome" over the top to give the illusion of a watch face. Using the radial gradient array you constructed earlier, create a new Shader and Paint object. Use them to draw a circle over the inner face that makes it look like it's covered in glass.

```
RadialGradient glassShader =
  new RadialGradient(px, py, (int)innerRadius,
                     glassGradientColors,
                     glassGradientPositions,
                     TileMode.CLAMP);
Paint glassPaint = new Paint();
glassPaint.setShader(glassShader);

canvas.drawOval(innerBoundingBox, glassPaint);
```

18. All that's left is to draw two more circles as clean borders for the inner and outer face boundaries. Then restore the canvas to upright, and finish the `onDraw` method.

```
// Draw the outer ring
canvas.drawOval(boundingBox, circlePaint);

// Draw the inner ring
circlePaint.setStrokeWidth(2);
canvas.drawOval(innerBoundingBox, circlePaint);

canvas.restore();
}
```

All code snippets in this example are part of the Chapter 15 Artificial Horizon *project, available for download at Wrox.com.*

Bringing Map Overlays to Life

In Chapter 8, you learned how to use Overlays to add annotation layers to Map Views. The Canvas used for annotating Map View Overlays is the same class as the one used to draw new View controls. As a result, all of the advanced features described so far in this section can be used to enhance map Overlays.

That means you can use any of the draw methods, transparency, Shaders, Color Masks, and Filter Effects to create rich Overlays using the Android graphics framework.

Touch-screen interaction in Map Views is handled individually by each of its Overlays. To handle map taps within an Overlay, override the `onTap` event.

Listing 15-22 shows an `onTap` implementation that receives the map coordinates of the tap and the `MapView` on which the tap occurred.

LISTING 15-22: Handling Map View Overlay touch events

```
@Override
public boolean onTap(GeoPoint point, MapView map) {
    // Get the projection to convert to and from screen coordinates
    Projection projection = map.getProjection();

    // Return true if we handled this onTap()
    return [ ... hit test passed ... ];
}
```

The `MapView` can be used to obtain the Projection of the map when it was tapped. By using it in conjunction with the `GeoPoint` parameter, you can determine the position on screen of the real-world longitude and latitude pressed.

The `onTap` method of an Overlay derived class should return `true` if it has handled the tap (and `false` otherwise). If none of the Overlays assigned to a Map View return true, the tap event will be handled by the Map View itself, or failing that, by the Activity.

Introducing the Surface View

Under normal circumstances, your applications' Views are all drawn on the same GUI thread. This main application thread is also used for all user interaction (such as button clicks or text entry).

In Chapter 9, you learned how to move blocking processes onto background threads. Unfortunately, you can't do this with the onDraw method of a View, as modifying a GUI element from a background thread is explicitly disallowed.

When you need to update the View's UI rapidly, or the rendering code blocks the GUI thread for too long, the SurfaceView class is the answer. A Surface View wraps a Surface object rather than a Canvas. This is important because Surfaces can be drawn on from background threads. This is particularly useful for resource-intensive operations, or where rapid updates or high frame rates are required, such as when using 3D graphics, creating games, or previewing the camera in real time (as shown in Chapter 11).

The ability to draw independently of the GUI thread comes at the price of additional memory consumption, so while it's a useful — sometimes necessary — way to create custom Views, Surface Views should be used with caution.

When Should You Use a Surface View?

A Surface View can be used in exactly the same way as any View-derived class. You can apply animations and place them in layouts as you would any other View.

The Surface encapsulated by the Surface View supports drawing, using most of the standard Canvas methods described previously in this chapter, and also supports the full OpenGL ES library.

Using OpenGL, you can draw any supported 2D or 3D object onto the Surface, relying on hardware acceleration (where available) to significantly improve performance compared to simulating the same effects on a 2D canvas.

Surface Views are particularly useful for displaying dynamic 3D images, such as those featured in interactive games that provide immersive experiences. They're also the best choice for displaying real-time camera previews.

Creating a New Surface View

To create a new Surface View, create a new class that extends SurfaceView and implements SurfaceHolder.Callback.

The SurfaceHolder callback notifies the View when the underlying Surface is created, destroyed, or modified. It passes a reference to the SurfaceHolder object that contains a valid Surface.

A typical Surface View design pattern includes a Thread-derived class that accepts a reference to the current SurfaceHolder and independently updates it.

Listing 15-23 shows a Surface View implementation for drawing using a Canvas. A new Thread-derived class is created within the Surface View control, and all UI updates are handled within this new class.

LISTING 15-23: Surface View skeleton implementation

```java
import android.content.Context;
import android.graphics.Canvas;
import android.view.SurfaceHolder;
import android.view.SurfaceView;

public class MySurfaceView extends SurfaceView implements
  SurfaceHolder.Callback {

  private SurfaceHolder holder;
  private MySurfaceViewThread mySurfaceViewThread;
  private boolean hasSurface;

  MySurfaceView(Context context) {
    super(context);
    init();
  }

  private void init() {
    // Create a new SurfaceHolder and assign this class as its callback.
    holder = getHolder();
    holder.addCallback(this);
    hasSurface = false;
  }

  public void resume() {
    // Create and start the graphics update thread.
    if (mySurfaceViewThread == null) {
      mySurfaceViewThread = new MySurfaceViewThread();

      if (hasSurface == true)
        mySurfaceViewThread.start();
    }
  }

  public void pause() {
    // Kill the graphics update thread
    if (mySurfaceViewThread != null) {
      mySurfaceViewThread.requestExitAndWait();
      mySurfaceViewThread = null;
    }
  }

  public void surfaceCreated(SurfaceHolder holder) {
    hasSurface = true;
    if (mySurfaceViewThread != null)
      mySurfaceViewThread.start();
  }

  public void surfaceDestroyed(SurfaceHolder holder) {
    hasSurface = false;
    pause();
  }
```

```java
      public void surfaceChanged(SurfaceHolder holder, int format,
                                 int w, int h) {
        if (mySurfaceViewThread != null)
          mySurfaceViewThread.onWindowResize(w, h);
      }

      class MySurfaceViewThread extends Thread {
        private boolean done;

        MySurfaceViewThread() {
          super();
          done = false;
        }

        @Override
        public void run() {
          SurfaceHolder surfaceHolder = holder;

          // Repeat the drawing loop until the thread is stopped.
          while (!done) {
            // Lock the surface and return the canvas to draw onto.
            Canvas canvas = surfaceHolder.lockCanvas();
            // TODO: Draw on the canvas!
            // Unlock the canvas and render the current image.
            surfaceHolder.unlockCanvasAndPost(canvas);
          }
        }

        public void requestExitAndWait() {
          // Mark this thread as complete and combine into
          // the main application thread.
          done = true;
          try {
            join();
          } catch (InterruptedException ex) { }
        }

        public void onWindowResize(int w, int h) {
          // Deal with a change in the available surface size.
        }
      }
    }
```

Creating 3D Controls with a Surface View

Android includes full support for the OpenGL ES 3D rendering framework including support for hardware acceleration on devices that offer it. The SurfaceView provides a Surface onto which you can render your OpenGL scenes.

OpenGL is commonly used in desktop applications to provide dynamic 3D interfaces and animations. Resource-constrained devices don't have the capacity for polygon handling that's available on desktop PCs and gaming devices that feature dedicated 3D graphics processors. Within your applications, consider the load your 3D Surface View will be placing on your processor, and attempt to keep the total number of polygons being displayed, and the rate at which they're updated, as low as possible.

Creating a Doom clone for Android is well out of the scope of this book, so I'll leave it to you to test the limits of what's possible in a mobile 3D user interface. Check out the `GLSurfaceView` API demo example included in the SDK distribution to see an example of the OpenGL ES framework in action.

Creating Interactive Controls

Anyone who's used a mobile phone will be painfully aware of the challenges associated with designing intuitive user interfaces for mobile devices. Touch screens have been available on mobiles for many years, but it's only recently that touch-enabled interfaces have been designed to be used by fingers rather than styluses.

Full physical keyboards have also become common, with the compact size of the slide-out or flip-out keyboard introducing its own challenges.

As an open framework, Android is expected to be available on a wide variety of devices featuring many different permutations of input technologies including touch screens, D-pads, trackballs, and keyboards.

The challenge for you as a developer is to create intuitive user interfaces that make the most of whatever input hardware is available, while introducing as few hardware dependencies as possible.

The techniques described in this section show how to listen for (and react to) user input from key presses, trackball events, and touch-screen taps using the following event handlers in Views and Activities:

➤ `onKeyDown`   Called when any hardware key is pressed

➤ `onKeyUp`   Called when any hardware key is released

➤ `onTrackballEvent`   Triggered by movement on the trackball

➤ `onTouchEvent`   The touch-screen event handler, triggered when the touch screen is touched, released, or dragged

Using the Touch Screen

Mobile touch screens have existed since the days of the Apple Newton and the Palm Pilot, although their usability has had mixed reviews. Recently this technology has enjoyed a popular resurgence, with devices like the Nintendo DS and the Apple iPhone using touch screens in innovative ways.

Modern mobiles are all about finger input — a design principle that assumes users will be using their fingers rather than a specialized stylus to touch the screen.

Finger-based touch makes interaction less precise and is often based more on movement than simple contact. Android's native applications make extensive use of finger-based touchscreen interfaces, including the use of dragging motions to scroll through lists or perform actions.

To create a View or Activity that uses touch-screen interaction, override the `onTouchEvent` handler.

```
@Override
public boolean onTouchEvent(MotionEvent event) {
  return super.onTouchEvent(event);
}
```

Return `true` if you have handled the screen press; otherwise, return `false` to pass events through a stack of Views and Activities until the touch has been successfully handled.

Processing Single and Multiple Touch Events

The `onTouchEvent` handler is fired when the user touches the screen, once each time the position changes, and again when the contact ends. Android 2.0 (API level 5) introduced platform support for processing an arbitrary number of simultaneous touch events. Each touch event is allocated a separate pointer identifier that is referenced in the Motion Event parameter.

 Not all touch-screen hardware reports multiple simultaneous screen presses. In cases where the hardware does not support multiple touches, the platform will return a single touch event.

Call `getAction` on the `MotionEvent` parameter to find the event type that triggered the handler. For either a single touch device, or the first touch event on a multitouch device, you can use the `ACTION_UP/DOWN/MOVE/CANCEL/OUTSIDE` constants to find the event type as shown in Listing 15-24.

LISTING 15-24: Handling single (or first) touch events

```
@Override
public boolean onTouchEvent(MotionEvent event) {
  int action = event.getAction();
  switch (action) {
    case (MotionEvent.ACTION_DOWN)   : // Touch screen pressed
                                       break;
    case (MotionEvent.ACTION_UP)     : // Touch screen touch ended
                                       break;
    case (MotionEvent.ACTION_MOVE)   : // Contact has moved across screen
                                       break;
    case (MotionEvent.ACTION_CANCEL) : // Touch event cancelled
                                       break;
    case (MotionEvent.ACTION_OUTSIDE): // Movement has occurred outside the
                                       // bounds of the screen element
                                       // being monitored
                                       break;
  }
  return super.onTouchEvent(event);
}
```

To track touch events from multiple pointers, you need to apply the `MotionEvent.ACTION_MASK` and `MotionEvent.ACTION_POINTER_ID_MASK` to find the touch event (either `ACTION_POINTER_DOWN` or

ACTION_POINTER_UP) and the pointer ID that triggered it, respectively. Call getPointerCount to find if this is a multiple-touch event as shown in Listing 15-25.

LISTING 15-25: Handling multiple-touch events

```
@Override
public boolean onTouchEvent(MotionEvent event) {
    int action = event.getAction();

    if (event.getPointerCount() > 1) {
        int actionPointerId = action & MotionEvent.ACTION_POINTER_ID_MASK;
        int actionEvent = action & MotionEvent.ACTION_MASK;
        // Do something with the pointer ID and event.
    }
    return super.onTouchEvent(event);
}
```

The Motion Event also includes the coordinates of the current screen contact. You can access these coordinates using the getX and getY methods. These methods return the coordinate relative to the responding View or Activity.

In the case of multiple-touch events, each Motion Event includes the current position of each pointer. To find the position of a given pointer, pass its index into the getX or getY methods. Note that its index is **not** equivalent to the pointer ID. To find the index for a given pointer use the findPointerIndex method, passing in the pointer ID whose index you need as shown in Listing 15-26.

LISTING 15-26: Finding screen touch coordinates

```
int xPos = -1;
int yPos = -1;

if (event.getPointerCount() > 1) {
    int actionPointerId = action & MotionEvent.ACTION_POINTER_ID_MASK;
    int actionEvent = action & MotionEvent.ACTION_MASK;

    int pointerIndex = findPointerIndex(actionPointerId);
    xPos = (int)event.getX(pointerIndex);
    yPos = (int)event.getY(pointerIndex);
}
else {
    // Single touch event.
    xPos = (int)event.getX();
    yPos = (int)event.getY();
}
```

The Motion Event parameter also includes the pressure being applied to the screen using getPressure, a method that returns a value usually between 0 (no pressure) and 1 (normal pressure).

 Depending on the calibration of the hardware, it may be possible to return values greater than 1.

Finally, you can also determine the normalized size of the current contact area using the getSize method. This method returns a value between 0 and 1, where 0 suggests a very precise measurement and 1 indicates a possible "fat touch" event in which the user may not have intended to press anything.

Tracking Movement

Whenever the current touch contact position, pressure, or size changes, a new onTouchEvent is triggered with an ACTION_MOVE action.

As well as the fields described previously, the Motion Event parameter can include historical values. This history represents all the movement events that have occurred between the previously handled onTouchEvent and this one, allowing Android to buffer rapid movement changes to provide fine-grained capture of movement data.

You can find the size of the history by calling getHistorySize, which returns the number of movement positions available for the current event. You can then obtain the times, pressures, sizes, and positions of each of the historical events, using a series of getHistorical* methods and passing in the position index, as shown in Listing 15-27. Note that as with the getX and getY methods described earlier, you can pass in a pointer index value to track historical touch events for multiple cursors.

LISTING 15-27: Finding historical touch event values

```
int historySize = event.getHistorySize();
long time = event.getHistoricalEventTime(i);

if (event.getPointerCount() > 1) {
  int actionPointerId = action & MotionEvent.ACTION_POINTER_ID_MASK;
  int pointerIndex = findPointerIndex(actionPointerId);
  for (int i = 0; i < historySize; i++) {
    float pressure = event.getHistoricalPressure(pointerIndex, i);
    float x = event.getHistoricalX(pointerIndex, i);
    float y = event.getHistoricalY(pointerIndex, i);
    float size = event.getHistoricalSize(pointerIndex, i);
    // TODO: Do something with each point
  }
}
else {
  for (int i = 0; i < historySize; i++) {
    float pressure = event.getHistoricalPressure(i);
    float x = event.getHistoricalX(i);
    float y = event.getHistoricalY(i);
    float size = event.getHistoricalSize(i);
    // TODO: Do something with each point
  }
}
```

The normal pattern used for handling movement events is to process each of the historical events first, followed by the current Motion Event values, as shown in Listing 15-28.

LISTING 15-28: Handling touch screen movement events

```java
@Override
public boolean onTouchEvent(MotionEvent event) {

  int action = event.getAction();

  switch (action) {
    case (MotionEvent.ACTION_MOVE)
    {
      int historySize = event.getHistorySize();
      for (int i = 0; i < historySize; i++) {
        float x = event.getHistoricalX(i);
        float y = event.getHistoricalY(i);
        processMovement(x, y);
      }

      float x = event.getX();
      float y = event.getY();
      processMovement(x, y);

      return true;
    }
  }

  return super.onTouchEvent(event);
}

private void processMovement(float _x, float _y) {
  // Todo: Do something on movement.
}
```

Using an On Touch Listener

You can listen for touch events without subclassing an existing View by attaching an `OnTouchListener` to any `View` object, using the `setOnTouchListener` method. Listing 15-29 demonstrates how to assign a new `OnTouchListener` implementation to an existing View within an Activity.

LISTING 15-29: Assigning an On Touch Listener to an existing View

```java
myView.setOnTouchListener(new OnTouchListener() {
  public boolean onTouch(View _view, MotionEvent _event) {
    // TODO Respond to motion events
    return false;
  }
});
```

Using the Device Keys, Buttons, and D-Pad

Button and key-press events for all hardware keys are handled by the `onKeyDown` and `onKeyUp` handlers of the active Activity or the focused View. This includes keyboard keys, D-pad, volume, back, dial, and hang-up buttons. The only exception is the *home* key, which is reserved to ensure that users can never get locked within an application.

To have your View or Activity react to button presses, override the `onKeyUp` and `onKeyDown` event handlers as shown in Listing 15-30.

Available for download on Wrox.com

LISTING 15-30: Handling key press events

```
@Override
public boolean onKeyDown(int _keyCode, KeyEvent _event) {
  // Perform on key pressed handling, return true if handled
  return false;
}

@Override
public boolean onKeyUp(int _keyCode, KeyEvent _event) {
  // Perform on key released handling, return true if handled
  return false;
}
```

The `keyCode` parameter contains the value of the key being pressed; compare it to the static key code values available from the `KeyEvent` class to perform key-specific processing.

The `KeyEvent` parameter also includes the `isAltPressed`, `isShiftPressed`, and `isSymPressed` methods to determine if the function, shift, and symbol/alt keys are also being held. The static `isModifierKey` method accepts the `keyCode` and determines if this key event was triggered by the user pressing one of these modifier keys.

Using the On Key Listener

To respond to key presses within existing Views in your Activities, implement an `OnKeyListener`, and assign it to a View using the `setOnKeyListener` method. Rather than implementing a separate method for key-press and key-release events, the `OnKeyListener` uses a single `onKey` event, as shown in Listing 15-31.

Available for download on Wrox.com

LISTING 15-31: Implementing an On Key Listener within an Activity

```
myView.setOnKeyListener(new OnKeyListener() {
    public boolean onKey(View v, int keyCode, KeyEvent event)
    {
      // TODO Process key press event, return true if handled
      return false;
    }
});
```

Use the `keyCode` parameter to find the key pressed. The `KeyEvent` parameter is used to determine if the key has been pressed or released, where `ACTION_DOWN` represents a key press, and `ACTION_UP` signals its release.

Using the Trackball

Many mobile devices offer a trackball as a useful alternative (or addition) to the touch screen and D-pad. Trackball events are handled by overriding the `onTrackballEvent` method in your View or Activity.

Like touch events, trackball movement is included in a `MotionEvent` parameter. In this case, the `MotionEvent` contains the relative movement of the trackball since the last trackball event, normalized so that 1 represents the equivalent movement caused by the user pressing the D-pad key.

Vertical change can be obtained using the `getY` method, and horizontal scrolling is available through the `getX` method, as shown in Listing 15-32.

LISTING 15-32: Using the On Trackball Event Listener

```
@Override
public boolean onTrackballEvent(MotionEvent _event) {
    float vertical = _event.getY();
    float horizontal = _event.getX();
    // TODO Process trackball movement.
    return false;
}
```

SUMMARY

This final chapter has served as a catch-all for some of the more complex Android features that were glossed over in earlier chapters.

You learned more about Android's security mechanisms, in particular, examining the permissions mechanism used to control access to Content Providers, Services, Activities, Broadcast Receivers, and broadcast Intents.

You explored the possibilities of interprocess communication using the Android Interface Definition Language to create rich interfaces between application components.

Much of the last part of the chapter focused on the `Canvas` class, as some of the more complex features available in the 2D drawing library were exposed. This part of the chapter included an examination of the drawing primitives available and a closer look at the possibilities of the `Paint` class.

You learned to use transparency and create gradient Shaders before looking at Mask Filters, Color Filters, and Path Effects. You also learned how to use hardware acceleration on 2D canvas-based Views, as well as some Canvas drawing best-practice techniques.

You were then introduced to the `SurfaceView` — a graphical control that lets you render graphics onto a surface from a background thread. This led to an introduction of rendering 3D graphics using the OpenGL ES framework and using the Surface View to provide live camera previews.

Finally, you learned the details for providing interactivity within your Activities and View by listening for and interpreting touch screen, trackball, and key press events.

You also investigated:

➤ How to use Wake Locks to prevent the host device from going into standby mode.

➤ Using the Text To Speech engine to add voice output to your applications.

➤ Some of the possibilities of using the Internet as a data source, or processing middle tier, to keep your applications lightweight and information-rich.

➤ How to animate Views and View Groups using tweened animations.

➤ How to create frame-by-frame animations.

➤ Which drawing primitives you can use to draw on a canvas.

➤ How to get the most out of the `Paint` object using translucency, Shaders, Mask Filters, Color Filters, and Path Effects.

➤ Some of the best-practice techniques for drawing on the canvas.

➤ How to apply hardware acceleration to 2D graphics drawing.

INDEX

S